The Construction of Authorship

Post-Contemporary Interventions

Series Editors: Stanley Fish and Fredric Jameson

The Construction of Authorship
Textual Appropriation in Law and Literature

Martha Woodmansee and
Peter Jaszi, Editors

Duke University Press   Durham and London 1994

© 1994 Duke University Press
All rights reserved
Printed in the United States of America
on acid-free paper ∞
Library of Congress Cataloging-in-Publication Data
appear on the last printed page of this book.

CONTENTS

ACKNOWLEDGMENTS

The papers collected in this volume grew out of a meeting sponsored by the Society for Critical Exchange. That meeting received the generous support of the School of Law and College of Arts and Sciences at Case Western Reserve University and the Washington College of Law at The American University. The papers first appeared in the *Cardozo Arts & Entertainment Law Journal*, volume 10, number 2. The editors of this volume would like to thank the *Journal*'s editorial board and staff for their dedication and hard work in preparing the papers for publication. The following individuals were particularly instrumental in bringing this project to a successful conclusion:

1991-92 Editorial Board	*1992-93 Editorial Board*
EDWARD J. KLARIS, *Editor-in-Chief*	GARY S. LUTZKER, *Editor-in-Chief*
FELICIA ENNIS, *Managing Editor*	MARC A. STADTMAUER, *Executive Editor*
DANIEL T. OSHATZ, *Production Editor*	

INTRODUCTION

PETER JASZI
MARTHA WOODMANSEE

Authorship does not exist to innocent eyes; they see only writing and texts. Back in 1991, a few weeks before the meeting at which these papers were presented, Sabrina Jaszi, then almost six, learned that her father would be going out of town to a meeting and wanted to know what it would be about. "Authors," her father told her. "What is an author, Daddy?" Sabrina responded. The ensuing attempt at a definition—that an author is the creator of unique, original works such as stories, plays, and poems—was evidently too abstract, but another tack suggested itself. Sabrina's favorite bedtime reading at the time was the Lambs' *Tales from Shakespeare*, so falling back on the arch-author, her father tried again: "Shakespeare was a famous author, Sabrina." This obviously struck home. "Oh!" Sabrina exclaimed, "was there a *person* called Shakespeare?"

Probably few of us recall the precise moment we learned that texts do not (literally) write themselves, but many of us recollect with painful clarity the second stage in our loss of innocence. This was when we learned that our habitual way of writing, with its emphasis on imitation and adaptation, was not legitimate authorship—or worse, that it transgressed the authorship of others. In his contribution to this volume, Jim Swan describes the aftermath of such an episode in the life of an eleven-year-old girl accused of plagiarizing a story that she presented to the beloved head of her school. Several years later, reflecting on the trauma of being called to account before an institutional court of inquiry, she unwittingly revealed how thoroughly she had learned her lesson: she disparaged her early compositions as mere exercises in "assimilation" and "imitation," and went on to regret that, try as she might, she still had not succeeded in producing truly original compositions:

> I [simply] cannot always distinguish my own thoughts from those I read, because what I read becomes the very substance and texture of my mind. Consequently, in nearly all that I write, I produce something which very much resembles the crazy patchwork I used to make when I first learned to sew. . . . But we keep on trying because we know that others have succeeded, and we are not willing to acknowledge defeat.

Many of us were called to task for some such early, and equally innocent, act of appropriative writing—say, for copying a school report too extensively, or too literally, or without proper attribution, from an encyclopedia. Long after the details of the incident fade in memory, the associated sense of shame and inadequacy audible in this young writer's recollections lingers on. So our hearts go out to her. They go out to her especially when we learn that the writer was Helen Keller; for blind and deaf from birth, Keller's chief access to nature and culture was quite literally through the texts that others signed into her palm.

Yet however much we regret the brutal circumstances of this lesson in the proprietary nature of authorship, we tend to think of the lesson itself as necessary. In our adult world words may not be appropriated at will, but "belong" to the individual who "originated" them. So important to us is this division of intellectual property into mine and thine that we have codified it in laws of copyright and authors' rights that enable us to prosecute trespassers. It was thus crucial to her very survival as a writer that Helen learn "to distinguish [her] own thoughts from those [she] read."

Such laws, and the tribunals where "crimes of writing"[1] are prosecuted, are only the final instance in a large and intricate system of institutions of authorship extending from grammatical and stylistic rules and conventions to pedagogies of literature and composition. It is to this system that Michel Foucault called attention in "What Is an Author?,"[2] and the essays collected here may be viewed as investigations of some of these institutions, their histories, and their future prospects. The essays grew out of a meeting of eighty scholars from the law, humanities, and social sciences who came together at the invitation of the Society for Critical Exchange to renew the kind of interdisciplinary exchange out of which our modern regime of authorship emerged and has derived its persistent power. In this introduction we will set forth only the bold outlines and broad implications of this development (elaborated in our own contributions to the volume) and will leave it to the other contributors both to enrich our narrative and to complicate it.

Taken as a whole these studies of writing practices from the Renaissance to the present suggest that the modern regime of

---

[1] The telling phrase is the title of Susan Stewart's important study, CRIMES OF WRITING: PROBLEMS IN THE CONTAINMENT OF REPRESENTATION (1991).

[2] *Qu'est-ce qu'un auteur?* 63 BULLETIN DE LA SOCIÉTÉ FRANÇAISE DE PHILOSOPHIE, (1969) translated in TEXTUAL STRATEGIES, 141-160 (J. Harari ed., 1979).

authorship, far from being timeless and universal, is a relatively recent formation—the result of a quite radical reconceptualization of the creative process that culminated less than 200 years ago in the heroic self-presentation of Romantic poets. As they saw it, *genuine* authorship is *originary* in the sense that it results not in a variation, an imitation, or an adaptation, and certainly not in a mere re-production such as Helen Keller's, but in an utterly new, unique—in a word, "original"—work which, accordingly, may be said to be the property of its creator and to merit the law's protection as such.

Prior to this apotheosis of authorship words and texts circulated more freely—in the sense at least that the kind of appropriation for which Keller was called to answer was common. This is not because surveillance was lax, but because more corporate and collaborative norms of writing prevailed. This is evident from the apparent indifference to attribution exhibited in the early printed texts of the dramatic works of Beaumont and Fletcher which Jeff Masten examines, as well as in the commonplace books that are the focus of Max Thomas's contribution. Thomas discerns there a (con)fusion of writer and reader that he considers characteristic of the Renaissance generally. The distance between such promiscuous textual practices and our own proprietary ones is inscribed in English grammar: today we use quotation marks to assign credit for a passage and cordon it off as another's property, but as Margreta De Grazia shows, as late as the eighteenth century such marks "flagged passages as property belonging to all—'common places' to be *freely* appropriated." By calling attention to passages worthy of inscription in the reader's own commonplace book, quotation marks facilitated the appropriation of others' writing.

It is not as if such communal and collaborative writing practices disappeared with the ascent of the originary genius-proprietor. They persisted not only in everyday and technical writing, but among the very writers who contributed most substantially to the Romantic reconceptualization of this activity. William Wordsworth's collaboration with Coleridge is legend, and his extensive reliance on the writing of his sister Dorothy is now also beginning to come to light. This is occluded, however, in the authorial persona he projects publicly—that of the secular prophet with privileged access to experience of the numinous and a unique ability to translate that experience for the masses of less gifted consumers. In this self-presentation Dorothy and even Coleridge figure primarily as sources of "inspiration," or encouragement.

Thomas Pfau locates the "causes and motives" for this preeminently authorial practice in the "crisis of the subject," and in this way helps to explain not only Wordsworth's self-aggrandizing tendency but also the continuing power of his misrepresentation of a collaborative creative process as a solitary, originary one.

It is noteworthy that Wordsworth attempted to enlist the law in support of his authorial vision by intervening directly in Parliamentary debates over copyright law reform. The episode merits relating briefly because it reveals so pointedly both the very material nature of the considerations that led Wordsworth to reconceptualize authorship and the way in which the law tended to collaborate in his project.[3] When Wordsworth began his career the first English copyright statute, the Statute of Anne of 1710, had been on the books for some eighty years. That statute may not have been an intellectual property law in the modern sense, but it did provide fourteen years of protection against unauthorized printing to the author of a new book—or, as was more likely in practice, to the bookseller who had purchased that author's right. The work could receive an additional fourteen years if the author survived the original term of protection. Although the term of protection had been extended in 1814, Wordsworth felt that the new term of the greater of twenty-eight years or the life of the author was still much too short to accommodate the work of true genius, which, to quote his "Essay, Supplementary to the Preface" (1815), is obliged to "*creat[e]* the taste by which [it] is to be enjoyed."[4] The great difficulty of such "original" writing forced its author to look to posterity for recognition, Wordsworth felt, while that of the "useful drudges," being "upon a level with the taste and knowledge of the age," turned over rapidly. The latter could thus recover their investment within the allotted twenty-eight years.

Initially Wordsworth argued for perpetual copyright, but after 1837, when his friend Thomas Noon Talfourd, a lawyer and legislator who ultimately "attained greater recognition as an essayist and dramatist,"[5] introduced a bill calling for extension of the term of copyright to sixty years, Wordsworth threw himself into lobbying for this compromise. In answer to the objection of publishers that the bill "would tend to check the circulation of

---

[3] Martha Woodmansee, THE AUTHOR, ART, AND THE MARKET: REREADING THE HISTORY OF AESTHETICS 145 (1993).

[4] William Wordsworth, *Essay, Supplementary to the Preface*, in 1 THE PROSE WORKS OF WILLIAM WORDSWORTH 62, 80 (W.J.B. Owen, ed., 1974).

[5] BIOGRAPHICAL DICTIONARY OF THE COMMON LAW 500 (A.W.B. Simpson ed., 1964).

literature, and by so doing would prove injurious to the public," he wrote:

> [W]hat we want in these times, and are likely to want still more, is not the circulation of books, but of good books, and above all, the production of works, the authors of which look beyond the passing day, and are desirous of pleasing and instructing future generations. . . . A conscientious author, who had a family to maintain, and a prospect of descendants, would regard the additional labour bestowed upon any considerable work he might have in hand, in the light of an insurance of money upon his own life for the benefit of his issue. . . . Deny it to him, and you unfeelingly leave a weight upon his spirits, which must deaden his exertions; or you force him to turn his faculties . . . to inferior employments.[6]

His exalted understanding of the author's calling led Wordsworth to advocate an expansive view of copyright protection. The new legislation he hoped for was not forthcoming until 1842, and even then the proponents of greater protection had to settle for forty-two years (or if the author survived that period, life plus seven years). Only gradually would the term of copyright edge toward the present basic formula of the life of the author plus fifty years, established in Britain in 1911 and in the United States only in 1978.

Today, more and more American copyright advocates urge a further term extension to life plus seventy years, already an accomplished fact in Germany and elsewhere. Such expansionism is difficult to square with an "economic model" of copyright, which justifies protection only insofar as it promotes social welfare by providing an incentive to create and/or distribute new works. It follows directly, however, from acceptance of what Alfred Yen terms the "natural law model," in which copyright merely confirms a preexisting entitlement. Informed by the Romantic belief that long and intense legal protection is the due of creative genius, this latter model dominates "authors' rights" discourse in Continental Europe, and it has also exerted consistent, shaping pressure on the Anglo-American law of copyright, at least since Wordsworth's time.

Although the notion of authorship that informs our modern law of copyright is a recent one, the impulses that nourished it have their roots in early modern times. Worth mentioning, in

---

6 William Wordsworth, *To the Editor of the Kendal Mercury*, in 3 THE PROSE WORKS OF WILLIAM WORDSWORTH 310 (W.J.B. Owen, ed., 1974).

particular, is the strain of "possessive individualism" that was responsible for the acquisitive, expansionist, and colonial activity that we associate with early capitalism in England, for the book trade was an important site of such activity. Although not yet the burgeoning industry it would become by the nineteenth century, the eighteenth-century trade was an arena in which entrepreneurial publishers collided with one another, and with increasingly entrepreneurial writers, as they played out their shared conviction that the "individual [is] essentially the proprietor of his own person or capacities"[7]—and thus of whatever can be made of them.

Until near the end of the seventeenth century the book trade was dominated by the Honorable Company of Stationers, a guild organized in 1557 along medieval lines, to which the Crown granted a collective general publishing monopoly in exchange for its promise of rigorous self-censorship. Toward the end of the seventeenth century, and particularly after the demise of official censorship with the lapse of the Licensing Act in 1695, these once-stable arrangements declined into general disarray. New competitive forces were at work within the little world of the Company itself and, fueled by the same entrepreneurial energies, outsiders also offered unprecedented threats to the businesses of established guild publishers. These "pirates," whose freebooting took the form of satisfying public demand by reprinting books first published by others, were practitioners of a strong form of possessive individualism: whatever books they could make with their hands and their presses were theirs to dispose of, the Company's notional royal monopoly notwithstanding.

The established book trade responded in kind: their claims of proprietorship extended not only to the particular books they published, but to the content of those books—if not to the very market itself. Although the London booksellers who were the remnant of the Stationer's Company pushed for reregulation to restore the old commercial order, their campaign invoked a new rhetoric of individual interest and individual entitlement—both their own and, somewhat curiously, that of the "authors" who provided them with manuscripts. Conveying the tone of that campaign, the preamble of the resulting law characterized the evil it was designed to redress as the "printing, reprinting, and

---

[7] C. B. Macpherson, THE POLITICAL THEORY OF POSSESSIVE INDIVIDUALISM: HOBBES TO LOCKE 3 (1962). See also DEMOCRACY AND POSSESSIVE INDIVIDUALISM: THE INTELLECTUAL LEGACY OF C. B. MACPHERSON (Joseph H. Carens, ed., 1993).

publishing of. . .books and other writings without the consent of the *authors or proprietors* [thereof]. . .to their very great detriment, and too often to the ruin of them and their families. . . ." Despite this rhetoric, as John Feather's investigation of publishing practice before 1710 demonstrates, the Statute of Anne functioned primarily as a codification of existing trade arrangements. In invoking authors' hardships as well as their own in their appeal for parliamentary sympathy, the publishers hardly risked unbottling the genie of "authors' rights," for in any future they could foresee the rights to print and reprint would continue to be routinely transferred by writers to publisher-proprietors. Only with time would the statute's formal innovation—the initial vesting of the "sole liberty" of printing a book in its "author"—take on practical or theoretical significance.

The booksellers' decision to invoke authorship in their campaign for the Statute of Anne was, then, an instrumental one, fueled in part perhaps by the projection of their own proprietary impulses onto writers. The latter were clearly also beginning to be infected by the entrepreneurial spirit that characterized the early eighteenth-century book trade. The number of individuals seeking to earn their living by the pen increased so dramatically that a new collective term, derived from the name of the London street in which many of them resided, entered English usage: Grub Street. In a pamphlet of 1704, Daniel DeFoe, whose succession of self-promoting ventures culminated in a career as a professional writer, became the first to suggest that the right to prosecute book piracies ought to belong, in the first instance, to authors themselves.[8] This is not to say that Defoe would have viewed himself as a proto-Wordsworthian author-genius. Peter Lindenbaum's examination of John Milton's publishing contracts reminds us that at least through the 1660s even the most distinguished literary figures did not view themselves as rights-bearing proprietors in this modern sense. Such an image is the making of later writers who projected their own proprietary aims back onto precursors like Milton, transforming them into iconic author-victims locked in struggle with grasping publishers. Just how pervasive this Romantic revisionism has been emerges from Martha Woodmansee's study of the strong *anti-authorial* impulses in Samuel Johnson's writing practices.

---

[8] Defoe's *Essay on the Regulation of the Press* is discussed by Peter Jaszi in *Toward a Theory of Copyright: The Metamorphoses 'of Authorship'*, 1991 Duke L. J. 455-502, at 470, and in this volume by Mark Rose.

Elizabeth Eisenstein has associated the beginnings of possessive individualism among writers with the rise of print.[9] In this
volume Marlon Ross's study of eighteenth-century writers'
changing self-conceptions locates in the very materiality of print
the source of the growing belief that one had a right to own what
"he created in words." According to Ross, printed utterances
demanded to be taken seriously, so that "with time, to be printed
[was] to be an authority"—both responsible for one's words and
the proprietor of them. Among the figures whose growing authorial self-consciousness Ross examines is Alexander Pope, and in
his contribution Mark Rose recounts how this "aggressive professional, . . . the first major author to use the Statute of Anne repeatedly to pursue his professional interests in court," made a
measured decision to sue an equally entrepreneurial publisher,
Edmund Curll, who had earned notoriety as a pornographer and
pirate.[10] The point of law established in the 1741 case of *Pope v.
Curll*—that rights in letters, considered as incorporeal texts
rather than physical objects, belong to the writer rather than the
recipient—marks this litigation as an important early exchange in
a conversation between law and literature that continued through
Wordsworth's time.[11]

Today, however, that conversation seems stalled. In particular, law has missed out on the contemporary "critique of authorship"—the impulse, especially in literary studies, to put in
question the naturalness and inevitability of Romantic ideas
about creativity. Umberto Eco's "open work" remains a closed
book to the law,[12] just as Roland Barthes' call in "The Death of
the Author"[13] for a reversal of the conventional relation of author and reader has gone unheard by intellectual property lawyers. However enthusiastically legal scholars may have thrown
themselves into "deconstructing" other bodies of legal doctrine,
copyright has remained untouched by the implications of the
Derridean proposition that the inherent instability of meaning
derives not from authorial subjectivity but from intertextuality.

---

[9] Elizabeth L. Eisenstein, THE PRINTING REVOLUTION IN EARLY MODERN EUROPE 84
(1983).

[10] For background on Curll, see David Saunders, AUTHORSHIP AND COPYRIGHT 45-56
(1992).

[11] For examples of similar interventions in Continental Europe, see Martha Woodmansee, *The Genius and the Copyright: Economic and Legal Conditions of the Emergence of the
Author*, 17 EIGHTEENTH-CENTURY STUDIES 425-48 (1984).

[12] Umberto Eco, OPERA APERTA (1962); translated as THE OPEN WORK (A. Cancogni,
trans., 1989).

[13] Roland Barthes, *La mort de l'auteur*, (1968), translated as *The Death of the Author*, in
IMAGE, MUSIC, TEXT 142-48 (S. Heath trans., 1977).

Above all, the questions posed by Michel Foucault in "What Is an Author?" about the causes and consequences of the persistent, overdetermined power of the author construct—with their immediate significance for law—have gone largely unattended by theorists of copyright law, to say nothing of practitioners or, most critically, judges and legislators.

The problem, at least in part, is that even as the notion of authorship is subjected to the scrutiny of critical theory, the teaching of literature and composition to which future lawyers are exposed continues to reinforce the Romantic paradigm. Most writing today—in business, government, industry, the law, the sciences and social sciences—is collaborative, yet it is still being taught as if it were a solitary, originary activity. Despite growing recognition of the socially constituted nature of the individual human subject, Andrea Lunsford and Lisa Ede explain that teachers too often remain loyal to a reductively "expressive" model of composition, which defines their task as one of helping students "find a voice"—articulate the authentic, originary selves that lie deep within, beneath the layers of cliché in which they write.

This unrealistic model of composition places extraordinary demands on students. Everyone fails to measure up, but the young writers whose shortcomings are most visible are those— often students with non-Western backgrounds—who have not internalized basic lessons of intellectual property early in their educational careers, and who neglect to employ conventional means to mark the boundaries between "original" and "derivative" material. The stakes are high in disciplinary actions against students accused of intramural offenses against authorship. Indeed, our institutions underline the seriousness of these proceedings by giving them the form, as well as some of the content, of legal actions for violations of copyright law.

After such early lessons in the requirements of authorship, students who enroll in advanced literature courses enter these with exaggerated respect for the "real" authors celebrated in the syllabi organized around their "great works." Even the recent canon busting by critics of such syllabi usually stops at adding to the existing canon of great authors token representatives of diversity—new "authors" assimilable to the Romantic vision of authorship rather than role models for alternative writing practices. Meanwhile the canonical approach colonizes new territory: as literary studies has assimilated film studies, it has imposed the decontextualized "cult of the cinematic author" considered in

Marvin D'Lugo's study of the career and reputation of director
Carlos Saura, obscuring the inherently collaborative nature of
the medium as well as the social and political context of film
production.

The hold of authorship on the American legal imagination
shows no sign of abating. If anything it would seem to be gaining
in strength. To mention but a single manifestation of this trend,
the United States recently ended its century-long holdout and
joined the Berne Convention for the Protection of Literary and
Artistic Works, an international agreement grounded in thoroughly Romantic assumptions about creativity. The first Act of
this preeminent "authors' rights" treaty in 1886 represented the
culmination of a process which got underway in the mid-nine-
teenth-century with Victor Hugo's vigorous campaign for the
rights of European writers and artists. Other famous "authors"
rallied to the cause: Gerhard Joseph suggests that the manic energy with which Charles Dickens championed international copyright stemmed from the novelist's private insecurities about his
own "originality." And N. N. Feltes demonstrates how early advocates of international copyright appropriated and manipulated
the rhetoric of authorship to create the preconditions of a "new
world market" in published books—not unlike the way the Company of Stationers had once invoked authorship in the stream of
pamphlets and petitions that led up to the Statute of Anne.
American assimilation of the resulting culture of Berne is certain
to reinforce our courts' tendency to decide hard cases by appeal
to a Romantically derived concept of authorship.

Even legal scholars like Monroe Price and Malla Pollack who
argue that public policy rather than aesthetic ideology should
dictate what objects merit protection as works of authorship, ac-
cede that such a fundamental change in orientation is easier to
imagine than to accomplish. Having called attention to the
Supreme Court's recent decision in *Feist Publications v. Rural Telephone Service* (1991) denying copyright to factual compilations like
ordinary telephone books because they lack the requisite "creative spark," Price and Pollack explain that the Court "wants a living, breathing author"—that, in short, it will not reward the
investment of time and effort alone. If phone books were the only
casualty of the law's author fixation, there would be little real
cause for concern. But this is not the case. Western copyright
laws—and the international copyright system derived from
them—are at once too broad and too narrow: they tend to deny
or marginalize the work of many creative people while providing

such intense protection to the works they cover that reasonable public access to these latter works is frustrated.

To merit copyright an "expression" must be "fixed," leading to the exclusion of a wide range of improvised works and works of oral tradition. Moreover, since copyright extends only to "original" works, it denies protection to folklore and items of cultural heritage that are valued chiefly for their fidelity to tradition rather than their deviations from it. Copyright also slights "basic" components of cultural productions, barring protection to things like the rhythms most characteristic of both traditional musical forms and certain contemporary forms such as rap and hip-hop. And although, as we noted above, some of the collaborative modes of production characteristic of the Renaissance persist, copyright doctrine tends to marginalize or deny these practices. No copyright can exist in a work produced as a true collective enterprise rather than by one or more identifiable or anonymous "authors." Thus, copyright has no place for works produced in polyvocal collaborative situations like the nineteenth-century women's groups described by Ann Ruggles Gere, in which texts were generated and revised in an atmosphere of sociable intertextuality.

At the same time, the intensity of protection extended to productions that qualify as works of authorship tends to bar their reuse for new creative purposes, making virtual outlaws of those who draw on such works for their raw material. Several essays in this volume document this consequence of copyright. In his study of digital sampling, a technique that facilitates the capture, manipulation, and re-production of recorded sounds, "elevating all consumers to potential creators," David Sanjek details the response of copyright proprietors and courts: to treat the resulting new works of unauthorized electronic pastiche not as independent creations but as civil and criminal wrongs. And this creeping enclosure of the informational "commons" is not being accomplished by means of copyright alone. As Rosemary Coombe points out, the discourse of new theories of entitlement like the so-called "right of publicity" also resonates with the rhetoric of Wordsworth: this new right in a persona or "image" arises as the legal reflex of a celebrity's self-fashioning. And the more such extensions of legal protection are rationalized by appeal to authorship, the more clearly they reveal an emerging irony of contemporary intellectual property law: many "authors" who invoke the law's protection against "unrespectable" users—like Michael Jackson in the "Plunderphonics" case described by Sanjek, or

Madonna in Coombe's example—are themselves practiced cultural *bricoleurs*.

Since it is derived from Western, especially Continental, "authors' rights" principles, the international copyright regime that governs relations between developed and developing nations inevitably exhibits much the same biases. Moreover the exclusive vision of authorship contained therein has been internalized in many developing countries as part of their post-colonial legal legacy. As a consequence, while the traditional, folkloric, and collaborative productions of these countries circulate internationally, becoming subject to appropriation by the culture industries of the developed world, they go for the most part unprotected by both national laws in their countries of origin and the international copyright system. This absence of protection implies, in the first instance, that the creators or cultural custodians of many works and traditions realize no financial benefit from their exploitation, no matter how profitable or widespread. Perhaps more to the point, it means that those creators and custodians have no say—and certainly no veto—over the ways and means by which such exploitation occurs. Meanwhile, the expansive tendency of author-centered international copyright helps ensure that consumers in developing countries pay the asking price for the characteristic cultural productions of developed ones, such as motion pictures. Even newer kinds of works originating in the developed world, such as computer software, have been shoehorned into the rubric of "works of authorship," which remains resolutely closed to so many comparably collaborative manifestations of creativity.

Copyright is emerging as the dominant mode of legal regulation in the new digital environment of "data networks," "information superhighways," and "electronic libraries." Such developments are altering traditional relationships between makers, distributors, and consumers of information products in ways that could mark the end of publishing as we have known it. While entrants into the new information environment may require some kind of legal security as an incentive to participate, they may not need the long, intense protection afforded by conventional copyright—no matter how much they would like to have it. In an essay with important implications for this new development, Thomas Streeter examines the way in which law responded to an earlier innovation in commmunications technology with a regulatory scheme that endowed broadcasting corporations with a form of authors' rights. He suggests that the ideology of individual creativity has helped to mask the essentially bureaucratic imperatives that dictate the content of broadcast programming. As information consumers we should thus beware of efforts to regulate the digital environment as if it were simply a new vehicle for individual "works of authorship" rather than a potential cultural "commons."

The essays collected here demonstrate that our construction of the author as the bearer of special legal rights and cultural privileges carries consequences for the ways in which power and wealth are distributed. As James Boyle has put it,

> we are driven by a number of factors to confer property rights in information on those who come closest to the image of the romantic author, those whose contributions to information production are most easily seen as original and transformative. [T]his is a bad thing for reasons of both efficiency and justice; it leads us to have too many intellectual property rights, to confer them on the wrong people and dramatically to undervalue the interests of both sources of and audiences for the information we commodify.[14]

Some critics of the "law and literature" movement have followed the lead of Richard Posner in questioning whether literary and legal studies can illuminate one another, stressing instead the "profound differences between the two fields."[15] However apt these cautions may be to the umpteenth investigation of the "legal meaning of *Billy Budd*," they would miss the point of the present project, which is to revive interdisciplinary investigation of our ways of conceptualizing creative production. Here at least, law and literature have much to say to one another, and there is an urgent need for discussion.

---

[14] James Boyle, A THEORY OF LAW AND INFORMATION: ROMANCE AND COMMODIFICATION FROM BLACKMAIL TO SPLEENS 1-2 (1994).
[15] Richard Posner, LAW AND LITERATURE: A MISUNDERSTOOD RELATION 13-14 (1988).

ON THE AUTHOR EFFECT: RECOVERING COLLECTIVITY

Martha Woodmansee*

I

Will the author in the modern sense prove to have been only a brief episode in the history of writing? By "author" we mean an individual who is the sole creator of unique "works" the originality of which warrants their protection under laws of intellectual property known as "copyright" or "authors' rights." The question is timely because research since the appearance in 1969 of Michel Foucault's essay, *What is an Author?*,[1] suggests not only that the author in this modern sense is a relatively recent invention, but that it does not closely reflect contemporary writing practices. Indeed, on inspection, it is not clear that this notion ever coincided closely with the practice of writing. Yet, as the papers which follow show clearly, this did not prevent the notion from becoming highly influential in promoting certain kinds of writing at the expense of others in our estimation. It has exerted this influence in no small measure by helping to shape the laws which regulate our writing practices.

In an earlier investigation of the evolution of authorship[2] I determined that as late as the 1750s in Germany the writer was still being represented as just one of the numerous craftsmen involved in the production of a book—not superior to, but on a par with other craftsmen. A "book," the *Allgemeines Oeconomisches Lexicon* for 1753 informs us, is

> either numerous sheets of white paper that have been stitched together in such a way that they can be filled with writing; or, a highly useful and convenient instrument constructed of printed sheets variously bound in cardboard, paper, vellum, leather, etc. for presenting the truth to another in such a way that it can be conveniently read and recognized. Many people work on this ware before it is complete and becomes an actual

* Associate Professor of English, Case Western Reserve University. B.A., 1968, Northwestern University; M.A., 1969, Ph.D., 1977, Stanford University. I would like to thank Peter Jaszi for the collaborative spirit in which he read earlier drafts of this paper.

[1] Michel Foucault, *What Is an Author?*, in Textual Strategies: Perspectives in Post-Structuralist Criticism 141-60 (Josué V. Harari ed., 1979)

[2] *See generally*, Martha Woodmansee, *The Genius and the Copyright: Economic and Legal Conditions of the Emergence of the "Author,"* 17 Eighteenth-Century Stud. 425 (1984).

book in this sense. The scholar and the writer, the papermaker, the type founder, the typesetter and the printer, the proofreader, the publisher, the book-binder, sometimes even the gilder and the brass-worker, etc. Thus many mouths are fed by this branch of manufacture.[3]

If the writer appears here as only one of the craftsmen responsible for the finished product, that is because he was viewed, and by and large still viewed himself, in much the same terms as they—that is, as master of a craft, master of a body of rules, or techniques, preserved and handed down in rhetoric and poetics, for the transmission of ideas handed down by tradition.

The notion that the writer is a special participant in the production process—the only one worthy of attention—is of recent provenience. It is a by-product of the Romantic notion that significant writers break altogether with tradition to create something utterly new, unique—in a word, "original." First sketched out in Edward Young's *Conjectures on Original Composition* (1759), this new way of thinking about writing was elaborated by an emerging profession of writers from Herder and Goethe to Coleridge and Wordsworth, who postulated in his *Essay, Supplementary to the Preface*:

> Of genius the only proof is, the act of doing well what is worthy to be done, and what was never done before: Of genius in the fine arts, the only infallible sign is the widening the sphere of human sensibility, for the delight, honor, and benefit of human nature. Genius is the introduction of a new element into the intellectual universe: or, if that be not allowed, it is the application of powers to objects on which they had not before been exercised, or the employment of them in such a manner as to produce effects hitherto unknown.[4]

We owe our modern idea of an author to the radical reconceptualization of writing which came to fruition in this essay of 1815. That it represents a mystification of an activity which is of necessity rooted in tradition emerges from those investigations of authorship contained, and alluded to, in this volume that make it

---

[3] GEORG HEINRICH ZINCK, ALLGEMEINES OECONOMISCHES LEXICON 442 (Martha Woodmansee trans., 3d ed. 1753). For the evolution of authorship in Germany, see generally Woodmansee, *supra* note 2; Martin Vogel, *Der literarische Markt und die Entstehung des Verlags- und Urheberrechts bis zum Jahre 1800*, in RHETORIK, AESTHETIK, IDEOLOGIE: ASPEKTE EINER KRITISCHEN KULTURWISSENSCHAFT 117-36 (1973); HEINRICH BOSSE, AUTORSCHAFT IST WERKHERRSCHAFT (1981).

[4] William Wordsworth, *Essay, Supplementary to the Preface*, in 1 THE PROSE WORKS OF WILLIAM WORDSWORTH 82 (W.J.B. Owen ed., 1974).

their object to explore the manifold social, economic, political, and legal impulses responsible for this development.

As we move backward in time, the collective, corporate, or collaborative element in writing, which is still apparent in the above definition of a book, becomes even more pronounced. From the Middle Ages right down through the Renaissance new writing derived its value and authority from its affiliation with the texts that preceded it, its derivation rather than its deviation from prior texts. For St. Bonaventura, writing in the thirteenth century, there were four ways of making a book, and none of them involved the kind of solitary origination which Edward Young sought to promote:

> A man might write the works of others, adding and changing nothing, in which case he is simply called a 'scribe' (*scriptor*). Another writes the work of others with additions which are not his own; and he is called a 'compiler' (*compilator*). Another writes both others' work and his own, but with others' work in principal place, adding his own for purposes of explanation; and he is called a 'commentator' (*commentator*). . . . Another writes both his own work and others' but with his own work in principal place adding others' for purposes of confirmation; and such a man should be called an 'author' (*auctor*).[5]

While Bonaventura's *auctor* seems to be making a substantial (original) contribution of his own, he does so as part of an enterprise conceived collaboratively. Nor is *this* mode of book production privileged over the other three—over transcription, compilation, and commentary.

II

But it is hardly necessary to go back to the Middle Ages to find so corporate a view of writing, for it was still shared by Samuel Johnson (1709-1784). Although official history presents Johnson as the very archetype of the modern author, the majority of his energies as a writer went into the kinds of activities Bonaventura identifies. The large projects to which he put his name, like the monumental *Dictionary of the English Language* (1755), the edition of *The Plays of William Shakespeare* (1765) and the *Lives of the Poets* (1779-81), were collective and collaborative. The last of these, a series of "prefaces, biographical and critical," for a multi-volume collection of England's "major" modern poets, was

---

5 1 Elizabeth Eisenstein, The Printing Press as an Agent of Change 121-22 (1979).

the inspiration of the London booksellers. It seems that an Edinburgh publisher had brought out just such a collection. Alarmed by this incursion on their virtual monopoly of the book trade, James Boswell reports, some forty of London's "most respectable booksellers," including in particular "all the proprietors of copy-right in the various Poets," met to devise a strategy for countering this "invasion" of their "Literary Property." To their great relief, the Edinburgh volumes had been carelessly printed in a type too small to be read with comfort. So "it was agreed that an elegant and uniform edition of *The English Poets* should be immediately printed, with a concise account of the life of each authour, by Dr. Samuel Johnson."[6]

The resulting *Lives of the Poets* contributed decisively to the differentiation of "authoring" from ordinary literary labor by establishing a pantheon of great authors whose "works" differ qualitatively from the sea of mere writing. Yet this multi-volume accomplishment was the product not of the solitary originary mode of composition whose myth it helped to foster, but of fruitful collaboration between Johnson, the poets he immortalized, the London booksellers—and countless others. To mention but one of these others: Johnson drew freely from another's work for his *Life of Pope*. The account of Pope's personal habits, which constitutes "one of the most interesting parts of that life," according to Bertram Davis, was incorporated without acknowledgment from either the *Universal Magazine* for August 1775 or the *Gentleman's Magazine* for September 1775 (it having appeared in both).[7]

But if Johnson freely received, freely did he also give. "Few friends who needed anything written were ever turned away, so long as what they wanted was in a genre in which Johnson felt comfortable"[8] (and during his long career he wrote in more of

---

6 JAMES BOSWELL, LIFE OF JOHNSON 802 (R.W. Chapman ed., 1980) (1791). I wish to thank my colleague William R. Siebenschuh for freely sharing his knowledge of Samuel Johnson.

7 BERTRAM H. DAVIS, JOHNSON BEFORE BOSWELL: A STUDY OF SIR JOHN HAWKINS'S "LIFE OF SAMUEL JOHNSON" 49 (1957). On Johnson's extensive "borrowing" from other writers, see WALTER JACKSON BATE, SAMUEL JOHNSON 220 (1977). It comes as a "jolt" to the modern reader, Bate writes, to learn how much in Johnson's earliest biographical writing is "direct translation or mere paraphrase of other works. Even if we remind ourselves that this was the common journalistic procedure of the time (and that all of these works—like his other writings in these years—were anonymous, and that he himself was far from claiming credit for them), we still feel a disappointment." *Id.* Such disappointment has its source in the Romantic expectations created, in the first instance, by Boswell. *See infra* at 287-88.

8 PAUL FUSSELL, SAMUEL JOHNSON AND THE LIFE OF WRITING 39 (1971).

them than probably any writer before or since).[9] Indeed, even as the *Lives of the Poets* was being planned, Johnson was involved in an elaborate ghostwriting exercise to save one of London's most popular preachers, the Reverend William Dodd, from execution. Dodd had been convicted of forgery, "the most dangerous crime in a commercial country," according to Boswell, and had appealed to Johnson for help in securing a royal pardon. Although they had barely even met, Johnson threw himself into the effort, "writing (as if from Dodd) letters to the Lord Chancellor, Henry Bathurst, and to Lord Mansfield, the Chief Justice; a petition from Dodd to the King and another from Mrs. Dodd to the Queen; a moving sermon preached by Dodd at the chapel in Newgate Prison . . . on the text 'What must I do to be saved?' and published with the title 'The Convict's Address to his Unhappy Brethren'; and several other pieces . . . ."[10] The effort was to no avail. Following a brief correspondence with Johnson, Dodd was executed on June 27, 1777.

This was no isolated incident. In the eighteenth century it was common for clergymen to "borrow" sermons from one another[11]—a practice that is becoming common again today, thanks to electronic networking. Johnson, who was no clergyman, carried the practice farther, ghost-writing sermons on a large scale: " 'I have begun a sermon after dinner, and sent it off by the post that night.' "[12] For his "pulpit discourses," we learn from his lifelong friend and early biographer John Hawkins, Johnson

> made no scruple of confessing, he was paid . . . and such was his notion of justice, that having been paid, he considered them so absolutely the property of the purchaser, as to renounce all claim to them. He reckoned that he had written about forty sermons; but, except as to some, knew not in what hands they were—"I have," said he, "been paid for them, and have no right to enquire about them."[13]

His eventual output may have exceeded the number claimed here,[14] but such was Johnson's discretion that only twenty eight have been identified with sufficient certainty to be included in his collected works.

---

9 *Id.*
10 BATE, *supra* note 7, at 524. *See also* BOSWELL, *supra* note 6, at 827-35.
11 Jean Hagstrum & James Gray, *Introduction* to SAMUEL JOHNSON, SERMONS xxvii-xxviii [hereinafter SERMONS].
12 *Id.* at xxi.
13 *Id.* at xxi-xxii.
14 *Id.* at xxii n.4.

In fact, Johnson's sermon production went beyond commercial ghost-writing, passing into the realm of true collaboration. The Reverend John Taylor was apparently a chief beneficiary of his efforts. One of Johnson's oldest and closest friends, Taylor left behind at his death in 1788 some twenty five sermons which appeared shortly thereafter in two volumes, bearing on their title page the equivocal statement that they had been " 'left for publication by John Taylor.' "[15] Johnson's involvement in the writing of the sermons had long been suspected, and while the details will probably never be known, it now seems likely that it took several forms. As James Gray puts it in his study, "sometimes Johnson composed a whole sermon for his friend; sometimes he dictated it, in whole or part; sometimes Taylor supplied the 'foundation' and Johnson the 'superstructure'. . . ; and sometimes . . . Taylor did most of the composition, using an occasional Johnsonian turn of phrase."[16]

Johnson's involvement in challenging the authenticity of the Ossian poems—the great prototype of modern literary hoaxes—shows that he continued to collaborate in this way until the very end of his career. This episode centered around the epic poems, *Fingal* (1762) and *Temora* (1763), which James Macpherson purported to have discovered and translated from the Gaelic of a third-century bard called Ossian. In fact, Macpherson had composed most of them himself. Despite this—or because of it—their abrupt vigor and haunting suggestiveness struck a chord with the younger generation, especially in Germany, helping to call the Romantic revolution into existence.

Although not the first to question the poems' authenticity, Johnson became "the major and most effective spokesman against them."[17] His contemptuous discounting of them as counterfeits in his *Journey to the Western Islands of Scotland* (1775) so angered Macpherson that he threatened physical retaliation, causing Johnson to arm himself with a large truncheon.[18] This much is well known. But Johnson's tendency to efface his participation in collaborative projects operated to conceal the full extent of his involvement in the Ossian affair. Only recently has it come to light that Johnson continued the attack on Macpherson,

---

[15] *Id.* at xx.

[16] JAMES GRAY, JOHNSON'S SERMONS: A STUDY 42 (1972).

[17] Thomas M. Curley, *Johnson's Last Word on Ossian: Ghostwriting for William Shaw*, in ABERDEEN AND THE ENLIGHTENMENT: PROCEEDINGS OF A CONFERENCE HELD AT THE UNIVERSITY OF ABERDEEN 375, 379 (Jennifer J. Carter & Joan H. Pittock eds., 1987) [hereinafter *JLW*].

[18] BOSWELL, *supra* note 6, at 577ff.

albeit covertly and collaboratively, until the end of his life through his patronage of a young Gaelic scholar by the name of William Shaw. Johnson appears to have played at least an advisory role in the composition of the pamphlet in which Shaw first made his own disbelief public, *An Enquiry into the Authenticity of the Poems Ascribed to Ossian* (1781), for the pamphlet contains numerous complimentary references to Johnson and frequent quotations from his *Journey to the Western Islands of Scotland*, as well as reverberations of Johnson's charges against Macpherson.

As battle was joined between Shaw and the poems' proponents, Johnson's participation became more active, although no more public. He contributed substantially to penning a rejoinder to the angry response which Shaw's pamphlet almost immediately precipitated. This twenty-nine page document, entitled *A Reply to Mr. Clark*, was appended to a new "corrected" edition of the *Enquiry* and published in 1782. From the internal stylistic as well as external evidence assembled by Thomas M. Curley, it appears that "Johnson not only supervised [the] entire argumentation" of the rejoinder, "but also largely composed half of it and polished portions of the rest."[19] Although Shaw does not appear to have acknowledged this assistance anywhere, he demonstrated his gratitude by producing the first biography of his silent collaborator, *Memoirs of the Life and Writings of the Late Dr. Samuel Johnson* (1785).

Even as he helped to create the modern myth that genuine authorship consists in individual acts of origination, by orchestrating from behind the scenes this exposé of a fraudulent attribution of it, Johnson was himself participating in a mode of writing which puts this notion of authorship in question.

Space permits mention of but one further example of Johnson's collaborative impulse:[20] his very substantial contribution to the Vinerian law lectures which Robert Chambers delivered at

---

[19] *JLW, supra* note 17, at 388.

[20] Johnson also wrote countless prologues, proposals, dedications, advertisements, and political speeches for others—that is, in their names. Of his numerous dedications, the best known are the ones he wrote for Charles Burney's *History of Music* (1776) and Sir Joshua Reynolds's *Seven Discourses [on Art] Delivered in the Royal Academy* (1778). He also wrote a number for Charlotte Lennox—as well as, quite possibly, the penultimate chapter of her novel, *The Female Quixote*. Also deserving of further attention are Johnson's efforts on behalf of the aging physician, Zachariah Williams, father of the talented scientific writer, Anna Williams, whom Johnson took into his household in 1752. After several letters and petitions to the Admiralty failed to secure the old man an audience for his discoveries relevant to navigation, Johnson went so far as to throw himself into the subject and write up Williams's ideas in a little book, *An Account of an Attempt to Ascertain the Longitude at Sea* (1755), which he arranged to have published with Williams on the title page as author. *See* BATE, *supra* note 7, at 318-19.

Oxford from 1767 to 1771.[21] The Vinerian Chair of English Law
had been established in 1758 "to redress serious deficiencies in
contemporary legal training by giving undergraduates a systematic introductory study of their country's laws."[22] Chambers was
the second to hold the chair, having succeeded his teacher William Blackstone, who, during his eight-year tenure, delivered the
lectures which formed the basis of his celebrated *Commentaries on
the Laws of England* (1765-1769). Less than a fluent writer under
the best of circumstances, the erudite Chambers was understandably intimidated at the prospect of following Blackstone—so
much so that he postponed the scheduled commencement of his
own series of lectures to March 1767. During the preceding fall,
Johnson came to Chambers's aid, inaugurating a collaboration
that would continue at irregular intervals for approximately three
more years, and would include several periods during which
Johnson was in residence at Oxford. Their joint labors yielded
fifty-six—later expanded to the mandatory number of sixty—lectures on "the fundamental concepts, traditions and statutes making up the British constitution."[23] Although some of Johnson's
intimates knew of his participation in the preparation of Chambers's lectures, it was a generally well-kept secret during their
lifetimes and beyond.[24]

Johnson's undisclosed participation certainly went beyond
simple encouragement and general supervision. The modern editor of the lectures, Thomas M. Curley, speculates that Johnson
and Chambers must have worked on the lectures, together and
apart, in various ways. In some instances, he suggests, Chambers
wrote independently, while in others "[t]he collaborators would
have pooled the results of their research and exchanged ideas
about complex legal issues before Chambers resumed drafting

---

[21] My discussion is indebted to Thomas M. Curley's introduction to his edition of 1
SIR ROBERT CHAMBERS, A COURSE OF LECTURES ON THE ENGLISH LAW DELIVERED AT THE
UNIVERSITY OF OXFORD 1767-1773, at 3-33 (1985) [hereinafter CURLEY, COURSE]. *See
also* Thomas M. Curley, *Johnson's Secret Collaboration in* THE UNKNOWN SAMUEL JOHNSON
91-112 (John J. Burke & Donald Kay eds., 1983) [hereinafter Curley, *JSC*]; Thomas M.
Curley, *Johnson, Chambers, and the Law, in* JOHNSON AFTER TWO HUNDRED YEARS 187-209
(Paul J. Korshin ed., 1986) [hereinafter Curley, *JCL*].

[22] Curley, *JCL, supra* note 21, at 189.

[23] *Id.* at 193.

[24] Chambers took full public credit for the lectures, which were prepared for oral
delivery and went unpublished during his lifetime, although he revised a portion of the
material for eventual posthumous publication. Curley believes that "[f]astidiousness
about the quality of the lecture series rather than a fear that somebody would uncover
Johnson's part in its composition restrained Chambers from sending it to press."
CURLEY, COURSE, *supra* note 21, at 68. Not until 1939 was a copy of the original lecture
series discovered—a scribal transcription that had been requested by King George III
for his private library—and the lectures were first published in 1985.

his course and incorporated any argumentation that Johnson may have dictated or written for the professor's use at strategic points."[25]

We do not know whether or not Johnson was paid for his work on Chambers's lectures. But, as in other instances of his self-effacing participation in the composition of works for which others took credit, we may speculate on his non-financial motives. From the social dimension of such secret collaborations Johnson found not only good fellowship, social entree, and intellectual stimulation, but also an impetus to literary production—to which he often found it difficult to motivate himself.[26] For the arch-author Johnson, the corporate mode of writing appears to have been the most accessible and perhaps the most satisfying.

In addition, like most of the individuals with whom Johnson shared his words and ideas, Chambers was a close and long-standing friend. They had become acquainted in 1754 when Chambers was only seventeen years old. Later, Johnson may have been further drawn to the much younger Chambers by "the promise of legal eminence that he once coveted for himself, the gracious breeding and academic excellence that he always prized, and the filial attachment that he may well have craved in lonely middle age."[27] Indeed, the preparation of the lectures may have represented a vicarious achievement of goals Johnson was unable to accomplish in his own career. Ultimately, his distinctly non-proprietary attitude towards his collaborative contributions may have reflected a real uncertainty as to where his intellect and personality left off, and those of his co-writers began.

It is the chief object of modern textual scholarship to identify in all of this writing those words that originated uniquely with Johnson so that they can be properly credited to him, and a definitive *oeuvre* can be established. I do not wish to suggest that there is anything wrong with such activities, only that they presume a proprietary authorial impulse which Johnson apparently did not himself feel. Johnson the author in this modern sense is Boswell's making. "Without Boswell," Alvin Kernan writes, "Johnson would surely have been an important writer, and an interesting, powerful personality, but probably not the literary

---

[25] CURLEY, COURSE, *supra* note 21, at 22. *See also* Curley, *JCL*, *supra* note 21, at 193ff.

[26] Johnson's "inner resistance" to writing is characterized as "massive" by Bate: With Johnson, writing "could [only] be done easily if one did not care too much, or when (as was the case with much of his writing) it was done anonymously as a favor for others." BATE, *supra* note 7, at 379.

[27] Curley, *JCL*, *supra* note 21, at 189. *See also* CURLEY, COURSE, *supra* note 21, at 12-13.

type that he is, the towering and highly charged image of the first writer in the industrial, democratic, rationalistic age of print."[28] Having called attention to the crucial role of Boswell in the making of the modern author, Kernan does not press his advantage, however, and instead of recreating the master wordsmith for us, he falls in with Romantic biographers from Boswell to Bate and evokes the precursor of Wordsworth. While "[m]any writers before Johnson may have, certainly did, write greater books," Kernan observes,

> even the most individualized of them, a Petrarch or a Milton, let alone the anonymous Shakespeare, seem alongside him pale, fading, a few thin lines without much depth, shading, or emotional color. His intense personality, in a way the first romantic artist, appears at exactly the right point in literary history in several ways, the kind of poor, strange, troubled person that the print business could attract and use as a Grub Street hack, and, at the same time, the type of individual who needed and could use print to satisfy certain existential needs of his own for bread, for status, for meaning. But it went beyond this, and in the end, out of their own needs, Johnson and Boswell together created a social role that transcended individual needs, giving writers an important social function and making books, even in the vast numbers now produced by the printing press, something more than mere information, amusement, and commodity.[29]

Kernan writes as if the author in the modern sense were the goal toward which history had always been striving. But as I have tried to suggest, Johnson's life contains another story—for readers disposed to attend.

III

The corporate attitudes which surrounded writing right down through Johnson seem to be reasserting themselves again today. In their recent study of professional writing practices, Andrea Lunsford and Lisa Ede have found that most of the writing that goes on today is in fact collaborative.[30] Indeed, one comes away from their investigation of how people actually write in business, government, industry, the sciences and social sciences

---

[28] ALVIN KERNAN, PRINTING TECHNOLOGY, LETTERS & SAMUEL JOHNSON 108 (1987).
[29] *Id.* at 114-15.
[30] ANDREA A. LUNSFORD & LISA EDE, SINGULAR TEXTS/PLURAL AUTHORS (1990) [hereinafter LUNSFORD & EDE, SINGULAR TEXTS]; *see also* Andrea A. Lunsford & Lisa Ede, *Collaborative Authorship and the Teaching of Writing*, 10 CARDOZO ARTS & ENT. L.J. 673 (1992).

with the impression that there is but one last bastion of solitary origination: the arts and humanities. What gives their study such urgency is the fact that, this powerful collaborative trend notwithstanding, the assumption that writing is inherently and necessarily a solitary, individual act still informs both the theory and practice of the teaching of writing. Writing is still being taught as if, "envisioning students' professional lives after graduation," composition teachers "imagine[d] them seated alone, writing in isolation, misplaced Romantic spirits still struggling in a professional garret to express themselves."[31] In a word, we are not preparing students for the real writing tasks that await them.

As the collaborative nature of contemporary research and problem-solving fosters multiple authorship in more and more spheres, electronic technology is hastening the demise of the illusion that writing is solitary and originary. Even in the still relatively primitive applications that are widely available—the communication networks and information services like Internet, Bitnet, and Compuserve—not to mention the more sophisticated hypertext applications that are just beginning to be developed, the computer is dissolving the boundaries essential to the survival of our modern fiction of the author as the sole creator of unique, original works. The dissolution of these boundaries is the subject of Jay David Bolter's recent investigation of the impact of electronic technology on writing. In his examination of the on-going discussions that are being conducted in so-called "newsgroups," Bolter notes that

> [w]hen one subscriber in a newsgroup "publishes" a message, it travels to all the dozens or hundreds of others who belong to that group. The message may elicit responses, which in turn travel back and forth and spawn further responses. The prose of these messages is almost as casual as conversation, precisely because publication in this medium is both easy and almost unrestricted. The transition from reader to writer is completely natural. The reader of one message can with a few keystrokes send off a reply. Readers may even incorporate part of the original message in the reply, blurring the distinction between their own text and the text to which they are responding. There is also little respect for the conventions of the prior medium of print. Subscribers often type newspaper articles or excerpts from books into their replies without concern for copyright. The notion of copyright seems faintly absurd, since their messages are copied and relayed

---

[31] LUNSFORD & EDE, SINGULAR TEXTS, *supra* note 30, at 72.

automatically hundreds of times in a matter of hours.[32]

In a variety of ways, electronic communication seems to be assaulting the distinction between *mine* and *thine* that the modern authorship construct was designed to enforce.

Bolter's book is also available on disk, and the electronic "hypertext" version differs from the hard copy in several ways which illustrate the point I am making. Hypertext consists of text with highlighted words and passages. By selecting one of them, the reader accesses a new window which displays an amplification or extension of the highlighted idea. This extension, which may be thought of as an extended footnote, albeit one that could as easily be musical or graphic, could itself include highlighted sections which invite the reader to pursue yet further extensions, to explore further tributaries of the main textual stream. In short, hypertext liberates the writer (and reader) from the kind of linear exposition that print requires. Bolter's eletronic book goes off on "tangents" which, in the interest of a linear coherence, have had to be omitted from the printed version.

More significant in the present context, however, is the fact that hypertext can be interactive; and when the reader begins actively to intervene in the text, adding to, subtracting from, and modifying it from his or her keyboard, the boundaries between author and reader disintegrate. A reviewer of Bolter's book for *Artforum* writes of how he has already modified his copy of the disk by adding a few notes here and there, with the result that

> I am now to some degree coauthor of *my* particular version of the electronic book called *Writing Space*. And when I copy that version and pass it on to my friends (as Bolter specifically invites readers to do), they will no doubt make their own modifications and additions. It's conceivable that, after a sufficiently long period, only a small fraction of the material on the disk will have originated from Bolter's keyboard.[33]

By contributing his or her commentary, the reader becomes an overt collaborator in an unending process of reading and writing which reverses the trajectory of print, returning us to something very like the expressly collaborative writing milieu of the Middle Ages and the Renaissance with which we began. Bolter likens this new incarnation of the book to a medieval manuscript the

---

[32] Jay David Bolter, Writing Space: The Computer, Hypertext, and the History of Writing 29 (1991).

[33] Brian Eno, *On Writing Space*, Artforum, Nov. 1991, at 14 (reviewing Bolter, *supra* note 32).

margins of which "belonged to the scholarly reader"—were for "conducting a dialogue with the text."[34] During generations of copying, this text could migrate from the margins into the center, as the glosses of readers made their way into the original text.[35]

But the Renaissance "commonplace book" may provide an even more suggestive analogy. These were the notebooks, so to speak, in which one both transcribed writings by others which held some special significance and collected compositions of one's own—usually without a governing plan or arrangement and without attribution. Sometimes even the compiler of these "books" remained anonymous. When names did become associated with individual texts, it was generally for reasons that had nothing to do with authorship in the modern sense. As Peter Beal writes,

> A man's name might become linked with a poem in the course of manuscript transmission because he was the copyist, or because it was written by someone in his circle, or because he added his own stanzas to it, or wrote a reply to it, or set it to music, and so on.[36]

The compiler of the Renaissance commonplace book composed, transcribed, commented on, and reworked the writings of others—all in apparent indifference to the identity of their originators and without regard for ownership. This quintessentially Renaissance form of reading and writing is rapidly being revived by our electronic technology.

At the outset of the discussion I suggested that one of the most powerful vehicles of the modern authorship construct was provided by the laws which regulate our writing practices. Our laws of intellectual property are rooted in the century-long reconceptualization of the creative process which culminated in high Romantic pronouncements like Wordsworth's to the effect that this process *ought* to be solitary, or individual, and introduce "a new element into the intellectual universe." Both Anglo-American "copyright" and Continental "authors' rights" achieved their modern form in this critical ferment, and today a piece of writing or other creative product may claim legal protection only insofar as it is determined to be a unique, original product of the intellection of a unique individual (or identifiable

---

[34] BOLTER, *supra* note 32, at 162.

[35] *Id.*

[36] Peter Beal, *Shall I Die?*, TIMES LITERARY SUPPLEMENT, Jan. 3, 1986, at 13. *See also* Max W. Thomas, *Reading and Writing the Renaissance Commonplace Book: A Question of Authorship?*, 10 CARDOZO ARTS & ENT. L.J. 651-57 (1992).

individuals).[37] In short, the law has yet to be affected by the "critique of authorship" initiated by Foucault and carried forward in the rich variety of post-structuralist research that has characterized literary studies during the last two decades. Indeed, from recent decisions like those examined in Peter Jaszi's contribution to this volume, it would seem that as creative production becomes more corporate, collective, and collaborative, the law invokes the Romantic author all the more insistently. There would thus seem to exist both considerable potential and a pressing need to reestablish communication between the two disciplines. This is the goal of the present volume.

---

[37] *See* Woodmansee, *supra* note 2, at 445; *see also* Mark Rose, *The Author as Proprietor: Donaldson v. Becket and the Genealogy of Modern Authorship*, 23 REPRESENTATIONS 51 (1988); Carla Hesse, *Enlightenment Epistemology and the Laws of Authorship in Revolutionary France, 1777-1793*, 30 REPRESENTATIONS 109 (1990); Peter Jaszi, *Toward a Theory of Copyright: The Metamorphoses of "Authorship,"* 1991 DUKE L.J. 455.

ON THE AUTHOR EFFECT: CONTEMPORARY COPYRIGHT AND COLLECTIVE CREATIVITY

PETER JASZI*

> Are there influences at work that will in time abate feelings of proprietorship and thus modify conceptions of copyright, especially those bearing on plagiarism? Probably so.
>
> Much intellectual work including the distinctively imaginative is now being done by teams, a practice apt to continue and grow. The French have a name for it—*travaux d'équipe*. Such collaboration, I fancy, may diffuse and diminish emotions of original discovery and exclusive ownership.
>
> —Benjamin Kaplan, *An Unhurried View of Copyright* [1]

As exemplified by the articles in this volume, recent scholarship on "authorship" reflects various influences. Among the most important are Michel Foucault's article, *What Is an Author?*,[2] and Benjamin Kaplan's book, *An Unhurried View of Copyright*. Since the late 1960s, these two texts have influenced work in literary and legal studies respectively. Only recently, however, have the lines of inquiry that Foucault and Kaplan helped to initiate begun to converge.

Foucault asked literary critics and historians to question the received modern idea of "authorship," and to reimagine its future by reunderstanding its past. For the first time, he located the emergence of the "author" in the cultural context of the eighteenth century, arguing that "[t]he coming into being of the notion of the 'author' constitutes a privileged moment of *individualization* in the history of ideas."[3] Moreover, he emphasized that the idea of "authorship" was neither natural nor inevitable, but represented only one possible means to the end of constraining the "proliferation of meaning."[4] In so doing, Foucault suggested

---

* Professor of Law, Washington College of Law, The American University. B.A., 1968, Havard College; J.D., 1971, Harvard Law School. This article is a small part of a larger collaborative project, and I gratefully acknowledge Martha Woodmansee's contribution to both.

[1] BENJAMIN KAPLAN, AN UNHURRIED VIEW OF COPYRIGHT 117 (1967).

[2] The essay first appeared in English a decade after its French publication in 1969. *See* Michel Foucault, *What Is an Author?*, in TEXTUAL STRATEGIES: PERSPECTIVES IN POST-STRUCTURALIST CRITICISM 141 (J. Harari ed., 1979).

[3] *Id.* at 141.

[4] *Id.* at 159.

(in general terms) the potential for research into how practices of writing and reading have been organized around the idea of the "author."[5]

Kaplan, for his part, expressed an invigorating skepticism about the inevitability of the legal rules that define copyright, pointing out the transformational changes to this field of law over its few centuries of history. He argued that, by demythologizing copyright doctrine, the legal community could make space for reasoned development of the law in a time of rapid technological change. Although he did not specifically anatomize the notion of the "author" around which copyright is organized, Kaplan noted certain corollaries of that notion. He called on lawyers to reconsider the trend in Anglo-American copyright toward ever-greater protection against unlicensed imitation,[6] the origins of which he located in the obsession with "originality" which marked Romantic literary criticism.

Over the past twenty five years, Kaplan's critique of basic copyright concepts has been influential in practical discussion of legal policy, while followers of Foucault have investigated the "construction of authorship" in the domain of literary culture. In retrospect, however, it is surprising how recently scholars have begun to attend to the ways in which the cultural figuration of the "author," as the inspired creator of unique works of art, has interacted with the legal notion of the "author" as the bearer of the portable rights in literary and artistic property.

In 1984, Martha Woodmansee began to construct the bridge to join literary and legal perspectives. She demonstrated how a new class of professional writers in eighteenth-century Germany, seeking to justify legal protection for their labors, "set about redefining the nature of writing," and thus helped to "give the

---

5

> Certainly it would be worth examining how the author became individualized in a culture like ours, what status he has been given, at what moment studies of authenticity and attribution began, in what kind of system of valorization the author was involved, at what point we began to recount the lives of authors rather than of heroes, and how this fundamental category of "the-man-and-his-work criticism" began.

Id. at 141.

6

> [I]f man has any "natural" rights, not the least must be a right to imitate his fellows, and thus to reap where he has not sown. Education, after all, proceeds from a kind of mimicry, and "progress," if it is not entirely an illusion, depends on generous indulgence of copying.

KAPLAN, *supra* note 1, at 2.

concept of authorship its modern form."[7] More recently, Mark Rose has explored the ways in which debates over the extent of rights in literary property in eighteenth-century England both fed and fed upon developments in literary theory. He has concluded that the reception of German Romanticism in England came only after "the ground had been prepared by the long debate over copyright," and that "the romantic elaboration of such notions as originality, organic form, and the work of art as the expression of the unique personality of the artist was in a sense the necessary completion of the legal and economic transformation that occurred during the copyright struggle."[8] And Carla Hesse has shown that in France, the idea of the individualistic "author" as the bearer of literary property rights was introduced as an instrument of monarchist repression—a "legal instrument for the regulation of knowledge"—and that the French revolutionaries later sought to "dethrone the absolute author . . . and recast him, not as a *private* individual (the absolute bourgeois), but rather as a *public* servant, as the model citizen."[9]

For my part, I have begun to trace some of the specific linkages between the ideology of "authorship" and the formation of particular doctrinal structures in the law of copyright.[10] In the quotation I chose to introduce this essay, Professor Kaplan looks forward to a reconfiguration of copyright to take fuller account of collaborative creative practices. In her contribution to this volume, Martha Woodmansee demonstrates that the Romantic notion of "author" handed down to us from the eighteenth century never has been particularly apt to the realities of the writing process.[11] In what follows, I have sought to demonstrate how the persistence of the notion of "authorship" in American copyright law makes it difficult for any new legal synthesis, which would focus on the reality of collective creativity, to emerge.

First, however, it may be useful to review how a particular

---

7 Martha Woodmansee, *The Genius and the Copyright: Economic and Legal Conditions of the Emergence of the 'Author'*, 17 EIGHTEENTH-CENTURY STUD. 425, 426 (1984).

8 Mark Rose, *The Author as Proprietor:* Donaldson v. Becket *and the Geneology of Modern Authorship*, 23 REPRESENTATIONS 51 (1988).

9 Carla Hesse, *Enlightenment Epistemology and the Law of Authorship in Revolutionary France, 1777-1793*, 30 REPRESENTATIONS 109 (1990).

10 *See* Peter Jaszi, *Toward a Theory of Copyright: The Metamorphoses of "Authorship,"* 1991 DUKE L.J. 455 [hereinafter *Metamorphoses*]. Other writers have expanded the discussion by analyzing the significance of the "authorship" concept in domains of law other than copyright. *See* James Boyle, *The Search for an Author: Shakespeare and the Framers*, 37 AM. U. L. REV. 625 (1988); James Boyle, *A Theory of Law and Information: Copyright, Spleens, Blackmail, and Insider Trading*, 80 CAL. L. REV. (forthcoming 1992).

11 *See generally* Martha Woodmansee, *On The Author Effect: Recovering Collectivity*, 10 CARDOZO ARTS & ENT. L.J. 279 (1992).

version of the idealogy of "authorship" informed English—and ultimately American—copyright doctrine. Unlike the events in late eighteenth-century Germany, the first introduction of the "author" into English law had not been the outcome of any philosophically-grounded argument for "authors' rights" as such. In fact, late seventeenth- and early eighteenth-century efforts to establish copyright reflected no concern whatsoever about the situation of working writers: The Statute of Anne of 1710 was the result of lobbying by and for established London-based publishers and booksellers seeking new legal weapons against down-market competition spawned by the proliferation of print technology. Even in its incomplete, pre-Romantic form, "authorship" had positive connotations as a designation for literary activity of special merit, and the booksellers co-opted the term to create a stable legal foundation for a market in texts as commodities.[12]

After its introduction into the law of copyright, even as it received new content from developments outside legal culture, "authorship" remained a malleable concept, generally deployed on behalf of publishers rather than writers.[13] Indeed, the interests most directly at stake in disputes over the content of copyright law usually are those of firms and individuals with capital

---

[12] In practice the rights thus created were unlikely to remain with the individual "author" for long. Long after the first copyright laws, writers generally continued to sell their rights, bundled with the manuscripts to which they pertained, to publishers for lump sum payments. See 1 VICTOR BONHAM-CARTER, AUTHORS BY PROFESSION 17-25 (1978). For the subsequent development of publishing practices and the market in commodity texts, see N.N. FELTES, MODES OF PRODUCTION OF VICTORIAN NOVELS (1986).

[13] Publishers' invocations of "authorship" as a rationale for the extension of their own effective monopolies did not always succeed: the idea of the "author" did not acquire its full cultural charge for some years after 1710, and (as Mark Rose has documented) in 1774 the London publishers lost their hard-waged battle to establish perpetual copyright as a kind of "natural right" of "authorship," though only barely. See Rose, supra note 8. A majority of the common law judges who advised the House of Lords in the case of Donaldson v. Becket, 2 Bro P.C. 129, 1 Eng. Rep. 637, 4 Burr. 2408, 98 Eng. Rep. 257 (1774) seem to have accepted the ahistorical proposition that there had been a perpetual common law copyright prior to the enactment of the Statute of Anne; however, a majority of the judges (and presumably of the law lords who took the final decision) appear to have believed that this common law right was superceded by that enactment. See GAVIN MCFARLANE, COPYRIGHT THROUGH THE CASES 15-16 (1986). For an alternate interpretation of the "holding" of Donaldson, see Howard B. Abrams, The Historic Foundation of American Copyright Law, 29 WAYNE L. REV. 1119, 1128-29 (1983). For additional discussion of the case and its implications, see Rose, supra note 8, at 51. In particular, Rose notes that as of the time of the debate over perpetual copyright, the "mystification of original poetic creation and the concept of the creative process as organic rather than mechanical . . . anticipated in [Edward] Young's Conjectures on Original Composition" enjoyed greater currency in Germany than in England. Id. at 75-76. Had the case been decided after the popularization of these ideas in England by Wordsworth, Coleridge and others, the outcome on the issue of perpetual copyright might well have been different.

investments in the means by which the productions of creative workers are distributed to consumers.[14] These distributors have reaped most of the benefits of copyright's cultivation of Romantic "authorship."

The story of "authorship's" instrumental role in the development of eighteenth-, nineteenth- and much of twentieth-century Anglo-American copyright doctrine has been told elsewhere.[15] It includes such notable episodes as a court's justification of copyright protection for commercial photography in the form of a studio portrait of Oscar Wilde. In that case, *Burrow-Giles Lithographic Co. v. Sarony*,[16] the Supreme Court concluded that such photographs should be viewed as "representatives of the original intellectual conceptions of the author."[17] Far more recently, lawyers and judges have invoked the vision of the Romantic "author-genius" in rationalizing the extension of copyright protection to computer software. The conceptual challenge to copyright posed by computer technology has been submerged in an insistence that programs are no less inspired than traditional literary works, and that the imaginative processes of the

---

[14] *See* CRAIG JOYCE ET AL., COPYRIGHT LAW § 1.05, at 19-20 (2d ed. 1991) [hereinafter COPYRIGHT LAW]. This is true despite the fact that doctrinal and policy conflicts in copyright law have come to be cast in terms of the notionally opposed interests of "authors" and "users," a binary approach to identifying the interests at stake typical of the Supreme Court's copyright jurisprudence. Justice Stewart, in Twentieth Century Music Corp. v. Aiken, 422 U.S. 151 (1975), put the matter this way:

> The immediate effect of our copyright law is to secure a fair return for an "author's" creative labor. But the ultimate aim is, by this incentive, to stimulate artistic creativity for the general public good.

Id. at 156.

[15] *See Metamorphoses, supra* note 10.

[16] 111 U.S. 53 (1884). In the first line of its opinion, the Supreme Court tellingly describes the defendant as "a photographer, with [a] large business in those lines in the city of New York." *Id.* In fact, that business entailed not only the taking of photographs, but the sale and distribution of copies to the public, and it was on this latter aspect of the business that the activities of the defendant company impinged.

[17] *Id.* at 58. Photography had perplexed nineteenth-century lawyers who saw the machine, rather than human agency, as the source of the photographic image. *See* BERNARD EDELMAN, OWNERSHIP OF THE IMAGE: ELEMENTS FOR A MARXIST THEORY OF LAW 43-47 (Elizabeth Kingdom trans., 1979). In *Burrow-Giles Lithographic Co. v. Sarony*, the court resolved the dilemma by stressing the analogies between photography and more traditional forms of creative enterprise. The court found that the image involved there was a

> useful, new, harmonious, characteristic, and graceful picture, and that said plaintiff made the same . . . entirely from his own original mental conception, to which he gave visible form by posing [the subject] in front of the camera, selecting and arranging the costume, draperies, and other various accessories in said photograph, arranging the subject so as to present graceful outlines, arranging and disposing the light and shade, suggesting and evoking the desired expression, and from such disposition, arrangement, or representation, made entirely by the plaintiff, he produced the picture in suit . . . .

Burrow-Giles, 111 U.S. at 54-55.

programmer are analogous to those of the literary "author."[18]

The so-called "work-for-hire" doctrine provides an even more dramatic example of the ways in which the ideology of "authorship" has been manipulated. This rule, which is most commonly part of the jurisprudence of countries which trace their laws of intellectual property back to Britain, awards ownership of a work produced within the scope of employment to the employer—as its "author-in law," so to speak. Although it is somewhat unusual in comparative law context,[19] this identification of employer as author is more than a crude, instrumental fiction—rather, it is a logical (if perverse) working out of the underlying assumption that the essence of "authorship" lies in original, inspired creative genius. Judicial opinions in these cases incorporate a characteristic move: If the essence of "authorship" is inspiration, then it is the "employer's" contribution as the "motivating factor" behind that work (in the words of one decision)[20] that matters, rather than the mere drudgery of the "employee."[21] The United States Supreme Court's most recent pronouncement on the subject makes the same point, although in different terms: In "work-for-hire" cases, the crucial inquiry is into "the hiring party's right to control the manner and means by which the product is accomplished."[22]

Over the history of Anglo-American copyright, Romantic "authorship" has served the interests of publishers and other distributors surprisingly well. Recently, however, it played a more unpredictable role in shaping legal doctrine, as is apparent from the recent upsurge in interest in "moral rights"—long a feature of continental legal culture with its unabashed adherence to the cause of "authors' rights,"[23] but a recent arrival on the scene in most common law countries.[24] As might be expected, publishers,

---

18 See Anthony Clapes et al., *Silicon Epics and Binary Bards: Determining the Proper Scope of Copyright Protection for Computer Programs*, 34 UCLA L. REV. 1493, 1510-45 (1987). The argument caters to firms that employ individuals to engage in this sort of "authorship." Ultimately, this appeal to notions of "authorial genius" may do more to obscure than to clarify the stakes in decisions about software protection. See Pamela Samuelson, *Creating a New Kind of Intellectual Property: Applying the Lessons of the Chip Law to Computer Programs*, 70 MINN. L. REV. 471 (1985).

19 SAM RICKETSON, THE BERNE CONVENTION FOR THE PROTECTION OF LITERARY AND ARTISTIC WORKS 1886-1986, at 158-59 (1987).

20 See Picture Music, Inc. v. Bourne, Inc., 457 F.2d 1213, 1214 (2d Cir.), *cert. denied*, 409 U.S. 997 (1972).

21 See *Metamorphoses, supra* note 10, at 485-91.

22 Community for Creative Non-Violence v. Reid, 490 U.S. 730, 751 (1989).

23 See Frederic Pollaud-Dulian, *Le Droit Moral en France, a Travers la Jurisprudence Recente*, [Moral Rights in France, Through Recent Case Law], 145 REVUE INTERNATIONALE DU DROIT D'AUTEUR 126, 126-32 (1990).

24 See, e.g., Copyright, Designs and Patents Act, 1988, ch. 48, §§ 77-89 (Eng.), re-

software manufacturers, and motion picture companies have been less than enthusiastic about new legal rules which would give "authors" the inalienable rights to insist on proper attribution of their works and to object when those works are modified or destroyed in connection with (or subsequent to) their commercial exploitation. But despite organized resistance from the latter-day counterparts of the eighteenth-century London booksellers, the idea of "moral rights" has gained a toe-hold even in the United States, though not yet with respect to literary works.[25] The development of "moral rights" is best understood in strictly ideological terms, and it should come as no surprise that legislators arguing in support of "moral rights" should unconsciously echo the rhetoric of William Wordsworth:[26]

> Artists in this country play a very important role in capturing the essence of culture and recording it for future generations. It is often through art that we are able to see truths, both beautiful and ugly.
>
> Therefore, I believe it is paramount to the integrity of our culture that we preserve the integrity of our artworks as expressions of the creativity of the artist.[27]

The instance of "moral rights" is but one example of how the Romantic conception of "authorship" is displaying a literally unprecedented measure of ideological autonomy in legal context.[28] Recent copyright decisions show that even as scholars in literary studies elaborate a far-reaching critique of the received

---

printed in 3 COPYRIGHT LAWS AND TREATIES OF THE WORLD (BNA) [hereinafter CLTW]; Copyright Act, R.S.C., ch. C42, §§ 12.1-.2 and 18.1-.2 (1985) (Can.), *reprinted in* 1 CLTW, *supra* (Canadian provisions adopted in 1988). "Moral rights" reasoning probably failed to penetrate the common law countries earlier because of the existence of a counter-motif, in tension with that of "authors' rights." The common law countries rationalized copyright to be a limited monopoly designed to serve the public interest by promoting investment in the creation and distribution of works of the imagination. This "incentive" theory—probably the most commonly articulated public policy underlying copyright—draws into question any proposal that would enhance protection at the public users' expense, including the restrictions on re-use of copyright works implied in any "moral rights" scheme. For the various rationales underlying copyright legislation, see COPYRIGHT LAW, *supra* note 14, at 14-21.

[25] Visual Artists Rights Act of 1990 § 603(a)(codified at 17 U.S.C.A. § 106A (West Supp. 1992)). For a discussion of this legislation, see COPYRIGHT LAW, *supra* note 14, at 621-27.

[26] *See* Woodmansee, *supra* note 7, at 280.

[27] 135 CONG. REC. E2227 (daily ed. June 20, 1989) (statement of Rep. Markey), *quoted in* Visual Artists Rights Act of 1990, H.R. 514, 101st Cong., 2d Sess. 1, 6 (1990).

[28] We can expect more jurisprudential developments to reflect uncritical faith in the concept of "authorship" in years and decades to come; the 1988 adherence of the United States to the Berne Convention inevitably will produce further assimilation of U.S. copyright culture to that of the Berne Union. *See* Peter Jaszi, *A Garland of Reflections on Three International Copyright Topics*, 8 CARDOZO ARTS & ENT. L.J. 47, 58 (1989).

Romantic concept of "authorship," American lawyers are reaching out to embrace the full range of its implications.

The latest copyright decision of the United States Supreme Court, *Feist Publications, Inc. v. Rural Telephone Service*,[29] decided in March 1991, is a striking manifestation of this ideological entrenchment. The numbingly mundane facts of the underlying dispute serve to display the legal issues in higher relief: Feist, a firm that specialized in publishing regional telephone directories, was refused a license to use Rural Telephone Service's "white pages" directory, which covered a small part of the larger geographic area to be encompassed in Feist's projected directory. Feist went ahead and copied Rural's alphabetically-organized listings and Rural sued for copyright infringement. The case raised questions about how much copyright protection a telephone book should receive—or whether it should receive any protection at all. Before the Supreme Court weighed in, most lawyers assumed that some degree of copyright protection was available to safeguard capital investments in comprehensive, predictably-organized compilations of uncopyrightable data, such as phonebooks, price lists, and legal databases. Courts and commentators had reasoned that the "skill and effort" or "sweat of the brow" that went into preparing such compilations was enough in the way of "authorship" to justify protection.[30] To the consternation of many, the Supreme Court held otherwise by a unanimous vote,[31] reasoning that, to pass the constitutional threshold, copyrightable works must possess "some minimal degree of *creativity*," and that, in producing its local telephone directory, Rural Telephone Service had "expended sufficient effort to make the white pages directory useful, but insufficient *creativity* to make it *original*."[32] Reaching back into the Court's store of

---

[29] 111 S. Ct. 1282 (1991).

[30] Before *Feist Publications, Inc. v. Rural Telephone Service*, the leading cases on the subject were Leon v. Pacific Tel. & Tel. Co., 91 F.2d 484 (9th Cir. 1937), and Jeweler's Circular Publishing Co. v. Keystone Publishing Co., 281 F. 83 (2d Cir.) (L. Hand, J.), *cert. denied*, 259 U.S. 581 (1922). These cases endorsed copyright protection based on capital investment in compiling "facts." In *Feist*, Justice O'Connor asserted that these earlier courts "misunderstood" the copyright statute. *See Feist*, 111 S. Ct. at 1291. Prior to *Feist*, copyright scholars were divided on the issue. *Compare* Robert C. Denicola, *Copyright in Collections of Facts: A Theory for the Protection of Non-fiction Literary Works*, 81 COLUM. L. REV. 516 (1981) *with* William Patry, *Copyright in Compilations of Facts (or Why the "White Pages" Are Not Copyrightable)*, 12 COMM. & THE LAW 37 (1990). For an extremely sophisticated discussion, ultimately favoring "sweat of the brow" protection, see Jane C. Ginsburg, *Creation and Commercial Value: Copyright Protection of Works of Information*," 90 COLUM. L. REV. 1865 (1990).

[31] Only Justice Blackmun declined to join in Justice O'Connor's opinion, concurring in the judgment without a stated rationale.

[32] *Feist*, 111 S. Ct. at 1296 (emphasis added).

historical precedents, Justice O'Connor recalled the language of *The Trade-Mark Cases* of 1879: Copyright should extend only to works that "are *original*, and are founded in the creative powers of the mind. The writings which are to be protected are *the fruits of intellectual labor*, embodied in the form of books, prints, engravings, and the like."[33]

The *Feist* decision raises more questions than it answers; it will take time to determine exactly what kind of intellectual steel will suffice to strike "the minimal creative spark required by the Copyright Act and the Constitution."[34] The likely answers, in turn, may depend on the values and beliefs underlying the Court's decision. Unlike many important copyright decisions, *Feist* cannot be explained as a more or less transparent concession to the interests of publishers and other distributors. Indeed, the decision runs directly counter to those interests, leaving valuable and vulnerable "information products" which represent considerable capital investments without clear protection against misappropriation.

As a matter of information policy, the Court may have been right to cut back on available grounds of legal protection for compilations of data;[35] perhaps the social benefits of making information more generally available outweigh the private costs of denying it protection. There is no indication, however, that members of the Court gave this rationale any consideration, let alone embraced it. So far as Justice O'Connor's opinion reveals, the Court was moved solely by its adherence to a vision of originality "distilled [in earlier opinions] from the Constitution's use of the word 'authors' "; an "author" being defined "to mean 'he to whom anything owes its origin; originator; maker.' "[36] The obvious criticism of *Feist*—that it embodies a barren jurispru-

---

[33] 100 U.S. 82, 94 (1879).

[34] *Feist*, 111 S. Ct. at 1297. Early articles discussing the implications of *Feist* include Michael Schwartz, *Copyright in Compilations of Facts: Feist Publications, Inc. v. Rural Telephone Service*, 13 EUR. INTELL. PROP. REV. 178 (1991); Michael R. Klipper & Meredith S. Senter, Jr., *The Facts After Feist: The Supreme Court Addressses the Issue of the Copyrightability of Factual Compilations*, in FACT AND DATA PROTECTION AFTER *Feist* 343 (Jon A. Baumgarten ed., 1991); and David Goldberg & Robert J. Bernstein, *The Fallout from "Feist": (Copyrightability of Telephone Listings)*, 206 N.Y. L.J. 3 (1991).

[35] *See* L. Ray Patterson & Craig Joyce, *Monopolizing the Law: The Scope of Copyright Protection for Law Reports and Statutory Compilations*, 36 UCLA L. REV. 719 (1989). Other recent Supreme Court intellectual property decisions have reflected concern over the potential of legal protection to restrict vigorous competition. *See, e.g.*, Bonito Boats, Inc. v. Thunder Craft Boats, Inc., 489 U.S. 141 (1989).

[36] *Feist*, 111 S. Ct. at 1288, (citing Burrow-Giles Lithographic Co. v. Sarony, 111 U.S. 53, 58 (1884)). The constitutional reference is to article I, Section 8, clause 8—authorizing congressional intellectual property legislation.

dence of rule formalism—is ultimately inapposite. In fact, the opinion wears its values on its sleeve; from first to last, its rhetoric proceeds from unreconstructed faith in the gospel of Romantic "authorship."

That Romantic "authorship" is alive and well in late twentieth-century American legal culture has consequences for the law's engagement with (or failure to engage) the realities of contemporary polyvocal writing practice—which increasingly is collective, corporate, and collaborative. In practice, the law often proves ungenerous to non-individualistic cultural productions, like "folkloric" works, which cannot be reimagined as products of solitary, originary "authorship" on the part of one or more discrete and identifiable "authors."[37] By the same token, the extension of copyright protection to new categories of works may entail reimagining them so as to suppress complicating details about their modes of production.[38] At base, however, the law is not so much systematically hostile to works that do not fit the individualistic model of Romantic "authorship" as it is uncomprehending of them. Such works are marginalized or become literally invisible within the prevailing ideological framework of discourse in copyright—even to the point of literal invisibility.

Feist, once again, provides an example of this process of marginalization. The Court's discussion of copyright in telephone directories takes off from what is, from the perspective of copyright doctrine, a non-controversial premise: "Facts" are natural and uncreated; they are not protectable in themselves:

> Census-takers, for example, do not "create" the population figures that emerge from their efforts; in a sense, they copy these figures from the world around them. Census data therefore do not trigger copyright because these data are not "original" in the constitutional sense. The same is true of all facts—scientific, historical, biographical, and news of the

---

[37] "Folkloric works," for example, are corporate productions which have no identifiable author(s), and their continual re-production through transmission within a cultural group makes it difficult to locate the moment at which any hypothesized individual can have made an "original," "authorial" contribution. See Marie Niedzielska, *The Intellectual Property Aspects of Folklore Protection*, 1980 COPYRIGHT 339.

[38] Thus, the extension of copyright to photographs both glorifies the camera operator as an "artist-genius" and suppresses the claims of the photographic subject to merely a part in the production of the image. See *Metamorphoses, supra* note 10, at 480-81 n.97. Jane Gaines recently has identified the ways in which the courts minimized or suppressed the "authorship" claims of photographic subjects—including those of Oscar Wilde in the *Burrow-Giles Lithographic Co. v. Sarony* decision. See JANE GAINES, CONTESTED CULTURE: THE IMAGE, THE VOICE, AND THE LAW 74-83 (1991). For a discussion of *Burrow-Giles*, see *supra* notes 16-17 and accompanying text.

day.[39]

Thus, any "authorship" in the "white pages" must be sought in the acts of collecting and (especially) presenting the unprotected data which make up the individual directory entries in which individuals' given (or self-elected) names are associated with their chosen addresses and assigned telephone numbers.

From another perspective the distinction between uncreated "facts" and created "works" is purely fictitious. As Stanley Fish has pointed out, no so-called "fact" is interpretation-free—ultimately facts are products rather than predicates of interpretation.[40] To revert to the Court's example in *Feist*, the preordained categories of the census form define the "data" to be reported, not the reverse. If we seek non-circular justifications for the law's refusal to extend protection to such information collections, we must look beyond the naive distinction between the pre-existent and the "original."

Thus, the real problem with the "facts" involved in *Feist* is not that they fail to reflect human agency, but that they have—in fact—an embarrassment of very human sources. A telephone directory listing sums up a complex amalgam of choices, to which the subject of a given entry, as well as her parents, friends, teachers, and others—such as various real estate developers and government employees—have made contributions over time. And to complicate matters further, all these have interacted in complex, webbed relational patterns in making their contributions.

There may be sufficient reasons why such data should be placed firmly and irrevocably in the "public domain." Indeed, the very multiplicity and interdependency of their "authors" may explain why we should treat name/address listings as common property.[41] But rather than engaging in a critical assessment of the utility or disutility of copyright protection for "facts," the

---

[39] *Feist*, 111 S. Ct. at 1288-89 (citations omitted).

[40] STANLEY FISH, DOING WHAT COMES NATURALLY: CHANGE, RHETORIC AND THE PRACTICE OF THEORY IN LITERARY AND LEGAL STUDIES 61 (1989). In the context of copyright, Jane Ginsburg has charcterized—and criticized—the argument that "facts and theories" simply "are" as "the Platonic fact precept":

> If an historical "truth" in the Platonic sense exists, it can never be discovered, because the same diversity of understanding, approach, and predilection which makes every personality unique precludes a unity of historical interpretation.

Jane C. Ginsburg, *Sabotaging and Reconstructing History: A Comment on the Scope of Copyright Protection in Works of History after* Hoeling v. Universal City Studios, 29 BULL. COPYRIGHT SOC'Y OF THE U.S.A. 647, 658 (1982).

[41] For the values associated with common rights in the real property context, and their gradual extinction through the rise of a strictly proprietary model of property law, see E.P. THOMPSON, CUSTOMS IN COMMON 97-184 (1991).

Court in *Feist*, like other courts in prior cases, put its wholly un-critical faith in one vision of the creative process—the Romantic ideal of "authorship."

In other doctrinal settings, faith in solitary, originary Romanic "authorship" blinds decision-makers to the advantages of non-conforming cultural production. Copyright law, with its emphasis on rewarding and safeguarding "originality," has lost sight of the cultural value of what might be called "serial collabo-rations"—works resulting from successive elaborations of an idea or text by a series of creative workers, occurring perhaps over years or decades. Before copyright law's acceptance of Romantic "authorship" was complete, for example, copyright actually en-couraged the creation of popular adaptations of preexisting works, on the ground that "[a]n abridgment preserving 'the whole' of a work 'in its sense' is 'an act of understanding,' 'in the nature of a new and meritorious work.' "[42] But where the law formerly envisioned the possibility of improving existing works by redaction or expansion, modern copyright is more myopic, fo-cussing exclusively on the potential for harm to the interests of the original "author." Today, the privilege of producing "deriv-ative works" that re-work or incorporate protected pre-existing texts generally is reserved to those who have obtained copyright permission.[43]

Among the array of doctrines that make up contemporary copyright law, however, there remain several which can be deployed to legitimate unauthorized borrowings from protected works by subsequent "authors." One of these teaches that in or-der to constitute an infringement of copyright, a new work must be "substantially similar" to that from which its "author" copied; where the material copied is itself in the public domain, or is too insignificant in quantity, or is altered beyond recognition, there can be no liability. In practice, the crucial question is how the courts will interpret "substantial similarity." Here, recent case law had tended toward what may be called "totality" analysis, which has had the effect of further restricting re-use of existing textual materials.[44]

---

[42] KAPLAN, *supra* note 1, at 12 (quoting Newberry's Case, Lofft 775, 98 Eng. Rep. 913 (Ch. 1773)). *See also Metamorphoses, supra* note 10, at 472.

[43] *See, e.g.*, 17 U.S.C. § 106(2) (1988). Even where a "derivative work" has been pro-duced with the permission of the owner of a copyrighted underlying work, contempo-rary copyright law favors the owner of the underlying work. *See Metamorphoses, supra* note 10, at 492-96 (discussing reversionary rights and the Supreme Court decision in Stewart v. Abend, 495 U.S. 207 (1990)).

[44] "Totality" analysis began in earnest with Sid & Marty Krofft Tel. v. McDonald's

"Totality" analysis is yet another doctrinal reflection of the ideology of Romantic "authorship." In this interpretation of copyright doctrine, "authors'" rights in their "works" extend not only to the content of their own devising, but also to what they have themselves borrowed from the intellectual "commons"—presumably because they subsequently have impressed their artistic personalities on these borrowed materials. This vision marginalizes yet other "authors," who arrive still later on the scene, and denies that they might have an equally important role to play in the continuing process of cultural transmission by which texts are reformulated and elaborated. In effect, "totality" analysis converts copyright into a textual Homestead Act.

A recent example of this tendency in copyright is provided by the recent trial and appellate court decisions in *Rogers v. Koons.*[45] The plaintiff, Art Rogers, had photographed a couple holding a litter of German Shepherd puppies. That black-and-white image had first appeared in Rogers's newspaper photography column. It was undisputed that the defendant, Jeff Koons, had employed the image as the basis for a large three-dimensional wood sculpture with a non-naturalistic color scheme. Indeed, Koons argued that his choice of that image was self-conscious: The theme of the exhibition in which the sculpture was displayed (the "Banality Show") necessarily entailed the re-use of images already in cultural circulation.

The district court granted summary judgment for the plaintiff on the issue of the defendant's liability for copyright infringement, and thereafter this ruling was upheld by the Second Circuit Court of Appeals. In each instance, the court's opinion reflects its writer's faith in the ideology of Romantic "authorship." Indeed, the outcome of Judge Cardamone's opinion on appeal could hardly be in doubt after the opening paragraph:

The key to this copyright infringement suit, brought by a

Corp., 562 F.2d 1157 (9th Cir. 1977), which proved (for better or worse) to be the most influential copyright infringement decision of recent times. The court's copyright infringement analysis was summarized in a phrase: "[The defendants'] have captured the 'total concept and feel' of the [plaintiffs'] show." *Id.* at 1167. Traditional copyright limitations, such as the rule that protection attaches only to "expressions" and not to "ideas," are inherently at odds with "totality" analysis; nonetheless, it has enjoyed considerable favor in the courts. For the subsequent rise of this approach to assessing "substantial similarity," as well as some indications that its validity is now being called into question, see COPYRIGHT LAW, *supra* note 14, at 687-91 and *Metamorphoses, supra* note 10, at 491 n.138.

45 751 F. Supp. 474 (S.D.N.Y. 1990), *modified,* 777 F. Supp. 1 (S.D.N.Y. 1991), *and aff'd,* 960 F.2d 301 (2d Cir. 1992). The Second Circuit affirmed summary judgment in favor of the plaintiff on the issue of liability.

plaintiff photographer against a defendant sculptor and the gallery representing him, is defendants' borrowing of plaintiff's expression of a typical American scene—a smiling husband and wife holding a litter of charming puppies. The copying was so deliberate as to suggest that defendants resolved so long as they were significant players in the art business, and the copies they produced bettered the price of the copied work by a thousand to one, their piracy of a less well-known artist's work would escape being sullied by an accusation of plagiarism.[46]

In this telling summary account, the conflict posed is not between the competing claims of two cultural workers, pursuing different objectives in different media, but between a pure "artist," on the one hand, and corrupt "players in the art business," on the other.[47]

---

[46] *Koons*, 960 F.2d at 303.

[47] Later in the opinion, in introducing basic concepts of copyright, Judge Cardamone notes that James Madison had supported a constitutional grant of congressional power to enact copyright laws on the basis that authors had enjoyed such a right at common law, citing to *The Federalist* and to Blackstone's *Commentaries on the Laws of England*. *See id.* at 306. In fact, the question of what rights British authors enjoyed before the enactment of the Statute of Anne is not free from doubt, and the content and context of the cited passage from Blackstone is revealing. In the *Commentaries on the Laws of England*, Blackstone argues not that English common law *did* recognize the common law rights of individual "authors" but that it *should* (or should have) done so, because copyright should be regarded as a species of natural rights based (like property in land) on "occupancy":

> When a man by the exertion of his rational powers has produced an original work, he has clearly a right to dispose of that identical work as he pleases, and any attempt to take it from him, or vary the disposition he has made of it, is an invasion of his right of property. Now the identity of a literary composition consists intirely in the *sentiment* and the *language*; the same conceptions, cloathed in the same words, must necessarily be the same composition: and whatever method be taken of conveying that composition to the ear or the eye of another, by recital, by writing, or by printing, it is always the identical work of the author which is so conveyed.

2 COMMENTARIES ON THE LAWS OF ENGLAND 405-06 (Photo reprint 1979) (1766). *See* the discussion of Blackstone in Rose, *supra* note 8, at 63-64. Blackstone was a near-contemporary of Edward Young, Woodmansee, *supra* note 7, at 280, and his vision of the source of authorial entitlements is bound up with the Romantic ideology of "authorship" of which Young was an early exponent.

The district court opinion in *Koons* also displayed an affinity for the vision of copyright as a natural or inherent right. In his introduction to copyright concepts, Judge Haight quoted at some length from a 1924 decision of the Second Circuit Court of Appeals, King Features Syndicate v. Fleischer, 299 F. 533 (2d Cir. 1924). *King Features* involved a three-dimensional reproduction of a two-dimensional work of graphic art in the context of commercial, (rather than fine) art—the imitation of a cartoon character in the design of a mass-produced children's toy. The appellate panel concluded that "[d]oing this is omitting the work of the artisan, but appropriating the genius of the artist," *id.* at 535, and had expressed the view that:

> A piece of statuary may be infringed by the picture of the statuary for the Copyright Act *secured to the author* the *original and natural rights*, and it is the intendment of the law of copyrights that they shall have a liberal construction in order to give effect to what may be considered as an *inherent right of the author* in his work.

The invidious comparison is reinforced in succeeding paragraphs that further characterize the parties: Rogers is presented as a generally acclaimed "artist-photographer,"[48] widely published and exhibited, whose photograph "Puppies" had come to the defendant's attention as the result of a notecard issued by a firm specializing in "high quality reproductions of photographs by well-respected American photographers including, for example, Ansel Adams."[49] Koons, although finally conceded the designation of "artist," is portrayed as a controversial figure, whose claims to artistry are tainted by acquisitiveness. Although the information may be legally irrelevant, strictly speaking, Judge Cardamone notes that "[w]hile pursuing his career as an artist, he also worked until 1984 as a mutual funds salesman, a registered commodities salesman and broker, and a commodities futures broker," and concludes the description by quoting a newspaper critic's assessment that "Koons is pushing the relationship between art and money so far that everyone involved comes out looking slightly absurd."[50] Clearly enough,

---

Id. at 536 (emphasis added). That Judge Haight, writing almost sixty years after the *King Feeatures* case, chose to ground his analysis in the quoted language is representative of copyright law's general devaluation of later-created "derivative" works in the ideology of Romantic "authorship."

[48] *Koons,* 960 F.2d at 303.

[49] *Id.* at 304.

[50] *Id.* The comment (attributed only to an unamed "New York Times Critic"), which concludes the introductory section of Judge Cardamone's opinion headed "Koons," can be found in Michael Brenson, *Greed Plus Glitz, With a Dollup of Innocence,* N.Y. TIMES, Dec. 18, 1988, § 2, at 41. The article, which, like the opinion, emphasizes Koons's background in financial markets, is generally critical of the ·sculptor and his productions, characterizing Koons as "wanting more money than any artist his age has ever made from art" and his works as "[f]antasies of American youth and adolescence [which] are embalmed, frozen into glamorous and deathless products." *Id.* at 44. Other passages help to illuminate Judge Cardamone's skepticism about artistic Koons:

> His art is largely strategic. Images have been appropriated from photographs of popular culture and then collaged together into spanking new commodities. *They were made collectively, even anonymously, by workshops in northern Italy. What seems to matter is not the originality of the artist, but rather images that belong to an entire culture and that everyone in that culture can use.*

Id. (emphasis added).

Koons certainly does not fit the stereotype of a Romantic "author," as the following comparison with another artistic rebel makes clear:

> In medium, method and response to the past, however, the Koons and the Manet could not be further apart. While Manet painted his work, Koons supervised the production of his statue. While Manet was making art that he hoped would speak on equal terms with Titian and Goya, Koons makes art that he hopes can speak on equal terms with Michael Jackson.

Id.

Judge Cardamone does not refer to the final paragraph of the article, which grants Koons the epithets "smart and inventive," and indicates that his work "helps define some of the deeper tensions within the contemporary art world." *Id.*

A subsequent journalistic treatment of Koons and his works, argues that the controversy surrounding the sculptor stems (at least in part) from the challenge he poses to the

Koons's worldliness in money matters does not weigh in his favor.

Nor does his way of working. Before comparing the two works at issue in the case, Judge Cardamone's appellate opinion emphasizes the differences between the working methods of the individuals who created them. Rogers is a complete artist, whose personal life and art are fully integrated: "[He] has a studio and home at Point Reyes, California, where he makes his living by creating, exhibiting, publishing and otherwise making use of his rights in his photographic works."[51] By contrast, Koons's production is characterized by extreme division of labor. Not only is he "represented" by sales galleries in various parts of the world, but he does not personally execute the projects he conceives for ultimate sale: In preparation for the Banality Show, "[c]ertain European studios were chosen to execute his porcelain works, other studios chosen for the mirror pieces, and the small Demetz Studio, located in the northern hill country town of Ortessi, Italy, was selected to carve the wood sculptures."[52]

Finally, in the treatment of the issue of "substantial similarity," judicial attitudes toward the competing visions of creativity represented by Rogers and Koons are brought to bear on the issue of liability.[53] The courts may well have been right to reject

---

vision of artistic purity, which is closely associated with the ideology of Romantic "authorship":

> But to many of the artists who toy with advertising, Jeff Koons among them, "selling out" is a virtue, a backhanded way of stirring artistic rebellion. It is a post-Pop, post-punk pose that defies the traditional notion of what artists and art should be—poor and unknown. Peddling an image of themselves in the the manner of a movie star not only promises to make artists famous; it also allows them to thumb their noses at the assumption that art is somehow above the marketplace.

Paul Taylor, *The Art of P.R., and Vice Versa,* N.Y. TIMES, Oct. 27, 1991, § 2, at 1, 35.

[51] *Koons,* 960 F.2d at 303.

[52] *Id.* at 304-05. Koons's working relationship with the Demetz Studio was independently relevant to the analysis of the liability issue, and Judge Cardamone's opinion emphasizes how Koons directed "his artisans" by specifying that various details of the sculpture were to be "like [the] photo" or "as per photo." *Id.* at 305. At the same time, however, the implicit contrast drawn between Koons's and Rogers's methods helps to show the judge's biases, as does the passage in Judge Haight's district court opinion, which emphasizes that "[q]uestions of size and color aside, the sculpture is as exact a copy of the photograph as [Koons's] hired artisans could fashion, which is precisely what [he] told them to do." *Koons,* 751 F. Supp. at 478.

In Romantic theory the "true" artist was one who had escaped the division of labor that characterized modern life generally, and who united "head and heart, shrewdness and ingenuity, reason and imagination in a harmonious alliance," thus restoring the *"whole person"* in us. FRIEDRICH SCHILLER, ON BÜRGER'S POEMS (1791), *quoted in* MARTHA WOODMANSEE, THE AUTHOR, ART, AND THE MARKET: REREADING THE HISTORY OF AESTHETICS, 72 (1993).

[53] *Rogers v. Koons* also involved a "fair use" issue, and the characterization of Koons's artistic activities as "commercial" figured significantly there: "[W]e note that Koons'[s]

the main lines of the sculptor's defense: that, in assimilating the image of the photograph, Koons had taken no more than unprotected factual information concerning the existence and appearance of the photographic subjects;[54] and that, at the same time, he had altered and embellished the image (by, among other things, inserting flowers in the hair of the human figures and providing the puppies with grotesque bulbous noses). After all, the arrangement of the furniture and figures *was* reproduced in the sculpture from the photograph. If it represented Rogers's copyrightable "authorship," then a legally significant taking of protected material probably *did* occur. For the purposes of the present discussion, however, the correctness of the outcome is less significant than the technique of decision.

Certainly, Judge Cardamone's opinion eschews naive "totality" analysis, acknowledging that "ideas, concepts, and the like found in the common domain are the inheritance of everyone," so that "in looking at these two works of art to determine whether they are substantially similar, focus must be on the similarity of the *expression* of an idea or fact, not on the similarity of the facts, ideas, or concepts themselves."[55] Despite its apparent sophistication,[56] however, Judge Cardamone's approach to sub-

---

substantial profit from his intentionally exploitive use of Rogers's work also militates against a finding of fair use . . . ." *Koons*, 960 F.2d at 309.

[54] In the district court opinion, Judge Haight stated that "Koons does not articulate what non-protectible factual expression he regards himself as having used," 751 F. Supp. at 477, perhaps because the sculptor also relied on the seemingly unpromising (and ultimately ill-fated) argument that "Rogers' copyright protection 'is strictly limited to the work *as a photograph.*' " *Id.* (quoting trial brief submitted by Koons). Koons could have argued, however, that Rogers did not "create" or "originate" the physical appearance of the photographic subjects, and that he had not borrowed elements of the photograph for which Rogers was responsible: the lighting scheme employed when the photograph was taken, for example, or the balance of tones achieved when it was processed.

[55] *Koons*, 960 F.2d at 308. It is less clear whether Judge Haight in the district court appreciated the importance of discounting copying of mere unprotected ideas in the course of substantial similarity analysis.

[56] In most respects, Judge Cardamone's opinion merely expands upon the analysis of the district court, as reflected in the following passage:

[T]he present test of substantial similarity in the Second Circuit is "whether an average lay observer would recognize the alleged copy as having been appropriated from the copyrighted work."

There is no question in the case at bar that "an average lay observer" would recognize the sculpture "String of Puppies" as "having been appropriated from" the photograph "Puppies." Questions of size and color aside, the sculpture is as exact a copy of the photograph as [the sculptor's] hired artisans could fashion, which is precisely what [he] told them to do. Indeed, [the puppies's owner's] friend, having observed a newspaper picture of the sculpture, assumed that it was [the original] photograph, having been "colorized."

Koons, 751 F. Supp. at 478 (citing and quoting Ideal Toy Corp. v. Fab-Lu Ltd., 360 F.2d 1021, 1022 (2d Cir. 1966)).

This passage incorporates the ideology of "authorship" and the cult of "originality"

stantial similarity analysis still reflects the tendency to lump together the clearly protected, arguably protected, and certainly even unprotected elements of a copyrighted work in comparing it to another, allegedly infringing work. In characterizing the protected elements of the photograph, Judge Cardamone notes that it is the "expression" that Rogers "caught in the placement, in the particular light, and in the expressions of the subjects—that gives the photograph its charming and unique character, that is to say, makes it original and copyrightable."[57] In the following paragraph, Judge Cardamone asserts that Koons overstepped the line when he used "the identical expression of the idea that Rogers created; the composition, the poses, and the expressions . . . ."[58]

It is instructive to set these two lists of elements—protected and copied—side by side. Notably, Judge Cardamone does not rely on the difficult notion that the "particular light" of the photograph somehow was reproduced in the sculpture. But, while this protected element drops out of the comparison, the element of "placement" is subdivided into "composition" and "poses" in the itemization of Koons's borrowings—although the distinction

---

in a number of reinforcing ways. For one, the totalizing tendencies of the quoted "standard," with its emphasis on "recognition" of "appropriation," necessarily privilege prior works over subsequent ones. The same language, which is drawn from Ideal Toy Corp. v. Fab-Lu Ltd., 360 F.2d 1021, 1022 (2d Cir. 1966), is identified by Judge Cardamone as a source of precedential guidance on the substantial similarity issue. 960 F.2d at 307. Judge Haight dismisses in passing the claimed differences (matters of "size and color") between the two works, implicitly applying Judge Learned Hand's famous observation that "no plagiarist can excuse the wrong by showing how much of his work he did not pirate." Sheldon v. Metro-Goldwyn Pictures Corp., 81 F.2d 49, 56 (2d Cir.), *cert. denied*, 298 U.S. 669 (1936). This *dictum* uncovers the preconception that the truly "original" is superior to the merely "derivative," which has its source in the ideology of "authorship." Notably, it is cited explicitly by Judge Cardamone. 960 F.2d at 308. (In other contexts, it should be noted, Hand's superficially attractive principle has proved difficult to uphold consistently. In Warner Bros. v. American Broadcasting Cos., 720 F.2d 231 (2d Cir. 1983), for example, Judge Jon Newman reconsiders the validity of the Hand *dictum* and concludes that differences may matter more where substantial similarity determinations involving "graphic or three-dimensional" works are involved. *Id.* at 241.)

As already noted, *see supra* note 52, Judge Haight makes much of the point that the sculpture was not executed by the sculptor who affixed his signature to it, but by mere "hired artisans"—thus marginalizing the sculptor's contribution and undercutting the claims of his work to independent legitimacy as a product of "authorship." In this, too, Judge Cardamone's opinion follows.

One important move in the passage just quoted from the district court opinion, however, is not reproduced in that of the court of appeals. Judge Haight trivializes the inquiry into substantial similarity by invoking the subjectivity of an individual (the "friend") who is in no sense representative of any real or hypothetical audience group. The absence of any equivalent passage in Judge Cardamone's opinion is a mark of its greater sophistication, but not necessarily of any basic difference in its orientation.

[57] *Koons*, 960 F.2d at 308.
[58] *Id.* at 308.

between the two is not specified. Finally, both lists refer to the "expressions" of the subjects, but nowhere is it indicated to what extent or in what way these reflected Rogers's agency, rather than that of the subjects themselves.[59] In effect, the case for substantial similarity is strengthened by a systematic inflation of the claims of "authorship." If this is not "totality" analysis in its pure form, it is the next best thing.

On the particular facts, Judge Cardamone may well have been correct to conclude that "no reasonable jury could have differed on the issue of substantial similarity."[60] Nevertheless, his opinion effectively embraces an approach to substantial similarity analysis that is structurally biased in favor of the claims of the "author" whose work has temporal priority—a standard that cannot account fully for the possibility that "recognizable" borrowings incorporated from preexisting works into new ones may be of elements that are in the public domain.

The Romantic vision of "authorship," in which this approach to "substantial similarity" analysis is rooted, informs other critical passages of the court of appeals opinion in *Rogers v. Koons*. Thus, Judge Cardamone finds a fatal flaw in Koons' defense that the sculpture was a satire or parody qualifying as a privileged "fair use": The "fair use" doctrine applies only when the copied work itself is, "at least in part, an object of the parody . . . ."[61] This limitation, he insists, is needed if we are to ensure "public awareness of the original work" in cases of "fair use" parody:

> By requiring that the copied work be an object of the parody, we merely insist that the audience be aware that underlying the parody there is an original and separate expression, attributable to a different artist.[62]

In this reasoning, parody can qualify as "fair use" only so long as it acknowledges its subordinate position in the hierarchy of works, and, by extension, the subordinate position of its creator

---

59 For the general tendency of copyright law to efface the role of the photographic subject in the production of images incorporating his or her likeness, see *supra* note 16.

60 *Koons*, 960 F.2d at 308.

61 *Id.* at 310 (citing MCA, Inc. v. Wilson, 677 F.2d 180, 185 (2d Cir. 1981)).

62 *Id.* The passage continues: "This awareness may come from the fact that the copied work is publicly known or because its existence is in some manner acknowledged by the parodist in connection with the parody." *Id.* at 310. Of course, it is not self-evident that had Koons acknowledged Rogers in connection with his sculpture, the outcome would have been different. Finally, Judge Cardamone's views on "fair use" are shaped in large part by his perception that the defendant's "commercial" exploitation of Rogers' photograph was a use of a kind which could prejudice the potential market for that work if it became "widespread."

in the hierarchy of "authors." This limit is required, Judge Cardamone indicates, because "otherwise there would be no real limitation on the copier's use of another's copyrighted work to make a statement about some aspect of society at large."[63] Like other features of the doctrine applied in *Rogers v. Koons,* this one operates to discourage artists whose methods entail reworking preexisting materials, while rewarding those whose dedication to "originality" qualfies them as true "authors" in the Romantic sense.

The outcome in *Rogers v. Koons* notwithstanding, an otherwise actionable appropriation of material from a preexisting work may be excused on the ground that it represents a privileged "fair use" rather than (as is usually the case) an "unfair" one. One persuasive ground on which a defense of "fair use" may be premised is a claim that the defendant not only took protected material, but somehow transformed it in the taking. Thus, in her recent decision in *Basic Books, Inc. v. Kinko's Graphics Corp.,*[64] District Judge Constance Baker Motley wrote:

> [T]he Supreme Court has found that "the distinction between 'productive' and 'unproductive' uses may be helpful in calibrating the balance [of interests]."[65]

The opinion continued, under the heading "Transformative use":

> It has been argued that the essence of "character and purpose" [one of the four considerations itemized in 17 U.S.C. § 107, which codifies the fair use doctrine] is the transformative value, that is, productive use, of the secondary work compared to the original. District Court Judge Leval has noted that, "[t]he use . . . must employ the quoted matter in a different manner or for a different purpose from the original."[66]

Where "fair use" is concerned, it seems, mere "users" need not apply. The doctrine may be invoked only by those who have special claims to "authorship" in their own work.

The *Basic Books* litigation involved another form of "serial collaboration"[67]—making anthologies of selections from pub-

---

[63] *Id.* at 310.

[64] 758 F. Supp. 1522 (S.D.N.Y. 1991).

[65] *Id.* at 1530 (quoting Sony Corp. v. Universal City Studios, Inc., 464 U.S. 417, 455 n.40 (1984) (alteration in original)).

[66] *Id.* (quoting Pierre Leval, *Toward a Fair Use Standard,* 103 HARV. L. REV. 1105, 1111 (1990)).

[67] For a definition and discussion of serial collaborations, see *supra* text accompanying note 41.

lished writings for use as textbooks in college courses. The suit was brought by publishers against a commercial photocopying service that had prepared anthologies including unauthorized excerpts from copyrighted works; the materials in these compilations had been chosen by instructors to suit their own courses, culled from books and various other publications which totalled (in each case) thousands of pages. The litigation turned on the photocopying company's defense of "fair use," and the finding for the publishers was justified, in significant part, on the grounds that the use in question was a mere "non-transformative repackaging":

> In this case, there was absolutely no literary effort made by Kinko's to expand upon or contextualize the materials copied. The excerpts in suit were merely copied, bound into a new form, and sold. . . . The copying in suit had productive value only to the extent that it put an entire semester's resources in one bound volume for students. It required the judgment of the professors to compile it, though none of Kinko's.[68]

This puzzling passage is open to two distinct interpretations. It may be that "literary effort" and mere "judgment" are two different things, and that selecting and collating the excerpts to be included in an anthology is not the kind of new "authorship" that Judge Motley believes deserves recognition.[69] Or perhaps the photocopying company should not have been given credit for any "literary effort" invested in the design of anthologies by others.[70] One way or another, the value added to the preexisting materials by the act of compiling them is lost in the economy of this decision. Either way, the intellectual contribution that went into the creation of the "secondary" works goes unacknowledged in the *Basic Books* case, and its significance remains unanalyzed. Cer-

---

[68] *Basic Books*, 758 F. Supp. at 1530-31 (citations omitted).

[69] Notwithstanding the language of the decision, the "selection, coordination and arrangement" of preexisting materials is considered a form of "authorship" where those materials are not copyrighted or are used with permission. *See* 17 U.S.C. § 101 (1988) (defining "compilation" as "a work formed by the collection and assembling of preexisting materials or of data that are selected, coordinated, or arranged in such a way that the resulting work as a whole constitutes an original work of authorship"); *see also* Feist Publications, Inc. v. Rural Tel. Serv., 111 S. Ct. 1282, 1289 (1991). Is there a double standard at work in *Basic Books* with one level of "authorship" being sufficient to form the basis of a claim to copyright, and another, higher level being necessary to qualify a use as "fair."

[70] The professors who used the "anthologies" involved in the *Basic Books* litigation were not defendants in the litigation. The defendant company's efforts to claim that its use was privileged—for educational purposes—were rejected by the court: "The extent of its insistence that theirs are educational concerns and not profitmaking ones boggles the mind." *Basic Books*, 758 F. Supp. at 1532.

tainly, the value of such compilations cannot be accounted for within the framework imposed by the ideology of "authorship."[71]

In *Feist*, the Supreme Court failed to recognize that "factual" data, like name/address listings in a directory, are themselves the products of complex processes of corporate writing. Similarly, the opinions in *Rogers v. Koons* and *Basic Books* came to their conclusions by marginalizing the cultural significance of what I have called "serial collaboration"—a writing practice that cannot easily be accommodated within the Romantic conception of "authorship."

We should also note that copyright fails to come to terms with the reality of even more obvious forms of literary and artistic collaboration. Although copyright law has a category for works created by several writers working together on a preconcerted basis, the consequences that flow from the categorization of a work as one of "joint authorship" reflect the individualistic bias of American copyright doctrine. In effect, "a joint work" has several individual "authors": Each "joint author" must possess the

---

[71] The dependence on Romantic ideas of "authorship" by copyright law limits the availability of the "fair use" defense in such a case as *Basic Books*. The same conception of "authorship," however, has been invoked to justify "fair use." In Wright v. Warner Books, Inc., 953 F.2d 731 (2d Cir. 1991), the most recent in a series of Second Circuit decisions involving the applicability of "fair use" to quotations from unpublished manuscripts, the court concluded that the defendant's unauthorized takings from the unpublished letters and diaries of the writer, Richard Wright, were privileged. One factor that a "fair use" analysis must address, according to section 107 of the Copyright Act, is "the amount and substantiality of the portion used." In setting the stage for the discussion of this factor in the *Wright* decision, Judge Meskill observed that not all the passages quoted by the defendant were the subject matter of copyright: "Of the ten quoted sections [from the letters], four bear Wright's stamp of creativity and meet the threshold test of copyright protection. The other six tersely convey mundane details of Wright's life . . . ." *Id.* at 736. This remarkable invocation of the concept of "authorship" to deny protection to merely "mundane" passages is echoed later in the opinion, in the discussion addressing "fair use." *See id.* at 736-40. In the "fair use" section of the opinion, Judge Meskill considered a fifty-five word quotation from an unpublished letter. Judge Meskill states that "[t]he quoted passage is indeed stylistic. However, it is the only quoted piece of expression that represents anything close to the central point communicated in any of the letters." *Id.* at 738.

In its early decision in Bleistein v. Donaldson Lithographing Co., 188 U.S. 239 (1903), the United States Supreme Court disclaimed any role for the judiciary in assessing the "worth" of works for which copyright protection is claimed, "outside of the narrowest and most obvious limits." *Id.* at 251. If the issue in Wright had been posed as a choice between characterizations of the passages in question as meritorious or meritless writing, conflict with the *Bleistein* principle would have been inevitable. By presenting the choice as being between the characterizations "stylistic" and "non-stylistic" writing, however, the conflict is avoided. The issue, as the court presents it, is not whether the passages are worthwhile, but whether they are the outcome of "authorship" in the first instance. In one respect, this treatment of the issue may represent a mere sleight of hand; in another, however, it accurately reflects the underlying assumptions of the copyright system. If a glorified vision of "authorship" animates our law of copyright, we should expect to find that works deficient in "authorship" are denied all protection or (at least) rendered particularly vulnerable to "fair use."

legal attributes and should retain the legal prerogatives associated with solitary, originary "authorship." Thus, only identified or identifiable individuals can receive legal recognition for their contribution to a "joint work,"[72] while the duration of protection for a "joint work" is measured in terms of the longest-surviving of its several "authors." Perhaps most critically, each of those "authors" is entitled to use and authorize the use of the work as though he or she were solely responsible for its creation.[73] Far from acknowledging the extent to which participation in a corporate, creative enterprise entails the surrender of individual prerogative, copyright law implicitly assumes the continued relevance of the Romantic vision of "authorship" to this domain.

The Copyright Act and case law thus tend to treat "joint authorship" as a deviant form of individual "authorship." Indeed, in many particular instances copyright refuses to acknowledge the existence of "joint authorship," or does so only grudgingly. Notably, one of the significant innovations of the major statutory revision of American copyright law completed in 1976 was its substantial narrowing of the range of circumstances in which

---

[72] American copyright law provides for anonymous works, "of which no natural person is identified as author." 17 U.S.C. § 101 (1988). However, the statute assumes that in such instances one or more potentially identifiable individuals created the work, and includes special provisions allowing them to come forward and declare their identities. *See* 17 U.S.C. § 302(c) (1988).

[73] The "joint author's" right to use or authorize use is subject to a duty to account to his or her collaborator(s) for the financial proceeds. It also is subject to a limited and ill-defined exception, derived from the general law of co-tenancy: Uses of the work that are deemed "destructive" require the general consent of all "joint authors" of the work. There was early support for the view that a transfer of rights by one joint owner which "practically precludes the other from a like use" should fall within the bar. *See* Shapiro, Bernstein & Co. v. Jerry Vogel Music Co., 73 F. Supp. 265 (S.D.N.Y. 1947). *But see* Herbert v. Fields, 152 N.Y.S. 487 (1915). But recent commentators have stated that "as a general matter [courts should] confine relief to situations in which a co-owner's conduct may place the work in the public domain." PAUL GOLDSTEIN, 1 COPYRIGHT § 4.2.2.2 (1989). Others have noted that "only in those limited circumstance [sic] where by its nature the work can be exploited in one and only one medium and that medium customarily does not use competitive versions of the same work . . . a most rare type of situation." MELVILLE B. NIMMER & DAVID NIMMER, NIMMER ON COPYRIGHT § 6.10[A], at 6-28 (1991).

Since American copyright traditionally has provided only for "economic" as distinct from "moral" rights, we have no guidance on the problems that could arise, under the recently-enacted Visual Artists Rights Act of 1990. Although the Visual Artists Rights Act, which is codified at 17 U.S.C. § 106A, does provide for joint ownership of moral rights, nothing in the statute or the legislative history specifies the result when one "joint author" of a qualifying work objects to a use proposed or undertaken by another on non-economic grounds. Although it states that "authors" of a joint work of visual art are co-owners of the rights to claim authorship and object to the distortion, mutilation, or other prejudicial modification of the work, the statute gives no guidance concerning how that right would be exercised between the "joint authors"—nor does the legislative history. If the treatment of "economic" rights is any guide, we may presume that when one "joint author" has authorized a particular use, the scope of another right to object will be limited.

what might be termed a "collaboration" in the lay sense is recognized as a "joint work" in the legal one. Before 1976, courts were content to hold that a work of "joint authorship" need not be the result of face-to-face collaboration: as when, for example, lyrics were added to an already-completed tune.[74] By contrast, Section 101 of the 1976 Copyright Act defines "joint authorship" so to require "the intention, *at the time the writing is done*, that the parts be absorbed or combined into an integrated unit."[75]

Law's insistence on formally disaggregating collaborative productions, rather than categorizing them as "joint works," is apparent in recent decisions concerning the vexed question of whether the contribution of each "joint author" must be one which would be considered a copyrightable "work" in itself.[76] Although many courts have dealt with this issue in recent years,[77]

---

[74] *See* Shapiro, Bernstein & Co. v. Jerry Vogel Music Co, Inc., 221 F.2d 569 (2d Cir.), *modified*, 223 F.2d 252 (1955) (the "Twelfth Street Rag" decision.)

[75] H.R. Rep. No. 1476, 94th Cong., 2d Sess. 103, 120, *reprinted in* 1976 U.S.C.C.A.N. 5659, 5736 (emphasis added) (glossing the definition of "joint work" in Section 101 of the 1976 Copyright Act). All questions of temporality aside, the requirement that contributions to a "joint work" be ones intended to be "merged into inseparable or interdependent parts of a unitary whole," *id.*, is notably restrictive in itself, although it is nothing new. Here, the hyperbolic language of a 1944 opinion of Judge Learned Hand is instructive. A work of "joint authorship" comes into being, he stated, because "when [both "authors"] plan an undivided whole . . . , their separate interests will be as inextricably involved, as are the threads out of which they have woven the seamless fabric of the work." Edward B. Marks Music Corp. v. Jerry Vogel Music Co., 140 F.2d 266, 267 (2d Cir. 1944). The continuing tendency of courts to disaggregate creative contributions wherever possible, on the grounds that the resultant product is not "unitary," or "integrated," or "undivided," is exemplified by such decisions as Weissman v. Freeman, 868 F.2d 1313 (2d Cir.), *cert. denied*, 110 S. Ct. 219 (1989).

[76] As detailed below, this problem usually arises when one collaborator is responsible for the basic idea of a project, while another has undertaken its actual execution. But it could arise in other contexts as well. Copyright law does not extend protection to words, individual musical notes or short phrases. Stratchborneo v. ARC Music Corp., 357 F. Supp. 1393, 1405 (S.D.N.Y. 1973); Shapiro, Bernstein & Co. v. Jerry Vogel Music, 161 F.2d 406, 409 (2d Cir. 1947). Obviously, however, we can imagine a literary or musical project realized by inviting large numbers of individuals to make separate, sequential, contributions, each consisting of sub-copyrightable expression. It seems unlikely that the whole would be considered more than the sum of the parts under prevailing copyright doctrine. (For this example, though not necessarily for the conclusion I draw from it, I am indebted to Bruce Joseph, Esq.).

[77] *See, e.g.*, S.O.S., Inc. v. Payday, Inc., 886 F.2d 1081 (9th Cir. 1989); Olan Mills, Inc. v. Eckerd Drug of Texas, Inc., 1989 Copyright L. Dec. (CCH) ¶ 26,420 (N.D. Tex. 1989); Ashton-Tate Corp. v. Ross, 728 F. Supp. 597 (N.D.Cal. 1989); Boggs v. Japp, 1988 Copyright L. Dec. (CCH) ¶ 26,347 (E.D. Va. 1988); Whelan Assocs., Inc. v. Jaslow Dental Lab., Inc., 609 F. Supp. 1307 (E.D.Pa. 1985), *aff'd*, 797 F.2d. 1222 (3d Cir. 1986), *and cert. denied*, 479 U.S. 1031 (1987); Meltzer v. Zoller, 520 F. Supp. 847 (D.N.J. 1981). The Ninth Circuit Court of Appeals summarized the prevailing view in *S.O.S.*:

> A person who merely describes to an author what the commissioned work should do or look like is not a joint author for purposes of the Copyright Act . . . . To be an author, one must supply more than mere direction or ideas: one must "translate[] an idea into a fixed, tangible expression entitled to copyright protection." [citing CCNV v. Reid, 846 F.2d 1485 (D.C. Cir. 1988), *modified on other grounds*, 490 U.S. 730 (1989)]. The supplier of an idea is no

and most have answered in the affirmative,[78] the most important precedent in the area is the recent decision in *Childress v. Taylor*.[79] *Childress* involved a dispute over ownership in a play about the legendary black entertainer "Moms" Mabley. Alice Childress was a veteran stage performer, who had conceived the idea of such a play as a vehicle for herself and had assembled extensive documentation of Mabley's life and career. Childress then persuaded a playwright, Clarice Taylor, to prepare a script embodying her ideas and incorporating her research.

After Taylor's script had been completed, Childress allegedly misappropriated its contents as the basis for a "Moms" Mabley play of her own, and Taylor brought suit. The issue of "joint authorship" was squarely presented—only if Taylor was found to be the sole "author" of the play did she have a claim against Childress. The trial court ruled in favor of Taylor, on the ground that Childress's "ideas and research" did not represent a copyrightable, and thus legally significant, contribution. The court of appeals revisited the issue in an opinion which conceded that the issue posed was "open in this Circuit" and "troublesome,"[80] both because it is one to which the statute does not speak in so many words[81] and because conventional policy justifications for

---

more an "author" of a program than is the supplier of the disk on which the program is stored.
886 F.2d at 1087 (alteration in original).

[78] The most important exception is the *dictum* in Judge Ruth Ginsberg's opinion in Community for Creative Non-Violence v. Reid, 846 F.2d 1485, 1497 (D.C. Cir. 1988), *modified on other grounds*, 490 U.S. 730 (1989). After disposing of the "work for hire" issue, Judge Ginsberg noted that the question of whether the statue at issue had been a "joint work" hadn't been before the court, but suggested that it "might qualify as a textbook example of a jointly-authored work," and that merely supplying the general idea or concept for the work might count toward a finding of "authorship" on the part of one of the claimants to ownership rights. *Id.* at 1497. She continued: "Its contribution to the steam grate pedestal *added to its initial conceptualization and ongoing direction of the realization [of the work].*" *Id.* (emphasis added). The emphasized contributions, of course, are not ones which conventionally would be regarded as copyrightable in themselves.

More recently, another federal appellate court has explicitly held that the issue is an open one. *See* Andrien v. Southern Ocean County Chamber of Commerce, 927 F.2d 132, 136 (3d Cir. 1991) (en banc). *See also* Steve Altman Photography v. United States, 18 Cl. Ct. 267 (1989) (suggesting that "conceiving the idea" for a photograph may be a legally relevant authorial contribution).

[79] 945 F.2d 500 (1991).

[80] *Id.* at 506.

[81] Judge Newman's opinion for the curcuit court notes that
[t]he textual argument from the statute is not convincing. The Act surely does not say that each contribution to a joint work must be copyrightable, and the specification that there be "authors" does not necessarily require a copyrightable contribution. "Author" is not defined in the Act and appears to be used only in its ordinary sense of an originator. The "author" of an uncopyrightable idea is nonetheless its author even though, for entirely valid reasons, the law properly denies him a copyright on the result.
Id. Although the passage demystifies the statutory terminology, its vision of the "ordi-

copyright protection do not dictate a clear answer:

> If the focus is solely on the objective of copyright law to en-
> courage the production of creative works, it is difficult to see
> why the contributions of all joint authors need be copyright-
> able. An individual creates a copyrightable work by combining
> a non-copyrightable idea with a copyrightable form of expres-
> sion; the resulting work is no less a valuable result of the crea-
> tive process simply because the idea and the expression came
> from two different individuals. Indeed, it is not unimaginable
> that there exists a skilled writer who might never have pro-
> duced a significant work until some other person supplied the
> idea.[82]

Indeed, such working relationships are more than "not
unimaginable." Our knowledge of contemporary writing practice, to say nothing of our reconstructions of historical instances
like Samuel Johnson's various "secret collaborations,"[83] suggests
they are common—if not typical—among collaborators.

The above quoted passage comes as close as anything in
copyright jurisprudence to acknowledging the complexities of
collaboration, and the difficulties inherent in a legal framework
shaped by the individualistic assumptions of Romantic "authorship." Unfortunately, having achieved this insight, Judge Jon
Newman, who wrote the opinion for the circuit court, turns away
from it. He discusses, instead, the various pragmatic justifications for insisting on copyrightable contributions from all "joint
authors,"[84] concluding, somewhat vaguely, that such a rule embodying such insistence "seems more consistent with the spirit of
copyright law."[85]

Ultimately, the *Childress* court fails to confront the issues it
identifies so clearly. Instead, it retreats into a restrictive vision of
"joint authorship," aligning itself with the general tendency of
American statute and case law. Once again, copyright law has
been baffled by its inherited vision of Romantic "authorship,"
and reconsideration of the law's uncomprehending treatment of
corporate creativity has been deferred. Rather than confronting
the reality of prevailing writing practice, another court has be-

---

nary sense" of the word "author" is dependent upon a set of assumptions inherited by
law from Romantic aesthetics.

[82] *Id.*

[83] *See* Woodmansee, *supra* note 7, at 281-88.

[84] These include the discouragement of fraudulent claims and the striking of "an
appropriate balance in the domains of both copyright and contract law." *Id.* at 507.

[85] *Id.*

come an active participant in the ongoing process of its mystification.

The revision of copyright concepts to take fuller account of collaborative cultural production, forseen by Professor Kaplan, has yet to occur. But what, one might fairly ask, are the implications of copyright's recursive insistence on forcing all writing into to the Procrustean doctrinal model shaped by the individualistic, Romantic concept of "authorship"? In closing, let me suggest one area (among many) in which the continuing failure of copyright to comprehend collective creativity may soon have real, adverse consequences.

As Martha Woodmansee has noted, electronic technology is playing a crucial role in promoting writing practices in which the identities of individual contributors to shared dynamic texts are deemphasized, and their useful contributions effectively merged.[86] One environment in which this trend is notable is that of the many loosely connected national and international computer networks that form, collectively, the so-called "Internet." To date, the Internet (with its bewildering array of available "bulletin boards," "newsgroups," and "electronic texts") has developed as a spontaneous, cooperative, non-governmental response to the potential of new technologies. Thus, activities in the Internet environment have been free (for the most part) from legal regulation.[87] Among other things, the Internet environment has fostered a class of new "infopreneurs," who gather available data from the network, augmenting and repackaging it for further distribution.[88]

Obviously, there are tensions between some practices the Internet facilitates and traditional notions of proprietary rights in writing. As one commentator has noted, "In this informal and often unpredictable intellectual collaboration, authorship is frequently unrecorded"[89]—not to say uncompensated! In many respects, the conditions of the Internet environment today resemble those which prevailed at other moments of polymorphous collaboration, unrestrained plagiarism, and extraordinary cultural productivity—such as the Elizabethan stage or Hollywood before 1915.

---

[86] *See* Woodmansee, *supra* note 7, at 289-91.

[87] *See generally Information Policy: Superhighway Bill Sketches Outline of Ubiquitous Computer Network*, DAILY REP. FOR EXECS. (BNA), § C-1, Nov. 26, 1991.

[88] *See* Bruce L. Flanders, *Barbarians at the Gate: New Technologies for Handling Information Pose a Crisis Over Intellectual Property*, 22 AM. LIBRARIES 668 (July 1991).

[89] *Id.*

These conditions, however, may not prevail for long. Last year's congressional enactment of the so-called "Information Superhighway" legislation, which calls for the creation of a new, federally-funded, high-speed network within the Internet (the National Research and Education Network, or NREN), may serve as the catalyst for bringing the electronic network environment as a whole under firmer legal control, through (among other means) the extension of copyright regulation to the activities of network users.

A battle is shaping over the future of the Internet. On the one side are those who see its potential as a threat to traditional notions of individual properietorship in information, and who perceive the vigorous extension of traditional copyright principles as the solution.[90] On the other side are those who argue that the network environment may become a new cultural "commons," which excessive or premature legal control may stifle.[91]

There will certainly be some need for regulation as the network environment evolves, and copyright will most definitely have a role to play.[92] The ideology of Romantic "authorship," however, has greater potential to mislead than to guide the decision-makers who will shape the legal regime for this new and promising communications technology.

---

[90] *See, e.g.*, *id.* (predicting "an information anarchy where current copyright law and policy is, to put it politely, ineffectual and outdated").

[91] The position is typified by the views of Mitchell Kapor, president of the Electronic Frontier Foundation, Inc., and Jerry Berman, director of the American Civil Liberties Union Information Technology Project, who argue for "open network architecture," and stress that

> [w]e know from past demand on the Internet and commercial personal computer networks that the network will be used for electronic assembly—virtual town halls, village greens, and coffee houses, again taking place not just through shared text (as in today's computer networks), but through multimedia transmissions, including images, voice and video. Unlike the telephone, this network will also be a publications medium, distributing electronic newsletters, video clips and interpreted reports.

Mitchell Kapor & Jerry Berman, Building The Open Road: The NREN as a Test-Bed for the National Public Network (1991) (on file with the Electronic Frontier Foundation, Inc.).

[92] *See, e.g.*, John R. Garrett, *Text to Screen Revisited: Copyright in the Electronic Age*, ONLINE, Apr. 1991, at 22 (describing activities of the Copyright Clearance Center in clearing rights for the distribution of copyrighted texts by electronic means).

TOUCHING WORDS: HELEN KELLER, PLAGIARISM, AUTHORSHIP

Jim Swan*

> The originals are not original.
> — Ralph Waldo Emerson[1]

> Something . . . may have eluded you in passing, namely, this *belong-to-me* aspect of representations, so reminiscent of property.
> — Jacques Lacan[2]

> We photograph things in order to drive them out of our minds. My stories are ways of shutting my eyes.
> — Franz Kafka[3]

I. HANDS

At age twenty-eight, Helen Keller, a recent graduate of Radcliffe College, *cum laude* in English, and already the author of two highly praised books, *The Story of My Life*[4] and *The World I Live In*,[5] is suspected once again of plagiarism. A letter to an editor complains that she has lifted a passage word for word from the work of the English Unitarian clergyman and philosopher, James Martineau. The reply made by this remarkable woman—deaf and blind since her second year—is forthright and sensible, explaining that friends often read "interesting fragments" to her "in a promiscuous manner," and that if she then uses them in her writing, it is difficult to trace the "fugitive sentences and paragraphs"

* Associate Professor of English, Center for the Study of Psychoanalysis and Culture, State University of New York at Buffalo. Ph.D., 1974, Stanford University. I am grateful to friends and colleagues who read and commented on earlier drafts: Joan Copjec, Margreta de Grazia, Peter Jaszi, Claire Kahane, Deidre Lynch, Irving Massey, Fred See, Madelon Sprengnether, Elisabeth Weston, Martha Woodmansee. I also wish to thank Kenneth Stuckey, research librarian at the Perkins School for the Blind, for his skilled and cordial assistance.

1 Ralph Waldo Emerson, *Quotation and Originality, in* 8 RALPH WALDO EMERSON, COLLECTED WORKS 175, 180 (Centenary ed., 1979).

2 JACQUES LACAN, *Of the Gaze as Objet Petit a, in* THE FOUR FUNDAMENTAL CONCEPTS OF PSYCHO-ANALYSIS 67, 81 (Jacques-Alain Miller ed., Alan Sheridan trans., 1981) [hereinafter, LACAN, *Gaze*].

3 GUSTAV JANOUCH, CONVERSATIONS WITH KAFKA, *quoted in* ROLAND BARTHES, CAMERA LUCIDA: REFLECTIONS ON PHOTOGRAPHY 53 (Richard Howard trans., 1981).

4 HELEN KELLER, THE STORY OF MY LIFE (1954) (1903).

5 HELEN KELLER, THE WORLD I LIVE IN (1908).

which have been spelled into her hand. But this is not the first time that her writing has aroused suspicion. She herself says she has been troubled by several such cases. "Sometimes I think I ought to stop writing altogether," she complains, "since I cannot tell surely which of my ideas are borrowed feathers, except for those which I gather from books in raised print."[6]

Helen Keller is aware that she reads books in two distinct modes. In one mode, she is an autonomous reader, her hand actively tracing and deciphering the braille code embossed on the page. In the other, she is the object of a "promiscuous" generosity, the hands of others signing into hers a mixture of discursive fragments, which she remembers but cannot place as having an origin or a source. In one mode, her fingers trace a linear sequence of signs across the ordered surface of a page, each word in its own place on its own line. In the other mode, her hand is itself the surface on which someone else's fingers imprint a sequence of tactile signs, a sequence that is not spatial but temporal, with letters, words, and sentences all spelled one after the other onto the same surface.

The hand becomes all-important to her. With it, she makes do in the absence of sight and sound, and it matters immensely that her access to language—and to knowledge in general—is channeled almost entirely through the sensuous and intimate medium of touch. The blind who have their hearing can still hear a book read to them, and in the United States the system of talking-book libraries furnishes the blind with recorded books free of charge. Similarly, the deaf who have their sight can read books directly, and for conversation they also have sign language, some dialects of which are wonderfully rich and subtle in chirographic expressiveness.[7] For the deaf-blind, however, the touch of the hand is the only way to read or converse, by touching a book, or by touching hands, or, as Helen Keller did very adroitly, by touching another person's mouth. In *The World I Live In*, Keller says, "In all my experiences and thoughts I am conscious of a hand. Whatever moves me, whatever thrills me, is as a hand that touches me in the dark."[8] Of course, the sense of touch is not limited to the hand, and Keller describes herself as possessing a

---

[6] JOSEPH P. LASH, HELEN AND TEACHER: THE STORY OF HELEN KELLER AND ANNE SULLIVAN MACY 342-43 (1980). Anyone who studies Helen Keller and Anne Sullivan owes a great debt to Lash for this biography.

[7] *See generally* OLIVER SACHS, SEEING VOICES: A JOURNEY INTO THE WORLD OF THE DEAF (1990).

[8] KELLER, THE WORLD I LIVE IN, *supra* note 5, at 6.

deliciously unbounded sensation of perceiving the world through the whole surface of her body. "Sometimes it seems as if the very substance of my flesh were so many eyes looking out at will upon a world new created every day."[9] Thus conceived, the mind realizes itself in a world unstructured by the hierarchy of visual perspective, in and as a body unstructured by the hierarchy of sight over the other senses: every moment is newly created and wholly perceived.

"Promiscuous" is Keller's word for an important mode of reading—it applies both to the person who reads and the mixed, indeterminate object of her reading. For the other mode important to her, the word that suggests itself as the opposite of promiscuous is "proper," signifying what is bounded and structured in the field of vision, what Lacan calls the "*belong-to-me* aspect of representations, so reminiscent of property."[10] Of course, for Keller it is not a *visual* field, but the perceptual field which she learns to construct for herself out of the experience of her hands: there, in an incident very early in her relationship with Anne Sullivan, she is forced to acquire a sense not only of the "belong-to-*me*" but of the "belong-to-*you*" aspect (what English lawyers used to call the *meum et teum*) of that space. Sullivan calls the incident a "battle royal." Helen's table manners, she says, were "appalling." "She puts her hands in our plates and helps herself, and when the dishes are passed, she grabs them and takes out whatever she wants."[11] After a struggle in a locked dining room, lasting two, maybe three hours, Annie succeeded in getting Helen to eat with a spoon, to eat from her own plate and not from others', and to use a napkin—*properly*. This was a necessary first step before Helen would be responsive to Annie's attempts to teach her language, but her lifelong experience of *touching* the world in order to "see" it makes it difficult for her to sustain a sense of the boundaries routinely respected by people with hearing and sight, boundaries defined by those absolutely fundamental rules which we teach our children: keep your hands to yourself and don't touch what isn't yours.

It is in the space between "proper" and "promiscuous" reading, then, that Helen Keller finds herself accused of plagia-

---

9 *Id.* at 41. Compare John Milton's Samson, a blind poet's blind hero: "why was the sight / To such a tender ball as th' eye confin'd? / So obvious and so easy to be quench't, / And not like feeling, through all parts diffus'd, / That she might look at will through every pore?" JOHN MILTON, *Samson Agonistes*, lines 96-100, *in* JOHN MILTON: COMPLETE POEMS AND MAJOR PROSE (Merritt Hughes, ed., 1957) (1671).

10 LACAN, *Gaze, supra* note 2, at 81.

11 KELLER, STORY OF MY LIFE, *supra* note 4, at 248.

rism, the space where she cannot tell for sure whether something is hers or someone else's, and where she feels at times that she ought to stop writing altogether. It is also here, in this space between the proper and the promiscuous, that I want to locate my exploration of Helen Keller and the question of plagiarism. As I have suggested already, with an allusion to Lacan, I proceed in the awareness of psychoanalytic as well as other modes of inquiry, all of which feature strongly visual concepts in their theoretical discourse. I want to try, as best I can as someone with sight and hearing, to understand what it is for someone deaf and blind to be an author.[12] What happens, for instance, to Foucault's concept of the "author-effect," when we factor out the visual and auditory dimensions of writing—when reading *and* writing are performed as *touch*, with its dual potential, both transgressive and proprietary.[13] Or, what happens to the intensely visual aspect of much psychoanalytic theory—Lacan's "mirror stage"[14] or Winnicott's "mirror role of the mother?"[15] Does a deaf-blind child experience a mirror stage? And, if she does, what is the mirror and its significance? Is it just a metaphor? Or, to cite Foucault again: what is the Panopticon to the blind, or, for that matter, to the deaf-blind? Foucault says of the Panopticon—for him the quintessential mechanism of social discipline—that its major effect is to induce "a state of conscious and permanent visibility that assures the automatic functioning of power" that "[he] who is subjected to a field of visibility, and who knows it, assumes responsibility for the constraints of power; he makes them play spontaneously upon himself; . . . he becomes the principle of his own subjection."[16] Can we locate Helen Keller in a social space theorized in this way? Assuming that she is subjected to a field of visibility, does she *know* she is so subjected? Is she aware of that visual dimension of herself which is available

---

[12] It is quite a different matter to try, as a *man* with sight and hearing, to understand what it is for a deaf-blind *woman* to be an author.

[13] MICHEL FOUCAULT, *What is an Author?*, in LANGUAGE, COUNTER-MEMORY, PRACTICE 113 (Donald Bouchard ed., 1977). Foucault distinguishes between the eighteenth- and nineteenth-century construction of discourse as property and an earlier construction of it as transgression: "In our culture . . . discourse was not originally a thing, a product, or a possession, but an action situated in a bipolar field of sacred and profane, lawful and unlawful, religious and blasphemous. It was a gesture charged with risks long before it became a possession caught in a circuit of property values." *Id.* at 124.

[14] JACQUES LACAN, *The Mirror Stage as Formative of the Function of the I* (1949), in ÉCRITS: A SELECTION (Alan Sheridan trans., 1977) [hereinafter LACAN, *Mirror Stage*].

[15] D.W. WINNICOTT, *Mirror Role of Mother and Family in Child Development* (1967), in PLAYING AND REALITY 111-18 (1971) [hereinafter WINNICOTT, *Mirror Role*].

[16] MICHEL FOUCAULT, DISCIPLINE AND PUNISH: THE BIRTH OF THE PRISON 201-03 (Alan Sheridan trans., 1979).

to others but not to her?[17]

These two terms of deaf-blind reading, the proper and the promiscuous, are chosen deliberately for their lack of a visual or auditory connotation. They are also understood to be related, not as polar opposites constituting a structure, but as terms of an asymmetrical semiotic relation: one term defines the other. The promiscuous is defined as such only from the standpoint of the proper. It bears the imprint of "proper" thinking, for the promiscuous is structured as a feared or censured *lack* of propriety, a lack of boundaries and names and ordered relations. Promiscuity is *in*-decent, *un*-seemly, *im*-proper. What the promiscuous actually "is," is a question that cannot be answered, for it can be posed only from a "proper" standpoint—although "standpoint" is a questionable term here, since the proper knows itself only in opposition to the promiscuous, constructing a difference as the "point" it "stands" on. Therefore, to say that it is in the space between proper and promiscuous reading that Helen Keller finds herself accused of plagiarism, is to locate her, not between polar opposites, but in a narrative and conversionary space, where an "I" structures itself by an act of appropriation, an act initiated in response to trauma in order to recuperate what is experienced as a shattered self. The trauma of the original accusation of plagiarism, when she was eleven years old, may have been cruel and unnecessary, but its ultimate effect is unavoidable. Like the "battle royal" in which Annie forces Helen to eat a proper meal, keeping her hands out of other people's food, the trauma of being accused of plagiarism forces Helen to become aware of where her hands have been in other people's words: only then does she begin to be an *author*.

Furthermore, her experience discloses a crucial relation between blindness and autobiographical narrative, a virtual imperative for narrative in blind experience. The visual field for sighted persons is a field of *kinetic* images—fluid, shifting, actively mobile and elusive, not to be pinned down, not by the unaided eye.[18]

---

[17] Compare Diderot, who reports of the blind man of Puisaux, that the spectacle of power (*les signes extérieurs de la puissance*) is nothing to him, and that he scoffs at the threat of being imprisoned in a dungeon. DENIS DIDEROT, *Letter on the Blind for the Use of Those Who See*, in DIDEROT'S EARLY PHILOSOPHICAL WORKS 77-78 (Margaret Jourdain trans., Open Court Pub., 1916) (1749). *But see* FOUCAULT, *supra* note 16, at 200, for whom the dungeon is the opposite of the Panopticon: Bentham's design for the ideal prison, a ring of cells open to a central observation tower, is not where one is shut away but where one is made *visible*: "[v]isibility is a trap."

[18] *See* JOHN HULL, TOUCHING THE ROCK: AN EXPERIENCE OF BLINDNESS (1990). In this extraordinary account of going blind, Hull finds that his way of remembering faces—even his own face—is not what he expected: "When I try to conjure up the memory of a

Looked at another way, it is precisely this kinetic quality of the visual that provides us with a continuously modulated three-dimensional map of ourselves in space, although we cannot *see* the process of this mapping, because it is not available to us to look "another way." As with Lacan's account of the gaze, it is the view of ourselves from the position of the other, a position which we can never occupy.[19] I am in a room and turn my head, and what I see is not just the movement of the room's features: what I also see, but without being able to see that I see it, is the continuously adjusted mapping of my own existence in the room, my relation to the chair (and you in it), a table, a window, the cat on the back of the sofa. I want to say that I *see* these features, that I actively focus my eyes and my mind and look at them, and as a consequence they become visible to me. But what is also happening is that I am seeing myself continuously represented and made visible where I am in the space of the room—although, again, this is

loved face, I cannot seem to capture it, but the straight edges of [a] photograph seem to fix the mobile features firmly in my mind, so that I can imagine myself gazing at the image." *Id.* at 19. This tells us a great deal about the place of the photograph in sighted as well as blind experience, and the way the technology of the camera has intervened over the last century and a half to transform our conception of the visual field. Hull understands acutely the effect on him of not being able to visualize space or visualize himself in space, and he comes to relish moments when the wind is blowing or when it rains. In wind and rain, sound performs the role of light in shaping for him an audible space where there was no space before. For a blind person in a space that is otherwise silent, there are only intermittent sounds that seem to come from nowhere and then disappear. There is no shape or continuity of space, no sense of things existing before or after they happen to announce themselves as sound. Opening the door one evening, he hears the rain in the garden, and in its varying sound he can make out even the contours of the lawn, the rain "shaping out the curvature" for him. *Id.* at 30. It is "an experience of great beauty . . . . I feel as if the world, which is veiled until I touch it, has suddenly disclosed itself to me. . . . I am no longer isolated, preoccupied with my thoughts . . . I am presented with a totality, a world that speaks to me." *Id.* at 31. At another time, in early morning rain, he listens for what it tells him of the many textures, layers and shapes of the world within earshot. Thinking of the common opinion that the blind live in their bodies rather than in the world, he compares his sense of his body to his sense of the rain. The body too is multi-layered and multi-textured, and he apprehends it not as an image but as multiple "arrangements of sensitivities, a conscious space comparable to the patterns of the falling rain. . . . My body and the rain intermingle, and become one audio-tactile, three-dimensional universe, within which and throughout the whole of which lies my awareness." *Id.* at 133. This blind epiphany is surprisingly like Helen Keller's sense of perceiving through the whole surface of her body a world that is in a continuous process of becoming. What Hull underscores is the sharp contrast between the simultaneity and totality of perception in a moment like this, its pleasure heightened by a feeling of recovered loss, and the very different experience of "the single-track line of consecutive speech which makes up [his] thoughts." *Id.* He imagines the rain stopping and his sense of the world shrinking to the surface of his own body. Then he goes a step further and imagines himself paralyzed from the neck down, deprived even of his body sense, and he wonders at what point he becomes "only a line of thought-speech." *Id.* It is this difference between the three-dimensional totality of perception in rare moments of fully realized acoustic space and the linearity of discursive thought that Hull comes back to again and again in his narrative.

[19] *See* LACAN, *Gaze, supra* note 2, at 72-75.

not something I can say I actually *see*. The blind tell us what it is like to live in the absence of this invisible dimension of the visible—the way, without our noticing, that it assures us moment by moment of our own reality in the space of appearance. Without such assurance, the blind woman's walk through the world is an intensely *narrative* activity. In a familiar space blindness means a continuous exercise of memory and prediction. In an unfamiliar space, it means getting other people's help to mark out a path, or it means constructing a narrative around the sounds and sensations (or, for Helen Keller, just the sensations) that come and go at will and without notice. This has a very specific consequence for Helen Keller as a writer. John Macy, the editor of her first book, *The Story of My Life*, says that, unlike a sighted person, Helen lacks the capacity to "go back over [her] work, shuffle the pages, interline, rearrange, see how the paragraphs look in proof, and so construct the whole work before the eye, as an architect constructs his plans."[20] Instead, Helen relies entirely on memory to construct her narrative as a whole, just as she must rely on narrative memory to fashion the coherence of herself from day to day. This ability to construct herself as narrative, though, is something that Helen does not achieve without considerable pain and trouble.

II. MY WORDS, YOUR WORDS

It is not the accusation of 1908 but an earlier one that constitutes a fundamental trauma for Helen Keller. In November, 1891, when she was eleven, she sent a birthday present to Michael Anagnos, head of the Perkins Institution (now "School") for the Blind. She had written a story for him titled "The Frost King." Annie, in a cover letter said, "We thought it pretty and original."[21] A rather conventional piece of narrative scene painting, the story tells how frost fairies accidentally transform the autumn landscape, coloring all the leaves crimson and gold. Anagnos was very pleased, calling the story a "precious gift," and immediately had it printed in the Perkins alumni magazine, *The Mentor*, rather than waiting for the appearance of the annual report several months later. From there it was picked up and published by *The Goodson Gazette*, a Virginia weekly for the deaf and blind. Within just a week, however, the editor of the weekly was shown a children's book by Margaret T. Canby, *Birdie and His*

---

20 KELLER, STORY OF MY LIFE, *supra* note 4, at 224.
21 LASH, *supra* note 6, at 132.

Fairy Friends, in which one of the stories was "The Frost Fairies."[22] The editor then published his findings along with parallel columns of matching phrases and paragraphs from the two stories. In the turmoil that followed, most of the accusations were directed at Anne Sullivan as the one who had attempted to "palm off" the story as Helen's own, but Annie and Helen both firmly denied that Canby's story had ever been read to Helen. Anagnos was embarrassed by the incident. Though he voted officially to clear them both of any dishonesty, he was apparently dissatisfied and remained suspicious. Years later, Helen recalled learning that Anagnos privately continued to accuse both Annie and herself of deceit, and once he was quoted as saying that Helen was "a living lie."[23] She and Annie were never to forgive him.

Helen Keller's story has been told many times, and the "Frost King" episode is usually presented as a decisive event in her early experience. However, until Joseph Lash researched the episode for his dual biography of Helen and Annie, everyone tended to repeat Sullivan's 1892 version that portrays Helen at the age of eight having Canby's story read into her palm by Mrs. Hopkins, Annie's friend from Perkins,[24] then forgetting it until three years later when she writes her own story as an unconscious copy of it. Typically, Helen's earlier biographers cite this extended process of forgetting and later recall as a sign of Helen's genius, "[h]er phenomenal power of concentration,"[25] her "remarkable" or "astonishing" memory.[26] But the evidence does not bear this out. Distributed in several parts of *The Story of My Life* and Michael Anagnos's lengthy account of Helen in the Perkins Institution *Annual Report* for 1891,[27] there are letters and narrative passages which, when gathered together, suggest several possibilities: either Helen simply remembered "The Frost

---

[22] MARGARET T. CANBY, BIRDIE AND HIS FAIRY FRIENDS (Philadelphia, Wm. F. Fell & Co. 1873).

[23] LASH, *supra* note 6, at 168.

[24] It was to Mrs. Sophia C. Hopkins, who had been her house mother at Perkins, that Annie addressed the letters she wrote from Alabama recording her early progress with Helen. In the summer of 1888, Helen and Annie visited Mrs. Hopkins at her home in Brewster, Mass. Annie, still having trouble with her eyes, asked Mrs. Hopkins to care for Helen while she sought treatment and some rest. In her explanatory letter in 1892 to John Hitz, Annie says that it was during her absence that Mrs. Hopkins probably read stories from Canby's book into Helen's hand. KELLER, STORY OF MY LIFE, *supra* note 4, at 343.

[25] VAN WYCK BROOKS, HELEN KELLER: SKETCH FOR A PORTRAIT 35 (1956).

[26] HELEN ELMIRA WAITE, VALIANT COMPANIONS: HELEN KELLER AND ANNE SULLIVAN MACY 145 (1959); EILEEN BIGLAND, HELEN KELLER 92 (1967).

[27] *Sixtieth Annual Report, Perkins Institution for the Blind* (1892) (reporting on academic year 1890-91) [hereinafter *Perkins Report*].

Fairies" *and* several other stories in Canby's book, or she had recent and frequent access to them, or she and Annie used key passages and phrases from the stories as a shared code for conversing about landscapes and seasons. Perhaps her relationship to Canby's book was a combination of these, continuing through the whole period, from the summer of 1888 to the fall of 1891, when Helen says she wrote "The Frost King." For instance, in early August 1891, well before any autumn change in the leaves, which Helen says inspired her story, she writes a letter vividly describing a thunderstorm, and the description matches a part of Canby's story, "The Dew Fairies," almost word for word: "Teacher and I watched from our window the great black clouds chasing one another swiftly across the sky, seeming to growl angrily when they met, and sending bright flashes of lightning at each other like swords."[28] (The key words here are "teacher and I"—for Helen, *watching* is an activity always mediated by other people's words, other people's hands.) Some weeks later, on September 29, she writes a letter to Anagnos, telling him how much she enjoys the books that Annie reads to her and their walks together in the autumn landscape:

> We were especially happy when the trees began to put on their autumn robes. Oh, yes! I could imagine how beautiful the trees were, all aglow, and rustling in the sunlight. *We thought the leaves as pretty as flowers, and carried great bunches home to mother. The golden leaves I called buttercups and the red ones roses.* One day teacher said, "Yes, they *are beautiful enough to comfort us for the flight of summer.*"[29]

The italicized words come from Canby's story, "The Frost Fairies."[30] In her later account, Helen alludes to this letter and others of the same period, acknowledging that phrases in them showed how saturated her mind was with Canby's language. In particular, she quotes the sentence she attributes to Annie, about the comfort given by autumn's beauty, and says it is "an idea direct from Miss Canby's story."[31] It is in fact an exact quotation, and it also appears word-for-word in "The Frost King." As an example of how Helen goes about adapting her model, she draws the phrases quoted together in the letter from different parts of

---

[28] *Id.* at 93.

[29] *Id.* at 79 (emphasis added).

[30] *See* KELLER, Story of My Life, *supra* note 4, at 349-50, 354. Anne Sullivan, in her statement about the incident, included by Macy as part of Keller's book, prints the two stories side by side in parallel columns. *Id.*

[31] *Id.* at 67.

Canby's story. Then, when she writes "The Frost King," she uses these phrases in virtually the same order as they appear in Canby, but with variations of context and phrasing. For instance, she includes the phrase about leaves as pretty as flowers, replacing "pretty" with "lovely," but says nothing about "mother" and omits the comparisons with buttercups and roses.

There are numerous, well documented instances where Helen adapts or copies from Canby's book—not just "The Frost Fairies" but other stories as well. How much is from long-term memory and how much from more recent "promiscuous" reading is an open question and, I think, unresolvable. Surely, this process of imitation and adaptation was a fundamental part of Helen's education. From the circumstances of the September 1891, letter to Anagnos, it seems that Annie understood what it would mean for Helen to learn about the world, particularly in its visual dimension: she would have to learn about it *as language*. According to Nella Braddy, who was Annie's biographer and talked with her about her methods:

> She had to get Helen's lessons out of the material at hand—they worked together—she asked Helen to write what she saw. Then Annie would give touches like color, then they would read stories in *Youth's Library* and notice what these had described that they hadn't. Then they would add those details to make it more interesting.[32]

The world as language comes to Helen largely out of books.[33] Coaxed to write what she "sees," she comes to "see" what she writes, which is the imagery and phrasing of nineteenth-century popular children's stories written in the tradition of Romantic landscape description. Language, for her, appears to be concrete more than for those with sight and/or hearing. Scenes are remembered directly as language, and her experience of the world as touch, taste and smell is largely muted by the visual and auditory force of the language she adapts herself to. It is entirely possible that when Helen writes "The Frost King," she is work-

---

[32] LASH, *supra* note 6, at 145.

[33] Anne Sullivan tells of an incident in the winter of 1891-92 when she took Helen outside during a light snow-fall. Helen was delighted to feel the cold flakes on her face and hands and, as they went back indoors, she said, " 'Out of the cloud-folds of his garments Winter shakes the snow.' " KELLER, STORY OF MY LIFE, *supra* note 4, at 338 n.*. Annie recognized the sentence as obviously literary but had no idea where it came from. No one at Perkins recognized it as coming from any of the available books in braille. One teacher did finally locate it in an ordinary printed book and identified it as coming from a poem of Longfellow's, but in Helen's memory it is quite transformed from what it was in the poem. *Id.*

ing entirely from memory, that she remembers it largely word-
for-word, because word-for-word is how she comes to know the
world beyond her intimate knowledge of it as touch, taste, and
smell. But then the evidence is not reassuring.

Did Helen plagiarize Margaret Canby's book? If we mean by
plagiarism a deliberate and conscious intent to steal someone
else's intellectual property, then the answer has to be *no*. She did
quote verbatim from the book, and she frequently adapted
Canby's language to her own uses, but it all seems to have been
done innocently and has to be understood in the context of her
relationship with Annie. Where the problem seems to have
arisen is in the way people wanted to see Helen as an original
genius. Annie herself often describes Helen's mind as "sensitive" and "philosophic," her work as "original," at exactly those
moments when Helen is repeating the language of another text.
Lash's chapter on the episode ends with the opinion that, when
the plagiarism crisis broke, Annie panicked and denied that
Helen had ever had Canby's stories read to her.[34] Lash is citing
an anonymous unpublished typescript in the archive at the Perkins School, "Miss Sullivan's Methods."[35] It is legalistic in manner and rather sarcastically mean-spirited in debunking Sullivan's
version of the incident. According to Lash, why it was written,
who wrote it, and why it ended up in the Perkins archive, have a
lot to do with the bad feeling that continued between Anagnos
and Sullivan long after the crisis and right up to his death in
1906.[36] The anonymous indictment is the only source of a particularly damaging statement by a Perkins teacher, which prompted
Anagnos to impanel a formal court of investigation. According
to the teacher, one day during a late afternoon dinner Helen confided to her that Annie had in fact read Canby's story to her when
she was writing her own. Their conversation was interrupted by
Annie, who took Helen upstairs. When Helen returned, she denied what she had said earlier and seemed quite troubled.[37]

---

[34] LASH, *supra* note 6, at 150.

[35] *Miss Sullivan's Methods* (n.d., anonymous unpublished typescript, bound in leather,
on legal sized paper 7.50" x 12.75", 171 pages numbered by hand; stored in the Samuel
P. Hayes Library at the Perkins School for the Blind, Watertown, Mass.) (used by permission) [hereinafter *Methods*]. Lash speculates that it was written in 1906, after the
death of Anagnos, by Julia Ward Howe's son-in-law, David Prescott Hall, countering
statements that reflected Annie's ingratitude toward Anagnos. LASH, *supra* note 6, at
134 n.*.

[36] *Id.*

[37] *Id.* at 136-38 (quoting *Methods*, *supra* note 35, at 142-50). Helen alludes to the
incident herself: "Something I said made her think she detected in my words a confession that I did remember Miss Canby's story of 'The Frost Fairies,' and she laid her
conclusions before Mr. Anagnos . . . ." KELLER, STORY OF MY LIFE, *supra* note 4, at 64.

Helen was made to appear before the court, without Annie, and recalled how panicked she felt in the face of determined questioning that seemed intended to make her confess. Later, Mark Twain sought to comfort her, laughing at the incident as a farce ("As if there was much of anything in any human utterance, oral or written, *except* plagiarism!") and portraying the court as a group of "solemn donkeys" and "decayed human turnips."[38] The court split, four to four, in its opinion, and Anagnos cast the deciding vote in Helen's favor. Helen was dazed by the ordeal and wept bitterly in her bed that night, wishing she were dead.[39]

III. PROPERTY

"Miss Sullivan's Methods" ends on a note of serious doubt and suspicion about Helen's book, *The Story of My Life*, questioning the way it combines Helen's own narrative with Anne Sullivan's letters and several other writings, all of it arranged with a commentary by the editor:

> One arises from a study of the Book in a questioning state of mind. He is inclined to ask himself, what in this book is Miss Sullivan's, what is the Editor's, and what is Helen Keller's? He feels as he does looking at a *composite photograph*—the book is such [a] *"composite reminiscence"* of so much else. One feels as a bank clerk must feel, who for many years has been falsifying his accounts, and who says to himself, "which figures are right, which are wrong, which are the genuine figures, which are those I have substituted? For the life of me I cannot tell."[40]

Three very telling concepts inform the writer's judgment. First, there is intellectual property: how does one decide what in the book belongs to Helen, what to Annie, and what to John Macy the editor. Second, there is the photograph, a "composite" photograph, and the anxiety that this medium, still new in 1906, with its promise of an unprecedented fidelity of visual representation, might also have the power to trick the viewer; as if the writer felt vulnerable in the very mode of perception in which he enjoys a distinct advantage over the two women. And finally, there is the figure of the embezzler, who has become confused about which are the real figures and which the false ones. Overall, this writer gives the impression of someone who desires strict accountability, a world of rigid distinctions between original and copy, au-

---

[38] *Quoted by* LASH, *supra* note 6, at 146-47.
[39] KELLER, STORY OF MY LIFE, *supra* note 4, at 65.
[40] *Methods, supra* note 35, at 171.

thentic and counterfeit, "genuine" and "substitute," although there is the curious moment at the end, when he shifts his point of view and identifies with the deceiver rather than the deceived ("One feels as a bank clerk must feel"). My guess is that, when the writer imagines a potentially deceptive photograph, and then identifies with an imagined embezzler, he is telling us of his own confusion and difficulty with the concept of intellectual property, even at the same moment when he emphatically declares his conviction that not only was "The Frost King" a plagiarism, but its true circumstances have been obscured and covered up.

Generally, our understanding of intellectual property derives from the Anglo-American tradition of thought about property. A leading authority on the subject, at the time when Helen Keller is accused of plagiarism, is Eaton Drone's *Treatise on the Law of Property in Intellectual Productions in Great Britain and the United States* (also known as *Drone on Copyright*), which was published in 1879, one year before Keller's birth.[41] Drone expounds the law of copyright at length, but he does so in the context of a fundamental argument about the meaning of intellectual property. In the 1870s American law was modeled, as it is today, on an early eighteenth-century British statute and subsequent court rulings, in both England and the United States, which declare that the common law right of authors to property in their intellectual productions is superseded by copyright statutes; that authors in fact have no rights except under the particular statute that applies.[42] Drone rejects this position, and sees it as his task to argue the case for the common law right to intellectual property as a right prior to, and surviving, any copyright statute. Consequently, he devotes an introductory section to delineating "The Origin and Nature of Literary Property," which he ultimately traces to the seventeenth-century social contract theorists, chief among them being John Locke.[43]

Locke's theory, which concerns men existing in a state of nature before their agreement to form a civil society, bases property on the presumed natural right that a man has in his own person. This is a theory of private possession, modeled on the privacy of the body, which Locke elaborates as a theory of private appropriation: for whatever a man creates or cultivates or im-

---

[41] EATON. S. DRONE, A TREATISE ON THE LAW OF PROPERTY IN INTELLECTUAL PRODUCTIONS IN GREAT BRITAIN AND THE UNITED STATES (1879) [hereinafter DRONE].

[42] *Id.* at 1.

[43] JOHN LOCKE, *Of Property*, SECOND TREATISE OF GOVERNMENT, ch. 5, §§ 25-51, *in* TWO TREATISES OF GOVERNMENT (Peter Laslett ed., 1960) (1690).

proves with the labor of his body becomes his property.[44] There is a deep and complex irony in this theory, because in Locke's seventeenth-century, social contract theory performs a radical act of social and political amnesia. Locke, and Hobbes before him, both base their accounts of the origin of civil society on an anthropology that erases the actual history of property in England, at least from the time of the Norman Conquest forward, and substitutes in its stead a theory about the origin of property in the prehistory of culture. With Locke, though, appropriation comes from a state of nature where everything is first "in *common*," so that Locke, more exactly, theorizes in a transitional zone between the traditional idea of a commonwealth and the modern concept of private property. Still, the erasure is itself a sign that Locke theorizes in order to prevail in a field of contested meaning; that the object of his theory is not so much nature as the still powerful, though altered, tradition of feudal property relations among lords, and their tenants and servants. It is a fact often overlooked, for instance, that Locke devotes the first of his *Two Treatises of Government* to demolishing the thesis of Robert James Filmer's *Patriarchia*,[45] a text written at the height of the revolution which beheaded the English king and abolished the crown. Filmer argued that all social and political authority derived from the supposedly "natural" authority of the father over his wife, children and household servants. This was an attempt to rationalize, by an appeal to origins, the feudal tradition of authority—a tradition which had *already* been dissolved from within by the development of a free market. The defining feature of this market was the institution of the legal contract, a device by which one man enters freely into agreement with another in pursuit of his own self-interest and is bound, not by an unwritten, supposedly "natural" bond between lord and servant, but by the mutually agreed upon terms of the written contract. That the two parties to a contract may in fact be unequal in property and power as a consequence of a prior unequal distribution of wealth, is a matter that Locke's theory is silent on, exactly as it works to secure that prior unequal distribution as a system of property rights.

---

[44] *Id.* § 27. "Though the Earth, and all inferior Creatures be common to all Men, every Man has a *Property* in his own *Person*. This no Body has any Right to but himself. The *Labour* of his Body, and the *Work* of his Hands, we may say, are properly his. Whatsoever then he removes out of the State that Nature hath provided, and left it in, he hath mixed his *Labour* with, and joyned to it something that is his own, and thereby makes it his *Property*." *Id.* (emphasis in original).

[45] SIR ROBERT FILMER, PATRIARCHIA, OR, THE NATURAL POWER OF KINGS (London, 1680). (Filmer died in 1653, and the first posthumous edition appeared in 1680.)

Social contract theory thus performs not so much an erasure as a radical rewriting of the origin of property. To theorize a state of nature is to think into nonexistence the present order of things in whose midst one theorizes. After all, virtually every square foot of land in England had been inventoried already, *as property*, as far back as the eleventh century in the Domesday Book of William the Conqueror. Locke theorizes, then, upon an origin that is itself insufficiently theorized, and in doing so he proposes a concept of property without debt or obligation. If what you acquire exists first, as Locke says, in "the state that nature hath provided and left it in," then to whom do you owe any obligation, to whom are you tied by the bonds of exchange? This is the kind of question raised by the tradition of classical liberalism and its inability to provide or even account for a society as a collective or cooperative venture, its existence as a *common*wealth. It is also the kind of question that has led Marxist readers, like C. B. Macpherson,[46] to argue that in Locke's state of nature there is already established a system of property relations prior to the social contract; that civil society is created as an agreement by an already existing class of major property holders for the purpose of justifying and protecting their disproportionate share of the world's natural and "common" wealth.[47]

However, it is not just Marxism or post-modernist theory that recognizes a political design in Locke's thinking about origins. Even his contemporaries could see ironies in this kind of thinking, which was pervasive a good deal earlier in the seventeenth century than when Locke writes his work on property. Andrew Marvell, for instance, imagines in his long country-house

---

[46] C.B. MACPHERSON, THE POLITICAL THEORY OF POSSESSIVE INDIVIDUALISM: HOBBES TO LOCKE (1962).

[47] We are not much concerned with the *history* of property today, either—or with economic history in general. Recently, a new chair was hired for an economics department which was getting added resources at a time when the rest of the university faced possible retrenchment. Asked why his graduate program offered no courses in economic history, he replied, "We can do economics without history," and the current practice of economists, with their focus on cost/benefit analysis, bears him out. Their key concern now is the "problem" of social cost. That is, does the cost to A of injury to her property (e.g., air or water pollution) from B's use of her property outweigh the cost to B of damages paid to A or of regulations restraining B from using her property in a way that injures A? According to the prevailing Coase theorem, if A and B are allowed to negotiate without legal or regulatory intervention, then the outcome will tend to maximize the social product and, consequently, minimize social cost—*even if it means that B continues to injure A*. To do economics like this, of course you don't need history. *See* R.H. Coase, *The Problem of Social Cost*, 3 J. L. & ECON. 503 (1960). *But see* Duncan Kennedy, *Cost-Benefit Analysis of Entitlement Problems: A Critique* 33 STAN. L. REV. 387 (1981); Mark Kelman, *Consumption Theory, Production Theory, and Ideology in the Coase Theorem*, 52 S. CAL. L. REV. 669 (1979).

poem, "Upon Appleton House," a moment in which the land,
deliberately flooded to increase its fertility, seems like both the
newly created world and Locke's original nature:

> A levell'd space, as smooth and plain,
> As Clothes for Lilly strecht to stain.
> The world when first created sure
> Was such a table rase and pure.[48]

The ironies are manifold. "Leveled" glances at the democratiz-
ing political agenda of the Levelers, whom Locke also rejected.[49]
In the agricultural context, flooding used for deliberate ecological management of an estate is read ironically by the poem's narrator as a scene of pure and original nature. This repeats exactly
the way in which most Europeans, without irony, read the New
England landscape, where the Indians made use of controlled
burns to create lush grasslands along forest edges so as to support the deer and other animals that they hunted, while the
Europeans saw the same landscape as an untouched nature that
new world "savages" were blessed with.[50] Characteristically,
Locke uses the figure of a lone American Indian killing a deer as
the model of man's original acquisition of property.[51] "[I]n the
beginning" says Locke, "all the world was *America*."[52]

These allusions in Marvell's poem to concepts of political
and ecological origins are coupled with important allusions to
concepts of psychological and aesthetic origins. For instance, the
phrase, "Table rase," sounds a lot like Locke's notion of the new-
born mind as it awaits the advent of sense-experience to write
upon it a knowledge of the world. Furthermore, the name
"Lilly" in the line about cloth stretched for him to paint on, is

---

[48] Andrew Marvell, *Upon Appleton House*, lines 443-46, *in* 1 THE POEMS AND LETTERS
OF ANDREW MARVELL 76 (H. M. Margoliouth ed., 1971) [hereinafter MISCELLANEOUS
POEMS]. Marvell's *Miscellaneous Poems* were first published posthumously in 1681; he
most likely wrote *Upon Appleton House* around 1650, only a year or so after the beheading
of Charles I, while serving as tutor for the daughter of Thomas Lord Fairfax, retired
commander of the revolutionary "New Model" army, at the Fairfax estate of Nun
Appleton.

[49] *See* CHRISTOPHER HILL, THE WORLD TURNED UPSIDE DOWN: RADICAL IDEAS IN THE
ENGLISH REVOLUTION (1972); MACPHERSON, *supra* note 46, ch. 3.

[50] WILLIAM CRONON, CHANGES IN THE LAND: INDIANS, COLONISTS, AND THE ECOLOGY
OF NEW ENGLAND 47-51 (1983).

[51] Locke, *supra* note 43, § 30. "Thus this Law of reason makes the Deer, that *Indian's*
who hath killed it; it is allowed to be his goods who hath bestowed his labour upon it,
though before, it was the common right of every one. And amongst those who are
counted the Civiliz'd part of Mankind, who have made and multiplied positive Laws to
determine Property, this original Law of Nature for the *beginning of Property*, in what was
before common, still takes place . . . ." *Id.*

[52] *Id.* § 49.

Peter Lely, the Dutch portrait painter who came to England in 1641: the idea of the blank canvas as an untouched nature, lying open for civilized man to inscribe himself onto it, is exactly the idea of the creation of intellectual property that Eaton Drone draws from his reading of Locke. For Drone all property—real, personal, or intellectual—is founded on the same principle: "there is no purer, stronger, better title to property than that acquired by production."[53]

It does not matter to Drone that the passages he quotes from Locke suggest a system of property relations already in place, as in the sentence, "The grass my horse has bit, the turfs my servant has cut, and the ore I have digged, in any place where I have a right to them in common with others, become my property."[54] That is, in imagining a horse that is *his* horse and, significantly, a servant who is *his* servant, Locke assumes an already functioning market economy based on a system of property that underwrites one man's ownership of another man's labor. Similarly, when Drone quotes Locke to the effect that a man acquires whatever he removes from the state of nature by reason of the labor he has invested in it,[55] Drone passes over the slippery patch in Locke's argument which assumes that laboring on something is the same as acquiring it, an assumption that simply buries the question of original acquisition, which Locke's treatise sets out to explain in the first place.[56]

In following Locke as his authority on property, Drone ignores fundamental difficulties in Locke's theory. As a result, he expounds what is essentially a free-market concept of intellectual and literary property for which language exists as so much raw material, untouched by any prior relation of production, exchange, or obligation, and simply waiting for the writer's labor to mine it and make it his own. According to this view, a writer acquires property in words by the distinctive order he bestows on them: that is what the law of copyright protects.[57] Writing is understood as something belonging exclusively to its author whose

---

[53] DRONE, *supra* note 41, at 4.

[54] LOCKE, *supra* note 43, at § 28.

[55] *See* LOCKE, *supra* note 44; DRONE, *supra* note 41, at 3 n.4.

[56] This slippery patch is exactly where the modern industrial laborer discovers that her labor does *not* entitle her to a property right in the product of her labor.

[57] Drone quotes a judicial opinion in a key British case: " 'The subject of property is the order of words in the author's composition; not the words themselves, they being analogous to the elements of matter, which are not appropriated unless combined, nor the ideas expressed by those words, they existing in the mind alone, which is not capable of appropriation." DRONE, *supra* note 41, at 5 n.3 (citing Jeffreys v. Boosey, 4 H.L.C. 814, 867 (1854)).

unique production it is. No discursive practice affects this property relation, either before something is written or after. Such is Drone's assumption when he argues against the doctrine that there can be no property in intellectual productions because they are "incorporeal" and therefore cannot bear "distinguishable proprietary marks." To refute this, Drone invokes the commonplace notion that "corporeal possessions perish; but time does not destroy or efface what is best in literature."[58] Thus the material monuments of antiquity have decayed and are no longer distinguishable, while the writings of Cicero and Horace endure, their unique identities preserved through the ages down to the present day. But it does not occur to Drone to question what cultural purpose is served in nineteenth-century England by their preservation, production, circulation, and consumption as the texts of an elitist educational practice. The way a culture exists, not prior to, but *in* and *as* its written productions, the way a text functions as a site of contested meaning, as both something written and something read—this is simply not available to Drone in the way he thinks. For Drone, writing is the uniquely personal property of its author in a free-market economy.[59]

This, then, is most likely the concept of intellectual property underlying the accusation of plagiarism against Helen Keller and all the deep hurt and embarrassment that it causes her and Anne Sullivan, as well as Michael Anagnos and the Perkins School. When we remember that Helen is only eleven years old, with just four years experience of language, when a court of inquiry examines her about "The Frost King," we might understandably think that all this concern for property law is misplaced, and that we ourselves are acting like Twain's "solemn donkeys" and "decayed human turnips" who constituted the plagiarism court. Were it not for the public nature of this sorry episode, which forced the principle actors to assume a formal posture about the plagiarism issue, we might actually question whether the concept of property law has anything to do with it at all.

---

58 DRONE, *supra* note 41, at 7.

59 Drone is arguing against the Anglo-American tradition of copyright, by which an author transfers her property right in her work to a publisher. He might have found support in the French tradition of the *droit d'auteur*, which reserves broad rights to the author over her work even after publication. *See* BERNARD EDELMAN, LA PROPRIÉTÉ LITTÉRAIRE ET ARTISTIQUE (1989). For the development of this right in Germany, see Martha Woodmansee, *The Genius and the Copyright: Economic and Legal Conditions of the Emergence of the 'Author,'* 17 EIGHTEENTH-CENTURY STUD. 425 (1984).

IV. A Gift for Mr. Anagnos

In fact, "The Frost King" starts out as something quite different from private property. It starts out as a *gift*, a birthday gift, which Helen sends to Michael Anagnos. It is important to understand the transformation which it undergoes from the time it leaves her hands until its publication, first in *The Mentor*, the Perkins alumni magazine, then in the *Goodson Gazette*, and finally in the Perkins *Annual Report*. A gift, after all, is not a commodity, nor is it given in expectation of something in return. In a gift culture, the gift keeps its status as a gift only when the recipient in turn gives it, or something of comparable worth, to another person. It ceases to be a gift when she keeps it as her own, adding it to her stock or capital; in a gift culture whoever does this and prevents the continued circulation of the gift is thought to be immoral and in serious debt. As Lewis Hyde puts it, "The only essential is this: *the gift must always move.* There are other forms of property that stand still, that mark a boundary or resist momentum, but the gift keeps going."[60] In its pure form, gift culture has existed among rural folk and primitive tribes-people, but it also exists within our own world of advanced technology, industrial capital, and commodity exchange. Hyde locates it on the margins of the mainstream economy, in what our culture constructs as a "feminine" economy of "child care, social work, nursing, the creation and care of culture, the ministry, [and] teaching."[61]

A perfect example of the "feminine" economy is the Perkins School itself. Just recently, in the fall of 1990, *Life* magazine published an article, "To Reach the Unreachable Child,"[62] on the education of deaf-blind children at Perkins. Both the writer and the photographer are women and, without exception, the text and photos feature children and the adult women who are their teachers and mothers. No men are present or even mentioned. Typical of the story is the way it describes the relationship between a seven-year-old and her teachers. The girl has not yet acquired language and, frustrated at her inability to communi-

---

[60] Lewis Hyde, The Gift: Imagination and the Erotic Life of Property 4 (1983).

[61] *Id.* at 106. Under the heading of culture comes writing, of course, and scholarly research. This essay of mine, though it will be added to the inventory of my own intellectual capital, my *curriculum vitae*, and hopefully will count toward enhancing my academic status and income—is still a gift, to be consumed and circulated in the gift culture of research and scholarship; no one will pay me for writing it, and I will not sell it—a fact that may lead to difficulties with the IRS about the deductibility of my expenses but nonetheless marks the essay as a gift.

[62] Lou Ann Walker, *To Reach the Unreachable Child*, Life, Oct. 1990, at 88 (featuring photography by Mary Ellen Mark).

cate, she throws a tantrum. The teachers, said to be "extraordinary," "take the screaming and thrashing calmly, trying to figure out what has caused the fury, and then they go back to work, tirelessly, lovingly providing Lindsay with language, the key to ending her agonizing frustration."[63] This surely is the "feminine" economy of gift culture in action; the rewards, often felt to be powerful, are not measured in the same terms as in the mainstream market economy. " 'Sometimes I can't believe I get paid for this,' teacher's aide Ashley Pope says without a trace of irony,"[64] and according to the article she is paid less than if she were teaching at a public school. Still, the actual costs of educating deaf-blind children are very high. The care of one student, a girl of seventeen, is put at $140,000 a year, with her home state of Indiana contributing half of it and Perkins absorbing the rest through its endowment. Again, this is where the *Life* magazine article comes in, for it circulates in more than just one medium of exchange. The form in which I received it, on a recent visit to the school, was a re-print that Perkins has packaged for mailings to current and potential supporters.[65] In this form the article includes a cover letter from the school's director, who happens to be a man, and who makes explicit what the article assumes: "The gifts that make Perkins the school it is come in many forms and from many sources. And it seems that everyone who gives a gift to Perkins also in some way receives a gift. A gift that comes from the children."[66]

A gift from one of the children is exactly what Helen Keller's

---

[63] *Id.* at 92.

[64] *Id.* at 98.

[65] "*To Reach the Unreachable Child,*" PERKINS SCHOOL FOR THE BLIND (reprinting *Life* article, *supra* note 62, as a brochure for publicity and fund raising) [hereinafter *Perkins Reprint*]. The extra pages that come with packaging the story as a Perkins publication make a lot more room for photographs, especially those that show cuddly children playing with the young women who are their teachers. An added two page spread features Lindsay romping with her teachers in deep grass filled with dandelions, and the cover photo shows her in the same setting, her face lighted by an open smile. Inside, there is a significant substitution. In the *Life* article, a large photo of Kenneth, a ten year old, shows him curled up alone inside a large playroom container wearing a protective helmet. The caption reads: "Some deaf-blind children develop 'stims,' reflexive habits for extra stimulation, like banging their heads against walls. That's why Kenneth wears his helmet most of the time." Walker, *supra* note 62, at 91. In the Perkins brochure, this image, suggesting the isolation and loneliness of a deaf-blind child, has been replaced, and the same caption stands next to a photo that shows Kenneth playing with his teacher, his head in her lap, a smile on his face, the helmet cast aside in the background. *Perkins Reprint, supra,* at 7.

[66] *Perkins Reprint, supra* note 65, at 3. Helen's story (and Canby's) is about making gifts. A figure of great wealth, King Frost is on the lookout for opportunities to bestow it on others. In Helen's words, "he does not keep his riches locked up all the time, but tries to do good and make others happy with them." What leads to the key incident of the story is King Frost's decision to send his wealth—large vases of brightly colored

story was, a gift for the school's director. As the current director's letter indicates, a director is an ambiguous figure on the boundary between two cultures, between the "feminine" economy of a gift culture and the market economy of risk and competition, profit and exploitation. Like university presidents and board directors for hospitals, museums, symphony orchestras, and other cultural institutions, the director stands at the boundary across which wealth accumulated in commerce and capital investment is translated into the form of a gift. The position requires skill, tact, and considerable powers of persuasion. Michael Anagnos, in his handling of Helen's story, performs this boundary function, but in reverse—by translating a gift into a form of wealth and institutional property.

When Helen Keller is accused of plagiarism, her accusers proceed on the basis of assumptions about property, and about intellectual property in particular, that apply to the story, not as a gift, but as a publication. Only in its published form does the story begin to matter as intellectual property and, decisively, it is not Helen Keller who publishes it but Michael Anagnos. In publishing the story in 1891, in the Perkins alumni magazine, Anagnos transforms it from a gift to an ornament of institutional prestige for his school. To be sure, his long, glowing account of Helen in the *Annual Report* for 1891, where he prints the story again, is filled with enthusiastic praise, much of it—astonishingly—for what he sees as her intellectual independence and self-sufficiency:

> Helen's mind seems almost to have created itself, springing up under every disadvantage, and working its solitary but restless way through a thousand obstacles. It is enriched with an extraordinary set of powers and capacities, which are ever on the alert to serve it at its bidding and minister to its functions with alacrity and efficacy. They enable her to receive, revive and modify perceptions; to analyze, sift, weigh and compare impressions; and to produce ideas which reflect not dimness or pale moonlight but effulgent solar splendor.[67]

About "The Frost King" itself, Anagnos exclaims, "If there be a pupil in any of the private or public grammar schools of New England who can write an original story like this, without assistance from any one, he or she certainly is a rare phenomenon."[68]

---

gems—to Santa Claus, "who loves to do good, and who brings presents to the poor, and to nice little children at Christmas." KELLER, STORY OF MY LIFE, *supra* note 4, at 350.

[67] *Perkins Report, supra* note 27, at 80.

[68] *Id.* at 98.

It is a measure of his extravagance that Anagnos can take a deaf-blind girl, who is wholly dependent on her teachers and friends for every visual and auditory perception, and describe her as one who writes a story in intensely visual language "without assistance from anyone." Still, even with such praise for Helen, his publication of the story assimilates it to the property of the institution. Helen wrote it, but she is a Perkins student. Though her mind may seem self-creating, its liberation is a product of the school and its educational program. Remarkably, there is no mention of Anne Sullivan and the "feminine" economy of teaching, caring for, and meeting the needs of a child. Instead, and quite ironically, the praise installs Helen as a paragon of independent mastery, self-creating and self-possessing, in the style of the narcissistic masculine ego, which is also the style of the Lockean and modern Anglo-American concept of property. The irony is one that Anagnos himself will complete in the same volume of the *Annual Report*, where a signed note is inserted, apparently just before the printed volume went to the bindery, in which Anagnos briefly describes the plagiarism and regrets the "mistake," though it is not clear whose mistake it is—Helen's in writing the story, or his own in publishing it.[69]

Just who was to take the credit for Helen's education was often a matter of dispute. Was it Anne Sullivan? Or the Perkins School, and Michael Anagnos its director? Or was it Helen alone who should take the credit? During the year just before the "Frost King" episode, differences between Anne Sullivan and the school over this question flared up and even made it into the newspapers. Sullivan, the half-blind Irish orphan girl who had been rescued from the Massachusetts almshouse by the school and its Boston Brahmin patrons, was, in their eyes, never grateful enough. The Howe family in particular showed her their disdain. Samuel Gridley Howe, the founder of Perkins, was world famous for his success in 1838, when he taught language to the deaf-blind girl, Laura Bridgman. Howe died in 1876, and Annie carefully studied the record of his work with Laura Bridgman in preparation for becoming Helen's teacher. But in a letter in 1887, just two months after she had led Helen Keller to the discovery of language, Annie confided to Mrs. Hopkins, "Something tells me that I shall succeed beyond my dreams. Were it not for some circumstances that make such an idea highly improbable, even absurd, I should think Helen's education would surpass in inter-

---

[69] *Id.* at 94-95.

est and wonder Dr. Howe's achievement."[70] In time Helen's fame, and Annie's too, did eclipse Laura Bridgman's and Samuel Gridley Howe's. But on one occasion when Annie ventured to ask Howe's widow, Julia Ward Howe, the celebrated poet, whether it were possible "that the almshouse ha[d] trained a teacher" Howe replied contemptuously that "it ha[d] nurtured the vanity of an ill-mannered person."[71] Years later, Annie recalled that the Howes always made her feel uncomfortable, and that she would be "painfully aggressive" when she was with them.[72] It also did not help her relationship with Michael Anagnos, the director of Perkins, that he was married to one of the Howe daughters. In 1890, Annie's aggression took the form of a newspaper interview, in which she declared, "Helen is not a regular pupil at the Perkins Institution . . . . I have the whole charge of her and my salary is paid by her father."[73] It all came down to a single question: who owned Helen Keller? This time it was resolved by Anne Sullivan being obliged to make a retraction of her public statement in a letter to Dr. Samuel Eliot, president of the Perkins board of trustees. The interview, she said, had misrepresented her by making it appear that she should get all the credit for Helen's education. "And much as Helen is indebted to the Institution," she wrote, "I am much more so, for as you know, I was educated there."[74]

V. Mirrored Selves

This contest over Helen Keller between Anne Sullivan and the Perkins School repeats a conflict over the relation between Helen and her teacher going back to the moment of the "mira-

---

[70] KELLER, STORY OF MY LIFE, *supra* note 4, at 265-66.

[71] LASH, *supra* note 6, at 116.

[72] *Id.*

[73] *Id.* at 117.

[74] *Id.* at 119. When Michael Anagnos died in 1906, Frank Sanborn, who had been an associate of Samuel Gridley Howe and played a central role in rescuing Annie from the Tewksbury almshouse, wrote a memorial tribute in the Boston *Transcript*. He praised Anagnos as the educator of Helen Keller, likening him to Howe as the educator of Laura Bridgman. This prompted an indignant reply from Helen: "Mr. Anagnos did not educate me. . . . He did not attempt to give me instruction in any subject, for he was never able to use the manual language fluently." *Id.* at 336. Apparently the Boston papers remained faithful to Anagnos and Perkins. A 1920 review of *Deliverance* in the *Boston American* shifts the site of the "miracle" from her Alabama home to Perkins:

The beginning of [her] career occurred here in Boston, . . . and largely through the solicitude of her teachers, under the direction of Mr. Anagnos, son-in-law of Julia Ward Howe, the helpless child grew into attractive womanhood. She was not the only child delivered from cruel fate at the Perkins Institution, but she was without doubt the most remarkable.

BOSTON AMERICAN, July 18, 1920.

cle" and Helen's discovery of language. Joseph Lash has noted the many times when Annie was suspected, and sometimes accused, of attempting to keep Helen unnecessarily under her control. An earlier writer, Thomas Cutsforth, was quite blunt in his assessment of the relationship. Blind himself, he was a psychologist who wrote an important book in the 1930s on the education of the blind.[75] He directly criticized Helen's education for having ignored and distorted her own experience in the service of the culture's ideals of genteel literary expression, and its normative standards of "auditory and visual respectability."[76] Cutsforth also specifically targeted the relationship between Helen and Annie, seeing in it an infantile "capitulation" of Helen's personality to her teacher's that continued throughout their lives together.[77] His criticism has much merit, but it also represents a conventionally masculine vision of a science of personality, with its ideals of "natural" and "independent" development, whereas Helen's experience is shaped largely by the conventions of the late nineteenth century women's culture of female friendships, shared sentiment, and social reform.

The nineteenth-century culture of separate spheres for the sexes, according to Carroll Smith-Rosenberg, provides the context for intense and passionate friendships among women, begun in many cases early in adolescence and continuing throughout their lives, undeflected by marriage or geographical distance. "Friendship," wrote one woman to her friend, "is fast twining about her willing captive the silken hands of dependence, a dependence so sweet who would renounce it for the apathy of self-sufficiency."[78] Such a sentiment seems altogether foreign to Cutsforth's ideals of rationalism and self-reliance. Though the archival evidence analyzed by Smith-Rosenberg reaches only to the 1880s, it is hard to believe that this style of feminine relationship did not continue, though in an altered form, into the early twentieth century. Still, the circumstances of Helen Keller and Anne Sullivan's relationship were largely unique: Annie was fourteen years older than Helen, and she played her crucial role in Helen's development when she was almost three times Helen's age. This would appear to distinguish their relationship from the friend-

---

[75] Thomas D. Cutsforth, THE BLIND IN SCHOOL AND SOCIETY: A PSYCHOLOGICAL STUDY (1933).

[76] Id. at 53.

[77] Id.

[78] Carroll Smith-Rosenberg, The Female World of Love and Ritual: Relations between Women in Nineteenth Century America 1 SIGNS 1, 25-26 (1975).

ships recorded by Smith-Rosenberg. However, as expressed in their letters and diaries, these friendships often played out the roles of mother-daughter dyads, and it would seem likely that this cultural tradition constructed a context in which Keller and Sullivan, as well as others, understood their relationship.

It is within her dyadic relationship with Annie that Helen's life unfolds, especially in the earlier stages of her development and acquisition of language. Psychoanalytic theory, in its growth since World War II, has sharpened our understanding of early human development and the role of language acquisition, particularly in the context of such a dyadic relationship between mother and child. This is particularly true of Lacanian psychoanalysis and also British object-relations theory, as represented by the work of D. W. Winnicott. Both Lacan and Winnicott address these issues in terms of an early moment characterized by the mother's mirror "role" (Winnicott) or as a mirror "stage" (Lacan), in which the infantile subject discovers itself reflected in the other. In this way both theorists locate the infantile (literally "not speaking") self in "transitional" (Winnicott) or "imaginary" (Lacan) relation with the other, such that the question, "Which is self, which is other?" does not arise. This understanding of the self has an important bearing on Helen Keller as accused plagiarist and "promiscuous" reader, at the moment just before the traumatic accusation, when the question does not yet arise for her, "Which are my words, which are yours?" Winnicott, in fact, is very explicit about this aspect of the transitional: "it is a matter of agreement between us and the baby that we will never ask the question: 'Did you conceive of this or was it presented to you from without?' . . . The question is not to be formulated."[79]

For both Lacan and Winnicott, the *visual* emphasis in the idea of the mirror is a decisive feature, because so much of the theoretical argument about narrative origins comes back again and again to an inaugural *scene*—itself a site for essential *looking*—whether it be a primal scene, or the mirror stage, or some crucial dream or vision. But what of the blind? Winnicott, in his paper on the mother's mirror role, says that "blind infants need to get

---

[79] D.W. WINNICOTT, *Transitional Objects and Transitional Phenomena*, in PLAYING AND REALITY 1, 12 (1971) (emphasis omitted) [hereinafter, WINNICOTT, *Transitional Objects*]. One way in which Lacan and Winnicott differ is that Lacan takes the standpoint of the adult psyche inscribed in the domain of the "Symbolic," while Winnicott, a pediatrician as well as an analyst, takes the standpoint of the infant at the threshold of a "transitional" space that is in the process of becoming a semiotic domain. Perhaps this is why Winnicott appears to be the least semiotic of analytic theorists.

themselves reflected through other senses than that of sight,"[80] and for Winnicott the other senses appear to be metaphors of the visual: the infant gets *reflected* by other means, as if the visual were taken for granted as truly mimetic, a privileged access to the real. That Helen Keller is both blind *and* deaf, and stricken at such an early age, adds a profoundly important difference. Though she is cut off from visual and auditory signs and from language itself, her experience suggests that even for a deaf-blind child the inaugural scene may be modeled relationally on what passes between mother and child in the mirror stage, but that it is finally a scene structured in and as language, according to the play and force of the signifier.

In this argument, I am following an important recent effort by Joan Copjec to rethink the specularized subject of film theory.[81] The tendency in film theory, says Copjec, has been to concentrate on the first half of Lacan's hyphenated term, "photograph," as in his statement that the gaze is "the instrument through which . . . I am *photo-graphed*,"[82] while ignoring the second half, the *graph* of photo-graph, and its implication that the visual is graphic, a field of writing:

> Semiotics, not optics, is the science that clarifies for us the structure of the visual domain. Because it alone is capable of lending things sense, the signifier alone makes vision possible. . . . And because signifiers are material, that is, because they are opaque rather than translucent, because they refer to other signifiers rather than directly to a signified, the field of vision is neither clear nor easily traversable.[83]

To an important extent, this understanding of the visual as something to be read is already present in Lacan's early paper on the mirror stage. "This jubilant assumption of his specular image by the child at the *infans* stage . . . situates the agency of the ego,

---

[80] WINNICOTT, *Mirror Role*, *supra* note 15, at 112.

[81] Joan Copjec, *The Orthopsychic Subject: Film Theory and the Reception of Lacan*, 49 OCTOBER 53 (1989). Much of today's film theory, even when it claims to be following Lacan, routinely uses the concept of the "gaze" as just the reverse of what Lacan intends. Copjec's essay is an extended critique of this reversal. In film theory the gaze shows up, for instance, in discussions of gendered spectatorship, as in the "male gaze," a term in the critique of the masculine ego; whereas in Lacan, the gaze is fundamentally a *superego* concept. The gaze, as Lacan says, is "outside." In Freud's early structural model, the ego and the id are intrapsychic functions. Freud adds the superego later, and conceives it as originating in a gesture that internalizes an object from "outside" the psyche, typically the voice of parental prohibition and demand. The theory of the superego marks the beginning of "object relations" theory which, in its fuller development, is Winnicott's point of departure.

[82] LACAN, *Gaze*, *supra* note 2, at 106.

[83] Copjec, *supra* note 81, at 68.

before its social determination, in a fictional direction. . . ."[84] That is, the mirror-image assumed by the child *anticipates* a future coherence and unity of the bodily self that it presently lacks, and anticipation implies thought, imagination, an ability—however rudimentary—to interpret. Though the child is *infans*, without speech, it does not mean that she is without a basic competence for responding to visual signs. The infant's primal appropriation of a self-image already indicates an ability to read and therefore recognize the self-as-image or self-as-sign. But this recognition is not once and for all: Lacan's mirror "stage" is not only a stage of development but also the stage on which the ego will continue to play at assuming a coherent, unified image of an otherwise fragmented body ego (*corps morcelé*). Lacan's attempt to locate this moment of play "even before the social dialectic"[85] cannot escape the shadow which that dialectic already casts across the imaginary relation of the mirror, imparting to the ego its "fictional" direction.

The importance of the visual in this experience, not just as a metaphor, but as a specific mode of perception, is borne out by Selma Fraiberg's work with congenitally blind infants. Some blind infants show signs of autism; typically, they form no attachments and appear to have no sense of *self* and *other*, no concept of an object, either in the "outer" world of people and material things or in the "inner" world of bodily function and feeling. One ten-year old boy repeats over and over again the question, "Where is . . . ?" referring to the names of various people and material objects. His questions, however, do not attribute an existence elsewhere to the people and things named. Instead, they function as incantatory demands for the reappearance of objects that are not so much absent as "lost."[86] Of course, blind infants do acquire a concept of an object, but it typically comes later in their development than for sighted infants, and it requires a conscious effort from parents to compensate for the blindness with an abundance of auditory, tactile, and kinesthetic communication.

VI. WATER AND A BROKEN DOLL

It is with this understanding that I want to read Helen Keller's dramatic moment of acquiring language as an inaugural

---

[84] LACAN, *Mirror Stage, supra* note 14, at 2.
[85] *Id.* at 4.
[86] SELMA FRAIBERG, INSIGHTS FROM THE BLIND: COMPARATIVE STUDIES OF BLIND AND SIGHTED INFANTS 37 (1977).

scene structured like—but necessarily and critically different from—the visual. After she was stricken, Helen lived in a world of silence and what she remembered years later as "a tangible white darkness."[87] Still, even before Anne Sullivan first started working with her, at age seven, Helen had acquired a limited sign language, a system for pointing to present objects and indicating immediate wants like eating. She seemed able to negotiate her world quite well, and to distinguish among different people and objects. Apparently, she was even aware of mirrors. Anne Sullivan's first letter, three days after her arrival in Alabama in 1887, tells how she let Helen put on her bonnet and then watched, amused, as the girl tilted her head from side to side in front of a mirror, "just as if she could see."[88] This does not mean, however, that she had learned to conceptualize the visual experience of the mirror, even before she learned language. It was mimicry, a game of repeating the postures and gestures of those around her, with no understanding of them as sight or sound or *sign*.[89] Helen recalls:

> Before my teacher came to me, I did not know that I am. I lived in a world that was a no-world. I cannot hope to describe adequately that unconscious, yet conscious time of nothingness. I did not know that I knew aught, or that I lived or acted or desired. I had neither will nor intellect. I was carried along to objects and acts by a certain blind natural impetus.[90]

In a letter to William James, she says she can remember acts from her pre-verbal days—"shedding tears, screaming, kicking"—but cannot recall any feelings that went with them.[91] Maybe this is why she does not recall the early "battle royal" with Annie over her eating habits. Cut off from sight and sound, Helen has no grasp of language as a conceptual medium, not until the famous moment in the well-house when Annie pumps water over one hand and spells the word "w-a-t-e-r" in the other. With the discovery that water is a word,[92] she turns jubilantly to the objects

---

[87] KELLER, STORY OF MY LIFE, *supra* note 4, at 35.

[88] *Id.* at 245.

[89] In a letter written a year later, Annie repeats the same incident but does not mention a mirror. Instead, she says what she learned later: that Helen tilted her head from side to side with a hat on in imitation of her aunt Ev. LASH, *supra* note 6, at 51.

[90] KELLER, WORLD I LIVE IN, *supra* note 5, at 113.

[91] LASH, *supra* note 6, at 346.

[92] Actually, "water" is one of a few words that Helen remembers having learned before her illness. "I continued to make some sound for that word after all other speech was lost. I ceased making the sound 'wah-wah' only when I learned to spell the word." KELLER, STORY OF MY LIFE, *supra* note 4, at 25. Significantly, she remembered the word but not its force as language.

around her, demanding their names, consuming the world as language. An exhilarating moment of discovery and liberation, it is, however, a good deal more complex than I have indicated so far.

Helen remembers that, just before the scene in the well-house, she grew frustrated at Annie's repeated attempts that day to get her to understand the word "water," and she angrily threw her doll on the floor. It was a porcelain doll, one that Annie had given her on her arrival in Tuscumbia, and it shattered into many fragments.[93] All that Helen says she remembers feeling at the time was the sadistic pleasure of sensing the fragments at her feet. However, when she returned from the well-house scene, filled with her discovery of language, she immediately remembered the doll, felt her way to it, and tried to piece it back together. "Then," Helen says, "my eyes filled with tears; . . . and for the first time I felt repentance and sorrow."[94]

As one thinks of how to read this scene, it is important to recognize how Helen herself does *not* read it. Though she is often sentimental, she does not say that a sense of loss was the price she paid as a child to acquire the power of language. She is not mourning a fall into language from the realm of the Lacanian "imaginary." On the contrary, according to her narrative, language is what enables her to feel loss and sorrow understood as a positive, civilizing experience. In a movement of deferred meaning, language abruptly restructures both the memory of a primally destructive act and the "I" that remembers it, an "I" precipitated at that moment as a speaking subject and propelled forward into narrative as she revises—or, more exactly, conceives—her past. Helen remembers in fact that she learned many words that day, among them mother, father, sister, teacher; and

---

[93] The doll appears only in Helen's version of the episode, not in Annie's. Helen's account of the whole episode is quite brief compared to Annie's in her letters to Mrs. Hopkins. Her three-page chapter in *The Story of My Life* omits the "battle-royal" in the dining room and condenses a month of intense work into just a few days. Annie's narrative in her letters, from the moment of her arrival to the miracle in the well house, fills almost fourteen pages. So, Helen's account may not be as reliable as Annie's, especially since Annie wrote hers immediately as events happened, while Helen wrote hers some thirteen to fourteen years later in 1900-01. (Helen did write an earlier autobiographical sketch which appeared in the January 4, 1894, issue of *The Youth's Companion*, but she does not mention breaking the doll there.) Still, even though the broken doll appears only in Helen's published account, it seems appropriate to take it as a significant element in her experience. If it is the doll she says it is, the one that Annie gives her when she arrives in Tuscumbia, then it serves to link Helen Keller with the young girls at Perkins, whose gift it was. It also serves to link Helen with Laura Bridgman, who was a sewing instructor at Perkins in her late fifties in 1887; she made the doll's dress and sent a note with it "to my sister in Christ." LASH, *supra* note 6, at 49.

[94] KELLER, STORY OF MY LIFE, *supra* note 4, at 36-37.

she remembers, too, that she went to bed that evening anticipating, for the first time, the arrival of the next day.

And what about the broken doll? It seems a likely strategy to interpret it as a Winnicottean transitional object, a sign of the child's capacity to symbolize continued union with the (m)other while that union is in the process of being broken. But if this doll functions as a transitional object, it does so in a special way. For it seems as if at the age of six or seven, Helen, because she lacks access to the signifying and conceptual properties of language, cannot move beyond the primitive phase of the transitional. And, indeed, her lack of language is an enormous frustration to her. Years later, she remembers how she would stand between two persons who were conversing and touch their lips. Unable to understand, she nevertheless tried moving her own lips but without effect, and she would end up kicking and screaming until she was exhausted.[95]

The fate of the transitional object, says Winnicott, is simply to be discarded: "It is not forgotten and it is not mourned. It [just] loses meaning, and this is because the transitional phenomena have become diffused, have become spread out . . . over the whole cultural field."[96] For Winnicott, the development out of the mirror stage is a direct line of growth, and transitional phenomena, as they continue to play out the mirror role of the mother's face, remain entirely dyadic in form: there is no gap, no disruption, no third term (which Lacan locates in language and the domain of the Symbolic). Nevertheless, Winnicott does offer another way to understand the process in his paper, "The Use of an Object." There he proposes a critical step in the child's development from relating to objects, to the *use* of an object, a step that means repositioning the object "outside the area of the subject's omnipotent control. . . ."[97] Significantly, such repositioning means the destruction of the object, a destruction occurring on the boundary between fantasy and reality, which the object either does or does not survive. As for Lacan, in his later statements about the gaze, he appears to revise his earlier theory of the mirror stage (or recognize, perhaps, a neglected dimension of it). The idea of the "photo-graph", as something at once visual and written, indicates that the imaginary is already configured

---

95 *Id.* at 27-28.

96 WINNICOTT, *Transitional Objects, supra* note 79, at 5.

97 D.W. WINNICOTT, *The Use of an Object and Relating through Identifications, in* PLAYING AND REALITY 86, 89 (1969).

in the shadow of the symbolic, and the mirror already traversed by the signifier.

Before Helen smashes the doll—and certainly before she returns to mourn it—the doll, I think, presents the possibility of something, or someone, existing in relation to her, from beyond the perimeter of her paranoid isolation, but it is not a truly transitional object. Winnicott makes a distinction, in fact, between the truly transitional object, which is always "more important than the mother, an almost inseparable part of the infant,"[98] and another object that acts as a comforter in the mother's absence but is readily discarded on her return. Helen's doll, I believe, does not function as a transitional object, at least not until she returns and tries to piece it back together. Only when she recognizes its brokenness as a sign of her brokenness, that is, only when she recognizes it *as a sign*, does the doll then become—retroactively and, in loss, irrecoverably—a transitional object. Grief and regret become possible, then, in a space made transitional by language. Annie, in a letter written the same day, in April 1887, records that the first thing Helen did after the moment of discovery was drop to the ground and ask for its name, as if moved to acknowledge for the first time that this most elemental substance, the ground as material and concept, might actually exist apart from her and have a name—or exist *because* it had a name. First water, then earth: one almost expects air and fire to follow. What does follow, according to Annie, are words denoting boundaries and ways of negotiating them: "[d]oor, open, shut, give, go, come."[99]

Regarding doors and their liminal properties, as both barriers and openings, Helen records important memories of two incidents before the well-house scene. When she was about four, she discovered the use of a key and one day locked her mother in the pantry. No one was nearby, and Helen remembers sitting outside on the porch steps laughing as she felt herself being jarred by her mother's pounding on the door. The incident lasted for three hours. Then, again, soon after Anne Sullivan arrived, Helen locked her in her room and hid the key, refusing to tell anyone where it was. Finally her father had to get a ladder and bring Annie out through a window. It seems as if only when Helen enters the world as language, which she does immediately after an act of violence akin to Winnicott's destruction of the ob-

---

98 WINNICOTT, *Transitional Objects, supra* note 79, at 7.
99 KELLER, STORY OF MY LIFE, *supra* note 4, at 257 (alteration in original).

ject and Lacan's castration of the subject, that she then gains access to others, as *other*, and thus also enters the terrain of desire.[100] In a note added to her letter the next day, Annie records that when she got in bed that evening, Helen came into her room and "stole into [her] arms of her own accord and kissed [her] for the first time. . . ."[101]

VII. THE STORY OF MY LIFE

In writing her chapter on "The Frost King" episode, Helen Keller tells how she has been changed by the trauma of being accused of plagiarism and compelled to appear before a court of investigation. Several years after the event, she can describe her younger efforts at authorship as exercises in "assimilation" and "imitation." As she writes, she locates herself in time, in the midst of a "not yet completed" process, between the traumatic past and a moment in the indefinite future when she might really become a writer, someone who has learned to "marshall the legion of words which come thronging through every byway of the mind:"

> It is certain that I cannot always distinguish my own thoughts from those I read, because what I read becomes the very substance and texture of my mind. Consequently, in nearly all that I write, I produce something which very much resembles the crazy patchwork I used to make when I first learned to sew. . . . Trying to write is very much like trying to put a Chinese puzzle together. We have a pattern in mind which we wish to work out in words; but the words will not fit the spaces, or, if they do, they will not match the design. But we keep on trying because we know that others have succeeded, and we are not willing to acknowledge defeat.[102]

Writing has become difficult, and Helen has come to understand how slippery and stubborn words can be, the impossibility of gaining a perfect fit. Not only is what she writes a "patchwork," but so is the text and "texture" of her mind: it too is the patchwork whose substance is language. Insofar as she grasps this truth, Helen Keller subverts Foucault's panoptic model of knowl-

---

[100] *Compare* Ovid's Narcissus and his lament about his image in the water:
  To make it worse, no sea, no road, no mountain,
  No city wall, no gate, no barrier, parts us
  But a thin film of water. (3. 448-450)
There is no way from the "I" *to* the beloved because there is nothing *between* them. OVID, METAMORPHOSES 71 (R. Humphries trans., Indiana UP, 1955).
[101] KELLER, STORY OF MY LIFE, *supra* note 4, at 257.
[102] *Id.* at 67-68.

edge and discipline. "The Panopticon," says Foucault, "is a machine for dissociating the see/being seen dyad: in the periperic ring, one is totally seen, without ever seeing; in the central tower, one sees everything without ever being seen."[103] The idea of being able to see *everything*, to achieve a *totality* of knowledge, is something that Helen's assent to the difficulty of language exposes as a characteristic Foucauldian hyperbole. In a diary entry for January 30, 1892, when Annie has just told her that her writing is suspect, Helen writes, "I thought everybody had the same thought about the leaves, but I do not know now."[104] Once again, in order to discover herself as a thinking subject, she must discover and acknowledge her difference and her incompleteness. For Helen this amounts to a liberating position of doubt, although in response to the pain and unease of it, she constructs a narrativized self located between a traumatic origin and a future perfection, between fall and recovery. It is on this basis that she constructs herself as a narrative subject, a subject of writing.

At the end of her chapter, after affirming that what she has just written is "all the facts as they appear to me,"[105] and after disclaiming any desire to defend herself, Helen begins a new chapter:

> The summer and winter following the "Frost King" incident I spent with my family in Alabama. I recall with delight that home-going. Everything had budded and blossomed. I was happy. "The Frost King" was forgotten.
>
> When the ground was strewn with the crimson and golden leaves of autumn, and the musk-scented grapes that covered the arbour at the end of the garden were turning golden brown in the sunshine, I began to write a sketch of my life—a year after I had written "The Frost King."[106]

Of course, "The Frost King" is not forgotten at all. In a typically expressive gesture, Helen appropriates the language of the purloined text, impossibly visual in its signification,[107] and begins to write what will be the text that the reader is in the process of reading. What she makes her own, and makes of herself as speaking and writing subject, is the threshold moment of her en-

---

[103] DISCIPLINE AND PUNISH, *supra* note 16, at 201-02.
[104] KELLER, STORY OF MY LIFE, *supra* note 4, at 356.
[105] *Id.* at 69.
[106] *Id.*
[107] Except for the one detail: the musk scent of the grapes (and possibly the warmth of the sun).

trance into language. That is "the story of [her] life." In fact, the first version of her autobiography, which she publishes in the January, 1894, number of *The Youth's Companion*, just two years after the "Frost King" incident, is given a very simple but definitive title: "My Story."[108] In the process, "Helen Keller" becomes the name for a liminal moment of transition from darkness to light, silence to speech, bondage to liberation, repeated and commemorated in both what she writes and what others write about her.

The relation, though, between what she writes about herself and what others write about her is not always clear, and this lack of clarity is fundamental to the construction of "Helen Keller." The decade or so of Helen's early experience with publication, from 1892 to 1903, traces a narrative of disclosure and concealment, acknowledgement and denial, in her project of authorial self-inscription. First, there is the involuntary publication of "The Frost King" in early 1892 followed by the traumatic accusation of plagiarism and her passionate denial. Then comes the publication of the brief autobiographical sketch, aggressively and recuperatively titled "My Story," as if declaring that her only real subject, the only subject no one could accuse her of plagiarizing, is her "self," which, paradoxically, is the self that she writes into existence in writing her autobiography. Tellingly, the editor of *The Youth's Companion* declares that the story was "[w]ritten wholly without help of any sort . . . and printed without change."[109] Next, after writing several further sketches as freshman compositions at Radcliffe for Professor Charles Copeland in 1900-01, Helen publishes "The Story of My Life" in six installments in the *Ladies Home Journal* in 1902,[110] which the *Journal* introduces as "Helen Keller's Own Story Of Her Life, Written Entirely by the Wonderful Girl Herself."[111] Then, with some revision, this is published in book form the following year with the same title, *The Story of My Life*. But the book is a composite, and the full story is a collaboration, such that the lines are blurred between biography and autobiography.[112] In addition to Helen's autobiography, the book has a section containing her letters and

---

108 Helen Keller, *My Story*, YOUTH'S COMPANION, Jan. 4, 1984, at 3.
109 *Id.*
110 Helen Keller, *The Story of My Life* (pts. 1-5) LADIES' HOME J., Apr.-Sept. 1902.
111 *Id.* pt. 1, at 7.
112 Joseph Lash, originally commissioned to write a biography of Helen Keller timed for the 100th anniversary of her birth in 1980, quickly determined that "[i]t is impossible to write a book about Helen Keller that is not also a book about Annie Sullivan. . . ." LASH, *supra* note 6, at 3.

another section put together by John Macy, the editor, including Anne Sullivan's all-important 1887 and 1888 letters to Mrs. Hopkins, plus Macy's own account of Helen. This is an expansion of two installments he contributed to *Ladies Home Journal* as a supplement to Helen's autobiography, under the title, "Helen Keller as She Really Is."[113] So, the change in titles, from "My Story" in 1894 to *The Story of My Life* in 1903 traces an important but subtle change in Helen's claim of authorial autonomy. The first title announces a story that belongs doubly to Helen Keller, as both a story *of* her and a story *by* her. The second title announces something more complex: a story *of* her but one for which the article "the" in the phrase, "The Story," fails to disclose an author. This change was no doubt too subtle to be noticed, perhaps not even by Helen and Annie themselves, for the public has tended to take at face value the inscription of "Helen Keller" as author on the title page.[114] Of course, the writer of the accusatory text, "Miss Sullivan's Methods," makes much of the book's status as a "composite reminiscence,"[115] but most readers, eager to see Helen as the heroine of her own narrative, have tended to overlook this and think of the whole book as Helen's own, thus confirming her status as *author* of the book that narrates her achievement of an author's status in the first place.

VIII. Deaf-Blind Writing and the Production of "Helen Keller"

In early 1905, anticipating her marriage to John Macy, Annie wrote a letter to a friend, in which she sums up the finances that supported Helen and herself. Besides a trust fund yielding them $840 a year, there was the income from Helen's books and articles. On this score, Annie feels it necessary to set the record straight:

> Of course you know that whatever Helen writes represents my labor as well as hers. The genius is hers, but much of the drudgery is mine. The conditions are such that she could not prepare a paper for publication without my help. The difficulties under which she works are insurmountable. Someone

---

[113] John Albert Macy, *Helen Keller as She Really Is* (pt. 1), Ladies' Home J., Oct.1902, at 11.

[114] John Macy, though, is quite clear about the implications: "She cannot know in detail how she was taught, and her memory of her childhood is in some cases an idealized memory of what she has learned later from her teacher and others." Keller, Story of My Life, *supra* note 4, at 224.

[115] *Methods*, *supra* text accompanying note 40.

must always be at her side to read to her, to keep her type-
writer in order, to read over her manuscript, make corrections
and look up words for her, and to do the many things which
she would do herself if she had her sight. I make this statement because Helen's friends have not always understood
what the relations between her and me really are. They have
thought her earning capacity independent of me, and one person at least has hinted that financially she might be better off
without me. Helen feels very differently and when the book
contracts were made, she insisted that they should revert to
me on her death. It is also her wish to divide equally with me,
during her life, all the money that comes to her as our joint
earnings. I am willing to accept one third.[116]

In this passage, Annie interprets the primary triangle that binds
Helen and herself together, underscoring what for her are its adverse implications: there is Helen the "genius," Annie the
"drudge," and a world that is bent on valuing them accordingly.
Her own estimate of Helen's genius is, in large part, what
prompted Annie to idealize Helen's youthful abilities as a writer,
and to stand unyieldingly by her denial that Helen was reading
Canby when she wrote "The Frost King." What comes through
in Annie's account, though, is the generosity of both women toward one another: Helen's wish to divide her income equally with
Annie, and Annie's deferential willingness to accept only a third
("Does this seem a just arrangement?" she asks in the letter).[117]
What also comes through is the sense that both women understood how they were collaborators in the production of "Helen
Keller," although the relative importance of each one was inevitably in question.

Responding to the public's variable estimate of the two women, John Macy sarcastically joked that one half the world "believes Annie Sullivan is just a governess and interpreter, riding to
fame on Helen's genius," while the other half believes Helen is
"only Annie's puppet, speaking and writing lines that are fed to
her by Annie's genius."[118] The two women were constantly negotiating the way they were perceived, and Helen was always
alert to correct any lack of recognition for Annie. When they met
Dr. Maria Montessori in 1914, and she told Helen that she had
learned from her "as [a] pupil learns from [a] master," Helen
quickly replied that the compliment should have been paid to An-

---

116 LASH, *supra* note 6, at 329.
117 *Id.*
118 *Id.* at 319-20.

nie.[119] Then, in 1931, when they were both to be awarded honorary degrees by Temple University, Annie stubbornly refused to accept hers, complaining that she was unworthy of the honor.[120] Years later, in the stage production of William Gibson's play, *The Miracle Worker*,[121] this dynamic had its effect even on the actresses playing the roles of Annie and Helen. Of course, the title of the play refers to Annie, not Helen, but this was often lost on a public eager to cast Helen as the heroine of her own drama. Many years later, Gibson remarked ironically that the play's reception was such that its title should have been *The Miracle "Workee."*[122] Ann Bancroft, who played Annie, became distressed by the way audiences at the final curtain barely noticed her after the first round of applause, while they continued to cheer Patty Duke for her performance as Helen.[123] Nella Braddy, Annie's biographer, sympathized with Bancroft, telling her how "people would trample [Annie] so as to get at Helen."[124]

Again, it is John Macy who cuts through the public's perception of rivalry, and identifies "the unanalyzable kinship" that was "the foundation of Helen Keller's career."[125] Writing in 1902, when he was already a collaborator in their enterprise, having served as editor and compiler of *The Story of My Life*, he saw in Annie a special skill:

> [Sullivan's] skill in presenting material, some of which she does not try to retain herself, but allows to pass through her to the busy fingers of her pupil; her instinct in striking out the inessential; her feeling, which is now a matter of long experience, for just the turn of thought that Miss Keller needs at the moment. . . . [126]

What is striking about this description, by a man who may have already been in love with Annie, is the way it recalls Winnicott's description of the mother's mirror role in meeting and reflecting the infant's needs. This is evidenced by the way Annie filters out the "inessential" and instinctively provides Helen with what she needs "at the moment," thus shaping and translating the world

---

[119] *Id.* at 418.

[120] *Id.* at 596.

[121] WILLIAM GIBSON, THE MIRACLE WORKER: A PLAY FOR TELEVISION (1957).

[122] WILLIAM GIBSON, MONDAY AFTER THE MIRACLE: A PLAY IN THREE ACTS viii (1983).

[123] LASH, *supra* note 6, at 762.

[124] *Id.*

[125] Macy, *supra* note 113, at 12.

[126] *Id. See also*, LASH, *supra* note 6, at 295-96. Macy omitted this passage from the version published in Helen's 1903 book, *The Story of My Life, see supra* note 4.

to correspond with the shape of it already implicit in Helen's unique perceptual capacity and her desire.

What is in question here is a rivalry between two different ways of reading this moment: Winnicott's and Lacan's. Or perhaps, rather than a rivalry, a complementarity.[127] On the one hand, it is as if Lacan's focus on the *otherness* of the specular image, its contribution to the paranoid development of the ego, positions him to account for the rivalry between Helen and Annie, a rivalry that finds resolution only in Annie's repeated gestures of deference and Helen's reciprocal (and reparative) insistence on full recognition for Annie. On the other hand, it is as if Winnicott's focus on the *sameness* of the specular image—the baby seeing herself in her mother's face, because what the mother looks like when she looks at the baby is related to "what she sees there"[128]—positions Winnicott to account for the enduring, intensely intimate and dyadic relationship between the two women. This is a relationship in which the absent visual modality is replaced by touch, what Helen describes as mediating all her thought and experience, the hand that touches her in the dark.[129] Although Winnicott and Lacan are describing virtually the same phenomenon, where they differ is that Lacan, in his account of the mirror stage, never describes the infant as touching or being touched or held by her mother. Lacan alludes to this mode of mother-infant relating only as the contrasting ground for the infant's perceptual precocity: her "motor incapacity and nursling dependence," or generally, her "organic insufficiency."[130] Maybe it is a question of developmental timing. Writing after Lacan, Winnicott acknowledges his influence but says that the mother's face is "*the precursor of the mirror.*"[131] Still, Lacan is clear about the imaginary, pre-Symbolic character of the mirror stage, to the extent that it *can* be described as pre-Symbolic,[132] and this would situate Lacan's and Winnicott's theories as both dealing with the same developmental phase. But it is Winnicott who ex-

---

[127] An alternative way to configure the relation between Winnicott and Lacan is, in Shoshana Felman's phrase, a "missed encounter" between languages. They are both "products of their respective languages. Each works with, and takes into account, the concrete functioning of his own language. That is to say that they are both effects of the knowledge of their own languages." SHOSHANA FELMAN, THE LITERARY SPEECH ACT: DON-JUAN WITH J. L. AUSTIN, OR SEDUCTION IN TWO LANGUAGES (Catherine Porter trans., 1983).

[128] WINNICOTT, *Mirror Role, supra* note 15, at 112 (emphasis omitted).

[129] *See supra* text accompanying note 8.

[130] LACAN, *Mirror Stage, supra* note 14, at 2, 4.

[131] WINNICOTT, *Mirror Role, supra* note 15, at 111 (emphasis in original).

[132] *See supra* text accompanying notes 81-85.

plicitly focuses on the mother's function in holding and handling the infant, and presenting objects to her, as he addresses the mother's mirror role. And, significantly, he limits his observations only to *sighted* infants.

The difference between the bodily presence of the mother in Winnicott's theory and her virtual absence in Lacan's theory is already well understood, as are the implications of this difference. Madelon Sprengnether, for instance, sees it as implying decisively different relationships between mother and infant.

> Whereas [Winnicott's] theory stresses maternal presence (and plenitude) through the concept of mother-infant fusion, Lacan downplays the role of the biological mother to the point where she barely seems to exist in a corporeal sense. . . . The mother's [Winnicottean] role as an agent in the process of reflection means that her responsiveness to her infant has a profound influence on its subsequent development. The more she resembles a [Lacanian] mirror, in fact—passive, distracted, or withdrawn—the less her infant is able to use the image she provides. Such a circumstance, according to Winnicott, fosters the emergence of pathology.[133]

An important aspect of Sprengnether's argument is that she clarifies the extent to which Winnicott's theory is a critique of Lacan's. The critical difference is between the *reflective function* of the mirror and its *material being*. If the mother does not just reflect her infant "like" a mirror, but also resembles the cold, material otherness of its surface, then for Winnicott the mother-infant relationship becomes alienating and paranoid.

However, as far as I can tell, it has not been adequately understood how important in Lacan's theory is the absence of the tactile, of mutual touching and holding, for the development of infantile perception and knowledge (it is crucial for blind infants).[134] Philosophically, it has always been the habit of skeptical theories of perception, which deny the reality of the phenomenal world, to emphasize touch and downplay sight. Typically, such theories use the scratch of a blade or the tickle of a feather as their example: what is perceived is not so much the object as the sensation that it excites on the surface of the body.[135] In con-

---

133 MADELON SPRENGNETHER, THE SPECTRAL MOTHER: FREUD, FEMINISM, AND PSYCHO-ANALYSIS 183, 185 (1990).

134 *See supra* text accompanying note 85.

135 *See* HANNAH ARENDT, THE HUMAN CONDITION 114 n. 63 (1958). Arendt argues that it is not just any instance of the sense of touch that a skeptic uses to disprove the reality of the perceived world, but the special instance in which the sensation of touch excites or pains the body to the extent that the mind is distracted from the object in question

trast, Lacan emphasizes the visual in his central concepts of the gaze and the mirror stage, and he is apparently indifferent to bodily modes of perception, the "proximity" senses of taste, touch and smell (which virtually excludes Helen Keller from his theory). In this way, he exchanges a modern philosophy of doubt for a post-modern philosophy of paranoia.

What this suggests, I think, is a fundamental relationship between sight and touch that the post-Saussurean—and Lacanian— theory of the sign does not account for. For the developing child, the word "dog" (or rather, "doggie") comes to be grasped and repeated from out of the surrounding envelope of sounds, images, textures, tastes, and smells within which a child awakens to herself as a subject of *this* culture and not another, a member of *this* family, a child of *this* mother—whose voice, worded or not, comes combined with the touch, taste, and smell of her body, and the kinesthetic pleasures of being held, rocked, and carried in her arms. Lacan, it seems, reads Saussure from the vantage of his earlier association with surrealist artists and photographers. Consequently, his theory of the sign or, more exactly, the *signifier* (with the signified not as the referent of the signifier but its effect), seems to be based on a visual aesthetics strongly inflected by a paranoid positionality. There is, in Saussure's theory, the familiar "arbitrariness" of the sign. That the furry animal which has four legs and wags its tail is named *dog* or *chien* or *hund* or *perro*, depending on the language, shows that the signifier has no natural connection with the signified, since what the sign unites is not a word and a thing, but a sound-image and a concept (signifier and signified). As Mikkel Borch-Jacobsen points out, however, the more consequential principle in Saussure is the "value" of the linguistic sign.[136] The value of the sign is understood as the sum of its divergences from other signs: meaning is determined by *difference*.

> [Moreover,] . . . there is strict adherence between the signifier and the signified, and if this is so, it is because, in accord with the theory of value, they vary in concert within a linguistic system with which they are in solidarity (hence the despair of

---

and focused instead on the sensation itself. So, she quotes Descartes, on the unreality of "secondary" qualities: " 'The motion merely of a sword cutting a part of our skin causes pain but does not on that account make us aware of the motion or the figure of the sword. And it is certain that this sensation of pain is not less different from the motion that causes it . . . than are the sensation[s] we have of color, sound, odor, or taste.' " *Id.* (quoting Descartes, *Principals, Part 4, in* PHILOSOPHICAL WORKS (Haldane & Ross, trans., 1911)).

[136] M. BORCH-JACOBSEN, LACAN: THE ABSOLUTE MASTER (Douglas Brick trans., 1991).

translators, who know only too well that [*boef*] will never have exactly the same *meaning* as [*beef*], even if they refer to the same *thing*.)[137]

The despair of the translator marks both the limit and the power of language—the weight and specificity of the culture that it speaks. Such despair points to the unique materiality of the culture, the voices and fragrances, textures and flavors, and the singular play of light and dark and color, that come to be recognized and named by the developing subject. At the beginning of such recognition, according to Winnicott, there is not just the image of the mother, as if in a mirror, but her body too, experienced with all the same specificity of the senses. Winnicott's model of the infant in her mother's arms, the two gazing into one another's eyes, portrays a simultaneously visual and tactile perception of the object. This is where language begins, where the infant begins to exercise a capacity to recognize the self-as-image or self-as-sign. The beginnings of language and knowledge are, at the very least, tactile as well as visual.

In Diderot's account of the blind man of Puisaux, the man often speaks of mirrors. Asked to define one, he offers the felicitous intuition that it is an instrument that enables us to touch our faces at a distance (says Diderot: "Had Descartes been born blind, he might, I think, have hugged himself for such a definition").[138] In this we are not far from the moment when Helen awakens to the fact and power of language, as she feels water flowing in one hand while in the other hand she feels Annie spelling the word for water. My guess is that maturation for the sighted means a fading of the connection between the tactile and the visual, with the tactile remaining as an unfelt but active grounding of knowledge, perception, and desire. For the blind, and specifically for the deaf-blind, like Helen, touch and perception remain strongly related: touch *is* perception; which means that for Helen it will take a "battle-royal" to get her, as an alingual child, to acknowledge the boundaries between self and other that her blind groping continually transgresses. Later, it will take the trauma of being accused of plagiarism to get her to acknowledge similar boundaries between her words and the words of others.

If Winnicott is the theorist of the moment when touch and

---

[137] *Id.* at 174.
[138] Diderot, *supra* note 17, at 71-72. *See also* HULL, *supra* note 18, at 65-66 ("I am often surprised that my sighted friends know something when it is still so far off. The blind have to remember that it is just as if the sighted were touching their faces all the time.").

sight are merged in the dual unity of the mother-infant mirror relationship, then Lacan is the theorist of the moment when touch and sight are divided and the subject, left on her own to experience the disparity between her perceptual and motor capacities,[139] discovers herself divided between her physiological incompleteness and the formal completeness anticipated in the mirror image. What Lacan says of this stage of infantile development applies directly to Helen's development as a speaking and writing subject. It "is experienced as a temporal dialectic that decisively projects the formation of the individual into history. The *mirror stage* is a drama whose internal thrust is precipitated from insufficiency to anticipation."[140] Hence Helen's sense of herself as a writer located between present incompleteness and future mastery. Hence also the fundamental theme of her writing, the liminal moment of liberation, from darkness to light, silence to speech—but mediated always by tactile signs, by *touch*. This is the "Helen Keller" that Helen and her collaborators produce in her writing and public appearances.

Helen's own performance as "Helen Keller" took many forms. Besides her fifty-year career as a public lecturer, she and Annie spent a year and more performing the well house "miracle" on the vaudeville circuit all across America, scoring a triumph at the Palace Theater in New York. She also starred in a movie, entitled *Deliverance*, which was produced in 1919 by Francis Trevelyan Miller, a man who was part historian, part P. T. Barnum. Early in the planning stages, he assured potential backers that "its possibilities far exceeded the *Birth of a Nation*."[141] Helen enthusiastically agreed with his conception as she expressed her hopes for the film:

> It will help me carry farther the message that has so long burned in my heart—a message of courage, a message of a brighter, happier future for all men. I dream of a day when all who go forth sorrowing and struggling shall bring their golden sheaves home with them in joy. I dream of a liberty that shall find its way to all who are bound by circumstances and poverty. As the dungeon of sense in which I once lay was broken by love and faith, so I desire to open wide all the prison-doors of the world.[142]

---

[139] Another crucial difference: for Winnicott there are no infants *per se*, only infants and mothers.

[140] LACAN, *Mirror Stage, supra* note 14, at 4 (emphasis in original).

[141] LASH, *supra* note 6, at 473.

[142] *Id.* With my attention concentrated on perception and language, I have had to neglect in this essay the fact that Helen was an active socialist during this period. *See*

In the movie, the young Helen's miracle moment in the well house is played by a child actress. Helen appears as herself in the later scenes, many of them offered as inspirational tableaux, capped by a final spectacle with Helen on a white horse, "blowing a trumpet and leading thousands of shipyard and factory workers, people of all nations, toward 'deliverance'."[143]

Clearly, what Helen writes herself into is the discourse of conversion narrative, which continually reaffirms her in the role of "Helen Keller," the subject of her own liberation. However, she always credits the aid and love of others, and of Anne Sullivan in particular (notably in *Teacher*, the clearly reparative biography that she published in 1955).[144] It is always the collaborative moment, symbolized by the touch of one hand to another between Anne Sullivan and the deaf-blind otherness of Helen Keller, that audiences and readers have warmed to. In a way, Steven Spielberg's E.T. functions for audiences today in much the same way as Helen Keller did for audiences in the first decades of the century—with the crucial difference that E.T. can see and hear. That Helen, in *Deliverance*, was not only the subject of a film but *played herself before the camera*, must seem strange if only because she was cut off absolutely from experiencing the film and its representation of her.[145] But the importance of Helen Keller for contemporary theory is not at all diminished by her lack of sight and hearing. Her lack, on the contrary, puts directly into question our thinking about the cultural consequences of the camera, which has transformed modern social life during the last century and a half.[146] Lacanian theory is especially well suited to under-

---

generally HELEN KELLER, OUT OF THE DARK: ESSAYS, LETTERS, AND ADDRESSES ON PHYSICAL AND SOCIAL VISION (1913).

[143] LASH, *supra* note 6, at 481.

[144] *See generally*, HELEN KELLER, TEACHER: ANNE SULLIVAN MACY (1955).

[145] Even more of a puzzle, perhaps, is how she thought of herself as posing or performing *for a camera*.

> The director together with Annie devised a system of stamping on the floor to convey his instructions to her. First Polly Thomson or Annie spelled into her hand what she was supposed to do in the next series of 'takes' and the effect they were trying for . . . . The director [George Foster Platt] often was unable to hold back his tears as he tapped out 'be natural' and Helen, who could not see the result, tried gamely to fulfill his wishes. . . . Frequent flickers and starts of feeling seemed to be registering little inner electric shocks. Her gestures were equally expressive. But to synchronize gesture and feeling was a laborious process.

LASH, *supra* note 6, at 480.

[146] The cinematic camera now combines the technology of sight *and* sound. For the occasion of this essay, however, the emphasis is on sight, even though this tends to do less than justice both to Helen Keller's experience and to our own experience of a culture immersed in film and video. *See generally* KAJA SILVERMAN, THE ACOUSTIC MIRROR: THE FEMALE VOICE IN PSYCHOANALYSIS AND CINEMA (1988).

standing a culture saturated by the technology of the visual and its political and commercial exploitation, its production of high-gloss figurations of an alienated, alienating, and paranoid ideal ego (what is the difference, on TV, between George Bush on the news and Joe Montana in an ad for Nuprin?). But Lacan's intense focus on the visual, and his relative indifference to the more directly bodily forms of perception and knowledge, the "proximity" senses typified by touch, make his theory less useful as a tool for *revising* the paranoid structure of contemporary culture. Helen Keller's experience as a deaf-blind writer offers a different perspective. As Kafka says, writing is a way of shutting our eyes and, under the circumstances, that may be a reasonable thing to do.

AUTHOR/IZING THE CELEBRITY: PUBLICITY RIGHTS, POSTMODERN POLITICS, AND UNAUTHORIZED GENDERS

Rosemary J. Coombe[*]

Who authors the celebrity? Where does identity receive its authorization? I shall argue that the law constructs and maintains fixed, stable identities authorized by the celebrity subject. In so doing, however, the law also produces the possibility of the celebrity signifier's polysemy. The celebrity image[1] is a cultural lode of multiple meanings, mined for its symbolic resonances and, simultaneously, a floating signifier, invested with libidinal energies, social longings, and political aspirations.

Focusing upon cultural practices that engage, reproduce, ironize and transform the meaning and value of celebrity personas to assert alternative gender identities, I shall argue that the celebrity is authored in a multiplicity of sites of discursive practice, and that in the process, unauthorized identities are produced, both for the celebrity and for her diverse authors. Through its prohibitions, the law produces the means by which unauthorized identities are both engendered and endangered.

I will very briefly summarize the legal doctrine of personality rights[2] and argue that the rationales traditionally offered for recognizing and protecting rights to the celebrity persona cannot be supported and do not justify the extent of the protections legally afforded celebrities, their estates, or their assignees. The social

* Assistant Professor of Law, University of Toronto. B.A., 1981, LL.B., 1984, University of Western Ontario; J.S.M., 1988, J.S.D., 1992, Stanford University. This paper was presented at the Society for Critical Exchange Conference, "Intellectual Property and the Construction of Authorship," April 19-21, 1991, as one of the Loewenstein Lectures on Law, Power, and Representation, at Amherst College, April 22, 1991 and at the Culture and Consumption Lecture Series sponsored by the Humanities Doctoral Programme at Concordia University, October 1, 1991. The author would like to thank Peter Jaszi, Martha Woodmansee, Austin Sarat and David Howes for enabling the critical participation of diverse audiences in the authorship of this paper.

1 I will use the term "celebrity image" to designate not only the celebrity's visual likeness, but rather, all elements of the complex constellation of visual, verbal, and aural signs that circulate in society and constitute the celebrity's recognition value. The term "persona" will also refer to this configuration of significations. I will also use the terms "celebrity" and "star" interchangeably.

2 I use the umbrella term, "personality rights," to encompass the tort of appropriation of personality as it has developed at common law, the proprietary right of publicity that has developed in American law, and rights to prevent the appropriation of, inter alia, names and likenesses that have been enacted in provincial and state statutes as well as federal trademark legislation.

and cultural value of the celebrity image will then be situated in the larger historical context of late capitalism and the related cultural conditions of postmodernism.

Popular cultural practices that engage celebrity images in innovative fashions will then be explored to demonstrate the vibrant role played by these cultural icons in the self-authorings of subaltern social groups. Gay male appropriations of female stars in camp subculture, lesbian reworkings of James Dean, and middle class women's use of the *Star Trek* characters in the creation of fan magazines (fanzines) are practices that rewrite media imagery in subversive but politically expressive fashions. Investing celebrity personas with new and often oppositional meanings, these subordinate groups assert unauthorized gender identities. They thereby affirm both community solidarity and the legitimacy of their social difference by empowering themselves with cultural resources that the law deems the properties of others.

Liberal notions of freedom of expression fail to grasp the nature of contemporary cultural politics of postmodernism, I suggest, because they are held hostage by the philosophical conceits of the Enlightenment. In conclusion, I propose that we situate these practices in an enlarged vision of contemporary democracy that recognizes—as political practice—dialogic cultural activities of articulating the social world and authoring politically salient forms of difference. In this context, we can begin to consider the political costs of granting the celebrity exclusive rights to authorize her (own) image.

I. THE LEGAL PROTECTION OF THE CELEBRITY PERSONA

Anglo-American legal jurisdictions recognize the right of individuals to protect publicly identifiable attributes from unauthorized and unremunerated appropriation by others for commercial purposes or economic benefit.[3] Originally developed primarily to deal with an unauthorized use of a person's name or picture in advertising that suggested the individual's en-

---

[3] In Canada and Britain this right developed at common law into a distinct cause of action known as the tort of appropriation of personality. In the United States, the right of publicity arose as a category of the right of privacy which protects the individual against misappropriations of her name or likeness, and is recognized as a common law tort. Various states have also incorporated these rights in privacy statutes and state constitutional provisions. The literature detailing the origins and developing scope of these rights is so voluminous that a 256 page bibliography of relevant American literature was published in 1987. *See* Lisa Lawrence, *The Right of Publicity: A Research Guide*, 10 HASTINGS COMM. & ENT. L.J. 143 (1987). Today the literature is even more extensive, and I make no effort to summarize all the nuances of the field here.

dorsement of a product, the right of publicity has been greatly expanded in the twentieth century. It is no longer limited to the name or likeness of an individual, but now extends to a person's nickname, signature, physical pose, characterizations, singing style, vocal characteristics, body parts, frequently used phrases, car, performance style, mannerisms, and gestures, provided that these are distinctive and publicly identified with the person claiming the right. Although most cases still involve the unauthorized advertising of commodities, rights of publicity have been evoked to prohibit the distribution of memorial posters, novelty souvenirs, magazine parodies, and the presentation of nostalgic musical reviews, television docudramas, and satirical theatrical performances. Increasingly it seems that any publicly recognizable characteristic will be legally recognized as having a commercial value that is likely to be diminished by its unauthorized or unremunerated appropriation by others.

The right is recognized as proprietary in nature and may therefore be assigned, and the various components of an individual's persona may be independently licensed. A celebrity could, theoretically at least, license her signature for use on fashion scarves, grant exclusive rights to reproduce her face to a perfume manufacturer, her voice to a charitable organization, her legs to a pantyhose company, particular publicity stills for distribution as posters or postcards, and continue to market her services as a singer, actor, and composer. The human persona is capable of almost infinite commodification, because exclusive, non-exclusive, and temporally, spatially, and functionally limited licenses may be granted for the use of any aspect of the celebrity's public presence. Furthermore, the right of publicity has been extended beyond the celebrity, her licensees, and assignees, to protect the celebrity's descendants and their assignees and licensees.[4]

---

[4] American courts are divided on the issue of whether a right of publicity survives the individual's death and in what circumstances. Some courts have refused recovery for the relatives or assignees of a decedent where the name or likeness has been appropriated for commercial purposes on the grounds that an individual's personal right of privacy does not survive his death. Others have allowed recovery for invasion of privacy in similar circumstances. Decisions predicated upon rights of publicity range from those that hold that the right survives death in all circumstances, those that require the celebrity to have engaged in some form of commercial exploitation during her life before the right will be descendible, and those which unconditionally oppose descendibility in any circumstances. The tendency, however, has been towards greater recognition of the descendibility of publicity rights, and state legislatures have also inclined towards statutory recognition of the descendibility of such rights. The issue has yet to be determined or even seriously addressed in Canadian or British courts because the right is still considered a personal rather than a proprietary one.

II. The Value of the Celebrity Image

It is impossible to deny the potential value of the celebrity persona in an age of mass production and communications technologies. The aura of the celebrity is a potent force in an era in which standardization, rationalization and the controlled programming of production characterize the creation and distribution of goods and the capacity of mass media communications to convey imagery and information across vast distances is harnessed to ensure consumer demand. As mass market products become functionally indistinguishable, manufacturers must increasingly sell them by symbolically associating them with the aura of the celebrity—which may be the quickest way to establish a share of the market. It is suggested that fame has become the most valuable (and also the most perishable) of commodities and that celebrity will be the greatest growth industry in the nineties.[5] "With its alchemical power to turn the least promising of raw material[s] into alluring and desirable artefacts" such as designer jeans, sunglasses, deodorants, architect's tea kettles, and coffee mugs, "[f]ame's economic applications are limitless."[6] The value that a famous name adds to a product may be astronomical; London outworkers knit pullovers for £6—with a Ralph Lauren tag they sell for $245 in New York—but Lauren does have a $17 million annual advertising budget to cover.[7]

Celebrities, then, have an interest in policing the use of their personas to insure that they do not become tainted with associations that would prematurely tarnish the patina they might license to diverse enterprises. This potential commercial value is generally offered as reason in itself to protect the star's control over his identity through the allocation of exclusive property rights; because such interests have market value, they deserve protection. Others, like myself, see this as "a massive exercise in question-begging."[8] Market values arise only after property rights have been established and enforced; the decision to allocate particular property rights is a prior question of social policy that requires philosophical and moral deliberations[9] and a consideration of social costs and benefits.

---

[5] Deyan Sudjic, Cult Heroes: How to be Famous for More than Fifteen Minutes (1989).

[6] Id. at 19.

[7] Id. at 83.

[8] David Lange, *Recognizing the Public Domain*, 44 Law & Contemp. Probs. 147, 156 (1981).

[9] See Margaret Radin, *Market Inalienability*, 100 Harv. L. Rev. 1859 (1987) and Elizabeth S. Anderson, *Is Women's Labor a Commodity?* 19 Phil. & Pub. Aff. 71 (1990) for

In determining whether to grant a property right in a celebrity's persona, we might consider traditional liberal justifications in support of private property. The idea that people are entitled to the fruits of their own labor, and that property rights in one's body and its labor entail property rights in the products of that labor, derives from John Locke[10] and is persuasive as a point of departure. It does not, however, advance the argument in favor of exclusive property rights very far. As Edwin Hettinger remarks, "assuming that labor's fruits are valuable, and that laboring gives the laborer a property right in this value, this would entitle the laborer only to the value she added, and not to the *total* value of the resulting product."[11]

Publicity rights are justified on the basis of the celebrity's authorship—her investment of time, effort, skill, and money in the development of the image. Such claims, however rhetorically persuasive, are rarely supported by any empirical data. How much of a star's celebrity and its value is due to the individual's own efforts and investments? Clearly, individual labor is necessary if the persona is to have value and we could not appreciate stars without their expenditure of effort. However, as Hettinger argues, "it does not follow from this that all of their value is attributable to that labor."[12]

Star images must be made, and, like other cultural products, their creation occurs in social contexts and draws upon other resources, institutions, and technologies. Star images are authored by studios, the mass media, public relations agencies, fan clubs, gossip columnists, photographers, hairdressers, body-building coaches, athletic trainers, teachers, screenwriters, ghostwriters, directors, lawyers, and doctors. Even if we only consider the production and dissemination of the star image, and see its value as solely the result of human labor, this value cannot be entirely attributed to the efforts of a single author.

Moreover, as Richard Dyer shows, the star image is authored by its consumers as well as its producers; the audience makes the celebrity image the unique phenomenon that it is.[13] Selecting from the complexities of the images and texts they encounter,

---

philosophical discussions of the factors we need to weigh in determining if commodification is an appropriate mode of valuation.

[10] JOHN LOCKE, SECOND TREATISE OF CIVIL GOVERNMENT, ch. 5 (Wm. B. Eerdmans Publishing Co. 1978) (1690).

[11] Edwin Hettinger, *Justifying Intellectual Property*, 18 PHIL. & PUB. AFF. 37 (1989).

[12] *Id.*

[13] *See* RICHARD DYER, HEAVENLY BODIES: FILM STARS AND SOCIETY (1986); RICHARD DYER, STARS (1979).

they produce new values for the celebrity and find in stars sources of significance that speak to their own experience. These new meanings of the star's image are freely mined by media producers to further enhance its market value. As Marilyn Monroe said in her last recorded words in public, "I want to say that the people—if I am a star—the people made me a star, no studio, no person, but the people did."[14]

The star image is authored by multitudes of persons engaged in diverse activities. Moreover, stars and their fame are never manufactured from whole cloth—the successful image is frequently a form of cultural *bricolage* that improvises with a social history of symbolic forms. Consider the Marx Brothers. Clearly their characterizations involved creative activity, but, as David Lange points out,

> what we cannot know in fact . . . is how much the characters created by the Marx Brothers owe to the work of tens, scores, perhaps hundreds of other vaudeville and burlesque performers with whom they came into contact . . . . What we do not know, in short, is how much of these characters the Marx Brothers themselves appropriated from others. All that is certain is that they created themselves, individually and collectively, as a kind of living derivative work. That much Groucho himself has told us . . . . To be sure, the Marx Brothers became celebrities as most vaudevillians did not. But surely we are not rewarding them on that ground alone.[15]

Publicity rights enable stars to "establish dynasties on the memory of fame."[16] In *Groucho Marx Productions, Inc. v. Day and Night Co.*,[17] those who held rights in the Marx Brothers made a successful publicity rights claim against the creators of the play *A Day in Hollywood, A Night in the Ukraine*. The play's authors intended to satirize the excesses of Hollywood in the thirties and invoked the Marx Brothers as characters playfully imagined interpreting a Chekhov drama. The defendants were found liable, and their First Amendment claim was dismissed on the ground that the play was an imitative work.

The Marx Brothers themselves might be seen as imitative or derivative works, whose creation and success as icons in popular culture derive from their own creative reworkings of the signifying repertoire of the vaudeville community. Contemporary stars

---

[14] Dean MacCannell, *Marilyn Monroe Was Not a Man*, 17 Diacritics 114, 115 (1987).
[15] Lange, *supra* note 8, at 161-62.
[16] *Id.* at 162.
[17] 523 F. Supp. 485 (S.D.N.Y. 1981), *rev'd*, 689 F.2d 317 (2d Cir. 1982).

are authored in a similar fashion. How much does Elvis Costello owe to Buddy Holly, Prince to Jimi Hendrix, or Michael Jackson to Diana Ross? Take the image of Madonna, an icon whose meaning and value lie partially in its evocation and ironic reconfiguration of several twentieth-century sex-goddesses and ice-queens (Marilyn Monroe obviously, but also Jean Harlow, Greta Garbo, and Marlene Dietrich) that speaks with multiple tongues to diverse audiences. Descriptions of the Madonna image as semiotic montage abound,[18] but this extract from the *Village Voice* is my favorite:

> What Madonna served up in the name of sexuality was not liberation as I'd known it, but a strange brew of fetishism and femininism. Only later would I understand that the source of her power is precisely this ambiguity. It's a mistake to think of any pop icon as an individual . . . . Madonna is a cluster of signs, and what they add up to is precisely the state of sex in the culture now: torn between need and rage and unable to express one without the other.
>
> . . . .
>
> Madonna raids the image bank of American femininity, melding every fantasy ever thrown onto the silver screen and implanting them in the body and voice of every-babe.[19]

In an era characterized by nostalgia for the golden age of the silver screen and an aging baby boom generation's fascination with the television culture of its youth, successful images are often those which mine media history for evocative signifiers from our past. This is not to deny that such appropriations are creative endeavours; it is to stress emphatically that they are and to assert that such authorial processes ought not to be frozen, limited, or circumscribed by the whims of celebrities or the commercial caprice of their assignees.

If the Madonna image appropriates the likenesses of earlier screen goddesses, religious symbolism, feminist rhetoric, and sadomasochistic fantasy to speak to contemporary sexual aspira-

---

[18] For one example, see Teresa Podlesney, *Blondes, in* THE HYSTERICAL MALE: NEW FEMINIST THEORY 82 (Arthur & Marilouise Kroker eds., 1991), where the author argues that "the blonde" is the perfect post-WWII product and the ultimate sign of U.S. global supremacy, white patriarchy and the triumph of American mass media and mass production. Madonna, she suggests, is the "blondest blonde ever . . . with forty years of the blonde phenomenon informing her every move." As Podlesney also notes, Madonna has frequently been "heralded for (mis)(re)appropriating the iconography of the blonde bombshell in a cynical defiance of the rules of sexuality codified by patriarchy." *Id.* at 84.

[19] Richard Goldstein, *We So Horny: Sado Studs and Super Sluts: America's New Sex'Tude*, VILLAGE VOICE, Oct. 16, 1990, at 36.

tions and anxieties, then the value of the image derives as much, perhaps, from the collective cultural heritage on which she draws as from her individual efforts. But if we grant Madonna exclusive property rights in her image, we simultaneously make it difficult for others to appropriate those same resources for new ends, and we freeze the Madonna constellation itself. Future artists, writers, and performers will be unable to draw creatively upon the cultural and historical significance of the Madonna montage without seeking the consent of the celebrity, her estate, or its assigns, who may well deny such consent or demand exorbitant royalties. As Lange argues, the proliferation of successful publicity rights claims occurs at the expense of our rights to the public domain.[20] Consequentially, access to the public domain is choked, or closed off, and the public "loses the rich heritage of its culture, the rich presence of new works derived from that culture, and the rich promise of works to come."[21]

Some celebrity images seem significant to the North American social imagination that they might be said to constitute parts of a collective cultural heritage. Such images should not be subject to control by the parochial interests of celebrity's estates. Elvis Presley provides an apt example. In the recent film *Mystery Train*, director and producer Jim Jarmusch explores the cultural and psychological significance of Presley in the depressed economy of Memphis, Tennessee and in the consciousness of those who live on its social margins. The film also addresses his charisma for those in other countries whose fascination with American media images manifests itself in pilgrimages that have turned Memphis into a late twentieth-century mecca. The possibility that Elvis Presley's estate might seek to prohibit the production and/or distribution of a film such as this,[22] while simultaneously arranging to market cologne designed "for all the King's men,"[23]

---

[20] Lange, *supra* note 8, at 163.

[21] *Id.* at 165.

[22] I have no idea whether Jarmusch sought the consent of the Presley estate or the corporate owners of his publicity rights and, if so, what royalties he agreed to pay. Nor do I know whether the Presley estate ever sought to enjoin the film's production or to demand royalties. The very possibility of such an injunction and its desirability is what is at issue here. Celebrities or their estates are not obliged to grant licenses for the use of their image regardless of the artistic or social merit of the work in which they are employed, and may withhold consent on any pretext. In this hypothetical scenario, *Mystery Train* might be privileged under the First Amendment, but then again, it might not. For a discussion of some of the problems with the concept of freedom of speech in the postmodern era, see *infra* at Part V. See also my extended discussion in *Publicity Rights and Political Aspiration: Mass Culture, Gender Identity, and Democracy* 26 NEW ENG. L. REV. (forthcoming 1992) [hereinafter *Publicity Rights*].

[23] A party launching the Elvis Presley cologne was held at the New York club Hot

indicates the parameters of the problem. The opportunity for the celebrity's assignees to behave this way has, in fact, been seized. When the City of Memphis decided to erect a bronze statue to memorialize Elvis as part of a city redevelopment scheme, a nonprofit city corporation offered pewter replicas of the King in return for donations to finance the monument. Owners of rights to commercially exploit the Presley likeness were quick to seek and obtain an injunction.[24]

A Lockean labor theory justifying property rights in the celebrity image is inadequate to establish a right to receive the full market value of the star persona or to support exclusive rights to control its circulation and reproduction in society. Liberal values protecting individual freedom guarantee the possession and use only of the product of one's personal labors and only insofar as the exercise of this right does not harm the rights of others. Enabling celebrities and their estates and assigns to exercise absolute rights to authorize the circulation of the celebrity image may have adverse consequences, both for the preservation of our collective cultural heritage and for our future cultural development.

The social value and cultural meaning of the celebrity image has its genesis in the same historical conditions that created the possibility of its economic value. In his illuminating essay "The Work of Art in the Age of Mechanical Reproduction," Walter Benjamin suggests that technologies of mechanical reproduction and systems of mass production changed modes of human perception and evaluation, fundamentally altering our aesthetic responses. These changes, I argue, are integrally related to the cultural value of the celebrity image in contemporary social life.

To reiterate Benjamin's central argument—the work of art traditionally had a tangible individuated presence in time and space, a singular history, and a situation in a cultural tradition. This notion of the original, necessary to the idea of authenticity and to the work's authority, increasingly becomes irrelevant in an age of technical reproduction. Mass reproduction creates copies that possess an independence from the original; they can transcend the limitations of the original's physical tangibility and susceptibility to age and deterioration. As the art work's substantive duration ceases to matter, the art object loses its authority or its aura—"[the] unique phenomenon of a distance however close it

---

Rod in early October 1990. Michael Musto, *La Dolce Musto*, VILLAGE VOICE, Oct. 26, 1990, at 44.

[24] Memphis Dev. Found. v. Factors Etc., Inc., 441 F. Supp. 1323 (W.D. Tenn. 1977).

may be."[25] The aura embodies the work's value by engaging the beholder's affective, reflexive relationship to the cultural tradition in which the work is situated. The artwork is unapproachable; both in its physically unique embodiment, and in its tangible history in a cultural tradition, it resists too intimate an appropriation by the beholder into his own physical and cultural lifeworlds.

The work of art's aura is lost in the age of mechanical reproduction because "the technique of reproduction detaches the reproduced object from the domain of tradition."[26]   By substituting a plurality of copies for a unique existence, it enables the consumer to position the reproduction in his own lifeworld without any necessary awareness of an original or its historical situation. The photograph and the film represent the culmination of the destruction of the aura because they are designed for reproducibility. "From a photographic negative, for example, one can make any number of prints; to ask for the 'authentic' print makes no sense."[27]   The criterion of authenticity ceases to be applicable to artistic reproduction. The uniqueness of a work of art was due to the work's situation in a traditional ritual context that defined its use value. Technologies of mass reproduction enabled copies to transcend the work's historical use value in social cults of ritual and become pure objects of exchange value or commodities.

Benjamin's reflections on the work of art and the decline of its aura may help us to understand the cultural significance of the celebrity image. Here I want to go beyond Benjamin's own disjointed observations of the screen actor as one who has his performance fragmented by the camera, is alienated from his audience, deprived of his corporeality, and dissolved into flickering images and disembodied sounds.[28]   He sees the effect of film as engaging the whole living person but destroying its aura and replacing the actor's aura with an artificially produced "personality" that is only the "phony spell of [the] commodity."[29]   Benjamin alludes to the possibility of another, alternative understanding of the celebrity with his reference to "the cult of the movie star"[30]—one that suggests that celebrities may repre-

---

25 Walter Benjamin, *The Work of Art in the Age of Mechanical Reproduction, in* ILLUMINA-TIONS 243 n.5 (Hannah Arendt ed. & Harry Zohn trans., 1968).
26 *Id.* at 221.
27 *Id.* at 224.
28 *Id.* at 228-29.
29 *Id.* at 231.
30 *Id.*

sent residual vestiges of the "auratic" in contemporary mass culture.

If the work of art's aura derives from its unique, embodied or tangible presence in time and space, an individual history, and a situation in a cultural tradition, then it is difficult to deny the aura of the celebrity. However often a celebrity's likeness is reproduced, there remains a social knowledge of the celebrity as an individual human being with an unapproachable or distant existence elsewhere, a life history, and a mortal susceptibility to the processes of heartache, illness, aging, and ultimately, death. It is difficult to envisage Elvis Presley without conjuring up images of health, vibrancy, and sexual energy followed by injury, gluttony, corpulence, and decay. Arguably, the celebrity evokes the fascination she does because however endlessly her image is reproduced, her substantive duration, that is, her life, never becomes wholly irrelevant. She never loses her autonomy from the objects that circulate in her likeness.

Moreover, the star is historically situated and lives her life in historical and social conditions that give her image its meaning, resonance, and authority. The celebrity image's value might also be seen to reside in its character as a particular human embodiment of a connection to a social history that provokes its beholder to reflect upon her own relationship to the cultural tradition in which the star's popularity is embedded. We all consider celebrities from different social positions. As a feminist and social democrat, for example, I cannot perceive Marilyn Monroe without reflecting upon my own troubled relationship to male definitions of female sexuality, the femininity of sexual innocence, the Playboy tradition, the Cold War and Monroe's own left wing politics.[31] Celebrity images, I would contend, always maintain their aura because they bind subjects in affective and historically mediated relationships that preclude their appropriation as pure objects.[32]

Stewart Ewen sees the power of the celebrity image as rooted in photography's simultaneous affinity to reality and fan-

---

[31] See GRAHAM McCANN, MARILYN MONROE (1988) for an extended elaboration of a male feminist's reflections on his relationship to the Monroe persona, and DYER, supra note 13, for an insightful discussion of her position in newly emergent discourses of sexuality in the 1950s. Monroe's ongoing dynamic presence in contemporary sexual politics is addressed in MacCannell, supra note 14, a perceptive and scathing review of biographies written by Norman Mailer, Gloria Steinem, Anthony Summers, and Roger G. Taylor.

[32] I am grateful to Kathleen Robertson for clarifying this point.

tasy,[33] and as a cultural response to modern social experiences of alienation, and anomie. The celebrity is an icon of the significance of the personal and the individual in a world of standardization and conformity—embodying the possibility of upward mobility from the mass, "[c]elebrity forms a symbolic pathway, connecting each aspiring individual to a universal image of fulfillment: to be someone, when 'being no one' is the norm."[34]

The seductive power of celebrity auras and their ubiquity in contemporary social life make the celebrity persona a compelling and powerful set of signifiers in our cultural fields of representation. Simultaneously embodying the fantastic and the real, utopian ideals and quotidian practices, and the realization of popular aspirations for recognition and legitimacy, the celebrity form attracts the authorial energies of those for whom identity is a salient issue and community an ongoing dilemma.

III.   "DOING GENDER": THE CELEBRITY FORM AND THE POLITICS OF POSTMODERNISM

What meaning do particular celebrities have in people's own social experiences? It is necessary to make philosophical arguments about the cultural losses contingent upon the commodification of the celebrity image socially concrete. In so doing, the political dimensions of this foreclosure on the use of cultural resources comes into relief. Marginal social groups are continually engaged in nascent constructions of alternative identities. The celebrity image plays a central role in many of these cultural practices.

The practices I will examine are those of gay male camp subculture in the pre-liberation era, lesbian refashionings of pop icons, and, finally, middle class women's engagement in the reading, writing, and circulation of *Star Trek* fanzines. These practices involve the redeployment of celebrity images—an aspect of that rearticulation of commodified media texts that has been defined as the essence of popular culture.[35] Theorists of postmodernism assert that contemporary cultural theory must come to terms with "the textual *thickness* and the visual *density* of everyday life . . ."[36] in societies characterized by pervasive media imagery and com-

---

[33] STUART EWEN, ALL CONSUMING IMAGES: THE POLITICS OF STYLE IN CONTEMPORARY CULTURE 90 (1988).

[34] *Id.* at 95-96.

[35] HAL FOSTER, RECODINGS: ART, SPECTACLE, CULTURAL POLITICS (1985).

[36] Angela McRobbie, *Postmodernism and Popular Culture, in* POSTMODERNISM: ICA DOCUMENTS 165 (Lisa Appignanesi ed., 1989).

modified forms of cultural representation. A central dimension of the study of postmodernism has therefore been a concern with the ways in which people "live and negotiate the everyday life of consumer capitalism"[37] and use mass culture in their quotidian practices. Cultural consumption is increasingly understood as an active use rather than a passive dependence upon dominant forms of signification. As Michel de Certeau and Paul Willis argue, consumption is always a form of production and people continually engage in cultural practices of *bricolage*—resignifying media meanings, consumer objects, and cultural texts in order to adapt them to their own interests and make them fulfill their own purposes.[38] These practices are central to the political practices of those in marginal or subordinated social groups who forge "subcultures" with resources foraged from the mediascape.[39]

Subcultural practices involve improvisational cultural appropriations that affirm emergent cultural identities for those in subordinate social groups.[40] Angela McRobbie argues that the frenzied expansion of mass media enables new alliances and solidarities across traditional spatial, racial, and cultural boundaries and resources for producing new meanings and new identities:

> Sontag's linking [of camp] with . . . gay men, is instructive because she shows how a relationship evolved around a social minority making a bid for a cultural form in which they felt they could stake some of their fragmented and sexually deviant identity. The insistence, on the way, on both style and pleasure made the product attractive to those outside as well as inside . . . she is describing how forms can be taken over,

---

[37] Andrew Ross, *Introduction* to UNIVERSAL ABANDON? THE POLITICS OF POSTMODERN-ISM at xv (1988). *See also* Rosemary J. Coombe, *Encountering the Postmodern: New Directions in Cultural Anthropology*, 28 CANADIAN REV. OF SOC. & ANTHROPOLOGY 188 (1991); Rosemary J. Coombe, *Beyond Modernity's Meanings: Engaging the Postmodern in Cultural Anthropology*, 11 CULTURE 111 (1991); Rosemary J. Coombe, *Postmodernity and the Rumor: Late Capitalism and the Fetishism of the Commodity/Sign*, in JEAN BAUDRILLARD: THE DISAPPEARANCE OF ART AND POLITICS (1991); LINDA HUTCHEON, THE POLITICS OF POSTMODERNISM (1989); PAUL WILLIS, COMMON CULTURE (1990).

[38] Ross, *supra* note 37, at xv; MICHEL DE CERTEAU, THE PRACTICE OF EVERYDAY LIFE (1984).

[39] The concept of the mediascape is borrowed from Arjun Appadurai, *Disjuncture and Difference in the Global Cultural Economy*, in GLOBAL CULTURE: NATIONALISM, GLOBALIZATION, AND MODERNITY 295 (Mike Featherstone ed., 1990). He asserts that we need to consider the complexity of the global flow of cultural imagery as producing new fields he defines as ethnoscapes, technoscapes, finanscapes, mediascapes, and ideascapes.

[40] STEVEN CONNOR, POSTMODERNIST CULTURE: AN INTRODUCTION TO THEORIES OF THE CONTEMPORARY 186 (1989). Dick Hebdige, for example, describes the manner in which music styles like rap and hip hop deploy existing cultural forms using principles of parody, pastiche, and irony to articulate and negotiate mixed, plural, or transitional identities for social groups at the margins of national or dominant cultures. *See* DICK HEBDIGE, CUT 'N' MIX: CULTURE, IDENTITY, AND CARIBBEAN MUSIC (1987).

and re-assembled . . . [which] often means outstripping their
ostensible meaning. . . . And if media forms are so inescapable
. . . then there is no reason to assume that consumption of
pastiche, parody or high camp is, by definition, without subversive or critical potential. Glamour, glitter, and gloss,
should not so easily be relegated to the sphere of the insistently apolitical.[41]

Mass media imagery provides people who share similar social experiences with the opportunity to express their similarity by imbuing with emotional energy a range of cultural referents to
which media communications have afforded them shared access.
It also enables them to author/ize their difference by improvising
with those images to make them relevant to their social experiences and aspirations.

If the celebrity is an image that is both fantastic and real,
embodying the realization of widespread aspirations for public
affirmation, it is especially likely to attract the authorial energies
of those in marginal groups for whom recognition, legitimacy,
and positively evaluated identity are compelling issues. Although
the "recoding" of celebrity images is in no way limited to a concern with gender identity, I will focus upon practices which question traditional formulations of gender and express desires to
construct alternatives.

The concept of alternative gender identities is borrowed
from Judith Butler's ovarian work, *Gender Trouble*, in which she
suggests that a feminist politics requires an inquiry into the political construction and regulation of gendered identities, a radical
critique of the limitations of existing categories of identity, and
an exploration of practices in which alternatively gendered
worlds are imagined. The practices I will be exploring are active
performances of gender "that disrupt the categories of the body,
sex, gender, and sexuality and occasion their subversive resignifi-
cation and proliferation beyond the binary frame."[42]

Feminist theory recognizes a distinction between sex and
gender, asserting "that whatever biological intractability sex appears to have, gender is culturally constructed."[43] As Butler suggests, the inevitability or objective facticity of the relationship
between sex, gender, desire, and sexual practice is potentially
contested by the idea of gender as an undetermined interpreta-

---

[41] McRobbie, *supra* note 36, at 174-75.
[42] JUDITH P. BUTLER, GENDER TROUBLE: FEMINISM AND THE SUBVERSION OF IDENTITY
at xii (1990).
[43] *Id.* at 6.

tion of sex. The recognition of gender as a cultural construct enables the possibility of a multiplicity of genders, and also raises the question of whether sex itself may not be produced through the limitations that restrict the performance of gender to a binary economy. Regimes of power institute, maintain, and try to stabilize naturalistic and causal relations of coherence among and between sex, gender, sexual desire, and sexual practice, but such correspondences are neither "natural" nor inevitable.[44] Other identities that express discontinuous relations between biological sex, cultural gender, and the "expression" or "effect" of these in sexual desire and practice are persistent and provide critical opportunities for contesting the dominant sexual economy.[45]

Identity is always a practice of articulation from within existing cultural forms; gender is performative, a doing and constituting of the identity it is purported to be. These performances are always constructed within the terms of discourse and power, and thus engage heterosexual cultural conventions.[46] Butler is interested in modes of "doing" gender that evoke, but do not constitute, simple reproductions of the terms of power that subvert the very constructs they mobilize, "displacing those naturalized and reified notions of gender that support masculine hegemony and heterosexist power."[47] For example, "numerous lesbian and gay discourses . . .[position themselves in] resignificatory relationships to heterosexual cultural configurations."[48] This repetition of heterosexual cultural forms may be the site of their denaturalization, bringing "into relief the utterly constructed status of the so-called heterosexual original."[49]

Celebrity images provide important cultural resources for many practices of "doing" gender that subvert and reconstruct dominant forms of gender identity. The denaturalization of heterosexual cultural forms is readily apparent in gay camp subculture, a phenomenon I have already alluded to as involving an engagement with media-disseminated celebrity images. Andrew Ross argues that gay camp has had a significant influence on

---

[44] *Id.* at 17.
[45] *Id.* at 17-23.
[46] *Id.* at 25-30. Butler's position here is congruent with my stance in Rosemary J. Coombe, *Room for Manoeuver: Toward a Theory of Practice in Critical Legal Studies*, 14 LAW & Soc. INQUIRY 69 (1989), where I argue that subjectivity is always constructed within the discursive forms of prevailing structures of power, through the creative process of *bricolage*—cultural practices that deploy existing cultural forms in ever emergent new fashions that may transform structures of power even as they evoke its significations.
[47] BUTLER, *supra* note 42, at 33-34.
[48] *Id.* at 121.
[49] *Id.* at 31.

changing social definitions of masculinity and femininity from the late fifties, working "to destabilize, reshape and transform the existing balance of accepted sexual roles and sexual identities."[50] Whatever its ultimate cultural effects, however, its origins must be understood in the context of gay urban life in the pre-liberation period.   In the 1950s and 1960s a sophisticated gay male subculture evolved around a fascination with classical Hollywood film stars like Judy Garland, Bette Davis, Mae West, Greta Garbo, and Marlene Dietrich.   In an age when their ability to be open about the fact that they were gay was circumscribed, gay men's use of certain star images constituted a kind of "going public" or "coming out."   Camp contained a kind of commentary on the ongoing feat "of *survival* in a world dominated by the tastes, interests, and definitions of others."[51]

This is explicated by Esther Newton, whose ethnographic study of drag queens and urban camp subculture in the late 1960s indicates that camp humor grew out of the incongruities of living gay and male in a patriarchal and heterosexist society during a period when the stigma of being gay was largely accepted and internalized rather than rejected as illegitimate.[52]   Drag queens were homosexual men performing the social character of "women" (that is, the signs and symbols of a socially defined American category) by artificially creating the image of glamorous women.   Drag performs a subtle social critique:

> The effect of the drag system is to wrench the sex roles loose from that which supposedly determines them, that is, genital sex.   Gay people know that sex-typed behavior can be achieved, contrary to what is popularly believed.   They know that the possession of one type of genital equipment by no means guarantees the "naturally appropriate" behavior.
>
>   . . . .
>
> [One of the] symbolic statement[s] of drag questions the "naturalness" of the sex-role system *in toto*; if sex-role behavior can be achieved by the "wrong" sex, it logically follows that it is in reality also achieved, not inherited, by the "right" sex. . . . [It] says that sex-role behavior is an appearance [or performance].[53]

The most popular stars in the camp pantheon, subject of most frequent impersonation, were "glamorous" in highly man-

[50] Andrew Ross, No Respect: Intellectuals and Popular Culture 159 (1989).
[51] *Id.* at 144.
[52] Esther Newton, Mother Camp: Female Impersonators in America 3 (1979).
[53] *Id.* at 103.

nered ways that indicated an awareness of the artifice in which they were engaged. This celebration of the personas of those who subtly mocked the corny flamboyance of femaleness "defetishize[d] the erotic scenario of woman-as-spectacle."[54] Thus, they explored the relation between artifice and nature in the construction of sexuality and gender long before these issues were recognized as part of the political agenda.

Camp lost its appeal with the arrival of a militant gay politics that asserted the "natural" quality of homosexuality, revived "masculine" styles, and sought to undermine the "effeminacy" of the stereotypical gay image. The finale of Michel Tremblay's acclaimed 1974 play *Hosanna*[55] well illustrates the new attitude towards camp. Hosanna, an aging drag queen who identifies with, and projects her identity upon, Elizabeth Taylor, is humiliated and forced to renounce her attachment to the star, and disarm herself of her Taylor impersonation. Stripped naked, he declares, "I'm a man," and (at long last, it is implied), allows his lover to embrace his "true" "masculine" self. Camp has, however, enjoyed something of a resurgence in the 1980's, confluent, perhaps, with the influence of Foucault, poststructuralism, and a revival of the credibility of the notion of the socially constructed subject.

Lesbian engagement with celebrity images is a less documented and more recent phenomenon. One lesbian challenge to the "truth" of sex, gender, and desire and the restrictions of a binary sexual economy is given voice and celebrated by Sue Golding in her discussion of a performative gender identity she calls lesbian hermaphrodism. This "erotic sensibility,"[56] worn, felt, and enacted by a number of lesbians, is a "fictionalized sexuality"[57] that finds its performative significations in mass media icons which it replicates in ironic, playful, and assertive reconfigurations:

> I know you've seen the type: no tits, no cock, oozing with a kind of vulnerable "masculinity," sheathed in a 50s style black-leather motorcycle jacket. Or to put it slightly differently, it's James Dean, with a clit . . . . What emerges is the 'virile girl', the butch baby, full of attitude but not of scorn, lots of street

---

54 Ross, *supra* note 50, at 159.

55 MICHEL TREMBLAY, HOSANNA (John Van Burek & Bill Glassco trans., Vancouver 1974).

56 Sue Golding, *James Dean: The Almost Perfect Lesbian Hermaphrodite*, in SIGHT SPECIFIC: LESBIANS AND REPRESENTATION 49 (Dionne Brand ed., 1988).

57 *Id.* at 50.

smarts and a bit of muscle. This new hermaphrodite embodies forever the image of the destructive adolescent dramatically and in one being, teeming with a creative, raw energy, and beckoning with the possibility of a new era. But she's public . . . [not] simply "out of the closet". . . . [S]he is the orphan of a people's imaginary . . .[including] that kind of feminism which knew above all that sexual difference was ever only a political and not biological category. She is public in the most profound sense of the term: a composite copy of a mass invention, a replica of our own societal icons which are themselves never anything other than a public fiction. She is James Dean over and over again: James Dean with his arrogant hair, James Dean with his tight black denims, James Dean with the bitter brat look, James Dean with the morbid leather boots, James Dean against the whole boring suburban middle class.[58]

As Golding makes clear, this is an erotic sensibility or sexual identity that rejects the truth of anatomical sex and goes well beyond the idea of gender as a cultural construction built upon a prediscursive or naturally sexed body that provides a politically neutral surface for multiple significations. Demonstrating that gender identity (construed as a causal or natural relationship among sex, gender, sexual practice, and desire) is the effect of a regime of power, this gender rebel without a cause also rejects those prior forms of "gender trouble" that accepted and worked within the terms of the natural sex/cultural gender dichotomy. This hermaphrodism bears no relation to biological chromosome content, nor is it a '60s "androgyny" that built a sexual aesthetic around an "absence" of the sexual organs, or a '70s sexual aesthetic that ironized the ways in which society enforces gender specific clothing.[59] Rather, this gender rebel performs with her body an erotic identity that is an embodied performative—"the defiant aesthetic of the erotic masculine shot through with the voluptuousness of the female sexual organs."[60]

An "erotic mutant," "a fractured playfulness of social icons (like the Dean image, although Elvis Presley offers other possibilities) copied over and over,"[61] by the lesbian hermaphrodite exemplifies the sex/gender/desire/practice matrix as a performatively enacted signification that parodies, proliferates, and subverts gendered meanings. "Doing gender," however, is

---

[58] *Id.* at 52.
[59] *Id.*
[60] *Id.*
[61] *Id.*

not the exclusive preserve of gays and lesbians, however more likely the social conditions of their existence are to incline them to contest hegemonic norms of gender identity. This is illustrated by the authorial activities of *Star Trek* fanziners, who construct communities and articulate new gender identities by literally re-writing their favorite television series characters.

Star Trek fans constitute a social and cultural network that is international in scope. Within this community, there are distinct groups of fans that organize around the production, circulation, and consumption of fanzines.[62] This subculture is explored with great sensitivity by Camille Bacon-Smith in her sparkling ethnography, *Enterprising Women*. The fanzine community is almost exclusively female and predominantly heterosexual. It involves middle class women who work as housewives and in nursing, teaching, clerical, and service occupations.[63] Fans exchange letters, distribute newsletters, create artwork, make videotapes, and produce and circulate fanzines that contain original fiction, poetry, and illustrations by women across North America, Britain, and Australia.[64] In 1988, it was estimated that there were 300 publications that enabled fans to explore aspects of television series; 120 of them centered on *Star Trek*,[65] a number which no doubt underestimates the production of fan literature because it does not include literature circulated only in photocopy circuits or more covertly circulated publications.[66]

In their creative endeavors, fanzine contributors employ images, themes, and characters from a canonized set of mass cul-

---

[62] For a discussion of the social and institutional structures of fan communities see, CAMILLE BACON-SMITH, ENTERPRISING WOMEN: TELEVISION, FOLKLORE, AND COMMUNITY at ch. 2 (1992).

[63] *Id.*; Henry Jenkins, *Star Trek Rerun, Reread, Rewritten: Fan Writing as Textual Poaching*, 5 CRITICAL STUD. IN MASS COMM. 85 (1988); Constance Penley, To Boldly Go Where No Woman Has Gone Before: Feminism, Psychoanalysis, and Popular Culture, Public lecture delivered at the Public Access series "Capital/Culture," Toronto (Apr. 24, 1990) and at the conference, "Cultural Studies Now and in the Future" sponsored by the Unit for Criticism and Interpretive Theory, University of Illinois at Urbana-Champaign (Apr. 5-9, 1990).

[64] Usually produced out of women's homes, fanzines are generally mimeographed or photocopied reproductions, but some have become more sophisticated with the introduction of computerized desktop publication technology; few issues are less than a hundred pages long.

[65] Jenkins, *supra* note 63, at 89.

[66] Penley, *supra* note 63, estimates that there are three to five hundred publishers of homoerotic fanzines alone (which would include those featuring characters from *Miami Vice, Simon and Simon, Starsky and Hutch*, as well as the *Star Trek* characters). These publications are sold at cost, relying upon subscriptions and often pre-payment to finance production and distribution costs. BACON-SMITH, *supra* note 62, at 3; producers are motivated more by the desire to express identity and establish community than any monetary interest and often operate at a loss.

ture texts (the *Star Trek* television series episodes, films, and commercially produced novels), to explore their own subordinate status, voice frustration and anger with existing social conditions, envision and construct alternatives, share new understandings, and express utopian aspirations. In so doing, they force media texts to accommodate their interests, to become relevant to their needs, and thereby empower themselves with mass culture images. Issues of gender roles, sexuality, and the tension between family obligations and professional ambition are explored in the *Star Trek* future world—one which holds out the promise of opportunities for nontraditional female pleasures, active involvement in central decision making roles, and a state of sexual equality in which emotional needs and professional responsibilities are taken seriously by men and women alike.[67]

In most stories, women are engaged in rewriting the masculine gender rather than in imagining alternative feminine ones.[68] Many stories involve male friendships: and two significant genres of fanzine fiction are "Slash" (or homoerotic) and "Hurt-Comfort"[69] stories, both of which center on relationships between the male characters. In all of these stories, the links between anatomy, gender, desire, and sexual practice are sundered. In the male friendship stories, the male characters are alternatively engendered. Stripping them of a rationalist, ego-centered individualism, the fans imbue them with emotionality and empathy, knitting them into close family and community relationships as well as intimate caring friendships which nurture and support them in their adventures.[70]

In "Slash" fiction, women write erotic stories and draw illustrations depicting a love relationship between Kirk and Spock.[71] Fearing social ridicule, loss of employment, and possibly legal repercussions[72] fanzine writers often write such stories under

---

[67] Jenkins, *supra* note 63, at 93-97.

[68] It appears that stories focusing on women represent less than a quarter of the stories fanziners read, according to a 1990 survey reported in *Enterprising Women*. BACON-SMITH, *supra* note 62, at 157.

[69] Hurt/Comfort stories are those in which one male character is hurt and suffers and the other comforts and nurses him. For a more in depth discussion of Hurt/Comfort stories, see BACON-SMITH, *supra* note 62, at Chapter 10.

[70] *Id.* at 212-18.

[71] Erotic fiction is also written about the characters in *Starsky and Hutch*, *Blake 7*, and *The Professionals*. For a longer discussion of Slash fiction writing, see Constance Penley, *Brownian Motion: Women, Tactics, and Technology?*, in TECHNOCULTURE 135 (1991) and Constance Penley, *Feminism, Psychoanalysis and the Study of Popular Culture*, in CULTURAL STUDIES (1991).

[72] Constance Penley told me in conversation that Lucasfilm threatened legal action—most likely an injunction on copyright grounds—when they discovered that fanzine writ-

pseudonyms. Much of this literature circulates only through complex subterranean photocopying networks in order to evade exposure outside of the group.[73] So well-hidden is the circuit that only the most experienced readers and writers have access to it. Bacon-Smith describes a number of tasks performed by the homoerotic romance and rejects the idea that the male characters are surrogate women—an idea popularized by Joanna Russ when she argued that because of the overriding importance of touch, to the slow thoroughness and sensitization of the whole body, the sexuality expressed is female.[74] Bacon-Smith, however, asserts that these women are writing consciously and deliberately about men, exploring who men are and reconstructing them into people with whom it might be more comfortable to share life, love, and sexual relationships. These women want to explore relationships between powerful equals while tearing "down the very institution of hierarchical power that constructs men as individuals"—reconstructing power itself as an integrated union of mutuality with full and open communication.[75]

In all of these stories the "male" characters are given a combination of gender traits—Kirk's "feminine" traits are matched to Spock's "masculine" ones and vice-versa. Each shares aspects of traditional gender roles. In this way, new genders are inscribed on "male" bodies, and new desires, experiences, feelings, and practices may therefore proliferate.[76] As well as being alternatively engendered, the male characters are freshly embodied; their bodies are inscribed with ranges of sensitivity, expanded zones of erogeneity and a heightened receptivity to tactile pleasures and physical comfort. Their heroes' pain, decontextualized in the mass media, is re-united by fanzine writers with both physical and psychological suffering. The male characters then,

---

ers had depicted Luke Skywalker and Han Solo in an erotic relationship. BACON-SMITH, *supra* note 62, at 251 n. 6, also notes that the fandom has had an uneasy relationship with Lucasfilm but does not elaborate.

[73] *Id.* at 314. Not all *Star Trek* fans share the same attitudes about this fiction. Some fans oppose these stories on religious or moral grounds, others find them "untrue" to the source or canon, some find them too explicit, and others worry about exposing the original actors to ridicule. *Id.* at 334-37.

[74] *See* BACON-SMITH, *supra* note 62, at 371.

[75] *Id.* at 379-81.

[76] This would help to explain why fans do not necessarily see the sexual relationship between Kirk and Spock as a homosexual one. Penley, *supra* note 63. As some fans see it, there are forms of love that defy description; the sexual orientation of Kirk and Spock is irrelevant because their love is a matter of cosmic destiny. *Id.* For similar reasons, fans don't see even the most sexually graphic material as pornographic. BACON-SMITH, *supra* note 62, at 369. Such categories are simply inappropriate in these alternative universes.

are reconstructed as fully emotional and sentient beings. Arguably, the fanzine writers perform the most thorough practices of "doing gender" that have been examined. Constructing new connections between novel (male?) bodies, new (masculinities?), erotic desires, and sexual practices, they simultaneously situate these newly engendered creatures in personal and social relationships, empowering themselves and their community as they do so.

IV.   JURIDICAL PRODUCTIONS OF CULTURAL SPACE(S)

Superficially, these subcultural practices seem distant, if not utterly divorced from the legal regime of personality rights, but they occupy a space intersected by a multiplicity of relations between law and cultural form. I am concerned here, not simply with law as a set of prohibitions, but with law as it is imbricated in the everyday life of cultural practice.[77] The risks these people run under legal regimes of prohibition are real ones—so are the ethical risks of writing about their practices. Bacon-Smith, Jenkins, and Penley have been very careful not to reveal details about, or examples of, particular fanzine writing, filming, and drawing practices or the identities of practitioners. I respect their circumspection and similarly will not, as a matter of ethical principle, delineate the precise ways in which fanzines or performers in gay and lesbian subcultures could be held to violate personality rights (as well as the copyright and trademark rights held by the commercial producers of the media products on which they draw). To do so would be to provide the legal resources with which to prosecute them, or with which they might be threatened with potential legal action.

Juridical powers, however, are productive as well as prohibitive; the law is generative of knowledges, spaces, categories, identities, and subjectivities.[78] The law of publicity rights, by prohibiting reproductions of the celebrity image for another's advantage, promotes the mass circulation of celebrity signifiers

---

[77] For longer discussions of this approach to thinking about law, see Robert Gordon, *Critical Legal Histories*, 36 STAN. L. REV. 57 (1984) and Coombe, *supra* note 46.

[78] In *History of Sexuality Volume I: An Introduction*, Michel Foucault argued that juridical regimes must be understood as productive rather than merely prohibitive—producing what they purport merely to represent. MICHEL FOUCAULT, HISTORY OF SEXUALITY VOLUME I: AN INTRODUCTION (Robert Hurley trans., Vintage Books 1980)(1976). For a general discussion of the socially constitutive character of law, see Christine Harrington & Barbara Yngvesson, *Interpretive Social Research*, 15 LAW & SOC. INQUIRY 135 (1990). For a discussion of the juridical production of class and gender subjectivities in the transition to industrial capitalism, see Rosemary J. Coombe, *Contesting the Self: Negotiating Subjectivities in Nineteenth Century Ontario Defamation Trials*, 11 STUD. L., POL. & SOC. 3 (1991).

by ensuring that they will have a market value. If the image were freely available for mass reproduction, there would, presumably, be less of an incentive to engage in the investments necessary to disseminate it through media channels. Ironically, then, the law creates the cultural spaces of postmodernism in which mass media images become available for signifying practices. It produces fixed, stable identities authored by the celebrity subject, but simultaneously creates the possibility of places of transgression in which the signifier's fixity and the celebrity's authority may be contested and resisted. Authorized and unauthorized identities are both, therefore, engendered in relation to this juridical regime. The law, however, lends its authority only to those meanings that the celebrity wishes to appropriate, attributing these to her own efforts, and implicitly denies that any cultural value is being produced elsewhere.

Power may produce resistance in the Foucauldian sense, but it does not determine the form or the content of the practices that transgress its strictures. Through its prohibitions, the law may produce the means by which unauthorized identities are both engendered and endangered, but these practices are not simply effects or consequences of juridical regimes. People's interests and inclinations to engage in the construction of alternative gender identities are shaped by multiple hegemonies. Performative enactments of erotic identity are unlikely to be univocal direct statements of opposition to any singular structure of power; more often they may engage multiple forms of cultural "resistance" to multiple instances of power. Through irony, mockery, parody, pastiche, and alternative modes of appreciation, activities of creative appropriation enable fans to comment indirectly on gender ideology, law, and the commodity form.

Such commentary is especially cogent in the fanzine context. Fans don't see *Star Trek* as something that can be reread, but as something that must be rewritten in order to make it more responsive to their needs and a better producer of personal and community meanings.[79] According to Henry Jenkins, fans expressly reject the idea that the *Star Trek* texts or the Kirk/Spock characters are a privileged form of exclusive property but at the same time they have developed a complex moral economy[80] in which they legitimize their unorthodox appropriation of the me-

---

[79] Jenkins, *supra* note 63, at 87.

[80] The term is borrowed from E.P. Thompson, *The Moral Economy of the English Crowd in the Eighteenth Century*, PAST AND PRESENT, Feb. 1971, at 76.

dia texts, characters, and personas. Despite the potential for legal prosecution, they see themselves as loyalists, fulfilling the inherent promise and potential of the series—a potential unrealized or betrayed by those who "own" the intellectual property rights in it. Fans respect the original texts and regularly police each other for abuses of interpretive license, but they also see themselves as the legitimate guardians of these materials, which have too often been manhandled by the producers and their licensees for easy profits.[81] As one fan writes: "[W]e have made [Star Trek] uniquely our own, so we do have all the right in the world . . . to try to change it for the better when the gang at Paramount starts worshipping the almighty dollar, as they are wont to do."[82] Fan writers exercise an ethic of care with regard to the characters—a care they fear commercially motivated parties frequently do not share.[83]

Although fanziners, gay camps, and lesbian hermaphrodites are not engaged in practices in direct opposition to the law (however they may unintentionally violate it), the law of publicity rights informs their performative activities. The knowledge that the cultural icons with which they express themselves do not belong to them, however affectionately they are adopted, is constitutive of these practices. The relationship of fans to the commodification of the signifiers whose meanings they create may be one of admiration or antagonism, irony, parody, fear, or complicitous critique.[84] In any case, the law generates the space for a proliferation of politics as well as identities, and polities as well as genders, as people create their own ethical distinctions between expression and theft. Communication always involves

---

[81] Jenkins, *supra* note 63, at 100.

[82] *Id.*

[83] In ENTERPRISING WOMEN, Bacon-Smith also illuminates the complexities of the attitudes fanwriters hold with regard to the legal status of the source product. On the one hand they are aware that the characters, plots, films, television episodes, videos, logos, and dialogues with which they work are the properties of others. On the other hand, they take quite seriously the philosophy of "IDIC" (Infinite Diversity in Infinite Combination), propagated by Gene Roddenberry, the originator of *Star Trek*. They respect the legal prohibition against profiting from their writing, tape-making, and artistic activities, but the possibility that their activities might still be enjoined on copyright, trademark, or publicity rights grounds does not appear to operate as a serious deterrent. These women know they assume risks of legal prosecution, but legal risks are only very few and possibly the most distant of the risks they face; indeed, Bacon-Smith implies that the assumption, management, and shared exploration of risk is the central ethos of the community, and constitutive of the construction and reconstruction of culture in which they engage. BACON-SMITH, *supra* note 62, at 302-452.

[84] For a discussion of complicitous critique as an attitude symptomatic of postmodernism, see LINDA HUTCHEON, THE POLITICS OF POSTMODERNISM (1989).

borrowing the images of alterity. Only recently has it become a form of trespass.

V. Infinite Diversity in Infinite Combination: Democracy as Dialogic Practice

The cultural politics of constructing alternative gender identities, through improvisations upon the celebrity image, are not readily appreciated using current juridical concepts or easily encompassed by the liberal premises upon which legal categories are grounded. The reasons for these difficulties, I believe, can be located within the contradictions, instabilities, and ambiguities of liberal legal discourse itself—contradictions that are becoming increasingly apparent in the condition of postmodernity.[85]

Liberal legal discourse addresses the expression of identity, community, and political aspiration under the rubric of free speech or freedom of expression, a field of doctrine that clings tenaciously to Enlightenment concepts in the face of late capitalist realities. As Owen Fiss notes, the constitutional protections of freedom of speech rest on increasingly anachronistic premises that do not address the salient characteristics or challenges of capitalist mass communications systems in North America.[86] Presupposing that the biggest threat to public discourse is the silencing of the individual speaker by the state, "the Free Speech Tradition can be understood as a protection of the street corner speaker."[87] Assuming a natural division between public and private actors, free speech simply protects all "private" actors, regardless of their power, against the evils of state intervention, notwithstanding that in an age of mass media conglomerates, threats to the autonomy of speech and public debate are more likely to come from extremely powerful "private" actors who control the most influential circuits and contents of communication.[88] Increasingly, a person's right to political speech may encroach upon another's rights of property (the need to picket in shopping malls, for example) and property rights generally prevail unless the property holding citizen is understood to hold the property for public use (and thus to exercise a "governmental" function so that she must be treated like a state).

Critics on the left argue that the public/private and state/

---

[85] I explore these contradictions in more detail in *Publicity Rights, supra* note 22.
[86] Owen Fiss, *Free Speech and Social Structure*, 71 Iowa L. Rev. 1405 (1986).
[87] *Id.* at 1408.
[88] *Id.* at 1410-13.

citizen dichotomies of freedom of speech law mystify and distort our understanding of contemporary political life

> because government is implicated in all activity that occurs within its territorial jurisdiction. As sovereign, the government is as responsible for its active decisions not to intervene and regulate as it is for its decisions to act affirmatively. . . . [T]he retention of an existing situation is also due to the efforts and actions of the state. . . . The protection of private property and the enforcement of private contracts by the government attests to the strong and necessary presence of government in private transactions. . . . Property and contract are creatures of the state and support for these allocative regimes is neither more nor less politically neutral or activist than opposition to them. The question is not whether government should intervene, but when and how . . . .[89]

When "public" speech interests come up against "private" property interests, the latter almost invariably triumph, ensuring that "the law insulates vast sectors of the social hierarchy from official scrutiny and public accountability."[90] Those who hold "private" property are not required to consider the "public" interest in free speech in their exercise of exclusive property rights. Once we break down this untenable distinction, however, and recognize the state's role in creating and enforcing property rights, "the question of whose entitlements are to be protected from whose interference becomes a contested matter of political choice rather than the correct application of abstract principle."[91]

Laws commodifying the celebrity image inevitably come up against concerns about freedom of expression, but they do so sporadically, yielding inconsistent and confused rationales that reveal the inadequacies of liberal discourse in the cultural conditions of postmodernism. It is generally accepted that rights of publicity must yield to social interests in freedom of expression, "when first amendment principles outweigh the celebrity's interest in compensation."[92] But when will this be the case?

Courts routinely assert that the First Amendment protects publication of news of a celebrity but does not protect commer-

---

[89] Alan Hutchinson, *Talking the Good Life from Free Speech to Democratic Dialogue*, 1 Yale J.L. & Lib. 17, 21 (1989).

[90] *Id.* at 22.

[91] *Id.*

[92] Lawrence, *supra* note 3, at 332.

cial uses of celebrity images.[93] Often this is premised on a distinction between fact and fiction—factual accounts about celebrity behavior do not violate their publicity rights because celebrities are the subject of legitimate news.[94] Newspapers, films, and documentaries are not understood to be engaged in commercial purposes when they publish news, notwithstanding that their production, distribution, and exhibition is a large commercial enterprise carried on for private profit.[95] Distinctions between fact and fiction, publishing news about a celebrity and commercially exploiting her image, are notoriously difficult to maintain in the promotional culture[96] of postmodernity. The courts' efforts to employ and maintain such distinctions yield contradictory and sometimes ludicrous results, as the following cases, drawn from the same jurisdiction, illustrate.

Ann-Margret sued *High Society* magazine for a violation of publicity rights for the unauthorized use of a semi-nude photograph taken from one of her films. The court dismissed the action on the basis that the photograph was newsworthy and its use protected.[97] The same year, a model brought legal action for the unauthorized use of a nude photograph in the same magazine. The court rejected the defendant's claim that the First Amendment protected use of the photos because the model was not shown participating in a newsworthy event; the photographs, therefore, were not a matter of public interest.[98] When a couple found their nude photographs in a commercially distributed mass market guide to nude beaches, however, a court denied them relief and upheld the publisher's right to disseminate information of public interest; the photographs were not being used for commercial purposes.[99]

Law students are trained to rationalize and distinguish such cases to show how categories like disseminating information in

---

[93] *See, e.g.,* Grant v. Esquire, Inc., 367 F. Supp. 876 (S.D.N.Y. 1973); Rinaldi v. Village Voice, 359 N.Y.S.2d 176 (Sup. Ct. 1974), *cert. denied,* 423 U.S. 883 (1975); Garner v. Triangle Publications, 97 F. Supp. 546 (S.D.N.Y. 1951).

[94] *Garner,* 97 F. Supp. at 549.

[95] University of Notre Dame du Lac v. Twentieth Century-Fox Film Corp., 256 N.Y.S.2d 301 (Sup. Ct.), *aff'd,* 259 N.Y.S.2d 832 (1965).

[96] The concept of promotional culture is developed by Andrew Wernick, *Promotional Culture,* 15 CAN. J. POL. & SOC. THEORY 260 (1991). He contends that North American culture has come to present itself at every level as an endless series of promotional messages. Advertising, besides having become a most powerful institution in its own right, has been effectively universalised as a signifying mode.

[97] Ann-Margret v. High Soc'y Magazine, 498 F. Supp. 401 (S.D.N.Y. 1980).

[98] Hansen v. High Soc'y Magazine, Inc., 5 Media L. Rep. (BNA) 2398 (Sup. Ct.), *rev'd on other grounds,* 76 A.D.2d 812, 429 N.Y.S.2d 552 (1980).

[99] Creel v. Crown Publishers, 115 A.D.2d 414, 496 N.Y.S.2d 219 (1985).

the public interest and commercial exploitation of another's name and likeness are rational, desirable, and necessary. Celebrities and the media industries reward them handsomely for their efforts. Even the most determined law student, however, might have difficulty supporting a decision which held that the unauthorized use of "before and after" photos of a girl in a teen magazine—replete with the brand names of the products used to effect the transformation—was a newsworthy use of her name and likeness rather than a commerical exploitation.[100]

The underlying distinction between fact and fiction that must provide the scaffolding for this conceptual structure becomes increasingly fragile in postmodernity as societies become saturated with signification and the value of the "hyperreal" accelerates.[101] Courts have found it increasingly difficult to distinguish truth from falsity, and fact from fiction, or to limit First Amendment protection to objective renderings that correspond to some knowable reality. They maintain, however, the philosophical edifice of "the mirror of nature"[102] by developing ever more distinctions within distinctions to keep its structure intact.

A defendant is held to forfeit the privilege of disseminating newsworthy information if her use is materially and substantially false and she has recklessly disregarded its falsity.[103] When a comedian ran a mock campaign for President as a publicity stunt, however, he was unable to prevent an entrepreneur from distributing a poster bearing his photograph with the caption, "For President."[104] The court determined that the poster was newsworthy and thus that the defendant was engaged in spreading information rather than in commercial exploitation. It did not address the issue of whether the "information" defendant disseminated was to be characterized as materially false (the comedian was not running "For President") or factual information about a fictitious candidacy (a true account of a falsity). When Elvis Presley died, however, those who held his publicity rights successfully stopped an entreprenuer from marketing a picture of

---

[100] Lopez v. Triangle Communications, Inc., 421 N.Y.S.2d 57 (1979).

[101] For discussions of "hyperreality," see UMBERTO ECO, TRAVELS IN HYPERREALITY (1989) and JEAN BAUDRILLARD, SIMULATIONS (1983). *See also* JEAN BAUDRILLARD, SELECTED WRITINGS 166-84 (Mark Poster ed., 1988); DOUGLAS KELLNER, JEAN FROM MARXISM TO POSTMODERNISM AND BEYOND 60-92 (1989).

[102] The phrase, of course, is borrowed from RICHARD RORTY, PHILOSOPHY AND THE MIRROR OF NATURE (1979).

[103] Lerman v. Flynt Distrib. Co., 745 F.2d 123 (2d Cir.), *cert. denied*, 471 U.S. 1054 (1984).

[104] Paulsen v. Personality Posters, Inc., 299 N.Y.S.2d 501 (Sup. Ct. Spec. Term 1968).

Presley "In Memorium."[105] Perhaps the New York courts, like the weekly tabloids, doubt that "the King" has truly departed.

Accomodating the immense potential value in fictionalizing the lifestyles of the rich and famous has provoked courts to articulate new distinctions within the fact and fiction dichotomy. A New York court held that a right of publicity will not be recognized where a fictionalized account of a public figure's life is depicted in such a way that the audience knows (truly?) that the events are falsely represented.[106] Another New York bench, however, decided that allowing the publication of a known fictional bibliography of a (factual) baseball player would take freedom of expression too far given the defendant's limited research efforts to verify his story.[107] The book was seen as a clear case of "a commercial exploitation."

The efforts of a film producer to verify his findings, however, were not investigated when he represented a deceased pilot's alleged reappearance as a ghost in his mass marketed movie. The pilot served as captain aboard an Eastern Airlines flight that crashed in 1972. After the crash, people reported that the captain and crew of the fated flight appeared as ghosts aboard other Eastern planes. Relatives of the deceased brought action for unauthorized commercial use of name and likeness against the maker of the film that reconstructed these events.[108] The filmmaker prevailed because of his right to disseminate information "of current and legitimate public interest" under the "newsworthiness" section of the Florida statute.[109] If the case were considered in New York, the following questions might have been addressed: Was the information "true"? Was it substantially "false"? Did the filmmaker recklessly disregard its falsity, or was he providing a fictionalized account of a real person's activities? Will a fictionalized version of a real person's activities, as imagined by other people, be protected? Perhaps it depends how carefully you've verified the falsity of your fabrication and how easily the audience can identify the activities as fictional. But what if most of them believe in ghosts? In any case, there is a

[105] Factors Etc., Inc. v. Creative Card Co., 444 F. Supp. 279 (S.D.N.Y. 1977), *aff'd sub nom.* Factors Etc., Inc. v. Pro Arts, Inc., 579 F.2d 215 (2d Cir.), *cert. denied*, 440 U.S. 908 (1978).

[106] Hicks v. Casablanca Records, 464 F. Supp. 426 (S.D.N.Y. 1978).

[107] Spahn v. Julian Messner, Inc., 250 N.Y.S.2d 529 (Sup. Ct. Spec. Term 1964), *vacated*, 387 U.S. 239 (1967).

[108] Loft v. Fuller, 408 So. 2d 619 (Fla. Dist. Ct. App. 1981).

[109] FLA. STAT. ch. 540.08 (1990).

legitimate public interest in disseminating (true?) information about (actual) ghost sightings in the state of Florida.

Attempting to limit freedom of speech defenses in publicity rights claims to the dissemination of factual information in the name of newsworthiness is conceptually boggling, culturally untenable, and politically pernicious. We value freedom of expression not as a means of spreading verifiable information about a world of brute fact, but as the activity with which we culturally construct worlds, create social knowledges, forge ethics, and negotiate intersubjective moral truths whose credence is never established by a measurable correspondence to an objective reality. Self, society, and identity are realized only through the expressive cultural activity that reworks those cultural forms that occupy the space of the social imaginary.[110]

Political theorists of the postmodern condition point to the necessarily cultural character of contemporary politics. The social and political orders in which we live are contingent creations that we ourselves discursively construct. It is through creative cultural practices of articulation that the social world is given meaning, and, hence, it is always contestable and open to re-articulations. Ernesto Laclau and Chantal Mouffe, in particular, see practices of articulating social difference as central to democratic politics.[111]

All knowledges of social identity are symbolic systems of difference, and representational structures of difference are, by their very nature, incapable of achieving closure. No structure of differential identity is ever final; new forms of difference are always emergent, and new social identities continually assert their legitimacy and presence. Indeed, advances in the democratization of Western societies are dependent upon "autonomous initiatives starting from different points within the social fabric,"[112] as new groups constitute themselves politically. Laclau and Mouffe refuse to privilege any particular subject positions, seeing

---

110 The concept of the social imaginary is developed in CORNELIUS CASTORIADIS, THE IMAGINARY INSTITUTION OF SOCIETY (Kathleen Blamey trans., MIT Press 1987) (1975).

111 See ERNESTO LACLAU & CHANTAL MOUFFE, HEGEMONY AND SOCIALIST STRATEGY: TOWARDS A RADICAL DEMOCRATIC POLITICS (Winston Moore & Paul Cammack trans., 1985); Ernesto Laclau & Chantal Mouffe, *Post Marxism Without Apologies*, NEW LEFT REV., Nov./Dec. 1987, at 79 [hereinafter *Post-Marxism*]; Chantal Mouffe, *Radical Democracy: Modern or Postmodern?*, in UNIVERSAL ABANDON? THE POLITICS OF POSTMODERNISM 31 (Andrew Ross ed., 1988); see also, Fred Dallmayr, *Hegemony and Democracy: On Laclau and Mouffe*, 1 STRATEGIES: J. THEORY, CULTURE, & POL. 29 (1988); FRED DALLMAYR, MARGINS OF POLITICAL DISCOURSE (1989); Bradley Macdonald, *Towards a Redemption of Politics: An Introduction to the Political Theory of Ernesto Laclau*, 1 STRATEGIES: J. THEORY, CULTURE, & POL. 5 (1988).

112 *Post-Marxism, supra* note 110, at 105.

the contemporary political world as one of multifaceted struggles amongst peoples continually articulating new social identities from discursive resources. Democratic politics is essentially a dialogic process whereby social identities are continually emergent in political articulation. A radical and plural democracy must maintain optimal conditions for encouraging such articulations.

Articulations of identity are possible only in conditions of polysemy, symbolic ambiguity, and a surplus of meaning, where the necessary cultural resources for contesting meaning and asserting identity are freely accessible. In the condition of postmodernity, our cultural resources are increasingly the properties of others, and meaning is the monopoly of an elite who control the commodified texts that pervade our social lives.[113] These are the cultural images with which politically salient forms of difference may increasingly be shaped. Whose identities will be authorized and whose authorship will be recognized? As the cultural cosmos in which we live becomes increasingly commodified, we will need to define and defend the cultural practices of articulation with which we author the social world and construct the identities we occupy within it.

---

[113] An extended version of this argument that draws its examples from the fields of copyright and trademark law may be found in Rosemary J. Coombe, *Objects of Property and Subjects of Politics: Intellectual Property Laws and Democratic Dialogue*, 69 TEX. L. REV. 1853 (1991).

THE PRAGMATICS OF GENRE: MORAL THEORY AND LYRIC AUTHORSHIP IN HEGEL AND WORDSWORTH

THOMAS PFAU*

> Moral conduct is agents related to one another in the acknowl-
> edgement of the authority of a practice composed of condi-
> tions which because of their generality attracts to itself the
> generic name, "practice": morality, *mos*. A morality is the *ars
> artium* of conduct, the practice of all practices; the practice of
> agency without further specification.[1]

The following remarks wish to complement the often pene-
trating and erudite case studies of the social, aesthetic, and legal
dimensions of text-production and ownership with an inquiry
into the ideological *pragmatics* of authorship. Critical investigations of copyright issues and fair use interpretation, the dynamics of literary collaboration, and the economics of author/
publisher relations have greatly advanced our understanding of
discourse by concentrating on the significantly *material* dimension
of authorship.[2] Arguably, though, the distinctly empirical nature
of such analyses has left the concept of a subject in which the
empiricity of authorial conduct converges theoretically un-
reflected, thereby inviting a variety of theoretically inspired critiques. The following observations do not wish to add to the now
predictable analyses of authorship, which "correct" or "sup-
plant" the empirical study of its subject with a theoretical critique
that offers what amounts to a formal-linguistic demonstration of
the "Death of the Author."[3] Rather than concentrating on the
problem of continuity between a generalized theory of the subject and the social and material manifestations of authorship, I
seek to examine the social *efficiency* of the writer's voice as *author*.

* Assistant Professor of English, Duke University. M.A., 1985, University of California at Irvine; Ph.D., 1989, State University of New York at Buffalo.

1 Michael Oakeshott, On The Understanding Of Human Conduct 60 (1975).

2 For representative approaches to authorship, specifically in the context of eighteenth-century and Romantic studies, see Martha Woodmansee, *The Genius and the Copyright*, 17 Eighteenth-Century Stud. 425-48 (1984); Susan Eilenberg, *Mortal Pages:
Wordsworth and the Reform of Copyright*, 56 ELH 351-74 (1989); Richard Swartz, *Wordsworth,
Copyright, and the Commodities of Genius*, PHILOLOGICAL Q. (forthcoming).

3 As archetypes of such inquiries, see Roland Barthes, *The Death of the Author*, in The
Rustle of Language (Richard Howard trans., 1986); Michel Foucault, *What is an Author?*,
in TEXTUAL STRATEGIES (Josué Harari ed., 1979).

The traditional, genetic paradigm posits authorship as the social effect of an inward subjectivity or, by holding fast to the notion of such an interior order, questions the concept of the author. Positively or negatively, subjectivity continues to determine our conceptions of authorship. I propose, then, to abandon the genetic paradigm on behalf of a teleological one, a procedure that will cause us to interrogate authorship in radically different ways. The trajectory of my argument is sketched out by the following questions:

1) What is the relation between morality—understood as an "inward" category such as "conscience," "conviction" and "duty"—and discourse, initially taken in its broadest sense as both, speech and writing?

2) If, as I intend to show, the causality between morality and discourse is neither contingent nor temporal, but co-instantaneous, what features of discourse insure the public acknowledgment of a purportedly inward-based discourse *as* socially and ideologically authoritative? What textual and rhetorical features effect the conversion of private meanings into social force or, shifting emphasis slightly, what do a text's form and genre contribute to the transfiguration of inward morality into a collective authority?

3) When confronting an essential, albeit *strictly undecidable*, causality between moral authority and authorial competence—*i.e,* between the inwardness of "spirit" and the purportedly contingent technologies of its public (moral) and authorial appearance—what further insight may such a scenario yield regarding the cultural logic and interpretability of discourse?

4) Finally, what significance does the "literary" hold within this larger context. That is, what features within a "literary" text's topical, generic, and rhetorical structure seduce us into identifying a *prima facie* authorial practice as an originary and self-identical subjectivity? Here I will concentrate on the genre most visibly concerned with the literary as a "moral" practice, and for that reason most insistent on the capacity for sublating an ostensibly inward and disinterested aesthetic sensibility into a social and moral force: lyric poetry and, specifically, the Romantic ode.

By suspending the assumption of an ontological "common ground" between an inward consciousness and the distinctly public figure of the author, we may be in a position to better understand the ideological "interest" or "motives" that govern the practice of social/authorial self-enactment. Indeed, I mean to demonstrate that one, arguably *the*, constitutive motivation of authorship as a socio-rhetorical practice involves its displacement or elision of precisely those epistemological tensions that have vitiated theories of self-reflection, self-reference, and inward self-presence for quite some time. While such theories continue to inform the empirical conceptions or post-structuralist critiques of authorship—namely, as their positive or negative presupposition, respectively—I would suggest that a "crisis of the subject," however we may choose to articulate it, is not a theoretical embarrassment, but is, instead, the cause and motive for authorial practice.

Understanding the displacement of selfhood or individuality by authorship as an integral moment in the speculative and ideological pragmatics of Romantic and post-Romantic writing, rather than as a contingent "de-facement" or "disfiguration" of a subjectivity posited *a priori*, is likely to enhance a 'positive' understanding of the social and ideological *pragmatics* of authorial practice. It is in Hegel that we witness the crisis of a genetic paradigm of subjective authority, which his considerations of moral "conviction" initially wish to retain under the title of an expressive conscience. To concentrate on the issue of morality, moreover, is not a haphazard or incidental gesture; for nowhere does the question concerning the relation between the private and the public, or between the inward authenticity of a "conscience" and the rhetorical competence of an author, prove as critical as in moral theory. To conceive of authorship as a pragmatic construction and affirmation of social and ideological *authority* will require us to scrutinize the relation between the presumed "inwardness" of a "voice" and the social and authorial power of a text. Indeed, it may be more than critical hyperbole to suggest that the practice of authorship, at least after its institutional definition in the late seventeenth and early eighteenth century, constitutes either an interpretive variation or (to use F. Schlegel's expression) a sustained footnote on the distinctly Occidental and Christian *Leitmotif* of morality.

The subsequent analysis of Hegel's moral agency and moral discourse theory demonstrates how the authorial and distinctly social self-enactment of a purportedly "inward" subjectivity (i.e., "conscience") hinges on that agency's performative mastery of a generically fixed type of rhetoric. In other words, the authorial transfiguration of an "inward" conscience into a social and ultimately ideological "force,"—of an "I" into a "We"—concerns a mastery of *form* rather than a verifiably authentic signification of *meaning*. Following our reconsideration of Hegel's moral theory, a reading of William Wordsworth's exactly contemporaneous *Ode to Duty*[4] will draw out the constitutive affinity between moral authority and authorship and the social pragmatics of *genre* or discursive *form*, respectively. What may initially seem a forced, or even frivolous, juxtaposition of rigorously systematic moral reflection and a perilously incidental lyric effusion, hopefully will acquire critical legitimacy as we begin to perceive the emphasis in both texts shifting from an order of ethical interiority to a concern with the mastery of highly formalized language. Firmly rooted in eighteenth century theories of lyric poetry, Wordsworth's ode offers us an emphatically visible (i.e., highly formalized) expression of inwardness designed to immunize it against the disturbingly complex social and ideological "motives" commonly attributed to Romantic authorship. To tip my hand once more, we will see that authorship, when analyzed as a rhetorical and textual practice, converts individuality into authority, not under the auspices of an expressivist interiority, which support the formalist paradigms of Saussure's language-as-signification legacy, but as a *pragmatic intervention* within a strictly social continuum of discursive practices and predecided meanings.

I

In an effort to reconfigure moral theories from Plato and Aristotle through Erasmus, Leibniz, Hume, Adam Smith and Kant, G.W.F. Hegel's *Phenomenology of Spirit*[5] devotes a significant and highly condensed chapter to redefining the question concerning the intelligibility of the social and the political as one of morality. Hegel views community and society as the consequence of individual acts whose authority is grounded in an essentialized and strictly inward form of consciousness. Hence, because community and moral order are posited as the semantic effects of private signification that is grounded in and legitimated by a form of moral authorship, a theoretical (dialectical) meta-discourse is called upon to verify and support the integrity of this relation between individual (moral) agency and social authority.

Hegel's *Phenomenology* posits the speculative progression of a "natural consciousness" whose "reflexive determinations" of its own concept [*Begriff*] successively "cancel" [*aufheben*] these empirical positions, and thus "sublate" [*aufheben*] the discrete indi-

---

    4 William Wordsworth, *Ode to Duty*, *in* POEMS IN TWO VOLUMES AND OTHER POEMS, 1800-1807, at 104 (Jared Curtis ed., 1983).
    5 G.W.F. Hegel, Phenomenology of Spirit (A.V. Miller trans., 1977).

viduality of consciousness into the inclusive authority of "spirit" [*Geist*].[6] Glancing ahead to the textual and cultural logic of lyric form, we can observe how Hegel's speculative "movement" coincides with the narrative progression of self-imagings in the classical and early Romantic ode. The latter also evolves the unfolding of a localized inward experience (not infrequently a crisis provoked by the sensuous/sensual foundations of subjective self-experience) into an exemplary and strictly conceptual, moral authority. What interests us about this progression, both in Hegel and Wordsworth, is its dynamic structure and troubled rationality.

Hegel's theory warrants this concern in that the *Phenomenology* from the outset casts the issue of morality as one of *relations*, not *essences*. The entire section C in Part BB of the *Phenomenology of Spirit*,[7] entitled "Spirit that is certain of itself. Morality," concentrates on the intersection of private conviction and social obligation, which converges in a speculative analysis of the concept of Duty. Initially, Hegel comments, "[s]elf-consciousness knows duty to be the absolute essence. . . . However, as thus locked up within itself, moral self-consciousness is not yet posited . . . as *consciousness*. The object is immediate knowledge, and, being thus permeated purely by the self is *not* an object."[8] In short, duty must mediate the positivity of its own, immediate "conviction" and the strict negativity of the worldly and sensuous "otherness" by which it is opposed. Hence, "moral consciousness as the *simple knowing* and *willing* of pure duty is, in the doing of it, brought into relation with the . . . actuality of the complex case . . . ."[9] A tension emerges between a consciousness characterized by a general and formal sense of morality (Duty) and another consciousness informed by the situational and contextual exigencies of a specific situation. "Thus it is postulated that it is *another* consciousness which . . . contains the equally essential relation to 'doing', and to the necessity of the *specific* content: since for this other, duties mean *specific* duties, the content as such is equally essential as the form which makes the content a duty."[10] Accord-

---

6 For particularly astute accounts of Hegel's dynamic of reflection, see Martin Heidegger, Hegel's Concept of Experience (Kenley Royce Dove trans., 1983), and Heidegger's lectures on *Hegels Phänomenologie des Geistes*, in 32 GESAMTAUSGABE (1980); *see also* ALEXANDRE KOJÈVE, INTRODUCTION TO THE READING OF HEGEL (James H. Nichols trans., 1969) and RODOLPHE GASCHÉ, THE TAIN OF THE MIRROR 23-59 (1986).

7 Hegel, *supra* note 5, at 364.

8 *Id.* at 365.

9 *Id.* at 369.

10 *Id.* at 370.

ing to Hegel, the quality of the spirit *qua* "conscience" will ultimately reconcile the universality of duty as a postulate directed at
all being, with the situational pragmatic and particularity of "duties," thereby mediating form and content. The need for such
reconciliation is more than a merely technical, philosophical exi-
gency, since the initial opposition comes down to one between
the transcendental (Duty) and the empirical (duties). It is a conflict between two ways (orthodox vs. pragmatic) of *meaning*; and,
as Hegel is well aware, conflicts of meaning ultimately become
conflicts of value.

Hence, what Hegel now refers to as "[t]his self of conscience" or a "*third self*" is also characterized as "[m]oral self-
consciousness having attained its truth."[11] To reveal the ground
that authenticates and authorizes this "truth" of conscience requires a paradigmatic shift from the merely individuated "(self-)
consciousness"—irrespective of whether its content be Duty as
form or duties as content—to something like our modern concept of "personality". As Hegel observes, "[t]he totality or actuality which shows itself to be the truth of the ethical world is the
self of the . . . person; its existence consists in its being acknowledged by others."[12] In other words, "[c]onscience is the common element of the two self-consciousnesses, and this element is
the substance in which the deed has an *enduring reality*, the moment of being *recognized* and *acknowledged* by others."[13] Hence,
moral authority emerges at, and indeed constitutes, the very intersection of cognition and politics. To note its bilateral structure, that is, for it to be "recognized" as *moral* authority and to be
"acknowledged" as moral *authority*, is to understand why morality
evolves as the integration of these potentially conflicting moments within a discursive-linguistic community.

With unfailing concentration, Hegel thus points out how
"here again we see language as the existence of Spirit. Language
is self-consciousness existing *for others*, self-consciousness which
as such is immediately *present*, and as *this* self-consciousness is universal."[14] Irrespective of its formal modes of appearance, language is categorically understood as the infrastructure for the
construction and manifestation of moral authority. Consequently, language must shoulder the burden of proving the truth
and "sincerity" of the speaker's collective and morally authorita-

---

[11] *Id.* at 384-85.
[12] *Id.* at 384.
[13] *Id.* at 388.
[14] *Id.* at 395.

tive "spirit" for others. While "moral consciousness" presents itself as "still *dumb*, shut up with itself within its inner life,"[15] Hegel now asserts that "language . . . emerges as the middle term, mediating between independent and acknowledged self-consciousnesses; and the *existent self* is immediately universal acknowledgment."[16] The social dimension to this inward paradigm of the "ethical spirit" emerges into full view with Hegel's qualification of it as "law and simple command."[17] For reasons soon to become apparent, it is important to stress that this kind of language is performative rather than (if the distinction retains any validity) referential; that is, it instantiates or enacts (rather than signifying or *re*presenting) moral meanings as social values.

> The content of the language of conscience is the *self that knows itself as essential being*. This alone is what it declares, and this declaration is the true actuality [*wahre Wirklichkeit*] of the act, and the validating [*das Gelten*] of the action. Consciousness declares its *conviction*; it is in this conviction alone that the action is a duty; also it is valid as duty solely through the conviction being *declared*. For universal self-consciousness is free from the *specific* action that merely *is*; what is valid for that self-consciousness is not the *action* as *existence*, but the *conviction* that it is a duty; and this is made actual in language.[18]

Regarding the concept of duty and its collective subjectivity, "conscience," the passage suggests that a successful performance of moral speech has at least three requisites. First, its discursivity is *necessary*, since it alone insures the existence of moral authority "*for* universal acknowledgment." Second, the sincerity of moral speech is strictly an effect of the rhetorical and generic *form* of such speech. Finally, therefore, the universality of moral speech proves contingent on the *felicity* of its performance rather than on the *intentionality* seemingly prepossessed by the "subject" of utterance.

What renders Hegel's argument so volatile, yet also productive, is its recognition of the undecidable causality between an inward moral conviction and "its" socially visible, discursive authorship. The performative and strictly rhetorical grounding of moral individuality indicates why "conscience" and "conviction" cannot be granted axiological or temporal priority over their discursive instantiation. To redescribe morality as social and discur-

---

[15] *Id.* at 396.
[16] *Id.*
[17] *Id.*
[18] *Id.*

sive practice rather than as an inward presence ("conviction") mandates a significant reconception of discursive practice *per se*; it is to be thought neither as a signification nor as an expression of an inward self-consciousness, but is rather an intervention within a social- and foreign-determined continuum of form- and genre-based practices of moral *meanings*.

Hegel is rather alarmed, however, as he witnesses how his "own" theory progressively reveals the sincerity and authority of moral conscience to be irreducibly *the effect* of its universal linguistic performativity as "declaration" (*Aussprechen*). Eager to reign in the deviant (i.e., undecidable) causality between the spirit and its word, Hegel now confronts the question as to "[w]hether the assurance of acting from a conviction of duty is *true*"[19] with categorical directness, namely, by declaring the question inherently illegitimate. To do so "would presuppose that the inner intention is different from the one put forward[,]" when in fact, "this distinction between the universal consciousness and the individual self is just what has been superseded, and the supersession of it *is* conscience."[20]

Hegel's insistence on the "truth" of conscience, even though it co-originates with its social practice as "declaration," problematically sidesteps the issue concerning the veracity of a moral conscience and its "universal" authority. By insisting, with uncharacteristic orthodoxy, that "whoever says he acts in such and such a way from conscience, speaks the truth," Hegel deflects the formal/performative structure and its culturally (rather than individually grounded) "motives" into the mere antithesis of conscience, a kind of "bad faith" or "false consciousness."[21] Precisely this unmisgiving conflation of moral sincerity and semantic/syntactic forms indicates, however, that the *Phenomenology*

---

[19] *Id.*

[20] *Id.* at 396-97.

[21] *Id.* at 397. My use of formal/performative, notions not infrequently opposed to one another, proceeds from the understanding that no performance is ever "free" in any empirical or transcendental sense. To stress that point, Michael Oakeshott observes that "[t]he so-called 'practical' is not a certain kind of performance; it is conduct in respect of its acknowledgement of a practice." Oakeshott, *supra* note 1, at 57. However, Oakeshott's conception of performance seems overly reductive, since "performance," at least in the way it is used here, is simultaneously "practical" in Oakeshott's sense—i.e., "composed of conventions and rules of speech, a vocabulary and a syntax" *id.* at 58—*and* "performative" (spontaneous or creative). For a practice is never merely enacted by an agent, but also has the agent display his or her mastery of this practice. This resonates in Oakeshott's and Hegel's insistence that a "practice" is to receive "acknowledgement" from its community. For a more extensive discussion of Oakeshott's neo-pragmatist theory of moral conduct, see Thomas Pfau, *Immediacy and Dissolution: Reflections on Moral Theory and the Logic of Critical Discourse, in* INTERSECTIONS: NINETEENTH-CENTURY PHILOSOPHY AND CONTEMPORARY THEORY (Tilottama Rajan & David Clark eds., forthcoming).

achieves its logical and systematic coherence at least in part by eliding a competing discursive paradigm, one in which the relation between linguistic form and social authority is grounded in a *pragmatics* (a cultural unconscious of sorts) rather than in an originary interiority. Indeed, Hegel's argument continues to invite that alternative when noting that

> it is *in the form of the act* that the universality lies. It is this form which is to be established as actual: it is the *self* which as such is actual in language, which declares itself to be the truth, and just by so doing . . . is acknowledged by [all other selves].[22]

The question regarding the grounds of moral sincerity thus is subtly being recast as a quest for a socially "acknowledged" form.

II

Hegel's paradigmatic discussion of morality yields some fundamental insights and conclusions. To begin with, the moral subject oscillates, both in theory and praxis, between the traditional, essentialist category of an originary self and a pragmatist agency that authorizes its social "personality," that is, between a genetic and a teleological causality.[23] To be sure, it would amount to very little, if we were merely to proclaim that the figure of the author can never be decisively tethered to a self as origin. For the same reason, it would also prove facile and ultimately trivial to deplore (strictly as a contingency) how the

---

[22] Hegel, *supra* note 5, at 397 (first emphasis added). A surprising yet characteristic configuration of lyric speech and moral speculation can be found in IMMANUEL KANT, CRITIQUE OF PRACTICAL REASON (Lewis White Beck trans., 1949). In an effort to counter moral relativism and its concurrent, discursive indeterminacy—summarized and sharply criticized as the spectre of "moral fanaticism" (191/A 150-52)—Kant insists on Duty as "the sole genuine feeling." *Id.* at 192. In making this argument, Kant reveals the *pragmatics* of lyric as genre as he suddenly interrupts his latinate prose with the idiom of a neo-classical ode:

> Duty! Thou sublime and mighty name that dost embrace nothing charming or insinuating but requirest submission and yet seekest not to move the will by threatening aught that would arouse natural aversion or terror but only holdest forth a law which of itself finds entrance into the mind . . . (though not always obedience)—a law before which all inclinations are dumb even though they secretly work against it: what origin is there worthy of thee, and where is to be found the root of thy noble descent which proudly rejects all kinship with the inclinations and from which to be descended is the indispensable condition of the only worth which men can give themselves?

Id. at 193.

[23] The distinction between genealogical and teleological causality, certainly rooted in Aristotle's distinction between *causa materialis* and *causa finalis*, reappears in Paul de Man, *Autobiography as De-Facement*, in The Rhetoric of Romanticism 67-81 (1985). De Man, in turn, borrows from Gérard Genette. *Id.* at 69.

sincerity of moral utterances tends to be obscured by their rhetorical conventionality. For, as Hegel's argument already suggests, it appears by now distinctly possible that *the contingency of moral meaning is structural rather than accidental.* Hence, too, our argument neither purports to uncover some false consciousness inherent in moral self-enactment, nor to expose moral practice as festering with subjective interest and teeming with ideological bias. Indeed, it is only when formal attempts at "grounding" or, alternatively, discrediting the category of the author in foundationalist or essentialist terms (i.e., terms relying on or directed against a "general" theory of the subject) have been decisively suspended, that we can begin to think again "positively" about the pragmatics of authorial, discursive conduct. Such a rethinking must acknowledge, before all else, that the customary oppositions of private/public, thought/discourse, pure/empirical, and of conviction/declaration no longer admit a reliable deduction (i.e., a "genetic" causality) of social authority from an inward, self-present moral essence. Yet, for the same reason, we cannot discredit morality as merely a "false consciousness" or an "unconscious" pathology (i.e., a "teleological" causality grounded in some essentialized conception of unconscious desire).

Alternatively, then, I propose that we conceive of social and ideological authority as semantic effects of a strictly rhetorical and discursive practice of "authorship" rather than grounding these notions in the hypostatized interiority of a private consciousness, no matter whether it is posited as authentic, false, or pathologically distorted. For it is the practice, rather than some hypostatized "essence," of authorship which generates the above oppositions by inviting and structurally engineering an affective interpretive response that will construe the semantics/values of moral discourse as the effects of a concealed, inward origin. In other words, rather than *suffering* from the constitutive opaqueness of its subject, moral discourse both *celebrates* and *recovers* from the epistemological crisis of the subject (manifest in the rhetorical figure of *humilitas* or self-effacement and in diegetic form as a *peroratio* of spiritual redemption), itself the very cause and substance of moral speech. That is, moral speech is practice in a constitutive rather than secondary sense (*cf.* epigraph), and its capacity to produce meaning proves incompatible with the formalisms of phenomenological intentionality and propositional logic. In fact, the pragmatics of moral discourse enlist the notional myth of such anterior, private self-presence ("conscience," "feeling," "conviction," etc.) in order to generate the social and communal authority commonly regarded as the "foundation" of Romantic and post-Romantic authorship.[24]

In order to consider not only the possibility but, indeed, the pervasiveness of a non-egological and a-intentional concept of authorial practice or agency, it will help to briefly recall that such a theoretical position has been available to us, albeit in highly problematic terms, for some time now. I am thinking of John L. Austin's influential and ground-breaking analyses of performative (illocutionary) utterances.[25] Such utterances, we recall, are quite simply statements where "[t]he uttering of the words is, indeed, usually a, or even *the*, leading incident in the performance of the act,"[26] such as betting, christening, exchanging marriage vows, promising, etc. Once the paradigm of true/false is replaced with that of successful/unsuccesful performatives, it becomes apparent that meanings are not so much signified as they are enlisted, cited or used, at least in situations such as those specifically favored by Austin. It follows that utterances whose efficacy is largely grounded in their subscription to predecided social and rhetorical conventions/meanings, will no longer support the traditional assumption of an inward, spiritual self-presence of the kind that supported the moral authority and self-identity of Hegel's speaker. "Surely," Austin notes,

> the words must be spoken "seriously" and so as to be taken "seriously"? . . . But we are apt to have a feeling that their being serious consists in their being uttered as (merely) the outward and visible sign, for convenience or other record or for information, of an inward and spiritual act: from which it is but a short step to go on to believe or to assume without realizing that for many purposes the outward utterance is a description, *true or false*, of the occurrence of the inward performance.[27]

Austin's reduplicative notation of words "*spoken seriously* and so as to be taken seriously*" already intimates that the motive of speech belongs to an altogether different (performative, pragmatist) order than the intention or conviction which such utterance is designed to render distinctly visible. Indeed, in an often misun-

---

[24] See Meyer H. Abrams, Natural Supernaturalism (1971) for a highly representative and symptomatic instance of reading the poet-author as the redeemer of both his private self and a larger collectivity.

[25] John L. Austin, How to Do Things With Words (1962). I can only offer a brief assessment of Austin's argument.

[26] *Id.* at 8.

[27] *Id.* at 9.

derstood passage, Austin offers a characteristically wistful and humorous description of the remarkable amalgam of profundity and mundaneness otherwise known as moral discourse:

> It is gratifying to observe . . . how excess of profundity, or rather solemnity, at once paves the way for immorality. For one who says "promising is not merely a matter of uttering words! It is an inward and spiritual act!" is apt to appear as a solid moralist standing out against a generation of superficial theorizers: we see him as he sees himself, surveying the invisible depths of ethical space, with all the distinction of a specialist in the *sui generis*. Yet he provides Hyppolitus with a let-out, the bigamist with an excuse for his "I do" and the welsher with a defence for his "I bet." Accuracy and morality alike are on the side of the plain saying that *our word is our bond*.[28]

In disrupting the speculative chain of essential causes and rhetorical effects (Emotion → Reflection → Conviction → Expression → Authority) Austin's observations require us to rethink the "motives" for utterance and, consequently, the conditions that determine its meanings *as encoded within* the *form* of utterance, rather than being granted axiological priority over their "expression".[29] The question arises again as to whether moral discourse

---

[28] *Id.* at 10. For a lucid discussion of this passage, including some of its mistaken interpreters who read it as evidence of Austin's endorsement of an inward and foundationalist theory of the subject, see Sandy Petrey, Speech Acts and Literary Theory 84-85 (1990). Austin returns later in his text to the ostensibly referential nature of moral pronouncements, i.e., referring to some anterior and inward "emotion." AUSTIN, *supra* note 25, at 78-79. It is important, however, to remember that the issue of intentionality and inward self-presence is not being resolved in the direction of a "false consciousness" either. For Austin's lucid critique of the epistemological difficulties posed by lying, see John L. Austin, *Pretending, in* PHILOSOPHICAL PAPERS 201-19 (1961).

[29] Austin's increasingly self-contradictory and self-defeating attempts at specifying and restricting the range and applicability of his insights into the nature of illocutionary speech-acts are largely responsible for the irreconcilable conflict of interpretations given his work by traditionalists on the one hand, with a strong investment in methodological appropriation of the performative, and by deconstructivists and neo-pragmatists on the other. For positions of a decidedly "conservative" and, at times, orthodox inflection, see JOHN R. SEARLE, SPEECH ACTS (1969), and CHARLES ALTIERI, ACT AND QUALITY (1981). Altieri's text, notwithstanding its professed interest in bridging the gap between Searle and deconstructionist interpretations of Austin's linguistic postulates, arguably goes more astray ultimately than either of the two schools which he purports to reconcile. For assessments more interested in the a-systematic and paradoxical nature of Austin's performative theory, see JACQUES DERRIDA, LIMITED INC. (Samuel Weber ed., 1988). This contains Derrida's earlier *Signature, Event, Context* and, responding to John Searle's critique of that essay, the title essay itself. Derrida, however, seems at times too invested in exposing Austin's fallacious conclusions regarding "fictional" or, in Austin's own exclusionary characterization, "parasitical" utterances. See also Stanley Fish, *With the Compliments of the Author: Reflections on Austin and Derrida, in* DOING WHAT COMES NATURALLY: CHANGE, RHETORIC, AND THE PRACTICE OF THEORY IN LITERARY AND LEGAL STUDIES 37-67 (1989), and SANDRA PETREY, SPEECH ACTS AND LITERARY THEORY (1990) for a recent reexamination of all these debates.

constitutes a practice merely circumscribed by a contextual conventionality while grounded in inward sincerity, or whether its linguistic mode of appearance *instantiates* that conventionality and authenticity.   Pondering John L. Austin's notion of the performative, Jacques Derrida thus remarks:

> Aside from all the questions posed by the very historically sedimented notion of "convention," we must notice here: (1) That . . . Austin seems to consider only the conventionality that forms the *circumstance* of the statement, its contextual surroundings, and not a certain intrinsic conventionality of that which constitutes the locution itself, that is, everything that might quickly be summarized under the problematic heading of the "arbitrariness of the sign" . . . . Ritual is not an eventuality, but, as iterability, is a structural characteristic of every mark. . . .
>
> . . . .
>
> [F]inally, is not what Austin excludes as anomalous, exceptional, "non-serious," that is, *citation* (on the stage, in a poem, or in a soliloquy), the determined modification of a general citationality—or rather, a general iterability—without which there would not even be a "successful" performative?[30]

Meaning has priority over textuo-rhetorical form neither in an intrinsic subjectivist and psychologizing sense nor in an extrinsic historicizing sense. Hence, to argue that authority is bound up with the discursive practice of authorship, rather than being grounded in inward intention and/or an independent contextual determinism, is to categorically dissociate the "motives" that inform such practice from the classical concept of a self-conscious intentionality.   To restate the issue in the terms of literary analysis, authorship is not a secondary effect of an "expressivity," but instead supplants that very concept.

   Yet how are we to discern the "motives" of authorial discourse independent of some hypostatized, subjectivist model of origination or extrinsic contextual determinism? What distinctive feature can replace the irremediable opaqueness of "intentionality" and the illimitable contextual determinacy of "meaning" in phenomenological and post-structuralist/historicist critique, respectively? The following reading of the later Wordsworth's dinstinctly moral idiom, as exemplified by his *Ode to Duty*, shall illustrate the import of discursive *form* in answering

---

[30] Jacques Derrida, *Signature, Event, Context, in* Margins of Philosophy 323-25 (Alan Bass trans., 1982) (footnote omitted).

this question. In speaking of "form", I am thinking, to put it in provisional and admittedly general terms, of a text's affiliation with a certain "iterable" rhetorical and authorial practice—itself something like a "genre".[31] Put differently, the consideration of a text's rhetorical *form* may offer us a distinctly more promising answer to the post-modern theoretical predicament elaborated above, and furthermore may help us elucidate the significance of Wordsworth's, and Romanticism's, increasing endorsement of formal and generic features in its overarching poetic and authorial effort at reconstructing a morally and socially effective concept of the human subject.

III

A sharp reversal of Wordsworth's earlier, predominantly autobiographical writings, the publication of his 1807 *Poems in Two Volumes*[32] marks a distinctive turn away from the often inconclusive attempts at demarcating the authority of the self in a genetic and narrative form. The significance of this reversal becomes apparent if we consider its institutional consequences for contemporary, interpretive and editorial practice. Beginning with Matthew Arnold's contention that in order "[t]o exhibit th[e] body of Wordsworth's best work" criticism must "clear away obstructions from around it, and . . . let it speak for itself," critics and philologists of Wordsworth's uniquely convoluted text have made "indisputable" progress toward an aesthetically and politically more unified "body" of Wordsworth's work.[33] While interpretive scrutiny has exposed the increasing conservatism in the

---

[31] *See* Carolyn R. Miller, *Genre as Social Action* 70 Q.J. Speech 151 (1984). In a very lucid essay, the author echoes these positions when speaking of genre as "pragmatic, fully rhetorical, a point of connection between intention and effect, an aspect of social action." *Id.* at 153. Given this thesis, the issue, naturally, becomes one of "clarifying the relationship between rhetoric and its context of situation." Following Kenneth Burke's concept of motive, Miller notes that to speak of a "relationship" in the first place is to assume a recurrence. Notwithstanding the fact that the material situation of any given instance of discourse must be considered unique, it is also true that "[s]ituations are social constructs that are the result, not of 'perception', but of 'definition.' " *Id.* at 156. Genre, which conceives of discursive practice as the iterability of forms, instantiates precisely this sense of recurrence, thereby carrying out social motives that are clearly not to be conflated with a self-present, individual consciousness or intentionality. Discourse, that is, is marked *prima facie*, not by intention, but by exigence. "The exigence provides the rhetor with a socially recognizable way to make his or her intentions known. . . . Exigence must be seen neither as a cause of rhetorical action nor as intention, but as a social motive." *Id.* at 158. And, as Miller goes on to state, "at the level of the genre, motive becomes a conventionalized social purpose, or exigence, within the recurrent situation." *Id.* at 162.

[32] Wordsworth, *supra* note 4.

[33] Matthew Arnold, Essays in Criticism: Second Series, *reprinted in* SELECTED PROSE, 366, 374 (1970).

evolution of Wordsworth's career from Jacobin writer to social reformer, to lyric poet, to aged author/poet-laureate, textual editorship has sustained this argument, albeit by means of a reversed chronology. Thus, for example, the *Prelude* and *The Ruined Cottage* have been traced from their last to their earliest versions, thereby sustaining the interpretive hypothesis of Wordsworth's authorial betrayal of what, between 1793 and 1805, had constituted his "greatness" as a writer.[34]

This transformation from the writer of a text to the author of "Two Volumes" implicates Wordsworth in an ethical dilemma of sorts, as he adopts traditional poetic forms, endorses an unmistakably nationalist and conservative political tone, and transfers the poetic authority that eluded him in the *Prelude* ("the hiding places of man's power / Open; I would approach them, but they close"[35] onto an array of aesthetic figures and motifs (naturalized, gendered, or mythical) whose authority is grounded in the very poetic tradition that Wordsworth's earlier poetics had expressly disavowed.[36] Not surprisingly, Wordsworth's authorial self-promotion of *Poems* (1807) is punctuated by an underlying rhetoric of apology that blends the spiritual and material rewards of his lyric productivity, both as regards himself and his reader; as his "Advertisement" to the *Poems in Two Volumes* comments:

> The short Poems, of which these Volumes consist, were chiefly composed to refresh my mind during the progress of a work of length and labour, in which I have for some time been engaged; and to furnish me with employment when I had not resolution to apply myself to that work, or hope that I should proceed with it successfully. Having already, in the Volumes entitled Lyrical Ballads, offered to the World a considerable collection of short poems, I did not wish to add these to the number, till after the completion and publication of my larger work; but, as I cannot even guess when this will be, and as

---

[34] Geoffrey Hartman, Wordsworth's Poetry 1787-1814 (1964). Following Matthew Arnold's remark that while "Wordsworth composed verses during a space of some sixty years . . . it is no exaggeration to say that within one single decade of those years, between 1798 and 1808, almost all his first-rate work was produced," ARNOLD, *supra* note 31, at 372, numerous critics have recently favored the early Wordsworth. *See, e.g.*, Stephen Gill, *Wordsworth's Poems: The Question of Text*, 34 REV. ENG. STUD. 172 (1983). *But see* Jack Stillinger, *"Textual Primitivism" and the Editing of Wordsworth*, 3 STUDIES IN ROMANTICISM 28,i (David Wagenknecht ed., 1989). *But see*, WILLIAM H. GALPERIN, REVISION AND AUTHORITY IN WORDSWORTH (1989) (attempting to resuscitate Wordsworth's late poetry).

[35] WILLIAM WORDSWORTH, XII THE FOURTEEN-BOOK PRELUDE 279-80 (W.J.B. Owen ed., Cornell U. Press 1985).

[36] Regarding Wordsworth's rejection, at issue are, of course, the 1798 *Advertisement* and 1800 *Preface*, in particular the 1802 "Appendix" on "Poetic Diction."

several of these Poems have been circulated in manuscript, I
thought it better to send them forth at once. They were composed with much pleasure to my own mind, and I build upon
that remembrance a hope that they may afford profitable pleasure to many readers.[37]

The relation between the *Prelude* and the present collection
of poems is conceived primarily in economic terms. Thus the
slow and sputtering "progress of a work of length and labour"
contrasts with the "profitable pleasure" which the present collection of "short poems" promises both to Wordsworth and his
"many readers." Arguing that lyrical productivity is to correct an
economic imbalance that has affected both the spiritual ("re-
freshing my mind") and monetary ("make it worth my while[,] I
mean in a pecuniary view") aspects of Wordsworth's career, the
"Advertisement" exposes the arguably indecorous proximity of
political, aesthetic, and economic ambitions and of a "pure" lyrical expressiveness, respectively. The legitimacy of publishing the
book ultimately derives from the temporary shelter that it offers
to the author as a proprietor of intellectual values, which "have
been circulated in manuscript," whose final cultural significance
is deferred indefinitely until the revelation of the work. The *book*
thus mediates between the strictly private text (the *Prelude*) and
the eventual, public *work* (the *Recluse*). This bilateral relation—
between the privacy of the subject's text and the social efficacy of
the completed work—defines the lyric *book* itself as the quintessentially performative moment in the construction of Romantic
authorship. Lyric productivity thus reconciles a private and intellectual ("inward") *property*, and a socially efficient *authority* under
the auspices of lyric and aesthetic *form*. Meanwhile, that this moment itself should remain so oblique, both for Wordsworth's
contemporaries and for his modern critics, involves the "Advertisement's" strained and paradoxical attempt to mediate a text
largely unknown and a work largely unfinished.

In the absence of any autobiographical frame of reference,
the intellectual authority of the 1807 collection will be based on
the *form* of spirituality *in general*. That is, the lyric predicates the
authority of the "spirit" not on its narrative mode of origination,

---

[37] Wordsworth, *supra* note 4, at 527. In a letter to the publisher John Taylor, dating
from June 15, 1806, Wordsworth assumes a confident tone about his poetic powers
while admitting at the same time that his lyric productivity should also "make it worth
my while I mean in a pecuniary view." *Id.* at 11. Asking for Taylor's advice on the risks
of publishing at his own expense, since Longman's initial offer for what was to become
Poems in Two Volumes had not been satisfactory, Wordsworth's notes that "in the present
state of my reputation there can be no risk with a 1000 Copies." *Id.*

but on the universality of its communicated poetic form, and it is precisely the trope of a "moral consciousness"—that is, "conscience"—which organizes this transition in Wordsworth's career.[38] *Ode to Duty*, a lyric often cited though seldom read, exhibits the essential role played by the genre of lyric in Wordsworth's transfiguration from writer to author, from an affective "individuality" to a literary "personality"—a reversal enacted through the construction of a quintessentially middle-class, bourgeois "moral community." For Geoffrey Hartman:

> The "Ode to Duty" is more in need of interpretation than the other poems so far considered . . . not only because it has failed to attract devoted attention, but also for an intrinsic reason. Wordsworth is speaking in the Ode in his "character of philosophical poet"; and our immediate difficulty with it stems from a diction of generality, not to say vagueness, which its "philosophical" character seems to have imposed.[39]

Expanding on the Ode's preoccupation with literary ancestry, Geoffrey Hartman thus notes that "[i]t is, most probably, the im-

---

[38] Highly instructive of the Ode's capacity to enact the sentiment of moral spontaneity and authenticity are Robert Lowth, Lectures on the Sacred Poetry of the Hebrews (1753-1756); JOHN NEWBERY, THE ART OF POETRY ON A NEW PLAN (1762); HUGH BLAIR, LECTURES ON RHETORIC AND BELLES LETTRES (1783). Newbery's classicist doctrine maintains that "[t]he Ode . . . was probably the first species of poetry [and] [i]t had its source, we may suppose, from the heart." 2 NEWBERY, *supra*, at 39. And yet, when discussing the linguistic infrastructure of the sublime (divinely inspired), Newbery discovers that moral sincerity is bound up with a precarious stylistic calculus that oscillates between hyperbole and humility. "Though the sublime style is bold and figurative, sublime thoughts may sometimes require only a plain and simple style." Effective poetic style, in Newbery's poetics no less than in Wordsworth's *Preface* (1800), must produce the effect of *authenticity*, which in turn requires verbal structures that will elide all reflective time. *Spontaneity* thus becomes the visible and legible signature of authentic "passion," and Newbery's principal objective lies in defining the formal and rhetorical features that inculcate this appearance. "The passions of anger, grief and joy . . . are not to be loaded with studied metaphors, similes, and descriptions . . . [I]n general, [passions are] better expressed by sudden starts, suppressions, apostrophes, exclamations, and broken and unconnected sentences . . . ." 1 *Id.* at 53.

[39] Hartman, *supra* note 34, at 277-78 (1964) (footnote omitted). To ask, "whose poem?" entails further, inherently theoretical, questions concerning the relation between subjectivity and revision and literary collaboration. For the "Ode" undergoes extensive and compulsive revision, including substantial alterations at the stage of page proofs, which Wordsworth received in early 1807. It is also something of a collaborative family project, with Mary and Sara Hutchinson copying versions and revisions of the poem and with Coleridge deleting and re-ordering the verse as well as providing instructions (though eventually disregarded) for Longman's typesetters. For a textual account of the poem, see WORDSWORTH, *supra* note 4, at 30-32. The textual reflexivity of the poem continues in later editions, as Wordsworth decides to cancel, beginning with the 1815 edition of his *Poems*, the one stanza (st. 6) that may be said to propose an argument about morality rather than be concerned with imaging the topic itself. Yet a later printing further continues to blend moral meaning and literary authority by adding an epigraph from Seneca's *Moral Epistles* (added at the suggestion of Barron Field in 1836).

age of Milton in Wordsworth's mind, rather than an abstract ethics, which determined his conception of Duty."[40] That the presentation of Duty should take shape as a voluntary, and allusively explicit, subordination of Wordsworth's poetic voice ("made lowly wise," line 61)[41] to Milton does not yet constitute an outright contradiction of the poem's avowed discovery of an ethical self-consciousness. While pointing to the apparent discrepancy between the "elevated style,"[42] the "invented ceremonial of the self giving the self away,"[43] and the trivial circumstantiality of "common household duties"[44] as the ostensible challenge posed to the moral consciousness thus presented, Hartman still insists on the coherence of the poem by acknowledging the respective coherence of stylistic form and intellectual content. "[I]t is quite possible that in his desire for a greater affiliation with the poets of the past or with the present public formed by them, Wordsworth slipped into a conflation of an original thought and the traditional perspective from which he wanted only the style."[45] Hartman is right, I think, in locating the source for the reader's bewilderment in the poem's "philosophical generality" and in the "poet['s] consciously fashioning his own diction of generality."[46] That is, the intellectual authority of the speaker's newly discovered moral exemplariness is potentially imperiled by the excessively general and formalized style, a style whose rich literary heritage (Horace, Milton, Gray) casts moral authority strictly as an effect of the diverse authoritative literary and intellectual traditions that underwrite the present meditation.[47]

Yet to perceive the intellectual and rhetorical dimensions as latently incompatible, which we take as a reason for the poem's relatively uneventful history of interpretation, is to situate the poem mistakenly within the traditional paradigm of an expressive and self-transparent lyric "I." In contrast, I would argue that such an expressive self—endowed with unlimited powers of configuring its intellectual materials with their corresponding aesthetic form, itself to be discernibly invoked and delicately

---

[40] Hartman, *supra* note 34, at 279.
[41] Wordsworth, *supra* note 4, at 107.
[42] Hartman, *supra* note 34, at 278.
[43] *Id.* at 280-81.
[44] *Id.* at 282.
[45] *Id.*
[46] *Id.* at 283.
[47] *See* Leslie Brisman, Milton's Poetry of Choice and its Romantic Heirs 239 (1973) (demonstrating "how interwined the problem of a moral 'daughter of the voice' is with the problem of poetic voice").

transgressed—constitutes the most entrenched and tenacious obstacle to reconception of the Romantic lyric as an instance of a distinctly *social* practice, and hence, predicated on preexisting social and economic paradigms of authorial identity and the circulation of intellectual property.[48] One of the first to rigorously question this notion of the lyric "I" is Theodor Adorno in his *Aesthetics*:

> The linguistic quality of art gives rise to the query of what exactly it is that art says. Linguisticality is the true subject of art, producer and recipient being false subjects. For centuries the "I" of the lyrical poet has been instrumental in distorting the true state of affairs by fabricating the illusion of a false poetic subjectivity. True poetic subjectivity is by no means the grammatical "I" that speaks in the poem . . . [The "I"] constitutes itself immanently through an act of language performed by a particular work. In this process the actual producer is a moment of reality like any other. Thus the private person is hardly decisive even when it comes to the actual production of art. The work of art intrinsically tends towards a division of labour, with the individual being part of it. As production gives itself over to the matter at hand, it results in a universal that is born out of the utmost individuation. The power behind this kind of externalization by the private ego into the matter at hand is the collective essence of the private ego; it is responsible for the fact that art works are linguistic in character. Even without being conscious of society, the labour that goes on in the art work through the medium of the individual is social labour, [perhaps the more so the less it is conscious of this connection].[49]

---

[48] Marjorie Levinson has hinted at the need for an understanding of the social dimension of the lyric "I" as its only conceivable, critical foundation. See Marjorie Levinson, WORDSWORTH'S GREAT-PERIOD POEMS (1986) for her readings of *Immortality Ode* and *Peele Castle. See also* Marjorie Levinson, *The New Historicism: Back to the Future, in* RETHINKING HISTORICISM: CRITICAL READINGS IN ROMANTIC HISTORY 18 (1989).

[49] Theodor W. Adorno, Aesthetics 239-40 (C. Lenhardt trans., 1984). The German text, ÄSTHETISCHE THEORIE 250 (Rudolf Tiedemann & Gretel Adorno eds., 1970), contains a subordinate clause in the last sentence of the passage cited that the translation accidentally omits, which I have reinserted in brackets. The German reads: "Die Arbeit am Kunstwerk ist gesellschaftlich durchs Individuum hindurch, ohne daß es dabei der Gesellschaft sich bewußt werden müßte; *vielleicht sogar desto mehr, je weniger es das ist*" (restored clause emphasized). Eventually, we will have to go beyond the essentialist rhetoric that informs Adorno's description of the relation between collectivity, production, and labor. Giles Deleuze and Félix Guattari rightly insist that if we view linguisticality as the only evidence for the social pragmatics of discourse, we must accept that it is the relational play of such discourse which generates the *appearance* of what orthodox Marxism continues to reify under the concepts of labor, matter, individuality, collectivity, and class. "The semiotic or collective aspect of an assemblage relates not to a productivity of language but to regimes of signs, to a machine of expression whose variables deter-

Wordsworth's *Ode to Duty*[50] offers concrete evidence for the linguistic instantiation of such a collective subjectivity, socially legitimized by the motif of morality and rhetorically configured by the subtly distributive play of pronominal references. Notably, the opening apostrophe is not overtly tethered to an expressive "I," though its addressee, Duty, is not consigned to the aesthetic autonomy of traditional allegory either. First invoked as "Stern Daughter of the Voice of God!", Duty appears the correlate of desires harbored by an appropriately self-effacing speaker.[51] Hence, its denomination causes Duty to oscillate between allegory and the proper name: "O Duty! if that name thou love."[52] This contingency of "Duty" on the rhetorical, specifically tropological, competence of the speaker results in the subsequent introduction of metaphors concerned with social organization, themselves alternatively of a retributive-martial,[53] spiritual,[54] or political kind.[55]

The principal task of the lyric lies in the creation of a rhetorical movement that the reader will interpret as the *expression* of an inward transformation. That is, through its careful invocation of discursive characteristics traditionally associated with a paradigm of morality and spirituality in general, the *Ode* aims at staging the inward drama of the speaker's transfiguration from an inward, self-conscious subjectivity into a social, and morally exemplary personality. It is from the "acknowledgment" of such a transformation as one precipitated by moral conviction that the inwardness of "conscience" derives its social force and authority. The traditional lyric "I" thus is displaced (in what was the first stanza composed) onto those "Glad Hearts" that cannot authoritatively represent "the genial sense of youth."[56] Between the "thou" of Duty and the "they [who] a blissful course may hold"[57] there opens the yet unclaimed sphere of authority for the poet as both social and moral practitioner.[58] That gap of authority is almost imperceptibly filled by the first person plural of the subsequent

---

mine the usage of language elements." GILES DELEUZE AND FÉLIX GUATTARI, A THOUSAND PLATEAUS 90 (Brian Massumi trans., 1988).

[50] Wordsworth, *supra* note 4, at 104.

[51] *Id.*

[52] *Id.* "Duty! if best that name thou love" (MS. 44) *Id.*

[53] "a Rod / To check the erring, and reprove; / Thou who art victory" *Id.* at lines 3-5.

[54] "a Light to guide" / "a glorious ministry" *Id.* at lines 3, 8.

[55] "Thou who art . . . law" *Id.* at line 5.

[56] *Id.* at 105 (lines 12, 13).

[57] *Id.* (1827-, line 21).

[58] Note Wordsworth's increasing pronominal foregrounding of the unreflective, affective "Glad Hearts" in later versions of the Ode: "Oh! if through confidence mis-

stanza, with the revisions of the passage in question exhibiting how such faith in the redeeming aspects of self-submission to an ethically figured authority *is itself an effect of the rhetorical pronouncement* of such faith.

> i l
> Serene ~~would~~ be our days and bright;
>
> ill
> And happy ~~would~~ our nature be;
>
> When love is our   l
> If ~~love were an~~ unerring   ~~right~~;
> And joy its own security.[59]

Social authority thus is instantiated as a voice of both stylistic and philosophical maturity, mediating between the self-sufficient "thou" of the "Daughter of the Voice of God" and the unreflective "they" who cannot *represent* their moral authority ("Who do thy work and know it not")[60] and thus have none. Adorno's notation of a "division of labor" constitutive of the ostensibly private and spiritual expressivity of the "lyric I" reflects in the collective pronoun ("our days . . . our nature . . . our light")[61] as well as in the subsequent conversion narrative of stanzas four and five.[62] For it is here that the sublation of a purportedly primordial, lyric self ("being to myself a guide")[63] into the moral authority of "conscience" reveals its inherently speculative character in terms strikingly cognate with Hegel's concept of morality. Stanzas four and five thus seek to mediate the contingency of a "natural" consciousness (the former 'I' that "[t]oo blindly" has "reposed [its] trust")[64] and the collective spirit whose identity, both for itself and for others, is beyond time and, both in Hegel's and Wordsworth's view, beyond question. "My hopes no more must change their name, / I long for a repose which ever is the same."[65]   In Hegel's view, the erasure of time and, by extension, of historical difference is the salient characteristic of the accomplished sublation of individual, narrative "meaning" [*Meinen*] into the collective authority of the

---

placed / *They* fail, thy saving arms, dread Power! around *them* cast." *Id.* (1836-, lines 15-16) (emphasis added).

[59] *Id.* at 304-05. I quote from the printer's copy for the 1807 collection, known as Longman MS., 10', lines 17-20.

[60] *Id.* at 105 (line 14).

[61] *Id.*

[62] *Id.* at 106.

[63] *Id.* at line 27.

[64] *Id.* at line 28.

[65] *Id.* at lines 39-40.

"we" and its corresponding "truth"; namely, the concept of the subject as "spirit" rather than individuality. "Spirit necessarily appears in Time," Hegel notes at the end of his *Phenomenology of Spirit* (published in the same year and month as Wordsworth's *Ode*): "and it appears in Time just so long as it has not *grasped* its pure Notion, i.e., has not annulled [*getilgt*] Time."[66]

Adorno recognized the constitutive dis-individuation that the rhetorical labor/performance of the lyric strongly implies. This recognition suggests that the "general" and "vague" diction, and the concomitant erasure of a private, inward subjectivity—at least in an ode concerned with ethics and, specifically, with the concept of Duty—is anything but the contingent aesthetic mishap that Wordsworthians have principally regarded this ode to be. On the contrary, the supplementation of the no longer sufficient, private "I" with a collective individuality (a certain "class" of readers, governed by the privileged voice of the author), is an altogether integral function of all moral utterance. That is, the performative dimension of the lyric needs to plot its authority in a form discernable and sufficiently general for its intended audience. The construction of moral authority ("conscience") not only requires the construction of authorship but, so as to legitimate the author as the collective spirit, effectively dissembles him in the ostensibly spontaneous, "timeless" practice of lyric speech.

Lyric poetry, then, is not to be regarded as a principally signifying or expressive structure but rather constitutes an intervention within an iterable and "acknowledged" practice of signification. Stabilized by its literary tradition—which is itself being reaffirmed in the curricular agenda of classical learning and by a pedagogy stressing mnemonic recitation—the lyric thus instantiates the general concept of a moral-spiritual authority rather than founding it. As regards its readers, the aura of the lyric, then, is principally one of recognition rather than discovery, and Stuart Curran correctly notes that "[b]y the time the history of the ode embarks on the century in which it was to become synonymous with lyric poetry, its greatest examples had already made conventional its nature as a dramatic, self-reflexive, and dialectical form."[67] The *Ode* thus does not "express" a newly discovered spiritual conviction but, instead, realigns (and thereby

---

[66] Hegel, *supra* note 5, at 487.

[67] *See* Stuart Curran, Poetic Form and British Romanticism 66 (1986); *see also* PAUL FRY, THE POET'S CALLING IN THE ENGLISH ODE 74-78 (1980) (for the most thorough consideration of the aesthetic tradition within which Wordsworth's *Ode* proceeds).

empowers as a cultural "authority") the self with a historically proven social value, here present as an "iterable" genre. It will be successful in this to the extent that its very form *recognizably* reaffirms a cultural value by *rhetorically* "expressing" the discovery of a collective moral value under the aegis of the speaker's inward and immediate "conscience". The positional stability of *form* remains predicated on its historical iterability and, precisely therefore, can afford to acknowledge its historicity through casual allusion and epigraphic framing.

Predictably, the pragmatics of lyric production reveal their efficacy in the commentaries by some of Wordsworth's first critics. While *Ode to Duty* appears to have elicited little commentary among Wordsworth's early reviewers, the chiasmic relation of statements made by two readers supports our earlier thesis regarding the intrinsic undecidable causality of moral speech. At issue is the following stanza of the *Ode to Duty*:

> Stern lawgiver! yet thou dost wear
> The Godhead's most benignant grace;
> Nor know we anything so fair
> As is the smile upon thy face:
> Flowers laugh before thee on their beds;
> And Fragrance in thy footing treads;
> Thou dost preserve the Stars from wrong;
> And the most ancient Heavens through Thee are fresh and strong.[68]

"The last two lines," Francis Jeffrey notes, "seem to be utterly without meaning; at least we have no sort of conception in what sense *Duty* can be said to keep the old skies *fresh*, and the stars from wrong."[69] Jeffrey's rejection of these statements as devoid of all meaning is balanced by his casual notation of the poem's "lofty vein," though it has been "unsuccessfully attempted."[70] Arguably, then, form could not succeed in seducing a reader as politically and aesthetically resistant to the 'Lakers' as Jeffrey. Yet, that Wordsworth's lyrics achieved at least limited success in seducing the reader into subscribing to the general spirit and moral authority of the lyric is evinced by another reviewer, Lucy Aikin. Having observed how "[t]he sonnets [dedicated to liberty] hold a severe and manly tone [and] bear strong traces of feeling and of thought," she goes on to note that "[o]ne of the Odes[,]

---

68 Wordsworth, *supra* note 4, at 107 (lines 49-56).
69 Francis Jeffrey, 11 Edinburgh Rev. 214 (1807), *reprinted in* ROMANTIC BARDS AND BRITISH REVIEWERS 18 (1971).
70 *Id.*

to Duty, is a meanly written piece, with some good thoughts."[71] The apparent confusion of standards in reading, betrayed by the alternative notations of a poem in "a lofty vein" yet "without meaning," or a lyric "meanly written" yet containing "some good thoughts," suggests that the authority of the lyric, in some respects, has already been affirmed by either critic. For both Jeffrey and Aikin base their critique or praise on a paradigm of lyric "expressivity", thus advancing their aesthetic qualifications on the grounds of an authentic, exemplary, and individual moral consciousness perceived to have struggled with configuring its inalienable spiritual content with the "proper" aesthetic form. Thus, both implicitly reinforce the autonomy of aesthetic form whose potential interference with the communication of moral value and spiritual authority remains a technical contingency rather than a constitutive aspect of authorial practice. That is, as *aesthetic* objections, both Jeffrey's charge of semantic opaqueness and Aikin's misgivings about a poem "meanly written" remain well within the interpretive space delineated by the pragmatics of a distinctly "literary" and formal lyric. With their critical intelligence fully enclosed by the unimpeachable tropes of aesthetics (*form*) and morality (*conscience*), they cannot but affirm the social authority, which apparently is itself the quintessential pragmatic effect of the cultural logic that circumscribes Wordsworth's lyric authorship in 1807 and beyond.

---

[71] Lucy Aikin, 6 Annual Rev. 521 (1808), *reprinted in* ROMANTIC BARDS AND BRITISH REVIEWERS 37 (1971).

Ode to Duty

Stern Daughter of the Voice of God!°
O Duty! if that name thou love
Who art a Light to guide, a Rod
To check the erring, and reprove;
Thou who art victory and law
When empty terrors overawe;
From vain temptations dost set free;
From strife and from despair; a glorious ministry.

There are who ask not if thine eye
Be on them; who, in love and truth,   10
Where no misgiving is, rely
Upon the genial sense of youth:
Glad Hearts! without reproach or blot;
Who do thy work, and know it not:
May joy be theirs while life shall last!
And Thou, if they should totter, teach them to stand fast!

Serene will be our days and bright,
And happy will our nature be,
When love is an unerring light,
And joy its own security.   20
And blessed are they who in the main
This faith, even now, do entertain:
Live in the spirit of this creed;
Yet find that other strength, according to their need.

I, loving freedom, and untried;
No sport of every random gust,
Yet being to myself a guide,
Too blindly have reposed my trust:
Resolved that nothing e'er should press
Upon my present happiness,   30
I shoved unwelcome tasks away;
But thee I now would serve more strictly, if I may.

Through no disturbance of my soul, ⎫
Or strong compunction in me wrought, ⎬
I supplicate for thy controul; ⎭
But in the quietness of thought:
Me this unchartered freedom tires;
I feel the weight of chance desires:
My hopes no more must change their name,
I long for a repose which ever is the same.   40

ODE TO DUTY

Yet not the less would I throughout°
Still act according to the voice
Of my own wish; and feel past doubt
That my submissiveness was choice:
Not seeking in the school of pride
For 'precepts over dignified,'°
Denial and restraint I prize
No farther than they breed a second Will more wise.

Stern Lawgiver! yet thou dost wear°
The Godhead's most benignant grace;   50
Nor know we any thing so fair
As is the smile upon thy face;
Flowers laugh before thee on their beds;
And Fragrance in thy footing treads;
Thou dost preserve the Stars from wrong;
And the most ancient Heavens through Thee are fresh and strong.

To humbler functions, awful Power!°
I call thee: I myself commend
Unto thy guidance from this hour;
Oh! let my weakness have an end!   60
Give unto me, made lowly wise,
The spirit of self-sacrifice;
The confidence of reason give;
And in the light of truth thy Bondman let me live!

THE INTERDISCIPLINARY FUTURE OF COPYRIGHT THEORY

ALFRED C. YEN*

I. INTRODUCTION

The proper scope of an author's property has long troubled copyright analysts. Most agree that authors should (and do) own the right to prevent others from literally duplicating original copyrighted material. Beyond that, the reach of an author's rights becomes very hazy. Can an author prevent the use of her plot or characters? What about the general appearance of sculpture, a painter's style or a photographer's perspective and choice of subject matter? One hundred and fifty years ago all of these items were part of the public domain.[1] Recent decisions, however, suggest that these items have now become private property.[2]

At first glance, extending authors' rights beyond literal reproduction seems like a good idea. As Judge Learned Hand stated, "It is of course essential to any protection of literary property . . . that the right cannot be limited literally to the text, else a plagiarist would escape by immaterial variations."[3] However, sober reflection indicates that too much of this good thing is undesirable. Authorship is possible only when future authors have the ability to borrow from those who have created before them.[4] If too much of each work is reserved as private property

---

* Associate Professor of Law, Boston College Law School. B.S., M.S., 1980, Stanford University; J.D., 1983, Harvard Law School. The author would like to thank Tracy Tanaka, Boston College Law School class of 1991, for her able research assistance. Some of the research reflected in this essay was supported by research grants from Boston College, Boston College Law School and the Boston College Law School Fellows.

[1] Early copyright decisions reflect a very narrow view of the kinds of appropriation which constitute infringement. *See* Stowe v. Thomas, 23 F. Cas. 201 (C.C.E.D. Pa. 1853) (No. 13,514) (refusing to find defendant's German translation an infringement of Harriet Beecher Stowe's Uncle Tom's Cabin).

[2] *See* Sid & Marty Krofft Television Prods., Inc. v. McDonald's Corp., 562 F.2d 1157, 1167 (9th Cir. 1977) (protecting "total concept and feel" of plaintiff's costumed characters and television series); Sheldon v. Metro-Goldwyn Pictures Corp., 81 F.2d 49 (2d Cir. 1936) (protecting plot of play); Steinberg v. Columbia Pictures, Inc., 663 F. Supp. 706, 709 (S.D.N.Y. 1987) (protecting plaintiff's perspective and style in illustration referred to as "a parochial New Yorker's view of the world"); Kisch v. Ammirati & Puris, Inc., 657 F. Supp. 380 (S.D.N.Y. 1987) (denying defendant's motion to dismiss copyright claim based in part on plaintiff's choice of camera angle, lighting, and subject matter).

[3] Nichols v. Universal Pictures Corp., 45 F.2d 119, 121 (2d Cir. 1930).

[4] *See, e.g.,* Emerson v. Davies, 8 F. Cas. 615, 619 (C.C.D. Mass. 1845) (No. 4,436):
In truth, in literature, in science and in art, there are, and can be, few, if any,

through copyright, future would-be authors will find it impossible to create. Society would presumably suffer from the decreased production of creative works. Proper construction of our copyright law therefore depends on striking a socially acceptable balance between the interests of authors and the public.

From a purely intuitive point of view, two issues certainly seem relevant. First, society would like to ensure the promotion of social welfare through the production of creative works. Second, society would also want to strike a just and fair compromise between authors and consumers of creative works. If we are to believe various statements made by the Supreme Court, however, the first issue is the only one which may be considered when interpreting American copyright law. For example, in *Sony Corp. of America v. Universal City Studios Inc.*, the Supreme Court wrote:

> The monopoly privileges that Congress may authorize are neither unlimited nor primarily designed to provide a special private benefit. Rather, the limited grant is a means by which an important public purpose may be achieved. It is intended to motivate the creative activity of authors and inventors by the provision of a special reward, and to allow the public access to the products of their genius after the limited period of exclusive control has expired.[5]

In my view, this one-sided approach to copyright cultivates an obviously cramped view of an area which is assuming ever-increasing importance for our society. After all, justice and fairness are key considerations in most areas of the law, especially property law.[6] Why should copyright be any different?

This Essay will briefly, but critically, examine the major reasons which have been given for why copyright should be different from other areas of the law. Part II will begin by sketching two copyright theories which follow the intuitions outlined above. The first theory justifies copyright as an economic incentive which advances social welfare. The second justifies copyright as the legal vindication of a person's moral right to property in the

---

things, which, in an abstract sense, are strictly new and original throughout. Every book in literature, science and art, borrows, and must necessarily borrow, and use much which was well known and used before. . . . No man writes exclusively from his own thoughts, unaided and uninstructed by the thoughts of others. The thoughts of every man are, more or less, a combination of what other men have thought and expressed, although they may be modified, exalted, or improved by his own genius or reflection.

[5] Sony Corp. of Am. v. Universal City Studios, Inc., 464 U.S. 417, 429, *reh'g denied*, 465 U.S. 1112 (1984).

[6] For an overview of various philosophies of property, see LAWRENCE C. BECKER, PROPERTY RIGHTS: PHILOSOPHICAL FOUNDATIONS (1977).

fruits of her labor. Part III will study the reasons for suppressing the discussion of justice and fairness in copyright jurisprudence. This Essay will show that these reasons are insufficient to support the suppression, and goes on to outline arguments which demonstrate that considerations of justice and fairness are essential to a complete copyright theory. The Essay concludes with some remarks about the future of copyright theory.

II.   Two Models of Copyright

Modern American copyright scholars recognize two apparently conflicting copyright theories. The first, and dominant, theory states that copyright exists solely to provide necessary economic incentives for the production of creative work. Under this view, copyright is necessary because in its absence those interested in using the author's work would simply copy the work instead of buying it from the author. Authors would then find their economic returns too small to justify the costs of authorship. In such a situation authors might not produce and social welfare would presumably suffer.[7] To remedy this problem, economic theory supports granting authors copyright in their works. However, those rights are necessarily limited in scope, because copyright imposes costs on society in exchange for the benefits of induced creative activity. First, the owner of copyright will charge a monopoly price for her work. The number of people who gain access to the work will therefore decrease.[8] Second, copyright raises the production cost of future works, because prohibiting borrowing from existing works makes it more difficult for future authors to create.[9] Thus, the proper degree of copyright protection is that which maximizes the difference between the benefits of induced creative activity and the costs of increased authors' rights.[10]

The second, and generally less well explored "natural law theory" considers copyright as the legal vindication of a person's moral right to property in the fruits of her labor.[11] Under this

---

[7] *See* William M. Landes & Richard A. Posner, *An Economic Analysis of Copyright Law,* 18 J. Legal Stud. 325, 328 (1989). In economic terms, an inefficiency, or "market failure," has occurred.

[8] William W. Fisher III, *Reconstructing the Fair Use Doctrine,* 101 Harv. L. Rev. 1659, 1700-02 (1988).

[9] Landes & Posner, *supra* note 7, at 332.

[10] Fisher, *supra* note 8, at 1717. *See also* Landes & Posner, *supra* note 7, at 326. This economic statement captures the conventional adage that copyright balances incentives for production against the need for free access to works.

[11] This theory descends from eighteenth-century concepts of property. These concepts are reflected in the writings of William Blackstone and John Locke. *See* 2 William

theory, copyright's justification does not rest upon any showing of economic necessity. Instead, copyright exists because society's failure to protect authors' property interests would result in the denial of a basic human right. Thus, the author rightfully gains copyright in her work to the extent that she can claim sole credit for the work's creation.

A.   *The American Choice*

Although both of the above described theories support copyright's existence and suggest its boundaries, American analysts generally insist that copyright rests solely on economics. Both the United States Supreme Court and Congress have stated that copyright exists only for the purpose of advancing social welfare through economic incentives for authorship.[12] Moreover, the Supreme Court has explicitly rejected natural law copyright arguments.[13] Analysts generally follow this lead by explaining copyright's basic doctrines such as originality and the idea/expression dichotomy in economic terms.[14] Two separate

---

BLACKSTONE, COMMENTARIES *8; JOHN LOCKE, TWO TREATISES OF GOVERNMENT at § 27 (Peter Laslett ed., 1970) (3d ed. 1698).

[12] *See supra* text accompanying note 5. *See also* H.R. REP. No. 2222, 60th Cong., 2d Sess. 7 (1909), *reprinted in* 6 LEGISLATIVE HISTORY OF THE 1909 COPYRIGHT ACT, at S7 (1976).

> The enactment of copyright legislation . . . is not based upon any natural right that the author has in his writings . . . but upon the ground that the welfare of the public will be served and progress of science and useful arts will be promoted by securing to authors for limited periods the exclusive rights to their writings.

[13] *See* Wheaton v. Peters, 33 U.S. (8 Pet.) 591, 654-68 (1834).

[14] These concepts are embodied in our present copyright code at 17 U.S.C. § 102 (1988). Together they define the existence and scope of copyright in a given work. Originality provides the basic requirement for copyrightability by providing that only "original works of authorship" are eligible for protection. 17 U.S.C. § 102(a). Copyright therefore does not protect works which lack minimal creativity or are simply copies of other preexisting works. *See* Toro Co. v. R & R Prods. Co., 787 F.2d 1208, 1213 (8th Cir. 1986) (denying protection to manufacturer's parts numbering system because of lack of originality); L. Batlin & Son, Inc. v. Snyder, 536 F.2d 486 (2d Cir.) (holding that a copy of preexisting work in public domain lacks sufficient originality), *cert. denied*, 429 U.S. 857 (1976); Magic Mktg., Inc. v. Mailing Servs. of Pittsburgh, Inc., 634 F. Supp. 769 (W.D. Pa. 1986) (advertising phrases on envelope lack originality).

However, the mere fact that a work is "original" does not mean that copyright prohibits all borrowing from that work. Instead, the idea/expression dichotomy permits some borrowing from every copyrighted work by specifically excluding ideas from an author's property. 17 U.S.C. § 102(b). Thus, even though a book is protected by copyright, a future author is free to borrow the ideas embodied in the book. Only the book's expression remains protected from copying. Landsberg v. Scrabble Crossword Game Players, Inc., 736 F.2d 485 (9th Cir.) (denying protection for instructions on how to play Scrabble), *cert. denied*, 469 U.S. 1037 (1984); Baker v. Selden, 101 U.S. 99 (1879) (idea of a double-entry bookkeeping system not protected by copyright).

For example, since originality defines the works eligible for copyright protection, its economic interpretation becomes an exercise in determining whether extending copyright to a given work promotes social welfare. Similarly, application of the idea/

lines of thinking support this choice.

The first rests on the descriptive claim that Americans have always viewed copyright as a matter of economics, and not a basic matter of fairness and justice. Proponents of this argument base their position on statements such as those noted in the preceding paragraph. They also point out that the Constitution explicitly contemplated an economic basis for copyright by authorizing Congress to "promote the progress of . . . the useful arts."[15] Departure from economic copyright theory therefore represents an unwarranted, and perhaps unconstitutional, change from established practice.

The second line of thinking rests on the normative claim that natural law copyright theory leads to dire consequences. As an initial matter, proponents of this view note that copyright lasts for only a limited duration.[16] By contrast, natural law principles would allow copyrights of unlimited duration. Furthermore, copyright sometimes allows individuals to borrow original material created by other authors.[17] They contend that a serious regime of property in the fruits of an author's labor would never allow such a result. Thus, adherents to the second justification

---

expression dichotomy becomes an economic cost-benefit calculation. If authors need more incentive to produce creative works, then fewer facets of works should be considered ideas, and more facets should be considered expressions. If society needs greater access to works, the converse is true. This vision suggests the use of economic analysis to strike the required balance between the interests of authors and the interests of society. See Whelan Assocs., Inc. v. Jaslow Dental Lab., Inc., 797 F.2d 1222, 1235 (3rd Cir. 1986).

> [P]recisely because the line between idea and expression is elusive, we must pay particular attention to the pragmatic considerations that underlie the distinction and copyright law generally. In this regard, we must remember that the purpose of the copyright law is to create the most efficient and productive balance between protection (incentive) and dissemination of information, to promote learning, culture and development.

cert. denied, 479 U.S. 1031 (1987).

Major articles which adopt a primarily economic view of copyright include Stephen Breyer, The Uneasy Case for Copyright: A Study of Copyright in Books, Photocopies, and Computer Programs, 84 HARV. L. REV. 281 (1970); Wendy J. Gordon, Fair Use as Market Failure: A Structural and Economic Analysis of the Betamax Case and its Predecessors, 82 COLUM. L. REV. 1600 (1982); Robert M. Hurt & Robert M. Schuchman, The Economic Rationale of Copyright, 56 AM. ECON. REV. 421 (1966); Landes & Posner, supra note 7; Peter S. Menell, An Analysis of the Scope of Copyright Protection for Application Programs, 41 STAN. L. REV. 1045 (1989). A recently published treatise by a leading copyright scholar, Professor Paul Goldstein, also reflects the current primacy of economic theories of copyright. PAUL GOLDSTEIN, COPYRIGHT: PRINCIPLES, LAW AND PRACTICE (1989). Although Professor Goldstein does not exclusively use economic terms to explain copyright principles, they certainly play a major role in many key areas of his work.

15 U.S. CONST. art. 1, § 8, cl. 8.

16 Copyright terms presently last for the life of the author plus fifty years. See 17 U.S.C. § 302 (1988). Additionally, the Constitution requires Congress to secure an author's copyright for only a limited period of time. U.S. CONST. art. 1, § 8, cl. 8.

17 For a description of the so-called idea/expression dichotomy, see supra note 14.

state that recognition of copyright's natural law basis destroys any balance between the interests of authors and the public.[18]

1.   Evaluation of the Descriptive Claim

As noted previously, the descriptive claim for suppression of copyright's natural law facets rests on constitutional language and a long string of statements which purportedly restrict copyright analysis to economics. Closer examination of the record shows, however, that the case for suppression is far from air tight. If nothing else, early Americans did not view copyright as a purely economic instrument. Instead, they referred explicitly to copyright's support in both economics and natural law. For example, no fewer than seven state copyright statutes contained preambles such as New Hampshire's, which read:

> As the improvement of knowledge, the progress of civilization, and the advancement of human happiness, greatly depend on the efforts of learned and ingenious persons in the various arts and sciences; as the principal encouragement such persons can have to make great and beneficial exertions of this nature, must consist in the legal security of the fruits of their study and industry to themselves; and as such security is one of the natural rights of all men, there being no property more peculiarly a man's own than that which is produced by the labor of his mind . . . .[19]

---

[18] See Howard B. Abrams, *The Historic Foundation of American Copyright Law: Exploding the Myth of Common Law Copyright*, 29 WAYNE L. REV. 1119, 1185-87 (1983); Lyman Ray Patterson, *Private Copyright and Public Communication: Free Speech Endangered*, 28 VAND. L. REV. 1161, 1210 (1975).

[19] Act of Nov. 7, 1783, 1783 N.H. Laws 305. The copyright statutes of Massachusetts and Rhode Island contained essentially identical preambles. *See* An Act for the Purpose of Securing to Authors the Exclusive Right and Benefit of Publishing their Literary Productions, for Twenty-One Years, ch. 26, 1783 Mass. Acts 236; An Act for the Purpose of Securing to Authors the Exclusive Right and Benefit of Publishing their Literary Productions, for Twenty-One Years, 1783 R.I. Acts & Resolves 6. Furthermore, the Connecticut statute provided:

> Whereas it is perfectly agreeable to the Principles of natural Equity and Justice, that every Author should be secured in receiving the profits that may arise from the Sale of his Works, and such Security may encourage Men of Learning and Genius to publish their Writings which may do Honor to their Country, and Service to Mankind . . . .

Act of Jan. 8, 1783, 1783 Conn. Pub. Acts 617. The New York statute is substantially identical. An Act to Promote Literature, ch. 54, 1786 N.Y. Laws 298. The New Jersey statute contained the following preamble:

> Whereas Learning tends to the Embellishment of Human Nature, the Honor of the Nation, and the general Good of Mankind; and as it is perfectly agreeable to the Principles of Equity, that Men of Learning who devote their Time and Talents to the preparing of Treatises for Publication should have the profits that may arise from the Sale of their Works secured to them . . . .

An Act for the Promotion and Encouragement of Literature, ch. 21, 1783 N.J. Laws 47. Finally, the North Carolina statute provided:

This thinking was echoed in Madison's support for the Federal Constitution's grant of congressional authority to enact copyright legislation:

> The utility of [the copyright power] will scarcely be questioned. The copyright of authors has been solemnly adjudged in Great Britain to be a right of common law. The right to useful inventions seems with equal reason to belong to the inventors. The public good fully coincides in both cases with the claims of individuals.[20]

Evidence of copyright's non-economic heritage exists in modern copyright as well. Despite ostensibly relying on a purely economic outlook, the Supreme Court occasionally adopts statements which reflect copyright's roots in fairness and justice.[21] From statements like these we can conclude that natural law actually motivates courts, despite protestations to the contrary. Furthermore, it has been suggested that modern copyright doctrine is entirely consistent with a regime constructed from natural law principles, and that economically interpreted concepts such as the idea/expression dichotomy actually owe their ancestry to natural law.[22] Finally, when one considers the existence of copyright protection for works which do not require economic incentives for production,[23] it is hard to believe that the repeated statements which restrict copyright theory to economics provide an accurate description of actual copyright thinking. The claim that

---

> Whereas nothing is more strictly a man's own than the fruit of his study, and it is proper that men should be encouraged to pursue useful knowledge by the hope of reward; and as the security of literary property must greatly tend to extension of arts and commerce . . . .

Act of Dec. 29, 1785, ch. 26, 1785 N.C. Laws 22.

For a more complete analysis of evidence that early Americans viewed copyright as a matter of natural law, see Gary Kauffman, *Exposing the Suspicious Foundation of Society's Primacy in Copyright Law: Five Accidents*, 10 COLUM.—VLA J.L. & ARTS 381, 403-08 (1986).

[20] THE FEDERALIST No. 43, at 279 (James Madison) (E.M. Earle ed., 1976). Madison's reference to common law copyright in Great Britain approvingly refers to the famous case of Millar v. Taylor, 4 Burr. 2303, 98 Eng. Rep. 201 (1769), which explicitly recognized and enforced a natural law copyright claim. Although *Millar v. Taylor* was overruled in 1774, Madison's reference still stands as an endorsement of its result and reasoning. For a discussion of common law copyright, see LYMAN RAY PATTERSON, COPYRIGHT IN PERSPECTIVE (1968); Abrams, *supra* note 18, at 1119.

[21] *See* Mazer v. Stein, 347 U.S. 201, 219 ("Sacrificial days devoted to such creative activities deserve reward commensurate with the services rendered."), *reh'g denied*, 347 U.S. 949 (1954).

[22] See Alfred C. Yen, *Restoring the Natural Law: Copyright as Labor and Possession*, 51 OHIO ST. L.J. 517, 529-39 (1990).

[23] For example, copyright protects theses papers written by graduate students in fulfillment of degree requirements. These works would be produced with or without copyright law. Thus, it is hard to see how copyright protection for such works increases the production of creative works. Their protection must therefore rest on something other than economic theory.

courts and legislatures never associate natural law principles with copyright is simply untrue. We should therefore criticize the extant purely economic copyright regime for its failure to recognize copyright's roots in both economics and natural law.

2. Evaluation of the Normative Claim

The second reason for suppressing copyright's natural law roots is the belief that consideration of natural law will destroy any balance between the interests of authors and consumers. This concern is certainly understandable. The idea that a person should have a property interest in the fruits of her labor is powerful. Since a copyrighted work is surely the product of an author's labor, it would seem that all borrowing from a copyrighted work violates the author's property in the fruits of her labor. Copyright would therefore necessarily have to prohibit any unauthorized use of a copyrighted work. Future authors would find no public domain from which to draw because everything (including language) would owe its existence to other human beings.

This fear is unjustified, for the notion that authors can claim creative responsibility for (and therefore property in) an entire work is simply false. Any frank appraisal of authorship must conclude that each author's work contains both the author's original creations and material drawn from other authors[24] and the society in which the author lives.[25] Authorship is therefore not the creation of works which spring like Athena from the head of Zeus, but the conscious and unconscious intake, digestion, and transformation of input gained from the author's experience within a broader society. This realization provides the factual basis from which the natural law theorist justifies a strong public domain.

The easiest case occurs when authors borrow material from society without restatement. In this situation, the natural law implication is clear. Since the author did not create the borrowed material, the author has no moral claim to property in it. Indeed,

---

[24] *See supra* note 4; Jessica Litman, *The Public Domain*, 39 EMORY L.J. 965, 1010-11 (1990). Brief consideration of one's own work should prove the essential truth of this proposition. The honest legal scholar must admit that his arguments, conceptions, methods of analysis, writing style, and terminology are heavily influenced, if not directly formed, by the writings of others. Similarly, composers use sounds they have heard before, writers recycle plots, and computer programmers use logic and techniques that they have seen before.

[25] A good example of this is our recognition of Mozart's music as both "Mozartean" and German in its personality. Similarly, the work of Renoir and Monet can be identified both individually and as French.

granting an author property in the material by prohibiting its use in future works would be unjust, for society would be deprived of material that it had created. Thus, to the extent that borrowed material already belongs to society, it should remain in the public domain.

When material is borrowed and restated, the case for a public domain is less clear, but equally sound. Consider a work in which an innocent person is convicted of a crime and imprisoned. Even if the work is fictional, it is not solely the product of the author's labor. Rather, the work captures the products of society (the plot) and the author (the rewriting of the plot). In effect, society and the author are jointly responsible for the work's creation, and both should own some property rights in the work. This implies putting part of the work into the public domain while allowing the author property rights in other parts through some sort of equitable division.[26] Thus, certain aspects of this material become the author's property even though some public property will be lost. More important, other aspects of the material become public property even though the author will lose property rights in some of her original creations. The point is that society and authors must each get a fair share of works for which they are jointly responsible.

Of course, the foregoing analysis leaves open the question of how copyright should treat material which can be separately identified as solely that of the author. A superficial natural law analysis might conclude that copyright protects all of this material. After all, if society did not create the material, it must have been created by the author, and she should be able to claim her property rights.

A closer examination, however, shows that this position actually understates the extent of a natural law public domain, which prefers including original creations rather than excluding them.

---

[26] In other words, others have the right to copy some portions of the author's work. In defining the scope of borrowing, courts must remain cognizant of the possibility that the author's original material may be inseparable from public domain material. In these cases, the so-called doctrine of merger should be applied so that the public domain is not privately appropriated through copyright. The public domain is actually augmented by denying property rights in original material. *See* Herbert Rosenthal Jewelry Corp. v. Kalpakian, 446 F.2d 738, 742 (9th Cir. 1971) (holding that defendants did not copy plaintiff's jeweled bee pin because it was not "an 'idea' that defendants were free to copy"). Additional natural law support for this proposition comes from the famous Lockean proviso. In that passage, Locke denies the existence of property in the fruits of a person's labor where the appropriation fails to leave "enough and as good" for others. LOCKE, *supra* note 11.

If the public domain only contained material for which no person could claim creative credit, authors would receive compensation from all who borrowed their original material. Concurrently, all authors who wanted to borrow from their predecessors would have to pay for the privilege of doing so. Although such a scheme seemingly gives each person the fruits of her labor, it would in fact create an unjustified windfall to authors fortunate enough to have already created copyrighted material.

If existing authors gained the power to prohibit all borrowing from their works, they would reap huge benefits from subsequent authors who borrowed from them. At the same time, however, they would probably never be forced to compensate prior authors from whom they had borrowed. In some cases the prior authors (and their heirs) may be dead. In other cases the prior works may never have been copyrighted. Worse yet, in some cases the prior authors might not be aware that borrowing had even occurred. Thus, present day authors would gain the fruits of their labors while never paying for their use of the labor of others.

By contrast, a vigorous public domain that contains original material avoids the problem of unjust enrichment. Since practically every author would both owe and be owed compensation under a complete property rights scheme, it would seem eminently fair to simply abandon the futile task of trying to reach a perfect accounting of compensation among all authors. Instead, society could "balance the books" in a more equitable manner by forgiving many of the "debts" owed by modern authors to their predecessors. In return for this windfall, modern authors should forgive similar debts to future authors by dedicating some of their material to the public domain. In other words, the public domain would be used as a device through which authors could both borrow from and compensate one another. The effect of such a scheme would be to place even original material into a public domain.[27]

---

[27] The equitable contribution of authors to the public domain could be achieved in two ways. First, portions of every work should be dedicated to the public domain immediately upon creation. These portions should include those which are both likely to have been borrowed (and therefore not original) and likely to be borrowed in the future. A good example in modern copyright is the doctrine of *scenes a faire*, which places trite plots, scenes, and sequences into the public domain. *See, e.g.*, Schwartz v. Universal Pictures Co., 85 F. Supp. 270, 275 (S.D. Cal. 1945); Cain v. Universal Pictures Co., 47 F. Supp. 1013, 1017 (S.D. Cal. 1942). Although these trite devices may sometimes be original, the likelihood of their having been borrowed and their use by future authors makes their immediate inclusion in the public domain fair. Second, all works should receive copyright protection for a limited time only, thereby ensuring eventual dedication to the

III.   THE NECESSARY CONSIDERATION OF FAIRNESS AND JUSTICE

So far this Essay has shown that the primary reasons for suppressing natural law theories of copyright are not compelling. Indeed, it seems that the use of a natural law theory would be consistent with present doctrine and would justify the existence of a healthy public domain which complements the property rights of authors. However, die-hard economic theorists will surely not give up so easily. They may contend that economics alone provides the best way to construct any system of rights, including copyright.[28] In my view, however, any attempt to construct a copyright regime solely on economics is likely to fail. The relevant problems can best be exposed by briefly setting forth the premises on which an economic copyright regime would stand.

As the reader is undoubtedly aware, a fundamental proposition of modern economics is that, under perfect conditions, the unregulated self-interested transactions of individuals maximize social welfare.[29] Of course, perfect conditions never exist. Government should therefore use the legal system to correct the misallocation of resources caused by the lack of perfect conditions. If one assumes that social welfare can be expressed in dollar terms, we should then select the copyright regime which maximizes society's wealth, where wealth is defined as "the value in dollars or dollar equivalents . . . of everything in society. It is measured by what people are willing to pay for something or, if they already own it, what they demand in money to give it up."[30]

In other words, government should correct misallocations of

---

public domain while providing a fair vindication of the author's creative labor. Such a result presently exists under 17 U.S.C. § 302 (1988), which terminates copyright fifty years after the death of the author.

[28] The pros and cons of such a proposition require a lengthy ethical and economic discussion which space will not permit. Suffice it to say that such theorists have grown numerous in recent years through the proliferation of the "Chicago School" of the law and economics movement. It should also be stated that not all economic analysts agree with the strong normative claims of the Chicago School. For defenses of an economics only approach to all of law, see A. MITCHELL POLINSKY, AN INTRODUCTION TO LAW AND ECONOMICS (1989); Richard A. Posner, *Utilitarianism, Economics, and Legal Theory*, 8 J. LEGAL STUD. 103 (1979). For criticisms of these defenses, see JULES COLEMAN, MARKETS, MORALS AND THE LAW (1988); ROBERT COOTER & THOMAS ULEN, LAW AND ECONOMICS 10 n.8 (1988):

> The claim that law can be reduced to economics is similar to the claim that used to be made in psychology that mind can be reduced to behavior. This proposition, called "reductivism" in philosophy, is dead in psychology, and it ought to be laid to rest in the economic analysis of law, too.

Id.; Ronald M. Dworkin, *Is Wealth a Value?*, 9 J. LEGAL STUD. 191 (1980).

[29] COOTER & ULEN, *supra* note 28, at 44-49 (describing economic efficiency theorems and defining conditions necessary for efficient operations of markets).

[30] Posner, *supra* note 28, at 119.

property rights by 1) determining the price each person sets for her property; and 2) reassigning each person's property to others whenever the amount others are willing to pay for the property exceeds the amount for which the individual is willing to sell that property.

Although quite brief, the foregoing is sufficient to expose two practical problems which make reliance on a purely economic copyright model highly questionable. First, the necessity of ascertaining prices means that courts require information they simply do not have. This lack of information causes two related problems for the economist. If economists do not have reliable data on individual preferences, their calculations are necessarily estimates. In an area such as copyright, the lack of information is so severe that economic recommendations become little more than random guesses about whether certain interpretations of copyright actually stimulate creativity.[31] Moreover, even if information related to copyright were available, the lack of information for other sectors of the economy would mean that recommendations that appear to increase welfare through copyright may in fact decrease social welfare overall.[32]

Even if these information problems could be overcome, sole reliance on economics to assign copyright rights would remain a highly dubious proposition, for economics is sometimes incapable of choosing among conflicting alternatives. For example, it is a well known fact that the price a person is willing to pay for a resource depends on what the person already owns. If a person owns very little, then she is unable to offer more than a small amount for a resource no matter how badly she desires it. By

---

[31] *See* George L. Priest, *What Economists Can Tell Lawyers About Intellectual Property: Comment on Cheung, in* 8 RESEARCH IN LAW AND ECONOMICS: THE ECONOMICS OF PATENTS AND COPYRIGHT 19, 21 (John Palmer & Richard O. Zerbe, Jr. eds., 1986).

  The inability of economists to resolve the question of whether activity stimulated by the patent system or other forms of protection of intellectual property enhances or diminishes social welfare implies, unfortunately, that economists can tell lawyers ultimately very little about how to enforce or interpret the law of intellectual property.

[32] *See* E.J. MISHAN, COST-BENEFIT ANALYSIS 98-101 (1976) (describing the problem of second best). This problem may be illustrated by the following example. Suppose that the available information suggests that an increase in copyright incentives would cause a net increase in productive works of $100 million. At first blush, such a change seems presumptively desirable. The net increase, however, occurs only by diverting capital and human labor from other sectors of the economy to the production of copyrightable works. The losses incurred in those other sectors must therefore be weighed against the gains in the copyright area before one can consider the change wealth maximizing. The difficulty of identifying all of the affected sectors and gathering the necessary information makes it extremely difficult, if not impossible, for the economist to make an unequivocal welfare maximizing recommendation.

contrast, if she is wealthy, she is able to offer a lot.[33] Further-more, the price a person is willing to pay for an entitlement is generally less than what she will sell the entitlement for once she owns it.[34] Since those who own entitlements such as copyrights are likely to value them more than those who do not, the wealth maximizer naturally prefers to assign rights according to the status quo. This turns wealth maximization into a normative principle which justifies whatever assignment of property rights is proposed.[35] The only way out of such a dilemma is to consider other reasons (such as fairness and justice) for assigning property rights to an individual.

V.   THE INTERDISCIPLINARY FUTURE OF COPYRIGHT THEORY

American copyright theory should thus be expanded to include the natural law model which has long been suppressed. This does not mean that we should discard the economic model. Copyright obviously functions as an economic instrument in our society, and we should continue to analyze it from that perspective. At the same time, however, we must realize that we cannot find all the answers to copyright's riddles in the discipline of economics. By restoring natural law thinking to copyright jurisprudence, we simply recognize that copyright exists not only to promote social welfare, but also to secure to each person a basic human right.[36] Proper construction of our copyright law there-

---

[33] One might be tempted to consider how much those who are not wealthy would pay for rights if they were. Economists ignore hypothetical preferences, however, based on unowned wealth. As Judge Posner states, "[t]he only kind of preference that counts in a system of wealth maximization is thus one that is backed up by money—in other words, that is registered in a market." Posner, *supra* note 28, at 119.

[34] MISHAN, *supra* note 32,, at 133-134 (1976); Cass R. Sunstein, *Legal Interference with Private Preferences*, 53 U. CHI. L. REV. 1129, 1151 (1986).

[35] MISHAN, *supra* note 32, at 140-141, 398-401. A similar problem is raised by the so-called Scitovsky Paradox. *See* Tibor Scitovsky, *A Note on Welfare Propositions in Economics*, 9 REV. ECON. STUD. 77 (1941). The problem noted in the text can be illustrated by the following example. Consider proposal A. If proposal A is adopted, the producers of records own the right to make cassette tapes from the records they produce. Producers value this right at $200 because this is the additional revenue that they can gain by making and selling cassette tapes to consumers. Suppose further that consumers would be willing to buy the rights of making cassette tapes, but only if the price were $190 or less. In this hypothesized situation, proposal A seems clearly wealth maximizing and should be adopted. Since producers value the right more than consumers do, wealth is maximized by assigning the right to producers.

For purposes of comparison, now consider proposal B, which is the opposite of proposal A. Consumers now have the right to freely make cassette tapes from records. Since they now own the right in question, consumers in situation B value the entitlement more than they did in situation A. Suppose that they consequently will not part with the right for anything less than $203. Under these facts, proposal B is preferable to proposal A, and should be adopted.

[36] This view is reflected in the Universal Declaration of Human Rights, G.A. Res. 217

fore depends on two separate inquiries. First, we must decide just how much property we think authors deserve. Second, we must decide how to structure the laws which secure those rights to take advantage of our economic system's ability to stimulate creative activity for our mutual benefit. The study of these questions forecasts a broad and interesting cross-disciplinary future for copyright theory.

For example, the question of how much property authors deserve starts with an attempt to separate original material from borrowed material in each work. Of course, the nature of authorship makes it likely that this attempt will only be partially successful in giving authors and society their just desserts. Borrowed material is often recast and reshaped to the extent that its identification or separation is impossible. Even seemingly original creations sometimes depend on borrowing which is not readily apparent. When this happens, society must construct an equitable division of property between the author and the public. Brief reflection shows how the legal theorist's conception of this division would benefit from cross-disciplinary inquiry. First, any separation of original material from borrowed material requires sophisticated notions of creativity and borrowing. Second, if we are serious about making an equitable division between authors and society on the basis of the author's debt to her predecessors, society's belief about the size of this debt becomes vitally important. Art historians, literary critics and authors themselves will undoubtedly have valuable insights to contribute to this debate.

Similarly, the question of how to structure legal entitlements to take advantage of our economic system also requires competence in areas often outside a lawyer's training. Regardless of how much property society thinks an author deserves, a wide range of legal tools will become available to secure the necessary rights. The obvious tool is the "breadth" of copyright's reach. If authors deserve a lot, even very faint borrowings might become actionable. However, other tools may secure for authors their just desserts equally as well. Changing the length of copyright's term, creating licensing schemes, or even making cash payments to authors would all affect the size of authorship's rewards. If society wants to structure its copyright rewards to take advantage of our capitalist system, economists will undoubtedly have help-

---

[III], U.N. Doc. A/810, at 76 (1948), which states, "[e]veryone has the right to the protection of the moral and material interests resulting from any scientific, literary or artistic production of which he is the author."

ful recommendations for choosing among the various alternatives. Since capitalism in turn depends on the cooperative behavior of individuals, psychologists may be able to suggest legal arrangements which facilitate bargaining.[37]

Without question, the future sketched out above will be difficult to explore. Few persons can claim expertise in all the disciplines relevant to copyright's construction. This problem may deter some from changing the monolithic economic inquiry which presently dominates copyright jurisprudence. Perhaps too many cooks will ultimately spoil copyright's broth. Although such a fear is perfectly understandable, I believe that we should nevertheless expand our copyright discourse. Copyright law gives individuals the power to control the future use of texts, paintings, compositions, and other forms of communication. It therefore fundamentally affects the kind of intellectual life each of us is able to lead. Everyone, regardless of perspective, should therefore be encouraged to participate in the ordering of that life.

---

[37] For example, economists often suggest that property rights exist for the purpose of facilitating the private bargaining which promotes social welfare. Since empirical research shows that bargaining is more likely to occur when the parties' rights are clear, it seems that a judge or legislature interested in using copyright to advance social welfare would select the least ambiguous rules possible. *See* COOTER & ULEN, *supra* note 28, at 99-100. This insight is noteworthy because the present trend permits plaintiffs to claim copyright in increasingly vague facets of their works. *See* Fisher, *supra* note 8, at 1659 (criticizing fair use doctrine as vague and uncertain); Alfred C. Yen, *A First Amendment Perspective on the Idea/Expression Dichotomy and Copyright in a Work's "Total Concept and Feel,"* 38 EMORY L. J. 393 (1989) (criticizing modern interpretation of the idea/expression dichotomy as vague). To the extent that these decisions are justified as welfare maximizing economic incentives for authors, the potential welfare benefits may be offset by the difficulty authors and potential consumers will face in bargaining over exploitation of these vague rights.

MILTON'S CONTRACT

PETER LINDENBAUM*

Speak with an author about his or her publisher and you are
likely to hear grousing about bad distribution, inadequate advertising, or the tardiness (or even non-existence!) of a paperback
edition. Speak with an editor or a publisher's representative and
you may well be regaled with accounts of high-strung prima don-
nas making totally inconsequential last-minute changes or insisting upon jacket-cover colors to match those of a favorite football
club. There has always, no doubt, been just such friction between parties entering into a relationship which is, after all,
designed for their mutual help, comfort, and of course profit.
The author-publisher relationship is in fact, as the wording of my
previous sentence is designed to suggest, a type of marriage.
Perhaps then, we ought not find it odd or ironic that in the various legal battles over copyright in eighteenth-century England, it
should have been the booksellers who, while looking to their
own best interests, assumed such a large role in helping to create
their modern counterpart, the economically independent author.
In presenting particularly strong arguments for perpetual copyright for authors, the booksellers defined the author as the proprietor of his own work, thus giving him a new and enhanced
status as a professional.[1]

But if we are accustomed to viewing the eighteenth century
as the period which institutionalized the concept of authorship as
we know it today (or at least did know it until the death of the
author began to be celebrated in France some twenty years ago),
we also recognize that such conceptions are not established overnight, or in one Parliamentary Statute of 1709, howsoever important. The modern idea of the author as a creative artist and
independent being with legal and proprietary rights in and to his
work, is among other things one of the long-term results of the
introduction of print into Western culture.[2] In the seventeenth

---

* Professor of English, Indiana University. B.A., 1960, Harvard University; B.A., 1962, Cambridge University; Ph.D., 1970, University of California at Berkeley.

[1] See Mark Rose, The Author as Proprietor: Donaldson v. Becket and the Genealogy of
Authorship, 23 REPRESENTATIONS 51 (1988); Martha Woodmansee, The Genius and the Copy-
right: Economic and Legal Conditions of the Emergence of the "Author," 17 EIGHTEENTH-CEN-
TURY STUD. 425, 425-48 (1984) (dealing primarily with conditions in eighteenth-century
Germany).

[2] See ELIZABETH L. EISENSTEIN, THE PRINTING PRESS AS AN AGENT OF CHANGE (1979);
ALVIN KERNAN, PRINTING TECHNOLOGY, LETTERS, AND SAMUEL JOHNSON (1987). Kernan's

century particularly, we find many examples of "the author" slouching towards 1709 to be born. Of these, Ben Jonson, with his careful editing of his own texts and the extraordinary self-consciousness with which he presented himself and his writerly concerns in both his poems and his plays, is particularly important.[3] Even more important is John Milton, both because of the way he insisted upon his identity as a major poet in his poetry and prose throughout his career (even before he was a major poet) and because of the way eighteenth- and nineteenth-century poets and critics consistently tended to take him at his word.

Yet to speak of authorial intention and posthumous reception and reputation is to conjure up the author in what we might call his ideal mode; there is of course a material dimension to authorship as well, to be seen in the author's dealings with members of the book trade, with those who produce the book and make their livings by it. In this essay, I shall focus on that latter realm, to see what contribution Milton, or the case of Milton, can be said to have made towards the conception of authorship there. In any such investigation, the one event that stands out as a turning point in Milton's own career and in literary history as well is the poet's act on April 27, 1667 of entering into a formal contract with printer Samuel Simmons for the publication of *Paradise Lost*.

The contract is evidently the earliest known such literary agreement to have come down to us, although, to judge both from the relatively sophisticated and detailed nature of its stipulations and from what we know of the particular character of the two men entering into it, it is by no means necessarily the earliest such contract ever written. Its details have long been known, but the document has not always been interpreted correctly. Milton

---

focus upon Johnson as the paradigmatic example of the writer in a print culture, at a time when print could be said "to affect the structure of social life at every level," *id.* at 48, and "print logic began to shape mental structures," *id.* at 51, necessarily tends to deemphasize the various important steps taken in the seventeenth century towards the modern conditions of authorship.

[3] *See* Richard C. Newton, *Jonson and the (Re-)Invention of the Book, in* CLASSIC AND CAVALIER: ESSAYS ON JONSON AND THE SONS OF BEN 31-55 (Claude J. Summers & Ted-Larry Pebworth eds., 1982); Joseph Loewenstein, *The Script in the Marketplace*, REPRESENTATIONS, Fall 1985, at 101. Jonson was, however, so deeply immersed in the patronage system that it remains difficult to talk of him as a figure of political, economic, and authorial independence. *See also* Arthur F. Marotti, *John Donne, author*, 19 J. MEDIEVAL & RENAISSANCE STUD. 69 (1989) (documenting how, in spite of Donne's own efforts to the contrary, that very different gentleman- or coterie-poet was in the course of time and by virtue of the posthumous publication of his works from the mid-seventeenth century on "absorbed into the evolving literary institution" so as "to emerge as an author in the modern sense of the term").

was to receive five pounds immediately, an additional five pounds at the end of the first edition (that edition or impression considered to be completed when 1300 copies had been sold off to "particular reading Customers"), and then five more pounds at the end of each of the second and third impressions (these, too, considered to be completed when 1300 copies were sold). In addition, the contract stipulated that none of the three editions was to run more than 1500 copies. In consideration of that £20, Milton on his part gave over to Simmons "All that Booke Copy or Manuscript" of the poem together "with the full benefitt proffitt & advantage thereof or which shall or may arise thereby," Simmons thus enjoying rights to the copy or manuscript and all impressions without let or hindrance from Milton; the poet also agreed not to allow or cause to be printed without Simmons's consent either the book or manuscript or any other work of the same tenor or subject.[4]

That much we know; what we don't know with enough assurance is what precisely to make of those sums mentioned and thus whether, for instance, Milton with his independent wealth (diminishing though it was in the 1660s) was shamefully underpaid for his work, as was so often argued by eighteenth-century biographers and critics. We do know that a playwright not formally connected with a dramatic company could make £6 from a play in Shakespeare's time and that Ben Jonson might make £40 from a court masque; but neither of these payments involved dealings with the book trade. There is some, though not much, evidence that authors may have been routinely paid by publishers in the course of the seventeenth century. The chaos brought on by the abolition of the Star Chamber and its licensing decrees in 1641 brought with it a threat to do away completely with the idea of copyright. This in turn prompted the Stationers' Company to issue a Humble Remonstrance in 1643 asking for a return to an

---

[4] The text of the contract is to be found in 4 THE LIFE RECORDS OF JOHN MILTON 429-31 (1956). The original is British Library Additional MS 18,861. *See also* LYMAN RAY PATTERSON, COPYRIGHT IN HISTORICAL PERSPECTIVE 71-77 (1968). Patterson notes that while the language of the contract suggests that Milton has given over complete ownership of the poem to Simmons, in actual fact the author retained certain implicit personal (or creative)—if not property—rights in his work even after the contract had been signed and payment received. This was also true in the whole system of copyright through entry by stationers alone in the Stationers' Register. The, as Patterson sees it, particularly significant promise on Milton's part not to interfere with Simmons's publishing of the poem "would hardly have been necessary if copyright had been deemed to give the copyright owner *all* rights in connection with the copyrighted work" (emphasis added). The rights Patterson sees Milton (and any other author in the Stationers' Register copyright system) as retaining are those to alter and revise his work and to protect its integrity; that is, to prevent unauthorized distortions and abridgments.

orderly system for regulating the press, claiming among other things that the elimination of private ownership of copy "as it discourages Stationers, so it's a great discouragement to the Authors of Books also; Many mens studies carry no other profit or recompense with them but the benefit of their Copies."[5] As part of the same campaign, a group of eminent Presbyterian divines of the time stated in a public declaration that to their knowledge "very considerable Sums of Money had been paid by Stationers and Printers to many authors for the Copies of such useful Books as had been imprinted."[6]

But we have very little record of what actual payments might have been made by stationers in the period around and immediately preceding the publication of *Paradise Lost*, when in fact it was the author being paid rather than he or she paying to have a work printed. George Herbert's widow evidently received nothing at all from the poet's posthumous *The Temple* of 1633,[7] while about the same time William Prynne received thirty-five or thirty-six copies of his *Histriomastix*, to dispose of as he saw fit, for sale or as presentation or patronage-seeking copies.[8] Closer to Milton's time, Richard Baxter received £10 from his printers *after* the publication of his *Saint's Everlasting Rest* in 1649, having left "the matter of profit, without any covenants to [his printers'] ingenuity," and then £10 from each of his two printers for every edition thereafter to 1665, evidently yielding him altogether a sum of £170 for that text over a thirteen to sixteen year period—all in all, an astounding sum.[9] And Dryden is reported to have re-

---

[5] *The Humble Remonstrance of the Company of Stationers*, British Library E.247 (THOMASON COLLECTION), *reprinted in* 1 EDWARD ARBER, A TRANSCRIPT OF THE REGISTERS OF THE COMPANY OF STATIONERS OF LONDON 1554-1640 A.D., at 584-88 (London, 1875-94). This Remonstrance is dated by Thomason as April 1643. For a convenient listing of the instances within the Stationers' Company records of the Company's recognition that authors had a right to payment for their work see PATTERSON, *supra* note 4, at 68-69. These were not, however, formal contracts between author and publisher.

[6] This document is described and quoted in two different pamphlets written in 1735, evidently by the historian Thomas Carte, in support of a bill in Parliament designed to strengthen the capacity of authors to combat piracies. *See* THE CASE OF AUTHORS & PROPRIETORS OF BOOKS; A SECOND LETTER FROM AN AUTHOR TO A MEMBER OF PARLIAMENT (Bodleian Library, MS Carte 114, ff. 336r and 332v). I have been unable to locate the actual document itself. It is also quoted (by way of earlier sources) in Leo Kirschbaum, *Author's Copyright in England before 1640*, 40 PAPERS OF THE BIBLIOGRAPHICAL SOCIETY OF AMERICA 79 (1946).

[7] *See* Daniel W. Doerksen, *Nicholas Ferrar, Arthur Woodnoth, and the Publication of George Herbert's The Temple, 1633*, 3 GEORGE HERBERT J. 22 (1979-80).

[8] *See* W.W. GREG, A COMPANION TO ARBER 277-78 (1967) (quoting State Papers Domestic, Charles I, Vol. 231, art. 77).

[9] Richard Baxter, *Reliquiae Baxterianae* pt. III, app. 7 at 117 (London, 1696). In that same letter, Baxter also reports that Dr. William Bates received above £100 for his *Divine Harmony* (i.e., the *Harmony of the Divine Attributes* (1674)) and "yet reserving the power for

ceived £20 (in borrowed funds) from Jacob Tonson for the play-wright's manuscript of *Troilus and Cressida* in 1679, but that report comes to us from Edmond Malone in 1800 and hence is unrelia-ble.[10] Such evidence, sparse as it is, is hardly enough upon which to base any conclusions as to whether or not Milton was fairly remunerated.[11]

If the sums stipulated in the contract cannnot in themselves provide grounds for determining whether Milton was treated fairly by his publisher, the other provisions and stipulations of the contract render more substantial help. For what placing an upward limit of 1500 copies on each impression—at first glance, an apparently odd or inconsequential stipulation—did was to en-sure that Simmons's profits would not increase inordinately in relation to the amounts Milton was to receive. And further, the contract contained the stipulation that Milton could demand an accounting of sales at reasonable intervals. If Simmons failed to provide the accounting, he was obligated to pay the £5 for the whole impression as if it were due. Such stipulations imply that the £5 installments were definitely not viewed as mere tokens by either party in the contract, and indeed that such sums seem to be about right. And if the £10 for the first edition and the £20

---

the future to himself." It would appear that Bates somehow arranged matters so that his publisher did not retain perpetual copyright in his work.

[10] Edmond Malone, *Some Account of the Life and Writings of John Dryden,* in 1 THE CRITI-CAL AND MISCELLANEOUS PROSE WORKS OF JOHN DRYDEN 522-23 (London, 1800).

[11] In great contrast to the limited evidence from the seventeenth century, we have a good number of contracts from the eighteenth century, thanks in large part to the efforts of the early nineteenth-century antiquary and autograph collector William Upcott. *See* WILLIAM UPCOTT, ORIGINAL ASSIGNMENTS OF MANUSCRIPTS BETWEEN AUTHORS AND PUB-LISHERS (on file with British Library Add. MS 38,728-30). The collection's earliest agreement, dated 1703, is for Joseph Trapp's tragedy *Abra-Mule,* which Trapp sold to Jacob Tonson for £21-10s. These collected conveyances unfortunately do not provide much help in interpreting the ten-pound sum Milton received for the first edition of *Paradise Lost.* All but three of them date from after the Copyright Act of 1709 (when the sums paid for manuscripts began to rise sharply) and they reveal a great amount of variation, depending presumably upon the prior reputation of the author, the genre of the work (plays seem generally to have brought in more than poems or novels), and, if it were a play, whether it had already been performed on stage and to what kind of suc-cess. Some examples: in 1715 Curll purchased the copy of Susannah Centlivre's play *The Wonder* for 20 guineas. In 1713, Bernard Lintot paid £50-15s to Nicholas Rowe for *Jane Shore, A Tragedy.* Also in 1713, Tonson paid Addison £107-10s for the copy of *Cato,* and in 1707 he paid £370-10s to Laurence Echard for his multi-volume *History of Eng-land.* In 1709, Curll purchased a nine-page Latin poem, *Muscipula,* from Edward Holds-worth for five guineas and 50 copies for Holdsworth's own use. Of some interest is the fact that the contracts of John Watts in the 1720s and 1730s often state that the author gives over all rights to his work *forever* "notwithstanding any Act or Law to the contrary," in what would appear to be defiance of the 1709 Act's stipulation limiting copyright in new works to a term of 14 years (renewable for another 14 years thereafter). I assume that this represents continued interpretation of the stipulations of the Act of 1709 in a way that best suited the bookseller's own interests.

altogether for three editions are in fact just or normal payments
for the time, what I think we must consider as most significant
about the payment to Milton is not so much the sum agreed upon
(which has proved so distracting to later critics), but that it was
agreed upon by means of a formal document between author and
publisher. For in that alone we see an author who is fully acknowledging the condition of authorship, viewing himself as the
possessor of property that gives him definite rights (for instance,
the right to demand an accounting of sales), even as he lives and
writes at a time when copyright is granted solely to stationers
through entry in the Stationers' Company Register. This is not
the off-hand agreement of someone affecting to be an amateur or
a gentleman-poet, anxious to avoid the stigma of print, or a figure using poetry for advancement in some other, non-literary,
realm.[12]

A contract is an agreement between two parties, and to be
able to make full sense of it, we need to know the particular concerns and prior history of *both* parties entering into it, not simply
the more famous figure. Those of us in literary studies are accustomed to viewing this particular contract simply from Milton's
point of view, or what we assume to be Milton's point of view.
But in fact, the full implications of the contract emerge most
forcefully if we view the document against a background of Simmons's career in the book trade, a career which, as it happens, is

---

[12] My phrasing here is designed to call to mind the studies of J.W. SAUNDERS, THE
PROFESSION OF ENGLISH LETTERS (1964); J.W. Saunders, *Milton, Diomede and Amaryllis*, 22
ELH 254-86 (1955); J.W. Saunders, *The Stigma of Print*, in 1 ESSAYS IN CRITICISM 139
(1951). Saunders recorded the move from a Renaissance literary system based on patronage where poets wrote as amateurs, using their poetry as means of advancement in
other realms, to a system in which the writer emerges as an independent professional.
But unfortunately, thrown off by the Milton-Simmons contract's reference to an upper
limit of 1500 copies per edition while payment was to be provided Milton when 1300
copies were sold, Saunders placed Milton incorrectly in his scheme. Saunders assumed
that 200 copies of each impression were put at Milton's disposal as presentation copies.
Were that true, Milton would indeed be the poet Saunders envisioned, a continuing
participant in the patronage system, writing if not for a social elite, at least for a *cultured*
"fit audience . . . though few." But William Riley Parker located 343 extant copies of the
first edition's original 1300 (or 1500), or approximately one in four from that edition.
See 2 WILLIAM RILEY PARKER, MILTON: A BIOGRAPHY 1109-12 (1968). If 200 of the original copies were presented to friends or potential patrons by the author, we would expect
some 50 of those copies to have survived, perhaps more, since it is fair to assume that a
recipient of such a copy (or his or her heirs) would be more likely than the regular buyer
to save it, particularly after the poem came to be recognized as a classic. But there does
not seem to be any reliable evidence in *any* extant copy of it having been such a gift. *Id.*
at 1116. That is, there is no evidence such as we have on the title page of John Morris's
copy of the *Pro Populo Anglicano Defensio* of it being "ex dono authoris." We have to
assume, then, that the number of presentation copies was very small and that Milton was
farther removed from conditions of earlier Renaissance authorship and closer to those
of the eighteenth-century professional than Saunders suggested.

relatively difficult to reconstruct. For Samuel Simmons was a very shadowy figure in his trade, both in his own time and ever since. That relative obscurity is in part a function of the single most important fact we need to keep in mind about him, and that is that Simmons, unlike the more famous members of the seventeenth-century book trade and those whose names are well known to students of the trade today—for instance, Humphrey Moseley, Henry Herringman, and Jacob Tonson—was primarily a printer rather than a bookseller (although he did some bookselling as well). As the many petitions by printers attest and complain from the end of the sixteenth century on, it was the booksellers who were rising steadily to positions of prominence in the Stationers' Company and to financial dominance in the trade generally, at the expense of both printers and bookbinders.[13] Yet even when we have allowed for this major distinction between printer and bookseller, we still have to acknowledge that Samuel Simmons's career in the book trade was far from brilliant or striking. There were printers who made a bigger immediate impact upon the trade—most notably perhaps (and very close to home), Samuel's own parents, Matthew and Mary Simmons.[14]

D. F. McKenzie has recorded Matthew Simmons's name on some 433 imprints in a printing career that spanned twenty years from 1635 to an early death in 1654, an average, then, of 21.7 items per year.[15] The name of Mary Simmons, who took over the business upon her husband's death and who bore sole responsibility for the shop until 1662 when son Samuel completed his apprenticeship, is to be found on some ninety-one items over the seven-year period from 1655 to 1661, or an average of thirteen items a year. Oddly, once Samuel finished his apprenticeship and his name began to appear on imprints along with Mary's and

---

13 *See* CYPRIAN BLAGDEN, THE STATIONERS' COMPANY: A HISTORY, 1403-1959, at 90, 122, 149-52 (1960). For an example of the evidence Blagden discusses, see A BRIEF DISCOURSE CONCERNING PRINTING AND PRINTERS (1663) (published by a Society of Publishers).

14 D. F. McKenzie has established that Samuel Simmons was the son of Matthew and Mary, not the nephew (as was previous assumed by both Milton scholars and students of the book trade). *See* D. F. McKenzie, *Milton's Printers: Matthew, Mary and Samuel Simmons*, 14 MILTON QUARTERLY 87-91 (1980).

15 These and the following figures on imprints are from the Appendix to the fourth of D.F. McKenzie's as yet unpublished Lyell Lectures. *See* D.F. McKenzie, *Bibliography and History: Seventeenth Century England, in* 4 LYELL LECTURES app. (Oxford 1988). I should like to acknowledge the considerable help of Professor McKenzie, now Reader in Bibliography at Oxford University, who kindly allowed me to read the manuscript of those lectures and thereafter answered a well-nigh endless number of questions on them. My debt to those lectures, and to a good deal else of McKenzie's work besides, will be clearly evident in the pages and notes to follow.

there were now two people who presumably could conduct business for the firm, the number of Simmons imprints goes *down*. For the period from 1662 until 1678 (the last year Samuel's name appears on a title page), there are fifty-eight items, or an average of 3.4 imprints a year. And once Mary's name ceases to appear on imprints altogether (after 1670) and only Samuel's name is indicated on new imprints, when it would appear that Mary has gone into partial or full retirement, the average number of imprints decreases farther yet, to fewer than three items a year (twenty-three new imprints in the eight years from 1671 to 1678).

Now, as McKenzie also demonstrates, the number of acknowledged imprints by no means represents the total output of a printing house's work. For instance, in 1668, 54 percent of the items published and still extant do not carry a printer's name.[16] The three new Simmons titles for that year listed in Wing's *Short-Title Catalogue*[17] could have supplied, McKenzie calculates, little more than six weeks' work for the firm's two proprietors, five workmen, one apprentice, and two presses.[18] There must, then, have been considerably more anonymous work printed in the shop, if the shop were to proceed at anything like its full capacity (and remain open for business the next year). But even if we take into account that—to assume the trade average—there must have been at least an equal number of unacknowledged works printed in Simmons's shop in the years from 1662 to, let us say, 1680, it is still difficult to see how Samuel Simmons was earning a decent living. Either he was not doing so very well, or he was an extraordinarily self-effacing figure in his trade. I suspect both.

If we look at the particular works that bear Samuel's name as printer, we are driven to much the same conclusion. In a printing career extending from 1662 to perhaps 1680 (when he sold the rights to *Paradise Lost* and there is no further record of his activity as a stationer), Samuel's name appears, either with his mother's or alone, on only eleven different works, although some of them in several editions or differing versions. Of these eleven items, four were continuations of ventures that one or both of his

---

[16] D.F. McKenzie, *The London Book Trade in 1668*, 4 Words: Wai-Te-Ata Studies in Literature 81 (Wellington, N.Z., 1974). In his fourth Lyell Lecture of 1988, McKenzie notes that similarly in 1644 only 46 percent of the items published and still extant carried a printer's name and only 32 percent a bookseller's; in 1688, the figures were 31 percent for printers and 32 percent for booksellers. McKenzie, *supra* note 15, at 10-11.

[17] Short-title Catalogue of Books Printed in England, Scotland, Ireland, Wales, and British America and of English Book Printed in Other Countries 1641-1700 (compiled by Donald Wing 1972).

[18] D.F. McKenzie, *Simmons*, *in* Lyell Lectures, *supra* note 15, at 6.

parents had printed before him.[19] Four we can identify as printing jobs for other stationers.[20] And at best, only three can be said to be efforts initiated by Samuel himself, works that he alone went out and sought (or which sought him out), one of these last three being *Paradise Lost*.[21] If we look at the seven items that involved some thought on Simmons's and his mother's part—that is, printing jobs for which there would not be immediate payment

---

[19] (1) John Speed's *A Prospect of the Most Famous Parts of the World* was printed with Mary in 1662, the early date suggesting that Mary was the main impulse behind its publication. (2) John Mennes's *Witts Recreations*, which was printed with Mary in 1663 and by Samuel alone in 1667 (in two different editions), had been published earlier by Matthew Simmons in 1650 and 1654. The Stationers' Register records Matthew as acquiring the rights to the work from Humphrey Blunden on 3 June 1654. (3) Thomas Shelton's *Tachygraphy or Short-writing*, published by Samuel in 1671 and 1674, had been published earlier by Mary in 1660 and 1668; Matthew obtained partial rights to the work on 25 January 1649/50 and Mary purchased Samuel Cartwright's original share on 19 April 1659. (4) Several parts of Joseph Caryl's *Exposition with Practical Observations upon the Book of Job* were published by Samuel alone (in 1664, 1666, and 1671) and by Samuel and Mary together (1666), and Samuel published the complete Caryl *Job* in a two-volume folio edition in 1676-77. Early parts of the *Exposition* had previously been published by Matthew as far back as 1650. When the parts of Caryl's work first began to appear in 1643, copyright was shared by several different stationers. The Stationers' Register reveals that Matthew and then Mary bought up the shares of those other stationers from the 1650s through the 1670s. *See* Stationers' Register, entries for 24 November 1651, 14 March 1656/7, and 15 November 1672. By the end of 1672, Mary evidently owned all rights to all 12 parts, whereupon she signed them over to Samuel on 5 May 1673. When Samuel came to publish the complete Caryl in 1676, he would (all going well) be following upon, and benefitting from, the earlier efforts and perhaps vision of his parents.

[20] (1) Thomas Goodwin's *Patience and Its Perfect Work* (1666) was, the title page tells us, "Printed by S. Simmons for Rob. Duncan," who had entered the work in the Stationers' Register on 21 February 1666/7. (2) Thomas Lye's *The Child's Delight* was printed in 1671 for Thomas Parkhurst, who had entered the work in the Stationers' Register on 1 March 1669/70. (3) Peter Heylyn's *Theologia Veterum* was printed in 1673 "for A. S.," who is presumably the widow Anne Seile whose husband Henry had published the first edition back in 1654. (4) Robert Clavel's *Catalogue of All the Books Printed in England Since the Dreadful Fire of London in 1666, to the End of Michaelmas Term, 1672*, printed in 1673 "by S. Simmons, for R. Clavel, in Cross-Keys Court in Little Britain," was plainly an advertising venture by Robert Clavel, who would simply hire a printer for the task; it is of some interest that Clavel did not stay with Simmons for the 1674 version of the *Catalogue*, switching to Andrew Clarke instead (and then to Samuel Roycroft for the 1680 version).

[21] Simmons entered *Paradise Lost* in the Stationers' Register on August 20, 1667 and entered Hugh Davis's *De Jure Uniformitatis Ecclesiasticae or Three Books of the Rights Belonging to an Uniformity in Churches* on October 9, 1668. There is no entry for the third item in this category, John Milton's *Accedence Commenc't Grammar*. I am giving Simmons the benefit of the doubt and assuming that it was he rather than bookseller John Starkey (who was later to enter *Paradise Regained* and *Samson Agonistes*) who is the publisher of the *Grammar*, that is, the person who took the financial risk in having it printed and thus the one who ordinarily *would* have entered the title in the Stationers' Register. Copies of the *Grammar* bear two different title pages, one telling us that the work was "Printed by Samuel Simmons next door to the Golden Lion in Aldersgate Street," and the other, that it was "Printed for Samuel Simmons and to be sold by John Starkey at the Miter in Fleet Street, near Temple Bar." The phrase "printed for" (particularly when a bookseller is also mentioned) is ordinarily, but not always, used to identify the copy holder.

It should be acknowledged as well that, given Milton's earlier association with Matthew Simmons in the 1640s, the two Milton titles on Samuel's list might also be considered mere continuations of earlier interests of his parents and thus rightfully belonging in the first category of items I have mentioned.

and therefore for which there was some monetary risk involved (the first and third categories just mentioned)—we find a reasonably varied list: two prose works of a religious nature, one religious epic poem, an anthology of light verse, two instructional works (a book on shorthand by Thomas Shelton and Milton's *Accedence Commenc't Grammar*), and one geographical survey. The list is suitably varied even if it does lean towards the religious (although much less so than a similar list we might construct for Samuel's father, Matthew). But the list remains undeniably short.

Simmons's career is alas all too easily summed up—for good and for ill—in his edition of the complete Joseph Caryl *Exposition with Practical Observations upon the Book of Job*, the individual parts of which seem to have been among the mainstays of the Simmons printing house for over twenty years and thus among the works handed on to Samuel by his parents. It is a magnificent two-volume work, running more than 2400 folio pages. Simmons put it forth as a subscription edition, partaking of that new method of marketing that was to prove increasingly popular and profitable in the next century.[22] And, in promoting it, Simmons reveals some flair for advertising. He announced the venture in the Michaelmas 1673 *Term Catalogue*, claiming that the true value of the work when completed and bound would be £4 and that the work would in fact be sold at that price in the future. Those who subscribed immediately, however, would pay only fifty shillings for the work in quires, twenty-five shillings now ("it being a work of great charge") and twenty-five for the second volume upon delivery of the first. Those who subscribed for six copies would get a seventh free.

But something seems to have gone wrong. In the Michaelmas 1677 *Term Catalogue* announcing the appearance of Volume II, Simmons acknowledges that the project has been "long a doing . . . to the great vexation and loss of the Proposer." Some

---

[22] It is an early example of such a venture but not necessarily to be viewed as a ground-breaking one. See the list of such projects in F.J.G. ROBINSON & P.J. WALLIS, BOOK SUBSCRIPTIONS LISTS: A REVISED GUIDE (1975). However, Robinson and Wallis only provide the titles of those works which included a published List of Subscribers along with the text (which Simmons's edition of Caryl did not). They list four such works before 1676. *But see* Sarah Clapp, *The Beginnings of Subscription Publishing in the Seventeenth Century*, 29 MODERN PHILOLOGY 199-224 (1931) (recording 54 instances of subscription publishing from 1617 to 1688); Sarah Clapp, *The Subscription Enterprises of John Ogilby and Richard Blome*, 30 MODERN PHILOLOGY 365-79 (1933). Using the work of Robinson/Wallis and Clapp, I count ten examples of subscription ventures (several were attempted but did not materialize) prior to 1676 and two more in that year (in addition to the Caryl *Job*).

critics, motivated by "malicious prejudice, others simply subject to imprudent mistake" have subjected his text to unjust carping. And Simmons seems to have made other miscalculations yet, to have misjudged his market. For, three years after his death, the Trinity 1690 *Term Catalogue* announced that the work was being remaindered; what Simmons originally announced would be worth £4 and which he was selling for only fifty shillings, had decreased in value and could be purchased for thirty shillings in quires, forty shillings bound, at W. Marshall's at the Bible in Newgate.

It could very well be that, as Harris Fletcher suggested forty-five years ago, the Caryl venture drove Simmons to virtual bankruptcy.[23] Or the miscalculations attendant upon that venture may have been more a symptom than the cause of what we have to see finally as an undistinguished and relatively quiet, probably even failing, career as a printer. It is possible, of course, that Simmons, like others in his trade, developed other business interests besides printing and bookselling. But as a stationer at least, as printer and publisher, he does not separate himself from number.

What I think we can conclude from even this brief examination of Simmons and his career is that when John Milton contracted with him for *Paradise Lost*, the poet was by no means in the hands of a sharper (Dryden's label for his publisher, Jacob Tonson, the poet being in a fit of pique over the financial arrangements for his *Virgil*).[24] Simmons was simply not the sort of figure to make a fast pound, either at an author's expense or indeed in any other way. And in view of the fact that Simmons revealed little of the entrepreneurial spirit of the more successful stationers of his time nor even the market aggressiveness of his parents (there is no sign, for instance, of his buying up the copy of other stationers' successful imprints, as his parents did), we are probably safe to assume that it was Milton who sought out Simmons rather than vice versa, and presumably because of the long-standing relationship Milton had established with the Simmons family back in the 1640s when Matthew printed a number of Milton's prose tracts. We have no idea, of course, whether Sa-

---

[23] 2 JOHN MILTON'S COMPLETE POETICAL WORKS, REPRODUCED IN PHOTOGRAPHIC FACSIMILE 109 (1945).

[24] Dryden comments on Tonson in his letter to the bookseller of December or January 1695/6: "Upon triall I find all of your trade are Sharpers & you not more than others; therefore I have not wholly left you." Letter from John Dryden to Jacob Tonson, *in* THE LETTERS OF JOHN DRYDEN 80 (1942).

muel Simmons would have been Milton's first or fourth choice as publisher, but what we have to assume is a relationship between relative equals, in which neither author nor printer/publisher comes before the other with cap in hand.[25]

The relationship between Milton and Simmons, in effect epitomized in the contract, is highlighted if we glance back at what we can construct of Milton's relations with the publisher of his first volume of poetry, the bookseller Humphrey Moseley, who brought out the *Poems of Mr. John Milton* in 1645. If Simmons was rather diffident and retiring among printers, Moseley was nothing if not flamboyant among booksellers. He plainly thrived in his trade, finding numerous opportunities for self-display, ranging from prefaces in which he praised himself, to service in high offices in the Stationers' Company (Stockkeeper, Renter Warden, Under Warden), to a will in which he left the Company £10 to buy a standing bowl or cup.[26] Moseley made no secret of his royalist sympathies in the period from 1641 to 1660 and even gives us something of himself in his book lists. In the latest such catalogue I have seen, one evidently from 1659 or 1660, he lists 363 items in various categories, the final grouping entitled *Books I Purpose to Print, Deo Volente.* Moseley thus posited not simply a potential clientele out there but one perhaps interested in Humphrey Moseley himself.[27]

Moseley was by no means necessarily a sharper either, but he certainly was an entrepreneur, with a good eye for what was likely to impress a reader. He states in his Preface to Milton's *Poems* that he has been so encouraged with the reception of Waller's late choice pieces among most ingenious men that he has been prompted to adventure forth once again in search of "evergreen, and not to be blasted Laurels" such as follow in the pres-

---

[25] There has been much speculation about Milton's possible dissatisfaction with Simmons as a publisher, since the poet did not return to Simmons with his later two volumes of poetry, the *Paradise Regained/Samson Agonistes* volume and the 1673 *Poems &c. upon Several Occasions.* But the spottiness of Simmons's career, the very evidence that prompts one to conclude he was not likely to take advantage of the blind, out-of-favor, 59-year-old poet, suggests further that Simmons himself may not have been greatly interested in publishing more of Milton's poetry (or indeed any poetry), or more simply that Simmons was not an obvious figure in the trade for Milton to return to.

[26] For Moseley's will, a brief biography, and a comprehensive list of books he published, see John Curtis Reed, *Humphrey Moseley, Publisher* (pt. 2), *in* 2 OXFORD BIBLIOGRAPHICAL SOCIETY PROCEEDINGS AND PAPERS, at 57-142 (1928).

[27] This list is inserted into a Bodleian Library copy of Waller's *Poems* (Shelf No. Don.f.144), published in 1645 but evidently not sold and bound until 1659 or 1660 since the inserted list contains titles from those years. For evidence of Moseley's royalism, see his *Prefaces* and *Dedicatory Epistles* to ARTHUR LAKE, TEN SERMONS ON SEVERALL OCCASIONS (1641); BEAUMONT AND FLETCHER, COMEDIES AND TRAGEDIES (1647); and JOHN SUCKLING, LAST REMAINS (1659).

ent volume. As part of the presentation of Milton's poems, he provides not only that self-congratulatory Preface, but a letter of commendation on *Comus* from Sir Henry Wotton (duly mentioned in the Preface), letters and poems of praise from Milton's Italian friends, and a dedicatory letter, again for *Comus*, from Henry Lawes to Vicount Brackley, heir apparent to the Earl of Bridgewater. It is possible of course that Milton originally volunteered such letters without any prompting, but they look more like responses on Milton's part to requests for such items by Moseley; or if not that, in view of the high-toned appeal of Moseley's other volumes, what Milton assumed Moseley and his projected readers would like to see gracing the pages of a Moseley volume.

Warren Chernaik has suggested rather wittily that in the 1645 *Poems*, Moseley kidnapped Milton and made a royalist out of him, much against the poet's will.[28] Richard Helgerson earlier pointed to the similar way in which Milton's, Carew's, and Shirley's volumes of poems appear next to each other in Moseley's book lists and with virtually the same title, variations upon *Poems with a Masque*.[29] We are informed on the title page of Milton's *Poems* that "Mr. Henry Lawes, Gentleman of the Kings Chappel, and One of His Maiesties Private Musick," set the songs to music, and we are given similar information on the title pages of the works of Waller, Carew, William Cartwright, and John Suckling as well—all Royalist poets. We know from the Greek verse added at the bottom of the frontispiece of his *Poems* that Milton did not think highly of William Marshall's artistry;[30] Moseley on the other hand evidently did, since Marshall's engraved portraits appear as frontispieces for the poems of Milton, Shirley, and Suckling, and for prose works of Robert Stapylton, Edmund Gregory, and no doubt others. The works of Milton, Waller, Carew, Shirley, Suckling, and Cartwright are by these various means made to look like part of a series: Moseley's English Poets. Marshall even succeeded in making Milton and Shirley *look* alike. We know nothing at all of possible payments Moseley might have made to his various authors, but what his prefaces, his standardized format and frontispieces, his various appeals to a common (and

---

[28] Warren Chernaik, *Books as Memorials: The Politics of Consolation*, 21 YEARBOOK OF ENG. STUD., 210 (1991).

[29] RICHARD HELGERSON, SELF-CROWNED LAUREATES: SPENSER, JONSON, MILTON, AND THE LITERARY SYSTEM 272 (1983).

[30] Milton, upon seeing the portrait, evidently asked Marshall to engrave beneath it a few lines in Greek, a language the engraver seems not to have understood since one of the lines translates as "Portraiture the fool pretends" *See* 1 PARKER, *supra* note 12, at 289.

mainly royalist) audience did was to make these authors *his* authors.

Milton's move from a publisher of the likes of Humphrey Moseley to the much more obscure Samuel Simmons is in large part no doubt dictated by political events of the 1660s. Closely connected with the Puritan cause, having justified the execution of King Charles in print after the fact, having served as Secretary for Foreign Tongues to the Council of State in both the Republican and Cromwellian governments, several of his tracts having been condemned to be burned by the common hangman, and himself having been jailed briefly in 1660, Milton had plainly fallen out of favor. It could very well be that Humphrey Moseley's fashionable successor in the book trade of the 1660s and the bookseller who took over most of Moseley's titles, Henry Herringman, would, if asked, have had nothing whatsoever to do with a figure such as John Milton.[31] But regardless of the immediate cause of Milton's having recourse to a printer/publisher such as Simmons, what we can see in the change is Milton in effect gaining more leverage in the relationship with his representative in the marketplace. The balance in the relationship was plainly shifting in the direction of the author, even if the author was not yet *explicitly* claiming proprietorship in his intellectual work in the form of authorial copyright. It could be, and this we do not and probably cannot know, that Milton was attracted to and felt comfortable with Samuel Simmons precisely because Simmons, unlike Moseley, was *not* a force in the book trade. Simmons was someone Milton could lean on or even bully a bit, could extract a fair contract from, could be assured would do his best by the poem's text, giving it careful and respectful attention (which in fact Simmons did do).

Alternatively, the case may be, as I have already suggested, that Milton was grateful to find *anyone* in 1667 who would be will-

---

[31] Herringman was what we might call Moseley's spiritual heir in the trade, buying up the large majority of Moseley titles in fashionable poetry. The Stationers' Register entry for August 19, 1667 (as it happens the entry immediately before that of Simmons for *Paradise Lost*), for instance, records the transfer from Moseley's widow to Herringman of the rights to the poems of Cowley, Donne, Davenant, Carew, Crashaw, Suckling, Denham, and Volume III of the Works of Jonson. Milton's *Poems* is not on that list, nor was it transferred on April 9, 1664 when Herringman assumed the rights in the copy of Moseley's other 1645 poet, Edmund Waller. When Milton's 1645 volume was reissued in 1673, it was under the imprint of quite a different bookseller, Thomas Dring. There is, however, no record of the transfer of the copy of that early volume of Milton's poems anywhere in the Stationers' Register and we do not know whether to assume Herringman did not want it or whether some other bookseller or printer (or perhaps even Milton himself) had made some other or prior special arrangement with Moseley for that particular item.

ing to risk publishing the work of an out-of-favor poet and a work unlikely to bring a publisher much profit, either late or soon. But even if Milton's choice of, or alighting upon, Simmons was an act of desperation rather than considered and willed authorly choice, the contract that arises from that act remains in itself a significant document in the history of authorship—largely because of the, I would argue, mistaken construction put upon it by Milton's eighteenth-century editors, biographers, and critics. Simmons's copy of the contract seems to have been passed on to bookseller Jacob Tonson when that marketing genius acquired the full copyright to *Paradise Lost* (in two separate steps, in 1683 and 1691). Thereafter, the contract remained, no doubt as proof of possession of the copyright, in the hands of the Tonson family until 1768, along with the manuscript of Book I of the poem. The third generation Jacob Tonson even used it as evidence in a court action to frighten off a prospective publisher of Milton's poem in 1739, well after the Copyright Act's prescribed twenty-one years had elapsed. But the Tonsons also made the contract available to the various editors who were bringing out editions under their aegis. And in 1725, Elijah Fenton, one of those Tonson editors, discussing the contract and the arrangements it stipulates, complained about the fact that Milton could get no more than £15 for his copy, which small sum Fenton saw as reflecting the political bias and bad taste of Restoration England: "So unreasonably may personal prejudice affect the most excellent performances!"[32] Thomas Newton, a clergyman and later a bishop and thus something in addition to a professional writer or editor, narrowed the attack from one on the age generally to one on publishers (Newton thereby biting one of the hands that was helping to feed him): "And how much more do others get by the works of great authors, than the authors themselves!"[33] It remained for Isaac Disraeli in the early nineteenth century to advance perhaps the most caustic attack upon booksellers in the context of this particular conveyance, singling out for abuse, not Simmons, but the subsequent owners of the copyright, the Tonsons: "Tonson and all his family and assignees rode in their carriages with the profits of [Milton's] five-pound epic."[34]

---

[32] Elijah Fenton, *Preface* to JOHN MILTON, PARADISE LOST at xxiii (London, Elijah Fenton ed., 1725). This is the first detailed reference to the contract and I assume Tonson either told Fenton of it or showed it to him; if the latter, Fenton did not quite look long enough to get the details straight.

[33] Thomas Newton, 1 JOHN MILTON, PARADISE LOST at xxxvii (London, Thomas Newton ed., 1749).

[34] ISAAC DISRAELI, CALAMITIES OF AUTHORS 28-29 (London, 1812).

The various eighteenth-century editors and writers who attacked Simmons, Tonson, and booksellers generally were plainly appropriating Milton in their own struggle for respectability (and cash), a struggle they viewed themselves as carrying on in part with their needed representatives in the marketplace. In mounting such attacks, they were viewing Milton as an unfairly treated author of their own eighteenth-century sort, making Milton one of their own. Whatever construction we wish to put on Milton's contract with Simmons then, that is, whether we view the poet (as I have argued here) as *not* treated unfairly by Simmons, or whether we prefer to say that he was, Milton has claim to be considered our earliest modern professional author.

FROM RIGHTS IN COPIES TO COPYRIGHT: THE RECOGNITION OF AUTHORS' RIGHTS IN ENGLISH LAW AND PRACTICE IN THE SIXTEENTH AND SEVENTEENTH CENTURIES

JOHN FEATHER*

An author's right to be treated as the creator and owner of literary property is not defined in any English statute before the Copyright Act of 1814.[1] That Act, however, was to some extent a formal codification of long-standing practices that had arisen partly because books are commercially viable properties only after they pass through the hands of publishers, printers, and booksellers. Indeed, the real history of copyright in Britain, as opposed to its formal legal history, can never be dissociated from the organization and structure of the book trade. That was as true in the sixteenth century as it was in the nineteenth, for it was in the sixteenth century that the concept of a book (or text or work) as property began to evolve. This paper traces one aspect of that evolution, and tries to discern what, if any, rights the author was deemed to have, or could abrogate to himself.

The traditional view among literary scholars, supported by many legal historians, is that authors' rights were non-existent in the sixteenth century. It is argued that, with the exception of a few cases of crown grants of patents to individual authors to protect their books, there is no evidence for authors' rights in any form. The earliest glimmering of recognition cannot be found until the 1640s, when some stationers began to pay authors for their books.[2] This argument is, in itself, clearly inadequate, if only because of its fallacious logic. If authors' rights were not recognized, why were the patents granted to authors? Moreover, if we are prepared to accept that payment to authors constitutes a *de facto* recognition of rights, we have to concede that there is evidence for payments before the 1640s. These caveats, however, are comparatively trivial. We cannot test the traditional

---

* Professor and Head of Department of Library and Information Studies, Loughborough University, United Kingdom.

[1] John Feather, *Publishers and Politicians: The Remaking of the Law of Copyright in Britain 1775-1842 Part II: The Rights of Authors*, 25 PUBLISHING HIST. 45-72 (1989).

[2] Leo Kirschinbaum, *Author's Copyright in England Before 1640*, 40 PAPERS OF THE BIBLIOGRAPHICAL SOCIETY OF AMERICA 79 (1989). *See also* Feather, *supra* note 1, at 43-80.

view of copyright evolution without looking in a little more detail at what rights were considered to exist and how they were established and protected.

In England, the legal basis for the granting of rights in copies was the Royal Prerogative. The extreme assumption in law was that all written works could be disposed of by the Crown, although in practice this came to be understood in a slightly different way. By the early seventeenth century, some authorities held that there were "prerogative copies," defined as those for which there is "no particular author." In such instances, " 'then, by the rule of our law, the King has the prerogative in the copy.' "[3] This particular case concerned almanacs,[4] but the same principle was applied to all the major patents, such as those in the English Bible, the Book of Common Prayer and indeed the Statutes of the Realm.[5] This interpretation, however, while it accurately reflects the practice of the early seventeenth century, was not universally accepted even then and certainly could not have been fully sustained a hundred years earlier.

There were, however, three distinct classes of privileged books protected by patents, although the distinction may be clearer in retrospect than it was at the time. First, there were patents that granted an individual, or group of individuals, the sole right to print a particular book of unknown or collective authorship, e.g., the Bible. The earliest patents, granted in the reign of Henry VIII, all seem to fall into this category. Secondly, some patents granted similar rights in whole groups of books on a particular subject or in a particular category, including those not yet written. The first significant grant of this kind was that made to Richard Tottel in 1553 for common law books.[6] Finally, there were patents granted to protect named books by named authors. These patents are more difficult to identify, but an indisputable example arose in 1563 when Thomas Cooper, at that

---

[3] Company of Stationers v. Seymour, 1 Mod. 257 (1677), *quoted in* 6 SIR WILLIAM HOLDSWORTH, A HISTORY OF ENGLISH LAW 373 n.6 (1924) (citation omitted) [hereinafter HOLDSWORTH].

[4] *Id.*

[5] There is no easily accessible complete list of the patents. All are, of course, on the copyright patent rolls ("CPR"), and can be most easily traced through the published Calendars. A few examples are: statutes and proclamations (to John Cawood, 1553), 1 CPR PHILLIP AND MARY 53 (1553-54); psalters and primers (to William Seres, 1559), 1 CPR ELIZABETH I 54-55; and the English Bible and other items (to Christopher Barker, 1557), 7 CPR ELIZABETH I 333-34. *See also* JOHN FEATHER, A HISTORY OF BRITISH PUBLISHING 17, 36-37 (1988) and references cited therein.

[6] *Id.* at 17.

time Master of Magdalen College School, Oxford,[7] was granted a patent to protect his revised edition of Eliot's Latin dictionary and his own *Thesaurus Linguae Romanae* for a period of twelve years.[8] Other examples follow, with increasing frequency, throughout the reigns of Elizabeth I, James I and Charles I. These are, of course, the books cited to support the view that this was the only form of author's copyright which was recognized before 1640.

In fact, when we look more closely at this third group of privileged books, a somewhat different picture emerges. Almost without exception they were learned works that had involved their authors in long periods of compilation, and sometimes great expense, or books for which the market was very limited and that needed protection in order to guarantee the publisher a reasonable chance of financial return. Several such patents were enrolled in the 1570s. In 1573, for example, Ludovick Lloyd was given an eight-year privilege for his translation of Plutarch's *Lives*, with the rider that no other English translation of the work was to be printed during that period.[9]

Gradually, the terms of such grants became less restrictive. In 1592, Richard Field was granted the sole right to print Sir John Harington's translation of Ariosto's *Orlando Furioso*, with no limitation of time.[10] Some of the grants became very broadly based indeed. When Cooper's privilege expired in 1580, it was partly renewed in the name of his publisher Henry Bynneman; this time it was for twenty-one years and included not only the latest recension of Eliot's dictionary, but also Cooper's continuation of Languet's *Chronicle* and all chronicles and dictionaries.[11] Thus, an individual patent had been changed into a class patent, analagous to Tottel's rights in common law books.

By the middle of Elizabeth I's reign, however, it was already recognized that the privileges granted by patent covered only a minority of books. An investigation into the patents in 1583 concluded that "[s]tationers hath diuers copies seuerall to them selues, wch they enioye as fully as if they had the Quenes preuilege for euerie of them. . . ."[12] No objection seems to have been raised to this at the time, but when Sir Thomas Coventry,

---

7 He subsequently became Bishop of Winchester. *See* DICTIONARY OF NATIONAL BIOGRAPHY.

8 2 CPR ELIZABETH I, at 518.

9 6 CPR ELIZABETH I, at 93.

10 CSPD ELIZABETH I 179 (1591-94).

11 8 CPR ELIZABETH I, at 210-12.

12 *See* SIR WALTER GREG, A COMPANION TO ARBER 127 (1967).

the Solicitor-General, investigated the matter again in 1618, he reported to James I that:

> Wee do not conceive that either the ordinans or the decree can restrein yor power and p^{r}rogative to grant privilege, where it shalbe needfull or convenient . . . but the Stacion^{r}s chiefly relye on this that the thinges are meane, and not worth of yor Maties priuelege especially, the printing of them being settled already.[13]

Coventry's implied claim of an absolute prerogative was typical of the times, but it did have some support in this instance. The Monopolies Act of 1614, intended to remedy the widespread abuse of the patent system for private profit, specifically exempted "grants of privilege heretofore made or hereafter to be made of for, or concerning printing" from its provisions,[14] and indeed James I had made a number of grants of privilege for individual books.[15]

In practice, as Coventry recognized, the use of the prerogative to grant rights in books was severely limited by established custom. The phrase "the printing of them being settled already" is the key to understanding this, for Coventry was here referring to the long-standing book trade practice of assigning *de facto* rights to the first publisher of a new book. This had been described more neutrally, and largely accurately, by the 1583 Commissioners:

> euerie of them [the stationers] hath of order seuerall to him self any boke that he can procure any learned man to make or translate for him, or that can come to his hand to be the first printer of it.[16]

This is by far the most succinct contemporary statement of the true situation in the late sixteenth and early seventeenth centuries, and a good deal more succinct and accurate than much subsequent academic writing on the subject.

How did the stationers come to occupy this special position? Who were the stationers? In answering these questions the historian of the book trade can perhaps help the literary scholar and indeed the legal historian to understand the origins and development of the copyright.

The "stationers" referred to both by the Commissioners in

---

[13] *Id.* at 165.
[14] 21 JAMES I, at ch. 3, § 10.
[15] GREG, *supra* note 12, at 50-52, 56-57, 72, 153-55, 157, 162-63, 236.
[16] *Id.* at 127.

1583 and by Coventry in 1618 were the freemen of the Company of Stationers of London, the trade guild, or livery company, to which members of the book trade belonged. The Stationers' Company had a very special and protected relationship both with the trade that it encompassed and with the Crown, and had powers and privileges far beyond those of other livery companies. Although it can trace its history back to the beginning of the fifteenth century,[17] the Company's most glorious era begins with its reorganization in 1557, the last year of Mary I's reign.[18] In that year, a Royal Charter granted it a virtual monopoly over printing and bookselling in London and throughout the kingdom. This was confirmed and amplified by Elizabeth I in 1558. The reason for granting such sweeping powers to the Stationers' Company was no mere benevolence. In 1559 Elizabeth I made the purpose quite explicit in a set of Injunctions on the book trade.[19] The Company's role was to control the output of the press, and to ensure that no book was printed unless it was properly licensed by the censors appointed by the Crown.[20] This gave the Company great responsiblity as a counterbalance to its great power, and during the first decade of its chartered existence it gradually evolved both regulations and practices to enable it to fulfill these obligations.

The details of the Company's internal organization need not detain us, but in one respect its arrangements are critical to our present subject, for it took its duties as surrogate controller of the press very seriously and tried to ensure that the Injunctions were fully enforced. To do so, it established a system of recording licenses in a volume known to scholars as the "Stationers' Register," although known at various times in history as the "Hall Book," the "Register Book," the "Entry Book," and probably other names as well. In 1557-1558, the first year of operation under Mary I's Charter, a list of titles was recorded in the Register with the annotation "lycensed to be printed by the master and

---

[17] For the history of the Stationers' Company prior to 1557, see Graham Pollard, *The Company of Stationers Before 1557*, 18 THE LIBRARY, 1-38 (4th ser. 1937-38).

[18] *See* CYPRIAN BLAGDEN, THE STATIONERS' COMPANY—A HISTORY 1403-1659 (1960). The Charter is printed in 1 EDWARD ARBER, TRANSCRIPT OF THE REGISTERS OF THE COMPANY OF STATIONERS OF LONDON 1554-1640, at xxvii-xxxii (Birmingham, 1875-94) [hereinafter ARBER]. *See also* Graham Pollard, *The Early Constitution of the Stationers' Company*, 18 THE LIBRARY, at 235-60 (4th ser. 1937-38).

[19] *See* W.W. GREG, SOME ASPECTS AND PROBLEMS OF LONDON PUBLISHING BETWEEN 1550 AND 1650, at 5-6 (1956).

[20] The relevant Injunction is printed in ALFRED W. POLLARD, SHAKESPEARE'S FIGHT WITH THE PIRATES AND THE PROBLEMS OF THE TRANSMISSION OF HIS TEXT 13-14 (1920).

wardens.''[21] There is a similar series of entries for 1558-1559,[22] and although the record may be incomplete, it is clear that the practice of entering licenses to print in the Register first became usual and then, very soon, compulsory. As early as 1557, a stationer was fined twenty shillings by the Company for printing a book before it had been entered,[23] and in December of the same year another stationer was fined four shillings for printing a book "contrary to our ordenaunces that ys not havynge lycense from the master and wardyns.''[24]

Again, some interpretation is needed. What are these ordinances? And what exactly are the licenses apparently being issued by the Master and Wardens? The first question can be easily, although not very satisfactorily, answered. As early as 1558-59, the Master and Wardens, the elected senior officers of the Company, and their immediate advisers later formalized into the Court of Assistants (who in due course became self-electing and the electoral college for the wardenships and mastership), were drafting regulations under which the Company might operate. Only a draft survives of this version, but the Ordinances were finally agreed upon in 1562, and revised from time to time thereafter.[25]

The Ordinances help us to understand the licenses, although they do not fully explain their force. In the 1558-59 draft, one clause reads: "Euery boke or thinge to be allowed by the stationers before yt be prynted.''[26]This clearly reflected earlier practices, as the fine in December 1557 shows. But what was the license? The form of words used varies, but it is clear that the Master and Wardens are granting it. It is equally clear that under the 1559 Injunctions the powers of censorship rested with the Privy Council and other designated officials of church and state. In practice, however, this crucial authority had been delegated to the Stationers' Company. The license granted by the Master and Wardens in effect signified their assent to the view that it was permissible to print the book. This was indeed an awesome responsbility, for in many cases, and soon perhaps in most, there was no formal permission from the censors.

The original purpose of the entries in Stationers' Register is

---

[21] 1 ARBER, *supra* note 18, at 74-75.

[22] *Id.* at 94-97.

[23] *Id.* at 45.

[24] *Id.* at 70.

[25] BLAGDEN, *supra* note 18, at 42-45.

[26] GREG, *supra* note 19, at 4.

clear: it was a record of the fact that, in the opinion of the Master and Wardens, the book had been properly licensed or could be printed without offense. It very soon, however, came to take on an entirely different meaning. At some time in the year 1563-64,[27] John Sampson was fined twenty pence by the Company for printing what are called "other mens copyes,"[28] a phrase that becomes familiar in the Company's records during the next eighty years, and that was used in each of the following two years to justify fines on other stationers.[29] Indeed, even before the 1562 Ordinances were adopted, something similar can be found. In 1558-59, William Copland was fined twenty pence for printing a book "of master Bradfordes."[30] These entries and others can only mean that as early as the late 1550s and certainly before 1565, it was accepted within the Company that the license was not merely a testimony to the right to print a particular book, but to the unique right to do so. Here we have, in all but name, the concept of copyright.

Within a very short time, we have every indication that "copies" were being treated as property. The justification for the fines was, of course, that the printing by one stationer of a copy that had been entered to another was an infringement of the latter's property rights. It followed therefore that copies could be traded, and in the late summer of 1564 we have the first record of such a transaction, when two copies were registered in the name of Thomas Marsh, "which he boughte of" Luke Harrison.[31] In 1566-67, we have the first example of a joint registration by two stationers of the same copy, in which they apparently owned equal shares.[32] Gaps in the records from the later 1560s through 1576 leave some questions outstanding, but by 1576 when the Register resumes and becomes more detailed, there can be no doubt that there is a well-established and generally accepted pattern of copy ownership, including transfers by purchase, inheritance and gift, subdivision into shares, and similar commercial activities. The evidence that copies were treated as property is scattered throughout the early records of the Stationers' Com-

---

[27] Entries were not precisely dated until 1576, and can only be assigned to a particular year.

[28] 1 ARBER, *supra* note 18, at 239.

[29] *See, e.g.*, 1 ARBER, *supra* note 18, at 274, 315.

[30] *Id.* at 93.

[31] *Id.* at 259.

[32] *Id.* at 329.

pany. As early as 1579, a copy was used as security for a debt;[33] similar practices at a later date include using copies to secure mortgages.[34]

The basic rules were very simple. Every copy had to be entered on the Register. This is apparent from fines for not registering,[35] although it was not made explicit until as late as 1637, when a decree of the Court of Star Chamber required that in addition to being licensed, every book "shall be also first entred in the Registers Booke of the Company of Stationers."[36] Once it had been registered, the copy was the sole property of the person who had registered it, provided that he had the right to make the entry in the first place. Indeed, a number of entries is conditional and the reservations expressed coincidentally reveal sharp practice and uncertainties.

These conditional entries are not uniform. In 1580, the Wardens, dissatisfied with the contents of a book, ordered it to be entered with the proviso that those in whose favor the entry was made "promese to bringe the whole impression thereof into the Hall in case it be disliked when it is printed."[37] This clearly arose from the Warden's fear of allowing a book to be printed that was religiously or politically unacceptable. Fear of annoying an influential author was equally potent. In 1581, a book on the education of children was entered with the reservation that if it had any contents "preiudiciall or hurtefull" to Roger Askham's *Schoolmaster* "then thys Lycence shalbe voyd".[38] Askham had been Elizabeth I's tutor and was highly regarded at court. Most interesting for our purposes, however, are those conditional entries where the concern was with the legalities of the ownership of the copy rather than its contents. A number of entries in the 1580s are made with such comments as "vpon condicon that no other man be interested in yt,"[39] and "soe much . . . as Doth not belonge to anie other of this Companie."[40] These cases, which are a few among many, clearly illustrate that the Stationers' pri-

---

[33] RECORDS OF THE COURT OF THE STATIONERS' COMPANY 1576 TO 1602, FROM REGISTER B, at 9 (W.W. Greg & E. Boswell eds., 1930) [hereinafter Greg & Boswell].

[34] RECORDS OF THE COURT OF THE STATIONERS' COMPANY 1602 TO 1640, at 217, 292 (William A. Jackson ed., 1957) [hereinafter Jackson]. *See also* 4 ARBER, *supra* note 18, at 377.

[35] *See, e.g.*, 2 ARBER, *supra* note 18, at 336 (entry of Sept. 2, 1578).

[36] 5 *id.* at 529-30.

[37] 2 *id.* at 366.

[38] *Id.* at 390.

[39] *Id.* at 416.

[40] *Id.* at 421.

mary concern was to regulate the trade to benefit its own members.

The origin of their power to do so lay in the state's perception of the need for censorship, but that power also conferred obvious economic benefits on the trade, or at least on certain members of it. For the book trade historian, the real significance of the early history of copy ownership is that it was the motive force for a critical change in the balance of power within the trade itself. For more than a century after the invention of printing, it was the printers, with their command of the limited technical facilities for book production, who controlled the trade. For example, it was the printers who dominated the Stationers' Company in the first ten or fifteen years after its Charter was granted. Gradually, however, the copy-owning booksellers took over from them. Printers came to be, as they have remained, the paid agents of the copy owners.[41] The copy owners reinforced their dominance through the Stationers' Company from the late 1580s onwards, and then began to exert political and legal influence outside the narrow circles of the book trade itself.

The Stationers' Company thus came to occupy the remarkable position of power and influence noted first by the 1583 Commissioners, and later and less objectively by Coventry, because it was a matter of mutual convenience to the trade and the state. The bargain was a simple one; in return for relieving the state of the day-to-day burden of censorship, the leading members of the Stationers' Company were guaranteed a virtual monopoly over the publishing of English books. This bargain was established in little more than a decade, and was to survive for over half a century. In essence, it even survived the destruction of the political system that created it.

The Stationers' position was further enhanced by their gradual absorption of the older system of copy protection by patent. This was a long and complicated business, whose details need not concern us. In summary, it is enough for our purposes to note that from the late 1570s onwards there was concern in the trade about the disproportionate wealth and power of those among its number who held the patents in the privileged books such as the Bible, the Statutes, and the common law books. The "class" patents, as they are sometimes called, were a particular grievance, because they included some of the most profitable copies in existence, whose publication involved far less financial

---

[41] FEATHER, *supra*, note 5, at 35-40.

risk than the speculative publishing of new and untried titles in a small and limited market. Piracy of patented copies was becoming a real problem by the early 1580s, but was ingeniously solved by Richard Day, who had inherited from his father a large group of patent rights including those in schoolbooks. Day reached an agreement with the principal pirate, John Wolfe, under which Wolfe became one of a group of shareholders in the schoolbook and other patents. This now became a complex piece of jointly-owned property, and to avoid disputes between the shareholders, its management was effectively delegated to the Court of Assistants, the governing body of the Stationers' Company. Other patents followed the same pattern of development, and by the 1590s, the whole operation had its own Treasurer, and a capital value assessed at the massive sum of nine thousand pounds. It was known as the "English Stock". Shares in the Stock were sold to Company members according to their rank and status. Regular annual dividends paid from the profits of publishing the Stock's copies ensured that the trade in general supported the system.[42] This was an even more astonishing coup than the Company's takeover of the crown licensing system, for it now controlled those copies that clearly did have their origin in the royal prerogative and existed only because of grants from the Crown.

It is clear that the idea of rights in copies, that is, the unique right to print a particular text, was well established before the end of the 1580s, and probably earlier. At the same time it was also claimed, and probably established *de facto*, that such rights could only belong to freemen of the Stationers' Company. In 1598, members of the Company were required by the Court of Assistants to desist from the practice of entering copies on behalf of non-members.[43] A later order, in 1607, was even more explicit: copies were to be entered only by freemen of the Company resident in London; no freeman was to help anyone else to enter a copy, and no copy was to be printed without entry.[44] The Company went to great lengths to prevent the ownership of copies outside its own membership. In 1605, ten copies were entered to Edmund Weaver that were alleged to be the property of Thomas Wight, who was not a member of the Company. This entry was,

---

[42] *See* Cyprian Blagden, *The English Stock of the Stationers' Company: An Account of its Origins*, 10 THE LIBRARY 163-85 (5th Ser. 1955); Cyprian Blagden, *The English Stock of the Stationers' Company in the Time of Stuarts*, 12 THE LIBRARY 167-86 (5th Ser. 1957).
[43] Greg and Boswell, *supra* note 33, at 59.
[44] Jackson, *supra* note 34, at 31.

however, only to allow Wight to "dispose of them to any freeman of this Companye."[45] These were, of course, only the internal rules of the Stationers' Company. In one commentator's view, the 1614 Monopolies Act made it possible for anyone to own a copyright,[46] but in practice the Act was only applied in the case of rights granted by patent. For the vast majority of copies which were not the subject of patents, entry in the Register by a free-man was the only way of establishing rights, whatever the niceties of legal theory. The intention was to ensure that the Company retained absolute control over the trade. The commercial advan-tages were obvious, but the case could always be made in terms of the need to protect the security of the state.

The key to enforcement was that entry in the Register was the only acceptable proof of copy ownership, as can be shown from a number of incidents. The case of Thomas Wight, seeking to have his copies entered even though he could never exploit them, exemplifies this, but there are more explicit cases of the Register being used to prove ownership. An interesting, if nega-tive, example is that of the rights in "the book of Dcor ffaustus;" the book is not Marlowe's play, but rather the English translation of the German "Faust Book," which was his source. On Decem-ber 18, 1592, the Court of Assistants ruled that the copy was owned by Abel Jeffes, if no entry could be found for it in the name of Richard Oliffe.[47] No such entry existed, and the copy was duly considered to belong to Jeffes; in 1596, he was able to transfer his share to Edward White. The full story is actually more complicated than this brief summary implies. No-one in-volved was an exemplary member of the Company, and there was almost certainly a good deal of sharp practice hidden beneath the curt entries in the Court Book and the Register.[48] Nevertheless, the principle is clear enough: Oliffe's claim had to stand or fall on the existence of a valid entry in the Register. Another case, and perhaps a less difficult one, occurred in 1603, when the late Rob-ert Dexter's copies were declared to be the common property of the Company, "according to a former constitution in suche cases."[49] Five copies were named, but there was the rider that

---

[45] 3 ARBER, *supra* note 18, at 288-89.

[46] HOLDSWORTH, *supra* note 3, at 366.

[47] Greg and Boswell, *supra* note 33, at 44.

[48] MARLOWE'S DOCTOR FAUSTUS 1604-1616, at 9-10 (1950).

[49] The "former constitution" embodied the rule that the unclaimed copies of a dead owner reverted to the company. It is not clear where this rule was actually written, but it was certainly the normal practice; it was referred to as the "Custom of the Company" in 1626, and the "antient Custome" in 1638. Jackson, *supra* note 34, at 188, 307.

the order included "all other copies and bookes wherein Robert Dexter Deceased had Right by entranc [*sic*] in the hall book."[50] Nothing could be more explicit.

Although entry was the only proof of ownership, it has to be remembered that the Register was merely a record of established rights; it did not, in itself, confer those rights. The conditional entries exemplify this, but a more surprising group of entries is of copies in which rights are clearly deemed to exist, and to be properly owned, but for which there had been no entry. On July 2, 1602, thirteen copies which had belonged to a deceased member of the Company were entered in the name of William Leake; of these, earlier entries can be found for nine only. Four of them had never been entered, and yet the ownership, and the right to transfer them, was not challenged.[51] In 1607, a similar transfer of a group of copies took place including several which had not previously been entered.[52] An even clearer case is that of Dekker's play *The Shoemaker's Holiday*, written in 1599, staged in 1600 and published in the same year by Valentine Simmes.[53] There was no entry in the Register, but in 1610 it was transferred by Simmes to James Wright, without any difficulty or challenge.[54] It is clear that Simmes's rights were accepted, and we can conclude from this that unchallenged publication in itself constituted the establishment of rights in the copy, at least so far as the trade was concerned. The entry in the Register merely confirmed those rights, after any member of the Company who denied them had the opportunity to prove his case.

A challenge to the right of publication might come from several sources. The Court of Assistants was concerned primarily with objections from within the Company's membership, since its first concern was to maintain good order in the trade by ensuring that its own decrees and ordinances were obeyed. The Court Books and the Hall Books are full of minutes and entries, some

---

[50] 3 ARBER, *supra* note 18, at 248.

[51] *Id.* at 210. The transaction was perhaps somewhat more complicated than I have implied. The entry was "by Direction from the wardens under their handes: after yt had ben agreed uppon at il last courtes." Unfortunately, Register B, Greg and Boswell, *supra* note 33, has nothing to say on the transaction. The two previous meetings of the Court of Assistants had been on May 8 and June 28, and, apparently, at neither meeting was this matter discussed. However, there are a number of minor errors and confusions in Register B in 1602, *id.* at 86-90, and some minutes may not have been written up properly at the time.

[52] 3 ARBER, *supra* note 18, at 365. There are no caveats and complications in this case, in which John Smethwicke entered sixteen copies "which dyd belonge to Nicholas Lynge."

[53] 3 E.K. CHAMBERS, THE ELIZABETHAN STAGE 291-92 (1923).

[54] 3 ARBER, *supra* note 18, at 431.

of them deeply obscure in their details, which reflect both the disputes that arose, and the Court's efforts to mollify everyone involved in them, while ensuring that its own authority was not blatantly flouted. The second source of objections, far fewer in number, but taken very seriously when they did arise, was the various official bodies which might object to the contents of a book rather than to the commercial arrangements made for its publication. These represent only a very small proportion of the cases that were heard, and as the number of internal trade cases increased with the great increase in the output of books in the later sixteenth and early seventeenth centuries, the proportion of cases promoted by outsiders became even smaller.

There was, however, also a third source of complaints, from outside both the book trade and the official circles concerned with the censorship of the press. This group of complainants, although the use of the word "group" implies a degree of cohesion which did not exist, consisted of those who argued that they had some prior claim on the ownership of whatever it was that was claimed as a piece of property by a Stationer. In dealing with this, we must first deal with a red herring which bedevils much of the writing on this subject by literary historians.

The serious study of most of the matters discussed in this paper had its origins in the study of the textual and theatrical history of the Elizabethan and Jacobean drama, and especially in the complex relationship which existed, or which was presumed to exist, between playwrights, theatrical companies and printers and publishers. We must necessarily generalize, and, as a generalization, it is not wildly misleading to say that plays were written by authors working on commission for theatrical companies. Some companies were effectively owned by an individual. One such was the Admiral's Men in the later part of Elizabeth I's reign, whose owner, Philip Henslowe, kept a detailed, if somewhat confused account, of his dealings with playwrights and others.[55] It is clear that Henslowe paid his dramatists, and that their plays then went into the repertory for as long as they could hold the stage. Other companies, of which the only significant example was the Chamberlain's Men (who became the King's Men in 1603) were, in effect, joint stock companies. The whole issue is confused by the fact that Shakespeare was a principal sharer in the Chamberlain's/King's company, and that his plays,

---

[55] HENSLOWE'S DIARY (R.A. Foakes & R.T. Rickert eds., 1961) [hereinafter Foakes & Rickert].

after 1598, belonged to that Company. There was nothing unsual about this arrangement; it was the standard pattern. The dramatist wrote for the Company that employed him, or of which he was a shareholder, and the play he wrote became part of the stock of plays owned and performed by that Company.[56]

None of this was of any significance to the book trade, except insofar as some plays were published. We must first put that statement in context. In a typical year, between June 1594 and June 1595, Henslowe's company, the Admiral's Men, introduced eighteen new plays into their repertory.[57] If we assume that a major professional company, such as the Admiral's, always worked at that rate, then we would expect it to introduce something of the order of 150 to 200 new plays a decade. Let us compare this with the rate of publication. In the fifteen years from 1590 to 1605, eighteen plays were published that can be definitely associated with the Admiral's Men;[58] in the period 1597 to 1612,[59] 32 plays belonging to the Chamberlain's/King's Men were printed.[60] It is not unreasonable to conclude that publication was of infinitesimal significance to playwrights and theatrical companies. Publication was the exception not the rule.

So far as the Stationers' Company was concerned, plays were copies like any other. Some plays were printed in texts generally recognized by later scholars to be deeply corrupt, and yet their publication was not itself irregular. The cases of 2 and 3 Henry VI illustrate this point. The first edition of 2 Henry VI (with the title The First Part of the Contention of York and Lancaster) was published in 1594, in a badly mangled text not entirely by Shakespeare.[61] This was entered in the Register on March 12, 1594, in a perfectly normal way, by Thomas Millington.[62] Millington, the publisher of the 1594 and 1600 editions, transferred his rights to Thomas Pavier in 1602.[63] Pavier published an edition in 1619, and the play, in a revised and more accurate text, was duly re-

---

[56] There is, of course, a vast literature on all of this, much of it of little relevance to our purposes. The organization of the theatrical companies does, however, have some bearing on the issue. CHAMBERS, supra note 52, is the standard and massively detailed (and virtually unreadable) source. For a useful summary, however, see ANDREW GURR, THE SHAKESPEARIAN STAGE 1574-1642, at 19-59 (1970).

[57] See Foakes & Rickert, supra note 55, at 21-30.

[58] Id. See also 3 CHAMBERS, supra note 53, passim; W.W. GREG, A BIBLIOGRAPHY OF THE ENGLISH PRINTED DRAMA TO THE RESTORATION (1939-59).

[59] The period from the formation of the Company to Shakespeare's retirement.

[60] See supra, note 54.

[61] For an exhaustive study, see PETER ALEXANDER, SHAKESPEARE'S HENRY VI AND RICHARD III (1929).

[62] 2 ARBER, supra note 18, at 646.

[63] 3 id. at 204.

printed in the First Folio of Shakespeare's works in 1623, an enterprise to which Pavier was almost certainly a consenting
party.[64] *3 Henry VI* has very similar legal and textual histories.
The key point here is that a corrupt text was treated as if it were a
perfectly normal copy. From the trade's point of view that was
precisely the case.

It is crucial to maintain a clear distinction between "piracy"
as it was understood in the book trade and "piracy" as it might
have been understood by the theatrical companies. So far as the
book trade was concerned, piracy could take place only if the established and proven rights of a Stationers' Company member
were infringed. The theatrical companies took a different view,
and on a few occasions intervened, or attempted to intervene, to
prevent the publication of plays from their repertory. The most
notorious case was in 1619, when the Court of Assistants ordered
as follows: "vppon a ler from the right ho[ble] the Lo.
Chamberleyne It is thought fitt & so ordered That no playes that
his Ma[tyes] do play shalbe printed w[th]out consent of some of
them."[65] The Court could hardly ignore an order from such a
source, and it should be seen in the context of interventions by
civil and ecclesiastical authorites to prevent undesirable publication in particular cases. Some such cases involved an author who
wanted to protect his work for some reason. The King's Men had
their own special reasons for seeking to protect their plays from
publication at that time, and merely followed the normal contemporary practice of turning to their most powerful patron in the
hope of obtaining his help, as indeed they did.[66] Earlier instances of alleged intervention by the theatrical companies to
prevent publication (usually, but not always, of apparently corrupt texts) have been discussed at great length,[67] but the case for
them remains unproven. In the last analysis, there is no real evidence that, except in the one instance just cited, there was any
significantly special relationship between the theatrical companies and the book trade. So far as the trade was concerned, plays
were just books like any other, waiting to be converted into cop-

---

[64] *See* W.W. GREG, THE SHAKESPEARE FIRST FOLIO: ITS BIBLIOGRAPHICAL AND TEX-
TUAL HISTORY 68 (1955).

[65] Jackson, *supra* note 34, at 110.

[66] This was part of the preliminary stages of assembling the rights that were needed
to produce the First Folio; *See* GREG, *supra* note 64, at 28-75.

[67] Pollard began the discussion in SHAKESPEARE'S FIGHT, *supra* note 20, at 42-44;
Greg judiciously ended it in ASPECTS AND PROBLEMS, *supra* note 19, at 112-22, where he
gives a much more measured account of the so-called "blocking" entries and related
issues.

ies and hence into profits. These interventions on behalf of the theatrical companies are not without parallel and precedent elsewhere. Although the majority of patents for books were granted by the Crown to members of the book trade, this was not invariably the case. Some went to Crown servants, as part of the normal process of rewards for services rendered, but even in the sixteenth century there are isolated examples of patent protection for authors and others involved in the writing, as opposed to the publishing, of a book. A very early example is found in Mary I's reign. It was not, however, until the reign of James I that the number of authorial patents became somewhat more significant. It was, on the whole, works of scholarship that were most fully protected, just as they had been in the middle decades of the sixteenth century. The difference was that it was now generally the authors and not the printers or booksellers who were recognized as needing this protection. Two examples are of particular interest: John Minsheu's *Glosson Etymologicon*, for which a patent was granted in 1611, and was ultimately to become the first book published by subscription in England,[68] and John Marriott's *Pharmocopoeia Londiniensis*, protected in 1616, which was the first of a long line of such books.[69] These and other examples all suggest that James I was exercising the prerogative as Coventry had defined it: that is, the law assumed that all copyrights could be granted by the Crown. In practice, however, these patents confirmed, rather than conferred, the rights of the creator of what would later be called a literary work. In the 1640s, this confirmatory grant of copyright was incorporated into the process of licensing by the House of Commons when it usurped the powers of the Crown, and there are enough examples of this practice to suggest that the concept of authorial rights was quite familiar.[70]

We must not push the evidence further than it will allow us to go, but even from the book trade we can find some limited recognition of authors' rights. We know, for example, that authors were paid for their copy. In itself this proves nothing, but it does at least suggest that the booksellers recognized that in acquiring a copy for entry and publication, they were acquiring something which had already taken on the status of property. In

---

[68] *See* GREG, *supra* note 19, at 51-52, 157; *see also* Sarah L. C. Clapp, *The Beginnings of Subscription Publication in the Seventeenth Century*, 29 MODERN PHILOLOGY 199-244 (1931-32).

[69] GREG, *supra* note 12, at 156, 162.

[70] *See* N. Frederick Nash, *English Licenses to Print and Grants of Copyright in the 1640's*, 4 THE LIBRARY, at 174-84 (6th Ser. 1982).

this matter, examples from the theatrical world are not without interest, although they must be used with caution. The playwright Robert Greene was once accused of selling the same play twice, once to the Queen's Men and then again to the Admiral's.[71] The facts are of less interest to us than the accusation, for clearly it was thought credible that a man should write a play and then sell it. We have here at least anecdotal evidence that an uncommissioned writing was regarded as its author's property in the late 1580s when this allegation was published.

Moreover, we can see the beginnings of a distinction between manuscript and printed works. In the 1590s, Thomas Nashe indicated that printed publication was one way to prevent further illicit copying of works by scriveners, at a time when the circulation of literary works in manuscript was still common.[72] In effect, an astute author could take advantage of the system established and controlled by the Stationers' Company. Once a book was in print, it was protected by the Company's regulations, and there is evidence for the exploitation of this fact by authors seeking to protect themselves against unauthorized printing or the printing of inaccurate or incomplete texts.[73] Again, the examples are few, and we know more about those of literary interest than about the great mass of ordinary books; but the signposts are there if we will only read them. Before the death of Elizabeth I, it was recognized that authors had some rights in the books that they wrote, and that those rights could be translated into money by the sale of the copy to a Stationer. The Stationer could then use the book trade's own system of copy protection both to protect his own investment and, if it were a matter of concern, the author's reputation.

The recognition of the essential uniqueness of each copy was implicit in the whole idea of copy protection, and as early as the mid-1580s, we find the Court of Assistants trying to regulate against plagiarism. In 1584, for example, *A book of cookery* was entered to Edward White, on the condition that no-one else owned the copy and that it was not "collected out of anie book already extante in printe in English."[74] This is the earliest explicit statement in the Register that an entry is conditional upon

---

[71] 3 CHAMBERS, *supra* note 52, at 325.

[72] This continued throughout the seventeenth century. *See, e.g.*, Harold Love, *Scribal Texts and Literary Communities: The Rochester Circle and Osborn b. 105*, 42 STUD. IN BIBLIOGRAPHY 219-35 (1989).

[73] *See* PERCY SIMPSON, STUDIES IN ELIZABETHAN DRAMA 186-92 (1955).

[74] 2 ARBER, *supra* note 18, at 438.

the copy having a degree of originality. It was not, however, the first time that the problem had arisen. Two years earlier Henry Denham was ordered by the Court of Assistants to pay the not inconsiderable sum of £ 4.6s.8d. to Edward White because of a book which he had published called *The Diamond of Devotion*, "pte whereof was taken out of a copie of ye said Ed. whites Called the footepath of faithe."[75] Similar cases are not numerous, but they did occur.[76] All point towards the same conclusion: that there was, probably unintentionally, a growing *de facto* acceptance that the protection of copy-owners' rights, which were the economic cornerstone of an organized and efficiently conducted book trade, would only be possible if the integrity of the copies themselves were subject to some similar, if less stringent, control.

It would be perverse to claim that authors' rights were widely recognized in pre-revolutionary England; it would be more accurate, although still perhaps a slight exaggeration, to suggest that they were dimly perceived. Nevertheless, the early history of rights in copies is critical to an understanding of the later development of the concept of copyright. English copyright has its origins in the Crown's need to control the press. This need led to the development of a system in which control could be exercised by restricting the number of printers and booksellers, and by ensuring that even within that number there were close controls on who might print what books. Such a system rapidly outgrew the capacity of the Crown to adminster it, so that it was, in effect, handed over to the book trade. The leading members of trade seized upon it for their commercial advantage, and in so doing confirmed the idea that a copy was unique and that the right to print it was also unique. This, in turn, led to the gradual realization that unique copies had unique creators, and that those creators also must be deemed to have some share in the rights which they had created.

In the later seventeenth century and beyond into the eighteenth, the rapid expansion of the book trade, and a changing cultural climate in which there was an insistent and almost insatiable demand for new books, created a situation in which authors were better placed to negotiate with their publishers. Even so, rights remained trade rights. The so-called Copyright Act of 1710 mentions neither copyright nor authors; it was little more than a codification, an inadequate and inaccurate codification as it

---

[75] Greg and Boswell, *supra* note 33, at 12.
[76] *See, e.g.*, Jackson, *supra* note 34, at 105, 207.

proved, of existing book trade practices. The power of the authors, however, was soon to be asserted. Men—and a very few women—had been living by their pens in England since the sixteenth century. By the middle of the eighteenth century, they were a large and growing, if not yet entirely respectable, class. That was possible only because the products of their pens commanded a market price, and that in turn was possible only because the commodity was protected against unfair competition. The origins of that protection can be seen dimly through the veils which will probably always divide us from a full understanding of the English book trade at the very beginning of its organized existence. Nevertheless, the ideas were there, and just as the 1710 Act was little more than a statutory recognition of the rights of the trade, the Act of 1814 was an even more belated recognition that authors had always played their part in the commerce of letters, and for nearly two hundred years had been rewarded, however inadequately, for their labors.

THE AUTHOR IN COURT: *POPE v. CURLL* (1741)*

MARK ROSE**

I.

On 4 June 1741 Alexander Pope, represented by his friend William Murray (later Lord Mansfield), filed a complaint in Chancery against his ancient enemy, the bookseller Edmund Curll. At issue was a volume of letters Curll had published five days earlier entitled *Dean Swift's Literary Correspondence*, which contained letters to and from Pope and Jonathan Swift, as well as letters from Dr. John Arbuthnot, Lord Bolingbroke, John Gay, and others. Pope filed his complaint under the terms of the Statute of Anne,[1] the world's first copyright statute, and claimed the rights, curiously enough by modern thinking, both in his own letters and in those sent to him by Swift. Pope sought, and was granted, an injunction to prevent Curll from selling any further copies of the book. After a response from Curll moving to dissolve, the injunction was continued by Lord Chancellor Hardwicke, but only for those letters written by Pope, not for those sent to him by Swift.[2]

Pope v. Curll, which established the rule that copyright in a letter belongs to the writer, remains a foundational case in English and American copyright law. It is also one of the first cases in which a major English author went to court in his own name to defend his literary interests. What *Pope* records, I shall suggest, is

* This article is printed by permission of Oxford University Press. A similar copy of this article will appear in a forthcoming edition of *Cultural Critique*.

** Director of the University of California Humanities Research Institute. He is currently completing a book-length study entitled *Authors and Owners: The Invention of Copyright*.

The author would like to thank Robert Burt, Robert Folkenflik, Paul Geller, Peter Haidu, Richard Helgerson, Robert Post, Ruth Warkentin and Everett Zimmerman for their comments and assistance of various kinds in connection with this essay.

[1] Act for the Encouragement of Learning, 1709, 8 Anne, ch. 19.

[2] *Pope v. Curll* is reported by J.T. Atkyns. *See* Pope v. Curll, 2 Atk. 342, 26 Eng. Rep. 608 (Ch. 1741). Pope's complaint and Curll's answer are in the Public Record Office in London. The case has been discussed in Harry Ransom, *The Personal Letter as Literary Property*, 30 STUD. IN ENGLISH 116-31 (1951). Ransom also discusses the later case of Thompson v. Stanhope, Amb. 737, 27 Eng. Rep. 476 (1774), which involved the posthumous publication of Lord Chesterfield's letters. In a series of hypothetical cases, Ransom further explores the complications that arise from the establishment of letters as copyrightable. *See also* David Foxon, *Pope and Copyright*, in POPE AND THE EARLY EIGHTEENTH-CENTURY BOOK TRADE app. (1991) (drawing together useful information on Pope's contracts, lawsuits, and plans for litigation); Pat Rogers, *The Case of* Pope v. Curl, 27 THE LIBRARY 326 (1972) (reporting on the materials in the Public Record Office).

an important transitional moment in the concept of authorship and of authors' rights, and a transitional moment, too, in the conception of literary property.

It is a striking fact that in England the legal empowerment of the author as a proprietor preceded the social formation of professional authorship, a development that, as Alvin Kernan has argued, is to be associated with Samuel Johnson.[3] In the first part of the eighteenth century, the values of the patronage culture of early modern England were still prevalent among respectable authors. Pope may have had commercial reasons for pursuing his action against Edmund Curll under the provisions of the new copyright statute, but he presented the issue less as a matter of commerce than of privacy. The unauthorized publication of a gentleman's private letters was, he felt, a violation of basic social principles. *Pope* suggests how from the very beginning of the story of authors' rights in England, issues of "propriety" in the moral sense became inextricably entwined with issues of "property" in the sense of economic interest. *Pope* also records an important moment in the development of the concept of intellectual property. Who owns a letter, the writer or the receiver? In the court's response to this question, the notion of the essentially immaterial nature of the object of copyright was born. This was, at the time, a novel doctrine. But the potential for its production was latent from the beginning in the provision of the Statute of Anne which transformed authors, as well as booksellers, into potential owners of literary property. Booksellers are concerned with material objects—books—whereas authors are concerned with compositions, and with texts. If the author were to be a proprietor and an agent in the literary marketplace, or were to appear in court in his own person to protect his own interests, then inevitably the conception of the property owned would be affected.

To understand the significance of *Pope v. Curll,* I will first discuss the Statute of Anne and the rights of authors in the period prior to its passage. Following this, I will consider the complex nature of Pope's motives in initiating this lawsuit. Finally, I shall consider the case itself and discuss its significance both in the context of Pope's life and career, and in the context of the development of legal doctrine.

---

[3] ALVIN KERNAN, PRINTING TECHNOLOGIES, LETTERS & SAMUEL JOHNSON (1987).

II.

Entitled "An Act for the Encouragement of Learning, by Vesting the Copies of Printed Books in the Authors or Purchasers of such Copies, during the Times Therein Mentioned," the Statute of Anne, which came into effect on 10 April 1710, was not quite the landmark recognition of authors' rights that it has often been claimed to be. As Lyman Ray Patterson has emphasized, the statute was essentially a booksellers' bill, a legislative continuation of the ancient trade regulation practices of the Stationers' Company, the London guild of printers and booksellers which had long controlled the book trade in Britain.[4] But unlike the traditional guild practice in which ownership of a "copy" continued in principle forever, the statute limited the term of copyright to fourteen years. An extension for a second fourteen-year term was possible if the author was still living at the expiration of the first term. And in a second departure from traditional guild practices, the statute established authors as the original holders of the rights in their works, thereby explicitly recognizing for the first time the author as a fully empowered agent in the literary marketplace.

Prior to the passage of the statute, authors could not be said to "own" their works. Indeed, the very notion of owning a text as property does not quite fit the conception of literature in the early modern period in which it was common to think of a text as an action rather than as a thing. Texts might serve to ennoble or immortalize worthy patrons, and in the process perhaps to win office or other favors for their authors; they might move audiences to laughter or tears; they might expose corruptions or confirm the just rule of the monarch or assist in the embracing of true religion, in which case their authors were worthy of reward. Alternatively, they might move men to sedition or heresy, in which case their authors were worthy of punishment. Thinking of texts in this way, valuing them for what they could do, was commensurate with the traditional society of the sixteenth and seventeenth centuries dominated by patronage structures, just as, later, treating texts as aesthetic objects was commensurate with the advanced marketplace society, founded on the notion of private property, as it developed in the eighteenth century.[5]

---

4 LYMAN R. PATTERSON, COPYRIGHT IN HISTORICAL PERSPECTIVE 143-50 (1968).

5 On occasion a state might grant an early modern author an exclusive right to print for a limited term. But these privileges should be thought of as forms of patronage, rather than private property rights, granted as rewards for notable services rendered.

A sixteenth or seventeenth-century author did, of course, own his manuscript, and this might be sold to a bookseller or to a theatrical company. Yet once the material object left his possession, the author's rights in it were at best tenuous. Still, to say that authors owned nothing more than the ink and paper of their manuscripts is not to say that they had no literary rights at all. In the early modern period, there seems to have developed in connection with the individualization of authorship the transformation of the medieval *"auctor"* into the renaissance "author," a general sense that it was improper to publish an author's text without permission. In sixteenth-century Venice, for example, the Council of Ten decreed that printers must not publish works without the author's written consent.[6] In sixteenth-century France, several cases were brought which sucessfully asserted the author's right to control the publication of his work.[7] In England, according to an edict proclaimed by the Long Parliament in the context of the flood of anonymous controversial publications that followed the abolition of the Star Chamber, the Stationers' Company was required to see that all books identified the author on the title page and that no book was published without the author's consent. If any printer failed to secure the author's consent, he would be treated as if he were the author himself.[8]

Issued in a moment of anxiety at the prospect of an uncontrolled press, the Long Parliament's decree was essentially an instrument for establishing criminal responsibility for books deemed libelous, seditious, or blasphemous. Aware that an unscrupulous printer might publish a book against the author's wishes, the House of Commons included a clause requiring authorial consent.[9] Parliament's concern was not with authors' economic rights, but with their potential vulnerability to prosecution merely for having held offending ideas, which was not in itself a crime.

The nature of the English decree suggests that in discussing the development of authors' rights it is important to distinguish between issues of "property" and issues of "propriety." The acknowledgement of the author's personal right to control the publication of his texts was a principle based on concepts of honor

---

[6] Horatio F. Brown, The Venetian Printing Press, 1469-1800, at 78-80 (Gerard Th. van Heusden ed., 1969) (1891).

[7] Marie-Claude Dock, Etude sur le droit d'auteur 78-79 (1963); Cynthia J. Brown, *Du manuscrit a l'imprime en France: le cas des Grands Rhetoriqueurs, in* 1 Actes du Ve Colloque International sur le Moyen Francais 103, 117 n.37 (1985).

[8] 2 Journals of the House of Commons 402 (1803).

[9] Act for the Encouragement of Learning, 1709, 8 Anne, ch. 19 (Eng.).

and reputation consistent with the traditional patronage society. It was not necessarily the same as the acknowledgement of a property right in the sense of an economic interest in an alienable commodity. In practice, of course, the right to control first publication had economic implications, and therefore, it could easily be treated as a property right. Indeed, in practice, English booksellers of the sixteenth and seventeenth centuries seem to have recognized an obligation to pay authors for their "copies."[10]

The parliamentary decree of 1641/2 is, so far as I know, the only state affirmation of any kind of authorial right in England earlier than the Statute of Anne and is essentially a criminal edict. It is probably not an inaccurate generalization, to say that before the statute, an English author effectively had no place in court except as a criminal defendant charged with libel, blasphemy, or sedition. Despite eighteenth-century assertions about authors' ancient common law property rights, no such authorial right was ever established or even, so far as I know, asserted by an author.[11] Indeed, what legal standing—other than under the edict of 1641/2 which was only briefly in force—an English author might have had to take action against a bookseller is unclear. In 1704 Daniel Defoe called for a change, complaining in his *An Essay on the Regulation of the Press*[12] that there was "no Law so much wanting in the Nation, relating to Trade and Civil Property," as one that would provide for authors. If an author could be punished for a libelous or seditious book, Defoe said, then it was only just that he also be permitted to reap the benefit of an excellent book: "For if an Author has not the right of a Book, after he has made it, and the benefit be not his own, and the Law will not protect him in that Benefit, 'twould be very hard the Law should pretend to punish him for it."[13] During the seventeenth century, England had become essentially a marketplace society and the values of possessive individualism were defined and promulgated. Defoe's call for the establishment of authorial property bears witness to the potential for the extension of the ideology of possessive individualism to authorship. We should note, how-

---

10 PATTERSON, *supra* note 4, at 64-77.

11 *See* Howard B. Abrams, *The Historic Foundation of American Copyright Law: Exploding the Myth of Common Law Copyright*, 29 WAYNE L. REV. 1119 (1983); Mark Rose, *The Author as Proprietor: Donaldson v. Becket and the Geneology of Modern Authorship*, 23 REPRESENTATIONS 51 (1988).

12 DANIEL DEFOE, *An Essay on the Regulation of the Press in* ON THE FREEDOM OF PRINTING AND SPEECH (1978).

13 *Id.* at 21.

ever, that his claim is not based on the modern principle that the author is entitled to exploit the product of his labor so much as on the notion of the complementarity of punishment and reward. Defoe was still thinking within the framework of traditional society, in which authority, transmitted through punishment and reward, was conceived as descending from above.

III.

The provision in the Statute of Anne that established the author as the first proprietor of his work did open the way for the author to appear in court in the novel role of plaintiff in a civil action. But in fact, nearly all the early litigation that arose under the statute involved booksellers seeking determinations against other booksellers rather than authors defending their rights against booksellers. The explanation for this is simple. During this period, authors were still, in large part, sustained by the ideology of the traditional patronage society in which gentlemanly honor was the crucial value, and reward, rather than profit, for worthy works was what one expected. The early eighteenth-century conception of respectable authorship as a learned and polite activity existed, at least in principle, apart from the marketplace and did not encourage authors to rush into litigation in defense of their literary properties.[14]

Alexander Pope was an exceptional figure, for more than any other writer of his day he behaved like a literary entrepreneur and made a fortune from his verse. Pope's prominence gave him enormous bargaining power, which he used to secure unusually favorable terms from his booksellers. Despite his involvement in the literary marketplace, Pope characteristically presented himself as a gentleman and a scholar rather than as a professional and was almost obsessively concerned with what we would today call image management. As part of his concern with image management, Pope resolved to make his correspondence public in the latter part of his career, in order, as Maynard Mack puts it, among other things, to "erect a monument to himself and the gifted writers he had known."[15] But for a gentleman to publish his own letters would have seemed inexcusably vain, and Pope

---

[14] The only case preceding *Pope* that I am aware of in which a specifically literary figure sued in his own name is *Gay v. Read* (1729) in which John Gay obtained an injunction to protect his rights in *Polly*, the sequel to *The Beggar's Opera*. For information about the case, see James R. Sutherland, *'Polly' Among the Pirates*, 37 MOD. LANG. REV. 291 (1942).

[15] MAYNARD MACK, ALEXANDER POPE: A LIFE 660 (1985).

had to arrange matters so that publication would seem to occur against his wishes. Therefore, in 1735, Pope tricked Curll into publishing his correspondence, thereby creating a situation which would allow him to protest against the indignity of being exposed in print and at the same time, open the way for an authorized version.

So much is familiar knowledge. As reconstructed by James McLaverty, however, the evidence suggests that Pope had a further purpose in the 1735 affair with Curll, one that illuminates his goal six years later in filing suit against Curll over the correspondence with Swift.[16] In the spring of 1735, the London booksellers were campaigning for a bill that would extend the statutory term of copyright. Pope did not appear to be particularly concerned with the term of copyright, but was determined that no bill for the benefit of booksellers be passed without also including a clause to protect authors. He therefore contrived to have the surreptitious edition of his letters appear while the bill was pending. Thus, Curll would serve as an example of an irresponsible bookseller in order to dramatize the bill's limitations and defeat it. The 1735 bill was indeed defeated, although not necessarily because of the affair of the letters as Pope claimed. Shortly after, Pope expressed the hope that if the booksellers' bill was again brought in, Parliament would not increase the term of copyright without also doing something for authors "Since in a Case so *notorious* as the printing a Gentleman's PRIVATE LETTERS, most Eminent, both *Printers* and *Booksellers*, conspired to assist the Pyracy both in printing and in vending the same."[17]

The incident of 1735 bears witness to Pope's genuine concern that there be a legal remedy for the unauthorized publication of letters. We should observe, however, that the issue as he presents it is a matter of personal right rather than of economic interest. Pope's point is that the unauthorized printing of a gentleman's "PRIVATE LETTERS"—the outraged capitals are expressive—is an offence against decency. In 1737 he repeats this same point in the preface to the authorized edition of his correspondence. The unauthorized printing of private letters, he says, is a form of *"betraying Conversation"* and is damaging to the social fabric:

---

[16] James McLaverty, *The First Printing and Publication of Pope's Letters*, 2 THE LIBRARY 264 (1980).

[17] 2 ALEXANDER POPE, *A Narrative of the Method by which Mr. Pope's Private Letters were procured and published by Edmund Curl, Bookseller* (1735), *in* THE PROSE WORKS OF ALEXANDER POPE 317, 345 (1986).

> To open Letters is esteem'd the greatest breach of honour;
> even to look into them already open'd or accidentally dropt, is
> held ungenerous, if not an immoral act. What then can be
> thought of the procuring them merely by Fraud, and printing
> them merely for Lucre? We cannot but conclude every honest
> man will wish, that if the Laws have as yet provided no ade-
> quate remedy, one at least may be found, to prevent so great
> and growing an evil.[18]

What I would suggest is that in the suit against Curll in 1741,
Pope was seeking to achieve in the courts what he had failed to
achieve in Parliament—that is, to secure protection for himself
and for others against the unauthorized procuring and printing
of private letters.

The correspondence with Swift was a set of letters that Pope
particularly wished to see published, and for many years he had
sought to get Swift to return his letters to him. When at last he
succeeded, Pope arranged through an elaborate ruse to have the
letters printed in Dublin. This made it possible for him to publish an authorized edition as part of his collected works.[19] Six
weeks after Pope's edition appeared, Curll released his volume,
which he claimed was a reprint of the Dublin edition. Pope, who
had anticipated Curll's action,[20] immediately brought suit. No
doubt commercial considerations figured in Pope's suit, for
Curll's cheap piracy represented a threat to the expensive authorized edition.[21] No doubt, too, Pope may have derived vindic-
tive pleasure from making Edmund Curll once again his target.
Whatever his other motives, the history of his passionate concern
over the previous six years with the impropriety of unauthorized
printing of letters, suggests that by suing Curll in 1741, Pope was
trying to answer his own call to find an "adequate remedy" for
"so great and growing an evil" by establishing that letters fell
under the statute. In *Pope v. Curll*, then, a commercial regulatory
statute was being employed to pursue matters that had as much
to do with "propriety"—with authors' personal rights—as with
authors' economic interests. In the context of the developing
marketplace culture, questions of authorial honor and reputation
were becoming entwined with questions of commercial law.

Let us return for a moment to Pope's preface to the 1737
edition of his letters. This preface is dominated by the genteel

---

[18] 1 ALEXANDER POPE, THE CORRESPONDENCE OF ALEXANDER POPE xl (1956).
[19] MACK, *supra* note 15, at 665-71.
[20] 4 POPE, *supra* note 18, at 343 (Letter to R. Allen).
[21] *Id.* at 350.

discourse in which Pope represents his outrage as a man of honor against unauthorized publication. But what we can call the "discourse of property" makes itself felt as well. For example, Pope complains that the booksellers' practice of soliciting copies of authors' letters leads to petty thievery: "Any domestick or servant, who can snatch a letter from your pocket or cabinet, is encouraged to that vile practise."[22] Moreover, if the quantity of material procured falls short, the bookseller will fill out the volume with anything he pleases, so that the poor author has "not only Theft to fear, but Forgery."[23] And the greater the writer's reputation, the greater the demand for his books and so the greater the injury to the author: "[Y]our Fame and your Property suffer alike; you are at once expos'd and plunder'd."[24] The blending of the discourse of propriety (marked by such terms as "honor," "generosity," and "fame") with that of property (marked by such terms as "theft," "snatch," and "plunder") produces a certain instability in the preface that is evidence of the way it inscribes a transitional moment in cultural history. My point is that Pope's suit against Curll was equally a mingled affair that took place between two worlds: the traditional world of the author as a gentleman and scholar and the emergent world of the author as a professional.

On 16 February 1742/3, a year and a half after the decision in *Pope v. Curll*, Pope was again in court filing complaints against booksellers. This time, he employed the statute in two actions that clearly pertained to his right to exploit his works for profit. Neither of these cases is reported, and neither seems to be as fascinating as *Pope v. Curll*. They do remind us, however, that although Pope always presented himself as a gentleman, he was also in practice an aggressive professional and the first major author to use the Statute of Anne repeatedly to pursue his professional interests in court.[25]

---

[22] 1 *id.* at xxxix.

[23] *Id.* at xl.

[24] *Id.*

[25] Both suits were related to the publication of the four-book version of the *Dunciad* in 1742. In one, Pope sued Henry Lintot in order to establish that after the initial fourteen-year period, the rights in the original version of the *Dunciad* reverted to himself as author. In the other, Pope sued Jacob Ilive, claiming that he had pirated the enlarged *Dunciad*. For the accounts of these cases, see John Feather, *The Publishers and the Pirates: British Copyright Law in Theory and Practice, 1770-1775*, 22 PUBLISHING HISTORY 1, 1-32 (1987); Howard P. Vincent, *Some Dunciad Litigation*, 18 PHILOLOGICAL Q. 285, 285-89 (1939).

IV.

Let us turn now to the issues litigated in *Pope v. Curll* and to their resolution. Pope's bill of complaint begins by invoking the Statute of Anne and its provision for authors. He states that between 1714 and 1738 he wrote various letters to Swift and specifies by date twenty-nine, asserting himself to be the sole author and maintaining that, having never disposed of his copyright in the letters, he possesses the sole right to print or sell them. He states that during the same period he also received various letters from Swift, and again specifies twenty-nine by date, saying that he had hoped that neither those letters in which property had vested in him by virtue of being their author, nor those letters which were addressed and sent to him, would ever have been published without his consent. He charges Curll with knowingly conspiring with certain unnamed confederates to defraud him of his rights by publishing these letters and complains that he is without remedy at common law. He waives the penalties allowed by the statute but asks for a disclosure of all agreements made with respect to the book and an accounting of the profits, which are to be paid to himself. Any unsold copies are to be delivered to the court and disposed of as the court shall direct. Meanwhile, Curll and his associates are to be restrained by an injunction from any further sales.

Pope's bill of complaint was entered on 4 June 1741 and shortly thereafter the requested injunction was issued. Curll swore to his answer on 13 June and moved to dissolve the injunction. In his answer, Curll acknowledges the statute and admits printing five hundred copies of the book and selling sixteen, but makes three principal points in his defense. First, he argues, that since

> all the letters mentioned in the Complainants said Bill of Complaint were as this Defendant verily believes Actually sent & delivered by and to the several Persons by whom & to whom they severally Purport to have been written & Addressed . . . the Complainant is not to be Considered as the Author & proprietor of all or any of the said letters.[26]

Second, he raises the question of whether, in any case, familiar letters fall under the terms of the statute, saying that he is advised "that the said letters are not a work of that Nature & sole

---

[26] The phrase "Author & proprietor" is, I take it, to be understood in the conjunctive: Curll is certainly not denying that Pope actually wrote the letters that he sent to Swift but only that Pope can claim a property in them.

Right of printing whereof was Intended to be preserved by the said Statute to the Author." Third, he says that he has reprinted the letters in question from the Dublin edition printed by George Faulkner under the direction, as he believes, of Dr. Swift, and it is his understanding that any book first published in Ireland may be lawfully reprinted in England.[27] In addition, Curll responds to particular assertions in Pope's complaint, denying that he has any direct knowledge of whether Pope is the sole author and proprietor of the letters or whether Pope ever disposed of whatever rights in the letters he might have had. Curll denies that he has made any agreements with anyone regarding the book except with his printer, and points out that the part of the published book to which Pope is laying claim amounts to only one-fifth of the whole. Curll therefore asserts that he has done nothing illegal in publishing the book and maintains that Pope is not entitled to an account of his profits.

Lord Chancellor Hardwicke's decision, handed down on 17 June 1741, addresses the principal points made by Curll in his defense. The first question, he says, is whether letters, not being intended for publication, fall within the framework of the statute, the purpose of which was defined, we recall, as the encouragement of learning. Hardwicke cites as a parallel the instance of sermons, "which the author may never intend should be published, but are collected from loose papers, and brought out after his death,"[28] and rules in the affirmative, stating that "it would be extremely mischievous[] to make a distinction between a book of letters, which comes out into the world, either by the permission of the writer, or the receiver of them, and any other learned work."[29] In response to Curll's argument that an author is no longer to be considered the owner of a letter if it has actually been sent—or, as Hardwicke summarizes the point, "that where a man writes a letter, it is in the nature of a gift to the receiver"[30]— Hardwicke again overrules the objection, by making a distinction between the physical letter and the copyright:

> I am of opinion that it is only a special property in the receiver, possibly the property of the paper may belong to him; but this does not give a licence to any person whatsoever to publish

---

[27] In fact Curll used Pope's own edition as copytext. Rogers observes that Pope probably did not realize this because it might have been an effective point to make in court. Rogers, *supra* note 2, at 329.

[28] Pope v. Curll, 2 Atk. 342, 26 Eng. Rep. 608 (Ch. 1741).

[29] *Id.*

[30] *Id.*

them to the world, for at most the receiver has only a joint property with the writer.[31]

As to whether a book originally printed in Ireland, where the statute did not reach, was a "lawful prize," Hardwicke points out that any affirmative would have pernicious consequences, for it would establish an easy way for booksellers to evade the statute by sending books over to Ireland to be printed first. Finally, returning to the initial matter of whether the contested material falls under the statute, Hardwicke notes that the defendant's counsel insisted that the exchange of letters between Swift and Pope "does not come within the meaning of the act of Parliament, because it contains only letters on familiar subjects, and inquiries after the health of friends, and cannot properly be called a learned work."[32] Again, Harwicke decides in the affirmative:

> It is certain that no works have done more service to mankind, than those which have appeared in this shape, upon familiar subjects, and which perhaps were never intended to be published; and it is this makes them so valuable; for I must confess for my own part, that letters which are very elaborately written, and originally intended for the press, are generally the most insignificant, and very little worth any person's reading.[33]

On the basis of his judgment that familiar letters do indeed fall under the statute, together with his distinction between the receiver's tangible property in the physical letter and the writer's intangible property in his copyright, Hardwicke rules that the injunction be continued, but "only as to those letters, which are under Mr. *Pope*'s name in the book, and which are written *by him*, and not as to those which are written *to him*."[34]

Hardwicke's decision on the question of Irish publication is comparatively straightforward and requires little comment. More interesting is his decision on the question of whether the Swift-Pope letters fell under the terms of the statute. What we should observe here is that the issue in the case led to a circumstance in which a legal question—were letters on familiar subjects protected?—required a judge to make a literary critical proclamation from the bench. If there was to be a statute protecting cer-

---

[31] *Id.*
[32] *Id.*
[33] *Id.*
[34] *Id.*

tain kinds of writings—those that contributed to the advancement of learning—then judges would perforce find themselves, like Hardwicke, making pronouncements on generic matters and on literary value. Hardwicke's judgment is rendered in the somewhat pompous language of refined taste, but the issue is nevertheless also one of commercial value. Under the aegis of the statute, literary and legal questions converged in such a way that significant sums of money might depend upon whether a particular kind of text was deemed "worth protecting" and admitted to the privileged category. Two senses of value—the literary and the commercial—were becoming entangled.

Perhaps the most interesting aspect of Hardwicke's ruling was his distinction between the receiver's special property in the physical letter and the writer's property in the copyright. The Statute of Anne, let us note, prescribed specific and concrete penalties for the invasion of literary property. It provided that all offending books were to be forfeited to the rightful proprietors of the copy to be destroyed, and furthermore that every offender was to forfeit one penny for every offending sheet found in his custody. Precisely what kind of property, tangible or intangible, Parliament supposed it was protecting in the statute is unclear, for in all likelihood such metaphysical questions about the nature of literary property never occurred to the legislators. As Benjamin Kaplan has remarked, the draftsman of the statute was "thinking as a printer would—of a book as a physical entity; of rights in it and offenses against it as related to 'printing and reprinting' the thing itself."[35] So, too, the defendant's counsel was thinking of a letter as a physical entity, an object which once "[a]ctually sent & delivered"[36] passed wholly to the recipient. Hardwicke's judgment, however, involved an important and novel abstraction of the notion of literary property from its material basis in ink and paper.

It is perhaps significant that in the years immediately preceding Hardwicke's decision, the new term "copyright" first came into general use. Indeed, appropriately enough, one of the earliest recorded uses of "copyright" occurs in a letter written by Pope to John Gay in 1732, in which Pope speaks of the bookseller Benjamin Motte together with some other "idle fellow" having

---

[35] BENJAMIN KAPLAN, AN UNHURRIED VIEW OF COPYRIGHT 9 (1967).
[36] Answer to Plaintiff's Complaint, Pope v. Curll, 2 Atk. 342, 26 Eng. Rep. 608 (Ch. 1741) (No. C11/1569/29) (on file with London Public Records Office).

written to Swift "to get him to give them some Copyright."[37]
The old stationers' term, "copy," was related to the use of copy
as the term for an original manuscript from which copies were
made. Thus, it retained some feeling for "copy" as a material
object, the manuscript on which the printed edition was based.
The new term "copyright" suggests an attenuation of this sense
of the material basis of the property. Its appearance at this moment is worth noting in the context of Hardwicke's decision,
where the author's words have now, in effect, flown free from the
page on which they are written. Not ink and paper, but pure
signs, separated from any material support, have become the
protected property.

V.   The Development of Intellectual Property

When they entered titles in the Stationers' Register, the English booksellers of the sixteenth and seventeenth centuries spoke
of "their copies" and "their books," but they could not really be
called owners of the texts in the absolute sense of property articulated for the marketplace society by John Locke. Rather the
stationers of the old order were participating, as guildsmen of
various kinds had done for hundreds of years, in a community
defined in terms of reciprocal rights and responsibilities. When
disputes between stationers arose, they were settled by the guild
court, which generally tried to arrange compromises rather than
lay down principles. Now that a statute was on the books, however, the need for the interpretation and articulation of principles
would inevitably arise. Furthermore, with the shift in jurisdiction
from the guild to the public courts, literary property would be
treated like any other form of private property, which was, after
all, what the courts were most familiar with. But in order to do
this, a new and abstract concept of precisely what an author
owned would have to be constructed. We can see this process at
work in Hardwicke's decision. We should observe, however, that
Hardwicke's judgment on this matter is couched in cautious language: "possibly the property of the paper" may belong to the
receiver, who "at most" has "only a joint property with the
writer."[38] The tentativeness with which Hardwicke proposes the
distinction between the receiver's tangible property and the author's intangible property is to be attributed, no doubt, to the

---

[37] Letters From John Gay to Jonathan Swift, 28 August 1732, *in* 4 The Correspondence of Jonathan Swift 64, 64-65 (1963-5) (quoting Letter from Pope to Gay).
[38] Pope v. Curll, 2 Atk. 342, 26 Eng. Rep. 608 (Ch. 1741).

fact that the notion of copyright as a wholly intangible property was still at this point novel and the theory of a property that inheres in words alone had not yet been worked out.

Could a text—as distinguished from a book—be a property? Did authors really have a "property" in their works, entitling them to general relief at common law, or did the statute merely grant them an exclusive privilege, a limited monopoly with penalties to give it force? In 1743, two years after the decision in *Pope v. Curll* and a year before Pope's death, a group of seventeen London booksellers, invoking the Statute of Anne, initiated a suit in the Scottish Court of Session against a group of twenty-four booksellers from Edinburgh and Glasgow that addressed these questions.[39] It was in the context of this long drawn out case that in 1747 William Warburton, Pope's friend and literary executor, published his *Letter from an Author Concerning Literary Property*, which provided the earliest theorization of copyright as a wholly intangible property.[40]

At the heart of Warburton's *Letter* is an analysis of the nature of property, designed to demonstrate that a text can indeed be property. Property, he says, can be divided into two classes— movables and immovables. Movable properties can in turn be divided into those that are natural and those that are artificially made. Artificially produced movables can be further divided into products of the hand and products of the mind, for example, "an *Utensil* made; a *Book* composed."

> For that the Product of the *Mind* is as well capable of becoming Property, as that of the *Hand*, is evident from hence, that it hath in it those two essential Conditions, which, by the allowance of all Writers of Laws, make Things susceptible of Property; namely common *Utility*, and a Capacity of having its Possession *ascertained*.[41]

We should note that Warburton never actually demonstrates that literary property has "a Capacity of having its Possession *ascertained*." This point, however, might be lost in the smooth development of his analysis, which, proceeding by progressive division into familiar binary oppositions (movable/immovable,

---

[39] For the fullest report of this complex case, known variously as *Booksellers of London v. Booksellers of Edinburgh and Glasgow* or *Midwinter v. Hamilton* or *Midwinter v. Kinkaid* or *Millar v. Kinkaid*, see LORD HENRY HOME KAMES, REMARKABLE DECISIONS OF THE COURT OF SESSION 154-61 (1766).

[40] WILLIAM WARBURTON, A LETTER FROM AN AUTHOR CONCERNING LITERARY PROPERTY (1747).

[41] *Id.* at 7.

artificial/natural, body/mind), makes the notion of intellectual property seem natural and inevitable.

What was the nature of the author's property? According to Warburton, property that was the product of the hand was "confined to the individual Thing made."[42] Like the instrument of its creation, the property was wholly material. "But, in the other Case of Property in the Product of the Mind, as in a *Book* composed, it is not confined to the Original MS. but extends to the *Doctrine* contained in it: Which is, indeed, the true and peculiar Property in a Book."[43]

Thus, the essence of the author's property was wholly immaterial, consisting solely of the "doctrine" or ideas that were the product of his mental labor. Six years earlier, Lord Chancellor Hardwicke had tentatively distinguished between the receiver's property right in the material basis of a letter and the author's property right in the words. Now, in Warburton's *Letter*, the notion of a property in pure signs, abstracted from any material support, was being systematically developed and promulgated.

The clincher in Warburton's argument was his distinction between literary property and patents. Warburton was arguing that since copyrights were property rights and not merely privileges, literary properties, unlike patents, were perpetual. But why should an author's rights be treated any differently from the rights that an inventor might have in a new and useful machine? Warburton's approach was to demonstrate that inventions were of a mixed nature, partaking of the characteristics of both manual and mental products. Thus, insofar as a machine was a kind of utensil, it was appropriate that the maker's property be located in the individual material object and be perpetual. Nevertheless, because the operation of the mind was so intimately concerned in inventions, it was appropriate to extend to inventors a patent that reached beyond the individual material object, but only for a limited term of years. Thus, patent protection was a special category of limited rights designed to accommodate the mixed nature of mechanical inventions, as distinguished from the purely intellectual nature of literary compositions. Rhetorically, then, the introduction of this third, mixed, category of property situated between products of the hand and products of the mind helped to confirm the idea of literary property as wholly immaterial.

The year after Warburton's *Letter* appeared, the Court of

---

[42] *Id.*
[43] *Id.* at 7-8.

Sessions issued a decision that in effect denied that a text could be a property. But the legal debate over the nature of literary property was just beginning. Warburton's theorization of copyright was to influence William Blackstone, who, when arguing for the plaintiff in *Tonson v. Collins*,[44] a suit between two booksellers over the right to print the *Spectator*, developed the notion of copyright still further. As Blackstone stated:

> "[A] literary composition, as it lies in the author's mind, before it is substantiated by reducing it into writing," has the essential requisites to make it the subject of property. While it thus lies dormant in the mind, it is absolutely in the power of the proprietor. He alone is entitled to the profits of communicating, or making it public. The first step to which is clothing our conceptions in words, the only means to communicate abstracted ideas.[45]

Words might be either spoken or written, Blackstone continued, but in any case the words were merely the vehicles of the author's sentiments. "The sentiment therefore is the thing of value, from which the profit must arise."[46]

Arguing for the defendant in *Tonson*, Joseph Yates accepted the principle "that the author has a property in his sentiments till he publishes them."[47] But Yates insisted that from the moment of publication the author's ideas ceased to be private property, and cited the limited protection afforded inventors under patent law as a parallel. In reply, Blackstone invoked Warburton's *Letter* on the difference between mechanical inventions and literary compositions, and reaffirmed the immaterial nature of literary property: "Style and sentiment are the essentials of a literary composition. These [elements] alone constitute its identity. The paper and print are merely accidents, which serve as vehicles to convey that style and sentiment to a distance."[48] Six years later in the second volume of his *Commentaries*, Blackstone refined the formulation he had made in *Tonson*. He discussed copyright as a species of property and insisted that, whatever might be the material method of conveying a text from one person to another, the identity of the composition itself "consists entirely in the *sentiment* and the *language*; the same conceptions, cloathed in the

---

[44] 1 Black. W. 301, 96 Eng. Rep. 169 (K.B. 1760), *reargued and dismissed*, 1 Black. W. 322, 96 Eng. Rep. 180 (K.B. 1761).

[45] *Id.* at 322-23, 96 Eng. Rep. at 180-81.

[46] *Id.* at 323-24, 96 Eng. Rep. at 181.

[47] *Id.* at 333, 96 Eng. Rep. at 185.

[48] *Id.* at 343, 96 Eng. Rep. at 189.

same words, must necessarily be the same composition."[49]

We should note that in the process of developing Warburton's theory of copyright—and under pressure from Yates's rejection of the notion that ideas might remain property once published—Blackstone significantly shifted the conception of literary property from Warburton's "doctrine" or his own equivalent "sentiments" to the conception of the essence of the property as a fusion of idea and language: "[T]he same conceptions, cloathed in the same words." Not ideas alone, but the expression of ideas: this, to put Blackstone's point in the familiar modern form which it anticipates, was what copyright protected. What was the nature of literary property as Blackstone formulated it? Paper and print—the material basis of publication— were to be regarded merely as "accidents." The bearer of meaning through which the writer's ideas were realized was language. Clothed in words, which Blackstone treated as if they were a kind of substance, the writer's sentiments became property. In the early modern period, it was, as I have noted, usual to think of a text as an action, as something done. Now, in the context of the developing marketplace society, the text was being represented as a kind of thing.

Warburton and Blackstone were arguing the case for copyright to be regarded as a common law property right and thus for copyright to be perpetual. The debate over this issue continued until 1774 when perpetual copyright was rejected by the House of Lords. But even though the claim for perpetual copyright was finally rejected, their representation of literary property—a representation that may be understood as an exposition of Lord Chancellor Hardwicke's opinion on the question of the ownership of letters—as essentially immaterial, endured and of course endures to this day.

Pope v. Curll, then, represents a significant transitional episode both in the history of authorship and in the conception of literary property. Pope himself is of course fascinating as a transitional figure: on the one hand, the last of the great poets in the Renaissance tradition and, as such, the courtly transmitter of received wisdom and the jealous guardian of his own and others' honor; on the other hand, the first of the moderns and, as such, a professional who was immersed in the production and exploitation of literary commodities and the jealous guardian of his finan-

---

[49] 2 WILLIAM BLACKSTONE, COMMENTARIES ON THE LAWS OF ENGLAND 406 (9th ed. 1978).

cial interests. And the case, with its complex blending and enfolding of motives and its fascinating dissolving of matters of propriety into matters of property, refracts both the peculiar nature of its eminent plaintiff and the earliness of its moment in the history of the author as a legally enfranchised figure.

Hardwicke's decision in *Pope v. Curll* has gone down in legal history as establishing that letters are subject to copyright and that an author has the right to withhold his texts from publication if he chooses. But perhaps even more fundamental than the ruling about letters coming under the statute was the distinction that Hardwicke drew between the receiver's property in the paper and the writer's property in the words, for in this moment the concept of literary property as a wholly immaterial property in a text might be said to have been born.

AUTHORITY AND AUTHENTICITY:
SCRIBBLING AUTHORS AND THE GENIUS
OF PRINT IN EIGHTEENTH-CENTURY
ENGLAND

MARLON B. ROSS*

I. INTRODUCTION

What qualifies a writer—one who writes out words—to be considered an author, one whose words demand attention? The answer to this question may seem self-evident, in that someone who writes but does not gain attention for what is written can hardly be called an author. The scribblings of a writer will remain locked up in a manuscript, somewhere in an attic, awaiting a dialogue with a public that does not exist. This conception of authorship that differentiates between the scribbling writer, who is locked in the experience within the self, and the author, who traverses the gulf between self and other, assumes and claims that we can transmit, and thus transmute, our experience of knowledge, by transporting that knowledge to a public space where experience itself is knowable, shareable, and answerable.

At first glance, this difference between scribbling writer and authentic author appears to be an intellectual, or more specifically a cognitive, distinction. As we think more clearly about it, however, it turns out to be a sociohistorical distinction, based on the technology of invention and the politics of intervention.[1] Early eighteenth-century writers, or should we say "authors," used the word "scribbler" to indicate the intrinsically wayward nature of producing script. To scribble is to make marks in a carefree or careless manner; usually illegible marks that are also

---

* Associate Professor of English Language and Literature, University of Michigan, Ann Arbor. Ph.D., 1983, University of Chicago.
[1] See Martha Woodmansee, *The Genius and the Copyright: Economic and Legal Conditions of the Emergence of the "Author,"* 17 EIGHTEENTH-CENTURY STUD. 425 (1984). In this influential essay, Martha Woodmansee traces the historical origins of modern authorship to a group of eighteenth-century English and German writers. In an attempt to make writing into a profitable profession, these writers justified a writer's "work" as property whose value is based on originality and whose profits belong to the author, rather than to printers and booksellers. By analyzing the legal battle that ensued in eighteenth-century England over copyright, Mark Rose builds on Woodmansee's study and explains "the way in its sometimes very abstruse course the modern system of the author and the 'work'. . . was institutionalized in the discourse of the law." Mark Rose, *The Author as Proprietor:* Donaldson v Becket *and the Genealogy of Modern Authorship*, REPRESENTATIONS, Summer 1988, at 51, 58-59.

unintelligible except to the mark maker in the moment of marking. The script will mean little to someone else or even to the scribbler at some future moment. With writing—that is, handwriting or manuscript—there is always a question of intelligibility foremost at the level of mere readability. The scribbling must be readable before it can be meaningful and meaningful before it can be significant. Handwriting or manuscript seems closer to the eccentricity of the individual whose steady or unsteady hand traces the marks. Manuscript would seem to bear the marks of the soul within itself, for the hand that scripts the text marks the frailty of all flesh in the very materiality of the text.

II.   The Derivation of Authority From Scribal Handwriting

When the medieval monks make handwriting into an art, they attempt to tame and to train this waywardness at the soul of scribbling. The legibility, the readable uniformity of their scribbling acknowledges that handwriting is a technology invented to stabilize meaning. This uniformity also asserts the intervention of divinity in transubstantiating mere material marks on a page into fully significant meanings that bear the weight of God's authority.

The texts that medieval scribes copy are often, though not always, sacred texts. But the mere act of copying these texts into manuscript confirms their status as authentic, universal, eternal authorities. The word "scribe" itself is used to translate the Hebrew concept of one who is an authority on the Jewish law, and the etymology of the word "scripture," holy text, takes us back to the same root in the Latin word meaning "to write." The correlation between scripting, or making a mark, and "scripturing," or making a holy mark, is hardly coincidental. As an etymological offshoot or byway of "to script," "to scribble"—that is, to make little marks carelessly—always threatens to divert us from the straight and narrow path that leads from script to scripture, from writing to authority. A monk should refuse to copy any scribbling that is not worthy of reproduction, preservation, and distribution. The art of making writing legible, then, is also a political act; the act of claiming or declaiming a culture's authorities. Any eccentricity in the script that distracts from the ability to read the writing also detracts from the centrality of the text, from the sanctity of its authoritative position, and threatens to degenerate into sinfully selfish scribbling. The script must be seen to author itself, for the scribe is merely a vehicular authority, a translator or medium of authority.

Elizabeth Eisenstein points out how difficult it is to assess authoritatively the habits of preprint and manuscript culture,[2] for that culture relies heavily on habits that were radically changed by the invention of print, while print itself enabled modes of knowing that were not available to scholars in preprint culture:

> Thus constant access to printed materials is a prerequisite for the practice of the historian's own craft. It is difficult to observe processes that enter so intimately into our own observations. In order to assess changes ushered in by printing, for example, we need to survey the conditions that prevailed before its advent. Yet the conditions of scribal culture can only be observed through a veil of print.[3]

I would hazard a hypothesis that given the ephemerality of unwritten words, even in a culture where memory might give a more intense life to what is spoken to be remembered, the handwritten word gains even more solidity as a source of authority.

Though it helps to make the word appear permanent, scribal solidity guarantees neither readability nor reliability. Eisenstein writes, "For the very texture of scribal culture was so fluctuating, uneven and multiform that few long-range trends can be traced . . . . Yet all library collections were subject to contraction, and all texts in manuscript were liable to get corrupted after being copied over the course of time."[4] Moving from word to script, or at best from script to word to script, the medieval scribe was certainly prone to error, and yet such error does not unsettle the system of textual authoritativeness that guides him faithfully, if not accurately, to copy holy script. When mid-eighteenth-century antiquarians look backward to this preprint culture, their task of historical reconstruction is aided, rather than hindered, by the "fluctuating, uneven and multiform" nature of the unprinted past.[5] The scholarly caution that Eisenstein practices, which lends authoritativeness to her monumental history, would only be a hindrance to eighteenth-century antiquarians who are themselves ushering in the age of historical anthropology. In other words, like the medieval scribe, the Enlightenment antiquarian must reconstruct full, authoritative meaning from methodically

---

2 *See* 1 Elizabeth Eisenstein, The Printing Press As An Agent of Change 8 (1979).
3 *Id.*
4 *Id.* at 10.
5 *Id.*

errant material artifacts. His capacity to do so is enhanced, perhaps even enabled, by a blindness to the inherent unreliability of
the method of reconstruction available to him. As we shall see
below in the cases of Thomas Chatterton and Horace Walpole,
the antiquarian relies on an absence of genuine knowledge about
the past he studies in order to construct a field of real knowledge
about that past.

As early eighteenth-century writers realized with profound
regret, it is impossible to purge the waywardness at the soul of
script; a waywardness that always diverts the bold power of script
into the diminished emasculation of scribbling. Even the authority of God cannot prevent the frailty of flesh that tempts a scribe
to miscopy his text. This waywardness lives in the manuscript of
the medieval scribe not only as the inherent errancy of miscopy-
ing, but also in the form of artful embellishment. From the view-
point of the medieval scholar, the soul of the text is its legibly
copied script; the body is its eccentric dress—the lavish decora-
tion of the scribe—just as the soul of the written word is its sacred unutterable meaning and the word itself merely the
embodiment of that meaning. Of course, that it is a monk who
does the copying contributes to the aura of authority that emanates from the script. It is the technology of handwriting itself,
however, that serves as the vehicle for this aura. Without the uniform script, and without the embellishment which constantly reminds the reader of the difference between soul and body,
between substance and instance, between public authority and
private apprehension of that authority, the manuscript would
lose its claim to our attention, respect, awe, and obedience.

Scribal embellishment is intrinsically artful, in that its aesthetic achievement is both illusory and artificial. While intending
to suggest that the monk's labor is produced solely for the glory
of God, embellishment duplicitously also enacts a tendency toward scribbling. This tendency brings attention to the prideful
self with its intrinsically fallible apprehension of divine authority
and its constant yearning to claim God's authority as its own.
Truth needs art only when it attempts to manifest itself in material form. Thus, authoritative knowledge is always artfully displayed because true knowledge is always tainted when touched
by human desire and perceived through human vision. Therefore, the scribe's unpaid labor for the profit of salvation contains
within itself the tendency to degenerate into paid labor for mere
profit, whether it be worldly fame or monetary gain.

III. THE INVENTION OF PRINT AND THE DEGRADATION OF NON-POSSESSIBLE KNOWLEDGE

As the extension of manuscript, the invention of print solidifies and intensifies the difference between the eccentric scribbling of individual experience and the shareable knowledge of identifiable authorities, and ironically creates even greater ambivalence about copying truth into text. But this does not happen overnight. As Walter Ong has noted, "Well after printing was developed, auditory processing continued for some time to dominate the visible, printed text, though it was eventually eroded away by print."[6] According to Ong,

> Print was a major factor in the development of the sense of personal privacy that marks modern society . . . . By removing words from the world of sound where they first had their origin in active human interchange and relegating them definitively to visual space, and by otherwise exploiting visual space for the management of knowledge, print encouraged human beings to think of their own interior conscious and unconscious resources as more and more thing-like, impersonal and religiously neutral. Print encouraged the mind to sense that its possessions were held in some sort of inert mental space.[7]

In fact, we could say that print gradually seduced the mind into thinking of mental experience in terms of individual possession. The medieval monk or scholar tended to conceptualize knowledge as that which was common to a culture; that which could be known and therefore certified by common culture. Knowledge could possess properties: it could be subtle or unsubtle, divine or secular, classical or Christian, refined or vulgar. And the origins of knowledge were attributable to identifiable sources such as Aristotle, Augustine, the pagans, and divine revelation. But knowledge itself was not property. Authority, in this sense, is always proper, always an order of truth gleaned by some individuals perhaps better than by some others, but not possessed solely by any individual. For an individual alone to possess such knowledge would make it purely private knowledge, purely private truth, a blatant self-contradiction. Possessible authority, on the other hand, is conceptualized as a personal acquisition, which the individual mind has earned as a result of knowledge or experience created by the individual as a private being.

---

[6] WALTER ONG, ORALITY AND LITERACY: THE TECHNOLOGIZING OF THE WORD 120 (1982).

[7] *Id.* at 130-32.

We could trace the emergence of possessive authority as far back as the twelfth century, keeping in mind the inherent duplicity always alive within scribal labor. As Eisenstein writes,

> With the so-called "book revolution" of the twelfth century and university supervision of copying, there came a "putting-out" system. Copyists were no longer assembled in a single room, but worked on different portions of a given text, receiving payment from the stationer for each piece . . . . The contrast between the free labor of monks working for remission of sins and the wage labor of lay copyists is an important one.[8]

Through a sort of guilt by association, we can see how wage labor might metonymically become associated with the capacity to possess the knowledge which is the source and aim of the labor. We can also envision how the "employer" of copyists might become a metonym for the owner of the knowledge and thus of the authority supposedly contained within the text. But this very indirect metonymy could not fully diminish the ideological constraints under which the early university scholar employs and the copyist labors. If knowledge is that which is worth knowing, and therefore worth teaching in a medieval university, and if all worthy knowledge is an extension of God's truth, then the university scholar is an ideological extension of the monk, and the texts he has copied are likewise such an extension. For the scholar to claim that the knowledge he gleans is solely his own, he would have to deny implicitly the ultimate source of all worthy knowledge outside the fallen flesh. He would have to deny that authority derives only from within the mind of God as mediated by the communal authority of the church. As the church begins to lose its authority during the Reformation, we realize what kind of consequences such a challenge to communitarian knowledge could bring to the secularizing scholar. Knowledge is by definition communal, just as authority is by definition external and resistant to privatization; all experiences that derive merely from the self are diversions and deceptions.

At first, uniform script is the effect of authority, not the cause of it. But as print gains ascendancy, this relation is reversed. Originally, to be an authority is to be scripted. But with time, to be printed is to be an authority. Early eighteenth-century writers are caught in the swivel moment of this process of reversal, not only when print begins to give the stamp of authority, but also

---

[8] EISENSTEIN, *supra* note 2, at 12-13.

when authority begins to become fragmented by the posses-sibility of private knowledge. For these writers, scribbling is both positive and negative, both necessary and impossible. It is posi-tive in the sense that writing in general is considered a positive activity. To scribble is to make a mark on the world that ties the private mind to public realities in a literally tangible way. Scrib-bling, in this positive sense, indicates how writing is a marginally central activity. It is what we must do in order to make sense of ourselves and of our world, but it should be done only in those moments of leisure, while reflecting on the central business of managing life, and should be done only by those who are leisured, those in the leisured class who have no other pressing obligations.[9]

On the other hand, scribbling is temporary madness. It rep-resents yielding to the temptation of individual whims at the ex-pense of commonsense understanding. In this negative sense, the scribbler is always self-deluded. Likewise, he is always delud-ing his audience by encouraging them to think that they can find truth in the nervously profuse markings that derive from the anx-ieties of their individual experience, rather than from the sane consensus of externally vested cultural authorities. The scribbler is the careless writer who claims cultural authority over his read-ers merely by virtue of the fact that he has written; that his scrib-blings have been scripted, that his script is made overly and overtly legible through the technology of print. Wouldn't it be better if this scribbler's quirks had remained in his own head, or at least in his own handwriting? At least then we would not for-get that these words come from the eccentric pride of a self-de-luded pretender to authority. At least then we would be less prone to confuse the false authority of that which commands our attention because it is accessibly legible, with the authentic au-thority of that which is printed because it commands our attention.

---

9 See MARLON B. ROSS, CONTOURS OF MASCULINE DESIRE: ROMANTICISM AND THE RISE OF WOMEN'S POETRY 57-68 (1989). Though leisured reading and writing were no doubt markers of status in the premodern period, they were not conceived as Arnoldian cul-tural obligations. Renaissance writers and readers approached texts as unfixed, variable artifacts that were to be engaged with, compiled and rewritten according to the instruc-tion of the reader's pleasure, rather than according to some notion of authorial authority emanating from an individually authorized text. See Coburn Freer, "Changing Concepts of Literary Ownership in the English Renaissance" (Apr. 1991) (unpublished manu-script, presented at the "Intellectual Property and the Construction of Authorship" con-ference); Max W. Thomas, Reading and Writing the Renaissance Commonplace Book: Question of Authorship?, 10 CARDOZO ARTS & ENT. L.J. 665 (1992).

IV. POSITIVE AND NEGATIVE SCRIBBLING: THE PROBLEMS OF DISTINCTION ILLUSTRATED IN *THE DUNCIAD*

The members of the early eighteenth-century Scriblerus Club joined together in order to protect themselves from the negative consequences of scribbling by scribbling in the positive sense. The Scriblerians, fearful of losing the cultural distinction between positive and negative scribbling, between the writer and the author, between false authority and authentic authority, set out to keep this distinction in tact. Whatever eccentricities may nervously twitch in their individual voices can be smoothed over by the give-and-take of group dynamics, from the consensus that naturally arises from communal efforts.[10] Through their communal scribbling, the Scriblerians can more easily claim that they together represent a continuous tradition of authority, recognizable, intelligible, and sustainable. Pope's *The Dunciad*[11] enunciates, on the one hand, the authorialness and authoritativeness of consensus that results from being able to make a distinction between forms of scribbling. On the other hand, it slips endlessly down that hill of ever-intensifying differentiation, a process whereby differences multiply upon differences until false scribbling and authentic scribbling are identically different, and all authority is falsely scripted.

We are confronted with this lucid contradiction on the very first page of *The Dunciad*. "The Dunciad IN FOUR BOOKS / PRINTED ACCORDING TO THE COMPLETE COPY FOUND IN THE YEAR 1742 WITH THE PROLEGOMENA OF SCRIBLERUS, AND NOTES VARIORUM / To which are added / SEVERAL NOTES NOW FIRST PUBLISH'D, THE HYPERCRITICS OF ARISTARCHUS, AND HIS DISSERTATION ON

---

[10] The dialectic at work between communitarian authority and authority as individual possession in the eighteenth century has a variety of cultural sources and consequences too numerous and complex to trace here. I do not want to suggest, however, that the ideological implications of communitarian authority are necessarily conservative. Throughout the eighteenth and nineteenth centuries, communal authority/authorship is exploited by marginal groups seeking greater sociopolitical power, as well as greater power of individual conscience, initiative, and inventiveness. This was especially true among middle-class religious dissenters in Britain, who formed such groups as the Lunar Society, the Society for Constitutional Information, and the many corresponding societies. Although these groups tend to conceptualize authority as radically individuated and possessible, they also envision a culture in which access to knowledge is mediated by a community of interested seekers after unmediated truth. An interesting analogue to such groups is the nineteenth-century women's clubs described in Anne Ruggles Gere, *Common Properties of Pleasure: Texts in Nineteenth Century Women's Clubs*, 10 CARDOZO ARTS & ENT. L.J. 647 (1992).

[11] ALEXANDER POPE, *The Dunciad*, in POEMS OF ALEXANDER POPE 709 (John Butt ed., 1963).

THE HERO OF THE POEM."[12] Of course, the 1729 edition of *The Dunciad* had also claimed or promised to be "a much more correct and compleat copy . . . than has hitherto appeared."[13] This promise of completeness is immediately countered by the hordes of prefaces, commentaries, notes, addenda, and appendices which weigh down the text, and which suggest that the obsessive process of revision is unceasing. With each new individual, claiming, from the quirkiness of his own little perspective, to have the final word, claiming to have the definitive view, claiming a direct line of descent from ultimate authority, the text becomes both larger, "more complete," and smaller, trivialized by the weight of undistinguished and nondistinguishable authorities. The text becomes a compendium of error, reminiscent of the famous lines about humanity itself in *Epistle II of Essay on Man*:

> Born but to die, and reas'ning but to err;
> Alike in ignorance, his reason such,
> Whether he thinks too little, or too much:
> Chaos of Thought and Passion, all confus'd;
> Still by himself abus'd, or disabus'd;
> Created half to rise, and half to fall;
> Great lord of all things, yet a prey to all;
> Sole judge of Truth, in endless Error hurl'd:
> The glory, jest, and riddle of the world![14]

By the end of *Essay on Man*, this mass of confusion and error has been proven a harmony of means and ends, knowable only by God, but intuitable by the good, sane, and skilled poet. Otherwise, Pope himself would not be able to give us a glimpse of this harmony. Theoretically, the poet's authority does not come from taking God's perspective—though in actuality Pope himself cannot help but do so in the poem—but instead from scanning humanity itself: "Know then thyself, presume not God to scan;/The proper study of Mankind is Man."[15] The obvious paradox is that Man cannot know Mankind's position, unless his eyes take him above and below that position. To look above or below our status is to vacate the only position of authority that we are collectively competent to hold. But in order to know our position, we have no choice but to vacate that position. The authentic authority of the eighteenth-century author hinges precariously—one

---

[12] *Id.*

[13] ALEXANDER POPE, *The Dunciad, in* THE POEMS OF ALEXANDER POPE, 317 (1729).

[14] ALEXANDER POPE, *An Essay On Man: Epistle II, in* THE POEMS OF ALEXANDER POPE, *supra* note 11, at 516.

[15] *Id.*

might even say vacuously—on this intrinsically self-vacating stance.

The Dunciad is harassed by this fear that authority is but the presumption of human error, that real authority is merely a vacuous metaphysical status in a chain of being that serves to enslave rather than to order humanity. *The Dunciad*, however, is assaulted by this obsessive fear without the final hope articulated by the self-contradictory paradoxes of the *Essay on Man*. Added to this fear of a self-vacating authority is an even more pronounced anxiety over self-vacating authority in relation to social status. From all sides, this authority is threatened with an energy as manic as that which claims that authority itself can be based on the social status of a scribbler. A genuine author needs time and resources to scribble. He needs to have history at his finger tips to avoid falling into the pit of eccentric auto-scribbling, writing out the anxieties of the private self as an automatic autobiographical reflex to the desire for attention. In addition, to access cultural knowledge (classical learning, the cabals that run the political establishment, court etiquette, the gossip of high society, the protocols of literary composition), an authentic author needs to have a stake in the operation and preservation of that knowledge. In *The Dunciad*, we discover, however, that to be on the inside of culture, shaping its contours, is to be shaped by the meanest displays of cultural presumptuousness. To be in the know is to come to know all of the peevish jealousies, ambitions, pretensions, and dissensions that drive the highest ranks of a society to sustain their power over culture.

By the end of *The Dunciad*, we are intensely aware that this found text is as incomplete as ever, not only in that there are literally pieces missing from it, but also in that the poem's closure leaves us thinking and feeling that the center cannot hold; Anarchy, and its attendant Error, rules. The anarchy of the text itself contributes to this sense. It is a heteroglossic poem, with many different voices speaking at once, or more accurately, many different scribblers vying for our attention and diverting us from any univocal authority which might be able to speak from a public, communal stance. The voice of authority, if it is found in the voices of those who represent that authority by virtue of their social status, appears here not lucid, univocal, and universal, but instead opaque, insular, and distressingly disputatious. The poem is preceded, however, with the stamp of authority, suggesting that it speaks from an univocal, unequivocal, hegemonic position. Following the seal of the Lord Chamberlain, this statement greets the reader:

> By virtue of the Authority in Us vested by the Act for subjecting Poets to the power of a Licenser, we have revised this Piece; where finding the style and appellation of KING to have been given to a certain Pretender, Pseudo-Poet, or Phantom, of the name of TIBBALD; and apprehending the same may be deemed in some sort a Reflection on Majesty, or at least an insult on that Legal Authority which has bestowed on another person the Crown of Poesy: We have ordered the said Pretender, Pseudo-Poet, or Phantom, utterly to vanish, and evaporate out of this work: And do declare the said Throne of Poesy from henceforth to be abdicated and vacant, unless duly and lawfully supplied by the LAUREATE himself. And it is hereby enacted, that no other person do presume to fill the same.[16]

Pope is satirizing the equivocal legal jargon whereby royal patents were granted to printers for a monopoly on the publication of certain texts and the pseudo-legal procedure whereby publishers had managed to take economic control over the administration of copyright through the Stationers' Company. The license granted here, however, is ironically the right of authors to revise their own production. Pope points to the ludicrousness of authorizing authors to produce, print, and distribute what they scribble, and the even more ludicrous idea of authorizing middle-class merchants, mere middling go-betweens, to fulfill this function for authors. Implicit in the rhetoric of *The Dunciad* is this constant upheaval, threatened by self-declared authors who impose their self-styled authority on the public. Even worse, the licensing laws and printing industry turn social status topsy-turvy, as genuine upper-class authors are expected to grovel before middle-class merchants and artisans in order to receive the stamp of state authority.[17]

---

[16] POPE, *supra* note 11, at 710.

[17] Like some other canonical writers of the late seventeenth and early eighteenth centuries, Pope displays intense ambivalence concerning the author's source of authority, whether that source derives from above or below. Yet to see the author as self-authorizing is in itself distressingly problematic for him. In Mark Rose, *The Author in Court*: Pope v. Curll, 10 CARDOZO ARTS & ENT. L.J. 475 (1992), the author stresses Pope's transitional status:

> On the one hand, the last of the great poets in the Renaissance tradition and, as such, the courtly transmitter of received wisdom and the jealous guardian of his own and others' honor; on the other hand, the first of the moderns and, as such, a professional who was immersed in the production and exploitation of literary commodities and the jealous guardian of his financial interests.

V. STATE AUTHORITY: LICENSING LAWS AND THE PRINTING PRESS

How is it that the author himself must be authorized? Is not the author by definition the authority who must authorize himself? The history of copyright was a history of control before it became a history of the individual's right to own what she or he created in words. As Annabel Patterson and Benjamin Moore have pointed out, the development of the modern conception of authorship is intimately linked to changing patterns of social control, rather than some sort of progress from monarchic state control to authorial individual freedom.[18] Just as medieval scribes developed the art of manuscript in order to perpetuate the authority vested in the church while diminishing the waywardness of fleshly threats to that authority, so the monarchic state developed the licensing system to control the authority that is transmitted through the medium of print. Writers may scribble in the privacy of their estates, but cannot become authorities unless authorized as such by the prerogative of the monarchy, representing the power of the state itself. As long as scribbling in private is an upper-class privilege which does not necessarily eventuate in print, the state's authority seems safe.

The problem is that print makes scribbling in private less desirable, while making print itself irresistible. Print enjoins others, in other classes, to be tempted by its irresistibility. And why not, since printing itself is a middle-class occupation? The problem for the state is that, unlike the manuscript, the printed text does not merely transmit the authority vested in it by the communal authority of the church and ultimately the external authority of God. The printed text acquires itself the imprimatur of authority, not only in that it can carry the royal stamp or the stamp of the Stationers' Company, but more importantly because print, even without these legal imprints, becomes the cause of authority. Once printed, the text possesses authority, and the writer,

---

Id. Milton is often referred to as the most prominent writer occupying this transitional juncture. *See* Peter Lindenbaum, *Milton's Contract*, 10 CARDOZO ARTS & ENT. L.J. 439 (1992).

   [18] *See* BENJAMIN MOORE, REFORMING AUTHORS: LITERARY PROPRIETORSHIP AND SOCIAL AUTHORITY IN EARLY MODERN ENGLAND, where the author provides the converse perspective from that of Woodmansee and Rose by viewing "authorship and publication as instruments of social control," emerging out of "the regulatory practices that were derived from royal proprietorship and directed at the threat of sedition," *id.* at 2; ANNABEL PATTERSON, CENSORSHIP AND INTERPRETATION: THE CONDITIONS OF WRITING AND READING IN EARLY MODERN ENGLAND (1984). *See* John Feather, *From Rights in Copies to Copyright: The Recognition of Authors' Rights in English Law and Practice in the Sixteenth and Seventeenth Centuries*, 10 CARDOZO ARTS & ENT. L.J. 455 (1992).

however lacking in knowledge or experience, becomes an author who possesses the authority imprinted in the text, whose words must be attended to because someone saw fit to print them. Ironically, the publicly accessible materiality of print encourages the privatization of possessible authority and the internalization of truth. The conspiracy between the printing press and the Reformation had already made this fact clear. Even the writer who has no claim to authority, or especially such a writer, in the eyes of the church or the state, must be attended to, in that he must be denounced. The more the state or church feels compelled to denounce such private authorities, the more they publicize the erosion of their own public authority.

A. *The Attack On State Authority: Pope and* The Dunciad

The ritual of poet laureate is an extension of the state's control of the writer's authority. The poet laureate's power to speak is granted literally by the state; his authority as a poet is reflected in his power to speak for the state; likewise, the power of the state is reflected in the power to authorize prophetically inspired writers when and how to speak. For Pope, the poet laureate is necessarily a "Pretender, Pseudo-Poet, or Phantom."[19] This is not because the power of the state is questionable, but rather because Pope wants to differentiate between legitimate state power and illegitimate authorial power, between the prerogative of the crown and the privilege of the author. By reducing state power—the whole range of cultural authority—to the existence or nonexistence of an actual stamp of authority, state authorities unintentionally reduce the question of authorial authority to the lowest level of either petty court politics or vulgar commercial economics. A poet laureate is not appointed for his skill as a writer, or for his authority as an author, but for his serviceability to the crown. By separating out the rites and rights of the author from the politics of authority, Pope seems to declare writers free from state manipulation and free to write what they please, according to their own inner light—a sort of writerly Reformation.

Of course, Pope is doing no such thing. In Pope's view, writers are neither free from state manipulation nor free to write what they please. Instead, in order to acquire authentic authority the writer must bind himself to an authoritative tradition and to the laws and rules that govern that tradition. Rather than being divorced from politics, the writer is wed to politics; a politics that

---

19 POPE, *supra* note 11, at 710.

emanates from the authority of the tradition from which the writer writes. There is a subtle difference between a state hireling, a Colley Cibber, whom Pope blasts in *The Dunciad*, and a genuine poet, who writes from a political position legitimated by the tradition which reflects his own voice. So subtle that it actually leaves the throne of authority vacated: "We have ordered the said Pretender, Pseudo-Poet, or Phantom, utterly to vanish, and evaporate out of this work: And do declare the said Throne of Poesy from henceforth to be abdicated and vacant . . . ."[20] If the state poet is always and necessarily a pretender, a phantom, occupying an illegitimate position of authority, then where does the authority of the author rest? If that authority cannot be licensed or granted directly from the power of the head of state, then who can license or grant it? If the author's authority cannot be mediated by the power of the state, then on what basis can any mediation of authority occur?

In banishing Lewis Theobald from the poem, Pope is enacting a ritual of authorial differentiation. Theobald easily becomes identifiable as a false authority; the pretender aiming for the crown. But, of course, Pope cannot banish Theobald from the poem, for Theobald is a phantom, an enemy who must be identified in order to claim the rightful authority of good poets. Once the throne is vacated, it must be reoccupied, whether by Colley Cibber or some other unsuspecting victim, for the only way Pope can assert the authority of the author is to denounce the constant usurpation of illegitimate authority by illegitimate heirs to the throne of poesy.

According to Peter Stallybrass and Allon White, Pope is attacking a sort of diversion or diminution of authorship through contamination with low culture at the very point when authorship is claiming its right as authority within high culture:

> The "crime" of Theobald, Cibber, Settle and others is the act of mediation: they occupy a taboo-laden space *between* the topographical boundaries which mark off the discrete sites of high and low culture. They transgress domains, moving between fair, theatre, town and court, threatening to sweep away the literary and social marks of difference at the very point where such differences are being widened.[21]

It is not social difference alone, however, that is at stake here;

---

[20] *Id.*

[21] PETER STALLYBRASS & ALLON WHITE, THE POLITICS AND POETICS OF TRANSGRESSION 113-14 (1986).

more fundamentally, it is authorial authority itself that is constituted both by the attacks on false authors and by the construction
of an empty, unmediated space, occupied only by phantom poets.

To emphasize authorial authority, Pope fills *The Dunciad* with
phantoms, shadows, and obscure allusions to half-forgotten per-
sonages. While there are many pretenders to the crown, no
rightful heirs exist, for any rightful heir would not need the
crown, and would not need state mediation. By proliferating his
satire with soon-to-be-forgotten pretenders, Pope reminds us
that genuine authority is never obscured by the years that intervene or the factious political intrigues that fall by the way. He
forces us to remember the names of those whom he wants forgotten, for those names become, in his authoritative rendering, exactly that; mere names, phantoms of voices, rather than real
voices that can command our attention.

In order to affect his satire, Pope also risks dimming his own
name into an ineffectual phantom. He risks becoming a pretender to the throne that he has declared intrinsically illegitimate
and inherently self-vacating. Literally, his name is blotted from
the authorial position. Pope becomes another name in the poem,
virtually exchangeable with those of the false poets and false authorities on poetry and politics. Martinus Scriblerus, the fictitious editor of and commentator on *The Dunciad*, takes over the
position of the real author, and numerous other commentators
and critics supplement the poetic text. All of these scribblers find
their way into print, claiming by virtue of being in print, that they
are authorities on that which they discourse.

B.   *The Effects of Print*

When print becomes the cause of authority rather than
merely its effect, what results is the compulsiveness of print.
Writers who scribble become automatically authors who are licensed to print, intensifying and proliferating the spiral of
pretenders to authorial authority. Ricardus Aristarchus, the
supercritic or hypercritic, must add his bid for authority to the
hyperactivity of the printed poem: "Of the Nature of *Dunciad* in
general," he scribbles, "whence derived, and on what authority
founded, as well as of the art and conduct of this our poem in
particular, the learned and laborious Scriblerus hath, according
to his manner, and with tolerable share of judgment, disser-
tated."[22] Aristarchus must comment on Scriblerus' comment on

---

[22] POPE, *supra* note 11, at 711.

the poem, calling into question Scriblerus' judgment, and implicitly his authority. The poem's communal authority is the tradition which authorizes it, "our" authority, the authority of the august members of the Scriblerus Club. The "our" in Aristarchus' words "our poem" becomes perversely communal, as one writer exploits the authority of another in order to establish his own. But isn't this the mirror image of Pope's own vision of authentic authority? Isn't the writer supposed to write out of an authoritative tradition that binds him to a network of principles that can be communally adhered to? It seems that the ideal of a community of voices speaking from a tradition of authority is itself easily warped by the hyperactivity of print, which enables anyone who can write to take a stab at joining this community.

The wonderful perversity of *The Dunciad* is exactly Pope's hyperawareness of this mirroring effect, a proliferation of mirrored phantoms. And typographically the poem mirrors this proliferation of phantoms. It hits the eye as a barrage of names, as a mob of notes appended by Pope to satirize these names, and appended by later, modern editors, who, in bringing light to all those forgotten names, satirize themselves just in the way Pope was satirizing his own phantoms. In the final book of *The Dunciad*, Pope addresses directly this tendency of poetic authority to desiccate into disputatious prose, the tendency of mighty authorities, like Aristotle, to waste into trivial allusions, becoming mere prosaic Aristarchuses, the tendency of authority itself to splinter into the factiousness of printed words and dead letters:

> Thy mighty Scholiast, whose unweary'd pains
> Made Horace dull, and humbled Milton's strains.
> Turn what they will to Verse, their toil is vain,
> Critics like me shall make it Prose again.
> Roman and Greek Grammarians! know your Better:
> Author of something yet more great than Letter;
> While tow'ring o'er your Alphabet, like Saul,
> Stands our Digamma, and o'er-tops them all.
> 'Tis true, on Words is still our whole debate,
> Disputes of *Me* or *Te*, of *aut* or *at*,
> To sound or sink in *cano*, O or A,
> Or give up Cicero to C or K. [23]

The authoritative community of authorized voices always threatens to become merely factions of competing authorities, disputing dead letters. If Pope's community of respected voices, in

---

[23] *Id.* at 778.

writing a satire against the mob of self-authorized authorities, falls into an anarchy of print, what hope is there for keeping the sheep in the gentle fold and the goats outside in the rugged terrain where they belong? If anarchy can break forth from the staunch and rigid harmony of the heroic couplet, where sense descends into senseless sounds, then there is little hope that the question of authority can be easily settled in an age when print itself is the only weapon.

If we return to the question that generated this discussion, then, we begin to realize how deceptive that question was. What qualifies a writer to be an author? Pope's answer to the question is that all writers are authors by virtue of the fact that all writers are licensed to scribble and all scribblers can easily find a license to print. In a culture where not even the crown can control print—even if it could retain the authority to do so—the waywardness of scribbling can always find ways of manipulating the uniformity of print. Once print supplants manuscript, it does not purge that waywardness, but rather authorizes it. The technology of print does not merely facilitate this process of giving the aura of authority to individual scribbling; it mandates this process. Ironically, as print makes the copying of manuscript easier, eventually leading to the accessibility of books and even to their affordability, it also makes the concept of individually possessed authority inevitable. Caught at this turning point of history, Pope helps to authorize the individual's possession of authority as an effect of print, even as he attempts to prevent this process by printing satires against individually possessed, self-proclaimed authorities. That the Scriblerus Club should take their name from the act of scribbling is itself a poignant reminder of their plight, for however much they cling to this ideal of a living tradition of authoritative writing, they in fact help to bring into ascendance the age of mechanical reproduction in print.

VI. Class Status: Identification With National Historic Culture-A Source Of Authority

It is sometimes difficult to distinguish gleeful laughter from nervous laughter, and so Pope and his coterie necessarily remain on that borderline between self-confident mastery based on univocal authority and panic-stricken satirical violence aimed at purging the convincing pretenders to an authority that is all too equivocal. This ambivalence is also indicated in the practice of fabricating history as fiction. After the middle of the eighteenth century, this elaborate game of fabricating authors and histories turns into a serious pastime and rather quickly into a serious profession. Men of letters become historians of literary artifacts, searching out and researching the primitive, founding texts of their national heritage. Lewis Theobald, the target of Pope's ire in the 1729 *Dunciad Variorum*, is a precursor to this movement with his studious reconstruction of Shakespearean texts. This interest in reconstructing a national past is, of course, part of a larger history of the emergence of the liberal bourgeois state. As such, it indicates a shift in thinking about the relation of the individual to the national whole, and the relation of the individual to the source of authority. With the emergence of the liberal state, the individual's source of authority begins to shift from a vertical emphasis on obedience to the rank above one's own to an emphasis on horizontal identity, not merely in terms of class identity, but more importantly for our purposes, identity across history. The source of authority becomes identified with the continuity of a national tradition and the wholeness of a national people, toward which each individual contributes, regardless of rank or class. In fact, with the construction of a national identity based on the similarity of all individuals in relation to the whole rather than the difference according to rank, status itself becomes a contested source of authority. For the writer who hopes to become an author, this means that there are two avenues to success: the old path of pursuing classical knowledge in preparation for sustaining and exploiting the authority vested in classical texts and a newer path of discovering one's own voice in relation to the originary documents of the culture.[24]

The authority of national origins bases itself on a naturalist paradigm, in which identity implies natural, blood identification and an authentic history that can verify this identification. The dominance of print plays a vital role in the construction of this authoritative national history. This is ironic because the authority of the past appealed to is an authority deposited in artifacts that both precede the era of print and resist desiccation to the dead letter of the press. In addition to medieval manuscripts on fragile parchment, these include old paintings, fragments of buildings, architectural designs, helmets, swords, shields, elaborate insignia, pottery, furniture, tapestries, and of course oral legends. We could read the passion for these artifacts both as a

---

[24] *See* OLIVIA SMITH, THE POLITICS OF LANGUAGE 1791-1819 (1984) (explaining the ideological contests that result from this classical versus native dualism).

resistance to the authority invested in print in the modern age and as a compulsion to translate the past into print and thus confirm the authority of that national past by printing it. In this sense, the Society of Antiquarians structurally functions in a similar manner as the earlier Scriblerus Club.

A.   *The Antiquarians*

Halfway between the Royal Society of Scientists, which was established as a formal institution to spread the authority of science through rigorous empirical methods, and the Scriblerus Club, an informal group of leisured writers hoping to foster good taste by scribbling hardhitting, playful literary satires, the Society of Antiquarians combined the drive for institutionalized scientific method and the playful mania of a leisured pursuit. On the one hand, the antiquarians pursued their interests as a sign of their leisured, elite status, or as an attempt to codify or to gain the cultural privileges promised by that status. In this sense, antiquarianism was viewed as an idle, eccentric avocation, whose purpose was to give occasional pleasure by enabling dabblers to fabricate fanciful genealogies of the self, the clan, and the nation. On the other hand, the antiquarians were early anthropologist historians methodically pursuing an interest which could yield facts about the development of a great civilized nation-state out of a bold primitive people. In this paradigm, status does not seem to matter. All one needs are the skills of antiquarian scholarship and the commitment to reconstruct one's relation to a real past out of the meanest surviving artifacts. Insofar as the antiquarians looked to the Royal Society as a model, they pushed their culture forward towards an ideal of a culture based on progressive knowledge and meritorious advancement of individuals. But insofar as they thought of themselves as a congenial group of genteel collectors with a dilettantish taste for gothic artifacts, they looked back nostalgically to a time when the authority of their status did not need to be bolstered by the trappings of past glory.

The antiquarian movement also makes explicit the split in authority that is present from the moment writing is invested with the power to transmit and transfer authority. On the one hand, antiquarianism was a nascent system of knowledge, which demonstrated how authority existed objectively and could be mastered by those who diligently searched for truth in the details of everyday life. On the other hand, antiquarianism was a private obsession, which indicated to what lengths self-aggrandizing individuals might go in order to create or sustain the myth that authority can be mastered by the acquisition of personal properties, both attributes and possessions, which reveal one's intimate relation to the origins of a nation's past.

1.   Profile of an Antiquarian: Horace Walpole—The Aristocrat

We do not have a better example of the midcentury antiquarian than Horace Walpole. The youngest son of the most powerful politician of the eighteenth century, Walpole occupies that crucial space between politics and pleasure, authenticity and artifice, the authentic scholar and the hoaxing saboteur, between authority as legitimate knowledge and authority as mere dilettantish taste that results from leisured status. Walpole represents the way in which authority-panic, with its emphasis on competing camps, ordained hierarchy, authoritative judgment, and cultivated refinement, can easily be stylized into "mere" gossip and intrigue, status and privilege, and the standard of taste turned into the acquisition of a fashion. According to R. W. Ketton-Cremer, Walpole "wished to write books on antiquarian subjects without becoming associated with the pedantry and dinginess of antiquaries; he vaguely thought that his books, the productions of a gentleman's leisure, ought to be exempt from the searching criticisms of professionals."[25] With Walpole, we witness the status of authority unintentionally reduced to the authority of status. In other words, just as print becomes the cause of authority, rather than merely its vehicular effect, so the status of a writer becomes a putative cause of authority, rather than merely its vehicle. Similarly, just as authority of print derives ironically from the fact that it becomes a contested source of power—a battleground on which monarchs, church leaders, protestant dissenters, levelers, court patrons, printers, booksellers, copyright pirates, independent writers all battle for authority—so status also becomes a contested battleground, or conquered territory, assaulted by writers from the middling ranks and weakened from within by the lack of inherent integrity.

One example will have to suffice. In printing his famous journals in which he hopes to record the definitive history of his age, Walpole exposes all of the petty intrigues of the upper classes, not only to the upper classes themselves, to whom it would come as no surprise, but also to the world at large. The

---

[25] R.W. KETTON-CREMER, HORACE WALPOLE: A BIOGRAPHY 155 (3d ed., 1964) (1940).

journals are full of collected artifacts—gossip, intrigue, namedropping, bon mots, anecdotes, etc.—all intended to suggest Walpole's right to scribble the journal and assume the authoritative mantle of historian of the age of George III. These precious journal tidbits, verbal artifacts collected in the same way that he acquired antiques for his mock-gothic Strawberry Hill, reveal how Walpole's authority to speak for his time is based solely on his status as a leisured, wealthy aristocrat. Walpole can assume that his journals are historically significant—indeed can assume that they are historical—because they record the daily intrigues of those who possess authority, whether political, social, aesthetic, or literary, since all of these merely reflect one another. No matter how trivially personal these entries become, they constitute the author's authority. More precisely, the more personal these entries become, the more they can claim authority as the effect of Walpole's status.

By this point, the possessibility of authority has been so privatized that politics itself—the sphere of public affairs—has become identified with the personal authority of individuals who influence politics through their personalities, and with the personal influence of the historian who is personally involved with those politics. The rise of the party system, with its Whig emphasis on coalitions of powerful men cemented by the personal charisma of an opposition leader capable of diminishing or subverting the personal power of the king and his insidious court cabals, encourages the personalization of the historian's authority. The very waywardness of eccentricity, which the medieval scribes attempted in theory to sublimate in their manuscript scribbling, is transformed by the political conditions of the state and of print, into the heart of authority. Perhaps Walpole's journals are the logical consummation of the attempt to write authority. We move from the personal embellishment of uniform script in order to enforce the authority of scripture by scribbling scribes, to the eccentric titillation of private journals printed by a man whose only claim to authority is the authority of the status from which he scribbles the foibles of his class. In the fountainhead of print, we find its tail.

Where does this leave the writer who has no authority by virtue of the fact that he does not possess proper status? Will classical learning, a knowledge of history, an awareness of the rules and kinds of polite literature, etc., enable him to possess the authority which Pope tries so hard to make unpossessible by the individual writer alone? Will the acquisition of aristocratic friends, patrons, and readers provide such authority? Or must one seek to create authority from the sheer power of print itself, and the number of readers that the technology of print enables? It is impossible for the middle-class writer, who may have property and skills but lacks status and connections, to invent his authority without first constructing a myth of his natural relation to the national origins of authority in the people or the folk. If it is the people who give a native character and integrity to the nation-state, then likewise it is the culture of the people—rather than the universalizing, transhistorical, transnational classical culture of the upper classes—that grants authority to the nation itself.

Though this scenario of the middle-class writer negotiating authority through a natural connection to the national past no doubt enacts itself in a variety of ways, the case of Thomas Chatterton is especially apropos.

2.   Thomas Chatterton—The Middle-Class Writer

When Chatterton constructs his myth of national authority, he does so by fabricating a fifteenth-century priest, whom he names Thomas Rowley. Rowley is a scribe who records for history not only the literature, architecture, art, and sociopolitical history of his own scribal time, but also the history of his country in a prescribal time, the eleventh century. He copies records left by an Anglo-Saxon monk Turgot, who lived during the time of the Norman invasion—a time when the native traditions of the English people are invaded and interrupted by a foreign aristocracy. And notably, a history of that invasion, a poem recording the Battle of Hastings, is one of Turgot's greatest achievements. Rowley mediates between the authentic national past, the prescribal and pre-Norman time of his own fictitious past and his own scribal present, in the same way that Chatterton himself, through the fabrication of this myth, mediates between his own age of print and the preprint era of his national culture, the time of the fictitious Rowley. As Louise Kaplan points out, Bristol in the eighteenth century was the epitome of the dingy, provincial, middle-class town, monied as a result of its wealth in trade and vulgar because of its monied origins. Kaplan writes:

> By filling the streets and walls of Redcliffe with more ancient history, monuments, and antiquities than any other section of Bristol, Chatterton establishes his birthplace as the first and culturally most superior neighborhood of the most important

city in England. And as supplemented by Rowley's footnotes, St. Mary's Church and her latest builder, Sir William Canynge, become the emotional and spiritual centers of that history.[26]

The bourgeois vulgarity of Bristol is magically transformed into the origin of native English civilization, just as Chatterton's own vulgar class origins are magically transformed by the history he fabricates.

The forged poems, histories, architectural drawings, and antiquities that Chatterton writes do not usurp Chatterton's own voice as an author; rather, they constitute that voice, as Chatterton turns the disadvantage of his middling status into an advantage. If he has no authority as a sixteen-year-old legal apprentice, without money, status, connections, or advanced classical learning, he must exploit the authority of the national origins from which he certainly descends. What better way to do this than by forging a genealogy that connects his family and his neighborhood to those origins. If Chatterton's forgeries had remained merely in his own hands, or merely in the hands of his bourgeois patron, the antiquarian William Barrett, who also lacked good taste, breeding, and connections, then he could never have traded in obscurity for fame, mere scribbling for the authority of print, a fictitious authority for real authorship.

The interchange between Walpole, the "authentic" authority, whose status guarantees his authorship (he even owned his own printing press) and authority, and Chatterton, the faker, forger, and pretender to authority, reveals the moment in which exchange value wins out over the value of status. Though we do not have time to analyze this moment in proper detail, one point must be made. Chatterton sends his Rowley forgeries to Walpole, partly because Walpole had already offered his own fictitious preprint document to the reading public in the form of *The Castle of Otranto*,[27] which met with great success, even after it was revealed that the "gothic tale" was actually the forgery of a clever writer. Fabricated history had paid off for Walpole and his ability to deceive was applauded as a sign of his superior skill, good taste, and knowledge of the medieval past. Chatterton also sends his forgeries to Walpole because he needs Walpole to certify his aspiration to authority, metonymically by being associated with someone of Walpole's rank and authority, and literally by provid-

---

[26] Louise Kaplan, The Family Romance of the Impostor-Poet Thomas Chatterton 88 (1988).

[27] Horace Walpole, The Castle of Otranto (Oswald Doughty ed., 1929).

ing access to a printing press. When Walpole first responds, he grants Chatterton all the civility, and even deference, accorded to someone who has merited the attention of a man of higher rank:

> I give you a thousand thanks for it, and for the very obliging offer you make me, of communicating your MSS. to me. What you have already sent me is very valuable, and full of information; but instead of correcting you, Sir, you are far more able to correct me. I have not the happiness of understanding the Saxon language, and without your learned notes should not have been able to comprehend Rowley's text.[28]

The irony here, of course, is that Rowley's "Saxon language" is really Chatterton's primitive and primal imitation of a language he had no real knowledge of. In relation to the construction of a native national tradition, the ambitious, middle-class Chatterton can appear to have an advantage over the classically trained Walpole, whose upper-class training would have stressed the need to Latinize English, rather than the glory of its native origins in low Anglo-Saxon tongues. Walpole concludes his letter thus:

> I will not trouble you with more questions now, Sir, but flatter myself from the humanity and politeness you have already shown me, that you will sometimes give me leave to consult you. I hope, too, you will forgive the simplicity of my direction, as you have favoured me with no other.
> I am, Sir,
> Your much obliged and obedient humble Servant,
> HOR. WALPOLE.[29]

Just as the difference between the playfulness and nervousness of early eighteenth-century satirical laughter is very subtle, so the difference between sincere patronage and a patronizing sneer is really merely a matter of tone or mood. The self-condescending patronage of this first letter turns into the condescension of a patronizing sneer in the next letter, after Walpole begins to think, on advice from Thomas Gray, that the Rowley manuscripts are forged:

> For myself, I undoubtedly will never print those extracts as genuine, which I am far from believing they are. If you want them, Sir, I will have them copied, and will send you the copy. But having a little suspicion that your letters may have been designed to laugh at me, if I had fallen into the snare, you will

---

[28] Letter from Horace Walpole to Thomas Chatterton (Mar. 28 1769), *in* A SELECTION OF THE LETTERS OF HORACE WALPOLE 196 (W.S. Lewis ed., 1926).
[29] *Id.* at 197.

allow me to preserve your original letters, as an ingenious contrivance, however unsuccessful.[30]

What is the difference between the way in which Walpole at first duped his readers in the *Castle of Otranto* and the way Chatterton first duped Walpole? Why does Walpole discount the worth and genius of these fabrications, having offered his own genius in the guise of a similar fabrication? The condescension and uneasiness that make their way into Walpole's tone in the second letter are already implied in the first letter, for the nature of the interchange is troubled by the levelling authority of print. If Walpole had printed Chatterton's forgeries, it surely would have brought fame to Chatterton, and infamy to Walpole, despite the respective social status of each man. Indeed, Walpole's social status is supposed to protect him from the ingenuity of a man pretending to authoritative knowledge. Furthermore, having printed Chatteron's work, Walpole would have given him a direct entryway into the fame and authority of print; Chatterton would no longer need Walpole's patronage, and likewise would no longer need the stamp of Walpole's authority.

That Walpole is conscious of this dynamic is revealed by the final sentences of his second letter to Chatterton:

> I own I should be better diverted, if it proved that you have chosen to entertain yourself at my expense, than if you really thought these pieces ancient. The former would show you had little opinion of my judgement; the latter, that you ought not to trust too much to your own. I should not at all take the former ill, as I am not vain of it; I should be sorry for the latter, as you say, Sir, that you are very young, and it would be pity an ingenious young man should be too early prejudiced in his own favour.[31]

Actually, the latter depends upon the former: if Chatterton has too high an opinion of his own authority, it will necessarily manifest itself as not having a high enough opinion in the putative authority afforded by Walpole's status. Walpole's opinion of himself, his vanity, is at stake; otherwise, he would not even hesitate to return the Rowley documents. Chatterton's ingenuity not only tears away the veil that is supposed to protect status-authority from the vulgar eyes of the mob but it also suggests how such status-authority is really a stage-prop; easily set up by those who

---

[30] Letter from Horace Walpole to Thomas Chatterton (Aug. 1769), *in* A SELECTION OF THE LETTERS OF HORACE WALPOLE, *supra* note 28, at 205.

[31] *Id.* at 205-06.

are supposed to be in the know as a result of their status, and easily torn down by those who merely pretend to be in the know, regardless of their status.

In other words, Walpole's status functions in relation to Chatterton not as a medium of authoritative value, determining and limiting Chatterton's assumption to authority, the way patronage is supposed to work, but rather as a medium of exchange, providing both the cultural capital and literally the start-up capital for Chatterton's publishing enterprise. The best evidence for the nature of this relation is the fact that Walpole's rejection of patronage contributes to Chatterton's success as an author. Chatterton can, and does, get into print by other means. Once he does, the authority of print is enhanced, rather than hindered, by the scandal of Walpole's rejection. Chatterton understood this dynamic well, as we see in his bitter poem addressed, but never sent, to Walpole:

> Thou, who in Luxury nurs'd behold'st with Scorn
> The Boy, who Friendless, Penniless, Forlorn,
> Asks thy high Favour,—thou mayst call me Cheat—
> Say, didst thou ne'er indulge in such Deceit?
> Who wrote Otranto? But I will not chide,
> Scorn I will repay with Scorn, & Pride with Pride . . . .
> Had I the Gifts of Wealth & Lux'ry shar'd
> Not poor & Mean—Walpole! thou hadst not dared
> Thus to insult. But I shall live & Stand
> By Rowley's side—when *Thou* art dead & damned.[32]

As the poem wavers between humiliation and scorn, between self-revealing vulnerability and self-confident bravora, it promises to match Walpole's pride of place with Chatterton's own pride of stance. Even Chatterton's awkward handling of the diction and forms of poetic address—a genre preserved for those of high status—is turned into a kind of self-mastery, as Chatterton matches each of Walpole's prerogatives of status-authority with his own presumptions of authority beyond status. Chatterton takes the ultimate stance, as he turns Walpole's insult into his own, being so generous as to refuse to "chide" Walpole, as though he has any right to chide in the first place, and despite the fact that Walpole has chided, and thus insulted, him. The fact that this poem, not published in Chatterton's lifetime, eventually finds its way into print and reprint fulfills Chatterton's prophecy

---

[32] EDWARD H. W. MEYERSTEIN, A LIFE OF THOMAS CHATTERTON 271 (1930) (quoting poem Chatterton addressed, but never sent to Horace Walpole).

at the end of the poem. It is not status, but print, that will have the final word, for authority itself is no more than a matter of who has the final word.

CHARLES DICKENS, INTERNATIONAL COPYRIGHT, AND THE DISCRETIONARY SILENCE OF *MARTIN CHUZZLEWIT*

GERHARD JOSEPH*

There is no binary division to be made between what one says and what one does not say; we must try to determine the different ways of not saying . . . things, how those who can and those who cannot speak of them are distributed, which type of discourse is authorized, or which form of discretion is required in either case. There is not one but many silences, and they are an integral part of the strategies that underlie and permeate discourses.
—Michel Foucault, *The History* of Sexuality[1]

Some architects are clever at making foundations, and some architects are clever at building on 'em when they're made.
—Charles Dickens, *Martin Chuzzlewit*[2]

After finishing *Barnaby Rudge* in 1841, Charles Dickens set off with his wife for the United States, full of enthusiasm for the young country, but he returned, so the well-known story goes, thoroughly disillusioned. The texts that evince the grounds of that disillusionment are of course the *American Notes* of 1842 and the novel *Martin Chuzzlewit* of 1843-44: the braggart insularity, the vulgarity of manner, the rapaciousness of real estate speculation, the political corruption, the unattractiveness of the landscape both urban and rural—all such reasons emerge clearly enough in the critical comments within both texts, if in the American section of *Martin Chuzzlewit* most virulently.

But even during his lifetime, the argument circulated that perhaps the primary and most personal cause of Dickens's bitterness concerned his disappointments surrounding the issue of copyright law. For one of the undeniable reasons Dickens had gone to America was to work for the acceptance of International Copyright so that his books, among those of others to be sure,

* Professor of English, Lehman College and the Graduate School, City University of New York. B.A., M.A., 1953, University of Connecticut 1955; P.h.D., 1966, University of Minnesota (1966).
    1 1 MICHEL FOUCAULT, THE HISTORY OF SEXUALITY 27 (Robert Hurley trans., 1978).
    2 CHARLES DICKENS, MARTIN CHUZZLEWIT 555 (Oxford University Press 1991) (1844).

would no longer be pirated by unscrupulous American publishers. It was a mission in which he entirely, humiliatingly failed, and a copyright agreement between England and the United States was not concluded until 1891.

But one has little direct sense of the authorial impact of that failure in reading either the *American Notes* or *Martin Chuzzlewit*. So, at any rate, James Spedding argued in an anonymous 1843 review of *American Notes* in the Edinburgh Review:

> [Dickens] went out there, if we are rightly informed, as a kind of missionary in the cause of International Copyright; with the design of persuading the American public (for it was the public to which he seems to have addressed himself) to abandon their present privilege, of enjoying the produce of all the literary industry of Great Britain without paying for it;—an excellent recommendation, the adoption of which would, no doubt, in the end prove a vast national benefit . . . . In this arduous, if not hopeless enterprise, Mr. Dickens, having once engaged himself, must be presumed, during the short period of his visit, to have chiefly occupied his thoughts; therefore the gathering of materials for a book about America must be regarded as a subordinate and incidental task—the produce of such hours as he could spare from his main employment. Nor must it be forgotten that in this, the primary object of his visit, he decidedly failed; a circumstance (not unimportant when we are considering his position and opportunities as an observer of manners in a strange country) to which we draw attention, the rather because Mr. Dickens makes no allusion to it himself. A man may read the volumes through without knowing that the question of International Copyright has ever been raised on either side of the Atlantic.[3]

As Alexander Welsh comments in his study of Dickens and copyright, there is a hidden, all but prosecutorial assumption in Spedding's argument[4] not unlike that of the psychoanalyst who argues doublebindingly that an analysand's reticence on a matter *must* be the sign of repression: Dickens's silence on the copyright issue in *American Notes* (and I would add in *Martin Chuzzlewit*) thus seems to Spedding, who did not know Dickens personally, to be an admission of some kind, most "decidedly" an admission of failure. But of course if Dickens failed, he must have intended to succeed in what Spedding insists was the "main employment" of

---

[3] James Spedding, *Dickens's American Notes*, 76 EDINBURGH REVIEW 500-01 (1843), *quoted in* ALEXANDER WELSH, FROM COPYRIGHT TO COPPERFIELD 36-37 (1987).
[4] WELSH, *supra* note 4, at 37.

his visit. And as Welsh comments upon such attribution of intention, "The positive argument from circumstances, that since Dickens spoke on behalf of copyright he probably intended to speak, is a strong one. Much weaker is the argument, from his silence [in *American Notes* and *Martin Chuzzlewit*], about his state of mind."[5] Welsh also adds, however, that Dickens's subsequent change from silence to fierce denial that he went to America to work for International Copyright serves "to etch [Spedding's] argument deeper."[6]

It is within such a context of the positive of Dickens's speech and negative of his silence that I would like to consider an incident in *Martin Chuzzlewit* which may or may not provide evidence of Dickens's novelistic voicing of a concern with copyright. I say "may or may not" since it is up to the listener to accept or reject the argument. That is another way of saying that what follows is an example of the positive of speech and the negative of silence, but now displaced onto the reader who "hears" or "does not hear" the voicing of what this reader takes to be the novelist's concern.

In chapter thirty-five of *Martin Chuzzlewit*, Martin and his servant Mark Tapley, having just disembarked in Liverpool from their American trip, seek out a cheap tavern in order to formulate plans for their immediate future. Their lodging is

> one of those unaccountable little rooms which are never seen anywhere but in a tavern, and are supposed to have got into taverns by reason of the facilities afforded to the architect for getting drunk while engaged in their construction. It had more corners in it than the brain of an obstinate man; was full of mad closets, into which nothing could be put that was not specially invented and made for that purpose; had mysterious shelvings and bulk-heads, and indications of staircases in the ceiling; and was elaborately provided with a bell that rung in the room itself, about two feet from the handle, and that had no connexion whatever with any other part of the establishment.[7]

The passage throws off a striking architectural metaphor and conceptual phrase for the structure of *Martin Chuzzlewit* as a whole: that novel too feels as if it were put together by a drunken architect—has more angles to it than the brain of an obstinate

---

[5] *Id.*
[6] *Id.*
[7] MARTIN CHUZZLEWIT, *supra* note 2, at 549.

man; is replete with mad closets, mysterious shelvings, and useless bells; is full of odd, discrete units (notably the disproportion-
ately long American section) that seem to have questionable
connection with anything else in the novel. The greatness of
Martin Chuzzlewit (and it is a great novel, arguably Dickens's fun-
niest) arises from a disjunctive fecundity of character and scene
rather than from the tight coherernce of its comic, melodramatic,
and romantic plots. For better and worse, it lacks what Coleridge
valorized as a unity of feeling; the qualities we admire are rather
its energy and variety, its sharp discontinuities—the newspaper
virtues of Dickens's early years. The novelist, that is, harks back
to—as he never will entirely disavow or escape—the tendencies
of the sketch-collector as he piles up memorable portrait after
portrait, self-contained scene after scene to generate the impression of a drunken architect's variegated but rather disorderly urban structure.

Of course, the question of what does and what does not constitute aesthetic order, of how much *discordia* Coleridge's *concors*
will allow, is always debatable once we get text specific. As lin-
guistically-inspired structuralists have taught us, all works of art
(i.e., buildings and novels for the sake of the present argument)
may be read like sentences with varying degrees of coherence.
The certainty that even the most apparently seamless of works
are marked by disruptions and redundancies, what Michael Rif-
fatere has called "ungrammaticalities,"[8] is the operative assumption of semiotic theory. In some cases such ruptures seem
momentarily healed when the work's grammar is construed from
a wider focus; in others, however, the effort to transcend ungrammaticalities of structure results in a specious papering-over
of a work's heterogeneity, in the falsification of parataxis into
syntax, of mere contiguity into analogy, of metonomy into metaphor. The appeal of some works—of some novels and some
buildings—is that they seem programmatically ungrammatical;
they stubbornly refuse to satisfy first the writer and then the
reader's profound psychological yearning for a stable integration
of part and whole. The arts—indeed, the human sciences as a
whole—may thus be seen collectively as a kind of "grammar
school" through which we readers and viewers move as children,
construing as best we can, accustoming ourselves to various sorts
of texts, learning "to cipher and to sing," as Yeats puts it so

---

[8] *See* Michael Riffaterre, The Semiotics of Poetry 1-22 (1978).

memorably in "Among School Children."[9]

Consequently, chapter thirty-five of *Martin Chuzzlewit*, which concerns itself with the disputed origin and hence the intellectual ownership of a grammar school, may be taken as yet another "allegory of reading," in Paul de Man's sense. For that chapter offers us a comic version of the structuralist's paradigm, the grammar of part for whole. To begin with, the "drunken architect's" room in which Martin and Mark plot their future seems a perfect architectural correlative for the idea of the "ungrammatical" in Riffaterre's sense. As I have said, the parts of the novel do not seem to cohere very well; they seem merely contiguous; no part of *this* structure leads very efficiently or directly to another, whatever the straightforward desires of its characters. As Mark and Martin are sitting in their tavern room, they are intent upon "losing no time," of "travel[ling] straight" to the Dragon Inn[10] where they hope to link up with the novel's other major characters, Tom Pinch and Mary Graham, in a meeting that will forward Dickens's plot. But in this leisurely, tangent-seeking, drunken idler of a novel, there are few straight lines: as Mark and Martin look out the window, their gaze is arrested by a figure that "slowly, very slowly" (and paratactically) passes:

> Mr. Pecksniff. Placid, calm but proud. Honestly proud. Dressed with peculiar care, smiling with even more than usual blandness, pondering on the beauties of his art with a mild abstraction from all sordid thoughts, and gently travelling across the disc, as if he were a figure in a magic lantern."[11] In their astonishment Mark and Martin make inquiries of the tavern's landlord and discover that they have indeed seen Pecksniff—that they have returned to England just in time for a momentous architectural event, the laying of the first stone of a new grammar school by the local Member of Parliament under the supervision of "[t]he great Mr. Pecksniff, the celebrated architect,"[12] whose design for the school has carried off first prize in a competition. As an interested onlooker to the subsequent ceremony, Martin, catching sight of the plans, realizes that Pecksniff had stolen *his* plans, ones that Martin had undertaken as an exercise during his architectural apprenticeship to Pecksniff. "My grammar-school. I invented it. I did it all," Martin exclaims at his discovery. "He has only put four

---

9 W.B. Yeats, The Poems 242-43 (1961).
10 Martin Chuzzlewit, *supra* note 2, at 549-50.
11 *Id.* at 550.
12 *Id.* at 551.

windows in, the villain, and spoilt it!"[13]

The false building of the House of Chuzzlewit throughout its history (one of the earliest of the Chuzzlewits may have been Guy Fawkes, the unsuccessful underminer of the Houses of Parliament) has all sorts of local expressions in the novel, though that architectural/dynastic theme achieves its most rhetorically overt and all-embracing form in Old Martin Chuzzlewit's climactic verdict upon the entire race of Chuzzlewits: "The curse of our house . . . has been the love of self; has ever been the love of self."[14] That English "false building" had had its American equivalent during Martin and Mark's disastrous cross-Atlantic journey in Mr. Scadder's description of the factitious Eden (Cairo, Illinois in Dickens's actual American odyssey) to which he sends the gullible pair as a "flourishing . . . architectural city," a thriving community of "banks, churches, cathedrals, market-places, factories, hotels, stores, mansions, wharves" and other public and private edifices.[15] The naive Martin discovers the reality beneath the verbal facade, the "paper city" of Phiz's illustration,[16] soon enough in the fetid wilderness that is all but the death of him; and of course his cocky certainty that he will make his fortune in America through the application of "ornamental architecture" to "domestic American purposes" is shown to be a ludicrous pipe-dream when exposed to the enterprising scams of America's real estate swindlers.

But it is in Pecksniff's professional deceit that the novel launches its initial, most blatant and most comic attack upon the "natural right" of property, for his appropriation of his students' architectural plans shows him to be the first and paradigmatic of the novels' believers that one can "own" a building—and by extension a House in the dynastic sense. I have asserted above that, as an example of the novel's "ungrammaticality," the laying of the grammar school's first stone in chapter thirty-five seems like a discrete, redundantly incremental instance of Pecksniff's villainy only loosely related to the larger plot. But that scene is at least prepared for by an earlier one in chapter six, where Pecksniff defines his aesthetic principles while offhandedly assigning Martin the exercise of designing a grammar school, precisely the design which Martin and Mark stumble on in chapter thirty-five:

---

13 *Id.* at 553.
14 *Id.* at 804.
15 *Id.* at 355.
16 *Id.* at 357 (illustration by Halbot K. Browne ("Phiz")).

"Stay," said [Mr. Pecksniff]. "Come! as you're ambitious, and are a very neat draughtsman, you shall—ha ha!—you shall try your hand on the proposals for a grammar school: regulating your plan, of course, by these printed particulars. Upon my word, now," said Mr. Pecksniff, merrily, "I shall be very curious to see what you make of the grammar-school. Who knows but a young man of your taste might hit upon something, impracticable and unlikely in itself, but which I could put into shape? For it really is, my dear Martin, it really is in the finishing touches alone, that great experience and long study in these matters tell."[17]

Such a master-apprentice procedure was typical enough for Pecksniff: to the preliminary sketch of his pupils he habitually added a "few finishing touches from the hand of a master . . . an additional back window, or a kitchen door, or half-a-dozen steps, or even a water spout"—and then claimed the design as his own work.[18] "[S]uch," says the Dickensian narrator, "is the magic of genius, which changes all it handles into gold."[19] And as a matter of fact, Pecksniff, hypocritical parasite that he is, is endowed with alchemical powers, if not quite of the sort that he believes he has. Rather his genius is that of a subversive absurdity capable of estranging both the conventional moral and aesthetic orders of the novel's surface—specifically, in the present emphasis, throwing into question nineteenth-century assumptions about the ownership of intellectual property. For no matter how virulent the attacks upon him, Pecksniff's confidence in the virtue of his procedures throughout the novel is absolutely unshakable: he is sincerely, unaffectedly, naturally pompous—the quintessential expression of an unimpregnable narcissism. For the rest of us, self-deception can never be complete because the reality principle will probably not allow it, but Pecksniff's self-deception is totally sincere and therefore perversely heroic, a comic exemplification of Romantic egoism.[20]

Pecksniff's invulnerable egoism carries over quite naturally from his ethics to his aesthetics. When in the speech quoted above from chapter six he avers that he habitually adds the "finishing touches" of the master to the apprentice efforts of his pupils, he is merely defining a time-tested guild ethos whose suc-

---

[17] *Id.* at 87-88.
[18] *Id.* at 88.
[19] *Id.*
[20] *See* Gerhard Joseph, *Pecksniff and Romantic Satanism*, 2 THE DICKENS WORLD 1-2 (1986).

cessful results we see celebrated in the stone laying ceremony of chapter thirty-five. We must assume that he sees nothing dishonest in that method, that were Martin to accuse him of plagiarism to his face, he would answer quite sincerely in the tones of martyred innocence with which he outfaces Old Martin in the novel's closing confrontation scene. And indeed we (or at least I) believe him and are tempted to come to his defense, if only because his "theft" of Martin's design raises—again, in a comic register, to be sure—questions of serious import to intellectual property rights in general and to the authorship of architectural and literary texts in particular. As Peter Jaszi has pointed out to me in correspondence, a strictly legal analysis of the competing claims to the architectural work in question between master and apprentice would, in the nineteenth century, have supported Pecksniff's claim to ownership: he is arguably the intellectual "owner" of the grammar-school twice over, by virtue of his status as Martin's master *and* by the addition of those marginal windows which by contemporary standards would have absolved him of any charge of plagiarism, a charge which has always been more common in a literary context than in an architectural craft anyway. Indeed, it was not until late in 1990 that changes in American copyright law for the first time embraced architectural designs (as distinct from plans and drawings) as copyrightable subject matter.[21]

Furthermore, while it is easy enough to laugh at the broad absurdity of Pecksniff's appropriation of his pupils' work in an extra-legal, moral context, what seems less obvious is that Martin's pride of invention ("*My* grammar-school. *I* invented it. I did it *all*.") is morally suspect in its turn.[22] Indeed, the combined activity of master and pupil highlights the controversial status of originality, both architectural and—by extension—literary, in the nineteenth century.

As the career of Coleridge among others makes clear, authorial plagiarism became a significant moral and aesthetic issue in the nineteenth century precisely because of the high premium put upon the ideals of "originality" and "invention" at the expense of classical "imitation." (Hence, Dickens's half-joking characterization of himself as The Inimitable—and the public acceptance of the tag). It is certainly not true, as one sometimes

---

[21] Architectural Works Copyright Protection Act of 1990, Pub. L. No. 101-650, 104 Stat. 5135 (codified at 17 U.S.C. §§ 101, 102(a), 106, 120 and 301(b)).

[22] MARTIN CHUZZLEWIT, *supra* note 2, at 553 (emphasis added).

hears, that writers before the nineteenth century were not concerned with originality: they were concerned, but not so deeply and urgently as the Romantics. The key document in the transvaluation of imitation and originality was of course Edward Young's *Conjectures on Original Composition*[23] in 1759. But as Thomas McFarland has recently shown, originality and imitation have never existed in isolation but have always been two terms of a ratio, two sides of a "paradox."[24] As originality is defined against its counter-ideal of imitation (and always involves a certain amount of it), so imitation is never merely slavish but always inclines toward its opposite, originality or invention.

All this sounds high-minded enough until we get to the dangerous ground of plagiarism, which is after all a dark variant of imitation and influence.[25] Because it brings the bourgeois conception of individual identity into conflict with itself, plagiarism tends to be easily dismissed from our cultural consciousness and has occasioned relatively little theoretical discussion, considering the number of writers who have been guilty or at least accused of it. At any rate, precisely because the honorific status accorded the concept of originality by Romantic writers came into conflict with their universal indebtedness, plagiarism is one of the central embarrassments of the ninteenth century—as the careers of Coleridge in a serious register and Pecksniff in a comic one demonstrate.

For Pecksniff's architectural plagiarism may within such a context be seen as a mock commentary upon the imitation/originality paradox that McFarland describes.[26] That is, we are no doubt meant to side with Martin in his outrage at Pecksniff's theft, but that theft also serves a critical function, putting into question the egoism and pride of ownership out of which such outrage arises. If *Martin Chuzzlewit* as a whole is meant to condemn the "love of self" that built the House of Chuzzlewit, that selfishness had been given an aura of theoretical respectability by the heroic egoism of post-Renaissance thought generally and the "egotistical sublime" of Romanticism in particular. Martin's in-

---

23 EDWARD YOUNG, CONJECTURES ON ORIGINAL COMPOSITION (Ewing J. Webb ed., 1969).

24 THOMAS MCFARLAND, ORIGINALITY AND IMAGINATION 1-30 (1985).

25 And Harold Bloom's "anxiety of influence" is arguably a disguised form of apprehension about plagiarism, the later writer's anxiety about his appropriation of an earlier one's intellectual property, so much so that McFarland suggests that plagiarism might well be added as an "ugly duckling" seventh to Bloom's six "revisionary ratios." *Id.* at 22.

26 *Id.* at 1-30.

sistence upon his originality does of course indict Pecksniff's knavery, his stealing of the sign of another's personality (not to mention whatever monetary theft is involved), which is what plagiarism attempts. But Pecksniff's theft serves in turn to question the pride of personality and ownership in Martin—and by extension in the entire graspingly individualistic House of Chuzzlewit.

Such an ambivalence swirls about the structure of a grammar-school whose lessons are instructively hard to construe. Affirming the psychic dangers of plagiarism for *both* the plagiarizer and his accuser,[27] that ambivalence captures the boundary of anxiety concerning the structure of a fragile, coherent self which is relatively muted in plagiarism's more respectable cousins, imitation and influence. Perhaps Mark Tapley's generous estimate of the combined work of Pecksniff and Martin is the most forgiving way to defuse the anxiety implicit in both sides of the originality paradox: "Some architects are clever at making foundations, and some architects are clever at building on 'em when they're made. But it'll all come right in the end, sir; it'll all come right."[28] Wise servant that he is, Mark may thus be said to anticipate a major thrust of postmodernist theory—the insistence upon the "intertextuality" and therefore the inter- or transpersonal nature of all intellectual enterprises.

On the grounds of such an argument it is now time to turn back to the subject with which we began, the silence of Dickens on the subject of International Copyright law in *American Notes* and *Martin Chuzzlewit*. And I trust the reader can anticipate what I am now going to say: the American piracy of Dickens's novels (as well as those of other English writers), arguably the primary reason for his American journey, gets displaced in *Martin Chuzzlewit* onto a meditation on Pecksniff's theft of Martin's grammar-school plans. On the face of it, such a connection may sound a bit bizarre; the differences between the two situations may at first glance seem more striking than the similarities, if only because the relationship between an architect and his apprentice in a comic fiction seems so very different from that between a master novelist and the publishers of his work in that more naturalized fiction, our construction of an author's life. And yet it is surely true that the dispute about authorial rights to an intellectual property within a fiercely individualist humanist/capitalist ethos

---

[27] For a discussion of the "scapegoating" of the plagiarist by his accuser in the "grammar school" of academia relevant to the novel's continuing scapegoating of Pecksniff, see NEIL HERTZ, *Two Extravagant Teachings*, in THE END OF THE LINE 144-59 (1985).

[28] MARTIN CHUZZLEWIT, *supra* note 2, at 555.

is what is at issue for both Martin the apprentice and Dickens the author. To be sure, there is no money involved for Martin (at least the text mentions no prize money for the grammar-school design) as there was for Dickens over copyright, but that just makes the psychic connection tighter because it is less exclusively mercenary: the very fact that intellectual rather than monetary rights are in dispute for Martin would seem to argue, in the displacement I posit, that for Dickens the money seemed (or so he would have told himself) less important than the principle of a creator's "natural rights" to his words subject to whatever contractual arrangements he might wish to make.[29] The high ground of intellectual more than financial rights was, at any rate, the position Dickens tried publically (and Pecksniffianly?) to occupy during his American journey—to the studied and deeply humiliating derision of American newspaper commentators.

The Inimitable Dickens no doubt felt he was entirely in the right in matters literary and financial—but why then the fierce denials once he returned from his American journey that International Copyright was a significant reason for the trip and why the discretionary silence about the matter in both *American Notes* and *Chuzzlewit*? Perhaps an oblique answer may be gained from the foregoing reading of the grammar-school episode: Dickens's text surely asks us to side with Martin's indignation at Pecksniff's highhandedness, and that authorial advocacy seems clear enough. But that text also, I would suggest, asks us to recognize the House of Chuzzlewit's "love of self" that taints, however slightly, Martin's self-affirming "My grammar-school. I invented it. I did it all."[30] The reason that Dickens was so perceptive about the corrupting egoism of the House of Chuzzlewit (and the way in which it frequently expressed itself through mercenary calculation) was that he was hardly a stranger to Pecksniffian hypocrisy, rampant egoism, and mercenary calculation himself. That was arguably the case in his reasons for the American journey, wherein he tended to mask a self-serving advocacy of International Copyright behind the less strictly commercial, more high-minded motives of gathering materials for a book. Peck-

---

[29] Marxist critics like Pierre Machery have of course long held that the theory of writer as an independent "creator" belongs to a historically specific humanist and capitalist ideology, to what Foucault would call an aspect of the "author function" within a modern, post-classical episteme. *See* MICHEL FOUCAULT, *What Is an Author?*, *in* LANGUAGE, COUNTER-MEMORY, PRACTICE 116-38 (Donald F. Bouchard ed. & Donald F. Bouchard & Sherry Simon trans., 1977); PIERRE MACHEREY, A THEORY OF LITERARY PRODUCTION 66 (Geoffrey Wall trans., Routledge & Kegan Paul eds., 1978).

[30] MARTIN CHUZZLEWIT, *supra* note 2, at 553.

sniff's theft of the grammar-school plans and Martin's response to it thus half reveal and half conceal Dickens's complicated, retrospective feelings about his reasons for the American journey.

INTERNATIONAL COPYRIGHT: STRUCTURING "THE CONDITION OF MODERNITY" IN BRITISH PUBLISHING

N.N. Feltes[*]

International copyright law, originating in the French revolutionary laws of 1791 and 1793, made no distinctions between French and foreign authors and freely granted French copyright to foreign works.[1] In the ensuing years, only Belgium followed the revolutionary French example of unilaterally protecting works published abroad.[2] Consequently, the number of bilateral agreements between individual European states, dealing particularly with translation rights, grew in the first half of the nineteenth century. By 1886, only Greece, Monaco, some of the Balkan states, and Asian and American states, including the United States, were without any international copyright agreements.[3] While the network of bilateral copyright arrangements which existed prior to 1886 was extensive, the protection it offered to authors in foreign countries was neither comprehensive nor systematic.[4] The pressure for a universal law of copyright, however, arose less out of a desire for juridical consistency than from the material contradictions of time and place for which "modernism" was the resolution elsewhere on the ideological level. This can be seen in the events leading up to the Berne Convention of 1887.[5]

In September 1858, a congress on Literary and Artistic Property was held in Brussels which passed resolutions constituting "a rudimentary outline of a programme for a universal copyright law."[6] During the Paris Exhibition in 1878, the French *Société des gens de lettres* held an international literary congress, presided over by Victor Hugo.[7] This congress passed further resolutions on international copyright and founded an International

[*] Professor of English & Social & Political Thought, York University. B.A., 1953, Notre Dame University; M.A., 1957, University College, Dublin; B. Litt., 1959, Oxford University.

[1] SAM RICKETSON, THE BERNE CONVENTION FOR THE PROTECTION OF LITERARY AND ARTISTIC WORKS: 1886-1986, at 5 (1987).
[2] *Id.* at 22.
[3] *Id.* at 30.
[4] *Id.* at 39.
[5] DAVID HARVEY, THE CONDITION OF POSTMODERNITY 218 (1989).
[6] RICKETSON, *supra* note 1, at 42.
[7] *Id.* at 46.

Literary Association to protect literary property and to organize regular relations between literary societies and writers of all countries.[8] Over the next few years the ALAI[9] held annual congresses and in 1883 it persuaded the Swiss government to sponsor a conference in Berne for the "formation of a Union of literary property."[10] This conference produced the draft of a "Universal Literary Convention, Scheme of Proposals,"[11] which became the basis for the successful negotiations between governments at the Berne Diplomatic Conferences of 1884, 1885, and 1886.[12] Meanwhile, in 1837 and 1844 the British Parliament had passed successive acts to protect books published in the United Kingdom and other artistic works imported from those countries which afforded reciprocal protection to British publications. By 1886, copyright agreements had been established by Orders in Council with sixteen European states.[13] As the negotiations proceeded in Berne during the 1880s, Britain, a participant at the Conferences, passed an act in anticipation of the International Copyright Act of 1886 that empowered the Queen to issue Orders in Council embodying the chief features of the new convention.[14] The United States, on the other hand, had sent only observers to the Berne conferences,[15] and while never joining the Convention, passed the "Chace Act" in 1891. This act granted copyright to authors of certain specified nationalities (including British subjects) whose work was first or simultaneously published or "manufactured" in the United States.[16]

The forces that drove the multilateral initiatives towards international copyright are perhaps not immediately clear. Nor does the jocular label, "piracy," meaning simply "free-booting with reference to literary property,"[17] provide a sufficient explanation. "Piracy," as Brander Matthews wrote, "is a term available

---

[8] *Id.* at 46-47.

[9] The International Literary Association changed its name to International Literary and Artistic Association (*l'Association littéraire et artistique internationale*), commonly known as ALAI. *Id.* at 48 (footnote omitted).

[10] *Id.* at 49 (quoting *Association Littéraire et Artistique Internationale—Son Histoire, Ses Travaux* (1878-1889), in BIBLIOTHÈQUE CHACONAC 122-23 (1889).

[11] RICKETSON, *supra* note 1, at 50.

[12] *See* RICHARD ROGERS BOWKER, COPYRIGHT, ITS HISTORY AND ITS LAW 311-21 (1912); WILLIAM BRIGGS, THE LAW OF INTERNATIONAL COPYRIGHT 237-39 (1906); RICKETSON, *supra* note 1, at 41-71.

[13] WALTER ARTHUR COPINGER, THE LAW OF COPYRIGHT 567, 578-80 (3d ed. 1893).

[14] *Id.*

[15] RICKETSON, *supra* note 1, at 56.

[16] BRIGGS, *supra* note 12, at 640-50; COPINGER, *supra* note 13, at 567, 578-80.

[17] BOWKER, *supra* note 12, at 251.

for popular appeal but perhaps lacking in scientific precision"[18] since most countries, while protecting works by their own authors, did not regard the unauthorized publication of foreign works as unfair or immoral.[19]

The exigencies of book production in the 1880s and 1990s were the determining factors in the pressure for international copyright. In his evidence before the Royal Commission on Colonial and International Copyright in 1876, Sir Charles Trevelyan made two statements which he presented as universal truths, but which clearly reflect the broadest historical pressures. Distinguishing the author's own pecuniary interest in his work from that of his publishers, Trevelyan stated that "the interest of the author consists simply in the remunerative sale of his works anywhere and everywhere, it matters not by whom, provided he gets his fair remuneration. But the interest of the publisher is quite different, it is local."[20]

And in the same testimony, Trevelyan remarked: "[I]t is of great consequence that books should reach the body of the people fresh and fresh."[21] A recently published book might be good, even "a classic," but its goodness would be enhanced, Trevelyan's archaism emphasizes, if it were "not deteriorated or changed by lapse of time; not stale, musty, or vapid."[22]

Trevelyan does not seem aware of his own assumptions about the contradiction between ubiquity and locality, or those in his notion of literary "freshness." Yet, it is precisely these conflicting ideologies of space and time that are the larger determinations of the debate over international copyright. For example, it was said to be a general feeling in the United States that international copyright was simply a scheme whereby British publishers might capture the American book market.[23] It was obvious, however, that any British publisher, even after 1891, "had to calculate costs, freight charges, insurance and import duty before deciding whether the American international copyright act was in any way beneficial to a particular book."[24] Earlier struggles con-

---

18 Brander Matthews, *The Evolution of Copyright*, in THE QUESTION OF COPYRIGHT 29 n.1. (London, G.H. Putnan ed., 1891).

19 RICKETSON, *supra* note 1, at 18.

20 *Report of the Commissioners Appointed to Make Inquiry with Regard to the Laws and Regulations Relating to Home, Colonial and International Copyrights: Minutes of Evidence, Session 17 January—16 August 1878, XXIV*, PARLIAMENTARY PAPERS, REPORTS: COMMISSIONERS, INSPECTORS AND OTHERS 260 [hereinafter *Report of the Commissioners*].

21 *Id.*

22 The Oxford English Dictionary (2d ed. 1989) (defining "fresh and fresh").

23 S.S. Conant, *International Copyright*, 40 MACMILLAN'S MAG. 153 (1879).

24 SIMON NOWELL-SMITH, INTERNATIONAL COPYRIGHT LAW AND THE PUBLISHER IN THE

cerning copyright in England had been determined by an insularity which confined the issues to the nature of a book or text and how that might most profitably be exploited in an English market. But by the late nineteenth century, the constraints of English space and (so to speak) Greenwich time had been superceded. As David Harvey has recently pointed out, "modernism"—the general ideological level of the capitalist social formation—assumes as one of its missions "the production of new meanings for space and time."[25] Railways, transatlantic steamships and telegraphy are the most obvious instances of the material pressures for new meanings for space and time in early modern book production. Simply to consider space raises concrete questions of domicile and nationality, whether of author or of publisher. Such questions may include the different kinds of geo-political borders, not only the Atlantic Ocean or the English Channel, but the long Canadian-American land boundary. Augustine Birrell, for example, wrote with mock querulousness about the Canadian "piracy" of English books for the American market: "So far as the United States were concerned, our authors had no remedy but abuse—but Canada, was it not, as it were, our own kail-yard? Did not the Queen's writs run there, and so on?"[26] And J. A. Froude wondered who could collect the sort of minimal royalty that was suggested as a "free trade" alternative to copyright in different countries under different governments, given the impossibility of collecting royalties on the introduction of foreign editions into the British Colonies.[27] Again, there was the problem of sheer geographical size in organizing existing or potential markets in these colonies. As one American wrote:

> Your Mudie can mail books at a cheap rate to subscribers in every part of the United Kingdom, and get them back from the farthest limit within a week or ten days. But a Boston or New York library could not lend books to subscribers in Nevada or Dakota, thousands of miles away.[28]

The size of the United States, as well as its socio-political and ideological divisions, engaged the question of copyright in yet another way:

REIGN OF QUEEN VICTORIA 77 (1968). *See generally* Arnold Plant, *The Economic Aspects of Copyright in Books*, 1 ECONOMICA 167-95 (May 1934).

[25] HARVEY, *supra* note 5, at 216.

[26] AUGUSTINE BIRRELL, SEVEN LECTURES ON THE LAW AND HISTORY OF COPYRIGHT IN BOOKS 213 (London, Cassel 1899).

[27] J.A. Froude, *Report of the Copyright Commission, in* 148 EDINBURGH REV. 329 (1878).

[28] Conant, *supra* note 23, at 153.

[T]wo years since certain persons in the West—publishers of Chicago and St. Louis—vindicated for themselves the original freedom of citizens of the United States to reprint the works of Englishmen, and they reduced their prices to make a market . . . . The publishers of Chicago threatened to destroy the trade of the publishers of New York . . . . At present the publishers of the older cities are principally, if not solely, affected, and it is they who have made the discovery that the question of International Copyright has become "pressing."[29]

Similarly, international copyright dictated that the dimension of time was no longer to be structured simply as duration—the length of copyright and its relation to an author's lifetime which would allow him a fair reward and produce a profit for the publisher. Furthermore, not only "freshness" but staying power (or "shelf-life") were commercial values. As J. A. Froude argued, "Books of real worth survive the copyright period, and, the verdict of continued demand being finally passed, they carry with them their own commendation and become the property of the public."[30] Unprecedented speedy communication could not only "boom" a book, but could introduce pressures on the time another book might need to become a critical and financial success. Politically, issues of precedence of date of publication, or alternatively, of simultaneity of publication, were crucial. For time and space were often intimately connected in copyright law. After the Chace Act, a book needed to be published in both countries simultaneously to conform with both United States and British copyright law.[31] Not even an author's twelve-month residence in the United States could earn copyright protection for a work without first obtaining United States citizenship.[32] Later, measures were adopted to grant *ad interim* copyright for a book first published abroad while it was being manufactured in the United States.[33]

The Berne Convention and the international copyright legislation which preceded it restructured the accepted understandings of time and space in the interest of capitalist publishing. The Convention established a "Union," ensuring reciprocity in

---

[29] L.H. Courteney, *International Copyright: II. An Englishman's View of the Foregoing*, 40 MACMILLAN'S MAG. 163 (1879). For a survey of the geographical and demographic determinations of late nineteenth-century American publishing, see WILLIAM CHARVAT, *The People's Patronage, in* THE PROFESSION OF AUTHORSHIP IN AMERICA, 1800-1870: THE PAPERS OF WILLIAM CHARVAT (Matthew J. Bruccoli ed., 1968).

[30] Froude, *supra* note 27, at 314.

[31] NOWELL-SMITH, *supra* note 24, at 65.

[32] *Id.* at 34-35.

[33] *Id.* at 65-66.

the treatment of authors, or most often, of publishers (the author's "lawful representatives") within the signatory nations. The Union proclaimed that it should "enjoy in other countries for their works, whether published in one of those countries or unpublished, the rights which the respective laws do now or may hereafter grant to natives."[34] The Berne Convention established that:

> The country of origin of the work is that in which the work is first published, or if such publication takes place simultaneously in several countries of the Union, that one of them in which the shortest term of protection is granted by law . . . .
> The enjoyment of these rights . . . cannot exceed in the other countries the term of protection granted in the said country of origin.[35]

The spatial and temporal dimensions of copyright and their interaction were thus recast. What characterizes this early modern social reconstruction of space and time in book production and distribution is a new ideology: the reduction of space (place of publication, nationality of author, etc.) to a category contingent on time (time of publication, duration of property rights, etc.), a change which facilitates the rapid turnover of capital. The old forms of spatialization in publishing had inhibited processes of change, underwriting the timelessness of a publisher's "list," or of the "hundred best books," in the face of entrepreneurial publishing practices. The Berne Convention established the precedence of time over space in publishing; it valorized not only "timing," but also Trevelyan's unspoiled "fresh and fresh," or what Froude less enthusiastically called the "prevailing and passing delirium,"[36] so as to hasten capital turnover. As David Harvey argues, "those who define the material practices, forms, and meanings of money, time, or space fix certain basic rules of the social game."[37] The rules fixed by the Berne Convention overcame those spatial barriers and temporal understandings which impeded the turnover of publishing capital. The institutional context was thus established for ideological, "literary" values which came to be associated with, for instance, the best seller, in competition with fixed investments in publishing "lists." As Harvey writes, "The incentive to create the world market, to reduce

---

[34] Articles of the International Copyright Union 20, 35 (London, Longman's Green 1887).
[35] Id.
[36] Froude, *supra* note 27, at 342.
[37] HARVEY, *supra* note 5, at 226.

spatial barriers, and to annihilate space through time is omnipresent . . . . Innovations dedicated to the removal of spatial barriers . . . have been of immense significance in the history of capitalism, turning that history into a very geographical affair."[38] Harvey's methods open the possibility of a detailed analysis of spatial and temporal practices of modern capitalist publishing. His "grid of spatial practices,"[39] for instance, allows one to analyze spatially the ideological position of late Victorian publishing: the Berne Convention as a "representation of space," a signification that allows "such material practices to be talked about and understood," or Free Trade as a "space of representation," a "mental invention," allowing one to "imagine new meanings or possibilities for spatial practices."[40] Harvey's use of "Gurvich's typology of social times" enriches the concepts of "list" and "entrepreneurial" publishing.[41]

The debate in Britain during the time of the Royal Commission on Copyright in 1875-76, had presented just these issues in its entrenched ideological positions. The Commission included among its members Fitzjames Stephen, and in its second year, J. A. Froude and Anthony Trollope. But the commissioners whose participation best reveals the ideological issues were the two civil servants from the Board of Trade, Sir Louis Mallet and Thomas Henry Farrer. In an article in the *Edinburgh Review*, Froude called the controversy over international copyright "the battle of the Board of Trade."[42] Both Commissioners from the Board of Trade were doctrinaire free traders: Mallet ("a Cobdenite pur sang," according to a friend)[43] was, after Cobden's death, "the chief official representative of free trade opinion,"[44] and Farrer, Permanent Secretary to the Board of Trade, was "a free-trader of unyielding temper" who was by far the most powerful member of the Inquiry. Farrer's "unseen and quiet influence," was so effectual that "between 1872 and 1886 almost all the reforms of and additions to our system of commercial law were only brought

---

[38] *Id.* at 232. This whole section, especially this paragraph, is heavily influenced by Harvey's discussion on space and time. *See id.* at Part III.

[39] *See id.* at 220-21 (drawing on HENRI LEFEBVRE, LA PRODUCTION DE L'ESPACE (1974)).

[40] *Id.* at 218-19.

[41] *Id.* at 218-25.

[42] Froude, *supra* note 27, at 309.

[43] Bernard Mallet, *Introduction* to SIR LOUIS MALLET, FREE EXCHANGE at vi (London, Kegan Paul, Trench, Trubner, 1891). Translated, a Cobdenite pure blood. Cobden was the Commissioner prior to Mallet.

[44] XII THE DICTIONARY OF NATIONAL BIOGRAPHY 872 (Sir Leslie Stephen ed., Oxford University Press 1901).

about with the concurrence of the secretary of the board of trade."[45]

Farrer was not to be so influential in the matter of copyright, and the circumstances of his defeat are historically significant. He did not sit on the Inquiry during its second session in 1876. He did, however, appear as a witness five times, was thoroughly interviewed by Mallet, and on his final appearance, was asked to submit a written summary of his evidence and suggestions.[46] Like Mallet, Farrer saw free trade as "merely the unshackling of powers which have an independent existence." "All it can do, and that all is much, is to leave the powers of nature and of man to produce whatever it is in them to produce unchecked by human restrictions."[47] And, again like Mallet, he asserted that a literary work produced by men and women with little or no copyright privileges would somehow be a "better" work.

At times during the Inquiry, Mallet's questions were so doctrinaire that the publisher, John Blackwood, who was called as a witness, could not understand him. When Mallet asked Blackwood about extending "the area of consumption and of profit" while reducing "the term of protection" so as to "obtain the same results in stimulating authors to their best efforts," Blackwood, balking at "the sort of abstract question," simply answered, "I cannot follow that."[48] While Farrer was more subtle in his presentation of the logic of political economy, even Herbert Spencer, another witness, considered Farrer's references to the issue of rival editions as "free trade" and his habit of calling copyright "monopoly" to be "question-begging."[49] Locked in his abstract categories, Farrer persistently argued for a tight restriction on "the abstract principle of monopoly" in copyright,[50] saying that the ideal copyright system "should be co-extensive with the English language, giving the author the benefit of an enormous market and the reader the benefit of a price proportionately reduced."[51] He claimed, like Mallet, that free trade in books would improve the quality of literary production: "on the whole we must trust to the public demand purifying itself."[52]

---

45 XXII *id.* at 627.
46 *Report of the Commissioners, supra* note 20, at 581.
47 T.H. Farrer, Free Trade Versus Fair Trade 86 (London, Cassell, Petter, Galpin & Co. 1882).
48 *Report of the Commissioners, supra* note 20, at 303-04.
49 *Id.* at 540.
50 *Id.* at 406, 460.
51 *Id.* at 468.
52 *Id.* at 520-21.

When Fitzjames Stephen asked him if the remuneration of English authors should be increased, he stipulated that they must be "good English authors," although he agreed that there could not be any "definite or assignable relation between the money payment made to an author and the permanent value of his book."[53] And under pressure from Stephen over his attempt to distinguish "good" authors, Farrer simply reasserted the free trade logic of his position, that "the author's remuneration must depend upon the public demand for his book."[54]

Only Mallet and Farrer attempted to make a case before the Commission of Inquiry that laws of international copyright would influence the quality or value of the literary works produced. As Froude said, "The movement against copyright has originated with, and been carried on by, two or three speculative gentlemen in a Government department, who cannot reconcile the existing book trade with the orthodox theory of the nature of *value*."[55] Stephen's cross-examination made it clear that their case was founded only on abstract political economic opinions about what might be "good" or "very rubbishy" in literature, based on analogy to the production of simple commodities.[56] After the Commission's Report, Farrer wrote in the *Fortnightly* (in a sort of confused rebuttal of the Arnoldian view of "the literary") that the "essence of a book" lies in the "facts" or "ideas" it contains, rather than in its "form" or arrangement of these facts, whereas copyright law protects not the "facts" but the "form of words": "Original thought and observation, the highest form of mental labour, go unprotected, whilst literary manufacture, a very inferior product of the intellect, alone obtains protection."[57]

Copyright thus has "a tendency to encourage bad writers at the expense of good ones," Farrer wrote.[58] "It tends to make books bad, numerous and dear."[59] But what the insular, outmoded free trade discourse of Sir Louis Mallet and T. H. Farrer could not accommodate, and what overrode their opposition, were the concrete spatial and temporal particularities of the book trade at the turn of the century. When Farrer speaks of an ideal copyright system, "co-extensive with the English language," he

---

[53] *Id.* at 520.
[54] *Id.*
[55] Froude, *supra* note 27, at 339 (emphasis in original).
[56] *Report of the Commissioners, supra* note 20, at 520; T.H. Farrer, *The Principle of Copyright*, 30 FORTNIGHTLY REV. 842-43 (1878).
[57] Farrer, *supra* note 47, at 843.
[58] *Id.* at 848.
[59] *Id.* at 846.

ignores the historical determinations of any such system. Indeed, while he means to encourage the "extension" of the market for books, his allusion to "the English language" is in fact, parochial, recalling the island language rather than its concrete, historical (not to say imperial) extensions beyond geographical, social, and political boundaries, and its interaction with foreign languages. To create a world market in English books required the reduction of spatial (not just "trade") barriers. The doctrines of free trade had become, by the 1870s and 1880s, so abstract and so removed from social and economic practice, that the Royal Commission on Copyright, for all the confusion and disagreement in its Report, rejected unequivocally a free trade in books which excluded International Copyright, despite the influence exerted by the free trade dogmatists of the Board of Trade. Simplistic ideologies of supply and demand could not dictate to the modern market in books, however much they might dictate a particular ideology of literary value. International Copyright, in fact, structured a new world market for English books, requiring ideologies of value to accommodate the work of not only familiar local writers, but also foreign writers—indeed, of "international" writers.

SANCTIONING VOICE: QUOTATION MARKS, THE ABOLITION OF TORTURE, AND THE FIFTH AMENDMENT

Margreta de Grazia*

On the face of things, it is remarkable that the courts have concerned themselves of late with something so punctilious as the use of quotation marks. One would expect their use, like that of all forms of punctuation, to be prescribed from the schoolroom rather than legislated in the courtroom. Formerly, a misquotation was judged a grammatical solecism; now, however, after the Supreme Court's decision of June 20, 1991,[1] it may be the basis for a civil action. This Article argues that there is nothing fastidious about the Court's focus on this grammatical device. Small ciphers though they are, quotation marks are critical in upholding the constitutional principles upon which American jurisprudence is based.

I

The legal discussion of quotations issued from a recent case in which the psychoanalyst Jeffrey Masson, former project director of the Freud Archives, brought a libel suit against the journalist Janet Malcolm (and her publishers, the New Yorker and Alfred Knopf) for an interview that allegedly misquoted him. Masson argued that numerous quoted passages ascribed to him were defamatory in "falsely portray[ing] him as egotistical, vain, and lacking in personal honesty and moral integrity."[2] He was, for example, quoted as having said that his colleagues considered him an "intellectual gigolo,"[3] that he was "the greatest analyst who ever lived,"[4] that he intended to turn the Freud estate into "a place of sex, women, and fun."[5] For reasons to be discussed below, a California Northern District court ruled that the alleged

---

* Associate Professor of English, University of Pennsylvania. B.A., 1968, Bryn Mawr College; M.A., 1970, Ph.D., 1974, Princeton University. For helping to formulate the issues in this essay and for reducing its implausibilities and inaccuracies, I wish to thank Stephen Greenblatt, Alexander Nehamas, Sandra Sherman and Peter Stallybrass.

[1] Masson v. New Yorker Magazine, 111 S. Ct. 2419 (1991). I would like to thank Monroe E. Price for urging me to consider this case.

[2] Masson v. New Yorker Magazine, 686 F. Supp. 1396, 1397 (N.D. Cal. 1987).

[3] Id. at 1400.

[4] Id. at 1405.

[5] Id. at 1404.

inaccuracies were not actionable as libel; the Ninth Circuit Court of Appeals affirmed this decision—though with a strong dissenting opinion;[6] and the Supreme Court reversed it, granting Masson the right to a jury trial.[7] At each level, the published interview was compared with the 1065[8] page transcript of the approximately forty[9] hours of taped interviews in order to determine the extent of the difference between what Masson said and what Malcolm quoted him as having said.

The defense countered Masson's complaint that the interview had damaged his reputation with an appeal to the First Amendment's protection of freedom of the press. In the interest of maintaining a free and robust press, the law does not bind reporters and journalists to strict accuracy. In quoting individuals, especially when the transcription of oral statements is involved, they are not liable for certain alterations such as minor inaccuracies, correction of grammar and syntax, and condensation of phrasing.[10] The 1964 *N.Y. Times v. Sullivan*[11] decision extends constitutional protection to the press by superimposing upon state libel law a limiting standard requiring a plaintiff to prove that the statement in question was made with " 'actual malice'—that is, with knowledge that [the defamatory statement] was false or with reckless disregard of whether it was false or not."[12] In applying this standard (and several state precedents) to the *Masson* case, the District Court denied the plaintiff's plea, ruling that "the alleged defamatory statements"[13] were not actionable: they were either "rational interpretation[s]"[14] of Masson's tape-recorded statements or else "substantially true."[15]

In reaching this decision, the Court overlooked the grammatical distinction that quotation marks function to sustain: the distinction between direct quotation and indirect quotation, between what one said and what another said one said; in this case, between what Masson said and what Malcolm reported he said. The Court recognized no semantic difference between Malcolm's third person claim about Masson, and Masson's first person claim

---

    [6] Masson v. New Yorker Magazine, 895 F.2d 1535 (9th Cir. 1989) (Kozinski, J., dissenting).
    [7] *Masson*, 111 S. Ct. at 2419.
    [8] *Masson*, 686 F. Supp. at 1397.
    [9] *Masson*, 111 S. Ct. at 2425.
    [10] *Id.* at 2431.
    [11] 376 U.S. 254 (1964).
    [12] *Id.* at 279-80.
    [13] *Masson*, 686 F. Supp. at 1407.
    [14] *Id.*
    [15] *Id.*

about himself—between, as Judge Kozinski's dissent later suggested, "Masson thinks he is the greatest analyst who ever lived," and as Masson declared, "I am the greatest analyst who ever lived."[16] The grammatical standard requiring that *words in quotation marks* be reproduced verbatim was tacitly dropped and replaced with the considerably looser journalistic standard that applies to *words outside quotation marks*. The district court's decision suggests that statements within quotation marks need not reproduce what was said word for word in order to be constitutionally protected as free speech. Like any type of reporting, the words within quotation marks need only constitute (1) a fair interpretation or (2) an approximation. As an example of the first, Malcolm can without liability quote Masson as having said his colleagues considered him "an intellectual gigolo"[17] not because Masson said so, but because it was "a rational interpretation of Masson's comments."[18] As an example of the second, Malcolm can quote Masson as having said, "I am the greatest analyst who ever lived," not because those were his words, but because they closely resembled his words—what the court termed "the many egotistical and boastful statements"[19] in the taped interview. According to this ruling, quotation marks no longer set off words a person said from words a person might have said. This slip from the realm of the actual to that of the possible itself suggests that much more is at stake here than grammatical correctness; the distinction signalled by quotation marks between direct and indirect speech—between quoting and paraphrasing—upholds an opposition fundamental to the press (and not only the press) between two kinds of writing: report and commentary. This is an epistemological as well as a generic distinction, for those two kinds of writing are produced by two kinds of knowing as distinct as objective observation and subjective opinion.

The Court of Appeals reviewed six of the quotations alleged to be defamatory and in each case affirmed the District Court's decision. Judge Kozinski, however, submitted a magisterial dissenting opinion in which he parted with the majority "on a simple but fundamental point: the meaning of quotations."[20] While Kozinski found both parts of the majority's test troublesome, he

---

16 *Masson*, 895 F.2d at 1549 (Kozinski, J., dissenting).
17 *Masson*, 686 F. Supp at 1400.
18 *Id*. at 1400-01.
19 *Id*. at 1406.
20 *Masson*, 895 F.2d at 1548 (Kozinski, J., dissenting).

objected particularly to its appeal to "rational interpretation"[21] protection, for it ignored the fact that a direct quotation is understood "to come directly from the speaker"[22] and therefore "to contain *no* interpretation."[23] The courts' failure to preserve the distinction between "[a] speaker's own words"[24] and "an extrapolation of the speaker's words"[25] stretched the First Amendment sanctions from "poetic license" to licentious and illicit "license,"[26] allowing reporters, in effect, to ventriloquize. If the courts were to include fabricated quotations among permissible deliberate alterations, "there are no words whatsoever that they cannot put into a subject's mouth."[27] It is the words a subject is made to speak against himself rather than those spoken against him by another that pose the greatest threat: "they can have a devastating rhetorical impact and thus carry a serious potential for harm."[28] As Judge Kozinski specified, "by putting words in his mouth[,]"[29] rather than making it clear that she was using her own, Malcolm "[made] Masson appear more arrogant, less sensitive, shallower, more self-aggrandizing, and less in touch with reality than he appears from his own [taped] statements."[30] In short, because the misquotations were self-incriminatory, they "caused Masson a serious injury and made it look like a self-inflicted wound."[31]

In reversing the ruling, the Supreme Court continued to stress the distinction between quoted and unquoted statements. Quotation marks guarantee a higher degree of accuracy ("[i]n general, quotation marks indicate a verbatim reproduction"[32]) in addition to conferring special authority upon a statement ("the quotation allows the subject to speak for himself"[33]). As in Judge Kozinski's opinion, the Court's discussion repeatedly returned to the particular danger posed by words that appear to be spoken in the speaker's own person. Were the Court to "assess quotations under a rational interpretation standard, [it] would give journalists the freedom to place statements in their subjects'

---

21 *Masson*, 686 F. Supp. at 1407.
22 *Masson*, 895 F.2d at 1549.
23 *Id*. (emphasis added).
24 *Id*. at 1548.
25 *Id*.
26 *Id*. at 1554.
27 *Id*. at 1553.
28 *Id*. at 1549.
29 *Id*. at 1554.
30 *Id*.
31 *Id*. at 1550.
32 *Masson*, 111 S. Ct. at 2422.
33 *Id*. at 2434.

mouths without fear of liability."[34] Once again, it is the damage of self-defamatory words that is most to be feared. While any inaccurate quotation "may be a devastating instrument for conveying false meaning,"[35] a self-incriminating one is particularly "damning."[36] As several published responses to the interview suggested, Malcolm's misquotation was so effective in discrediting Masson "because so much of it appeared to be a self-portrait, told by petitioner in his own words."[37] As the elemental rule of evidence confirms, "[a] self-condemnatory quotation may carry more force than criticism by another."[38] It is precisely to prohibit the press from fabricating self-defamatory quotations that the Court retained only the "substantially true" defense applied in various previous rulings; it ruled out the "rational interpretation" protection, maintaining that "interpretative license" is applicable when the ambiguity of a statement (or event) requires interpretation; but the mere conveyance of a statement ordinarily involves no ambiguity, especially, it might be added, when it has been taped. With this stricter standard, the Supreme Court reversed the decisions of the lower courts, finding five of Malcolm's six fabricated quotations actionable as libel. Justice White, joined by Justice Scalia, filed a partially dissenting opinion calling for even tighter strictures on published quotations.[39] Appealing to the *Sullivan* standard that, as we have seen, equated "malice" with a deliberate falsehood or "reckless disregard" for truth or falsity,[40] they contended that *any* deliberate alteration of what a speaker said constitutes "malice," not just one that materially alters its meaning; *all* of the misquotations would, therefore, be actionable.[41]

II

What is remarkable about the legal discussion surrounding the issue of libel in *Masson v. New Yorker*, is how close quotation marks came to being rendered obsolete (or at least insignificant) in the first two rulings, before being firmly reinstated by the Supreme Court's reversal. The first two rulings extended to quo-

---

[34] *Id.*
[35] *Id.* at 2433.
[36] *Id.*
[37] *Id.*
[38] *Id.* at 2430.
[39] *Id.* at 2437 (White, J. & Scalia, J., dissenting).
[40] N.Y. Times v. Sullivan, 376 U.S. 254, 279-80 (1964).
[41] *Masson*, 111 S. Ct. at 2437-39.

tations the same "rhetorical license"[42] that applies to all other forms of reporting. By eliminating "the rational interpretation"[43] standard, however, the Supreme Court, following Kozinski, restored to them a unique standard of accuracy.

What is still more remarkable about the case is the prospect that compelled the Supreme Court to tighten constraints: the fear, for Judge Kozinski, that "there are no words whatsoever that [journalists] cannot put into a subject's mouth";[44] the dread, for the Court, that reporters would be free "to place statements in their subjects' mouths."[45] Lax use of quotations summons up the grisly shadow of compulsory self-incrimination, of being forced to bear witness against oneself, in this instance by being made to speak (or, more precisely, by being made to *look in print* to speak) self-condemnatory words. The extreme epithets that emerge in this context—misquotation is a "devastating instrument"[46] and "damning"[47] device producing "serious injury" and "a self-inflicted wound"—bring to mind the atrocious contraptions by which such self-incriminations were once legally extorted: racks, strappados, wheels. Lurking behind the Courts' dread of misquotation is, I would like to suggest, a long history of the gruesome inquisitorial procedures deployed in Europe and England to exact self-incriminating testimonies. Defamatory misquotation and coerced confessions are both procedures for putting self-incriminating words into another's mouth. This suggestion should not blur the vast phenomenological differences between the two: between a journalist making a public figure *appear in print* to speak in self-condemnation (for purposes of engaging her readership) and a torturer's or inquisitor's making a suspect *in deed* speak in self-condemnation (for legal, political, religious, or even sadistic purposes). Misquotation belongs in the realm of the representational, while torture exists in that of the experiential. All the same, both practices produce the same effect: the takeover of another's voice.

The Fifth Amendment to the U.S. Constitution[48] was drafted to guard against the juridical horror of coerced confessions and testimonies, guaranteeing that no defendant "shall be compelled

---

42 *Masson*, 895 F.2d at 1554.
43 *Masson*, 686 F. Supp at 1407.
44 *Masson*, 895 F.2d at 1553.
45 *Masson*, 111 S. Ct. at 2434.
46 *Id.* at 2433.
47 *Id.*
48 U.S. CONST. amend. V.

... to be a witness against himself."[49] As is indicated by several references in the debates leading to the Constitution's ratification in 1787, the right against involuntary self-incrimination was intended to protect the individual against the state's power to coerce confessions through torture and inquisition, a power exercised by European states up through the eighteenth century.[50] In Roman canon-law, torture had been integral to the juridical process: a conviction required a declaration, either in the form of the testimony of two witnesses, a voluntary confession, or a coerced confession (in conjunction with circumstantial evidence).[51] In the absence of the first two proofs, torture was applied in order to exact both a confession and corroborating details. Juridical procedures, then, depended upon torture not for punishment, but to produce the evidence required by law. Even in England, where jury trials based convictions on other standards, prisoners were tortured for confessions and information in cases of treason and heresy.[52] The abolition of juridical torture in Europe at the time of the French Revolution was attended by the recognition on this side of the Atlantic of the right against compulsory self-incrimination. In the summary of one Constitutional historian, "The disappearance of torture and the recognition of the right against compulsory self-incrimination were victories in the same struggle."[53]

III

Emerging at the time of this same struggle was the very feature under review in the *Masson* case. Not until the end of the eighteenth century, was the use of quotation marks made mandatory in the duplication of the spoken or scripted words of another.[54] While they appear sporadically in earlier manuscripts

---

[49] *Id.*

[50] George Mason, for example, urged the Virginia delegation to adapt prohibitions against compulsory self-incrimination (as well as against "cruel and unusual infliction of punishment") in order to distinguish the emergent nation from "those countries where torture [was] used [and] evidence was extorted from the criminal himself." 3 ELLIOT'S DEBATES 452 (2d ed. rev., J.D. Lippincott 1941) (1787). *See also* LEONARD W. LEVY, THE ORIGINS OF THE FIFTH AMENDMENT: THE RIGHT AGAINST SELF-INCRIMINATION 418-19 (2d ed. Macmillan 1986) (1968).

[51] JOHN H. LANGBEIN, TORTURE AND THE LAW OF PROOF: EUROPE AND ENGLAND IN THE ANCIEN REGIME 4-5 (1977).

[52] *Id.* at 73-138. *See also* Elizabeth Hanson, *Torture and Truth in Renaissance England,* 34 REPRESENTATIONS 53, 58-62 (1991).

[53] Leonard W. Levy, *The Right Against Self-Incrimination,* 3 ENCYCLOPEDIA OF THE AMERICAN CONSTITUTION 1575 (1986).

[54] For a list of late eighteenth-century grammar books that prescribe quotation marks, see C.J. Mitchell, *Quotation Marks, Compositorial Habits and False Imprints,* 5 THE LIBRARY 377 n.50 (1983). For the relation of quotation marks to various forms of edito-

and printed materials before then, they were not standardized until near the close of the century.[55] Only then did they assume their routine modern function of guaranteeing that the passage within quotes has been accurately reproduced and correctly ascribed. Before this period, grammar books prescribed no rules on the use of quotation marks. Nor was it customary in printing houses to bracket statements with quotes in order to indicate that they belonged to a given speaker or writer. While books printed in the sixteenth and seventeenth century did not use quotes for this purpose, quotation marks are edited in when the same books are reprinted in the nineteenth century.

This is not to say that quotation marks were not used before the eighteenth century. They existed in both manuscript and print, but served a different and even antithetical function. A single or double quotation mark, generally in the margin, was interchangeable with the pointing finger or indices: it pointed to or indicated an authoritative saying like a proverb, commonplace, or statement of consensual truth.[56] Marginal quote ciphers indicated that a passage possessed authoritative status, commonly derived from a classical (Aristotle, Seneca) or patristic (St. Augustine, St. Thomas) author or authority who was, in most cases, dead. By highlighting an utterance that was of potential interest and use to all readers, quotation marks facilitated the "lifting" of the passages they marked. Renaissance readers, it can be assumed, routinely scanned the margins for quote marks in order to spot passages suitable for inscription in their own personalized common-place books.[57] In brief, rather than

---

rial ascription, see MARGRETA DE GRAZIA, SHAKESPEARE VERBATIM 214-18, 220 (1991) [hereinafter DE GRAZIA, SHAKESPEARE VERBATIM]. For a condensed history of the bibliographic forms in which Shakespeare has been quoted, see Margreta de Grazia, *Shakespeare in Quotation Marks*, in THE APPROPRIATION OF SHAKESPEARE 57-71 (Jean Marsden ed., 1991).

[55] Sandra Sherman has drawn my attention to an interesting (and, I would maintain, idiosyncratic) early use of quotes in DANIEL DEFOE, THE HISTORY AND REALITY OF APPARITIONS (n.p. 1720). In a text intent on establishing belief in supernatural phenomena, Defoe uses quotation marks to enhance his credibility, announcing that he will enclose the reports of others to enable readers both to verify his sources and to discern between his own first-hand and their second-hand accounts.

[56] For the use of quotations to signal the words of authorities in the Middle Ages, see ARTHUR J. MINNIS, MEDIEVAL THEORY OF AUTHORSHIP 10 (2d ed. 1988). On "gnomic pointing" in Renaissance texts, see George K. Hunter, *The Marking of Sententiae in Elizabethan Plays, Poems, and Romances*, 6 THE LIBRARY 171-88 (1951).

[57] On the relation of "reading" in the early modern period to various forms of transcription, see Max W. Thomas, *Reading and Writing the Renaissance Commonplace Book: A Question of Authorship?*, 10 CARDOZO ARTS & ENT. L.J. 665 (1992). For a peculiar modern analogue that transforms the reader from passive consumer to active producer, see MICHEL DE CERTEAU, *Reading as Poaching*, in THE PRACTICE OF EVERYDAY LIFE (Steven Rendall trans., 1984).

cordoning off a passage as property of another, quotation marks flagged the passage as property belonging to all—"common places" to be freely appropriated (and not necessarily verbatim and with correct authorial ascription). Not until after the seventeenth century did quotation marks serve to enclose an utterance as the exclusive material of another which could be borrowed only if accurately reproduced and ascribed.[58]

As this short history indicates, the use of quotation marks in the modern period was not simply revised but reversed. No longer highlighting authoritative words to be profitably used by all readers and writers, quotation marks came to privilege and protect words belonging to the individual who produced them. The double brackets announce that words belong to their utterer and can be "borrowed" only on certain conditions. In tethering words to their utterer, rather than to transpersonal or traditional truth, they work to the same effect as the legal and hermeneutic ascriptive practices which fasten works to authors in this same period.[59] In the same way that copyright legislation and textual criticism ascribe works to their authors, so too quotation marks ascribe words to their utterers. All three practices depend on a reconceptualizing of language as a discursive field capable of being portioned into assignable private tracts or lots over which proprietary and usufructuary rights prevail. Indeed, quotation marks bear striking and pervasive witness to this reconfiguration of language as property, fixing discursive boundaries on the page between the *meum* belonging to the author and the *suum* "bor-

---

[58] For a discussion of the prevalence of quoting in the post-seventeenth-century forms of the novel and Romantic verse, see HERMAN MEYER, THE POETICS OF QUOTATION IN THE EUROPEAN NOVEL (Theodore & Yetta Ziolkowski trans., 1968) and JONATHAN BATE, SHAKESPEARE AND THE ENGLISH ROMANTIC IMAGINATION (1986).

[59] On the legal debates leading to the copyright laws which tie works to authors, see Mark Rose, *The Author as Proprietor:* Donaldson v. Becket *and the Genealogy of Modern Authorship*, 23 REPRESENTATIONS 51 (1988) [hereinafter Rose, *Donaldson v. Becket*] and MARK ROSE, THE AUTHOR AS PROPRIETOR (forthcoming 1992). For the hermeneutical consequences of this tie, see Foucault's canonical discussion of how the more or less psychological configuration of "author" tends to regulate textual meaning. Michel Foucault, *What is an Author?*, LANGUAGE, COUNTER-MEMORY, PRACTICE, 113 (Donald F. Bouchard trans. & ed., 1977). My *Shakespeare Verbatim* examines how the textual apparatus that is constructed around Shakespeare's works in 1790 grounds his works in what can be objectively documented of his life and subjectively inferred as his responses to that life, through such practices as the establishing of an authentic text, the devising of a chronology, the assembling of historical background, the cross-referencing of words and passages, etc. DE GRAZIA, SHAKESPEARE VERBATIM, *supra* note 54. For a discussion of how the author figure comes to curtail and regulate the semantics of Shakespeare's two most ostensibly interiorized works (the Sonnets and *Hamlet*), see Margreta de Grazia, *The Motive for Interiority*, 23 STYLE: TEXTS AND PRETEXTS IN THE ENGLISH RENAISSANCE 430 (1989).

rowed" from other authors.[60]

The shift in the function of quote marks provides a tidy example of a development crucial to a more complex history: the emergence of the concept of intellectual property. Mark Rose has discussed how the concept of literary property depended on an important transformation in the notion of "text"—from a gesture or act to be performed within a patronage system to a thing or commodity to be owned within a marketplace structure.[61] The writing process was rendered into an object capable of being owned in order to be commercially negotiated and legally regulated—in other words, in order to qualify as literary property.[62] This transformation needs to be stressed as the precondition for the concurrence we have already noted: the simultaneous codification of the right against compulsory self-incrimination in the U.S. Constitution and of the rules for correct quoting in English grammars. Both developments presuppose that words are, like property, assignable. A citizen or subject must be assumed to own words before being granted the right to keep them, even when it means withholding them from the legal process that seeks their disclosure. Ownership must also be assumed before written words are bracketed in proprietary markers. The legal right and the grammatical rule, therefore, depend on the same conferral of ownership over one's words; so too does their violation.

Quotation marks punctuate a page with sanctions—enclosing private materials from public use. When those enclosed words are about the very speaker who speaks them—when he is both the subject speaking and the subject spoken—they may be

---

[60] Even when quotation marks are used as an ironic device, to distance the writer from the quoted material, property determinations come into play. Disowning a statement is a form of ascribing it, i.e., the *non meum* is simply a more alienated form of the *suum*. Theodor W. Adorno cryptically but relevantly refers to the "abundant ironic quotations marks" in Marx and Engels as "shadows that totalitarian methods cast in advance upon their writings." Theodor W. Adorno, *Punctuation Marks*, in NOTES TO LITERATURE 94 (1991). Also germane is Michel de Certeau's discussion of quotation in terms of Friday's footprint on Crusoe's island, an encroachment or displacement on the latter's discursive turf that is both *"le texte propre"* and *"le discours du proprietaire."* Michel de Certeau, *Quotations of Voices* in THE PRACTICE OF EVERYDAY LIFE 155. Still more to the point of this study is ANTOINE COMPAGNON, LA SECONDE MAIN OU LE TRAVAIL DE LA CITATION (1979), which discusses the shift in the use of quotation in France (and the corresponding requirement of *"la perigraphie"*) as a kind hypostatized property dispensation that immobilizes the text. *See id.* at 349-356.

[61] Mark Rose, *The Author in Court: Pope v. Curll*, 10 CARDOZO ARTS & ENT. L.J. 475 (1992).

[62] For a survey of the complex history of copyright that involves repeated reconceptualizations of both 'work' and 'authorship,' see Peter Jaszi, *Towards a Theory of Copyright: The Metamorphoses of Authorship*, 1991 DUKE L.J. 455.

said to be doubly his and, therefore, to possess a double indemnity against preemption: hence the magnitude of Malcolm's injury to Masson in attributing to him not only words he did not speak, but derogatory words about himself he did not speak; hence, too, the atrocity of a juridical system that wrests self-condemnatory statements from a defendant. For the Fifth Amendment[63] (as well as its equivalents in common and state law) could be said to extend to the courts the proprietary sanctions represented by quotes on the page, with hugely heightened consequences to be sure. The prosecution is prohibited from forcing the accused to speak against himself, thereby preventing reversion to an early juridical system that allowed for, indeed depended upon, the separation of voice from agency. Quotes function as an ubiquitous caveat against prying words out of or putting words into the mouth of another, the objective of inquisitional torture. In writing, conventional punctuation suffices to caution against such appropriation; but in the courts where innocence and guilt are determined, the Constitution itself defends against it. It is, then, perfectly appropriate that the highest court in the land should trouble itself over minutiae like quotation marks. These grammatical ciphers support, however superficially, the Bill of Rights' protection of the individual, placing protective warranties around the individual's words, pervasive reminders integral to writing itself that words belong to their utterer. The Fifth Amendment protects that ownership precisely when an individual might be most pressured to relinquish it: even when bound "to tell the whole truth," a defendant is entitled to remain silent. The choice of what to say and what not to say abides with the speaker, even when under prosecution, assuring that speech remains under the defendant's control . . . as inalienably as life, liberty, and property—the other rights of the prosecuted safeguarded by the Fifth Amendment.[64]

IV

In the conclusion to *The Origins of the Fifth Amendment*, Leonard W. Levy endorses an earlier study of the Amendment which

---

[63] U.S. CONST. amend. V.

[64] "Nor shall [any person] be compelled in a criminal case to be witness against himself, nor be deprived of life, liberty or property, without due process of law; nor shall private property be taken . . . ." U.S. CONST. amend. V. Miranda v. Arizona, 384 U.S. 436 (1966), expanded Fifth Amendment protection during the trial stage of a prosecution to the earliest stage of a criminal action; in addition, *Miranda* specifies that a defendant must be informed upon arrest of his legal right to refuse to answer, *id.*, whereas the Fifth Amendment established only the defendant's right to invoke it.

stresses its importance in establishing the superior (indeed sovereign) claims of the individual over those of the state:

> [The state] has no right to compel the sovereign individual to surrender or impair his right of self-defense. . . . *Mea culpa* belongs to a man and his God. It is a plea that cannot be exacted from free men by human authority. To require it is to insist that the state is the superior to the individuals who compose it, instead of their instrument.[65]

But suppose the relation were precisely reversed: suppose the state sovereign and the individual subject to that sovereign. Suppose, in other words, an absolutist state prevailed rather than a liberal democracy. Would the sovereign then have a right to assert his authority, in this instance, to the end of compelling confession from accused subjects? However schematic, the reversal does enable us to look back to the period prior to the late eighteenth century. We have found that the modern use of quotations correlates with the U.S. Constitution's sanctioning of individual property. Might, then, the earlier use of quotes to sanction authorities be related to the Crown's prerogative to extend its power through its courts, even to the point of coercing voice? We have seen how the use of quotation marks to rope off statements coincides historically with the codification of a right against compulsory self-incrimination: both developments secure an individual's ownership over his words. Does the fact that such security was needed suggest an earlier distribution in which that ownership was maintained by another? In a period in which torture was not only legitimate but a part of the legal procedure itself, how could the state's or Crown's appropriation of voice be a crime? Did truth, wherever it resided, belong to the king, like the royal deer that ranged widely through other men's domains yet remained Caesar's property?

There may be no more awesome display of an absolutist state's power over its subjects than its violent confiscation of their voices. By inflicting pain to coerce confession, the state seizes the faculty associated with free will, the very site where agency is posited. As patristic exegetes pointed out, Genesis represented Creation as an act of speaking ("And God said, Let there be light") in order to establish that God created freely—of his own accord—and not by compulsion or necessity. Yet torture is designed to snap the connection between voice and will, to dis-

---

[65] Abe Fortas, *The Fifth Amendment: Nemo Tenetur Prodere Seipsum*, 25 CLEVELAND BAR Ass'n J. 91 (1954), *quoted in* LEVY, *supra* note 50, at 431.

empower a prisoner's agency by abolishing his or her exercise of not only movement but also speech. Will perforce surrenders to pain its control over voice, abandoning it to the torturer's instruments, the instruments whose use up through the seventeenth century was considered a royal prerogative.[66]

Elaine Scarry, in her arresting analysis of torture in *The Body in Pain*, lists the tactics torturers used to take possession of the prisoner's voice, the final and most extreme of which results in a form of coerced self-condemnation "by temporarily breaking off the voice, making it their own, making it speak their words, making it cry out when they want it to cry, be silent when they want its silence, turning it on and off, using its sound to abuse the one whose voice it is."[67] In her account, it is the volition of the torturers rather than of the speaker that controls voice, *their* instruments of torture wielding *his* or *her* instrument of voice. The extremity of the dislocation is stressed when Scarry imagines the unimaginable, what consciousness would register if not lost to pain: "The sounds I am making no longer form my words but the words of another."[68] Torture, in her account, effects a sadistic redistribution of voice as the prisoner's loss becomes the torturers' gain: "while the prisoner has almost no voice . . . the torturer and the regime have doubled their voice since the prisoner is now speaking their words."[69] In torture, then, the prisoner is dispossessed of the very faculty associated with agency. And since agency is power, the dispossessed prisoner is also disempowered and, conversely, the possessing torturers empowered.

The language of possession invites the association of torture with not only the inhumane but the demonic—with the forces believed capable of taking over voice, similarly depleting human agency to augment their own dark powers. It is important, however, to keep torture in the realm of the human, and even, in respect to the greater portion of European history, the legal. Scarry, who focuses on present political rather than past juridical torture, insists that there can be only a fraudulent relation between the physical act of inflicting pain and the verbal act of exacting information. While interrogation is made to appear the motive for inflicting pain, it is in fact no more than a gratuitous

---

[66] LANGBEIN, *supra* note 51, at 130-31.

[67] ELAINE SCARRY, THE BODY IN PAIN: THE MAKING AND UNMAKING OF THE WORLD 54 (1985).

[68] *Id.* at 35.

[69] *Id.* at 36.

flaunting of the torturers' power. Michel Foucault in *Discipline and Punish* provides a very different account of the practice on which justice depended for so many centuries, emphasizing its deep implication in the court's responsibility of finding and also publishing the truth.[70] In his description of what he terms the "classical penal tradition" that prevailed in early modern Europe, pain and interrogation, body and voice, power and knowledge are not so easily parted. The state deployed body and voice in order to establish both knowledge and power as the exclusive prerogatives of the sovereign and his delegated magistrates. The responses tortured out of prisoners by the juridical process itself yielded evidence contributing to the state's "production of truth," the truth of the crime and its retribution. The state required the confession of the accused, free or compelled, in order to verify its judgment, thereby establishing the univocality of its power. A protracted ritual of promulgation followed the sentence—in private among the magistrates and in public before a crowd—for purposes of confirming the "truth" of the sentence through multiple repetitions and reenactments of the crime. The court's verdict was borne out by the accused's confession, forced if necessary (and later repeated spontaneously), and its multiple reiterations during the procession to the scaffold through various rites (amendes honorables, penance at the scaffold) and signs (the placard born by the convicted, the display of the punished body, subsequent narrations and chronicling of the event). The self-condemnation of the accused was enlisted to authenticate the production of juridical truth: "Through the confession, the accused himself took part in the ritual of producing penal truth";[71] the accused was called upon "if necessary by the most violent persuasion—to play the role of voluntary partner in this procedure."[72]

English jurisprudence is the exception to Foucault's account, for, from as early as the fifteenth century, England prided itself in a jury system based on laws of evidence that required no coerced confessions. Records attest, however, that torture did occur, however unsystematically, in cases of the highest crimes in the

---

[70] MICHEL FOUCAULT, DISCIPLINE AND PUNISH: THE BIRTH OF THE PRISON (Alan Sheridan trans., 1979). JOHN H. LANGBEIN & EDWARD PETERS, TORTURE 79-89 (1985) and Hanson, *supra* note 52, similarly argue for the torture's importance to the epistemology of the early modern period, i.e., its definition of what constitutes evidence and proof.

[71] *Id.* at 38.

[72] *Id.* at 39.

land: sedition and heresy.[73] In addition, there was one form of torture that the English *did* systematically apply, at the very threshold of criminal prosecution. Upon being arraigned, a prisoner was asked to enter a plea (of guilty or innocent) so that his trial could proceed; if he refused, he was tortured by the *peine forte et dure*. As late as 1769, Blackstone described the "cruel process" of "penance for standing mute":

> the prisoner shall be remanded to the prison from whence he came; and put into a low, dark chamber; and there be laid on his back, on the bare floor, naked, unles where decency forbids; that there be placed upon his body as great a weight of iron as he can bear, and more . . . .[74]

The torture, the pressing to death by the gradual loading of heavy weights on the body, was applied until the prisoner assented—or died. Like juridical coerced confession, this procedure attempted the same seizure of the prisoner's voice; in both cases, the state expropriated (or destroyed) the voice it needed in order to conduct its procedures, in this instance pressuring the body to release the consent of the accused. If a prisoner persisted in "standing mute" to the death, he avoided trial and conviction. As a result, he was exempted, not from death, but from the penalties a conviction would have brought upon his descendants, those through whom he lived on. By refusing trial and thereby avoiding conviction, he held on to both his property and his good name, avoiding the forfeiture of his lands and the attaint of his person or "corruption of blood" that barred his descendants from inheritance "even to the twentieth generation."[75] Withstanding the will of the state by withholding consent to trial, the suspect retained a will or testament of his own—the right to bequeath to his descendants an untainted name and intact property. *Peine forte et dure* enacts a contest between the Crown and the arraigned, specifically over voice: if the Crown succeeds in extorting it, a trial follows; if the arraigned succeeds in retaining it, his inheritance and name will pass successively to his descendants.

In addition to "penance for standing mute," England had

---

[73] On the discrepancy in theory and practice on the issue of torture in England, see LANGBEIN, *supra* note 51, at 73-74 and Hanson, *supra* note 52, at 56-62.

[74] 4 WILLIAM BLACKSTONE, COMMENTARIES ON THE LAWS OF ENGLAND *322. Until 1772, a trial by jury could not proceed without the consent of the accused. LANGBEIN, *supra* note 51, at 75. In 1827, the refusal to plead was entered as a plea of not guilty. *See* LEVY, *supra* note 50, at 18.

[75] 4 BLACKSTONE, *supra* note 74, at *381.

another method of coercing words, not through instruments of torture but through a strategy of inquisition. While requiring no physical torture, the method exacted involuntary confession in cases of heresy and sedition through what was termed the oath *ex officio*. Instituted by the Crown in the ecclesiastical courts as an instrument for maintaining religious uniformity, the oath required the accused to swear to tell the truth before the inquisitorial process began, without knowing either the identity of his accusers or the nature of the accusation.[76] The procedure was calculated to result in self-condemnation whether the prosecuted refused to take the oath (a refusal interpreted as guilt) or whether he took it and was forced either to incriminate himself by telling the truth or else to perjure himself by lying. Like coerced confession and pressing to death, the *ex officio* accusation worked to induct the accused's voice into the juridical process.

The oath *ex officio* is of particular importance to our subject in that it was to protest this oath that the right against compulsory self-incrimination was urgently raised. Religious dissenters, the Puritans and particularly the Levellers, appealed to the common law principle "nemo tenetur seipsum prodere" ("no man is bound to accuse himself"), tracing the right as far back as the Magna Carta.[77] Levy is certainly correct in his *Origins of the Fifth Amendment* to discuss these sixteenth and seventeenth century appeals as precedents for the Fifth Amendment. It must be noted, however, that the right was not invoked in the name of individual sovereignty but, rather, in the name of religious faith.[78] Certain similarities dim a radical difference. Both the "nemo tenetur" and the Fifth Amendment claim a right to a private inner sanctum secure from state intervention. But that sanctum in the former case sheltered non-conformist faith, while in the latter it

---

[76] The procedure was used to prosecute Catholics, *cf.* Hanson, *supra* note 52, at 68-77, but also identified with Catholic prosecution of Protestants, as in the exceptionally popular JOHN FOXE, BOOK OF MARTYRS. *See* LEVY, *supra* note 50, at 79. Donna Hamilton discusses the relevance of the oath in relation to issues of privacy in SHAKESPEARE AND THE POLITICS OF PROTESTANT ENGLAND (forthcoming 1992). The oath was declared illegal in 1641 with the abolition of the ecclesiastical Court of High Commission. *See* LEVY, *supra* note 50, at 281-82.

[77] *Id.* at 246-47. *See also* Levy, *supra* note 53.

[78] Talmudic law has also been considered a precedent for the right against compulsory self-incrimination. *See generally* LEVY, *supra* note 50, at 433-41. But it appears to have forbidden such testimonies not out of respect for the rights of the accused, but rather, either because it deemed the accused incompetent to bear witness (as too much "his own relative," *id.* at 438) or because it considered no one to be entitled to dispose of what did not belong to him (while he could dispossess himself of the goods and estate which properly belonged to him, "his life is not his private property" to dispose). *Id.* at 439.

protected individual autonomy. In the earlier instance, heterodoxy claimed against orthodoxy the right to freedom of religion or conscience; in the latter, the individual asserted against government the right to self-defense. The distinction is crucial for the "nemo tenetur" was evoked to sanction not the personal sovereignty of the accused (his relation to himself, as it were) but rather what the accused believed to be transpersonal truth (his relation to God)—the truth of a dissident faith.

Even in regard to the clearest precedent for the Fifth Amendment, then, it is unclear that any special legal privilege shielded a subject's voice before the eighteenth century. Juridical torture, *peine forte et dure*, and the oath *ex officio* were all procedures by which the voice, through the instruments of torture or stratagems of inquisition, was legitimately seized by the state. The state, it appears, was entitled to demand and then coerce, ask and then take, the voice of its subjects, legitimately wresting voice from the subject's body in order to press it into the service of the body politic. Nor have all vestiges of this prerogative disappeared from our present court system. Indeed, the earlier coercive procedures might be seen as extreme versions of the swearing ceremony by which the court enlists the voices of all trial participants. The oath by which witnesses are sworn to tell the truth binds their voices to the objectives of justice, and any departures from that truth are penalized as perjury or contempt of court.

There is one extraordinary exception, however. By constitutional provision, witnesses and defendants are entitled to withhold speech in self-defense even when it blocks the interest of justice.[79] The Fifth Amendment offers indemnity from its own proceedings to a witness at risk of self-incrimination. The witness is entitled, by law, to withhold the evidence that it is the court's function to obtain—evidence, it might be added, of the most conclusive order. For unlike circumstantial evidence, a confession or self-accusation amounts to conviction. Ironically, to prevent the accused from self-accusation, the law legislates against itself, offering refuge to the very voice it would procure.[80]

---

[79] In the interest of protecting its own proceedings, the court can grant a witness immunity, require testimony, and charge him or her with contempt of court for refusing to give it. Such a procedure, in the terms of this paper, looks like Indian-giving: the court gives a witness control over his voice through the Fifth Amendment and then takes it back.

[80] In his entry on the *Right Against Self-Incrimination*, Levy notes the possible tension between the claims of justice and of the defendant on this issue: "Law should encourage, not thwart, voluntary confessions" and "History surely exalts the right . . . ."

Regardless of the court's objectives, voice remains the individual's domain, exclusively under his or her control—so exclusively that it complies with Blackstone's comprehensive definition of private property: "[Property is] that sole and despotic dominion which one man claims and exercises over the external things of the world in total exclusion of the right of any other individual in the universe."[81] Indeed, the right against self-incrimination is even more exclusive, for it excludes appropriation not only by "any other individual in the universe" but by any power whatsoever, including that of the state.

V

We have come a long way from the *Masson* rulings, having jumped centuries, continents, regimes, and disciplines. Yet always in sight has been the issue of voice. At a certain historical point, grammar and law track each other in placing sanctions on individual voice, as if to protect it from appropriations which were before then customary and legal. A transfer of property appears to have taken place: at one time the possession of cultural or political authority, voice later becomes the inalienable property of the autonomous individual. Quotation marks and the Fifth Amendment attend the transfer, offering voice asylum in writing on the page and in testifying at court respectively.

Having remarked this shift in proprietorship, we return to *Masson* with a new vantage. If quotations mark off the exclusive verbal property of another, would it not have been possible to consider a suit, over what does and does not belong in quotes, not as a libel case but as a property dispute, an intellectual property dispute? Encouraging the reclassification is the fact that copyright legislation privileging the author emerged at the same time as quotation marks privileging the utterer.[82] Copyright functions like quotation marks writ large to guarantee correct assignment and accurate reproduction. Furthermore, in copyright,

---

History does not, however, exalt the right against the claims of justice." LEVY, *supra* note 53, at 1576-77.

[81] 2 BLACKSTONE, *supra* note 74, at *2.

[82] As Martha Woodmansee has demonstrated in relation to Germany, and Mark Rose has demonstrated in relation to England, it is in the last decades of the eighteenth century that the author becomes the legal proprietor of his work. Martha Woodmansee, *The Genius and the Copyright: Economic and Legal Conditions of the Emergence of the "Author,"* 17 EIGHTEENTH-CENTURY STUD. 425 (1984); Rose, *supra* note 59, at 51-85. For a discussion of quotation marks in the context of copyright, see DE GRAZIA, SHAKESPEARE VERBATIM, *supra* note 54, at 214-19. Both copyright and quotation are ascriptive practices that fasten the work to the author—a function crucial to the modern conception of authorship and the hermeneutic on which traditional literary criticism is based.

as well as in quoting, misattribution and misrepresentation constitute violations. In Blackstone's seminal formulation, the author has the exclusive "right to dispose of that identical work as he pleases, and any attempt to take it from him [to misattribute], or vary the disposition he has made of it [to misrepresent], is an invasion of his right of property."[83] When another takes credit for an author's work, it is *plagiarism*; when another's work is credited to an author, it is *forgery*.[84] If Malcolm had quoted Masson without crediting him, she would have been plagiarizing; when she misquoted him and credited him, she forged. Forgery would then be her "crime of writing," to borrow Susan Stewart's recent category.[85] Indeed the lower courts's defense of her misquotations as inferences or extrapolations drawn from what he did in fact say could be used to defend a forgerer: though the author (be it Shakespeare, Ossian or Hitler) *did not write* the counterfeited work, he *might have* (as correspondences and continuities with his authentic works would indicate).[86]

There may have been too many complications for the courts to have treated misquotation as an intellectual property violation rather than libel.[87] (To begin with, Masson never committed his

---

[83] 2 BLACKSTONE, *supra* note 74, at *405.

[84] In conversation, Peter Jaszi has suggested an unusually apt analogy to the difference between plagiarism and forgery in the two categories of "reversed passing off": when a new product passes itself off as a patented one (e.g. a new soda bottled as Coke) or when a patented product passes itself off as a new one (e.g. Coke bottled as a new soda).

[85] SUSAN STEWART, CRIMES OF WRITING: PROBLEMS IN THE CONTAINMENT OF REPRESENTATION (1991).

[86] Both the district court and the court of appeals found the passages at issue nonactionable, not because Masson said them, but because taking into account what he *did* say, he *might* have said them: "In light of the many egotistical and boastful statements that Masson made in tape-recorded comments . . . ." Masson v. New Yorker Magazine, 686 F. Supp. 1396, 1406; "Given . . . the many provocative, bombastic statements indisputably made by Masson." Masson v. New Yorker Magazine, 895 F.2d 1535, 1541.

[87] Peter Jaszi has referred me to a possible precedent to *Masson* which was tried as a literary property violation, Hemingway v. Random House, Inc., 23 N.Y.2d 341, 244 N.E.2d 250, 296 N.Y.S.2d 771 (1968). The Hemingway Estate claimed that Hemingway's biography contained lengthy quotations his biographer noted and remembered from conversations with Hemingway that by common-law copyright belonged to the author (and his estate): "[H]is directly quoted comment, anecdote and opinion were [Hemingway's] 'literary creations', his 'literary property', and [the biographer] only performed the mechanics of recordation." *Id.* at 345, 244 N.E.2d at 253, 296 N.Y.S.2d at 776. The complaint was denied on the grounds that Hemingway in no way indicated "that he intended to mark off the utterance in question from the ordinary stream of speech, that he meant to adopt it as a unique statement and that he wished to exercise control over its publication." *Id.* at 349, 244 N.E.2d at 256, 296 N.Y.S.2d at 779. In other words, there are no conventions in conversation like those of writing to mark off private property; compare John Oswald's similar observation on musical performance: "Musical language has an extensive repertoire of punctuation devices but nothing equivalent to literature's "quotation marks," " quoted in Sanjek. John Oswald, *Bettered by the Borrower: The Ethics of Musical Debt*, WHOLE EARTH REV., Winter 1987, at 106, *quoted in*

comments to the tangible or fixed form required for copyright protection.[88]) For heuristic purposes, however, the possibility is worth entertaining, for it suggests still broader implications to the Supreme Court's decision. If misquotation is considered libel, the guidelines for quotation have important consequences for public figures and for the press, setting limits on how the latter can represent the former. Considered as intellectual property, however, their importance may bear on the principles of liberal democracy itself. For like any form of property arbitration, quoting involves drawing lines between *meum* and *suum*; between what belongs to Masson (his words) and what belongs to Malcolm (her words). Furthermore, the settlement they effect stakes out graphically not only one individual's claim against another's, but also any private discursive lot against the free and open public domain. The relation of quotations to copyright fully emerges here, for copyright arises precisely to mediate the conflicting claims between the individual (whose work needs protection in order to be profitable) and the public (which thrives on free access to discourse). In discussing how various kinds of "property in information" resolve tensions between the private and public, James Boyle has hailed copyright as "a *tour de force* of ideological mediation" because it deftly divides a work between the two contenders, offering *expression* to the private author and *ideas* to the public domain.[89] The same arbitration is maintained through quotation marks that close off the exclusive utterance while leaving open the common field of discourse. By insisting on the unique status of words within quotes, the Supreme Court has put linguistic property boundaries securely back in place—

David Sanjek, *"Don't Have to DJ No More": Sampling and the "Autonomous" Creator*, 10 CARDOZO ARTS & ENT. L.J. 607 (1992). In spoken presentation, "scare quotes" have been devised to supply this need.

88 The current copyright statute (17 U.S.C. §§ 101-810 (1988 & Supp. II)) vests copyright in eligible works the moment they are fixed in tangible form. The Copyright Act of 1976 extended tangibility, formerly limited to sheet music and scores, to include sound recording, but it was Malcolm who committed Masson's words to tangible form, on tape (later transcribed) and in notes (subsequently destroyed). Such a division of labor might require ownership to be divvied up as it is among song writers, performers, and technical producers in the case of recordings. On these issues, see JANE GAINES, CONTESTED CULTURE: THE IMAGE, THE VOICE, AND THE LAW (1991). Additional problems with charging Malcolm with intellectual property violation, briefly considered in *Hemingway*, 23 N.Y.2d at 341, 244 N.E.2d at 250, 296 N.Y.S.2d at 771, include undue restriction on freedoms of speech and press. *Hemingway* mentions, for example, the inhibiting effect protecting conversation as property would have on such historical and biographical works as Boswell's *Life of Johnson*. *Id.* at 347, 244 N.E.2d 255, 296 N.Y.S.2d 777-78. Another difficulty lies in discriminating between a self-sufficient (and original) contribution to a conversation from a responsive (and therefore derivative) one.

89 James Boyle, A Theory of Law and Information: Copyright, Spleens, Blackmail and Insider Trading (1991) (unpublished manuscript, on file with author).

assuring through graphic markers that what belongs to *him* remains distinct from what belongs to *her*, and that what belongs to *each* remains apart from what belongs to *everyone*—a conservative measure, to be sure, quite literally so.

And yet those first two court rulings, as we saw, came so close to disturbing this settlement, in effect preparing the way for the collapse between words inside and words outside quotation marks. If held to no stricter standards than unquoted words, quoted words might have lost their special status as accurate and authoritative utterances. No longer functioning as proprietary signs, they might have become superfluous ciphers—distracting page ornaments perhaps. Property divisions, then, would have ceased to be so clear-cut: one person's words would have run into another's, private plots and the public domain would have coalesced, and the page would have turned into an uncharted no-man's-land. The possibility of such a page brings to mind the question cited repeatedly in post-structuralism, appropriately without quote marks, unascribed, and in several variants: What does it matter who is speaking? We conventionally think that the origin of words is important and assign credit and blame accordingly. But post-structuralism does away with origins, positing all verbal formulations in the ubiquitous realm of the *always already*. Thus, writing can be nothing more than a tissue of quotations, a pastiche of passages possessing no authorial affiliation and therefore belonging to no one. To quote Roland Barthes (and advisedly): "The quotations from which a text is constructed are anonymous, irrecoverable and yet *already read*: they are quotations without quotation marks."[90] Needless to say, such a theory would pose radical problems for a regulatory system that protects original rather than derivative works.[91]

It would be bizarre to suggest that the decision of the California Court and Court of Appeals is even remotely, much less causally, connected to post-Heideggerian Continental theory. Yet a plausible link may be found in another more concrete area of contemporary activity: the new technologies of reproduction. Photography, tapes, videos, and xerography have blurred, if not dissolved, proprietary boundaries, allowing for the ready appro-

---

90 ROLAND BARTHES, THE RUSTLE OF LANGUAGE 49 (Richard Howard trans., 1989). For an extraordinary book that might be considered a 406 page elaboration on, and demonstration of, this passage, see COMPAGNON, *supra* note 60. "Toute ecriture est glose et entreglose, toute enonciation repete. Telle est la premisse de ce livre, qu'il met a l'epreuve de la citation, la forme simple de la repetition, l'amorce du livre." *Id.* at 9.

91 *See* Woodmansee, supra note 82 (discussing how the Romantic construction of authorial originality justified the claim to property in an author's work).

priation of materials. These technologies have quite literally turned "borrowing" and "lifting" into an art, the Postmodernist aesthetic of eclecticism that makes no pretense of inventing or creating its components and instead unabashedly draws them from elsewhere. Indeed, the terms "borrowing" and "lifting" prove anachronistic here, belonging to an earlier Modernist aesthetic whose appropriations—whether quotations, allusions, or echoes—remained in some sense identifiable as such, if not acknowledging their original context at least bearing its recuperable traces. Fredric Jameson, in his formative discussion of Postmodernist art, substitutes for "quotation" terms of "incorporation" and even "cannibalism" to describe more accurately processes that absorb the very materials they compile—themselves originating, as it were, in the very materials of their own unoriginal constituents.[92] Pastiche, therefore, emerges as the "well-nigh universal practice today,"[93] a form of imitation which, unlike modernist parody, presupposes no model. In referring to the present age as "the culture of the simulacrum,"[94] Jameson makes assimilative imitations the defining symptom of the age, manifested first and foremost by an architecture that builds itself by pillaging past edifices, but also in films and in novels that constitute the present out of the past and in music that snatches at dead styles, or at what used to be termed "styles" before their sheer and absolute imitability called for their reclassification as codes.[95] The wide availability of instruments for reproducing images, sounds, and words—to consumers as well as producers of culture—raise tremendously complex issues of how to commodify products that are partially or entirely derivative of other products. In an age of mechanical and electronic reproduction, voice, like any other property, is subject to various appropriative tactics—modern forms of exaction and coercion—that raise in their own way questions of ownership. In the context of such technologies, the strict upholding of quotation marks might appear quaint and outmoded, an anxious gesture against an onrushing future.

---

[92] FREDRIC JAMESON, POSTMODERNISM OR, THE CULTURAL LOGIC OF LATE CAPITALISM (1991).

[93] Id. at 16.

[94] Id. at 18.

[95] Id. at 15-17.

BROADCAST COPYRIGHT AND THE BUREAUCRATIZATION OF PROPERTY

THOMAS STREETER*

I. INTRODUCTION

Television as we know it is in several senses authorless. Many of its most conspicuous formal textual features are determined by the impersonal bureaucratic demands of the industrial system of which television is part. Stories are dramatically structured to be conducive to the insertion of commercials, for example, and rigidly restricted to half- or hour-long blocks; one can accurately predict whether or not the hero will get the bad guy at the end of a scene by looking at one's watch. Television ("TV") scriptwriters typically work in teams, according to strict formulae and production schedules, not isolated in moonlit towers and freezing garrets. They recognize the sharp contrast between what they do and the traditional model of the creative process associated with the literary ideal of the author. As one experienced television writer put it, " 'You don't have to have a talent to write for television . . . . I thought it was writing, but it's not. It's a craft. It's like a tailor. You want cuffs? You've got cuffs.' "[1] When TV entertainment does produce moments of insight and originality—and it has many such moments—they are often the product of TV's anonymous assembly line nature, such as the juxtaposing of unrelated images that results from inserting strings of commercials into the middle of programs.[2]

---

* Assistant Professor of Sociology, University of Vermont. A.B., 1977, Brown University; M.A., 1982, Ph.D., 1986, University of Illinois at U-C. The author thanks Peter Jaszi for his helpful comments on a draft of this paper.
    [1] TODD GITLIN, INSIDE PRIME TIME 71 (1985). The use of the word "writer" in this quote illustrates the continued presence of the Romantic construct of authorship—writing is not putting words on paper, but is an act of highly individual unique expression—even in conditions that contrast sharply with that construct.
    [2] Raymond Williams was one of the first to call attention to the centrality of juxtaposition to television aesthetics with his concept of "flow." RAYMOND WILLIAMS, TELEVISION: TECHNOLOGY AND CULTURAL FORM (1977). For a further discussion of this phenomenon, see Jane Caputi, Charting the Flow: The Construction of Meaning through Juxtaposition in Media Texts, 15 J. OF COMM. INQUIRY 32 (1991). It is not just television texts that differ from the traditional model of a linear, coherent book. For reasons linked, but not reducible, to the bureaucratic structures of the television industry, television audiences also use and experience the medium in a thoroughly non-book-like way. As every network executive knows only too well, the bulk of the audience turns on the set to watch television itself, not programs; their channel choice is simply a matter of finding the least objectionable of what's available at the time. People seldom turn to television to watch a particular program; even less often do they seek out the "work" of the televi-

In spite of its relatively authorless character, commercial television could not be what it is without copyright law, a legal institution that rests solidly on the principle of authorship as individual creation of unique works. As Martha Woodmansee,[3] Peter Jaszi,[4] and several of the contributors to this issue of the *Cardozo Arts & Entertainment Law Journal* have pointed out, since the eighteenth century, authors have been generally thought of as individuals who are solely responsible for originating unique works. The conceptual system of copyright relies heavily on this construct.[5] Although the individuality of the author seems obscured by the commercial concerns of Anglo-American copyright law, the categories associated with this law, such as originality and the distinction between an idea and its expression, are derived from the romantic image of authorship as an act of original creation whose uniqueness springs from, and is defined in terms of, the irreducible individuality of the writer.[6]

Ever since the publication of Michel Foucault's *What is an Author?*, the principal question for the institution of authorship has been "What matter who's speaking?"—the query that concludes Foucault's essay.[7] In radio and television, on one level, it seems to matter no longer who's speaking, and yet on the level of legal discourse, it most certainly does. This Article seeks to contribute

---

sion equivalent of an "auteur," such as a TV producer or writer. The evidence suggests, furthermore, that many, perhaps most, of the audience uses television as an accompaniment to other activities; thus, the attention the audience gives to television is selective, idiosyncratic and deliberately divided. For the classic description of this pattern, see Paul L. Klein, *Why You Watch What You Watch When You Watch*, in TELEVISION TODAY: A CLOSE-UP VIEW—READINGS FROM TV GUIDE 214 (Barry G. Cole ed., 1981). *See also* JOHN FISKE, TELEVISION CULTURE 66-83 (1987)(discussing television audiences).

  [3] *See* Martha Woodmansee, *On The Author Effect: Recovering Collectivity*, 10 CARDOZO ARTS & ENT. L.J. 279 (1992).

  [4] *See* Peter Jaszi, *On the Author Effect: Contemporary Copyright and Collective Creativity*, 10 CARDOZO ARTS & ENT. L.J. 293 (1992).

  [5] *See* Martha Woodmansee, *The Genius and the Copyright: Economic and Legal Conditions of the Emergence of the "Author,"* 17 EIGHTEENTH-CENTURY STUD. 425 (1984); Peter Jaszi, *Towards a Theory of Copyright: The Metamorphoses of "Authorship,"* 1991 DUKE L.J. 455 (1991).

  [6] John Frow, *Repetition and Limitation: Computer Software and Copyright Law*, SCREEN, Winter 1988, at 4.

  [7] Michel Foucault, *What is an Author?*, in LANGUAGE, COUNTER-MEMORY, PRACTICE: SELECTED ESSAYS AND INTERVIEWS 138 (Donald F. Bouchard et al. trans., 1977). Foucault's question can be interpreted two ways. Most obviously, the question nicely summarizes Foucault's challenge to the traditional literary and legal obsession with the author-creator; in response to all the worrying about who is the real author of a work, who deserves credit for it, what are the sources of his or her genius, and so on, Foucault cavalierly replies, "Who cares?" But the question is also a serious one. If the answer to "What matter who's speaking?" is no longer "because the author-genius is the source of originality," then the issue is still open: Foucault is asking "Why, in what circumstances, and how does it matter to us who's speaking?" This Article is informed by this second sense of Foucault's query.

to an understanding of how, in our day and age, it does and does not matter to us "who's speaking" by exploring copyright and the commercial broadcast media, focusing particularly on the mixture of indifference and obsession with "authorship" that media such as television embody.

II.   Authorship, Copyright, and Bureaucratic Culture

What is to be made of the fact that the relatively authorless medium of television is constituted in part by a set of legal practices that nominally rest on a romantic notion of literary authorship? It need not suggest, as does the Frankfurt School, that the genuine individual autonomy and creativity of authors has been perversely supplanted by a nightmarish, depersonalized and undifferentiated culture.[8] The belief that television has eliminated individuality and creativity is no more true than the belief that the creations of nineteenth century authors had nothing to do with the social and economic conditions under which they were produced. There were institutional and structural constraints then, and there is individuality, and creativity now.[9] The relations, however, between individuality, creativity and their institutional contexts have undergone conceptual transformations since the time the modern institution of authorship first appeared.

Certainly, part of the explanation for those transformations must come from the labyrinthine history of copyright itself. The experience of a tension between the romantic image of creativity in copyright and the un-romantic results of copyright's application is by no means unique to television and radio. It has been pointed out, for example, that the author-associated concept of the work in nineteenth-century copyright law served paradoxically to transfer power away from authors.[10] This trend was en-

---

[8] For the classic statement of this dystopian view of mass media and modern society, see Theodor W. Adorno & Max Horkheimer, *The Culture Industry: Enlightenment as Mass Deception, in* DIALECTIC OF ENLIGHTENMENT 120-67 (1972).

[9] Some viewers, such as certain kinds of media-literate fans or industry insiders, take genuine pleasure in the undeniable personal stamp of particular living, unique human beings—usually executive producer-writers—on TV programs. Some TV producers such as Norman Lear are fond of pointing out the personal visions and experiences they bring to their television creations. Recent scholarship has begun to capitalize on these possibilities by advancing an "auteur theory of television." *See, e.g.*, ROBERT J. THOMPSON, ADVENTURES ON PRIME TIME: THE TELEVISION PROGRAMS OF STEPHEN J. CANNELL (forthcoming 1992); ROBERT J. THOMPSON & DAVID MARC, ARCHITECTS OF THE AIR: THE MAKERS OF AMERICAN TELEVISION (forthcoming 1992). These approaches are limited, not because the personal stamp of individual "authors" is an illusion—the stamp is quite real—but because it cannot begin to explain either the character of television texts or the full range of cultural experiences associated with those texts, both of which are only minimally shaped by the peculiarities of individual producer-writers.

[10] *See* Jaszi, *supra* note 4, at 471-80.

hanced by the extension of copyright to non-artistic works and reached an extreme in the doctrine of works-for-hire.[11] In view of these and related trends, it can be argued that copyright as a whole serves the interests of publishers and distributors more closely than it serves the interests of either authors or users of copyrighted works. Yet these apparently anti-authorial effects are born of a legal regime that nominally exists to reward individual authors. The dependence of authorless television on authored legal constructs, therefore, may be simply an acute example of tendencies that are as old as copyright itself.

This Article cannot solve the entire riddle of copyright's obtuse relation to the ideal of authorship, but it can perhaps shed a little light on the matter by focusing on a related trend: the tendency of liberalism to rely on and, over time, engender bureaucracy.[12] Copyright law matured in the classical era of liberalism, which formally enshrined the ideal of the abstract individual freely exercising his or her creative capacity protected by a neutral system of natural rights, the most important of which was the right of property. The figure of the romantic author-genius was, to an extent, an offshoot of the figure of the free, property-holding, individual capitalist entrepreneur (even if the former figure embodies a criticism of the latter's calculating rationality). The development of authorship and copyright is intertwined with the complex historical career of liberalism.[13]

Liberalism expects to enable individual freedoms, yet it produces bureaucratic culture. Roberto M. Unger describes bureaucracy "as the characteristic institution that is the visible face of

---

[11] *Id.* at 485-91.

[12] I am using the term *liberalism* here in the sense developed by Roberto Unger, where liberalism is not just a philosophy or an attitude, but one of the dominant forms of Western social consciousness. ROBERTO M. UNGER, KNOWLEDGE AND POLITICS 18 (1975).

[13] Liberalism is not just a preference for things like individual freedom, a market economy, or the rule of law. It is the dream that such things can be happily integrated; that, for example, individual freedom can be reconciled with a market economy by recourse to formal procedures like the rule of law. This hope of transcending tensions between apparently opposed tendencies is what I assume Unger is describing when he writes that liberal consciousness "represents the religiosity of transcendence in secular garb." *Id.* at 163. Copyright law, in this light, is not intended solely to protect the authors' freedom, nor simply to encourage the public distribution of culture and information. It is not intended to turn intellectual products into marketplace commodities, nor to serve the interests of corporate publishers and distributors; it is the enactment of the dream that all of these disparate goals and values can be reconciled in law. Copyright expresses the hope that the freedoms of individual authors can be protected in a way that simultaneously ensures the open distribution of ideas and the healthy functioning of a marketplace in reproduced texts.

liberalism's hidden modes of consciousness and order."[14] In a sense, bureaucracy is an unexpected outcome of the enactment of liberal hopes. Largely because of liberalism's reliance on formal rules and procedures, the effort to reconcile disparate goals in legal and political structures tends over time to breed burgeoning bureaucratic institutions and logics.

The turn to bureaucracy in the name of liberal goals is a characteristic trend of the last hundred years. The historian Robert Wiebe has pointed out that "[b]ureaucratic thought filled the interior" of our dominant social consciousness beginning in the early decades of this century.[15] As bureaucratic terms and procedures repeatedly have been invoked in the service of classical values, bureaucracy has come to fill a shell of traditional liberal ideals.

What Unger describes theoretically and Weibe recounts historically, radio and television illustrate in the concrete. This Article's central argument is, in brief, that the effort to make broadcasting commercial, to turn the electronic dissemination of disembodied sounds and pictures into something that can be bought, owned and sold, has occasioned a pronounced bureaucratization of intellectual property. More precisely, throughout the institutional and legal history of broadcasting and copyright law from the 1920s to the present, the legal, business and political communities have repeatedly turned to twentieth century bureaucratic terms, institutions and procedures as a means to enact the nineteenth century liberal values associated with traditional private property rights and free markets.[16]

This Article suggests that the bureaucratization of broadcast copyright has taken three principle forms. First, the legal fiction of the corporate individual has turned industrial bureaucracies into legal stand-ins for the individual author.[17] Second, property has been simulated in the statistical formulae of blanket licensing organizations.[18] Third, ownership boundaries have been attenu-

---

[14] *Id.* at 20. *See* Gerald E. Frug, *The Ideology of Bureaucracy in American Law*, 97 HARV. L. REV. 1276 (1984).

[15] ROBERT H. WIEBE, THE SEARCH FOR ORDER: 1877-1920, at 162-63 (1967).

[16] An important issue here is technology. John Frow, Bernard Edelman, and others have explored how the rise and institutionalization of new technologies of reproduction such as photography, video tape, digital sampling and computer software have brought to the surface contradictions in copyright that were present but institutionally hidden in the medium of print on which copyright was based. *See, e.g.,* BERNARD EDELMAN, OWNERSHIP OF THE IMAGE: ELEMENTS FOR A MARXIST THEORY OF LAW (Elizabeth Kingdom trans., 1979).

[17] *See infra* at Part III.

[18] *See infra* at Part IV.

ated by an elaborate labyrinth of industry-inspired federal regulations that shape and channel the production and distribution of television programs.[19] In each case, it could be said that depersonalizing bureaucratic relations have been created in the name of personalizing legal institutions. This pattern is symptomatic of a general trend in twentieth century American laws and institutions identified by a variety of historians and legal scholars: a shift from classical, formal liberalism towards a revisionist, corporate liberalism.

III.   FROM CLASSICAL TO CORPORATE LIBERALISM

An emerging consensus among historians suggests that United States society underwent a major transformation around the turn of the twentieth century, resulting in new patterns of legal and political thought called "revisionist" or "corporate" liberalism.[20] Due to changes in society and the economy in the late 1800s, the classical legal regime became increasingly awkward. Repeatedly, classical liberal principles such as the abstract individual and natural property rights have conflicted with contemporary institutions and social relations such as corporations or electronic reproduction of texts. In this century, the characteristic response to such dilemmas has been not to abandon classical liberal principles, but to qualify them by turning to quasi-scientific tools such as bureaucracy, expertise, and statistics.

The modern industrial corporation has been at the center of this transformation. The corporations or trusts that began to appear in the last decades of the 1800s were complex social organizations that interwove the interests and decision-making activities of numerous individuals such as stockholders, managers, and boards of trustees.[21] The conflict between the liberal ideal of the entrepreneurial individual and the impersonal, collective nature of corporations was obvious, and generated considerable de-

---

[19] *See infra* at Part VII.

[20] *See, e.g.,* MARTIN SKLAR, THE CORPORATE RECONSTRUCTION OF AMERICAN CAPITAL-ISM, 1890-1916: THE MARKET, THE LAW, AND POLITICS (1988); WIEBE, *supra* note 15; R. JEFFREY LUSTIG, CORPORATE LIBERALISM: THE ORIGINS OF MODERN AMERICAN POLITICAL THEORY 1890-1920 (1982). For a summary of the change in legal logic in particular, see Elizabeth Mensch, *The History of Mainstream Legal Thought, in* THE POLITICS OF LAW: A PROGRESSIVE CRITIQUE 13, 18-39 (David Kairys ed., 1982). *See also* James Boyle, *The Politics of Reason: Critical Legal Theory and Local Social Thought,* 133 U. PA. L. REV. 685 (1985).

[21] ALFRED D. CHANDLER, JR., THE VISIBLE HAND: THE MANAGERIAL REVOLUTION IN AMERICAN BUSINESS (1977).

bate.[22] The efforts towards reconciliation of the corporation with liberal laws and ideologies have centered on two legal innovations: the legal fiction of the corporate individual, and a legal rationale that rests on a social-engineering vision of general standards flexibly applied according to questions of efficiency and fact as determined by experts. The key role of the fiction of the corporate individual in the production of broadcasting is fairly obvious. In the framework of copyright, giving corporations the status of persons under the law grants them the ability to stand in for authors, thus transferring the bulk of control over media works from individual creators to large bureaucratic institutions. TV programs are thus created, produced, owned, and exchanged by corporate bureaucracies. The television industry's notorious penchant for crassly formulaic thinking in broadcast programming is largely the product of this bureaucratic organization.[23]

In a very real sense, the classical discourse of unique individual creativity is not abandoned in this framework, but rearticulated within a new economic form. The authorless character of broadcast programs, a by-product of the bureaucratic social organization of broadcast corporations, is thus maintained by, and, at least symbolically, reconciled with copyright and the notion of authorship that underlies it. To a large degree, the bureaucratization of intellectual property in broadcasting is a product of the simple fact that large industrial bureaucracies have taken the place of individuals both in law and in the process of cultural production.

The fact that the legal construct of the corporation has taken the place of the individual in Anglo-American law, however, need not mean that faceless, impersonal structures have taken the place of living human beings in controlling cultural production, or that the Romantic notion of true creativity of individual authorship has been replaced by mindless imitation. The institution of authorship and the corporate form are both ways of organizing complex human activities. They differ only in the particular configurations of human activity, the habits of thought and practice, that give them their distinctiveness. The corporate form, in other words, is less a replacement of the individual than

---

22 Morton J. Horwitz, *Santa Clara Revisited: The Development of Corporate Theory*, 88 W. VA. L. REV. 173, 173-224 (1985).

23 The corporate character of the television industry is discussed at some length in Thomas Streeter, *Beyond the Free Market: The Corporate Liberal Character of U.S. Commercial Broadcasting*, 11 WIDE ANGLE 4, 4-17 (1989).

a different way for individuals to think and act in relation to one another.

The remainder of this Article, therefore, will focus not on reified institutions but on the patterns of thought and action, the imaginative workings, that help constitute those institutions in the corporate era. Central to the corporate imagination is the legal logic of corporate liberalism. Under classical liberalism, legal thought rested on a rigid, formal model, based on a geometric ideal of axiomatic deduction from rules and unequivocal, bright-line legal distinctions. Corporate liberalism, on the other hand, rests on a social-engineering vision of general standards flexibly applied according to questions of efficiency and fact. In twentieth century law, notions of property, individual autonomy, and rights, once thought of as absolute rules, have been increasingly interpreted as guidelines that can be qualified by the complexities of individual cases.[24] As a result, questions about the legal status of corporations and corporate activity can be treated as matters of degree: corporations can be private in many circumstances but public in others, and control can be defined in a number of different ways depending on context. Decisions about specific instances can be deferred to bodies of experts, independent regulatory commissions and other administrative bodies.

The legal rationale of corporate liberalism is particularly evident in two related practices associated with broadcast copyright: the blanket copyright license[25] and the use of federal administrative agencies to manage relations within industrial systems and mediate industrial disputes. The technique of the blanket license erects a bureaucratic system such as the American Society of Composers, Authors and Publishers ("ASCAP") that statistically approximates a system of market exchanges of copyrighted goods in situations where such exchanges are unworkable. The use of federal agencies to mediate relations within industries, on the other hand, displaces classical notions of ownership with standards such as industry profitability and the public interest. Adjudicating the distribution of control between, for example, cable operators and over-the-air broadcasters, therefore, is not a

---

[24] *See, e.g.,* Basic, Inc. v. Levinson, 485 U.S. 224 (1988), where the Supreme Court rejected the "agreement-in-principle as to price and structure" as the bright-line rule for materiality in cases involving the Securities and Exchange Commission Rule 10b-5, 17 CFR § 240.10b-5 (1991). Although the Court noted the ease of applying a bright-line rule, it noted that "[a]ny approach that designates a single fact or occurrence as always determinative of an inherently fact-specific finding such as materiality, must necessarily be overinclusive or underinclusive." *Id.* at 236.

[25] Blanket licensing is discussed at length, *infra* at Part IV.

matter of determining, once and for all, who owns what. Rather, the problem becomes a short term practical matter of negotiating a workable arrangement between competing parties or a series of tradeoffs that keep the various businesses happily involved and profitable without fully resolving the question of who, in the last instance, has proprietorship of the programs that reach home television sets.

IV. STATISTICAL SIMULATION OF PROPERTY AND THE BLANKET LICENSE

The property status of broadcast material was first raised by the question of radio and recorded music. In 1914, sheet music publishers founded ASCAP largely to effectuate the right granted composers by the 1909 Copyright Act to demand payment for public, for-profit performances of their compositions.[26] In the 1917 case of *Herbert v. Stanley*,[27] the Supreme Court decided that payments could be demanded, not just in cases of actual commercial concerts, but in the case of any performance that was part of a profit-making operation, such as musicians hired by a restaurant to entertain its diners. This decision created a potentially vast field for ASCAP to comb for royalties. ASCAP thus was faced with the simultaneously tantalizing and daunting task of trying to collect royalties from huge numbers of often small and casual performances of copyrighted works in nightclubs, restaurants and other commercial establishments across the nation.

Actually collecting payments for each individual performance of copyrighted works from, for instance, every piano player in every bar in the United States was thoroughly impractical. Instead, ASCAP turned to the device of the blanket license, which has since become a central feature of contemporary cultural production. Each establishment would pay a fee akin to an annual subscription, determined by things like the size of the establishment but not by the specific content of the performances. The money thus collected would then be distributed to copyright holders according to a statistical formula designed to approximate the actual, but unknown, number of performances of each work.

The blanket license is set up to maintain a system of market relations in copyrighted works, to ensure that composers and other artists get paid for the use of their property. At first glance,

---

[26] 17 U.S.C. §§ 1-215 (1909).
[27] 242 U.S. 591 (1917).

this appears to be its function. Money flows from users of copyrighted works to copyright holders, and works—in the form of sheet music or recordings—flow the other way. At second glance, however, certain constituent features of market relations are missing. Goods, even intangible goods, are not actually exchanged. Copyright holders do not get paid and users of those works do not pay for individual performances of works. Both parties deal primarily with a bureaucracy. On a day-to-day basis, both copyright holders and users experience a process more like paying taxes or procuring welfare: amounts are determined by formulae and bureaucratic procedure. The technique of the blanket license, therefore, does not so much enable a full-fledged market exchange of goods as it creates a statistically grounded, bureaucratically implemented abstraction of that exchange.

The blanket license thus illustrates the tendency of corporate liberal institutions to turn to bureaucracy, statistics, and expertise as an abstract means to uphold liberal standards of property and individualism in conditions that would seem to conflict with those standards. When faced with dilemmas, in other words, our corporate liberal imagination often turns to bureaucratic institutions and statistical abstractions as a means to uphold the general principles—not the full concrete reality—of a system of property rights and market exchange.

V.   CENTRAL TENSIONS: EXPANSION VS. CONTROL

In a general way, techniques such as the fiction of the corporate individual and revisionist legal reasoning have quite successfully served to keep alive the liberal ideal of autonomous, individual creator-entrepreneurs. Simultaneously, that ideal is safely adapting to apparently conflicting twentieth-century economic and technological circumstances. Corporations have taken the place of individual authors and thus generally control program production and distribution and mold programming to internal bureaucratic requirements. Conflicts or contradictions that might emerge from this system can be dealt with on a case-by-case basis by various private and public bodies of experts, such as ASCAP, the National Association of Broadcasters ("NAB") or the Federal Communication Commission ("FCC").

As with most ideological structures, however, the fit has been neither seamless nor frictionless; maintaining it has required considerable institutional and ideological effort. Much of the activity surrounding broadcast copyright in this century has involved a kind of negotiation of the tensions and contradictions inherent to corporate liberal thought and legal institutions.

Concerns specific to corporate, economic, and social organization have had an important impact on the implementation of copyright in the broadcast field. In contrast to nineteenth-century entrepreneurial businesses, corporations are structures, not isolated elements. They are administrative systems that coordinate and rationalize the activities of numerous units of production and distribution.[28] The concerns that dominate corporate decision-making, therefore, typically involve ensuring the smooth coordination of the different parts of complex vertically integrated industrial systems. The desire for system-maintenance, for stability and the smooth coordination of different parts of the processes of production and distribution, permeates corporate decision-making.

At the same time, however, corporations desire autonomy from other institutions—such as other corporations or the state—and the growth and profits that such autonomy can enable. They are thus constantly negotiating tensions between a drive towards stability and coordination, and a drive towards growth and autonomy. Furthermore, as creatures of capitalism in a politically liberal society, corporations are limited in their drive towards stability by concerns about political legitimacy and by the need to conform to antitrust principles.

ASCAP was, in a sense, the sheet music industry's response to this tension. The use of a bureaucratic organization and statistical approximation of market exchange was a means of encouraging wide dissemination and sales of sheet music while, at the same time, maintaining control, that is; maintaining the ability to recoup profits.

VI. RADIO AND RECORDED MUSIC: THE HISTORY OF BMI

The tensions between stability, coordination, growth and autonomy are particularly evident in the case of broadcasting. When broadcasting first appeared as an industrially-backed fad in the early 1920s, it presented both an opportunity for outward expansion and serious problems of maintaining control. From a corporate point of view, broadcasting's ability to cast broadly, to instantly disseminate messages to vast but unseen audiences, is a two-edged sword. On the one hand, broadcasting seems a corporate manager's dream: it can help proliferate both consumer

---

[28] *See* Streeter, *supra* note 23.

products and advertising-laden messages to potentially enormous audiences, thus expanding markets, sales, and the general penetration of consumer habits into the everyday life of the population. On the other hand, that very same tendency towards indiscriminate proliferation of products and messages poses a very real threat to general corporate stability and coordination. If messages and products are freely disseminated, the corporate system can succumb to problems of low profits, competition from small entrepreneurs, or a simple loss of control. New legal and institutional arrangements are necessary in order both to tame and to exploit broadcasting, to negotiate the tension between an expansionary, centrifugal push outwards and a centripetal pull towards limitation and control.

ASCAP helped inaugurate the search for a stable solution. In 1922, prominent commercial and government radio interests held a gathering, the first Washington Radio Conference, to develop procedures for coordinating their rapidly expanding but as yet untamed industry. ASCAP sent the Conference a message urging the creation of a blanket license system for radio performances of music.[29] When a response from the broadcast industry was not forthcoming, ASCAP began demanding royalties from several broadcast stations for the live and recorded musical performances that were beginning to be heard over the airwaves.[30] While at least one prominent station privately worked out a blanket license deal with ASCAP,[31] most broadcasters balked at the prospect of yet another expense in a field that was largely unprofitable. ASCAP then helped to secure its position with the court decision of *Witmark & Sons v. L. Bamberger & Co.*[32] that declared that an over-the-air performance of "Mother Macree" during a program sponsored by L. Bamberger and Company ("One of America's greatest stores") was not eleemosynary.[33]

The music copyright problem led to the formation of the National Association of Broadcasters (NAB) in April of 1923.[34] The

---

[29] ERIK BARNOUW, A TOWER IN BABEL: A HISTORY OF BROADCASTING IN THE UNITED STATES TO 1933, at 119 (1966).

[30] CHRISTOPHER H. STERLING & JOHN M. KITTROSS, STAY TUNED: A CONCISE HISTORY OF AMERICAN BROADCASTING 88 (2d ed. 1990).

[31] AT&T's pioneer station WEAF quickly negotiated an arrangement to pay ASCAP $500 annually, largely for public relations reasons. AT&T was at the time struggling to enforce radio patents over the objections of much of the rest of the radio industry, and could hardly afford to appear insensitive to intellectual property rights. *See* BARNOUW, *supra* note 29, at 120.

[32] 291 F. 776 (3d Cir. 1923)

[33] *Id.* at 779; *see also* BARNOUW, *supra* note 29, at 120.

[34] STERLING & KITTROSS, *supra* note 30, at 88-89.

NAB quickly became the commercial broadcast industry's principal tool for exerting the centripetal pull towards coordination, both within the industry and in relations with other industries. An immediate solution to the copyright problem, however, was not forthcoming from the April meeting. Instead, as broadcasting quickly evolved from an experimental fad into a central component of the consumer economy and as profits rose, broadcasters acquiesced to ASCAP's annual blanket licensing fees. ASCAP, in turn, became increasingly dependent on the broadcast industry for its revenues: in 1930, forty percent of ASCAP's income was from radio music performance fees; in 1937, sixty percent, and in 1939, sixty-six percent.[35]

For most of the decade of the 1930s, this relatively happy arrangement between ASCAP and the broadcasters satisfactorily negotiated the tension between expansion and control felt by both industries; profits and the proliferation of electronically-reproduced music expanded annually, but control was maintained. The only problem was a by-product of the fact that the relation between copyright holders and broadcasters was a bureaucratic stand-in for market exchange, not an actual market. In a classical market, when people raise their prices too high, competition either forces them to lower prices or causes them to go out of business. In the case of ASCAP's blanket license, market regulation was absent. What was to prevent ASCAP from raising its prices? The problem was not one of monopoly: there were plenty of buyers and sellers—in a sense, too many of them. The problem was that prices were being set according to a theoretical model of a market where no real market existed against which to test the theoretical model's accuracy.

Thus, it was predictable that ASCAP would raise its fees. Early in 1932, ASCAP asked for a royalty increase of "an estimated 300 percent."[36] In spite of a struggle from the NAB, the increase stuck, perhaps because the initial rates had been low and broadcast profits were at the time growing dramatically. However, when ASCAP in 1937 announced a further increase of seventy percent to be implemented in 1939, the NAB responded by organizing a competing licensing organization, Broadcast Music Incorporated ("BMI"). A large fund was established to attract copyright holders to sign on with the new organization. BMI also neatly exploited the indeterminacy of the process of distributing

---

[35] *Id.* at 193.
[36] *Id.* at 132.

fees by statistical approximation. ASCAP's formula for fee distribution favored older, established composers; BMI sought to attract disaffected newer song writers by adopting a formula favoring new entrants into the business.[37]

In spite of these efforts, BMI's library of licensed music remained slim at first. Between January and October of 1941, BMI's first year, broadcast listeners were treated to the unending repetition of the few available BMI and public domain songs. During this time, for example, the BMI-licensed "Jeannie with the Light Brown Hair" was forever engraved on American popular memory.[38] Control and limitation were being exerted at the expense of expansion. Instability ensued as listeners grew weary and various broadcast organizations considered defecting to ASCAP. To further complicate matters, the Department of Justice filed suit against both ASCAP and the broadcast networks for antitrust violations. Stability did not return until a compromise with ASCAP was reached in conjunction with an antitrust consent decree that caused license fees to return to old rates and allowed BMI to remain in existence and share the business of blanket licensing with ASCAP.[39] With small modifications, the arrangement the Justice Department and ASCAP reached in 1941 has survived to this day.

What happened to the categories of property and copyright in this process? At first glance, it seems that copyright was enforced, property rights in broadcast music created, and capitalist market relations successfully extended into the sphere of broadcast culture. At second glance, however, the situation appears more complicated. The struggles between ASCAP and the NAB were not manifestations of straightforward marketplace competition. Rather, they were more like the political struggles that often occur within or between rival bureaucratic institutions: the rivalry was expressed in terms of statistical formulae, membership lists, and general legitimacy. Profits were certainly at stake in the struggle, but profit was determined by the relative political strength of the institutions in question, not by buying more cheaply or selling more dearly. The blanket licensing organizations are bureaucratic, political entities and they behave accordingly.

Copyright, in this light, has taken on a new role in relation to

---

[37] 2 Erik Barnouw, The Golden Web: A History of Broadcasting in the United States 110 (1968).
[38] Sterling & Kittross, *supra* note 30, at 193.
[39] *Id.*

the process of cultural production. In classical liberal legal practice, copyright's role was formal. It was used to draw boundaries in a marketplace: one person's property rights, vis-a-vis a book or an article, began and ended at a certain specific point, determined by the criteria of originality, expression, etc. In the corporate technique of blanket licensing, copyright's role is less formal and more like a functional standard: copyright acts as a general bureaucratic guideline, signifying the general goals of the system (capitalist profitability and expansion) to those inside it. The specific implementation of those goals depends less on boundary-setting than on bureaucratic arrangements that keep the system running, even if boundaries are allowed to grow quite blurry in the process. The question of who in the final instance authored a broadcast song, or more importantly who owes whom what for it, is often left open, but this is unproblematic as long as the general goals of the system are served and as long as the industries involved are profitable, expanding, and relatively stable.

VII.   FCC REGULATION OF PROGRAM OWNERSHIP AND CONTROL

Another transformation in the role of intellectual property is evident in the elaborate role of federal broadcast regulation in shaping the control and ownership of broadcast programs. The common sense view of private property suggests that ownership confers a kind of sovereignty, the right to do whatever one wishes with the thing owned. This notion was reflected in nineteenth-century industrial disputes, which were most often treated as a matter of locating the formal boundary between the property rights of the parties involved. If the effluent from a coal mine spilled into a neighboring farmer's field, for example, the courts would set out to find the line between the farmer's and the mine's property rights. Were the farmer's property rights being violated by the spill or would forcing the mine to limit operations violate its property rights?

Today, in contrast, blurry boundaries are often treated as a natural part of doing business. Network executives regularly force changes in plots and lines of dialogue in programs owned by nominally independent program producers. And producers, via the FCC, prohibit networks from owning properties that are available to anyone else on the open market. Television corporations, in fact, face an elaborate labyrinth of regulations that shape and channel the production and distribution of program property. Television stations, for example, cannot broadcast network entertainment programs between 7:30 and 8:00 pm; networks cannot contractually obligate their affiliates to broadcast network programs; program producers and distributors cannot grant networks distribution rights for program reruns; cable operators must blank out certain cablecast programs that duplicate local over-the-air offerings. All of these rules have generated vociferous debate over the rules' fairness and efficiency, yet few object to them on the grounds that they violate property rights.

In the day-to-day workings of the television industry, the concepts of ownership, property, and copyright have become increasingly residual categories, supplanted by considerations of efficiency, fairness, and the overall functionality of the system. Although broadcast executives and lobbyists are fond of publicly bemoaning their second class status under the First Amendment, implicit in this system of regulation, at regular intervals throughout the system's history, they also have embraced it with quiet enthusiasm. Most of the existing regulations, in fact, originated in suggestions or complaints from industry members.

Both this maze of regulations and the industry's deeply ambivalent attitude towards it can be best understood in terms of the highly bureaucratic nature of broadcasting, particularly broadcast television, as a system of production and distribution.[40] Before the networks can compete with each other, an elaborate smoothly flowing system of program production and distribution first must be in place. Relations between networks and affiliates, advertisers and broadcasters, and independent producers and broadcasters all need to become formalized and regularized, and the values of stability and predictability prevail. For example, it is extremely rare for a broadcast station to change its network affiliation; however, when a station does jump ship, the event prompts the question: "What went wrong?" It is treated, in other words, as an exceptional matter for concern throughout the industry, not as normal marketplace behavior. The concerns that dominate decision-making in the industry tend to involve, not just short-term profits, but ensuring the smooth coordination of the different parts of a complex, vertically integrated industrial system. This internal focus on system-maintenance helps to ac-

---

[40] *See* Streeter, *supra* note 23. The main economic and structural causes of television's corporate character are: 1) extremely high capital intensivity and the resulting problem of overcapacity, 2) the social structures associated with the presence of professionalism and a "managerial class" in television management, and 3) the linked decline of classical economic competitive relations and their replacement with oligopoly relations.

count for what Bernard Miege has characterized as television's "flow culture," the character of a system where "programming must be uninterrupted, constantly renewed and therefore produced on an unbroken conveyer belt."[41]

Government regulation of broadcast program production and distribution has proven useful as a means for system-maintenance and coordination, and dates back to the beginning of broadcasting. When hobbyists, entrepreneurs, and corporations first began using radio to send news, music, and entertainment to mass audiences in 1920, there was considerable confusion—both technical and institutional. Not only was the interference between transmitters growing, but there were a broad variety of competing visions about what this new practice was for. Was broadcasting for hobbyists, religious groups, schools, entrepreneurs or corporations? Was it for serious discussions, music, proselytizing, propagandizing, or advertising?

The Department of Commerce ("DOC") was initially responsible for regulating the airwaves. The DOC helped resolve the institutional questions in the process of solving the interference problem. Then Secretary of Commerce Herbert Hoover firmly established broadcasting as a commercial, corporate activity by directly and indirectly determining what kinds of materials could be sent over different channels. One of his first regulatory acts was to forbid radio amateurs—hobbyists operating on a nonprofit basis who had done much to develop and popularize the technology—from "broadcast[ing] weather reports, market reports, music, concerts, speeches, news or similar information or entertainment."[42] Later commercial broadcasters themselves were located on separate zones of the spectrum so as to favor larger, well funded organizations, particularly electronics corporations.[43] By limiting the participants in broadcasting and the rules under which they operated, the government cleared the ter-

---

[41] Bernard Miege, *The Logics at Work in the New Cultural Industries*, 9 MEDIA, CULTURE, AND SOC'Y 276 (1987).

[42] Marvin R. Bensman, *Regulation of Broadcasting by the Department of Commerce, 1921-1927*, in AMERICAN BROADCASTING: A SOURCEBOOK FOR THE HISTORY OF RADIO AND TELEVISION 548 (Lawrence W. Lichty & Malachi C. Topping eds., 1975).

[43] In August of 1922, a distinction between A and B broadcast licenses was created, where A stations at 360 meters had less power, and B stations at 400 meters had more power and were expected to broadcast original programming. *See id.* at 550; *Radio Control Hearings on S. 1 and S. 1754 Before the U.S. Senate Comm. on Interstate Commerce*, 69th Cong., 1st Sess. 42 (1926). On March 21, 1923, the Department of Commerce created a third category, a "C" class of stations which were under 500 watts of power and were assigned to (and thus forced to share) a single frequency. Class A and B stations, on the other hand, began to receive exclusive frequencies, giving them prominent places in the broadcast world. That same year, the Westinghouse Corporation proposed and re-

rain and provided a stable foundation on which commercial corporations could work out the network-dominated, advertising-supported system of broadcast entertainment that survives to this day. The 1927 Radio Act, the legislation which laid out the basic terms and principles that have governed broadcasting ever since, served to legitimize and formalize this arrangement.

Since the 1920s, U.S. Government involvement in regulating programming generally has concerned the linked flows of program goods and profits among the principal institutional elements in the system: program producers, networks, and network affiliated stations. Predictable and relatively stable relations among these three different elements are necessary to the profitable operation of the system, and yet, given the numerous players and interests involved, difficult to maintain. Over the years, as minor disputes among participants in the system have erupted, the industry has become accustomed to turning to the FCC to serve as a moderator.

This process began to assume its contemporary form during an FCC investigation of network broadcasting that began in 1939. During the 1930s, the two largest radio networks, NBC and CBS, established an overwhelmingly dominant position in the broadcast business, controlling the lion's share of program production, station ownership, and advertising revenue.[44] Unable to break the network stranglehold and eager to gain a share of the broadcast profit pie, fledgling networks, such as Mutual, complained to the FCC. In response to these complaints (and to Congressional trustbusting sentiments) the FCC held hearings and promulgated rules designed to limit network power. Although the rules that had the most impact focused on station and network ownership, some were directed at the flow of programming and profits as well. Networks were prohibited from controlling an affiliate's advertising rates and from contractually obligating affiliates to broadcast network programs. Affiliates, in turn, were required to allow other stations to broadcast network

---

ceived its own exclusive, interference-free classification, class D, for its flagship station. Bensman, *supra* note 42, at 551-52.

[44] By 1938, the total number of radio stations was no larger than it had been shortly after the beginning of broadcasting in 1927. The percentage of existing stations affiliated with the major networks had climbed to 52 percent, up from 32 percent in 1934. Moreover, all but two of the thirty very profitable high-power broadcast stations in the country were owned by either NBC or CBS; about half of the industry's net income went to the networks and their twenty-three controlled stations, leaving the other half to be divided among 637 independent and affiliated radio stations. *See* STERLING & KITTROSS, *supra* note 30, at 634-35; FCC, REPORT ON CHAIN BROADCASTING, Docket No. 5060, Commission Order No. 37, 99 (1941).

programs that the affiliates refused to air. Control and profits would thus remain, not evenly distributed among affiliates and networks, but adequately distributed to maintain a steady flow of programming through the system.

After a brief confrontation between the FCC and the networks reflecting the waning New Deal political climate, FCC regulation of program and profit flow among industry participants settled into a relatively quiet, ongoing, and routine pattern. Industry leaders and lobbyists for broadcast industry factions became accustomed to using the FCC as a forum for settling factional disputes and pie-sharing struggles. In the late 1950s, for example, squabbles between Hollywood program producers and the networks set off hearings and rulemakings that eventually led to a series of regulations governing ownership and distribution of programs. The producers' complaint was that the networks, as sole buyers of prime time programming, exploited their power unfairly. To redress this perceived imbalance, in 1970 the FCC enacted two rules: first, it forbade networks from syndicating independently produced programs (the syndication rule); second, it forbade networks from obtaining any financial or proprietary rights in independently produced programming beyond the right for first-run network broadcast (the financial interest rule). That same year, networks were prohibited from broadcasting more than three hours of entertainment programming during prime time (the prime time access rule), which effectively created a half-hour slot between 7:30 and 8:00 pm reserved for non-network, syndicated programs.[45]

The 1970 rules did not dramatically change the character of the system. Networks continued to dominate the system long after the rules were in place, and to this day network executives exert detailed, line-by-line control over the scripting and production of television programs. The rules did, however, shift some of the profits to the Hollywood producers, and create space for low budget independent programs such as *Wheel of Fortune* and *PM Magazine* in the prime time access slot. The rules, in sum, helped maintain equilibrium in the system.

The rise in this century of the use of federal administrative bodies as inter-industry dispute resolution mechanisms is a long and elaborate story. What is significant is the transformed role of

---

[45] FCC, NETWORK INQUIRY SPECIAL STAFF, *Evolution of Rules Regarding Network Practices*, in FINAL REPORT, NEW TELEVISION NETWORKS: ENTRY, JURISDICTION, OWNERSHIP, AND REGULATION 451 (Oct. 1980).

copyright and the principle of intellectual property. Through blanket licensing, bureaucracies simulate intellectual property principles. In FCC regulation of program flows among industry subdivisions, on the other hand, the question of property is very nearly abandoned and replaced by the goal of a smoothly functioning and profitable system for program production and distribution, measured by standards such as efficiency and the "public interest."

VII.   Combining Federal Regulatory Management with the Blanket License: Cable Television and the Copyright Royalty Tribunal

The television industry's biggest equilibrium-upsetting event in the last twenty years has been the appearance of cable television as a fourth element of the system.[46] When cable first began to grow in small markets in the 1960s, the FCC, under pressure from over-the-air broadcasters, put a halt to cable's expansion: at the time, the new technology seemed too threatening to the existing system's stability. As the FCC began to reverse itself in the early 1970s, and cable began to expand again, numerous questions of program and profit flow arose: if a cable system carries a local TV station, is some form of payment called for, and if so, should the cable system pay the TV station for the signal, or does the local station owe the cable system for the privilege of being retransmitted? What if a cable system imports a distant signal to compete with local TV channels, perhaps with some of the same programs that local stations contracted for an exclusive right to broadcast? The history and nature of the regulations dealing with these issues is too complex to detail here, and they are, in any case, still developing. The important point is that the underlying regulatory patterns (if not always the official rhetoric) followed the general principle of negotiating differences and maintaining overall profitable functioning within the television industry.

In cable, however, the question of copyright has resurfaced as a central issue, with the more traditional questions of system maintenance. The programs that appear on a local cable system typically have had multiple owners and have passed through many hands along the way. Syndicators, sports and music inter-

---

[46] For a history and analysis of the growth of cable, see Thomas Streeter, *The Cable Fable Revisited: Discourse, Policy, and the Making of Cable Television, in* 4 Critical Stud. in Mass Comm. 174-200 (1987).

ests, local stations, and others all can be thought to have property rights associated with the material distributed on cable systems. Given the huge volume of programming that fills a typical cable system, however, most seem to feel that regular direct payments to the thousands of individual copyright owners would be a practical impossibility.

As a result, when Congress rewrote the Copyright Act in 1976, they created the Copyright Royalty Tribunal ("CRT"), one of whose functions is to operate a blanket licensing system for cable television.[47] The CRT, a part of the Library of Congress, collects money from cable operators, puts that money into a pot, and then redistributes it to program copyright holders. Cable operators pay an amount set by a formula based on their subscriber rate, and program copyright holders receive payments according to a similar formula. The CRT, in sum, combines the strategy of the blanket license with the use of Federal regulation as a form of system-maintenance.

As with ASCAP and BMI, the CRT is set up to maintain a system of property rights and market exchange relations for the ephemeral, electronically reproducible good of television programming. And as with the music licensing agencies, in a general way, this appears to be what it does. Money flows from cable operators to program producers, and programs flow the other way. Again, however, many of the constituent features of classical market relations are absent. Costs and payments are set, not by supply and demand, but by politically established bureaucratic formulae. Entry into this particular market involves having the appropriate qualifications and filling out the appropriate forms, not offering to buy or sell a product. Increasing one's profit is a matter of lobbying Congress, not of buying more cheaply or selling more dearly. The CRT, furthermore, has numerous "side effects" uncharacteristic of markets but characteristic of bureaucracies. First, nonmarket rationale often play a crucial role in the process. In a frank, if modest, redistributive effort, for example, Congress allocated an extra-large percentage of the CRT pot to the Public Broadcasting System and none to the three networks. Even when market criteria are used to make decisions, the formulae used to calculate payments inevitably favor some at the expense of others, and thus become matters for intra-industry

---

[47] The cable television compulsory licensing scheme has been described as "undoubtedly the most complicated provision of the new [1976] Copyright Act." EDWARD W. PLOMAN & L. CLARK HAMILTON, COPYRIGHT: INTELLECTUAL PROPERTY IN THE INFORMATION AGE 104 (1980).

political disputes. The CRT is a bureaucratic, political entity and behaves like one; it just so happens that one of its directives, one of its administrative functions, is to simulate a system of private property and market exchange.

The CRT has been heavily criticized from a number of angles. Copyright holding organizations have predictably lobbied and litigated for higher rates and higher shares of the distributed royalties. These efforts, in turn, have made the workings of the CRT convoluted and lumbering. Between 1979 and 1982, for example, squabbles between industry groups and the CRT's ensuing tinkering with distribution formulae postponed finalized distributions for this period until 1986, in spite of the fact that the amounts involved were often relatively small.[48] As of 1989 the CRT had not yet completed its distribution proceedings for 1987.[49] Noting the perhaps predictable tendency of the CRT's bureaucratic machinery to generate an ever burgeoning and, on the surface, inefficient series of proceedings and hearings, some critics have called for the creation of a more "pristine" form of property relations based on simple direct contractual relations between copyright owners and cable operators.[50]

Alternatives to the CRT could undoubtedly be developed that are more fair or efficient, according to one or another definition of those words. What seems unlikely to change in the foreseeable future, however, is the habit of turning to bureaucratic practices as a means of achieving goals such as fairness, efficiency, and "free" markets.

IX.   CONCLUSION: THE BUREAUCRATIC SIMULATION OF PROPERTY

In concluding this Article, I review a hypothesis that I have developed in another context.[51] It has been said that we live in a time in which "all that is solid melts into air," in a "postmodern condition" in which life seems to be characterized more by the dizzying manipulation of words, signs, and symbols than by the iron necessities characteristic of nineteenth-century industrial society.[52] We no longer deal with things themselves, the consensus

---

[48] Fred H. Cate, *Cable Television and the Compulsory Copyright License*, 42 FED. COMM. L.J. 191, 211-12 (1990).

[49] *Id.* at 214.

[50] *Id.* at 222 *passim.*

[51] *See* Streeter, *supra* note 23.

[52] MARSHALL BERMAN, ALL THAT IS SOLID MELTS INTO AIR: THE EXPERIENCE OF MODERNITY (1982); JEAN-FRANÇOIS LYOTARD, THE POSTMODERN CONDITION: A REPORT ON KNOWLEDGE (1984).

seems to be, but with what Baudrillard calls simulations.[53]

The postmodern experience might be historically related to the sometimes tense relations between the liberal exterior and bureaucratic interior of our political economic system. This relation can be usefully illuminated by way of a modified version of Baudrillard's notion of "simulation," where simulation is taken to mean, more or less, a representation once removed, a representation that has taken on a life of its own, divorced from its referent. Without subscribing to Baudrillard's entire intellectual framework, I would like to suggest that intellectual property, and the ideology of individual creation that goes with it, is not so much eliminated by contemporary conditions as it is simulated.

The rapprochement between bureaucratic practice and liberal thought expressed in institutions like the FCC and the CRT has not been frictionless; the incongruity of authorless television being made possible by the authored legal construct of copyright is an example of the friction that results. The notion of the bureaucratic simulation of property helps specify the character and historical context of that friction. Bureaucracies invariably define themselves as neutral and transparent, as simply the most rational means to collective ends. Alternatively, bureaucracies might be understood as systems of signification or representation, as means of *simulating* aggregate goals or purposes. This would then dislodge bureaucracy's self-definition by loosening the mechanistic link between the bureaucratic "signifier" (administrative means) and the bureaucratic "signified" (collective goals). The current state of property might then be understood by combining the notion of bureaucracy as a means for simulating goals with the nominally liberal political system whose legitimacy rests on an ideology of private property and free markets. The creation of intellectual property in broadcasting, in this view, is neither a matter of simply extending property relations into the sphere of culture, nor replacing it with monopolies. Rather, property and markets can be seen as bureaucratically simulated.

When faced with the absence or breakdown of traditional market relations, our bureaucratically structured business world sometimes sets out to establish an administrative counterpart to property, a *simulation* of property using the language and procedures of bureaucracy. The discourse of the corporate individual allows a simulation of the individual author-owner. The practice

---

[53] Jean Baudrillard, *Simulacra and Simulations, in* SELECTED WRITINGS 166-84 (Mark Poster ed., 1988).

of blanket licensing in its various forms erects, in lieu of a system of actual market exchange for goods, a bureaucracy (ASCAP or BMI) whose function is to simulate the ownership and exchange of goods. Federal administrative mediation of industry disputes similarly inserts bureaucracies (the FCC and the CRT) into the middle of the processes of program exchange and distribution, supplanting market mechanisms with bureaucratic regulatory procedures, all in the name of upholding free enterprise.

The point here is not that commercial broadcasting is merely a colossal ruse, that corporations essentially dupe themselves and the general populace into falsely believing they are engaged in market relations when they are not. The corporate environment is complexly structured in a way that encourages some procedures and strategies, discourages others, and generally sets boundaries to what can and cannot be done. Mastering the structure of that environment, its grammars and codes, its pressures and limits, is a large part of what managerial skill is all about. The structure of that environment, its discursive economy, is such that bureaucratic practices are favored in day-to-day procedures, and yet on a broader level pressures are exerted and limits are set by the basic terms of liberal capitalism. The bureaucratic simulation of property, in other words, is the product of intelligent and skilled managers, lawyers, and politicians steering a course through the treacherous shoals of the corporate capitalist political environment. It is an accomplishment, not a falsehood.

Much more research would need to be done to substantiate the notion of the bureaucratic simulation of property. Here I can only offer it as a heuristic that provides a way of making sense of some eccentricities of the legal framework surrounding contemporary cultural production. Current discussions of property tend to oscillate between naive acceptance of the dominant discourse (*e.g.*, the CRT upholds property relations) and a sweeping dismissal (the CRT represents the disintegration and meaninglessness of property). The notion of bureaucratic simulation, I hope, suggests a more fruitful approach to the problem of intellectual property.

AUTHORSHIP AND THE CONCEPT OF NATIONAL CINEMA IN SPAIN

MARVIN D'LUGO*

In a recent issue of *Film Quarterly*, James Naremore observes the ironic state of film studies when referring to the question of cinematic authorship:

> [E]ven though the generation of '68 produced some of the most valuable and brilliantly iconoclastic writing in the history of film, they never really dispensed with authorship. They may have tried, in Foucault's famous phrase, to "imagine a world in which it does not matter who is speaking," but clearly they didn't live in such a world. For every "great man" they tried to kill off in the realm of naive consumption, they created another in the realm of theory, producing a kind of academic star system. Meanwhile, figures like Hitchcock and Sirk continued to serve important functions for [the British film journal] *Screen*, just as Balzac and Flaubert served important functions for Roland Barthes.[1]

It is this "function" of authorship that, as Naremore says, has been largely ignored in critical discourse on film, giving the false impression that the cinematic author is a "dead subject."[2] Pointing to the international contexts within which certain aspects of the issues of film authorship arise, Naremore notes the essential contradictions that appear to lie at the heart of authorship and which therefore sustain it as a theme of film scholarship.[3] The objective of this essay is to explore some of those contradictory spaces within which the cultural politics of authorship have operated, and to delineate an area that film theory has conveniently suppressed from consideration. My specific objective is to draw attention to the ways in which the idea of cinematic authorship may be applied productively to a rigorous revaluation of the concept of national cinema.

As Foucault argues in his seminal essay, *What is an Author?*,[4]

---

* Professor of Spanish & Director of Screen Studies, Clark Unviersity. A.B., 1965, Brooklyn College; A.M., 1967, Ph.D., 1970, University of Illinois.
[1] James Naremore, *Authorship and the Cultural Politics of Film Criticism*, FILM Q., Fall 1990, at 20.
[2] *Id.*
[3] *Id.* at 21.
[4] Michel Foucault, *What Is An Author?*, in LANGUAGE, COUNTER-MEMORY, PRACTICE 113 (Donald F. Bouchard ed. & Sherry Simon et al. trans., 1977).

[T]he author's name characterizes a particular manner of existence of discourse. Discourse that possesses an author's name is not to be immediately consumed and forgotten; neither is it accorded the momentary attention given to ordinary, fleeting words. Rather, its status and its manner of reception are regulated by the culture in which it circulates.[5]

The author's name is what Foucault would call a "discursive function," privileging certain categories of textuality over others, imbuing those privileged texts with a value that, as he observes, has a particular function and modality within the cultures where those discourses circulate:

[U]nlike a proper name, which moves from the interior of a discourse to the real person outside who produced it, the name of the author remains at the contours of texts—separating one from the other, defining their form, and characterizing their mode of existence . . . a private letter may have a signatory, but it does not have an author; a contract can have an underwriter, but not an author; and, similarly, an anonymous poster attached to a wall may have a writer, but he cannot be an author. In this sense, the function of an author is to characterize the existence, circulation, and operation of certain discourses within a society.[6]

In film studies, the critical attention paid to theories of authorship has almost never confronted with any seriousness either the issue of such discursive privilege, or the matter of that process of circulation of which Foucault speaks. Rather, it has emphasized issues of textuality over the contexts of cinematic discourse. The history of the idea of authorship, or auteurism, has been marked by a pendulum swing away from an initial romanticized cult of individual authors to efforts aimed at the analysis of the cinematic apparatus and its mobilization of subjectivity derived from Sausserian linguistics, Althusserian Marxism, and Lacanian psychoanalysis, leading finally to the apparent disappearance of the author from film scholarship. But in fact, as Naremore contends, the author has never really disappeared but has been metamorphosed into other types of critical discourse.

The "golden age" of much of the theoric discussion of authorship in film runs from the mid-1960s well into the 1970s. The product of that scholarship was a canon of auteur studies focusing primarily on a number of directors identified with the

---

[5] *Id.* at 123.
[6] *Id.* at 123-24.

Hollywood studio system or with European or "art" cinema. The notion of cinematic authorship first gained currency in France during the period immediately following World War II, in the pages of *La Revue de Cinéma*, and was followed in the 1950s by the rise of a polemical movement in favor of auteur criticism launched by the editors of *Cahiers du Cinéma*. In the second issue of *La Revue*, an article appeared entitled *"La création doit être l'ouvrage d'un seul."*[7] As Edward Buscombe points out, part of the project of *La Revue* was to raise the cultural status of cinema by making the case that film was an art form and, like painting, offered the possibility of individual expression.[8]

François Truffaut's 1954 essay in *Cahiers du Cinéma*, entitled *"Une certaine tendance du cinéma français,"*[9] advocated an even more strident attitude that Truffaut called *"la politque des auteurs."* Focusing on the unity of a cinematic work produced by the personality of its creative auteur, the *Cahiers* position, as elaborated by Truffaut, was an attack on the tradition of French "cinema of quality," which stressed the importance of script writing and literariness as central to the cinematic enterprise, thereby eclipsing other elements specific to the cinematic medium. The politics of authorship was intended to redress this imbalance by focusing on the centrality of more cinematically specific qualities. Thus, the *Cahiers* group opposed the tradition of French art cinema by emphasizing the achievement of decidedly populist and popular Hollywood film directors: Alfred Hitchcock, Howard Hawks, John Ford, and Orson Welles. In the hands of the editors of *Cahiers*, auteurism was, as Buscombe points out, somewhat less than a theory.[10] It was, rather, a polemical position that served to engage other critics and audiences in the appreciation of the cinematic qualities of films.

On this side of the Atlantic, Andrew Sarris's hyperbolic embrace of *"la politique des auteurs"* did as much to popularize the idea of auteurism as to mystify it.[11] It was Sarris, for example, who, in his essay *Notes on the auteur theory in 1962*,[12] first coined the phrase "auteur theory." This theory consists of a number of ten-

---

7 Edward Buscombe, *Ideas of Authorship*, SCREEN, Autumn 1973, at 75, *reprinted in* THEORIES OF AUTHORSHIP 22 (John Caughie ed., 1981).

8 *Id.* at 22-23.

9 François Truffaut, *Une certaine tendance du cinéma français*, CAHIERS DU CINÉMA, Jan. 1954, at 9.

10 Buscombe, *supra* note 7, at 22-23.

11 *See* Andrew Sarris, *Notes on the Auteur Theory in 1962*, FILM CULTURE, Winter 1962-63, *reprinted in* THEORIES OF AUTHORSHIP 64 (John Caughie ed., 1981).

12 *Id.* at 62.

ets. First, "[o]ver a group of films, a director must exhibit certain recurring characteristics of style, which serve as his signature. The way a film looks and moves should have some relationship to the way a director thinks and feels."[13] Secondly, "[t]he *auteur* theory values the personality of a director precisely because of the barriers to its expression. It is as if a few brave spirits had managed to overcome the gravitational pull of the mass of movies."[14]

Of the many romantic notions of cinematic authorship to which Sarris's theory lay claim, the most interesting from the standpoint of the subsequent circulation of authorial discourse was his view of the cinematic author as an oppositional figure. Sarris recognized the industrial structure of the film industry not merely as an "interference" to the filmmaker's creativity, but as an essential element in a tension between the author and his material, a tension that, as John Caughie says, "comes to structure the 'interior meaning' of the film."[15] Sarris writes: "Because so much of the American cinema is commissioned, a director is forced to express his personality through the visual treatment of material rather than through the literary content of the material."[16]

In the post-1968 period, the idea of the cinematic auteur was increasingly seen as an embarrassingly romantic indulgence. As students of film looked for a more intellectual, if not a more scientific, approach to the cinema, the auteur theory underwent a series of transformations that finally yielded a methodologically more respectable, and presumably more coherent, approach to cinematic analysis. The principal apologist of this new auteurism was the English theorist and film writer, Peter Wollen, whose treatment of auteurism in the 1972 postscript to his book, *Signs and Meaning in the Cinema*, marked the conversion of the idea of cinematic author into something akin to a theory. Wollen wrote:

> To my mind, the *auteur* theory actually represents a radical break with the idea of an 'art' cinema, not the transplant of traditional ideas about 'art' into Hollywood. The 'art' cinema is rooted in the idea of creativity and the film as the expression of an individual vision. What the *auteur* theory argues is that any film, certainly a Hollywood film, is a network of different

---

[13] *Id.* at 64.
[14] Andrew Sarris, *Toward a Theory of Film History*, FILM CULTURE, Spring 1963, *reprinted in* THEORIES OF AUTHORSHIP 65 (John Caughie ed., 1981).
[15] *Id.*
[16] Caughie, *supra* note 7, at 64.

statements, crossing and contradicting each other, elaborated into a final 'coherent' version. Like a dream, the film the spectator sees is, so to speak, the 'film facade,' the end-product of 'secondary revision,' which hides and masks the process which remains latent in the film 'unconscious'. . . by a process of comparison with other films, it is possible to decipher, not a coherent message or world-view, but a structure which underlies the film and shapes it, gives it a certain pattern of energy cathexis. It is this structure which *auteur* analysis disengages from the film.

The structure is associated with a single director, an individual, not because he has played the role of artist, expressing himself or his own vision in the film, but because it is through the force of his preoccupations that an unconscious, unintended meaning can be decoded in the film, usually to the surprise of the individual involved. The film is not a communication, but an artefact which is unconsciously structured in a certain way. *Auteur* analysis does not consist of retracing a film to its origins, to its creative source. It consists of tracing a structure (not a message) within the work, which can then *post factum* be assigned to an individual, the director, on empirical grounds.[17]

Wollen's view of auteurism wrested away from the text the very condition of creativity that had for the French cinephiles established the basis of the film as a work of art, namely the status of the filmmaker as artist. In its place, the apparent subjectivity of the artist was transformed into a range of cultural and ideological codes whose decipherment was achieved through recourse to the systematicity of particular methodological practices: Saussurian linguistics, Marxism, or psychoanalysis. In principle, such a revision would appear to posit the question of the relation of textual practices, here codified in the name of the author, to the larger ideological framework of the social order within which such texts arise and circulate. But in Wollen's approach, and that of others who followed his lead, questions of cinematic authorship henceforth became almost exclusively questions of institutional or textual practice informed by a progressively more elaborate theoretic apparatus that either ignored or supressed the name of the author. The critical animosity to the "name of the author" is perhaps most pointedly expressed in Stephen Heath's 1972 essay in *Screen*, "Comments on the 'Idea of Author-

---

17 PETER WOLLEN, SIGNS AND MEANING IN THE CINEMA 167-68 (1972), *reprinted in* Caughie, *supra* note 7, at 146.

ship,' "[18] which is a response to Edward Buscombe's earlier essay on *auteurism*. Heath observes:

> The function of the author (the effect of the idea of authorship) is a function of unity; the use of the notion of the author involves the organisation of the film (as 'work') and, in so doing, it avoids—this is indeed its function—the thinking of the articulation of the film text in relation to ideology . . . (the modes of subject-ivity); it thus allows at once the articulation of contradictions in the film text other than in relation to an englobing consciousness, in relation now, that is, to a specific historico-social process, and the recognition of a heterogeneity of structures, codes, languages at work in the film and of the particular positions of the subject they impose.[19]

Ironically, as the critical practice of auteurism came under increasingly more strident attack during the 1970s, the intensive critical and theoretic revision of the films of Alfred Hitchcock began to emerge around psychoanalytic feminist film theory.[20] Such critical discourse, while seldom acknowledging its relation to auteurism, effectively resemanticized auteur studies into a broader critical discourse. Canonical film theory thus succeeded in the seemingly contradictory task of suppressing auteurism while salvaging the author. While the critical dissent against the earlier notion of the cinematic auteur had largely been silenced, the very idea of film authorship had obviously not abated and, according to Naremore, even seemed to flourish.[21]

Since the seventies, the exploration of authorship appears to have resurfaced in film scholarship in a variety of ways. Thomas Schatz, in *The Genius of the System*, proposed that the critical focus in American film history should be on the role of the movie mogul in the development of studio styles.[22] Another example is the study of independent filmmakers and theorists, such as Jean-Luc Goddard and Pier Paolo Pasolini, who represent alternatives to dominant American cinema. Finally, there has been a growing awareness of major figures in Third World cinema such as Tomás Gutiérrez Alea of Cuba and Ousmane Sembene of Senegal, whose works reveal notions of the cinema's relation to society

---

[18] Stephen Heath, *Comments on the Idea of Authorship*, SCREEN, Autumn 1973, *reprinted in* Caughie, *supra* note 7, at 214-20.

[19] *Id.* at 217.

[20] *See generally* TANIA MODLESKI, THE WOMEN WHO KNEW TOO MUCH: HITCHCOCK AND FEMINIST THEORY (1988)(offering a detailed examination of the polemical issues of feminism and authorship that have focused on Hitchcock's films over the last two decades).

[21] Naremore, *supra* note 1, at 20-21.

[22] THOMAS SCHATZ, THE GENIUS OF THE SYSTEM (1988).

that is at radical variance with the traditions of European and American film culture.[23]

The insistence upon the author in critical discussion leads to the question that lurks at the root of Naremore's discussion: What is the fundamental attraction of the idea of the author in film scholarship? To come to grips with that question, one needs to return to Foucault, whose original interrogation of "What is an author?" moved him to formulate a series of new questions about the discursive formations of authorship. "What are the modes of existence of this discourse? Where does it come from?; how is it circulated; who controls it? What placements are determined for possible subjects?"[24]

As I have indicated, the principal debates over auteurism were centered around what is known in film studies as the "classical text," that is, the Hollywood style of narrative cinema. To consider these new questions of circulation and control, I want to shift to a relatively uncharted area of cinematic geography in which the idea of the author continues, in Foucault's words, "to circulate," and thus to pose some of the suppressed questions of why that circulation continues. In Latin America, as a telling example, "author cinema" has a special connotation as opposition cinema. Numerous filmmakers have received critical attention for those films that challenge the political repression and excesses of authoritarian regimes. Related to this project of opposition cinema have been filmmakers' efforts to develop "alternative" styles of filmmaking that oppose what they see as the cultural colonialization of their film industry by the aesthetic and economic pressures of Hollywood cinema.

Author cinema in Latin America has often been called "second cinema." This term is derived from the classification first espoused by Fernando Solanas and Octavio Getino, two Argentine theorists of revolutionary filmmaking in the Third World. Solanas and Getino identified three major currents in world cinema. The classical cinema of Hollywood and the major European industries they designated as "First Cinema." Author cinema that emerged in opposition to the dominant forms of neocolonial filmmaking identified with the Hollywood model was designated "Second Cinema." "Third Cinema" was theorized as a militant, antihegemonic cinema aimed at bringing an audience of peasants and workers into a direct confrontation with the real-

---

23 Foucault, *supra* note 4, at 138.
24 *Id.*

ity of their political and cultural dependency, thereby moving them to revolutionary action.[25]

According to Solanas and Getino, Second Cinema was an effort, albeit a limited one, at cultural and political decolonization. They observed: "This alternative [cinema] signified a step forward inasmuch as it demanded that the filmmaker be free to express himself in non-standard language and inasmuch as it was an attempt at cultural decolonization."[26] In this context, we can readily discern how in Latin America the status of the author and of author cinema is linked to the concept of the nation. By breaking with the dominant Hollywood style of cinematic form and production, filmmakers seek alternative filmic practices that will align them with the aspirations of authentic and liberated national cultures.

Roy Armes has studied the careers of a number of Third World auteurs,[27] and has found a marked tendency for these filmmakers to define their own activity as auteurs in relation to nationalist movements opposed to neocolonialism. These include men like Fernando Birri in Argentina, Tomás Gutiérrez Alea in Cuba, and Satyajit Ray in India. According to Armes, in the 1950s and 1960s a generation of Third World filmmakers took direct inspiration from the Italian neorealist movement; others, however, simply read in the example of their Italian counterparts—a startling example of alternative strategies that seemed remarkably apt for the context of their own cultural circumstance. [28]

---

[25] Octavio Getino, *Some Notes on the Concept of a "Third Cinema,"* reprinted in ARGENTINE CINEMA 99 (Tim Barnard ed., 1986).

[26] Fernando Solanas & Octavio Gettino(sic), *Towards a Third Cinema,* reprinted in MOVIES AND METHODS 51 (Bill Nichols ed., 1976).

While acknowledging the project of author cinema in the Third World, Solanas and Getino are extremely critical of the potential such an enterprise affords filmmakers: "[S]uch attempts have already reached, or are about to reach, the outer limits of what the system permits. The *second cinema filmmaker* has remained 'trapped inside the fortress' as Goddard put it, or is on his way to becoming trapped." *Id.* at 51-52.

[27] ROY ARMES, THIRD WORLD FILM MAKING AND THE WEST, 80-85 (1987).

[28] *Id.* at 80. Armes describes the ideal of Italian neorealism conception and praxis this way:

The creators of neorealism had all worked in the mainstream of Italian commercial cinema during the early 1940s, and when they began making their own films in the early postwar years, not only did they inherit their equipment and commercial outlets from a fascist cinema they wished to supercede, but they also had to confront an audience shaped by the escapist entertainment cinema of the Mussolini years. Neorealism was a cinema made with limited means: often the rushes could not be viewed because there was no money to pay for prints, and films were shot silent (and post-synchronized) to allow shooting on location in the streets. But the resultant films were neither amateurish nor avant-garde: thanks to their professionalism and

Armes notes how:

> the processes of national independence and popular struggle and a growing awareness of a distinctive Third World identity can bring [these filmmakers], as intellectuals, into a new relationship with the mass of their fellow countrymen, and they show in their films a similar desire to uncover a hidden reality—in their case, the world concealed beneath the distortions and lies of colonial or neocolonial cultural dominance. Realist film making—for which the neorealists in Italy could serve as exemplars—set itself a number of tasks that distinguish it from mainstream entertainment cinema.[29]

With Armes we thus return to the notion that was originally expressed by Sarris, that the American filmmakers evolved their auteurist identities in opposition to the production system imposed by the Hollywood studios.[30] Sarris's sense of the auteur as opposition figure was defined as an emotional and creative tension with the system. But in societies on the margin of European and American film culture we can discern how the identity of the individual film author is inextricably bound to the question of national identity in ways that define a radically different kind of study of cinematic authorship.

It is in this context that I want to consider the case of authorship in Spanish cinema. Though obviously not a Third World culture, historically, Spanish cinema has occupied roughly the same position as culturally colonized national cinemas in the Third World. That culture of dependency has contributed in no small way to the emphasis upon author cinema as perhaps *the* single dominant feature of film production in Spain for the last four decades. Its emergence in the early 1950s was the direct result of the discovery of the Italian neorealist film movement by students of Spain's National Film School. Long dissatisfied with official cinema, controlled and regulated through elaborate censorship and subsidy systems, the young men of the National Film School of the 1950s were looking for ways to express Spain's social reality that had been systematically blocked by the patterns and ideology of national cinema. For the reasons that Armes described in relation to Latin American cinema, neorealism seemed to provide at least the strategies, if not the substance, of what these

---

artistic quality, they succeeded in conveying the truths of contemporary poverty, unemployment, and old age to audiences throughout the world. *Id.* at 81.

[29] *Id.* at 82-83.

[30] Sarris, *supra* note 11, at 64.

men sought: a re-engagement with Spanish cultural reality and the embrace of an anti-hegemonic style that was a rebuke of the Francoist ideology of representation.

As in the romantic notion of the author as rebel, the men who emerged as authors in the Spanish cinema of the 1950s were nearly all opponents of the status quo cinema and the imposter culture it purveyed. In a famous critique of the effects of governmentally coerced film production, the outspoken Juan Antonio Bardem described the relation of Spanish film to its audience in these terms:

> Living with its back to Spanish reality, our cinema has not been able to show us the true face of the problems, the land, or the people of Spain. This atemporal, hermetic, and false creation of a supposedly Spanish reality, such as it appears in our films, totally distances itself from the rich realist tradition of the Spanish novel. Right here and now, the spectator of Spanish cinema is unable to learn from a Spanish film about the Spanish style of living, how Spaniards revel, or how they suffer. . .The vision of the world, of this Spanish world, portrayed in Spanish film is false![31]

Bardem's denunciation of Spanish film under Francoism is inseparable from his broader rejection of the cultural politics of the Franco regime, which, since the end of the Civil War in 1939, had cleverly used the film industry to its own propagandistic and ideological ends. The rise of author cinema in Spain, which Bardem's position heralded, thus became inevitably aligned with the project of redefining Spanish national culture.

During the 1950s a number of young directors rose to prominence as opposition filmmakers. Their work was perceived in official circles and received by Spanish audiences as a rejection of the policies and ideology of Francoist "official culture." Of these, Bardem himself cut the most striking figure. He gained notoriety for his critical presentation of social repression in his films, and was, in his published articles on Spanish cinema in the counter-cultural journal *Nuestro cine*, an outspoken critic of the Spanish film industry. Bardem's aggressive positions led to continual difficulties with both the censors and the government. While publicly martyred at home (he was even arrested for a short while by the Civil Guard while shooting a film that was said to have displeased government authorities), the publicity he and

---

[31] Marvin D'Lugo, The Films of Carlos Saura: The Practice of Seeing 21 (1991) (quoting Emmanuel Larraz) (citation omitted).

his films enjoyed at European film festivals was as much a rebuke of fascist Spain as it was the recognition of the individual artist.[32]

Bardem's early career thus mirrors a paradigmatic situation as it recurs throughout much of Third World cinema: the alienation of individual filmmakers within a repressive culture and their eventual encounter with a form of popular filmmaking that effectively critiques the official construction of the nation as a means of connecting with the popular will; subsequently the international "ghettoization" of such films and their creators, which leads to their "appreciation" at foreign festivals as "authors" closely identified to national causes. Inevitably, this national/international interface reveals the insistent alignment of certain types of national cinema with the external "construction" of the author.[33]

The cult of the cinematic author gained force throughout the late 1950s and 1960s in Spain through a variety of additional channels. One of these was the direct influence of European journalistic support of auteurism in magazines such as *Cahiers du Cinéma* which, in turn, led to the development in Spain of cognate journals with a similar auteuristic bent. Such publications, though small in circulation, became the catalyst for the increased consciousness of the idea of cinematic authorship as a potent weapon in the counter-cultural movement against Francoism. They brought to the attention of a generation of aspiring filmmakers the work of foreign auteurs—Rossellini, De Sica, the Italian neorealists, the recently emergent French New Wave, and finally even their own fellow countryman, Luis Buñuel who, in

---

[32] The position of Bardem's work at home and abroad confirms Paul Willemen's observation the Third World Cinema's shifting semantic field as viewed by European audiences:

> In Europe, most Third Cinema products have definitely been consumed in a Second Cinema way, bracketing politics in favour of an appreciation of the authorial artistry. A pessimist might argue that the deeper a film is anchored in its social situation, the more likely it is that it will be 'secondarised' when viewed elsewhere or at a different time unless the viewers are prepared to interest themselves precisely in the particularities of the sociocultural nexus addressed . . . .

Paul Willemen, *The Third Cinema Question: Notes and Reflections*, reprinted in QUESTIONS OF THIRD CINEMA 9 (Jim Pines & Paul Willemen eds., 1989).

[33] Much of what is said here of Spanish cinema can easily be applied to any of a number of Third-World cinemas. Armes, for instance, draws particular attention to the 1960s Brazilian Cinema Novo movement which, like "New Spanish Cinema," evolved from young opposition filmmakers embracing neorealism and attempting to cultivate ties with populist anti-colonial aspirations. As such, Cinema Novo increasingly came to identify with the ideal of the nation, and the works of movement members, especially Glauber Rocha, gained prominence at foreign film festivals as auteurs whose productivity was aligned with the popular aspirations of the Brazilian people. *See* ARMES, *supra* note 27, at 71-85.

exile since the 1930s, was one of the favorites of the French film press but whose work had been all but unknown in Francoist Spain.

To these external influences upon the formation of the institution of Spanish cinematic authorship must be added two other seemingly contradictory forces that emanated from the government. The first was the censorial apparatus itself. The continual coercion of the film industry by the government through the elaborate system of pre-shooting and post-production censorship led a number of filmmakers intuitively to attempt a quasi-symbolic and seemingly hermetic mode of cinematic expression that, it was believed, could somehow fool the censors and yet communicate with the Spanish public. In advancing such a project, the filmmaker became an ingenious double scriptor of the film.

Here perhaps the case of Bardem's colleague and sometimes collaborator, Luis García Berlanga, is most telling. Berlanga's 1953 comedy, *Welcome Mister Marshall,* is a biting attack on the Francoist idealization of Spanish folkloric culture posed as merely a comedy about life in a sleepy, backward Castilian town. The suggestive textual system of the film, replete with dialogue and plot situations that mocked the regime's cultural policies, surprisingly, was able to pass the censors and achieve a wide popular success. Other less explicit examples abound throughout the final decades of the dictatorship in which the ingenuity of the filmmaker circumvented the censors' scissors and thereby established a distinctive signature as a critical voice of dissent.

A period of liberalization in the bureaucratic handling of the film industry occurred during the 1960s in which the government attempted to appropriate for its own advantage the promotion of the cult of authorship. The underlying premise of their packaging of "New Spanish Cinema" (the generation of young filmmakers, many of whom had recently emerged from the National Film School) was to show the outside world that Franco's Spain repudiated its belligerent origins and was opening itself to new ideas, even to internal political opposition.[34] Even as the censorship system continued to impose upon given filmmakers' works often severe restrictions on their power of expression, other government offices were providing subsidies and even special festival screenings for these films.

---

[34] In their critique of the idea of Second Cinema, Solanas and Getino speak of the ways in which "the system" often exploits to its own advantage the voices of opposition film authors as these authors remain naive about the flexibility of the system in assimilating their opponents. Nichols, *supra* note 26, at 52.

In following the course of one of these Spanish auteurs, Carlos Saura, along with Pedro Almodóvar, the best known of Spanish filmmakers, one can more precisely chart the politics of Spanish cinematic authorship. Saura's work becomes emblematic because it dramatizes, as the work of few other authors does, the critical bridge between the construction of the author as an external, contextual practice and the interior discursive practices that similarly define cinematic authorship. It suggests to us, as well, a type of textual praxis that is faithful to the post-structuralist goal of examining the ideological uses of cinematic textuality while recognizing the historical and political circulation of the name of the author as a privileged discursive formation.   Saura is, to a degree, a product of the peculiarly politicized cultural environment of the Franco dictatorship. His increased awareness of the possibility of authorial identity as a filmmaker was nurtured by a critical view of the repressive and anachronistic state of Spanish culture and, as well, a growing resentment of the intimidation and coercion of the censorship system. During the formative period of his career, from 1959 to 1963, Saura's first two films, *Los golfos* (*Hooligans*) and *Llanto por un bandido* (*Lament for a Bandit*), were severely treated by the censors. Not only were shooting scripts of these films rejected, forcing massive rewrites, but the final copies of both works were cut up by the censors who objected to specific scenes and dialogue. Understandably, Saura sought some sort of authorial control over the material aspects of film production that might guard against such incursions. He would eventually find such control through his collaboration with Elías Querejeta, the producer of his next film, *The Hunt* (1965), who would collaborate with Saura in a dozen more films over the next seventeen years.

Querejeta's plan was to develop an "international" style for Saura's films that would acknowledge the national and international contexts that define Spanish film. He proposed a strategy that would enable them to get the support of the government subsidy office and address two well-defined audiences, one Spanish and the other a limited cosmopolitan public abroad. Querejeta well understood that while a domestic audience was the prime target of a Spanish film, foreign festival recognition was essential if a Spanish film was to attract an audience at home. Querejeta understood, as well, that Bardem's appeal to foreign audiences in the 1950s was the result of that director's cinematic denunciations of the Francoist regime. Recognizing these textual and contextual parameters, Querejeta proposed to redefine what Saura had previously viewed as an adversary relation with the censorship boards into a more constructive collaboration.

Still opposing the regime, Querejeta was looking for a way to "negotiate" a film through the bureaucratic machinery so that it might actually receive the necessary support of the government while, in effect, critiquing from within the very system that supported it. The result of this strategy was a series of films that stylistically shifted focus from a neorealist to a seemingly more modernist cinema; that is, from an overtly political cinema of denunciation to a much more cerebral one that sought to expose the ideological deceits of Francoism. The effectiveness of this strategy may be gauged by the fact that in their first collaboration, *The Hunt*, Saura won the Silver Bear at the 1966 Berlin Film Festival for Best Direction, with the head of the jury, Pier Paolo Passolini, citing him for "the courage and indignation with which he presented a human situation characteristic of his timed society."[35]

Yet, ironically, while actively pursuing such authorial control over the material aspects of film production, Saura revealed within his films clear evidence that the notion of authorship remained for him a problematic issue. Running parallel to nearly every one of his films is what might be termed the narrative "allegory of authorship." That is, symbolic plots that place under the mark of suspicion the very presumption of the characters' individuality that, outside the fictionality of the film, Saura appears to pursue. His filmography, in effect, evolved as a double-tiered configuration of dramatized "authors-in-the-text" and the biographical "author-outside-the-text" as described by Kaja Silverman,[36] each in apparent conflict with the other. As he achieves progressively more authorial control, his protagonists seem more emphatically locked in the trap of discovering the social and historical constraints of Spanish culture that have denied them their true autonomy.

No more than a half dozen of the protagonists of Saura's films are literal authors-in-the-text. Yet, throughout his other films the paradigm evolves of individuals who strive to achieve a figurative authorship, that is, as the external author has done, to become originators of discourse. That authorial discourse is most often expressed within Saura's films through a scopic regis-

---

[35] D'LUGO, *supra* note 31, at 67 (quoting Roman Gubern)(citation ommitted)(translated from Spanish).

[36] KAJA SILVERMAN, THE ACCOUSTIC MIRROR 193-212 (1988).

ter. The characters are often portrayed as spectators, viewing the world around themselves and, through their gaze, attempting to reason the logos of this world as well as their own position in it. Seemingly unobtrusive, these on-screen spectators fulfill a double role within the cinematic narrative. They function as the on-screen agency of visual narration, an insistent trope of classical narrative cinema. They enact a form of discursive resistance to the dominant forms of representation, however, by questioning what they see.

The function of Saura's specularized authors-in-the-text is to place in question the larger relation of cinema to the dominant forms of cultural and political imaging that spectators have internalized. Such patterns of figuration within the cinematic text are aimed at exposing for the audience the discursive practices that shape their own sight and, consequently, their knowledge and understanding of the world. In *The Imaginary Signifier*, Christian Metz argues that "the cinematic institution is not just the cinema industry . . . it is also the mental machinery—another industry—which spectators 'accustomed to the cinema' have internalized historically and which has adapted them to the consumption of films. The institution is outside us and inside us, indistinctly collective and intimate, sociological and psychoanalytic. . . ."[37] With Saura, therefore, the question of extratextual authorship is always linked intimately with the interior textual construction and deployment of allegories of authorship.

The restaging of spectatorship within Saura's filmic narrative expresses in its most basic form the filmmaker's distrust of the simple visual dictation of social reality that many of his contemporaries during the Franco years were clamoring for in the name of social realism. We find evidence from the very start of his professional career that Saura preferred to use the cinematic medium to map the emotional and spiritual relation of Spaniards to the dubious projections of a mythologized Spain that had "Francoized" Spanish culture. Central to his development, therefore, was the intense scrutiny of the socially determined ways of seeing that the characters in any given film had absorbed as part of their formation as Spaniards. Against the normative patterns of institutionalized social sight, Saura depicted other characters who "mirrored" the position of the real spectator of the film, but who, unlike the spectator, paused to gaze and interrogate the social *mise-en-scène* in which they found themselves.

---

[37] CHRISTIAN METZ, THE IMAGINARY SIGNIFIER 19 (Celia Britton et al. trans., 1982).

Through this interrogative practice of seeing, Saura was able to question the discursive practices that had naturalized the various myths of "Spanishness" that had formed and deformed the contemporary Spaniard.

To repeat the forms of intelligibility of a repressive and backward society was, to his thinking, a futile task. His intuitive response to this circumstance of constraint was to look outside the illusionist frame of the cinematic apparatus to the place of the spectator, and, from there, to conceptualize his films within an intertextual mode, that is, the folding back upon itself of the discourse of Spanishness, postulating the narrative and its telling as a "textual rewriting or restructuration of a prior historical or ideological *subtext*."[38]

Although developed as a necessary response to the constraints of state censorship during the final fifteen years of the Franco dictatorship, Saura's elaboration of an author's cinema has continued well beyond that period, principally as he has increasingly come to see in the figure of authors-in-the-text a way of bringing a larger audience to question hegemonic patterns of culture that have shaped individual and cultural identity. In continually positing the questions of authorship "in-the-text," Saura's films suggest the richness and complexity of the concept of cinematic authorship that challenges the notions of "culture-blind" theoreticians of cinema. Authorship, as Saura's work attests, is not simply a reified figure external to the textual practices that define a given film. When fully realized within textual and cultural practice, the notion of the author can become the cipher of a series of discursive resistances to the ideological as well as industrial patterns that shape the cinematic institution.

As we attend to the modes of existence and circulation of authorial discourse in cinemas that lie on the margins of the sphere of domination defined by the Hollywood film industry, we may begin to discern the condition of authorial cinema as a part of an insistent strategy of cultural resistance. As Foucault's model of interrogation of the idea of authorship suggested to us, we need to begin the process of recognizing the multiple histories—social and political as well as personal—that traverse the figure of the author.

---

[38] FREDRIC JAMESON, THE POLITICAL UNCONSCIOUS 81 (1981).

"DON'T HAVE TO DJ NO MORE": SAMPLING AND THE "AUTONOMOUS" CREATOR

DAVID SANJEK*

"[T]he street finds its own use for things—uses the manufacturers never imagined."

—William Gibson[1]

Musical language has an extensive repertoire of punctuation devices but nothing equivalent to literature's " " quotation marks. Jazz musicians do not wiggle two fingers of each hand in the air, as lecturers sometimes do, when cross-referencing during their extemporizations, as on most instruments this would present some technical difficulties.

—John Oswald[2]

Get hyped, c'mon we gotta
Gather around—gotcha
Mail from the courts and jail
Claim I stole the beats that I rail
Look at how I'm livin' like
And they're gonna check the mike, right? Sike
Look at how I'm livin' now, lower than low
What a sucker know
I found this mineral that I call a beat
I paid zero
I packed my load cause it's better than gold
People don't ask the price but its [sic] sold
They say I sample but they should
Sample this my pit bull
We ain't goin' for this
They say I stole this
Can I get a witness?

—Public Enemy, "Can We Get A Witness"[3]

It is a longstanding practice for consumers to customize their commodities, command their use and meaning before they are commanded by them. The Puerto Rican poet, Víctor Her-

---

* Director of Broadcast Music Inc. Archives. B.A., 1974, Connecticut College; M.A., 1979, Ph.D., 1985, Washington University.
[1] MIRRORSHADES: THE CYBERPUNK ANTHOLOGY at xiii (Bruce Sterling ed., 1988).
[2] John Oswald, *Bettered by the Borrower: The Ethics of Musical Debt*, WHOLE EARTH REV., Winter 1987, at 104, 106.
[3] PUBLIC ENEMY, *Caught Can We Get a Witness*, on IT TAKES A NATION OF MILLIONS TO HOLD US BACK (Def Jam/Columbia Records 1988).

nandez Cruz, comments on this practice in his prose poem *The Low Writers*, where he describes how the inhabitants of the San Jose barrio inscribe meaning upon their vehicles:

> When I am in this room that flies it is as if I invented rubber. Like San Jose Low riders interiors, fluffy sit back, unwind, tattoo on left hand, near the big thumb a cross with four sticks flying, emphasizing its radiance, further up the arm skeletons, fat blue lines, Huichol designs on the copper flesh, the arm of the daddy-o on the automatic stick. A beautiful metal box which many call home. It doesn't matter if the manufacturer was Ford or General Motors, their executives in the suburbs of Detroit watching home movies, vacationing in weird Londons, when the metal is yours you put your mark on it, buying something is only the first step, what you do to it is your name, your history of angles, your exaggeration, your mad paint for the grand scope of humanity, the urbanites will see them like butterflies with transmissions.[4]

Similarly, the consumers of recorded music possess a range of options for the recontextualization of preexisting compositions: they can take material from one format and transfer it from a given context to another, thereby creating their own "mixes"; alter speed or pitch or juxtapose distinct recordings through mixers, variable speed turntables, or filters; or manipulate the recording on an adaptable turntable. Without doubt, while "[p]assivity is still the dominant demographic," a recording can be "played like an electronic washboard."[5] As Cruz states, the purchase of a commodity is only the first step; it can become the means of declaring your "exaggerations," your "mad paint for the grand scope of humanity."[6]

The range of options available either to the consumer or the creator for the recontextualization of existent recordings has been substantially enlarged by computer technology, specifically the Musical Instrument Digital Interface, or MIDI. A MIDI converts any sound into a series of retrievable signals which, since they can be stored on a computer, may be manipulated as one would manipulate any computer program. In effect, if one can type, one can compose; the programmer and the composer are now synonymous. Since one is able to retrieve any compositional element at will, as well as store any musical phrase, rhythmic de-

---

[4] VICTOR HERNÁNDEZ CRUZ, *The Low Writers*, in BY LINGUAL WHOLES (1982).

[5] John Oswald, *Plunderphonics: Or, Audio Piracy as a Compositional Prerogative*, 34 MUSICWORKS 5, 7 (1986).

[6] Cruz, *supra* note 4.

vice, or vocal effect one desires, the range of compositional possibilities is endless. This has undeniably enlarged, if not "democratized," the ranks of potential creators. Instrumental dexterity is no longer a prerequisite for creation. As John Leland has written:

> The digital sampling device has changed not only the sound of pop music, but also the mythology. It has done what punk rock threatened to do: made everybody into a potential musician, bridged the gap between performer and audience . . . . Being good on the sampler is often a matter of knowing what to sample, what pieces to lift off what records; you learn the trade by listening to music, which makes it an extension more of fandom than musicianship.[7]

However, it should be evident that the elevation of all consumers to potential creators thereby denies the composer or musician an aura of autonomy and authenticity. If anyone with an available library of recordings, a grasp of recorded musical history, and talent for ingenious collage can call themselves a creator of music, is it the case that the process and the product no longer possess the meanings once assigned them? Also, how is one to guarantee the livelihood of the composer of the sampled material, and insure that it is accorded the protection of copyright, if the sampling does not appear to infringe upon the original material under the protection of the "fair use" clause of the 1976 Copyright Act? The question of sampling's propriety remains open, but it is a process whose presence in the recording of music is increasing, not decreasing. It is my purpose, therefore, to address three questions. First, what is sampling's history and how is it connected to other common practices in the recording process; are the ideological presuppositions of rock history, which see technology as directly opposed to self-expression, no longer operative? Second, how has the sampling process necessitated a reexamination of copyright law and infringement litigation; has the "fair use" clause been rendered more elastic or called into question altogether? Finally, is sampling the postmodernist artistic form par excellence, and, if so, does it demand that we reexamine certain ideologies of performance, composition, and authenticity that have driven rock history for most of its duration? And, when considering these questions, we must not forget the dominant society's demonization of much contempo-

---

[7] John Leland, *Singles*, SPIN, Aug. 1988, at 80.

rary popular music as well as the fact that the very technology that permits the process of sampling is manufactured by conglomerates that demean their employees and pollute our environment.[8] It is all too easy to fall prey to a vision of a technological utopia of unfettered creativity while forgetting the workers who construct the chips that drive MIDI synthesizers, or that the dominant culture feels it needs to defend itself against the ideological contestation in some sampled music.

While sampling is most often associated with the genre of rap and hip-hop, it has in fact become common in the recording of all forms of music. Sampling is a process with a distinct history, a developed aesthetic, and a set of auteurs who have defined the parameters of its use. Rather than engaging in rock's traditional distinction between technology and art, the romantic assumption that any overindulgent use of technology diminishes not only individual "feel" or "touch" but also the very idea of self-expression, sampling proceeds from a belief in the innovative potentialities of technology and the use of a recording *itself* as a musical instrument. It legitimizes the belief that technological devices can be utilized by musicians and audiences alike (two distinguishable constituencies that sampling effectively unifies, as the technology can make any audience member a potential musician) to appropriate the products of capital and the recording industry to serve their own devices.

Sampling began as a manual procedure and gained in sophistication and precision with the invention and marketing of inexpensive computer technologies that transferred the work of the DJ to the programmer. The performing modes it largely, but not exclusively, serves—rap and hip-hop—have their origins in various black vocal performance styles including acapella work songs, skip-rope and ring game songs, doo-wop vocalizing, Cab Calloway and other jazz vocalists (including Leo Waton and Slim Gaillard), and the aggressive braggadocio of Bo Diddley.[9] However, technique and technology came together in Jamaica when portable sound systems allowed DJs such as Prince Buster, Duke Reid, Sir Coxsone, and Lee "Scratch" Perry to establish mobile discotheques and, using records by all manner of Jamaican and non-Jamaican artists alike, engage in audio combat with one another. They began to chant over the records, scatting or toasting

---

[8] For documentation of the hazards to the environment, their workers, and the economy wrought by the computer manufacturers of Silicon Valley, see DENNIS HAYES, BEHIND THE SILICON CURTAIN: THE SEDUCTIONS OF WORK IN A LONELY ERA (1989).

[9] DAVID TOOP, THE RAP ATTACK: AFRICAN JIVE TO NEW YORK HIP-HOP 83 (1984).

improvised sets of lyrics. At first, this was an exclusively live phenomenon. Later, producer/engineer King Tubby discovered that by manipulating the elements of a recording through reverb and echo or emphasizing bass tracks and phasing elements of the vocal in and out of the mix, one could create a multitude of versions from the raw components of any given recording.[10] Henceforth, what was once a purely vocal performance-based form became a technological creation, *dub*. It allowed for the process Dick Hebdige has called "versioning," whose beauty is that "it implies that no one has the final say. Everybody has a chance to make a contribution. And no one's version is treated as Holy Writ."[11] Performers adapted King Tubby's discovery to their own ends, and dub performers such as U Roy, I Roy, Big Youth, Tapper Zukie, Dr. Alimentado, Prince Far I, Augustus Pablo, and Eek a Mouse chanted their lyrics over the booming bass and echoing guitar and drums of the dub mix.

Dub most likely made its way to the United States through the Kingston, Jamaica-born Kool DJ Herc who emigrated in 1967 and purchased a sound system in 1973.[12] He soon, along with such other early key DJs as Theodor, Afrika Bambaataa, and Grandmaster Flash, began to establish the techniques that would lead to sampling: emphasizing the "break-beat" passages of a given record by cueing and extending a particular rhythmic break until the crowd was virtually exhausted; spinning or "scratching" a record very quickly on a single groove so that the vinyl itself becomes a percussion instrument; switching adeptly from one record to another or "punch phasing" so one musical passage flows seamlessly to the next; and emphasizing the pulse of the records by adding an electronic beat box. DJs engaged in style wars, a veritable form of aesthetic combat in which the audio auteurs attempted to outdo one another by providing the freshest sounds, the hardest beats, and the widest range of tracks. The result was, in the words of Houston A. Baker, Jr.:

> Discotechnology was hybridized through the human hand and ear—the DJ turned wildman at the turntable. The conversion produced a rap DJ who became a postmodern, ritual priest of sound rather than a passive spectator in an isolated DJ booth making robots turn. A reverse cyborgism was clearly at work in the rap conversion. The high technology of advanced

---

[10] Dick Hebdige, Cut 'N' Mix Culture, Identity, and Caribbean Music 83 (1987).
[11] *Id.* at 14
[12] Toop, *supra* note 9, at 19; *see also* B. Adler, Rap! - Portraits and Lyrics of a Generation of Black Rockers 15 (1991).

sound production was reclaimed by and for human ears and the human body's innovative abilities. A hybrid sound then erupted in seemingly dead urban acoustical spaces.[13]

However, as DJing was a manual technology, its range of effects was as limited as the manual dexterity of a lone individual. That all changed with the MIDI synthesizer, first engineered by the American company Sequential Circuits in 1981 and marketed by Sequential in conjunction with Roland and Yamaha in 1983. The MIDI works by taking an analog audio signal and converting it into a string of computer digits which can be held in random-access memory, retrieved, and introduced into a given recording. The process of recording a sample requires only that one set a level and press a record button. Playback is accomplished by connecting a piano-style keyboard to the sampler; striking a key on the keyboard "triggers" the sample.[14] Anything can be sampled, from a melody to a rhythmic accent, or even a vocal ejaculation. At first, a MIDI synthesizer unit could cost as much as $20,000, and, therefore, its use was beyond the economic reach of the live DJ. However, as prices fell (the unit nowadays costing as little as $2,000) the technology not only fell into the hands of a wider range of individuals but also cost far less to maintain and took far less time to master than standard instruments. Thus, it has led us to enter what some have called an Age of Plunder and Orgy of Pastiche, as the MIDI permits the possibility of deconstructing any available recording or any recordable material into a novel construction. It furthermore permits "the increasingly oligopolistic control of musical media [to be] countered by the consumer preference for devices that can, in some sense, increase their control over their own consumption."[15]

The range of possible uses for sampling is wide, but the forms it has taken can roughly be broken down into four general areas, each of which is distinguishable by the amount of sampling included, its placement in the material, and the effect the sampler has accomplished by the use of computer technology.

First, there are those records which sample known material of sufficient familiarity so that the listener may recognize the quotation and may, in turn, pay more attention to the new material as a consequence of that familiarity. Examples of the practice in-

---

[13] Houston A. Baker, Jr., *Hybridity, the Rap Race, and Pedagogy for the 1990s, in* TECHNOCULTURE 197, 200 (Constance Penley & Andrew Ross eds., 1991).

[14] J.D. Considine, *Larcenous Art,* ROLLING STONE, June 14, 1990, at 107-09.

[15] Simon Frith, *Art Versus Technology: The Strange Case of Popular Music,* 8 MED., CULTURE & SOC'Y 263, 275 (1986).

clude Run DMC's "Walk This Way," which incorporates Aerosmith's original recording; Hammer's "U Can't Touch This," which is built around a repeating riff from Rick James' "Super Freak"; and Vanilla Ice's "Play That Funky Music," which incorporates as its bridge that line as sung in the song of the same name by Wild Cherry. In addition, there is the quoting of material not immediately recognizable to the listener, but whose sampling is so frequent and widespread that it attains a measure of familiarity to the listener. The chief example of this practice is the drumming of Clyde Stubblefield, percussionist for James Brown from 1965 to 1971; his playing on the 1971 minor hit "Funky Drummer" has been sampled by various artists including Sinead O'Connor, Fine Young Cannibals, Big Daddy Kane, the Good Girls, Grace Jones, Mantronix, Michel'le, Seduction, Todd Terry Project, Alyson Williams, and most notably at the beginning of Public Enemy's "Fight The Power," on which Chuck D. raps "1989 the number another summer/Sound of the funky drummer."[16]

Secondly, there are those records which sample from both familiar and arcane sources, thereby attracting a level of interest equal to the lyrical content. Most often the amount of sampling, particularly on rap recordings, is minimal, the emphasis being laid on the rap itself and the beat supporting it; excessive sampling might be felt to intrude upon the vocal performance. However, other artists crowd their work with an intentional and at times oppressive amount of sound, sampled and otherwise. They act as what Simon Reynolds has called "chaos theoreticians," for their work reflects the chaos of society by metronomically replicating the din and collisions of a traumatized civilization.[17] Principal amongst these artists is Public Enemy, whose three albums to date—"Yo! Bum Rush the Show," "It Takes A Nation of Millions To Hold Us Back," and "Fear Of A Black Planet"—pile up layers of ingenious wordplay, ideological agitation, and some of the densest mixing imaginable to "Bring The Noise" to a resistant public. Their records, like Radio Raheem's boom box in Spike Lee's "Do The Right Thing" (itself playing Public Enemy's "Fight the Power"), are meant to be aurally agitating. Of equal interest is the work of the British producer/mixer and director of the On-U Sound record label, Adrian Sherwood. In addition to

---

[16] Harry Weinger, *The Ghost in the Machine is a Drummer*, ROLLING STONE, June 14, 1990, at 105.

[17] SIMON REYNOLDS, BLISSED OUT: THE RAPTURES OF ROCK 160 (1990).

found sound and polemical quotations from various sources, Sherwood's releases (over forty in all) incorporate and sample materials and performances from the realms of rock, reggae, dub, punk, and hip-hop. In his work with the performer Gary Clail and the ensemble Tackhead (which includes the rhythm section, Keith LeBlanc and Doug Wimbush, that propelled the recordings of one of the pioneering rap labels, Sugarhill Records), Sherwood aims for what has been called "sonic terrorism."[18] However, not all these samplers, who maximize their use of appropriated materials, aim to antagonize their listeners. A number of them playfully and wittily utilize the technology to more peaceful ends, including De La Soul, A Tribe Called Quest, and Digital Underground. They make it clear that one is able to maintain street credibility without losing a sense of humor. Like the technology it employs, sampling can be adaptable.

Finally, in a process dubbed "quilt-pop" by critic Chuck Eddy, recordings can be constructed wholecloth from samples to create a new aesthetic.[19] The landmark recording that laid the groundwork for this form was the 1980 "Adventures Of Grandmaster Flash On The Wheels Of Steel" on which the DJ joined together elements of Chic's "Good Times," Queen's "Another One Bites The Dust," Blondie's "Rapture," and three raps, Sugarhill Gang's "8th Wonder," Furious Five's "Birthday Party," and Spoonie Gee's "Monster Jam." The result was a recording about "taking sound to the very edge of chaos and pulling it back from the brink at the very last millisecond. On this record Flash is playing chicken with a stylus."[20] The technology Grandmaster Flash used to create these audacious and spectacular results is primitive compared to that available to contemporary samplers. Today, more sophisticated forms of montage encompass not only musical sources, but all manner of sounds in what might be described as instances of musical onomatopoeia. These would include S'Express, M/A/R/R/S, Cold Cut, and the Jams, whose album "The History Of the Jams a.k.a. The Timelords" sarcastically details on its sleeve all the legal and journalistic brouhaha left in their wake.[21] Certainly one of the most exciting and prolific creators of sampled collage is the young mixer/producer

---

[18] MC, *Chaos Theory: Tackhead*, I-D MAGAZINE, Oct. 1990, at 73-74.

[19] Chuck Eddy, *Quilt-Pop: Reap What You Sew*, VILLAGE VOICE, Oct. 24, 1988, at 86.

[20] Hebdige, *supra* note 10, at 142.

[21] A striking illustration of how rich and complex mixing can be is the transcription of M/A/A/R/S's re-mix of Erick B. & Rakim's "Paid in Full - Seven Minutes of Madness." *See* MARK COSTELLO & DAVID FOSTER WALLACE, SIGNIFYING RAPPERS: RAP AND RACE IN THE URBAN PRESENT (1990).

Todd Terry. Under various names, including Masters at Work, Black Riot, Swan Lake, and Royal House, Terry's "aggressive appropriation and recycling of breaks, hooks, shouts, and choruses from all corners of clubland combine with a rhythmic propulsion for another sort of postrap noise: raw, reckless, risky jams as exhilarating as they are brutal."[22]

Finally, sampling has been utilized in the ever proliferating domain of "mixes." As new dance forms or performance styles come into fashion, mixers—many of whom began, and on occasion still act as club DJs—are hired to produce alternate versions of a given recording in that style. Now it is uncommon to find a 12-inch release that does not include any number of versions, including the dance, dub, acid, house, and new jack swing mixes in addition to the ubiquitous bonus beats. (One wonders which amongst the various versions would be considered the Ur-Mix?). Mixers such as Arthur Baker, Trevor Horn, Rick Rubin, and Jellybean Benitez (in whose footsteps younger mixers such as Scott Blackwell, "Little" Louis Vega, and Freddie Bastone hope to follow) have found that their careers as DJs opened the path to full-time producing.[23] The degree to which these individuals deconstruct the original texts they mix can be so extreme that Arthur Baker was once named "Rock Critic Of The Year."[24]

It should come as no surprise that the practitioners of sampling have been accused of sheer pilferage, of appropriating the work of others because they are incapable of creating any of their own. Jon Pareles, popular music critic of the New York Times, in a piece entitled "In Pop, Whose Song Is It, Anyway?" wrote, "[I]t sometimes seems that sophisticated copying has overtaken innovation, that an exhausted culture can only trot out endless retreads."[25] He and other critics would like us to believe that if, as Marvin Gaye and Tammi Terril sang, "Ain't Nothin' Like The Real Thing," then sampling is a mere reflection of the real thing.

However, it is absurd to assert that we are living in an audio echo chamber, cycling and recycling the same sounds without adding to our stock of materials. Samplers engage in the practice for a number of reasons, only one of which (and any honest sampler will admit to it) is their lack of instrumental expertise. Part

---

[22] Vince Aletti, *The Single Life: Can We Party?*, VILLAGE VOICE, Jan. 10, 1989, at 67.

[23] Rusty Cutchin, *The Sons of Jellybean*, WORKING MUSICIAN, Aug. 1989, at 81-82, 84, 86, 116.

[24] Andrew Goodwin, *Sample and Hold: Pop Music in the Digital Age of Reproduction*, 30 CRITICAL Q. 34, 47 (1988).

[25] Jon Pareles, *In Pop, Whose Song Is It, Anyway?*, N.Y. TIMES, Aug. 27, 1989, (Arts & Leisure), at 1.

of it is surely their fascination with a form of technology whose cost and use is easily within their grasp. Additionally, technology is now so developed it has made the manual practice of DJing outmoded. But, even more important is the belief that sampling is not so much ransacking the past as reanimating it. As Greg Tate writes, "[M]usic belongs to the people, and sampling isn't a copycat act but a form of reanimation. Sampling in hip-hop is the digitized version of hip-hop DJing, an archival project and an artform unto itself. Hip-hop is ancestor worship."[26] No better illustration of hip-hop's sense of its own geneology exists than the persistent inclusion of lists of inspirations of the genre as well as those current practitioners who are hardcore and those who deserve to be dissed. Self-serving as the posture may seem to some, sampling in many cases resurrects material the conglomerates in charge of record companies have allowed to languish in their back catalog (those recordings kept in print but not customarily released to record sellers unless upon request) or taken out of print. As Stetsasonic argue in "Talkin' All That Jazz," "James Brown was old/Till Eric & Rak came out with 'I Got Soul'/Rap brings back old R&B."[27] Sampling, one could also argue, only benefits the conglomerates, as much of the CD market has been dedicated to just that archival material. However, one final reason individuals sample, as I was told by Prince Paul, former member of Stetsasonic and producer of De La Soul, is that the advances in recording technology have not necessarily improved the sound of recording, and he, therefore, often samples older records because, despite the resources available to him in the contemporary studio, he cannot recreate that original sound. Therefore, rather than denigrate the practice of sampling as Jon Pareles does, calling it "appropriationist art," we might instead examine what it allows artists to accomplish.[28]

We need also to realize that, while writers like Pareles focus almost exclusively upon rap and hip-hop music, sampling practices now pervade all elements of modern music recording. The magnetic recording tape that recording companies began to use in the 1950s has, from the start, made possible all manner of cutting/splicing/dubbing/multi-track recording. To assume that studio-produced recording is "natural," while the sampling of recorded material is "artificial," is splitting hairs. Producers and

---

[26] Greg Tate, *Diary of a Bug*, VILLAGE VOICE, Nov. 22, 1988, at 73.

[27] STETSASONIC, *Talkin' All That Jazz*, on IN FULL GEAR (Tommy Boy Records 1988).

[28] Pareles, *supra* note 25, at 1.

artists who belittle sampling see nothing wrong in availing themselves of the same technological resources—which range from digital delay to string and drum machines, emulators, and synclaviers—when it will save them the cost of hiring a live string section. As Evan Eisenberg has written, "The word 'record' is misleading. Only live recordings record an event; studio recordings, which are the great majority, record nothing. Pieced together from bits of actual events, they construct an ideal event. They are like the composite photograph of a minotaur."[29]

And yet, if one may not photograph a minotaur, one can market a recording and sample it too; but what then is the legal status of that sampled record? Is it now a new composition and how should its authorship be credited, royalties be judged, and proper monetary distribution of earnings be made? Such questions are complex and it must be admitted that the Copyright Act of 1976 fails to apply in any direct way to the administration of sampled material.[30] Furthermore, it can be argued, and samplers have done so, that the very nature of copyright is inexorably West European, in that it recognizes the melodic and lyrical components of any given piece, but fails to encompass its rhythmic components. And if rap and hip-hop are, like all Afro-American music, rhythmic in nature—as Max Roach states, "The thing that frightened people about hiphop was that they heard people enjoying rhythm for rhythm's sake"—can a rhythm be protected under the statutes as they now stand?[31] Charles Aaron focuses on the legal peculiarity of sampling's status when he writes:

> An experienced lawyer would advise any sampler to ask himself the following questions before seeking a license or selling a composition: Is the sample melodically essential to both the original and new work? Is it readily recognizable in its new context? Is it crucial to the financial success of both the original and the new work? But questions based on melodies or "hooks" or "key phrases" often don't apply to hip-hop, which is a *rhythmic* construct of patched-together drum beats and bass fragments, animated by snatches of melodic figures.[32]

What then is the legal status of a sampler and his use of digi-

---

[29] Evan Eisenberg, The Recording Angel: The Experience of Music from Aristotle to Zappa 109 (1987).

[30] *See generally* Copyright Act of 1976, Pub. L. No. 94-553, at 101, 90 Stat. 2541 (1976).

[31] Tate, *supra* note 26, at 73.

[32] Charles Aaron, *Gettin' Paid. Is Sampling Higher Education, or Grand Theft Audio?*, Village Voice Rock & Roll Quarterly, Fall 1989, at 22, 23.

tal technology for the appropriation of other artists' material? Is it merely, as J. C. Thom asserts, "[N]othing but old fashioned piracy dressed in sleek new technology"?[33] Clearly, any number of performers and writers have felt themselves to be abused, and therefore, pressed their cases in the courts. The most publicized of cases have been the Turtles' $1.7 million suit against De La Soul for using part of "You Showed Me" in the rappers' "Transmitting Live From Mars" and Jimmy Castor's suit against the Beastie Boys for using drum beats and the words "Yo Leroy" from his hit recording "The Return of Leroy (Part I)." Both suits were settled despite the heated publicity, yet not all negotiations have been acrimonious. Hammer split his publishing royalties 50-50 with Rick James for the use of the passage from "Super Freak," and 2 Live Crew worked out an arrangement for a payment of 5.5 cents per sale with Bruce Springstein for material incorporated in "Banned in the USA."[34]

Despite the variety of settlements, the legal status of a sample involves three key issues: the nature of the appropriation, the amount in bars or length in number of seconds, and the intention of use, either to compliment or parody and in some way damage the status of the original recording. At present, any legal resolution of these questions must refer back to the 1971 Sound Recording Act,[35] as a sample is always the transfer of an element of a recording to another recording. The 1971 Act, itself enacted in response to the marketing of audio cassettes and the recording industry's panic over home taping,[36] supplemented the 1907 Copyright Act[37] which did not legislate protection of recordings. Its writers felt they were not tangible entities, as is a piece of sheet music or a score, and they received no protection until the 1971 Act. However, due to a mistake, the Act protects only those recordings made subsequent to 1972, any earlier recording being protected by individual state statutes.[38]

The 1971 Act protects the work of the writer, the artists, and all performers, engineers, and manufacturers involved in a recording. Under the Copyright Act, authors control how their work is used, and any individual who wishes to appropriate the

---

[33] J.C. Thom, Comment, *Digital Sampling: Old-Fashioned Piracy Dressed Up in Sleek New Technology*, 8 Loy. Ent. L.J. 297, 336 (1988).

[34] Jeffrey Resner, *Sampling Amok?*, Rolling Stone, June 14, 1990, at 105.

[35] Sound Recording Act of 1971, Pub. L. No. 92-140, 85 Stat. 391 (1971).

[36] *See* H.R. No. 92-487, 92d Cong., 1st Sess. 2 (1971).

[37] The Copyright Act of 1907, ch. 320, 35 Stat. 1075 (codified as amended at 17 U.S.C. §§ 1-215 (1909)).

[38] See Thom, *supra* note 33, at 308.

piece in some fashion must apply for a mechanical license through the Harry Fox Agency, sole agent in charge of such transactions, at the rate of 5.25 cents per composition per record sold or one cent per minute, whichever is larger. The 1971 Act extends the protection from the writer to include the other prior mentioned individuals involved in the recording of that piece of material. It asserts a recording to be as much a "work" as a documented composition, thereby updating the 1907 law.[39] Although the recording industry customarily pays each of the "authors" of a recording, thereby allowing the record label to be the sole possessor of copyright, the Act nonetheless names performers, engineers, and manufacturers as co-authors. In the Senate Committee hearings drafting the 1971 Act, the following statement was made:

> The copyrightable elements in a sound recording will usually, though not always, involve "authorship" both on the part of the performers whose performance is captured and on the part of the record producer responsible for setting up the recording session, capturing and electronically processing the sounds, and compiling and editing them to make the final sound recording. There may be cases where the record producer's contribution is so minimal that the performance is the only copyrightable element in the work . . . . [T]he bill does not fix the authorship, or the resulting ownership, of sound recordings, but leaves these matters to the employment relationship and bargaining among the interests involved.[40]

The problem with this supposed resolution of the issue of pirated recordings, the immediate worry being the practice of home taping, is that it is meant to protect the reproduction of a whole recording, not the appropriation of separate sounds on that recording which digital technology permits. As is often the case with copyright legislation, the law must catch up with advancing technology. Nonetheless, the burden of proof of piracy is upon the plaintiff, who must prove that the accused party had access to the recording and that the new work is "substantially similar" to the original. Proving this can be difficult if the original work has been so mechanically altered as to be unrecognizable. The defendant can try, in turn, to apply the "fair use" component of copyright law and assert that he appropriated

---

[39] *Id.* at 306-07.
[40] H.R. REP. No. 487, 92d Cong., 1st Sess. (1971), *reprinted in* 1971 U.S.C.C.A.N. 1566, 1570.

neither the "hook" nor the "essence" of the original composition, that his borrowing of a sound, rhythm, or stock musical phrase is so insignificant or *de minimus* as not to damage the original recording, make light of its substance, or affect its marketability. Aside from these qualitative measures, he may also apply the quantitative tests posited in legal decisions but which are not necessarily outcome determinative. These include the limits to infringement stated in the 1915 *Boosey v. Empire Music Co.*[41] settlement that indicated that borrowings of six notes or more are an infringement when accompanied by phraseology similar to that sung in the original and the 1952 *Northern Music Corp. v. King Record Distribution Co.*[42] settlement that indicated that the appropriation of any more than four bars can indicate piracy. However, these presumed precedents were complicated by the 1974 case, *United States v. Taxe*,[43] that involved a defendant who pirated tapes of hit records produced and distributed by major record companies; the defendants changed the originals through alteration of speed, frequencies, or tones and addition of echoes or other sounds produced by a Moog synthesizer. They claimed the result was a "derivative" work, but the court was not persuaded by that defense. One commentator summarized the holding of the case as stating that "even though the right to reproduce is limited to the recapture of original sounds, that right can be infringed by an unauthorized re-recording which, despite changes in the sounds duplicated, results in a work of substantial similarity."[44] The significance of the *Taxe* decision can be found in the court's instructions to the jury which seemed to foreshadow the type of problem that would crop up repeatedly with the advent of digital technology. Thus the court instructed the jury that "[a]n infringement which recaptures the actual sounds by re-recording remains an infringement even if the re-recorder makes changes in the speed or tone of the original or adds other sounds or deletes certain frequencies, unless the final product is no longer recognizable as the same performance."[45]

Clearly, the law has begun to reflect the possibilities open to creators through digital technology, but it has not yet fully resolved the substance of sampling. A possible solution is for Con-

[41] 224 F. 646, 647 (S.D.N.Y. 1915).
[42] 105 F. Supp. 393, 397 (S.D.N.Y. 1952).
[43] 380 F. Supp. 1010 (C.D. Cal. 1974), *aff'd, vacated, and remanded in part*, 540 F.2d 961 (9th Cir. 1976), *cert. denied*, 429 U.S. 1040 (1977).
[44] Thom, *supra* note 33, at 327.
[45] *Id.* at 328 (quoting *Taxe*, 380 F. Supp at 1017).

gress to amend copyright legislation to establish some specific restrictions on duration, but this might affect the mechanical rate structure and raise the wrath of music publishers and songwriters. Another alternative is for the record companies to establish an industry-wide rate structure for licensing of and royalty payments for samples, but that could lead to complaints of price fixing. The likely resolution is outlined in the proposals of Steven R. Gordon and Charles J. Sanders.[46] Samplers should apply for the appropriate licenses, respect the rights of copyright holders, and be respected in turn as equal creators. Responsibility for obtaining clearance should fall to either the artist, the label, or both. Samplers realize that in the litigious environment of the United States, there is nothing to be gained and much money potentially to be lost by being a renegade. Surely some obscure materials will be sampled and overlooked, but the process should proceed devoid of recrimination and with the opportunity for money to be made by both the sampler and those whom he samples.

However, all too often the process has become embroiled in accusation and litigation even when the sampler operates outside

---

[46] "Practical Guidelines of Phonorecord Sampling Etiquette and Ethics"

1. Samplers should apply for mechanical and master licenses for any sample whose source is in any way recognizable by an informed listener as it appears on the new recording.

2. Copyright owners of both the sampled underlying musical composition and the master sound recording should give due consideration to licensing requests made by samplers, and if no philosophical or practical bar to such licensing is harbored by the petitioned licensor, license the use at a fair and reasonable rate.

3. Samplers should respect the rights of copyright owners both to receive fair compensation for sampling uses, or to deny the use if the owner so sees fit. In instances in which the material being sampled may not be copyrightable, but the final sampling use represents a recognizable taking of the style of the particular artist who created the sound which was sampled, similar consideration should be extended to such artist.

4. Sampling license applications should be made by samplers in writing "without prejudice," and potential licensors should accept the "without prejudice" nature of the request in all cases, in order to encourage the licensing process on the whole.

5. Mutual respect for the artistic integrity of both the sampler's work and the work being sampled should characterize all negotiations and discussions between the parties.

- Edward P. Murphy, president and CEO of The National Music Publishers' Association, Inc. and The Harry Fox Agency, Inc., in New York, reports that the Fox Agency is always willing to pass along licensing requests from samplers to the Agency's publisher principals, and to issue such licenses for use of the underlying song being sampled on instructions from the publisher, in a timely manner.

- Joel Schoenfeld, general counsel to the Record Industry Association of America in Washington, D.C. states that RIAA staff are available to help samplers seeking licenses to get in contract with the master licensing departments of its record company members in order to speed the licensing request process.

Steven R. Gordon & Charles T. Sanders, *The Rap on Sampling: Theft, Innovation, or What*, *in* ENTERTAINMENT, PUBLISHING, AND THE ARTS HANDBOOK 211 (1988).

the commercial mainstream, acknowledges his sampling, and in no way intends the new work to act as a detriment to that which it appropriates. Such was the case for John Oswald, a Canadian musician, operator of the Mystery Laboratories project, and a professor of music at York University, Toronto. Over the last several years, Oswald has spoken and published about the sampling process as a means of composition he calls "Plunderphonics," the practice of "electroquoting" or "audioquoting." Although Oswald uses sampling techniques, he has always been entirely aboveboard in his procedures and has in no way attempted to hide behind fair use protection. He stated in an interview, "My overall game plan was to try not to be covert about anything," and further indicated he wished all records came with footnotes or bibliographies of who they quoted.[47] Oswald saw his work as being in the avant-garde tradition that treated all forms of sound, recorded and otherwise, as potential compositional elements. In a March 1988 guest editorial in *Keyboard* Magazine he wrote:

> If creativity is a field, copyright is the fence. . . . When writers borrow ideas, they enclose the material in quotation marks and credit the source by name. There's a similar solution for musicians: credit all sources in print on albums and recital programs. . . . By definition, sampling is a derivative activity. Samples won't replace all pianos; they will continue to refer to pianos. Similarly, a sample or quote from an existing composition refers to, rather than steals from, the original. It's not necessary to tear down the copyright fence when you can enter from the gate.[48]

Despite Oswald's straightforwardness about his practices, he had the gate rather rudely slammed behind him. In 1987 he released a vinyl EP of four treated pieces by Stravinsky, Count Basie, Elvis Presley, and Dolly Parton that was followed by the 24 piece, 73 minute Plunderphonics CD with its sampled cover design of the head of Michael Jackson attached to a scantily clothed female body. As stated on the packaging, "Any resemblance to existing recordings "—or existing individual—" is unlikely to be coincidental. This disc is absolutely not for sale."[49] Furthermore, it includes a circled S, the computer term for programs

---

[47] Mark Hosler, *Plunderphonics*, MONDO 2000, Summer 1990, at 102, 103-04.

[48] Gerry Belanger, *Plunderphonics—Who Owns the Music?*, OPTION, Jul./Aug. 1990, at 16 (citing John Oswald's guest editorial, Neither a Borrower nor a Sampler Prosecute, Keyboard, Mar. 1988).

[49] JOHN OSWALD, PLUNDERPHONICS (Mystery Laboratories 1987).

that can be reproduced indefinitely by anyone with access to them. Unfortunately, the Canadian legislation against duplication and piracy is staggering, and when Bruce Robertson, president of the Canadian Recording Industry Association (CRIA) was presented with the CD, he responded by stating, "My immediate and deep reaction was not to the music, but to the gross distortion of Michael Jackson's image. . . . It was the combination of the music being played around with that only added insult to injury."[50] Yet, in the end, the injured party was not Jackson, but Oswald, for Robertson threatened to prosecute him to the full extent of the Canadian law despite the CD's disclaimer, its being not for sale, and general lack of publicity (until the prosecution that is) outside the avant-garde music community. Oswald was threatened with exorbitant infringement fines, a six year prison term, and required to surrender all remaining CDs and master tapes. He did so, and, in a compromise, agreed to surrender all materials, thereby erasing the master tapes and ceasing distribution of the materials, which one can only obtain through copies being made of the original CD. What Jackson and others gained from the action is vague, but what is lost is the work of a thoughtful artist who may well be extending the potential uses of recorded sound.

Oswald's fate brings us to the question of how sampling has transformed our notions of composition and authenticity. Some have designated sampling, with its emphasis upon appropriation, replication, and simulation, as the Postmodernist artistic form par excellence. Others less rhapsodically remind us that our emphasis upon the autonomous creator might well be a romantic artifact, and technology has so pervaded the creative process that the rhetoric of co-option lacks substance. True, sampling disrupts our long-cherished notions of the autonomous creator, but the technology that permits it allows consumers to appropriate not only the technology of mass culture but also the ideology that surrounds it for their own purposes. Sampling reminds us that our notions of mimesis have an aural component, for when we distinguish between "real" and sampled sound, it forces us to reconsider notions we have lazily allowed to abide in a virtual pre-technological avoidance of what sound means.

Furthermore, the fury sampling has given rise to in some people must be connected to the demonization of much popular music, particularly the rap and hip-hop genres. When *Newsweek*

---

[50] Belanger, *supra* note 47, at 18.

denigrates the "attitude" of much contemporary Afro-American music as a debasement of civilized standards, we must not only recognize that a diverse and complex community is being painted with too broad a brush but also wonder how much of its work the dominant society has sampled?[51]

Finally, sampling must be seen as a tactic, not the means of a technological utopia of unfettered creation by disenfranchised cultures. Is it as important to focus upon the process of pastiche as the ends which pastiche might serve? Too often the discussion of sampling has led to either exaggerated cultural pessimism or a facile polemical overenthusiasm. While too many voices bemoan the process of pop eating itself, might it be better to turn to the work and recognize that we have only begun to discover the potential sampling holds for the disposition of sound rather than focus on whose music is this anyway?

---

[51] The questionable analysis of rap and hip-hop music was included in two articles, Jerry Adler et al., *The Rap Attitude*, NEWSWEEK, Mar. 19, 1990, at 56-59, and David Gates, *Decoding Rap Music*, NEWSWEEK, Mar. 19, 1990, at 60-63. The best judgment of these two pieces is contained in the January 1991 issue of *The Source. The Magazine of HipHop Music, Culture & Politics*, the principal journal on that scene, where it states:

DON'T BELIEVE THE TYPE: The good news is that Tone-Loc was on the cover. The bad news is everything else inside. *Newsweek*'s March 19 issue fronted as a fair representation of our art form and our culture but really was a one-sided, vicious attack which ignored the positive value of rap and portrayed rappers and rap fans as threatening to mainstream culture. With this story, *Newsweek* confirmed that much of the media has *no clue* about what rap music really is.

The 1990 Hip-hop Year in Pictures, THE SOURCE, Jan. 1991, at 48.

BEAUMONT AND/OR FLETCHER: COLLABORATION AND THE INTERPRETATION OF RENAISSANCE DRAMA*

JEFFREY A. MASTEN**

It were . . . wisdome it selfe, to read all Authors, as *Anonymo's*, looking on the Sence, not *Names* of Books . . . .[1]

" 'What does it matter who is speaking,' someone said, 'what does it matter who is speaking.' "[2] It is perhaps writing against the grain of this Essay to begin by quoting Foucault's quotation of Beckett in his essay *What Is an Author?*, elaborately framed by the technologies keeping in place the Author whom Foucault critiques—the quotation marks, the citation. To follow this genealogy of quotation back further is to reach Beckett's ambivalent "someone," though even here I would want to note the attribution of these words to an authorial presence. *Someone*, like *anonymous*, denotes the insistence of the authorship question; though it does not identify, it marks a space for identity, a need to know "who is speaking."

The historicity of that need is registered in the word *anonymous*, which supports Foucault's contention that the author has a particular point of emergence as a cultural fiction. *Anonymous* does not take on its recognizably modern sense in English ("bearing no author's name; of unknown or unavowed authorship") until the late seventeenth century; earlier, around 1600, the word signifies "a person whose name is not given, or is unknown," but does not connect persons with texts.[3] Beginning

---

* This article is printed with permission of the Johns Hopkins University Press. *See* 59 ELH 337 (1992).

** B.A., 1986, Denison University; A.M., 1987, Ph.D. 1991, University of Pennsylvania. Professor Masten is currently Assistant Professor of English and American Literature and Language at Harvard University.

[1] RICHARD WHITLOCK, ZOOTOMIA, OR OBSERVATIONS ON THE PRESENT MANNERS OF THE ENGLISH: BRIEFLY ANATOMIZING THE LIVING BY THE DEAD 208 (London, Tho. Roycroft & Humphrey Moseley 1654) (emphasis added).

[2] MICHEL FOUCAULT, *What Is an Author?*, in THE FOUCAULT READER 101 (Paul Rabinow ed., 1984).

[3] 1 THE OXFORD ENGLISH DICTIONARY 493 (2d ed. 1989) [hereinafter OED]. A survey of seventeenth-century reference materials shows that, even in this limited meaning, *anonymous* rarely appeared in hard-word-lists and translation dictionaries.

An exception, the scholarly RIDERS DICTIONARIE (Oxford, 3d. ed. 1612), translates the English *Namelesse* into the Latin *Anonymus*, but, significantly, not vice-versa—a sug-

around 1676, however, *anonymous* begins to signal the author-iza-
tion of a text, the importance of someone, anyone, speaking.[4]
The author's emergence is marked by the notice of its absence.

My *its* here remarks on the author's singularity, for as modern usage makes clear, *anonymous* emerges with the author as a
singular entity; *anonymity*, the *Oxford English Dictionary (OED)*
notes, is a property of *"an* author or *his* writings."[5] There is a
moment in history, in other words, when it becomes important to
know not only that someone is speaking, but also that some *one* is
speaking. Unlike the *OED*, my *its* also avoids the normative seventeenth-century gendering of authorship; though this Essay addresses this issue only obliquely, it will suggest the inextricability
of the question of authorship from patriarchy's obsession with
knowing the identity of the father.[6]

The singular author and its twin, anonymous, are in a sense
my subject in this essay, but I am most interested in what preceded their "birth." There was, as my epigraph from 1654 suggests, a period of transition in early modern European history—a
time when both reading "Names" and reading "Sence" existed
as interpretive methodologies—preceded by a time when interpretation proceeded without an author. My project here is thus
the genealogist's: to trace back beyond the impasse of Beckett's
pronoun the seemingly natural connection between the author
and the text—the some/one and the speaking—in order to
demonstrate that interpretation has not always proceeded on the
basis of that relation (and thus need not always). Barthes fa-
mously noted the author's "death," and what I hope to elaborate
here is the author's "birth." I hesitate over these metaphors de-

---

gestion that the word had not gained currency as an English word beyond a scholarly,
latinate context. This is the case as late as 1677, in COLES, A DICTIONARY, ENGLISH-
LATIN, AND LATIN-ENGLISH (London, John Richardson et al. eds., 1677). In MINSHEU,
DUCTOR IN LINGUAS, THE GVIDE INTO TONGVES (London, Iohn Browne ed., 1617), the
Latin *Anonymus* is translated into English as "Vnnamed." In none of the other "dictionaries" in which it appears does the word connect persons with texts; the unanimous gloss
is simply "nameless."

4 OED, *supra* note 3, at 493. For methodological reasons (the *OED*'s limited quota-
tion-sources) as well as theoretical reasons (the notion of word "coinage" is readily his-
toricized within a capitalist context), we must read *OED*'s dates not as solid markers of a
word's invention or origin but, more flexibly, as an indication of meanings in circulation
at any given time. The related forms of *anonymous* (*anonymity, anonymously, anonymousness*)
emerge even later, in the eighteenth and nineteenth centuries.

5 *Id.* (emphasis added).

6 In the project from which this work derives, I explore the intersection of discourses of writing, sexuality, and reproduction in Renaissance drama and its early
printed apparatus. *See* Jeffrey A. Masten, Textual Reproduction: Collaboration, Gender,
and Authorship in Renaissance Drama (1991) (unpublished Ph.D. dissertation, University of Pennsylvania). On the issue of paternity, see MARJORIE GARBER, SHAKESPEARE'S
GHOST WRITERS: LITERATURE AS UNCANNY CAUSALITY (1987).

liberately, for (as I think Barthes would appreciate) "birth" natu-
ralizes and makes inevitable an event—or rather, set of events—
that were, as I will suggest, contingent and by no means biological, transcultural, or even uniformly-occurring across discourses
and genres within a given culture. To do this, I want to consider
a set of texts that consistently defy our (modern) sense of both
authorship and anonymity, texts generated in the predominantly
collaborative dramatic practice of early modern England. Most
of these texts began as productions in the theatre, where their
writers were not known, and many of them first appeared in print
without ascription of authorship (or anonymity); they are thus
"pre-anonymous"—that is, "anonymous" only in a sense that existed before the word itself emerged with the author to describe
their condition. *Anonymous*, in other words, only assumes its textual associations as a marking of difference from a new concept of
authorship. These texts also defy modern anonymity in another
crucial way, for their authorlessness is plural and collaborative.[7]

Collaborative dramatic texts from this period thus strikingly
denaturalize the author-text-reader continuum assumed in later
methodologies of interpretation. Located both at a historical
moment prior to the emergence of the author in its modern form
and as a mode of textual production that distances the writer(s)
from the interpreting audience, dramatic collaboration disperses
the authorial voice (or rather, our historically subsequent notion
of the authorial voice); it instead exhibits the different configuration of authorities controlling texts and (as we shall see) constraining their interpretation. In such a context, interpretation
(and here I mean both our methods for interpretation and our
sense of what an interpretation is) can be radically different.

In a scholarly field dominated by the singular figure of
Shakespeare, it is easily forgotten that collaboration was the Renaissance English theatre's dominant mode of textual production.
In his ground-breaking study of the profession of dramatist from
1590-1642, Gerald Eades Bentley notes that nearly two-thirds of
the plays mentioned in Henslowe's papers reflect the participation of more than one writer. Furthermore, of all the plays writ-

---

7 For a characterization of anonymity related but alternative to the one I have
sketched above, see Virginia Woolf, *ANON.*, 25 TWENTIETH CENTURY LITERATURE 382-98
(1975) (posthumously published). Although Woolf too identifies a shift in English culture from nameless to named texts, her construal romanticizes *Anon* as a free and nameless individual; the central strategy of the essay is in some sense to identify and
individualize the writer she identifies as nameless. In Woolf's scheme, the named author *replaces* (rather than emerges with) *Anon*.

ten by professional dramatists in the period, "as many as half . . . incorporated the writing . . . of more than one man." Printed title-page statements of singular authorship "tended . . . to simplify the actual circumstances of composition" when compared with other records.[8] There is also ample evidence of the frequent revision of play-texts, itself a diachronic form of collaboration. It was common practice for the professional writers attached to a given theatrical company to compose new prologues, epilogues, songs, characters, and scenes for revivals of plays in which they did not originally have a hand—*Doctor Faustus* and *Sir Thomas More* are famous examples. Thus "almost any play first printed more than ten years after composition and . . . kept in active repertory by the company which owned it is most likely to contain later revisions by the author or, in many cases, by another playwright."[9]

In a broader sense, theatrical production was itself a sustained collaboration, "the joint accomplishment of dramatists, actors, musicians, costumers, prompters (who made alterations in the original manuscript) and . . . managers."[10] That is, the construction of meaning by a theatrical company was polyvocal—often beginning with a collaborative manuscript, which was then revised, cut, rearranged, and augmented by prompters, copyists, and other writers, elaborated and improvised by actors in performance, accompanied by music and songs that may or may not have originated in a completely different context.[11] Furthermore, the larger theatrical enterprise, situated in the marketplace, was the highly lucrative, capitalist collaboration of a "company" of "sharers," in commerce with their audience—in Jean-Christophe Agnew's useful phrase, "a joint venture of limited liability."[12] Plays' prologues and epilogues, those liminal

---

[8] GERALD EADES BENTLEY, THE PROFESSION OF DRAMATIST IN SHAKESPEARE'S TIME 1590-1642, at 199 (1971).

[9] *Id.* at 263. Recent considerations of revised texts in the Shakespeare canon have effectively dissolved the notion of the single text, but they insist anachronistically upon the notion of a singular revising authorial consciousness. *See* THE DIVISION OF THE KINGDOMS: SHAKESPEARE'S TWO VERSIONS OF *King Lear* (Gary Taylor & Michael Warren eds., 1983). *But see* SCOTT MCMILLIN, THE ELIZABETHAN THEATRE AND *The Book of Sir Thomas More* 153-59 (1987) (author usefully explores revision as a deconstruction of authorial individuality in the Sir Thomas More manuscript).

[10] BENTLEY, *supra* note 8, at 198. *See also* Stephen Orgel, *What is a Text?*, *in* STAGING THE RENAISSANCE (David Scott Kastan & Peter Stallybrass eds., 1991) (elaborating on Bentley).

[11] This is to say nothing of the manifold collaborations that generated a play-text when/if it was eventually printed.

[12] JEAN-CHRISTOPHE AGNEW, WORLDS APART: THE MARKET AND THE THEATER IN ANGLO-AMERICAN THOUGHT, 1550-1750, at 111 (1986). *Compare* Woolf, *supra* note 7, at 395 (stating that "the play was a common product, written by one hand, but so moulded in

textual spaces between the play and the playhouse, stage the intersections of acting company and audience in the language of commerce; the prologue to *Romeo and Iuliet* (1597) emphasizes this trans/action when it speaks of "the two howres traffique of our Stage."[13] Human hands—hands that applaud, but also the hands that pay to see the play, the hand-shaking that seals the bargain, the collaborating hands of exchange and commerce—make repeated appearance in this framing material: "Do but you hold out/Your helping hands," the prologue to *The Two Noble Kinsmen* asks, "and we shall . . . something doe to save us."[14]

Including theatrical production in a discussion of "collaboration" may risk an excessive broadening of the term, but it is important to suggest (as I think the play-texts themselves do) the inseparability of the textual and theatrical production of meaning in a context that did not carefully insulate the writing of scripts from the acting of plays. (Actors William Shakespeare and William Rowley can serve as figures for this convergence.) The commonplace editorial concern over a play's "date of composition," which assumes a relatively limited amount of time during which a text was fully composed and after which it was merely transmitted and corrupted, is obviously problematic in this broader understanding of collaboration. What does "composition" include in such a context? (Re)writing? Copying? Staging? The addition of theatrical gestures? Typesetting (which, after all, is called "composing")? When is [the writing, staging, printing of] a text complete?

Censorship—in Annabel Patterson's extended sense, an activity that both silences discourses and generates others[15]—is a further participant in the production of theatrical meaning in this period. To choose two relatively simple examples: In *Sir Thomas More*, the censor writes in the manuscript along with the collaborating writers, making changes and demanding others. The suppression of *A Game at Chess* from the public stage occasioned the proliferation of widely variant printed and manuscript versions of

---

transition that the author had no sense of property in it. It was in part the work of the audience."). It is important to notice that (in a way to which I will return below) Woolf insists upon the singlehandedness of textual production in this period, even as she stresses the collaborative role of the audience.

13 William Shakespeare, An Excellent conceited Tragedie of Romeo and Iuliet (Q1) (London, Iohn Danter 1597).

14 John Fletcher & William Shakespeare, The Two Noble Kinsmen (Prologue) (London, Tho. Cotes for Iohn Waterson 1634). For a discussion of the handshake's emerging contractual significance, see Agnew, *supra* note 12, at 86-89.

15 *See* Annabel Patterson, Censorship and Interpretation: The Conditions of Writing and Reading in Early Modern England (1984).

the play.[16]

Despite this broad range of figures and forces collaborating in play-texts, later considerations of Renaissance drama have nevertheless worked to construct an authorial univocality. Viewing these texts as literature in the library rather than as working documents in the playhouse, criticism has read them primarily as written communications between writers and readers.[17] Such an approach privileges "writer" and "reader" according to their value in modern literate, literary culture and elides both the prior textual exchange between writers and actors and the oral/aural transaction between actors and audience, the more prominent participants in the initial and most prolific form of these texts' public/ation. Theatrical practice reserved no place for the writer in performance except as an actor in the company, and these texts were generally made accessible to readers only as an afterthought capitalizing on their theatrical popularity. It is crucial, in other words, to consider the social production of different genres and the ways in which they reach print. *The Faerie Queene* and, say, *Romeo and Iuliet* may both appear to be texts designed for reading (especially as edited for modern consumption); however, the former exhibits the apparatus of both the book and the author, while the latter (in quarto form) presents itself not as a communication between writer and reader (or even as a book, in the modern sense), but rather as a representation/recapitulation of a theatrical experience, a communication between actors and audience—the text "*As* it hath been often (with great applause) plaid publiquely. . . ."[18] Only by eliding or ignoring the theatrical as a mode of (re)production can these texts can be read from the post-Enlightenment perspective of individual authorship, the now-victorious mode of textual production and the site of Foucault's critique.

Traditionally, the criticism has viewed collaboration as a mere subset or aberrant kind of individual authorship, the collusion of two unique authors whom subsequent readers could discern and separate out by examining the traces of individuality and personality (including handwriting, spelling, word-choice, imagery, and syntactic formations) left in the collaborative text.[19]

---

[16] *See, e.g.,* T.H. Howard-Hill, *The Author as Scribe or Reviser?: Middleton's Intentions in A Game at Chess,* 1987 TRANSACTIONS OF THE SOCIETY FOR TEXTUAL SCHOLARSHIP 305-18.

[17] *See* McMILLIN, *supra* note 9, at 15.

[18] SHAKESPEARE, *supra* note 13 (emphasis added).

[19] THE LIBRARY OF CONGRESS SUBJECT HEADINGS reflects and perpetuates this paradigm by listing "collaboration" as a sub-heading only under the larger rubric of "authorship."

The work of Cyrus Hoy, to choose the most prominent and influential example of such studies, attempts to separate out the collaborators in "the Beaumont and Fletcher canon" on the grounds of "linguistic criteria";[20] however, there is a repeated conflict in Hoy's project between his post-Enlightenment assumptions about authorship, textual property, and individuality of style, and the evidence of the period texts he analyzes. Hoy wishes "[t]o distinguish any given dramatist's share in a play of dual or doubtful authorship" by applying a "body of criteria which, derived from the unaided plays of the dramatist in question, will serve to identify his work in whatever context it may appear."[21] His studies thus begin with the presumption of singular authorship ("unaided plays") and proceed to collaboration (tellingly glossed as "dual or doubtful"). Furthermore, his results assume that a writer's use of *ye* for *you* and of contractions like *'em* for *them* is both individually distinct and remarkably constant "in whatever context."[22]

These assumptions are challenged by evidence Hoy himself adduces. Problematically, as Hoy realizes, "there is no play that can with any certainty be regarded as the unaided work of Beaumont,"[23] and he admits that "Beaumont's linguistic practices are themselves so widely divergent as to make it all but impossible to predict what they will be from one play to another."[24] Beaumont's presence will thus be ascertained as that which remains after Fletcher, Massinger, *et al.* have been subtracted. Further, because he finds *The Faithful Shepherdess*, though "undoubtedly Fletcher's own," linguistically at odds with his other unaided works, Hoy omits it from his tabulation of evidence establishing Fletcher's "own" distinctive style.[25] Hoy's results are, furthermore, rendered problematic by the frequency of revision in these texts and the mediation of copyists, actors, compositors, and their "linguistic preferences" between Hoy's hypothetical writers' copy and the printed text he actually analyzes.[26] Additional

---

[20] Cyrus Hoy, *The Shares of Fletcher and his Collaborators in the Beaumont and Fletcher Canon (I),* 1956 STUDIES IN BIBLIOGRAPHY 130.

[21] *Id.*

[22] *Id.* at 130-31.

[23] *Id.* at 130.

[24] Cyrus Hoy, *The Shares of Fletcher and his Collaborators in the Beaumont and Fletcher Canon (III),* 1958 STUDIES IN BIBLIOGRAPHY 86.

[25] Hoy, *supra* note 20, at 142.

[26] Though he is largely engaged in the same project as Hoy, R.C. Bald demonstrates that distinguishing ostensible scribal and authorial pronoun preferences is fraught with difficulties. *See* R.C. Bald, BIBLIOGRAPHICAL STUDIES IN THE BEAUMONT AND FLETCHER FOLIO OF 1647, at 93-102 (1938).

questions arise when we consider the complexities at the outset
of collaborative writing, which may have included, according to
Sheldon P. Zitner, "prior agreement on outline, vetting of successive drafts by a partner, composition in concert, brief and possibly infrequent intervention, and even a mutual contagion of
style as a result of close association."[27]

This last item in Zitner's series highlights the extent to which
he remains in Hoy's paradigm, in which one writer's healthy individual style must be protected from infection by another's.
Zitner thus exhibits Hoy's problem at a more theoretical level.
We might note that the presumed universality of individuated
style depends on a network of legal and social technologies specific to post-Renaissance capitalist culture (e.g. intellectual property, copyright, individuated handwriting).[28] Furthermore, the
collaborative project in the theatre was predicated on *erasing* the
perception of any differences that might have existed, for
whatever reason, between collaborated parts. Moreover, writing
in this theatrical context implicitly resists the notion of monolithic personal style Hoy presumes: a playwright im/personates
another (many others) in the process of writing a play-text and
thus refracts the supposed singularity of the individual in language. At the same time, he often stages in language the *sense* of
distinctive personae, putting "characteristic" words in another's
mouth. What Hoy says of Beaumont—

> His linguistic "preferences"—if they can be termed such—are,
> in a word, nothing if not eclectic . . . . [i]t is this very protean
> character which makes it, in the end, quite impossible to estab-
> lish for Beaumont a neat pattern of linguistic preferences that
> will serve as a guide to identifying his work wherever it might
> appear

— might apply to all playwrights in this period.[29] Indeed, the
playwright of this era often thought to be most individuated—
Shakespeare—has likewise been characterized by the diversity,
protean quality, and expansiveness of "his" language.[30]

---

[27] FRANCIS BEAUMONT, THE KNIGHT OF THE BURNING PESTLE, THE REVELS PLAYS 10
(Sheldon P. Zitner ed., 1984).

[28] For an indispensable consideration of these issues, see Martha Woodmansee, *The
Genius and the Copyright: Economic and Legal Conditions of the Emergence of the "Author,"* 17
EIGHTEENTH-CENTURY STUD. 425 (1984). For a brilliant revisionist history of handwrit-
ing and the signature, see JONATHAN GOLDBERG, WRITING MATTER: FROM THE HANDS OF
THE ENGLISH RENAISSANCE (1989).

[29] Hoy, *supra* note 24, at 87.

[30] On the individuation of Shakespeare, see MARGRETA DE GRAZIA, SHAKESPEARE
VERBATIM: THE REPRODUCTION OF AUTHENTICITY AND THE 1790 APPARATUS (1991).

A more detailed critique of Hoy's attributions is required and might investigate the extent to which Hoy's specific linguistic criteria (the pronominal forms *ye/you*, for example) are, as *OED* suggests, actually class-related differences—that is, the extent to which they reflect not an individual's linguistic preference or habit, but rather a subject inscribed in and constituted by specific linguistic practices. (This is an issue of some complexity, for *ye* rather than *you* may announce the writer's own inscription in class-coded language, and/or may be the writer's ascription of that language to characters within the text.) I cite here some of the more obvious difficulties of Hoy's work because he is considered both an exemplary pioneer of, and a reliable model for, twentieth-century considerations of collaboration. He illustrates both the distinctly modern notions of individuality and authorial property underlying such considerations, as well as the corresponding sites for a post-structurally informed historicist critique. Above all, we can see in his work the insistence with which modern scholarship has asked the author question; the ultimate object of this quest is to know "who is speaking" each and every word of the canon.

That an historically inappropriate idea of the author here effectively constrains interpretation is best illustrated by the modern bibliographical fact that Hoy's authorial attributions in the *Beaumont and Fletcher* canon, a series of seven articles published in *Studies in Bibliography* from 1956-1962, prepared the way for, and are the basis of, the "standard" edition of those texts, *The Dramatic Works in the Beaumont and Fletcher Canon*, which began to appear in 1966 under the general-editorship of Hoy's dissertation adviser Fredson Bowers (who also edited *Studies*).[31] The collaborative plays in this influential edition, Bowers remarks, "have been grouped chiefly by authors,"[32] and Hoy himself argues elsewhere that "[s]cholarly investigation of the authorial problems posed by collaborative drama is . . . a *necessary precondition* to criti-

---

Shakespeare's style (whether protean or utterly, brilliantly predictable) figured prominently—and was deployed by all sides—in the controversy surrounding Gary Taylor's (re)attribution of the ms. poem *Shall I die?* to Shakespeare. *See* Gary Taylor, *A new Shakespeare poem?* TIMES LITERARCY SUPP., December 20, 1985, at 1447-48; Gary Taylor, *Shall I die? immortalized?*, TIMES LITERARY SUPP., January 31, 1986, at 123-24. For responses, see Times Literary Supp. *letters*, December 27, 1985-March 7, 1986. *See also* Stephen Orgel, *The Authentic Shakespeare* REPRESENTATIONS, Winter 1988, at 1-25.

[31] *See* Cyrus Hoy, *The Shares of Fletcher and His Collaborators in the Beaumont and Fletcher Canon (VII)*, 1962 STUDIES IN BIBLIOGRAPHY 88 n.10.

[32] 1 Fredson Bowers, *Foreword* to THE DRAMATIC WORKS IN THE BEAUMONT AND FLETCHER CANON vii (Fredson Bowers ed., 1966).

cal and aesthetic considerations of such drama."[33]   Collaborative texts must submit to an editorial apparatus founded on singular authorship, their "authorial problems" solved, before interpretation is permitted to proceed.

What I want to suggest here is that Hoy's mode of reading collaboration in early modern English drama merely as a more multiple version of authorship—a mode reproduced in editions and criticism of plays not only in the Beaumont and Fletcher canon, but also in the intersecting canons of Shakespeare, Massinger, Middleton, et al.—does not account for the historical and theoretical challenges collaboration poses to the ideology of the Author. Collaboration is, as we shall see, a dispersal of author/ity, rather than a simple doubling of it; to revise the aphorism, two heads are different than one.[34]

Such a reconceptualization of Renaissance dramatic collaboration has profound implications for the way we interpret these plays. Bibliographical attention to a text is often considered to be prior to interpretation—establishing a definitive, authoritative set of words for subsequent hermeneutic explication—but shifting the focus from authorship to collaboration demonstrates the extent to which twentieth-century textual criticism has itself been an elaborate interpretive act framing all its efforts with Foucault's constraining author.[35]   Bowers's prefatory words describing his general editorship of *The Dramatic Works in the Beaumont and Fletcher Canon* suggest, furthermore, that modern textual criticism reproduces in its own practice the privileging of author-based interpretation over collaboration:

> The texts . . . have been edited by a group of scholars according to editorial procedures set by the general editor and under his close supervision . . . . We hope that the intimate connexion of one individual, in this manner, with all the different editorial processes will lend to the results some uniformity not ordinarily found when diverse editors approach texts of such complexity. At the same time, the peculiar abilities of the sev-

---

[33] Cyrus Hoy, *Critical and Aesthetic Problems of Collaboration in Renaissance Drama*, 1976 RESEARCH OPPORTUNITIES IN RENAISSANCE DRAMA 4 (emphasis added).

[34] *Compare* WAYNE KOESTENBAUM, DOUBLE TALK (1989) (unwilling to engage collaboration's potential for unsettling the unitary author (or the humanist subject of psychoanalysis)).

[35] For a critique of the editing/interpreting distinction, see THE MONKS AND THE GIANTS: TEXTUAL AND BIBLIOGRAPHICAL STUDIES AND THE INTERPRETATION OF LITERARY WORKS, TEXTUAL CRITICISM AND LITERARY INTERPRETATION 180-99 (Jerome J. McGann ed., 1985). De Grazia brilliantly demonstrates how the editorial apparatus itself functions to shape and constrain interpretation in editions of the Shakespeare canon. *See* DE GRAZIA, *supra* note 30.

eral editors have had sufficient free play to ensure individuality of point of view its proper role; and thus, we hope, *the deadness of compromise that may fasten on collaborative effort* has been avoided.[36]

As in Zitner's rhetoric of collaborative "contagion," Bowers here seeks to protect from the deadly grasp of collaboration the "peculiar abilities" of the individual working in its "proper role." The danger collaboration poses to this editorial paradigm is likewise figured in the notion of "corruption" so important to twentieth-century editing of Renaissance texts, for "corruption"—the introduction of non-authorial material into a text during the process of "transmission"—is "collaboration" given a negative connotation. If the making of play-texts and theatrical productions was a collaborative enterprise, how can we edit out of the first folio version of *Hamlet*, for example, the "corruption" of "actors' interpolations"?[37] To do so is to deploy authorship as a constraint on interpretation in a way the text itself warns against:

> *Ham.* And could'st not thou for a neede study me
> Some dozen or sixteene lines,
> Which I would set downe and insert?
> *players* Yes very easily my good Lord.[38]

This exchange, which I quote from the first quarto, is itself "set downe" and "inserted" differently in the folio and second quarto versions of the play (the latter described on its title-page as "enlarged to almost as much againe as it was").

Like bibliography, much of the more self-consciously interpretive "literary criticism" continues to rely implicitly on the assumption that texts are the products of a singular and sovereign authorial consciousness, and a reconception of collaboration also has manifold implications here. Emphasizing collaboration in this period demonstrates at the level of material practice the claim of much recent critical theory: the production of texts is a social process. Within Hoy's paradigm of collaboration, language is fundamentally transparent of, because it is produced by, the individual author; the language one uses is (and identifies one as) one's own. But if we accept that language is a socially-produced (and producing) system, then collaboration is more the

---

36 1 Bowers, *supra* note 32, at vii (emphasis added).

37 On "verbal corruption" and actors' "interpolations" in Hamlet, see HAMLET 62 (Harold Jenkins ed., 1982).

38 WILLIAM SHAKE-SPEARE, THE TRAGICALL HISTORIE OF HAMLET: PRINCE OF DENMARKE (Q1) at sig. E4v (London, for N.L. and Iohn Trundell 1603).

condition of discourse than its exception.[39] Interpreting from a
collaborative perspective acknowledges language as a process of
exchange; rather than cordoning discourse off into agents, origins, and intentions, a collaborative focus elaborates the social
mechanism of language, discourse as intercourse.[40] "[I]f literature were as original, as creative, as individual, as unique as literary humanists are constantly saying it is," Morse Peckham has
noted, "we would not be able to understand a word of it, let
alone make emendations."[41] A collaborative perspective also
forces a re-evaluation of (and/or complicates) a repertoire of familiar interpretive methodologies—most prominently, biographical and psychoanalytic approaches—based on the notion of the
singular author. Other traditional critical categories policing the
circulation of language become problematic as well—for example, "plagiarism," "borrowing," "influence" (and its "anxieties"), "source," "originality," "imagination," "genius," and
"complete works."

The collaborative production of play-texts, as I have begun
to suggest, was manifold, and it is important to note that collaborations between (or among) writers had differing valences. We
will in the future want to investigate in more detail both the differences and the similarities of collaborations (between Beaumont and Fletcher, and, say, Chapman, Jonson, and Marston)
that resulted from different positionings within the institutions of
the theatre and outside it; crucial to such an analysis are Bentley's distinctions between "regular attached professional" playwrights and those like Jonson situated between the theatre and a
patronage network with significantly different socio-economic in-
flections. My point here, however, is to call for a revision in the
way we have read Renaissance dramatic collaboration *generally*,
and the ways we have deployed it in our readings of Renaissance
dramatic texts. That is, I am contending that collaborative texts
produced before the emergence of authorship are of a kind dif-

---

[39] McGann points out that even the text that seems to have been materially produced
by one person exists fundamentally in the realm of the social; revision in authorial manuscripts, he argues, "reflect[s] social interactions and purposes." *See* JEROME J. McGANN,
A CRITIQUE OF MODERN TEXTUAL CRITICISM 62 (1983).

[40] Stephen Greenblatt makes a related point in his discussion of "the collective making of distinct cultural practices and inquiry into the relations among these practices,"
though in the next sentence he returns to singular "making" in labelling his subject
"plays by Shakespeare." STEPHEN GREENBLATT, SHAKESPEAREAN NEGOTIATIONS: THE CIR-
CULATION OF SOCIAL ENERGY IN RENAISSANCE ENGLAND 5 (1988).

[41] 1 Morse Peckham, *Reflections on the Foundations of Modern Textual Editing*, 1971 PROOF
122, 144.

ferent (informed by differing mechanisms of textual property and control, different conceptions of imitation, originality, and the "individual") from collaborations produced within the regime of the author. I want to show more fully the implications of a collaboratively attuned (rather than authorially based) interpretation by examining a particular text in the Beaumont and Fletcher canon, a text of which the author-question has been often asked and (ostensibly) answered definitively: *The Knight of the Burning Pestle*.

We can take as a guide to a collaborative reading the sustained ambivalence the early printed texts of *The Knight of the Burning Pestle* demonstrate toward authorship. *The Knight*, probably initially performed between 1607-1610, was first printed in a 1613 quarto, the title-page of which mentions no writer(s). The dedicatory epistle, however, notes:

> [T]his vnfortunate child, who in eight daies . . . was begot and borne, soone after, was by his parents . . . exposed to the wide world, who for want of iudgement, or not vnderstanding the priuy marke of *Ironie* about it (which shewed it was no offspring of any vulgar braine) vtterly reiected it . . . .[42]

The play, apparently unparented on its title page, is here the offspring of both a singular "braine" and plural "parents." (Further, it bears publicly a "priuy" birth-"marke" of this ambiguous lineage.) This situation is only complicated by the second and third quartos of the play (both dated 1635); these title pages announce that *The Knight* was "Written by Francis Beaumont, and Iohn Fletcher. Gent.," but they include a different prefatory letter, "To the Readers of this *Comedy*," which cites a singular "Author [who] had no intent to wrong any one in this Comedy . . . which hee hopes will please all."[43] Finally, in these subsequent quartos there also appears *The Prologue*, a speech transferred into this text from an earlier play, which explains, in the only sentence it alters from its 1584 precursor, that "the Authors intention" was not to satirize any particular subject.[44] Most modern editors emend "the Authors intention" to "the author's intention," but

---

[42] THE KNIGHT OF THE BURNING PESTLE (Q1) at sig. A2 (London, for Walter Burre 1613) (emphasis in original).

[43] FRANCIS BEAUMONT & IOHN FLETCHER, THE KNIGHT OF THE BVRNING PESTLE (Q2) at sig. A3 (London, N.O. for I.S. 1635). The third quarto, often supposed to be a later reprint despite its stated date of 1635, is most easily distinguished from the second quarto by its spelling of "Beamount" on the title-page. FRANCIS BEAMOUNT & IOHN FLETCHER, THE KNIGHT OF THE BVRNING PESTLE (Q3) (London, N.O. for I.S. 1635).

[44] BEAUMONT & FLETCHER (Q2), *supra* note 43, at sig. A4.

we would want to note in this context the fertile ambiguity of early modern orthographic practice, which does not distinguish genitive singular from plural or genitive plural—that is, it does not use another of authorship's more recent technologies, the apostrophe, to separate the writer's/writers' propriety from his/their plurality.

A look at the preliminary material of these quartos demonstrates that, though authorship is intermittently present, it does not appear in anything approaching a definitive or monolithically singular form; all three quartos, like many others of this period, instead foreground in their apparatus a different network of textual ownership and production. Unlike the writer(s), the publisher Walter Burre does appear on the title-page of the first quarto, and he also signs the dedicatory epistle (quoted above) to Robert Keysar, the manager of the Blackfriars theatre where the play was first performed and the previous owner of the text. The epistle establishes an extended filiation for this child/text, arguing that, despite "his" failure in the theatre, he is "desirous to try his fortune in the world, where if yet it be welcome, both father and foster-father, nurse and child, haue their desired end."[45] If the "father" here is the play's writer (with Keysar as foster-father and Burre as nurse), his singularity jars with the "parents" noted above—although the parents who first "exposed" the text might also be read as the (boy) players. In sum, though no author (certainly no single author) emerges from these initial references to the play's origins, the quartos' preliminary materials do display a complex and shifting network of other authorities: the publisher Burre, the printer N.O., the acting-company manager Keysar, the inhospitable theatre audience, the players and their royal patron (the second and third quartos advertise the text "[a]s it is now acted by her Majesties Servants at the Privatehouse in *Drury lane*"), the writers Beaumont/Beamount and Fletcher (eventually, after both are dead), the "gentlemen" readers, and the unnamed writer of another play whose "intentions" are transferred over and now said to apply to the "Authors" or "author" of this play.

Later in the century (concurrent with the shift I earlier located in *anonymous*) the play's authorial lineage becomes more important, but it is by no means more fully stabilized. A speech that probably served as a prologue to a revival between 1665-1667, for example, assumes that the play is solely Fletcher's;[46] pub-

---

[45] The Knight of the Burning Pestle (Q1), *supra* note 42, at sig. A2v.
[46] *See* Beaumont, *supra* note 27, at 163-64.

lished in 1672, this prologue precedes by only seven years the ascription of the play as collaborative in *Fifty Comedies and Tragedies Written by Francis Beaumont And John Fletcher, Gentlemen* (the second folio).

I am obscuring from this textual history the fact that virtually all the recent editions of *The Knight* now place Francis Beaumont *solus* on their title pages.[47] Though the quartos situate the initially unauthored, eventually collaborated play within a collaborative network, these editions deploy an army of editorial glosses to contain the subversive ambiguities cited above, proceed to interpret the play via its relationship to Beaumont's other plays (no easy task, given the paucity of this canon) or to his class-position and family history, and separate it off from (to name some other possible contexts) other plays performed by the Children of Blackfriars, or other plays associated with the name "Beaumont and Fletcher."[48]

The irony of reducing *The Knight of the Burning Pestle* to a single author is that it is perhaps the most wildly collaborative play of this period. By this point, it should be clear that I do not here mean "collaborative" merely in the usual, restricted sense of two or more writers writing together; this play exposes—in a way that we lose when we read it as the creation of particular individuals acting (as Bowers might say) in their "proper role"—the more broadly collaborative enterprise of the Renaissance English theatre.

From the moment the Citizen interrupts the actor speaking the prologue in his fourth line and climbs onto the stage, *The Knight of the Burning Pestle* stages the somewhat contentious collaboration of an acting company and its audience. The audience becomes, literally, a part of the play, as the boy actors reluctantly agree to improvise, at the request of the Citizen and Wife, a play called *The Knight of the Burning Pestle*—starring the Wife's serving-boy Rafe—along with their rehearsed production of *The London Merchant*. This odd juxtaposition of genres—romance-quest and city-comedy—becomes increasingly complex, as the players at-

---

47 For example: John Doebler's edition in the Regents Renaissance Drama series (1967); Andrew Gurr's edition for Fountainwell Drama Texts (1968); Michael Hattaway's New Mermaids edition (1969); and Zitner's 1985 Revels Plays edition. All of these followed the 1966 publication of the play's "standard" edition (as edited by Hoy) in *The Dramatic Works* supervised by Bowers. *See The Knight of the Burning Pestle* (Cyrus Hoy ed.) *in* 1 BOWERS, *supra* note 32 at I.

48 For example, in EUGENE M. WAITH, THE PATTERN OF TRAGICOMEDY IN BEAUMONT AND FLETCHER (1969), the author of this now-classic study discounts *The Knight* as uncharacteristic before he proceeds to an analysis of the rest of canon 5.

tempt to accommodate and fuse the divergent plots. Like the framing prologues and epilogues of other plays, *The Knight's* opening lines (as well as its sustained amalgamation of plots) suggest the general situation of acting companies attempting to sell their representations within the proto-capitalist marketplace of Renaissance London: they are (in a sense that is constantly being re-negotiated) bound by the desires of their audience, at the same time that they participate in the construction of those desires. The economic valence of this transaction is foregrounded at several points in the play, as in the episode where the Citizen gives money to the actor playing the innkeeper for accommodating Rafe and thus for accommodating (literally and figuratively) the audience and its desire to see a knight-errant.

The boy who speaks for the players and negotiates with the citizens, like most prologue-emissaries between acting company and audience, invariably uses the plural and collaborative "we" to represent the company[49] and establishes joint ownership in "the plot of our Plaie."[50] A more comprehensive view, however, would see the entirety of the play's production (that is, the intersections of the "actors' " *The London Merchant* and "citizens' " *The Knight of the Burning Pestle*) as the corporate effort of the players—the collaboration of actors-acting-as-actors and actors-acting-as-citizens. This negotiation in turn brings into view another, silent collaborator in the larger production, the gentlemanly audience of the private theatre where the play is presented. No representative of this audience speaks, but the Boy, and occasionally the citizens, gesture toward its ostensibly more refined tastes:

> *Cit.* Boy, come hither, send away *Raph* and this whoresonne Giant quickely.
> *Boy.* In good faith sir we cannot, you'le vtterly spoile our Play, and make it to be hist, and it cost money, you will not suffer vs

---

[49] THE KNIGHT OF THE BURNING PESTLE (Q1), *supra* note 42, at sig. B1. *See also, The Knight of the Burning Pestle, supra* note 47, at 1-4 (Induction).

For reasons explored above, I quote not from an edition of *The Knight* governed by anachronistic notions of authorship, but rather from the first quarto, providing both page references to that text and the corresponding line numbers in the more accessible Hoy/Bowers edition cited *supra* note 47. Joseph Loewenstein notes acting companies' use of the first-person plural in *The Script in the Marketplace, in* REPRESENTING THE ENGLISH RENAISSANCE 266 (Stephen Greenblatt ed., 1988). My understanding of drama's eventual emergence as textual property is greatly indebted to this article.

[50] THE KNIGHT OF THE BURNING PESTLE (Q1), *supra* note 42, at sig. D4v. *See also The Knight of the Burning Pestle, supra* note 47, at III.259.

to go on with our plot, *I pray Gentlemen rule him.*[51]

The play here suggests what must have been the more complex task of accommodation facing the players: negotiating between the desires of the private theatre's gentlemen-patrons and the citizens eager for "something notably in honour of the Commons of the Citty,"[52] a process with economic ramifications, as these lines make clear.

This negotiation draws into play a number of divergent discourses, as I have already noted in passing; *The Knight of the Burning Pestle* is quite literally, in Barthes' famous phrase, "a tissue of quotations drawn from the innumerable centres of culture."[53] The range of the play's "quotation," its discursive diversity, is immense in a way that I can only suggestively summarize; this is nevertheless another important way in which the play figures the collaborative enterprise of theatrical writing in this period.[54] Rafe's improvised adventures in *The Knight of the Burning Pestle* appropriate and play with the discourse of romance-epic: he reads aloud an extended passage from *Palmerin de Oliva*, a romance translated into English in 1581; his subsequent adventures gesture toward episodes of *Don Quixote*, *Arcadia*, and *The Faerie Queene*; and he trains his "squire" and "dwarf" (two serving-boys) to speak in the antique chivalric discourse of those familiar texts.[55] Rafe's adventures also draw on a genre of plays about "prentice worthies."[56] The "actors'" *The London Merchant* is a similar pastiche of genres ("prodigal" plays, romantic-comedies, city-comedies), and Jasper's appearance as the ghost of himself deploys a revenge-tragedy convention in the service of a marriage-plot. Furthermore, the play's collation of romantic comedy eventuating in marriage with Rafe's romance-quest ending in his own

---

[51] THE KNIGHT OF THE BURNING PESTLE (Q1), *supra* note 42, at sig. F4v. *See also The Knight of the Burning Pestle, supra* note 47, at III.292-96 (final emphasis added).

[52] THE KNIGHT OF THE BURNING PESTLE (Q1), *supra* note 42, at sig. B1v. *See also The Knight of the Burning Pestle, supra* note 47, at 25-47 (Induction).

[53] Roland Barthes, *The Death of the Author, in* Image, Music, Text 146 (Stephen Heath trans., 1977).

[54] The source-tracing textual glosses and commentary in the editions mentioned above—upon which I rely heavily in the discussion of "quotation" that follows—are themselves voluminously symptomatic and constitutive of the twentieth-century preoccupation with authorship and the transmission of textual property. For an important critique of the traditional relation of "source" to play-text, see Jonathan Goldberg, *Speculations: Macbeth and source, in* SHAKESPEARE REPRODUCED: THE TEXT IN HISTORY AND IDEOLOGY 242-64 (Jean E. Howard & Marion F. O'Connor eds., 1987).

[55] The relation of *The Knight of the Burning Pestle* to *Don Quixote* is a matter of some controversy, especially if one is concerned about "Beaumont's" "originality." For a summary of the issues, see BEAUMONT, *supra* note 27, at 39-42.

[56] *See id.* at 28-31.

death may figure the emergent genre which the team of playwrights subsequently attached to this play were to make famous: tragicomedy.[57]

At a more local level, the play continually exhibits its allusive permeability. Figuring the larger theatrical practice of importing music "originating" elsewhere to fit the current production, Master Merrythought's lines are virtually all quotation/revisions of contemporary ballads and madrigals—some of which circulated orally, others in print. Modern editions attempt to separate these texts out of the texture of the play by italicizing them, labelling them "song," and devoting appendices to their special status as music. As Zitner, with evident frustration, notes in his appendix "The songs": "There are perhaps forty-one passages to be sung in *The Knight*. One says 'perhaps' since it is sometimes difficult to distinguish what is to be sung from what is to be spoken."[58] (A variation on the theme with which we began: what does it matter whom one is singing?)

A similar difficulty of distinguishing parts within the collaborated texture character-izes the serving-boy/hero Rafe. As already noted, he speaks in chivalric discourse as "the Knight of the Burning Pestle," and his first sustained utterance in the play is a recitation from *1 Henry IV*. Likewise, his speech at the end of Act IV parodies both the septenary meter of Elizabethan verse-narratives and May Lords' May-Day speeches. The generic attentiveness of Rafe's "tragic" death speech—about which the boy-actor complains, " 'Twill be very vnfit he should die sir, vpon no occasion, and in a Comedy too"[59]—signals Rafe's own construction out of allusion: the long narrative rewrites passages from *The Spanish Tragedy*, *Richard III*, and *Eastward Ho!* Furthermore (and potentially more subversive to an author-based notion of this text), Rafe's last words, "oh, oh, oh, &c.,"[60] are the same as Hamlet's in the Folio version of that play, where they are often presumed by modern editors to be excisable from the "author's" text as "actor's interpolation."[61] Rafe's final "&c." succinctly

---

[57] Waith quarantines the play from this possibility by labelling it "Beaumont's." *See* WAITH, *supra*, note 48.

[58] BEAUMONT, *supra* note 27, at 173.

[59] THE KNIGHT OF THE BURNING PESTLE (Q1), *supra* note 42, at sig. K2v-K3. *The Knight of the Burning Pestle*, *supra* note 47, at V.273-74.

[60] THE KNIGHT OF THE BURNING PESTLE (Q1), *supra* note 42, at sig. K3v. *The Knight of the Burning Pestle*, *supra* note 47, at V.327.

[61] HAMLET, *supra* note 37, at 62. Hamlet's Arden editor, Harold Jenkins, calls these O's "theatrical accretions to Shakespeare's dialogue." *Id.* at n.1. Terence Hawkes's perceptive essay *That Shakespeherian Rag*, in THAT SHAKESPEHERIAN RAG: ESSAYS ON A CRITICAL PROCESS (1986), first brought Hamlet's dying O's to my attention.

marks his last moments as the actor's improvisatory collaboration with, and beyond, the script.

Lee Bliss has argued that "Rafe becomes of necessity [*The Knight's*] self-appointed dramatist: he must create dialogue and motivation that will give life and shape to . . . rather skimpy situational cues" and "labors manfully to impose narrative coherence."[62] This is, she argues, "the young playwright's own situation."[63] While we might agree that Rafe is the central improvisatory, creative figure of *The Knight of the Burning Pestle*, to construct him as a type of the "presiding dramatist" (in Bliss's view, the young Beaumont) is to impose a constraining coherence on interpretation that the text militates against. For if Rafe is the author, he is the author as collaborator, improviser, collator of allusion—the locus of the intersection of discourses, but not their originator. More importantly, like the musical Merrythought, he does not exist outside, or independent of, the text; he is himself a construction of those discourses, the author as staged persona, "a tissue of quotations." Furthermore, like the "text" Barthes theorizes, a "multi-dimensional space in which a variety of writings, none of them original, blend and clash,"[64] Rafe is without origin—as the Wife puts it in her epilogue, "a poore fatherlesse child."[65] And to this extent he reproduces the troubled patrilineage of the text that begets him.

According to Foucault, "the author is the principle of thrift in the proliferation of meaning . . . a certain functional principle by which, in our culture . . . one impedes the free circulation, the free manipulation, the free composition, decomposition, and recomposition of fiction."[66] And though, as we have seen, a dispersal of the author in *The Knight of the Burning Pestle* does allow fiction to circulate more freely, we would be mistaken to think that the fatherless status of both the Knight (Rafe) and *The Knight* figures the freeing of fictions. *What Is an Author?* proceeds to such a visionary close, evoking a future in which fiction seems to circulate unlimited by authorial or other constraints, but Foucault himself acknowledges earlier in the essay that a culture devoid of

---

62 Lee Bliss, *"Plot Mee No Plots": The Life of Drama and the Drama of Life in* The Knight of the Burning Pestle 45 MODERN LANGUAGE QUARTERLY 3, 13 (1984).

63 *Id.* at 3.

64 *See* Barthes, *supra* note 53, at 146.

65 THE KNIGHT OF THE BURNING PESTLE (Q1), *supra* note 42, at sig. K4. *See also The Knight of the Burning Pestle, supra* note 47, at Epi.4.

66 FOUCAULT, *supra* note 2, at 118-19.

all such mechanisms is "pure romanticism."[67] This is a romanticism I do not want to reproduce in speaking of the early modern period. *The Knight of the Burning Pestle*, we remember, has an extended filiation, which includes a "foster-father" and "nurse," and the quarto preliminaries exhibit a network of constraining figures, including the previous owner of the text, the publisher, the actors, the theatre audience, and the readers of the printed texts—as well as the "author(s)," whose status is by no means fixed. Rafe may be "a poore fatherlesse child," but he is also a servant/apprentice shown quite clearly to be constrained by a particular class-position and, in his adventures (however freely they may seem to proliferate), by the desires of his master and mistress.[68] Fiction in this play is also all too obviously limited by the discourses available to the Citizen and Wife, the generic repertoire of the actors, and their location within the competitive theatrical market.

As I've argued implicitly in the interpretation outlined above, all of these constraints are more relevant to an interpretation of this text than the author(s). Even such rigorous theorizations of the author as Wayne Booth's "implied author" and Alexander Nehamas's "postulated author" are problematic when applied to the interpretation of collaborative dramatic texts from this period. Nehamas, for example, writes that "[i]n interpreting a text . . . we want to know what *any* individual who can be its subject must be like. We want to know, that is, what sort of person, what character, is manifested in it."[69] The need to postulate such an author—even (only) as "a hypothesis . . . accepted provisionally [that] guides interpretation"[70]—is specific to certain historical moments and genres.

While these observations are obviously indebted to Foucault's conceptual shift, I would at the same time want to interrogate his imagination of a post-authorial "constraining figure," for it seems to register both a residue of intention left by the de-

---

67 *Id.* at 119. Again, comparison with Woolf's romanticized character *Anon* is instructive. *See* Woolf, *supra* note 7.

68 The complexity of social class in this play is often too easily simplified by critics siding unselfconsciously with the actors and upper-class audience against the citizens' supposed lack of sophistication and their "naive" interventions in "art." Bliss, for example, derides the citizens because "they demolish the independent aesthetic status of the playwright's work and overturn the traditional ideal of drama as a clarifying mirror of men and their relation to their world." Bliss, *supra* note 62, at 4.

69 Alexander Nehamas, *Writer, Text, Work, Author, in* LITERATURE AND THE QUESTION OF PHILOSOPHY 286 (Anthony J. Cascardi ed., 1987).

70 Alexander Nehamas, *The Postulated Author: Critical Monism as a Regulative Ideal*, CRITICAL INQ., Autumn 1981, at 145.

ceased author and a singularity that the above discussion seeks to complicate. We might speak instead of "constraining contexts" for the play; as I have argued, a more appropriate interpretation of *The Knight* is one guided and constrained by what we know about the discourses, figures, locations, and cultural practices participating in its emergence. The ambivalence of this text and this culture toward the author is itself one of those contexts.

My terms here are plural, for, as we have seen, this text defies even the ideally liberal constraint Foucault imagines, "fiction . . . passing through something like *a* necessary or constraining *figure*."[71] It may be that we will not be able to emerge from the Enlightenment legacy of that necessary individual. However, our attempts to do so in our investigations of the past—to see figures (plural) rather than the singular reflections of our authorial selves, to note for example that my writing and citing in the present essay collaborate with, among other things, the Chicago manual that prescribes "my" "style"—can be instrumental in that emergence. To revise the position from which we began: What, or rather how, does it matter who are speaking?

---

[71] FOUCAULT, *supra* note 2, at 119 (emphasis added).

COMMON PROPERTIES OF PLEASURE: TEXTS IN NINETEENTH CENTURY WOMEN'S CLUBS

ANNE RUGGLES GERE[*]

By the latter half of the nineteenth century, the concept of intellectual property had gained currency, and the construction of authorship had been largely accomplished. Sixteenth century rights accorded to publishers to print books "without consent of the authors or against their will"[1] had been replaced by copyright laws that affirmed the unique role of writers in creating texts. The 1710 Statute of Anne established, in England at least, the centrality of protecting the rights of the author,[2] and, as Martha Woodmansee has explained, subsequent debates about the concept of intellectual property in Germany helped define the modern concept of authorship.[3] Elaboration of the concept of genius in aesthetic discussions during the romantic period affirmed the importance of the writer's relationship to the text. The conflation of aesthetic and economic/legal arguments created a context in which copyright laws protecting authors became commonplace and the "man-and-his work" view of texts could emerge.

To be sure, copyright law for literary works, particularly that dealing with texts circulated internationally, was still evolving in the early part of the twentieth century; but by the 1870s the concept of intellectual property was firmly established in the United States, and the construction of authorship had been effected to the extent that literary criticism lavished considerable attention on the background and intentions of authors, and authors became more powerful advocates for their own rights. As Coultrap-McQuin notes, "After the Civil War, authorship began to shed the characteristics of genteel amateurism and increasingly assumed the appearance of modern professions."[4] Writers saw themselves as producing literary commodities. "[P]rofessional authorship at the end of the century adopted some of the trap-

---

[*] Professor of English, University of Michigan. B.A., 1966, Colby College; M.A., 1967, Colgate University; Ph.D., 1974, University of Michigan.
[1] RICHARD R. BOWKER, COPYRIGHT: ITS HISTORY AND ITS LAW 15 (1912).
[2] Statute of Anne, 1710, 8 Anne, ch. 19 (Eng.).
[3] See Martha Woodmansee, The Genius and the Copyright: Economic and Legal Conditions of the Emergence of the "Author," 17 EIGHTEENTH-CENTURY STUD. 425 (1984).
[4] SUSAN COULTRAP-MCQUIN, DOING LITERARY BUSINESS: AMERICAN WOMEN WRITERS IN THE NINETEENTH CENTURY 194 (1990).

pings of modern businesses, among them market orientation and competitiveness, emphasis on skills rather than inspiration, accommodation to editors' and publishers' wishes, and 'masculine' aggressiveness."[5] During the last decades of the nineteenth century, when pseudonyms such as "a concerned reader" were replaced by the writer's name in magazine articles, and texts came to be viewed as commodities to be bought and sold, the concept of authorship achieved its contemporary contours.

Yet, I maintain that, even as the interrelated concepts of intellectual property and authorship were solidifying their positions in the dominant culture, alternatives to these concepts were being developed by the women's clubs that began to emerge during the last three decades of the nineteenth century. On the surface, these clubs looked benign enough. They maintained a long-standing American tradition of self-improvement. From the colonial period forward, beginning with Benjamin Franklin's Junta, Americans had enacted their egalitarian view of knowledge—a view that contrasted sharply with the European dependence on "the monumental accomplishments of the few"—by joining together in mutual improvement societies.[6] The Lyceum, a mutual education system created in 1826 to promote "the universal diffusion of knowledge" continued the tradition,[7] and after the Civil War, the Chautauqua movement fostered the continuing impulse toward self-improvement. Founded in 1874, Chautauqua sponsored large summer assemblies, as well as small locally-based study groups. The latter, institutionalized as Chautauqua Literary and Scientific Circles in 1878, claimed more than 100,000 members by 1891.[8]

Women, in the company of husbands, brothers, or fathers, participated in the Lyceum, in Chautauqua, and in other mutual improvement groups, but beginning in 1868, they began to establish their own clubs separate from men. To be sure, occasional groups of women had formed self-improvement organizations earlier in the century. Subscribers to Margaret Fuller's "Conversations" for women in Boston in the 1830s discovered the depth of intellectual work a single-sex group could attain;[9] and women who worked in Massachusetts textile mills during the 1800s miti-

---

[5] *Id.*

[6] DANIEL J. BOORSTIN, THE AMERICANS: THE COLONIAL EXPERIENCE 150 (1958).

[7] DAVID C. MEAD, YANKEE ELEGANCE IN THE MIDDLE WEST 15 (1977).

[8] HUGH ORCHARD, FIFTY YEARS OF CHAUTAUQUA 189 (1923).

[9] *See generally* CAROLINE WELLS HEALEY DALL, MARGARET AND HER FRIENDS (1895) (describing the composition and meeting habits of the group and presenting a complete account of a series of group meetings).

gated the drudgery of their daily tasks by forming reading groups.[10] Despite these occasional outcroppings, women's clubs, the organizations that wove themselves into the fabric of nearly every American city, town and village, did not really emerge until after the Civil War. During the period between 1870 and 1920, women's clubs expanded widely, manifesting diverse forms and purposes. Some, like Sorosis, the New York City contender for first club in the nation, emerged out of a specifically political agenda to provide professional women writers a forum similar to that of the all-male Press Club. Founder Jane Cunningham Croly, having been denied admission to a Charles Dickens reading held at the Press Club, sought members who were hungry for the society of women, "that is, with those whose deeper natures had been roused to activity, who had been seized by the divine spirit of inquiry and aspiration, who were interested in the thought and progress of the age, and in what other women were thinking and doing."[11]

The New England Women's Club, established in Boston in 1868, the same year as Sorosis, announced its purpose in these terms: " 'Its plan involves no special pledge to any one form of activity, but implies only a womanly interest in all true thought and effort on behalf of woman, and of society in general, for which women are so largely responsible.' "[12] The feminism implicit in these and similar statements of purpose for women's clubs was softened by the care which clubs took to portray themselves as affirming, rather than undercutting, domestic values. According to this view, women who met to discuss religion or literature or art would be more effective moral guardians of their homes. Most women's clubs carefully distanced themselves from suffragist groups, thereby preserving club membership as socially acceptable for ordinary women.

Framing women's clubs as socially acceptable for ordinary women unwilling to pay the social costs associated with radical behavior and specifically linking the clubs' mission to women's domestic role no doubt contributed to their dramatic growth. By 1906, 5000 clubs had joined the General Federation of Women's Clubs, and it has been estimated that this number represented

---

10 Lucy Larcom, A New England Girlhood 240-42 (1889).

11 Jane Cunningham Croly, The History of the Women's Movement in America 15-16 (1898).

12 Karen J. Blair, The Clubwoman As Feminist: True Womanhood Redefined 1868-1914, at 32 (1980).

only five to ten percent of the clubs in existence.[13] Precisely because clubs portrayed themselves as furthering domestic aims, clubwomen often naturally fell into the role of "municipal housekeepers," concerning themselves with libraries, kindergartens, sanitation, parks, and a variety of other public issues. Patriarchal culture came to expect this kind of "service" from women's clubs, as the following excerpt from The Reverend Harvey Colburn's history of the Ladies Literary Club of Ypsilanti illustrates. Colburn begins by explaining that in the early days of the town, the church was the center of social activities, but with the advent of the Literary Club in 1878, a "decided change" began to be felt.[14] The club applied to the National Federation of Women's Clubs and joined in 1896. Thereafter, there was a "noticeable change in programs and methods . . . from a purely self-centered club, they began to work along civil and social lines."[15] The fact that a man was authorized, in 1922, to recount the history of a woman's club, one that had been conducting its own business for over forty years, had purchased its own house, and had become an institution within the community, raises complicated questions. We might assume that the Ladies Literary Club, having achieved its own status, turned to Colburn as a representative of a peer institution. Alternatively, we might assume that just as many women's clubs sought approval, tacitly or overtly, from religious leaders when they initially organized themselves, so too the Ladies Literary Club still felt compelled to seek the "blessing" of that most patriarchal of institutions, the church. Whatever the explanations behind it, Colburn's history demonstrates the public expectation that women's clubs should assume the kinds of civic and social responsibilities that would justify the accolade "municipal housekeepers."

Historians of women's clubs have emphasized this connection between private and public life. Karen Blair, for example, describes clubwomen as domestic feminists (women who redefined idealized ladydom to give themselves access to public life) for whom clubs provided a kind of waystation between private and public life. She explains:

> [Clubs] provided a meeting place for women, allowing them to
> know each other, to develop pride in their strengths, to grow
> sensitive to sexism, and to become aware of the possibilities

---

[13] *Id.* at 96.

[14] Papers of Ladies Literary Club of Ypsilanti (on file with the Bentley Historical Archive, University of Michigan).

[15] *Id.*

for abolishing inequities through Domestic Feminism. In addition, club life taught women the speaking and organizing skills which they later applied to civic reform.[16]

In this view, women's clubs provided the necessary abilities and confidence for women who wished to assume the civic and social responsibilities that Reverend Colburn urged upon them. In this view, clubs served as a means to the end of public service and public life.

Writing about women's study clubs of the same period, Theodora P. Martin paints a more complicated picture. While acknowledging that some women's clubs did enable women to "turn[] from the realm of abstract thought to the arena of practical action, from education for self to education for service,"[17] Martin observes that clubs true to the "original purpose of self- and mutual education, remained on the scene to become a permanent part of informal adult education."[18] These organizations, which Reverend Colburn would categorize as "self-centered," were not conceived as waystations or as a means to any other kind of existence. They existed as ends in themselves.

My own research indicates that these so-called "self-centered" clubs, clubs that resisted joining the General Federation of Women's Clubs, or adding large numbers to their membership, or participating in public service projects, may have had as profound an effect on those outside their realm as their more public-oriented sisters. Specifically, in fostering literary activities that resisted the concepts of intellectual property and authorship as defined by the dominant culture, these "self-centered" clubs offered an alternative way of thinking about writers and texts.

These types of women's clubs resisted both the aesthetic and legal/economic dimensions of the concepts of intellectual property and authorship. One form of resistance appeared in communal rather than individual ownership of texts, texts both used and produced by the club. It was very common for club members to subvert the economics of text commodification by purchasing a single text and passing it around among members. The Chautauqua Institution, which operated its own printing house and developed curricular materials for its Chautauqua Literary and Scientific Circles, was often a source of materials used by women's clubs. The annals of the Chautauqua Institution are filled

---

[16] BLAIR, *supra* note 12, at 118.

[17] THEODORA PENNY MARTIN, THE SOUND OF OUR OWN VOICES: WOMEN'S STUDY CLUBS 1860-1910, at 4 (1987).

[18] *Id.*

with complaints regarding the difficulty in determining how many people were actually using Chautauqua materials because it was so common for women's clubs to purchase Chautauqua texts and circulate them among the membership.[19]

This economic subversion took aesthetic shape in the ways women's clubs used their texts. In many clubs reading aloud was a common practice, and, at the same time that it offered another kind of resistance to the economic forces that commodified texts, this practice redefined the nature of reading to make it more communal and corporeal. Rather than interacting in isolation with a written text, club members shared responses, frequently inserting their own voices into the reading. They interrogated texts, laughed at them, and felt free to disagree with them. This excerpt from the March 26, 1897, records of the Friday Club of Jackson, Michigan, illustrates:

> Mrs. Robb began the afternoon by reading in a half-hearted way from that most unsatisfactory essay of Emerson's—as she thinks—"Love," interrupting herself every three sentences by protests against the truth of the statements. . . . But the battle of the afternoon was fought over the story "Where Ignorance is Bliss" by Margaret Deland, which Mrs. Root placidly called into our midst—the variety of ethical opinions of the Friday Club is only limited by its number of members, and the joyous part of all is that we are so satisfied that we are right, secretly excusing our sisters' lack of accord with us—with the charitable thought "that though a dear woman she is a little narrow-minded," in a word, we have reached a higher moral plane of development—this makes us all happy and hurts nobody. We decided once or over again, singly, doubly, in groups, all together by turn in season and out of season (especially sister Ruth) that the hero was a fool and so was she, that the hero was indeed a moral hero, but the girl a fool, that the hero was a fool and the girl wise.[20]

When we compare this response to a reading with the kinds of responses encouraged in literature classes of the same time period, we see just how subversive the Friday Club's manner of reading was. Dominated by a combination of historical and philological approaches, the study of literature in schools and colleges allowed little room for affective responses and multiple

---

[19] *See* Charles Robert Kniker, *1978—Centennial of a Forgotten Giant: The Chautauqua Literary and Scientific Circle, in* CHAUTAUQUA LITERARY AND SCIENTIFIC CIRCLE HISTORY AND BOOK LIST 1878-1985, at 3 (1985).

[20] Minutes of the Friday Club of Jackson, Michigan (Mar. 26, 1897) (on file with the Bentley Historical Archive, University of Michigan) [hereinafter Friday Club].

interpretations. At the secondary level, teachers frequently used school editions edited by William Rolfe. The following questions from a Rolfe examination on Milton suggest the approach to literature encouraged by these texts:

1) Write a sketch of Milton's life to 1638.
2) Briefly outline L'Alegro.
3) Give examples of obsolete words in the poems.
4) Give examples of words used in a different sense than they are used today.
5) Which of these words (a list follows) are from Anglo Saxon and which are from Latin?[21]

On college campuses, where departments of English were not yet two decades old, the same combination of history and philology (linguistics) dominated the classroom. Writing in the *Dial* in 1894, Wright Martin Sampson, chair of the English department at the University of Indiana, asserted this about teaching literature:

> There are many methods, but these methods are of two kinds only: the method of the professor who preaches the beauty of the poet's utterance, and the method of him who makes his student systematically approach the work as a work of art, find out the laws of its existence as such, the mode of its manifestation, the meaning it has, and the significance of that meaning—in brief, to have his students interpret the work of art and ascertain what makes it just that and not something else. Literature, as every reader profoundly feels, is an appeal to all sides of our nature; but I venture to insist that as a *study*—and this is the point at issue—it must be approached intellectually.[22]

Sampson's distinction between response and study, between feeling and intellect, reflects a view common in the nascent college English departments of this period. Struggling against the idea that the study of literature could not possibly be intellectually challenging enough to justify college instruction, English professors, particularly those trained in philology, espoused a "scientific" approach to the field, one designed to emphasize intellectual rigor. Along with the emphasis on the rigors and difficulties associated with studying literature came a denial of feel-

---

[21] William Rolfe, *Examination on Milton, reprinted in* Arthur Applebee, Tradition and Reform in the Teaching of English 37 (1977).

[22] Martin Wright Sampson, *English at the University of Indiana, in* The Origins of Literary Studies in America: A Documentary Anthology 53 (Gerald Graff & Michael Warner eds., 1989).

ing or anything that might be perceived as "soft." Sampson's insistence on the "study" of literature, as opposed to mere apprehension of it, reflects this perspective.

Given this larger context of an emphasis upon philological and historical structures, and classrooms where readers assumed that they were to learn what the text had to teach them and to control passion with reason, the proceedings of the Friday Club are all the more remarkable. In insisting on the possibility of pleasure, of "liking" a text, members of the Friday Club demonstrate an affective investment in the system of signification and allow for a multiplicity of meanings to emerge from that signification. In so doing, they disrupt the "classroom" intellect of the dominant culture.

In a related way, reading aloud, thereby infusing the text with breath, voice and presence, invested texts with a corporeal dimension. As Derrida reminds us, the figure of the book has dominated our thinking and our educational institutions, making texts the transcription of something prior.[23] The effect of this concentration on the book has been to subordinate the physical. What McLaren calls the "schooled body" participates in the "liturgy of the everyday" in schooling, a liturgy that ritualizes discursive practices.[24] In the late nineteenth century, as now, the discursive practices of schooling privileged the book. The reading aloud of women's clubs offered resistance to the book-dominated view of discourse, at the same time that it offered an alternative erotics of learning. The following excerpt from E. G. Loomis's account of the meeting of the Friday Club for September 20, 1889, suggests the effect of this resistance:

> I confess to having been more interested in the sight of the dear familiar, new-old faces than at first in the reading, and to have paid very little attention to the selection from Lubbock, read by Mrs. Root. About the usual quota of Emerson was read and comments made over some knotty passages. It seemed to me that we as a club have benefitted by our association, in the matter of conversation—or of being able to think aloud with less timidity and with more directness.[25]

E. G. Loomis's clear affection for the members of the club, ex-

---

[23] *See* JACQUES DERRIDA, OF GRAMMATOLOGY (Gayatri Chakrovovty Spivak trans., 1974).

[24] Peter McLaren, *The Schooled Body*, in CRITICAL PEDAGOGY, THE STATE, AND CULTURAL STRUGGLE 190 (Henry Giroux & Peter McLaren eds., 1989).

[25] E.G. Loomis, Comments on a Meeting, Friday Club, *supra* note 20 (Sept. 20, 1889).

pressed as it is in physical terms, demonstrates how feeling takes precedence in the Friday Club where the schooled body is released from its liturgy of the everyday. This sentence could be dismissed as mere sentimentality were it not followed by the one in which Loomis describes the benefits conferred by the club—the ability to "think aloud (or participate in intellectual discourse) with less timidity and with more directness."[26] Loomis thus shows how the physical affection expressed in the first sentence contributes to the intellectual development of clubwomen.

The production of texts in women's clubs likewise resisted dominant concepts of intellectual property and authorship. Collaboration played a major role in writing. Members shared their personal libraries (a practice that accounts for the majority of public libraries in this country being established by women's clubs) as they gathered material for writing. Frequently, women's clubs institutionalized collaboration by requiring members to consult with one another before presenting a paper. Boston's Saturday Morning Club, for example, stipulated this: "Papers shall be read to the president (or to someone designated by her) at least a week before the discussion date."[27] The Friday Club of Jackson, Michigan kept records of its meetings in a series of "little books." Because the club had no hierarchy of officers, the little books were passed from one member to another after each meeting, and the recorder for the week, who would later read her "composition" aloud to the club, was free to draw upon other entries in the little book. As Zellie Emerson, writing in November of 1889, expressed it, writers created texts that benefitted from what we would call intertextuality:

> Shall I allow myself to be carried away by the poetic fancies and melodious measure of a Carlton, or imitate the quaint humorous style of a Robb, steal the deep wisdom and philosophy of a Gibson, or making *their* best my own, fuse the whole into one gigantic and glorious production, or thus cast suspicion on the originality of their matter and style, since mine must necessarily be the *epitome* of what is best in all?[28]

The intergenerational structure of women's clubs contributed directly to this kind of intertextuality. It was very common for several generations of the same family to belong to a given women's

---

[26] *Id.*

[27] Procedures of the Saturday Morning Club (on file with the Schlesinger Library, Radcliffe College) [hereinafter Saturday Club].

[28] Zellie Emerson, Friday Club, *supra* note 20 (Nov. 1889).

club. As they joined one another in consuming and producing club texts, mothers and daughters embodied the continuity and connection that psychologist Nancy Chodorow has described.[29] Rather than perceiving themselves as differentiated individuals, mothers and daughters in clubs defined themselves in relationship to one another. Terms such as fusion, fluidity, mutuality and continuity defined their relationships and shaped their use of texts as they borrowed language across generations.

Not surprisingly then, clubwomen resisted the boundaries between texts with acts of appropriation, imitation, and general playfulness. Club anniversaries frequently prompted appropriation of texts across generations. Frances Darling's 1968 paper about Maud Ward Elliot includes a long excerpt from a letter written by Maud to the club in 1946.[30] Maud, the daughter of Julia Ward Howe and one of the charter members of the Saturday Morning Club when it was founded in 1871, wrote her letter to the club on the occasion of its sixty-fifth anniversary. Maud, then ninety-two years old, recounted how she had, when she was seventeen, chided her mother about her frumpy friends ("the bonnets of some of those early suffragists were fierce" she claims) and suggested that it might be worthwhile to have a club for young women such as herself.[31] Frances Darling, writing twenty-two years later, incorporated a good deal of Maud's text into her own.

Separated from what we might describe as the agonistic kingdom of inscription, where writers struggle against the power of one another's texts, women in clubs moved freely from their own texts to those of others, participating in a shared world they created. Unlike the dominant culture, where ownership created boundaries between one text and another,[32] the boundaries between texts written in women's clubs were often more blurred. In contradistinction to the dominant culture's ethos of individual ownership, clubs assumed communal ownership of texts. This community-property view of texts was expressed most often in the requirement to submit a copy of one's paper to the club archive. The record book of Seattle's Century Club includes this statement: "Papers read before the club will become the prop-

---

[29] *See* NANCY CHODOROW, THE REPRODUCTION OF MOTHERING: PSYCHOANALYSIS AND THE SOCIOLOGY OF GENDER (1978).

[30] Letter from Maud Ward Elliot to Saturday Morning Club (1946), Saturday Club, *supra* note 27.

[31] *Id.*

[32] The possessive form *'s* derives from the male form, e.g., "John his hat" became "John's hat."

erty of the club, and a fair copy on sermon paper must be filed with the Corresponding Secretary."[33] Members of the Ladies Literary Club of Ypsilanti, Michigan made decisions about the disposition of papers. In the fall of 1898, for instance, the minutes include this: "It was moved and supported that Mrs. Dickinson's paper on the telegraph be printed in the local papers."[34] Presumably, Mrs. Dickinson had no objection to this publication of her work, but it was a decision of the club rather than her own choice. In 1897, the president of this same club admonished members to "be more careful in preserving club papers than heretofore"[35] and on another occasion in this year, the same president urged members to "notice particularly the papers as they are read at each meeting"[36] so they could vote on which papers to set aside for Reciprocity Day the following year. Reciprocity Day, an occasion when two or more clubs came together to share their best work, provided a wider audience for club papers. Clearly, members of the Ladies Literary Club saw papers written by individual members as club property to be disseminated as the club saw fit.

In the early days of Boston's Saturday Morning Club, one of the highest compliments that could be paid to a member was to request that she put a copy of her paper in the club's Green Trunk. The Green Trunk served as the club archive before the Saturday Morning Club established its collection at Radcliffe's Schlesinger Library in 1976. Actually, there were several green trunks. Minutes for the April 26, 1958, meeting of the Saturday Morning Club include this:

> At the Annual Meeting held at the apartment of Mrs. Rugg, the members of the Saturday Morning Club were invited to examine the contents of the famous "Green Trunk," a very small affair indeed, that contained the earliest records of the Club. As the records multiplied, another larger trunk was procured to hold the "Green Trunk" itself, plus the overflow, and later a third still larger one to hold these two. And still our records accumulate.[37]

The green trunk symbolized the importance of preserving club

---

[33] Record Book of the Seattle Women's Century Club (on file with the Northwest Collection of the Suzallo Library, University of Washington) (1901).

[34] Minutes of the Ladies Literary Club of Ypsilanti (Fall 1898) (on file with the Bentley Historical Archive, University of Michigan).

[35] Id.

[36] Id.

[37] Minutes, Saturday Club, *supra* note 27 (Apr. 26, 1958).

texts. The fiftieth anniversary celebration in 1929 featured a play written by club member Abbie Farwell Brown entitled *The Masque of the Green Trunk*. In addition to recounting some of the club's history, this play underscored the importance of preserving club texts by making the club archive—the green trunk itself—the star of the drama. When the "Mother" character presented the green trunk to the "Daughter" character in the play, she said:

> Take with you the little Green Trunk and the materials that I have used to start with. Truth (*puts in a tape measure*), and Thoroughness (*scissors*), and Sympathy (*needles*), and Loyalty, (*thread*) and Tact (*wax*) and Humor, (*a red pincushion*), mustn't forget that! (*Chuckles.*) There you are! Therefrom will the Tradition grow.[38]

The attributes of truth, thoroughness, sympathy, loyalty, tact and humor suggested ways of approaching club texts, as well as dealing with individual club members, but tradition was the most important feature, and the texts the club held in common created this tradition.

Owning texts in common did not mean that access to them was entirely open. Many clubs specified who might look at club records. A 1921 letter from one Saturday Morning Club member to another discusses who may gain access to the trunk and specifies that a letter of permission is required for anyone wanting to look at texts contained in the trunk.[39]

Clubs did not limit access to their texts because they were inferior. Indeed, many clubwomen were professional writers. A majority of the members of New York's Sorosis Club made their living by writing. Julia Ward Howe and Ednah Dow Cheney, Louisa Mae Alcott's biographer, were both well-known writers, but the texts they wrote for the New England Women's Club remained the property of the club. Abbie Farwell Brown, author of *The Masque of the Green Trunk* as well as of many other Saturday Morning Club papers, published a number of books and many articles; however, the texts she wrote for the Saturday Morning Club did not enter the commercial world.

The view of intellectual property that commodified texts gave little quarter to the pleasure to be derived from texts. In contrast, pleasure took a central place in the way women's clubs saw and dealt with their texts. As the Mother character in *The Masque of the Green Trunk* makes clear, clubs placed a high value on

---

[38] Abbie Farwell, *The Masque of the Green Trunk*, Saturday Club, *supra* note 27 (1929).
[39] Eleanor W. Allen, *Letter*, Saturday Club, *supra* note 27 (1921).

humor and the pleasures associated with it, and this was particularly true for their texts. Clubwomen especially valued texts that made them laugh. Papers that gave members special pleasure were designated for club archives and became part of the collective consciousness of the club, as this entry from the October 19, 1970 minutes of the Saturday Morning Club illustrates: "It was agreed that Miss Tetlow could read an old paper rather than write a new one. This gives the club a particular treat because her papers are ageless in their interest and stimulating."[40]

Not only did clubwomen adopt a stance quite different from that of the dominant culture so far as ownership of their own texts was concerned, they also extended this subversive view to texts produced by the dominant culture by imitating or parodying them. Many of the entries in the record book of the Friday Club of Jackson, Michigan were playful imitations, and the Bible provided a ready model. The minutes for March 20, 1891, read:

> And behold all the women were sore afraid, and again they said one to another of a surety, this is the place of departed spirits—for we hear sounds of instruments which are not, and we see the form of one who is afar in a distant city. But behold there was one among the women who had much wisdom, and she cried out in a loud voice saying—fools and unbelievers. Know ye not of one Edison who has learned the secrets of the lightning and who can shut up sounds of stringed instruments and of song, that one can command the sounds at will, and the sounds will come forth freely, even as water from a jug?[41]

Bakhtin describes parody as introducing the "permanent corrective of laughter"[42] with "a critique on the one-sided seriousness of the lofty direct word, the corrective of reality that is always richer, more fundamental and most importantly *too contradictory and heteroglot* to be fit into a high and straightforward genre."[43] Playful parodies abound in the records of women's clubs. Texts, ranging from poems by Whittier and essays by Emerson, served as the object of mimicry for writers in women's clubs. These texts, like the Biblical parody quoted above, undercut some of the "seriousness of the lofty direct word" in texts privileged by the dominant culture.

Clubwomen often appropriated texts from the dominant cul-

---

[40] Minutes, Saturday Club, *supra* note 27 (Oct. 19, 1970).
[41] Minutes, Friday Club, *supra* note 20 (Mar. 20, 1891).
[42] MIKHAIL M. BAKHTIN, THE DIALOGIC IMAGINATION 55 (Caryl Emerson & Michael Holquist trans., 1981).
[43] *Id.*

ture to create dramatic productions. Over the years, the Saturday Morning Club staged a number of plays. Several of them were based on texts written by club members (such as *The Masque of the Green Trunk*), but many others were based on texts produced outside the club. The Saturday Morning Club produced *In a Balcony* in 1889, *Antigone* in 1890, *A Winter's Tale* in 1895, and *Pride and Prejudice* in 1904, adapting each text to their own purposes.

Club records indicate that the most prized of its productions was *Antigone*. In addition to cutting Sophocles' text, Saturday Morning Club members adapted the text in several ways. The cast was composed entirely of women and both public productions were open to women only. Because the women's voices were lighter and did not carry as well as those of the men, the Saturday Morning Club's members decided to augment the Chorus of Theban Elders with a Chorus of Maidens. At a celebratory breakfast held a few days after the final presentation of *Antigone*, club members appropriated other texts as they relished their success. The record of the breakfast meeting includes the following:

> Miss Quincy responded for the Elders with some very amusing verses in the style of Hiawatha. Ellen Dennie (one of the directors) responded to the toast in her honor with a poem that began:
>
>> Theban Elders! Theban Elders
>> Are there, in the English language
>> Fitting words for just this moment
>> To express the joy and rapture
>> Which I owe to your great kindness
>> For a gift so rare and perfect,
>> Full of generous thought and feeling;
>> Thing of beauty, joy forever,
>> Keeping fresh in mem'ry's vision
>> Beauty evanescent, fleeting?
>> If so, I have failed to find them.[44]

Most of the toasts and poems read at this celebration borrowed, as this one does from Keats' *Endymion*, freely from texts circulating in the dominant culture. As would befit a group subverting the commodification of texts, the Saturday Morning Club donated the several thousand dollars of profits on *Antigone* to charity.

In both their consumption and production of texts, clubwomen subverted the concepts of intellectual property and

---

[44] Minutes, Saturday Club, *supra* note 27 (1891).

authorship. In valuing pleasure over economic profit and emphasizing aesthetics over functional concerns, they posited texts as communal property rather than economic commodities. They wrote with a playful intertextuality that undercut the ideology of authorship.

In one way, all this might seem of little consequence. After all, we are talking about a marginal group, one that enjoyed less than full participation in the dominant culture. So what if these quaint groups of women were enacting alternatives to dominant conceptions of intellectual property and authorship? I want to argue that these alternatives did have larger consequences.

The immediate response of the dominant culture provides one measure of the power attributed to women's clubs. Almost from their inception, women's clubs were ridiculed and belittled in the popular press. Cartoons lampooned them, articles questioned their motives and accomplishments, and the very phrase "woman's club" became a term of ridicule. Newspaper accounts of the Saturday Morning Club's all female production of *Antigone* demonstrate the alternately patronizing and hostile responses evoked by this production. Only women were allowed to purchase tickets to the production, a show so popular it ran two extra performances to accommodate all who wished to see it. Here are some excerpts from newspaper accounts of the production:

> The attention to detail was seen in pretty feminine touches . . . in the remarkable fact that every actor was letter-perfect in the hard text . . . it being generally understood that the author was dead, there were no calls for him, but an enthusiastic ovation was given the actors after the play . . . . The doorkeepers were women, the ushers were women, and a low-toned request at the door made most of the women of the audience take off their hats and bonnets. In consequence, the differing types of the Boston feminine head might be studied to better advantage than is usual in our audiences . . . . To the onlooker, the procession was a veritable beauty show . . . .[45]

Perhaps the most telling of all the newspaper accounts was this one:

> A Boston woman entered a Washington Street bookstore the other day and asked for a copy of "Antigone." The salesman replied that the demand had been so great of late that they

---

[45] Excerpts from several 1890 newspapers including the *Boston Post*, *Boston Herald*, and *Journal* (on file in Minutes, Saturday Club, *supra* note 27).

hadn't a copy of any edition left in the store. Whereupon she
retorted angrily, "Well, I do think, since I buy so many books
here, you might send me the new stories which you know I
shall want to read as fast as they come out."[46]

Just as the male response to women's inherent power over life
(through giving birth) has been to constrain and circumscribe
that power by deprecating women, so these commentaries suggest fears and anxieties about the power manifested by women
who mount their own productions without the aid of men.
Although men were quite accustomed to excluding women from
education, social gatherings, and a variety of other spheres, the
idea that women should be similarly exclusionary posed a real
threat, especially since fundamental concepts such as intellectual
property and authorship were subverted within that sphere.

More complicated and compelling evidence of the consequences of the literary activities of women's clubs is suggested by
considering the literacy activities common in women's clubs.
Jean Wyatt argues that reading and writing play a major role in
changing one's mind, and changing one's mind means giving up
traditional orientations to reality and abandoning reliance on distinct categories.[47] In the ways they read and wrote, clubwomen
called the traditional relationships among writer, text and public
into question. They inscribed themselves in unconventional and
playful ways, blurring dominant categories of author and text as
they did so.

The self-reflexive practices of writing and reading texts in
women's clubs gave participants an unusual opportunity to develop subversive thought. It is worth noting, in this regard, that
the unofficial and often-repeated motto of the Friday Club was
"Men may come and men may go but we go on forever." Writing
and reading statements like this one became what Patricia Yeager
calls "emancipatory strategies."[48] Precisely because they were
playful in consuming and producing texts, clubwomen took
power from their literary activities. Play is, as Schiller has explained, an inherently liberating force because it causes "reality
to lose [its] seriousness."[49] Playfulness in literary activities thus
enabled clubwomen to change their minds, to develop what Wy-

---

[46] Id.

[47] See JEAN WYATT, RECONSTRUCTING DESIRE: THE ROLE OF THE UNCONSCIOUS IN WO-
MEN'S READING AND WRITING (1990).

[48] See PATRICIA YEAGER, HONEY-MAD WOMEN: EMANCIPATORY STRATEGIES IN WOMEN'S
WRITING (1988).

[49] FRIEDRICH VON SCHILLER, THE AESTHETIC LETTERS, ESSAYS AND THE PHILOSOPHI-
CAL LETTERS 71 (J. Weiss trans., 1845).

att calls "new fantasies."[50] These new fantasies, or reconstructed desires, became the first step toward effecting changes in the material world.

---

[50] WYATT, *supra* note 47 at 219.

READING AND WRITING THE RENAISSANCE COMMONPLACE BOOK: A QUESTION OF AUTHORSHIP?

MAX W. THOMAS*

What can the material features of a text tell us about its status as something "authored"? What, more particularly, do those features reveal when the text in question predates a modern notion of copyright and occupies a liminal position with respect to the material system of reproduction (printing) fundamental to that notion? This basic question impels the present study—not as a problem to be solved, but as a *modus operandi*, a way to avoid relying upon modern notions of authorship when approaching texts to which they might not be applicable. In so doing, developing a model of the discursive conditions of poetic production more appropriate to such texts may be possible.

My concerns are particularly related to Renaissance poetry, especially the Renaissance practice of keeping a poetic commonplace book, in which a variety of poetic texts might be "gathered and composed," as Arthur Marotti puts it, typically in a blank "table book," often received as a gift, "in which poems or poems and prose were meant to be transcribed by its owner—usually without a governing plan or arrangement."[1] Most of the time, these poems were transcribed without attribution; sometimes even the compiler of the commonplace book remained anonymous. Peter Beal writes that when names do "become associated with poems" in manuscripts, it is

> for a variety of reasons besides simple authorship. A man's name might become linked with a poem in the course of manuscript transmission because he was the copyist, or because it was written by someone in his circle, or because he added his own stanzas to it, or wrote a reply to it, or set it to music, and so on. There is usually a reason for the association—scribes were not wont to pluck names out of the air at random . . . .[2]

* Assistant Professor of English, Univ. of Iowa; B.A., 1988, M.A., 1989, Case Western Reserve University; Ph.D. 1993, University of Pennsylvania. I wish to thank Margreta de Grazia for her trenchant comments on this essay, and Martha Woodmansee who made possible the discursive conditions of its production. I would also like to acknowledge the Bodleian Library, Oxford, for permission to quote from Rawlinson Poetry MS 148.

[1] ARTHUR MAROTTI, JOHN DONNE: COTERIE POET 5-6, 7 (1986).

[2] Peter Beal, *Shall I Die?*, TIMES LITERARY SUPP., Jan. 3, 1986, at 13.

Attribution clearly has different significance for Renaissance poetic practice than for modern textual scholarship and for modern
readers of Renaissance texts. After all, most twentieth-century
readers approach Elizabethan poetry through single-author editions (Donne, Shakespeare, Marlowe, Jonson, and so forth) or
through anthologies, which are also organized by author. An
Elizabethan reader's approach to that poetry would be significantly different from a modern reader's approach, even in the
poetry's most basic material dimensions. Not only attributions,
but also the texts of the poems themselves remained highly variable. As Gerald L. Bruns argues, the manuscript text remains
open, malleable, and therefore "tacitly unfinished: it is never
fully present but is always available for a later hand to bring it
more completely into the open."[3] As a result, poems might exist
in several different versions, some produced by deliberate alterations, others by errors in transcription. If collected, the poems
would be copied among a variety of other, unrelated poems, and
sometimes among non-poetic texts as well.

To account for these features of commonplace books simply
as the side-effects of a system of manuscript transmission, however, is to overlook the extent to which they may constitute material traces of textual practices and the conditions which make
possible the production of poetry during the Renaissance.   In
the first section of *A Theory of Literary Production*,[4] Pierre Macherey
formulates a theoretical project in which he argues that "in order
to identify a form of knowledge, . . . we must seek the conditions
which make the emergence of this knowledge possible."[5] He further argues that "the conditions that determine the production of
the book also determine the forms of its communication."[6]
Macherey traces the complex way in which the material operations of reading and writing help produce the ideologies of
knowledge and interpretation, and how those ideologies in turn
constrain the praxis of reading.[7] Moreover, he defines a "condition" of production as "the principle of rationality which makes

---

[3] Gerald L. Bruns, *The Originality of Texts in a Manuscript Culture*, 32 COMP. LITERA-
TURE 113, 126 (1980). Arthur Marotti discussed this issue at length in a paper entitled
"Malleable and Fixed Texts: Manuscript and Printed Miscellanies and the Transmission
of Lyric Poetry", presented at the 1988 MLA Session "Is Typography Textual?" (Sponsored by the Renaissance English Text Society).

[4] PIERRE MACHEREY, A THEORY OF LITERARY PRODUCTION (Geoffrey Wall trans.,
1978).

[5] *Id.* at 8.

[6] *Id.* at 70.

[7] *Id.* at 49.

the work accessible to thought";[8] his project is the recovery of a kind of *mentalite* through consideration of an abstract and ideal principle.

Conditions of production, however, can be material as well. When what is being produced is a text, those conditions can include the physical activities by which writing is produced (by hand or by press) and the manner in which written matter is consumed in the process of reading. These material conditions of poetic production in the Renaissance and their implications for a conception of authorship are what I wish to explore in the remainder of this paper. In order to be able to address these issues with some specificity, I will focus on a single commonplace book, now on deposit in the Bodleian Library, Oxford: Bodleian MS Rawlinson Poetry 148 ("Rawlinson 148").[9]

The manuscript was compiled between 1589 and 1621 by John Lilliat, an Anglican clergyman and cathedral musician. In 1589, it appears, Lilliat received a gift of a blank book, for recorded on the verso of the first leaf of the present manuscript, in a large italic hand, is the inscription:

> *Liber Lilliati.* Anno. 1589. *Maii.* 3.
> *Ex dono Roberti Sharpe./*[10]

At some point, however, Lilliat had the manuscript rebound,[11] and included in the midst of sixty-five leaves of poems copied out in his own careful secretary hand an almost complete printed copy of *The Hekatompathia or Passionate Centurie of Loue.*[12] There is no sharp boundary between the "printed" and "manuscript" portions of Rawlinson 148. The first four leaves contain brief poems and sententiae in manuscript; *The Hekatompathia*, begin-

---

8 *Id.*

. 9 LIBER LILLIATI: ELIZABETHAN VERSE AND SONG (BODLEIAN MS RAWLINSON POETRY 148) (Edward Doughtie ed., Univ. Del. Press 1985).

10 *Id.* at 43.

11 Edward Doughtie notes in his edition of the manuscript that the binding "is similar to other sixteenth- and early seventeenth-century bindings," which leads me to suspect that Lilliat had the manuscript rebound. *Id.* at 33. Whether all the handwritten poems had already been transcribed or whether the rebinding included blank leaves cannot be known.

12 "THE / EʹΚΑΤΟΜΠΑΘΙΑ / OR / PASSIONATE / *Centurie of* / Loue, // *Diuided into two parts: where-* / *of, the first expresseth the Au-* / *thors sufferance in Loue: the* / *latter, his long farewell to Loue* / *and all his tyrannie.* // Composed by *Thomas Watson* / Gentleman; and published at/the request of certaine Gentle- / men his very frendes." was entered into the Stationers' Register in 1582 and printed the same year. THOMAS WATSON, THE HEKATOMPATHIA OR PASSIONATE CENTURIE OF LOUE (Burt Franklin Press 1967) (1582). "[T]he first (presumably blank) leaf, the fourth leaf (in the first of two signatures marked A), and the last leaf (unprinted, sig. N4) are missing in Lilliat's copy; sig. I is misfolded." LIBER LILLIATTI, *supra* note 9, at 33. The missing leaves are not unusual; quartos often lost the outer leaves (and, as in the case of A4, their conjugates) to wear and tear.

ning with its title page, commences on the fifth leaf. The handwriting, however, does not stop there. More brief poems and sententiae cover the verso of the title page and the bottom margins of the next two leaves, on which the prefatory letters for *The Hekatompathia* are printed. In addition, the printed text has been annotated, marked with indices (pointing fingers: ☞), and heavily underlined. Although the next fifty-six leaves (the printed text of *The Hekatompathia*'s poems) contain no further manuscript poems, the underlining and indexing continues to appear, albeit infrequently. The printed text is then followed by sixty-one leaves of manuscript poetry. Lilliat's hand is literally present throughout Rawlinson 148, writing out poems, underlining printed text in *The Hekatompathia*, or adding annotations and indices alongside printed and handwritten texts alike.

Does the pervasive presence of that hand qualify the copy of *The Hekatompathia* included in Rawlinson 148 as part of the "commonplace book"? There are a few other manuscript commonplace books which incorporate a leaf or two of printed matter,[13] but nothing, to my knowledge, on this scale. Because Rawlinson 148 contains text produced by two different technologies and belongs to what we would define as two different "genres" ("commonplace book" and "sonnet sequence"), for us not to conceive of the sections as discrete texts is difficult. This difficulty is felt even at the level of bibliographic description, where it would be considered inaccurate not to distinguish between the two portions of the volume. Indeed, that the printed text and manuscript text belong to distinct conceptual categories seems self-evident. This assumption is at work in the historical scenario I suggested above (the gift of a table book, subsequently rebound); it is also present in the description of the manuscript by its modern editor, Edward Doughtie:

> The manuscript, now in the Bodleian Library at Oxford, consists of a printed copy of Thomas Watson's *Hekatompathia* (1582) bound with additional leaves on which a number of English poems, some songs with music, a letter, some Latin verses and phrases, and other items have been copied. A fair amount of this material has not been published.[14]

It is interesting that even in an edition devoted to the manuscript "items," Doughtie's description conceives of those materials as distinct from and supplementary to the printed text. Further-

---

[13] Marotti, *supra* note 3.
[14] LIBER LILLIATI, *supra* note 9, at 15.

more, Doughtie's edition is not the first time that the printed
portion of Rawlinson 148 has been privileged over its "additional" manuscript poems. When the "enthusiastic antiquarian
and collector"[15] Thomas Hearne acquired the manuscript, he
wrote his name and the date on the title page of *The
Hekatompathia*.[16] It seems likely that he acquired the volume because of the rarity of the printed collection (eleven copies are
extant). (Coincidentally, Hearne acquired the volume in 1709,
the year in which the Statute of Anne first legislated copyright.)

The economics of modern editing continue to reinforce a
division between the printed and handwritten portions of the
manuscript. It would be pointless and expensive for Doughtie to
reproduce the text of *The Hekatompathia* since it is available in edited and facsimile versions. Doughtie is not concerned with
presenting a facsimile of Rawlinson 148; rather, his aim is to
make available a manuscript "in some respects representative of
a large body of material which was at times more important for
some levels of literary culture than printed books."[17] The inclusion of printed matter in Rawlinson 148 is not representative of
the commonplace book tradition, and so, it seems, need not be
included in a modern edition.

This observation is not made to fault Doughtie or Hearne,
but rather to indicate the extent to which the requirements of
reproduction, the categories which govern modern textual practice, lead, not to a reproduction of a certain artifact (the collection of paper and ink that bears the shelfmark Rawl 148), but to
its disappearance. Moreover, because those categories (print and
manuscript) seem so self-evident, modern textual practices do
not address the possibility that a remarkably different textual
practice produced the Renaissance textual artifact. In Lilliat's
handwriting, however, is the evidence for such a practice, evidence that the "difference" we so readily detect might not have
been evident in the same way for a Renaissance compiler. In order to understand those practices, it is necessary to examine
more carefully what the process of compilation entailed. Rawlinson 148 is particularly helpful in this examination, for the process
of compilation is played out both in Lilliat's assembly of a com-

---

15 *Id.* at 34.
16 "MSS Rawl. Poet. 148" is also written on the title page. This notation may be
Richard Rawlinson's own catalogue number or a later addition. The page is also marked
with the stamp of the Bodleian Library and with two other apparent catalogue numbers:
"MS. num. 50" in Hearne's handwriting immediately beneath his name and date and "E.
Pr. 37.," which I have not been able to identify (Doughtie does not mention it).
17 LIBER LILLIATI, *supra* note 9, at 16.

monplace book and in the material he incorporated in it, particularly in *The Hekatompathia*.

The title page of *The Hekatompathia* reads approximately as follows:

T H E

E' Κ Α Τ Ο Μ Π Α Θ Ι' Α

O R

P A S S I O N A T E

Centurie of

L o u e,

*Diuided into two parts: where-
of, the first expresseth the Authors sufferance in Loue: the
latter, his long farewell to Loue
and all his tyrannie.*

Composed by *Thomas Watson*
Gentleman; and published at
the request of certaine Gentlemen his very frendes.[18]

First, the catchy, classicized, title is given prominence, then there is an italicized precis of the contents, in which a generic "Author" is mentioned. But that "Author" is not given agency: the text itself "expresseth the Author's sufferance."[19] The "Author" is a kind of main character, whose adventures with love will be set forth.[20] Thomas Watson's name appears in the following paragraph, which figures him as the *composer* of the "two parts,"[21] not as their author.

To be "composed," in the sixteenth century, is to be made up of parts or to be elaborately or artificially put together; it also

---

[18] WATSON, *supra* note 12. I have not reproduced the ornament and printer's information which follow the text quoted, nor the elaborate classical border which surrounds it. A naked Venus stands to the left of the title, an armored Mars to the right; cupids with drawn bows and phoenix birds appear across the bottom of the page, and at the top is an elaborate ornament in which the letter "A" (for Amor?) is entwined. The top and bottom borders have symmetrical right and left halves.

[19] *Id.*

[20] A similar analogue might be "Master F.J." in Gascoigne's *Hundreth Sundry Flowres*, whose adventures provide a loose narrative frame by which sonnets are presented. GEORGE GASCOIGNE, A HUNDRETH SUNDRIE FLOWRES (Ruth Loyd Miller ed., Kennikat Press 2d ed. 1975) (1573). What it might mean to be called an author is a question I take up later in this essay. *See infra* discussion accompanying notes 37-38.

[21] From this title page, there is no reason to assume that the contents will be poems. Indeed, the suggestion is that one will find songs and music inside. Lilliat's commonplace book fulfills that expectation, insofar as it includes six musical settings.

means to possess a "settled countenance," according to the *Oxford English Dictionary* ("OED").[22] Thus, the composer arranges and subdues the "sufferance" of the "Author." Composition is a process of mediation as well as a process of production. *The Hekatompathia* makes this mediation clear in its organizational principles. After the prefatory material, each page is composed of a roman numeral; an editorial comment upon the poem which follows, including verses in foreign languages upon which the poem is based or translated; the poem itself; and a printer's device to fill out the page. There are often marginal glosses alongside the poems as well.

Watson's role as a composer subsumes his role as an author. The "louepassions" or "sonnets," which present the stylized fiction of the conventional frustrated lover, are attributed to the "Author" by the title page and by the headnotes. The "Author," who is the speaker in the poems, refers only to the fictive discursive frame, which addresses the beloved or bemoans its condition to itself. The "Author" remains oblivious to the material conditions of his discourse: he could never know that his words exist only as black-letter type on a page. It is the composer who, like the reader, is insistently aware of the materiality and textuality of the "Author's" poetic utterances. The headnotes to poems XI to XVII demonstrate this awareness:

> XI: In this sonnet is couertly set forth, how pleasaunt a passio[n] the Author one day enioyed, whe[n] by chance he ouerharde his mistris, whilst she was singinge priuately by her selfe . . . .[23]
>
> XII: The subiect of this passion is all one with that, which is next before it . . . .[24]
>
> XIII: The Authour descanteth on forwarde vpon the late effect, which the song of his Mistres hath wrought in him . . . And in this passion after he hath set downe some miraculous good effectes of Musicke . . . .[25]
>
> XIIII: The Authour still pursuing his inuention vpon the song of his Mistres, in the last staffe of this sonnet he falleth into this fiction . . . .[26]
>
> XV: Still hee followeth on with further deuise vppon the late Melodie of his Mistres: & in this sonnet doth namelie preferre

---

[22] 3 OXFORD ENGLISH DICTIONARY 622 (2d ed. 1989).

[23] WATSON, *supra* note 12, at 25.

[24] *Id.* at 26.

[25] *Id.* at 27.

[26] *Id.* at 28.

her before *Musicke* her selfe . . . .[27]
XVI: In this passion the Authour vpon the late sweete song
of his Mistres, maketh her his birde . . . .[28]
XVII: The Author not yet hauing forgotten the songe of his
mistres, maketh her in this passion a seconde *Phoenix* . . . .[29]

One can imagine the composer becoming increasingly exasper-
ated with the absurdity of the conventional conceits (comparing a
woman to "Musicke," making a woman into a bird) to which the
"Author"/poet clings so tenaciously in poem after poem. The
composer is thus presented as a kind of reader, going through
the poems one by one and commenting upon them. This commentary, however, is not neutral, for it situates the text within a
particular discursive context and thus constrains the reader's encounter with the text. In the examples quoted above, that constraint is relatively simple, insofar as it reminds the reader of
what has already transpired. Elsewhere they are concerned with
more complex dimensions of the discursive practices at work in
the text:

> XL: The sense contained in this Sonnet will seeme straunge
> to such as neuer haue acquainted themselues with *Loue* and his
> Lawes, because of the contrarieties mentioned therein. But to
> such, as Loue at any time hath had vnder his banner, all and
> euery part of it will appeare to be a familier trueth. It is almost
> word for word taken out of *Petrarch*, (where hee beginneth,
> *Pace non truouo, e non ho da far guerra*; *E temo, e spero, &c.?*) All,
> except three verses, which this Authour hath necessarily ad-
> ded, for perfecting the number, which hee hath determined to
> vse in euery one of these his Passions.[30]

The "Author" himself never mentions the "determination" referred to above. The composer extrapolates volition from the
uniform appearance of the poems because the composer fore-
grounds the formal materiality of the poem. The extent to which
the headnotes call attention to the Latin, Italian, and French
sources for the poems, combined with this foregrounded materiality, suggests the extent to which the poems are not merely the
products of writing, but of reading as well. *The Hekatompathia* is
full of readings and readers. There is the "Author"/poet, who
reads and translates Petrarchan love poetry; the composer, who
reads the "Author's" poems, as well as their sources, and com-

---

[27] *Id.* at 29.
[28] *Id.* at 30.
[29] *Id.* at 31.
[30] *Id.* at 54.

ments upon them; the slough of readers who have written commendatory verses for the volume—and, in the case of Rawlinson 148, Lilliat, whose reading leaves textual traces as well, in his underlinings, annotations and indices.

The "reader" of poetry is conditioned by his/her "writing" practices because they are what articulate and implement the conditions of production: writing teaches one what to read for, whether that writing is as brief as the demarcation of a sententiae worth committing to memory, or as lengthy as a response to, alteration of, or translation of a poem encountered and re-produced. The extent to which the writing in *The Hekatompathia* is produced by and presented in the context of reading is one example; the way in which *The Hekatompathia* can be absorbed into a commonplace book is another. Lilliat's annotations to the second dedicatory letter in *The Hekatompathia*, "Iohn Lyly to the Authour his friend,"[31] are particularly instructive. The letter itself is highly metaphoric, and what Lilliat re-marks in his reading are individual tropes, which need have nothing to do with a dedicatory letter. Nonetheless, they are curiously appropriate, for Lily's letter suggests the extent to which it is the reader, not an author, who experiences the (almost orgasmic) pleasure of textualized passion:

> My good friend, I haue read your new passions, and they have renewed mine old pleasures, the which brought to me no lesse delight, the[n] they haue done to your selfe commendations. And certes had not one of mine eies about serious affaires beene watchfull, both by being too too busie had beene wanton: such is the nature of persuading pleasure, that it melteth the marrowe before it scorche the skin, and burneth before it warmeth: Not vnlike vnto <u>the oyle of Ieat, which rotteth the bone and neuerranckleth the flesh, or the Scarab flies, which enter into the roote and neuer touch the rinde.</u>[32]

(This passage is marked not only by underlining, but also by a small index in the right hand margin, pointing to the word "which.") The reader signals, and even participates in, this pleasure by taking pen in hand and writing upon the text. Indeed, amorous pleasure and the "commendations" earned by writing well are conflated both in the passage and in Lilliat's response.

That conflation of reading and writing is not restricted to textual "passion," but is, in fact, a condition of a more general

---

[31] *Id.* at 7.
[32] *Id.*

textual practice. Near the end of Lily's letter, Lilliat marks the following passage:

> Whereby I noted that <u>young swannes are grey, & the olde</u> white, you[n]g trees tender, & the old tough, young me[n] amorous, & growing in yeeres, either wiser or warier. The Corall in the water is a soft weede, on the land a hard stone . . . .[33]

In the right hand margin there is a vertical line which extends from the phrase underlined to the line on which the reference to "corall" ends, and in the margin Lilliat has written "The Corall." Yet the attention conferred on the coral and the swans by the marginal notation has little to do with their intrinsic meaning or their function in the letter as a whole. Rather, the attention is bound up with their status as memorable, re-markable, rhetorical figures. To understand a reading practice for which this re-markability is central, the reader must move into a text such as Erasmus' *De ratione studii ac legendi interpretandique auctores liber*,[34] which trains the reader to "take careful note in your reading of striking words; archaic or novel expressions; cleverly devised or neatly turned arguments; and any outstanding elegance of style, any adages, historical parallels, and general statements that are worth remembering. These passages should be indicated by some appropriate mark. (You should use several specially designed marks to indicate points of interest.)"

Commonplace books are about memory, which takes both immaterial and material form; the commonplace book is like a record of what that memory might look like. Commonplace books are also about the intimate connection between remembering and re-marking a text—about, that is, a practice of reading contingent upon writing. In turn, as Macherey suggests, the reading mind becomes attuned to sententiae; material praxis produces an ideological formation which then reflects back upon praxis.[35]

---

[33] *Id.*

[34] Erasmus, De ratione studii ac legendi interpretandique auctores liber, *reprinted in* 24 The Collected Works of Erasmus: Literary and Educational Writings 2, at 670 (Craig R. Thompson ed. & Brian McGregor trans., U. Toronto P. 1972).

[35] Macherey, *supra* note 4, at 92. Moreover, the act of recording the sententiae supposedly inscribes them in the mind as well; not only does this inscription add the figures to a stock available for further reproduction, but it also simultaneously constitutes the "character" of the reader/writer. Jonathan Goldberg discusses in much greater depth the extent to which the inscription of a person's "character" is bound up with the inscription of the grammatical character. *See* Jonathan Goldberg, Writing Matter: From the Hands of the English Renaissance (1990).

Particularly important in the context of the material praxis of reading is Lilliat's reaction to the end of Lyly's letter:

> And seeing you haue vsed mee so friendly, as to make me acquainted with your passions, I will shortly make you pryuie to mine, which I woulde be loth the printer shoulde see, for that my fancies being neuer so crooked he would put the[m] in streight lines, vnfit for my humor, necessarie for his art, who setteth downe, *blinde, in as many letters as seeing*.

Farewell.

John Lilliat.

[flourish][36]

Watson's jibe marks the materiality and textuality of his passion, which is visually apparent not in his person, but in the words which express it. Although he makes a conventionally self-deprecatory remark about the crookedness of his own "fancies," he also berates the printer's material practice, which occludes the crooked evidence. Lilliat's marks at this point reinforce the extent to which the evidence of writing is contingent upon its specific material format. Not only has he underlined the clever jibe, but in fact his own name appears stamped in a large italic hand at the end of the letter, a signature produced with a similar technology of imprinting. Is this a claim to authorship? If so, it seems (at least to us), absurd—the epistle is clearly attributed to Iohn Lyly in the title. But Lilliat has a large index pointing to "Iohn Lyly." Coupled with the stamp at the end of the letter, the signature suggests that Lilliat is responding to the homophony between the two names and taking advantage of their similarity to ventriloquize his own praise for Watson through Lyly's words. Moreover, he may be responding to a visual homology, insofar as the printed text and the letters of the stamp bear a distinct resemblance. He signs the words not so much because he claims ownership of them, or claims them as his original discourse, but because he uses *the same physical words* to praise Watson.

The practice of reading, then, is concomitant with and shaped by the practice of writing, and vice-versa. Both of these practices are necessary to the production of the commonplace book, which culls and reproduces already-written material as an integral part of the process of composition, which cobbles together new texts from words others have used. Indeed, the structure of poetic authority is based on a reading practice in

---

[36] WATSON, *supra* note 12, at 8.

which authority is derived from other writers. In the Middle Ages, that authority was associated exclusively with ancient writers, who were "to be respected and believed. . . . The writings of an *auctor* contained or possessed *auctoritas* in the abstract sense of the term, with its strong connotations of veracity and sagacity. In the specific sense, an *auctoritas* was a quotation or an extract from the work of an *auctor*."[37] By the Renaissance, however, the authority resides in non-classical authors as well, and also in general sententiae, as Erasmus' *De ratione studii* suggests. As Minnis puts it,

> the term *auctor* denoted someone who was at once a writer and an authority, someone not merely to be read but also to be respected and believed. . . . The term *auctor* may profitably be regarded as an accolade bestowed upon a popular writer by those later scholars and writers who used extracts from his works as sententious statements or *auctoritates*, or employed them as literary models.[38]

The status of *auctor* or author, it seems, can only be bestowed posthumously. Moreover, this status is not merely related to the production of texts, but to their consumption as well, because it is a notion which regulates the way in which a text is treated by later readers. Moreover, both writing and reading are processes of selection and collection, as a poetic collection such as *The Hekatompathia* makes explicit. And as the material evidence of Lilliat's writing/reading practice suggests, neither writing nor reading can be identified as the "primary" activity involved in the composition of a commonplace book; they operate simultaneously and interactively as constituents of the conditions of poetic textual production.

What role, then, does authorship, as we might understand it today, play in this model of textual production? Within the commonplace book, Lilliat includes "authorial" markers: Lilliat has signed a number of the poems with his initials (most frequently as "q^d Iω.λ."; a curious mixture of the Latin "quod" and Greek initials), and occasionally with his full name; he uses the stamp after several poems; and he attributes a number of other poems to their "authors," sometimes by initials and sometimes by full name, but not always "correctly." A full exploration of the force of ascription and attribution in the commonplace book is beyond

---

[37] ALISTAIR J. MINNIS, MEDIEVAL THEORY OF AUTHORSHIP: SCHOLASTIC LITERARY ATTITUDES IN THE LATER MIDDLE AGES 10 (2d ed. 1988).

[38] *Id.*

the scope of this paper; but by concentrating on two of the poems signed "Ιω.λ.," some idea can be gained of what is at stake.

The poems occur on folios 108r-v and 109r. The first of them, entitled *Dauids Dumpe,*[39] is a version of Psalm 130. It might appear as if Lilliat, or at least .Ιω.λ, is claiming the prophetic authority of David; he is certainly incorporating the words of the Biblical source. Moreover, Lilliat does not try to hide this fact; there is no intent to deceive here. *Dauids Dumpe* would surely have been recognizable to Lilliat's friends as a translation of Psalm 130. The poem, indeed, is not unlike Watson's translations in *The Hekatompathia*; it even includes a marginal gloss (although nothing like the copious commentary that precedes Watson's poems) to the left of the antepenultimate and penultimate lines, which reads "psal.132.11." The poem's rendering of Psalm 130 is far from literal (it is, for example, over three times as long, and in rhymed pentameter couplets), and yet this loose rendering does not seem to produce anxiety—until the poem incorporates another biblical text. The form of the "Dumpe" itself, it seems, is subject to extreme variations, but the marginal gloss marks the limit of those liberties, as it works to prevent confusion between Biblical texts, and thus to keep the utterances distinct.

This textual anxiety becomes important in the poem which follows *Dauids Dumpe.* This poem, which is called a "Prophesie"[40] in the title, articulates an unspecific anxiety that upon the death of "good *Elizabeth*" the church will fall, to be replaced by "*Pride,* so hie proceedinge,/Wherin ech state exceedinge,/To Common wealth a foyle"[41] (lines 11-13)—a catastrophe that will eventuate in bloody civil war. Since the poem depends upon the legitimacy of the prophetic voice, the question of authorship becomes an important issue. That need for legitimation literally frames the poem. The title was first written "*Lilliat,* his Prophesie. October 2. 1599." in a particularly careful blend of italic and secretary hand. But in an effort to secure the position, and hence authority, of the prophetic voice, the word "Minister," in a more cramped (perhaps hastier) secretary hand, was inserted after the proper name. Coming from someone ordained to pass along the word of God, the prophecy would carry more weight. The poem

---

[39] LIBER LILLIATI, *supra* note 9, at 125.
[40] *Id.* at 125.
[41] *Id.*

is doubly, multiply signed: to the left of the usual "q^d Iω.λ." Lilliat's stamp has been applied three times. "The self-guaranteed mark must be guaranteed by the situation in which one signs. . . . It will always be *where* the signature is, more than what it looks like, that serves to authenticate it," according to Jonathan Goldberg.[42] The force of the stamp impressed upon the page (and looking at the stamps counterclockwise from the left, the force of the stamp and the quantity of ink seem to increase, producing a more and more blurred name) does not seem to me to betoken ownership or authorship of the poem, but rather bears witness to the occasion which produced it. "Lilliat was *here*," it seems to announce, "and saw that this shall pass."

The force of the "q^d Iω.λ." is particularly strong in this poem: it means *said*. Not "wrote," not "according to," not "by." Said. The Latin and Greek letters mark the discursivity of the poems and the fact that they exist within an atmosphere of circulating texts. Other poems in the book are marked with other proper names: "qd Mr Dier," "qd D *Latwoorth*," "qd *Thomas Watson*." Lilliat's own name is attached in this way to texts he did not write, particularly to translations of sententious sayings and of passages from Ovid. Other texts are not marked at all, yet it seems reasonable to assume that Lilliat wrote at least some of them.[43] Why did he not sign those texts as he did so many others? Perhaps he never found occasion to release them into the current of circulating manuscripts or never found the need to authenticate his own voice. Ultimately, "Quod" points to the performative existence and iterability of Elizabethan poetry.

It is perhaps common knowledge in recent literary history that the eighteenth century saw the emergence of the notion of the author as an introspective, self-inspired creator; a notion which has been retrospectively applied to previous authors as well.[44] The function of the writer before this eighteenth century development is too often formulated with "a decided absence of positive propositions:"[45] it is easier to say what the writer was not

---

[42] GOLDBERG, *supra* note 35, at 247-48.

[43] Particularly poems which are extant only in this manuscript. *See generally* MARGARET CRUM, *First Line Index of English Poetry 1500-1600 in* Manuscripts of the Bodleian Library (1969) and Doughtie's thorough notes in LIBER LILLIATI, *supra* note 9. Moreover, Lilliat usually marks poems attributable to other poets with a proper name, if not always with the "correct" name.

[44] *See* Martha Woodmansee, *The Genius and the Copyright: Economic and Legal Conditions of the Emergence of the "Author"*, 17 EIGHTEENTH-CENTURY STUD. 425, 427 (1984).

[45] Michel Foucault, *What Is an Author?*, *in* LANGUAGE, COUNTER-MEMORY, PRACTICE 113, 136 (Donald F. Bouchard ed. & trans., 1977).

than what s/he was. However, the evidence of Rawlinson 148 suggests some positive propositions.

Much of Watson and Lilliat's literary production consists of reworking already extant poetry. Sometimes this reworking takes the form of translations from Latin (or Greek, Italian, and French, in Watson's case); at other times it consists of collections of sententious material. Often, Lilliat combines the two modes:

> *Quiere quisque diu quaerit, bene viuere nemo: Ast bene quisque potest viuere, nemo diu.*
> To liue *Longe* evry Man desires, but to liue *WEL*, no Man: Yet eury Man (loe) may liue *Well*, but to liue *Longe*, none can.[46]

Reading and writing seem to have focused on the gathering of sententiae. Lilliat is by no means atypical in his marginal indices and underlinings. The impulse to the sententious is an impulse to gather *auctoritas*, to tap into its didactic power. Perhaps it is that power to which the insistent signing of the "Prophesie" aspires.

In these material practices of composition, as it operates in Rawlinson 148, lie the traces of an epistemological structure, in which reading and writing are both constituent elements in what Macherey would call the "conditions"[47] for the production and consumption of the poetic commonplace book. Ascription, then, becomes important not just as a means to identify the "source" or "author" of the poem, but as a particular manifestation of those writing/reading strategies, for the production of poetry is an act of intervention in a larger discursive realm. It might even be possible to see the compiler of the commonplace book as the paradigm for reading/writing practices in the Renaissance, insofar as the two practices cannot be separated and operate in tandem. The compiler, then, operates in ways similar to Barthes' notion of a reader: "someone who holds collected into one and the same field all of the traces from which writing is constituted":[48] not as someone who acts as a terminus; rather someone who channels the energies of poetic discourse and then reintroduces them into the cultural flow from whence they were written/read.

---

[46] LIBER LILLIATI, *supra* note 9, at 43.
[47] MACHEREY, *supra* note 4.
[48] Barthes, *The Death of the Author, in* THE RUSTLE OF LANGUAGE 54 (Richard Howard trans., 1989).

COLLABORATIVE AUTHORSHIP AND THE TEACHING OF WRITING

ANDREA A. LUNSFORD* AND LISA EDE**

The concepts of author and authorship, so radically destabilized in contemporary literary theory—and in current discursive practice in fields as far removed as engineering and law—have also been problematized in the field of rhetoric and composition studies, where scholars have challenged the traditional exclusion of student writing from claims to "real writing" and "authorship," explored the ways in which *author*ity is experienced by student writers, and increasingly sought to map various models of composing processes.

Beginning with a 1983 essay called *Why Write . . . Together?*,[1] we have attempted to add to this conversation by probing the concept of authorship that informs the teaching of writing in the United States. We began this research guided by the following questions:

1. What specific features distinguish the processes of collaborative authorship from those of single authorship? Can these features or processes be linked to any features of the resulting products? In short, how can we best *define* collaborative authorship?

2. Is there a limit to how many people can write together? Are projects such as the *Oxford English Dictionary*, the *Bible*, the *Short Title Catalogue*, elaborate computer programs, encyclopedias—all often involving more than 100 authors—examples of collaborative authorship?

3. In what ways, if any, does collaborative authorship affect the way we view the traditional writer-audience relationship?

4. What epistemological implications does collaborative authorship hold for traditional notions of creativity and originality?

5. How might the ethics of collaborative authorship be examined and defined? In cases of group authorship, where

* Professor of English, Ohio State University. B.A., 1963, M.A., 1965, University of Florida; Ph.D., 1977, Ohio State University.
** Professor of English, Oregon State University. B.S., 1969, Ohio State University; M.A., 1970, University of Wisconsin; Ph.D., 1974, Ohio State University.
[1] Lisa Ede & Andrea A. Lunsford, *Why Write . . . Together?*, 1 RHETORIC REV. 150 (1983).

does the responsibility lie? Who stands behind the words of a report written by fifteen people?

6. Is the emphasis on or weight of various cognitive and rhetorical strategies different when co-authoring than when writing alone?

7. What are the pedagogical implications of collaborative authorship? What do we know about the advantages or disadvantages of having students participate in collaborative writing? If advantages do exist, don't they in some ways contradict our profession's traditional insistence on students working alone? And perhaps most importantly, do we have ways to teach students to adjust readily to collaborative writing tasks?

After a lengthy research project and eight years of study, we feel confident in saying that the traditional model of solitary authorship is more myth than reality, that much or most of the writing produced in professional settings in America is done collaboratively, and that, in fact, much of what we call "creative" writing is collaborative as well, though it almost always flies under the banner of single authorship.[2] But what of the college classroom and the teaching of writing that takes place there? That is to say, how may we best answer the last major research question, the one that challenges our pedagogy? While we will touch on those ways in which we have attempted to address all our original research questions, in the space provided here, we wish particularly to focus on writing pedagogy, relate its current forms to an epistemology that reifies radically individual forms and ways of knowing, and explore the potential for a reconstructed pedagogy that will allow for collaborative authorship.

I. HISTORICAL PERSPECTIVES ON COLLABORATION

In composition studies, interest in "discourse communities" has gone hand in hand with growing interest in social construction theories of knowledge, theories which attempt to situate the known in communal contexts. "Writing as a social process" has, in fact, become something of a buzz- or catch-phrase, as articles on small-group collaborative efforts, peer-response techniques, and the social nature of writing and reading appear in growing numbers. We may best examine this movement, generally referred to as collaborative learning, by situating it in an historical

---

[2] *See, e.g.*, ANDREA A. LUNSFORD & LISA S. EDE, SINGULAR TEXTS/PLURAL AUTHORS: PERSPECTIVES ON COLLABORATIVE WRITING at ch. 3 (1990).

context that represents one playing out of a persistent tension in American culture—that between the individual (the isolated Cartesian self)—and the community. This tension is vividly captured by Alexis de Tocqueville in his analysis of the American character. To describe this character, he uses a newly-coined word, *individualism* (which he differentiates from *egoism*): "Individualism is a calm and considered feeling which disposes each citizen to isolate himself from the main of his fellows and withdraw into the circle of family and friend; with this little society formed to his taste, he gladly leaves the greater society to look after itself."[3] As such an individualism increases, Tocqueville notes:

> More and more people who though neither rich nor powerful enough to have much hold over others, have gained or kept enough wealth and enough understanding to look after their own needs. Such folks owe no man anything and hardly expect anything from anybody. They form the habit of thinking of themselves in isolation and imagine that their whole destiny is in their hands . . . . Each man is forever thrown back on himself alone, and there is danger that he may be shut up in the solitude of his own heart.[4]

Tocqueville feared the results of unmediated growth of "individualism" and argued that it could be best countered by a strong tradition of community and public discourse: "Citizens who are bound to take part in public affairs must turn from private interests and occasionally take a look at something other than themselves."[5] This strong civic involvement with public discourse was, in Tocqueville's view, the balancing factor that would keep America from developing into a society of naturally exclusive, autonomous individuals, a society which would not, he feared, easily be able to resist totalitarianism or despotism.

In part, the founding document of America, The Declaration of Independence, reflects both the profound drive toward individualism and the commitment to community and public discourse that Tocqueville found in the American character, dual ideals which are inscribed in our history and which are often seen as being in constant tension with one another.[6] We might expect

---

[3] ALEXIS DE TOCQUEVILLE, DEMOCRACY IN AMERICA 506-08 (J.P. Mayer ed. & George Lawrence trans., 1969).

[4] *Id.*

[5] *Id.* at 510.

[6] See ROBERT N. BELLAH ET AL., HABITS OF THE HEART: INDIVIDUALISM AND COMMITMENT IN AMERICAN LIFE (1985) and ROBERT N. BELLAH ET AL., THE GOOD SOCIETY (1991), for an examination of the ideals related to tensions in contemporary America.

to find evidence of this tension in American education and in the teaching of writing. And indeed we do. As Michael Halloran[7] has demonstrated, the earliest rhetorical instruction in America was influenced by Cicero and Quintilian, and the Roman concept of the "ideal orator" as the public-spirited person speaking well animated such instruction. But this essentially rhetorical emphasis on the Greek and Roman "commune," on communal values and shared meanings, diminished in the nineteenth century as oral discourse was displaced by writing, as new "objective" methods of testing arose, and as the academy emphasized competition over cooperation, autonomous electives over the classical "core" curriculum, and the autonomous individual over the social. By the end of the nineteenth century, traditional rhetorical instruction had been largely displaced by emerging English departments heavily imbued with romantic theories of "genius" and originality, with a concept of writing as an individual solitary act, and with philological and exegetical traditions that emphasized the autonomous writer and the text as individually held intellectual property.[8]

Nevertheless, some educators resisted the trend toward individualism and isolation in English instruction. Anne Gere's monograph on the history of writing groups in America reveals that peer response techniques and small group collaboration have been advocated and enjoyed by some citizens and teachers since the colonial period—in mutual improvement groups such as Benjamin Franklin's Junto, in the Lyceum- and Chatauqua-generated societies, and in the women's clubs and literary societies.[9] In nineteenth-century schools, Michigan's Fred Newton Scott and his student Gertrude Buck both advocated more natural social conditions for composition instruction *and* evaluation,[10] while Alexander Bain's *On Teaching English* praised the practice of writing with an eye toward reading draft versions to a society of peers and revising on the basis of discussion.[11] And in the colleges and universities, the great popularity of literary and other

---

[7] *See* Michael Halloran, *Rhetoric in the American College Curriculum: The Decline of Public Discourse*, 3 PRE/TEXT 245 (1982).

[8] See GERALD GRAFF, PROFESSING LITERATURE (1987) for a recounting of this history, which treats English departments but not rhetorical instruction and/or theory.

[9] ANNE R. GERE, WRITING GROUPS: HISTORY, THEORY, IMPLICATIONS 32-54 (1987). *See also* David Potter, *The Literary Society, in* HISTORY OF SPEECH EDUCATION IN AMERICA: BACKGROUND STUDIES 238-58 (Karl R. Wallace ed., 1954).

[10] FRED NEWTON SCOTT, COMPOSITION-RHETORIC, DESIGNED FOR USE IN SECONDARY SCHOOLS (1897); Gertrude Buck, *The Metaphor—A Study in the Psychology of Rhetoric, in* 5 CONTRIBUTIONS TO RHETORICAL THEORY (Fred Newton Scott ed., 1899).

[11] *See* ALEXANDER BAIN, ON TEACHING ENGLISH (1901).

speaking societies offered an opportunity for cooperation and extensive collaboration.

As Mara Holt has demonstrated, collaborative pedagogy—while never dominant—has a rich history and tradition.[12] Basing her study on an examination of academic journals from 1911 to 1986, Holt traces this collaborative thread, arguing that "the rationales and practices of collaborative pedagogy consistently reflect social and intellectual and economic trends of the sociohistorical movement in which they are located.[13]

As the twentieth century proceeded, the dominant emphasis on individualism, on writing as an individually creative act, and on "objective" testing as a means of evaluating the intellectual property of solitary writers, continued to be questioned by a marginal collaborative pedagogy. Most influential was the work of educational philosopher John Dewey, who argued tirelessly for seeing the education of each individual in a social and communal *context*. As he notes in *The Public and its Problems* "Individuals still do the thinking, desiring, purposing, but *what* they think of is the consequence of their behavior upon that of others and that of others upon themselves."[14] Dewey's calls for "new" or "progressive" education began early in this century. Throughout his career he insisted that learning occurs in *interaction*, that social context is of utmost importance in the classroom, and that we should reform our traditional model (which privileges the individual) by enhancing "the moving spirit of the whole group . . . held together by participation in common activities."[15]

Dewey influenced generations of teachers and scholars, among them Sterling Andrus Leonard, who argued as early as 1916, in *Two Types of Criticism for Composition Work*, that "oral and written composition are developed in a socially organized class to carry out real projects . . . in a spirit of hearty cooperation."[16] In his 1917 *English Composition As a Social Problem*, Leonard goes on to say:

> We must not make the mistake of assuming that training in composition is purely an individual matter. Most self expression is for the purpose of social communication . . . . Our whole use of language has a social setting. The futility of

---

12 Mara Holt, Collaborative Learning From 1911-1986: A Sociohistorical Analysis 235 (1988) (unpublished Ph.D. dissertation, University of Texas (Austin)).
13 *Id.* at 235.
14 JOHN DEWEY, THE PUBLIC AND ITS PROBLEMS 24 (1927).
15 *Id.* at 54-55.
16 STERLING A. LEONARD, TWO TYPES OF CRITICISM FOR COMPOSITION WORK 509 (1916).

much of our past teaching has been due to our mental blinders to the social function of language. One has only to compare the situation of ordinary conversation with that of a class exercise in oral composition to realize how far we have forgotten the social genesis of speech. Worthy social conversation cannot be made at command of any person in authority. Ordinary human beings would not endure hearing the same item of discussion repeated by each person present. Nor would one care to say what everyone else had already said. Yet these are some of the striking characteristics of a composition exercise. If we are to make our training real, we must naturalize it, which is to say we must socialize our teaching of composition.[17]

Dewey's interactionist or constructivist approach to learning and knowledge gained increasing support in the 1930s from the work of George Herbert Mead, who argued that meaning is not individually wrought but is instead constructed through social interaction.[18] In *Invention as a Social Act*, Karen Burke LeFevre cites Mead's work as providing a theoretical foundation for a view of invention as collaborative, noting that "other social thinkers, such as Martin Buber and Ludwig Wittgenstein, [move from] what have traditionally been regarded as private psychological entities out into the realm of social interaction and contextualization of knowledge."[19] In addition, Piaget's work with children took a social constructivist approach to knowledge and learning as he demonstrated that children learn through *interaction* with others and with things in their environmental contexts.[20]

Dewey devotees[21] did much to rigidify and trivialize his original arguments; his influence faded during the exigencies of the war years. The critique of traditional education, with its teacher-centered classrooms and its emphasis on "working alone" and on "originality" continued, however, primarily in Britain. M. L. J. Abercrombie's *Anatomy of Judgment*[22] and her later *Aims and Techniques for Group Teaching*,[23] for instance, evolved from work with medical students. Abercrombie was convinced that small-group

---

[17] STERLING A. LEONARD, ENGLISH COMPOSITION AS A SOCIAL PROBLEM at viii-ix (1917).

[18] GEORGE H. MEAD, MIND, SELF & SOCIETY FROM THE STANDPOINT OF A SOCIAL BEHAVIORIST (1970).

[19] KAREN B. LeFEVRE, INVENTION AS A SOCIAL ACT 63 (1987).

[20] JEAN PIAGET, THE CONSTRUCTION OF REALITY IN THE CHILD (1954).

[21] Reductivist renderings of Dewey's work seem to have been uncritically accepted by E. D. Hirsch. *See* E. D. HIRSCH, CULTURAL LITERACY: WHAT EVERY AMERICAN NEEDS TO KNOW (1987). Hirsch uses Dewey as a whipping boy in his cultural literacy argument.

[22] M.L.J. ABERCROMBIE, THE ANATOMY OF JUDGMENT: AN INVESTIGATION INTO THE PROCESS OF PERCEPTION AND REASONING (1969).

[23] M.L.J. ABERCROMBIE, AIMS AND TECHNIQUES FOR GROUP TEACHING (1970).

discussion provided the most effective way to help those students become more sophisticated and accurate at diagnosis and, hence, better physicians. Reacting to a Report of a Committee of the Royal College of Physicians, which argued that "the average medical graduate . . . tends to lack curiosity and initiative; his powers of observation are relatively undeveloped; his ability to arrange and interpret facts is poor; he lacks precision in the use of words,"[24] Abercrombie devised an experimental teaching course that would help students, through collaboration, learn to recognize diverse points of view, diverse interpretations of the results of an experiment, and thus to form more useful and accurate medical judgments:

> My hypothesis is that we may learn to make better judgements if we can become aware of some of the factors that influence their formation. We may then be in a position to consider alternative judgements and to choose from among many instead of blindly and automatically accepting the first that comes; in other words, we may become more receptive or mentally more flexible. The results of testing the effects of the course of [collaborative group] discussions support this hypothesis.[25]

Abercrombie's emphasis on contextualizing knowledge and her realization that communally derived diagnoses are generally more accurate and effective than those of a single medical student served as a direct challenge to the traditional individualism and isolated competitiveness endemic to most medical school curricula and higher education.

At roughly the same time, Edwin Mason, in his book, *Collaborative Learning*, presented a strikingly similar challenge to British secondary schools and, along the way, coined the phrase "collaborative learning." Charging that "to work in a school day after day and feel that we are doing more harm than good, and that with the best will in the world, is too much to bear,"[26] Mason set out to reform the school system, which he believed was "meeting neither the needs of the young nor the demands of the world."[27] As a result, Mason proposed a radical restructuring of this system, one which would replace the current competitive, authoritarian, overly specialized or departmentalized and hence "alienated" program with one emphasizing interdisciplinary

---

[24] ABERCROMBIE, *supra* note 22, at 15-16.
[25] *Id.* at 17.
[26] EDWIN MASON, COLLABORATIVE LEARNING 7 (1970).
[27] *Id.* at 8.

study, small group work, collaboration, and dialogue—largely in the spirit of John Dewey. The remainder of his remarkable book describes such a curriculum and advises teachers on how best to implement it.[28]

As Abercrombie's and Mason's work began to have at least a small impact on pedagogical thinking, so too did that of the Brazilian teacher Paolo Freire, whose *Pedagogy of the Oppressed* appeared in 1968.[29] Arguing that literacy is best taught in the social contexts of people's own lives, Freire faulted traditional education with promoting not genuine public literacy, but passivity, alienation, and conformity instead. In his work, Freire aims to empower his student-colleagues to reclaim, reinterpret, and hence reenact their own lives and to gain growing awareness of how social forces work in dialogic relationship with individual experience to enslave—or to liberate—and to create the realities they inhabit *communally.* Freire's work has most recently been presented as a challenge to the traditional teaching of writing in Ira Shor's *Freire in the Classroom,* which calls for a commitment to social and political contextualizing of all learning and on a renegotiation of power and authority in all classrooms.[30]

These examples demonstrate that the drive toward radically individual autonomy, competitiveness, and isolated selfhood has always been countered, often only in a whisper but at other times in a louder, clearer voice, by a call for community, for shared public discourse, for working together for some common good. And, as Anne Gere has shown, we could write part of the history of writing instruction in the twentieth century in just such terms.[31]

II.   CONTEMPORARY WRITING PEDAGOGY AND COLLABORATIVE LEARNING

The last twenty years are generally regarded as having witnessed a large shift in writing pedagogy, sometimes as a growing awareness of process and context, sometimes (following the work of pioneers like Moffett, Emig, and Britton)[32] as a move from teacher-centered to student-centered learning models. Cer-

---

[28] *See generally* MASON, *supra* note 26.

[29] PAOLO FREIRE, PEDAGOGY OF THE OPPRESSED (Myra B. Ramos trans., 1970) (1968).

[30] FREIRE FOR THE CLASSROOM: A SOURCEBOOK FOR LIBERATORY TEACHING (Ira Shor ed., 1987).

[31] GERE, *supra* note 9.

[32] *See* JAMES MOFFETT, TEACHING THE UNIVERSE OF DISCOURSE (1968); JANET EMIG, THE WEB OF MEANING (1983); JAMES N. BRITTON, LANGUAGE AND LEARNING (1970).

tainly, we wish to acknowledge the effects of these largely positive shifts, most of which in our view run counter to the traditional valorization of autonomous individualism, privately held intellectual property, competition, and hierarchy. But in spite of these largely pedagogical efforts, most day-to-day writing instruction in American colleges and universities still reflects traditional assumptions about the nature of the self (autonomous), the concept of authorship (as ownership of singly-held property rights), and the classroom environment (hierarchical, teacher-centered).

We may look to contemporary composition studies as an illustration in point. Over the past few years, a number of scholars have attempted to understand this emerging field of study by, essentially, a naming of parts, by a taxonomizing. Thus, Richard Young identifies as the two major "groups," the "new Romanticists," and the "new Classicists," the former stressing the interiority and essential mystery of writing, the latter stressing exteriority and structured procedures for composing.[33] Patricia Bizzell modifies and amplifies this distinction, grouping composition studies into two camps—those who view writing primarily as "inner-directed" and "prior to social influence" and those who view writing as "outer-directed" and based on "social processes whereby language-learning and thinking capacities are used and shaped in . . . communities."[34] In several essays and a monograph on twentieth-century writing instruction, James Berlin offers another taxonomy, contrasting what he calls "objective" and "subjective" rhetorics with a tripartite division of "transactional" rhetoric.[35] Similar arguments are advanced, though from differing perspectives, by several others, including Lester Faigley and Stephen M. North,[36] but are probably put most strongly by LeFevre. In *Invention as a Social Act*, LeFevre contrasts what she calls the Platonic view of inventing and composing ("the act of finding or creating that which is . . . written as individual introspection;

[33] Richard Young, *Arts, Crafts, Gifts, and Knacks: Some Disharmonies in the New Rhetoric*, in REINVENTING THE RHETORICAL TRADITION 53-60 (Aviva Freedman & Ian Pringle eds., 1980).

[34] Patricia Bizzell, *Cognition, Convention, and Certainty: What We Need to Know About Writing*, 3 PRE/TEXT 213, 215 (1982).

[35] *See* James Berlin, *Contemporary Composition: The Major Pedagogical Theories*, 44 COLLEGE ENGLISH 765-77 (1982). *See also* JAMES BERLIN, RHETORIC AND REALITY: WRITING INSTRUCTION IN AMERICAN COLLEGES, 1900-1985 (1987) [hereinafter BERLIN, RHETORIC AND REALITY]; James Berlin, *Rhetoric and Ideology*, 50 COLLEGE ENGLISH 477-94 (1988) [hereinafter BERLIN, RHETORIC AND IDEALOGY].

[36] *See* Lester Faigley & Thomas P. Miller, *What We Learn from Writing on the Job*, 44 COLLEGE ENGLISH 557-69 (1982). *See also* STEPHEN M. NORTH, THE MAKING OF KNOWLEDGE IN COMPOSITION: PORTRAIT OF AN EMERGING FIELD (1987).

ideas begin in the mind of the individual writer and then are expressed to the rest of the world") with a social view of inventing and composing.[37] This social view takes a constructivist approach to knowledge and posits that the "self," in some ways similar to Wayne Booth's "range of selves" or Foucault's "subject positions,"[38] is socially constituted and that, hence, writing is essentially a social and collaborative act. Interestingly, in his recent essay *On the Very Idea of a Discourse Community,*[39] Thomas Kent argues that social constructionists such as LeFevre are, from the perspective of Donald Davidson's coherence theory of truth and knowledge, internalists, not externalists.

These taxonomies of composition studies overlap and differ in a number of ways and, as all taxonomies inevitably do, they limit—indeed they often distort—what we perceive about our own field of study. We mention them here, therefore, not to endorse any particular taxonomy of rhetoric and composition studies but to make one point that strikes us as particularly telling: the composition theorists and teachers most often identified with collaborative learning and peer response techniques—James Moffett, Donald Murray, Peter Elbow, Ken Macrorie—are also usually identified with Bizzell's "inner-directed" group,[40] Berlin's "expressionist" group,[41] or LeFevre's Platonic group,[42] which posits the uniqueness of individual imagination and sees writing as a means of expressing an autonomous inner self. Ironically, then, the very scholars most often associated with collaborative learning hold implicitly to traditional concepts of autonomous individualism, authorship, and authority for texts. In addition, their versions of collaborative learning generally fail to problematize the role of the teacher/authority in the writing classrooms.

The work of Peter Elbow provides perhaps the best example of the tension and potential contradictions we have been describing. For years, Elbow has encouraged writers to work in groups, reading their work aloud for oral responses, out of which revisions grow. Many of his recommended classroom activities rely on free-wheeling collaboration, and he continues to champion

---

[37] LeFevre, *supra* note 19, at 1.

[38] *See* WAYNE BOOTH, CRITICAL UNDERSTANDING: THE POWERS AND LIMITS OF PLURALISM (1979); Michel Foucault, *What Is an Author?*, *in* TEXTUAL STRATEGIES: PERSPECTIVES IN POST-STRUCTURALIST CRITICISM 141-60 (Josue V. Harari ed., 1979).

[39] Thomas Kent, *On the Very Idea of a Discourse Community*, 42 CCC 425 (1991).

[40] *See* Bizzell, *supra* note 34.

[41] *See* BERLIN, RHETORIC AND REALITY *supra* note 35, at 756.

[42] *See* LeFevre, *supra* note 19.

the use of collaborative learning. Yet in spite of this emphasis on the importance of audience response to revision and its advocacy of some form of collaboration, Elbow's work rests on assumptions about individualism and individual creativity that fail to sufficiently problematize traditional conceptions of "author" and that in fact come close to denying the social nature of writing. For Elbow, expressing personal authenticity requires not social interaction but mining the depths of the self, searching inside the self for a unique voice. As he says in *Writing Without Teachers*, "The mind's magic. It can cook things instantaneously and perfectly when it gets going. You should expect yourself at times to write straight onto the paper words and thoughts far better than you knew were in you."[43] In his more recent books, Elbow continues to represent the individual self as the essentially mysterious source of creation, frequently calling on the "magical" ways writers discover their unified voices.[44] *Writing with Power*, in fact, ends with a chapter on "Writing and Magic."[45] As Greg Myers notes in a critique of Elbow, "Magic is the only possible source for such [individual] ineffable energies . . . [such] metaphors prevent any analysis of the social conditions of our writing."[46] Such a stance is reflected in Elbow's more recent essays, in which he argues that writers often must ignore audience (or any "others") in order to get to the heart and soul of what they want to say.[47]

The composition theorist most closely associated with social construction and collaborative learning theories in general and peer group response in particular is Kenneth Bruffee, who became interested in peer tutoring as a means of helping students "practice judgement collaboratively, through a progressive set of analytical and evaluative tasks applied to each other's academic writing in a context which fosters self-esteem."[48] Yet in his early work on peer tutoring and in his text, *A Short Course on Writing*,[49] Bruffee also holds to the concept of single authorship and individual creativity (students write alone and then *revise* after getting

---

[43] PETER ELBOW, WRITING WITHOUT TEACHERS 69 (1973).

[44] *See* PETER ELBOW, EMBRACING CONTRARIES: EXPLORATIONS IN LEARNING AND TEACHING (1973); PETER ELBOW, WRITING WITH POWER: TECHNIQUES FOR MASTERING THE WRITING PROCESS (1981) [hereinafter ELBOW, WRITING WITH POWER].

[45] *See* ELBOW, WRITING WITH POWER, *supra* note 44.

[46] Greg Myers, *Reality, Consensus and Reform in the Rhetoric of Composition Teaching*, 48 COLLEGE ENGLISH 154, 165 (1986).

[47] Peter Elbow, *Closing My Eyes as I Talk: An Argument Against Audience Awareness*, 44 COLLEGE ENGLISH 50 (1987); Peter Elbow & Jennifer Clark, *Desert Island Discourse: The Benefits of Ignoring Audience*, THE JOURNAL BOOK 19 (Toby Fulwiler ed., 1988).

[48] Kenneth A. Bruffee, *The Brooklyn Plan*, 64 LIBERAL EDUCATION 447, 450 (1978).

[49] KENNETH BRUFFEE, A SHORT COURSE IN WRITING (2d ed. 1980).

peer response, much as in the Elbow method[50]) even while acknowledging the degree to which "knowledge is a social phenomenon, and the social context in which we learn permeates what
we know and how we know it."[51] In addition, the mode of collaboration demonstrated in Bruffee's text is generally teacher-centered: the activities are set by a higher authority (the teacher) and
the focus is on the revised end product—the intellectual property—of a text produced individually.

As Bruffee readily notes, only in the last few years has he
come to contemplate the full theoretical significance of such an
epistemology for the teaching of writing and reading.[52] Drawing
on the work of scholars in a number of disciplines[53]—Bruffee argues that what and who we are and write and know is in large
part a function of interaction and of community.[54] Thus writing
and reading are, essentially and naturally, collaborative, social
acts, ways in which we understand and in which "knowledge is
established and maintained in the normal discourse of communities of knowledgeable peers."[55] As Berlin points out, Bruffee's
later works have been "from the start based on a conception of
knowledge as a social construction—a dialectical interplay of in-
vestigator, discourse community, and material world, with language as the agent of mediation. The rhetorical act is thus
implicated in the very discovery of knowledge—a way not merely
of recording knowledge for transmissions but of arriving at it mutually for mutual consideration."[56] But Bruffee's emphasis on
collaboration and consensus continues to stand in contradiction
to his implicit romanticist views of creativity and authorship.
These views have been criticized most recently by Mas'ud
Zavarzadeh and Donald Morton, who say that

> [t]here is in Bruffee no sense of the politics of cognition that
> organizes this socially constructed knowledge. Society and the

---

[50] See ELBOW WRITING WITH POWER, supra note 41, at 20-24, 139-45.

[51] See BRUFFEE, supra note 48, at 116.

[52] See Kenneth A. Bruffee, Collaborative Learning and the "Conversation of Mankind," 46 COLLEGE ENGLISH 635 (1984).

[53] See, e.g., STANLEY FISH, IS THERE A TEXT IN THIS CLASS? (1980) (literary studies); LEV VYGOTSKY, THOUGHT AND LANGUAGE (Eugenia Hanfman & Gertrude Vakar, trans., 1962) (psychology); THOMAS KUHN, THE STRUCTURE OF SCIENTIFIC REVOLUTION (2d ed. 1979) (philosophy); RICHARD RORTY, PHILOSOPHY AND THE MIRROR OF NATURE (1979) (philosophy); CLIFFORD GEERTZ, LOCAL KNOWLEDGE: FURTHER ESSAYS IN INTERPRETATIVE ANTHROPOLOGY (1983) (anthropology).

[54] Bruffee, supra note 52, at 641-47. "[W]riting always has its roots deep in the acquired ability to carry on the social symbolic exchanges we call conversation." Id. at 641-42.

[55] Id. at 640.

[56] BERLIN, RHETORIC AND REALITY, supra note 35, at 175-76.

social for him (as for Rorty) are cognitive domains—areas of such apparatuses as agreement and convention and so forth. As a result of such a conservative (cognitive) theory of knowledge . . . the subject is presented as an uncontested category . . . . Bruffee's collaborative learning/teaching is, in other words, the latest reproduction of the "management" of the subject and the latest effort to save it through "collaborative learning and the *Conversation of Mankind.*" The teacher in this model is the manager of the classroom—an agent of social coalescence.[57]

Bruffee's particular brand of collaborative consensus has also been criticized by Greg Myers, who charges that

while Bruffee shows that reality can be seen as a social construct, he does not give us any way to criticize this construct. Having discovered the role of consensus in the production of knowledge, he takes this consensus as something that just is, rather than as something that might be good or bad[58]

Myers is insisting that those interested in collaborative learning step back and ask *what* such practices will be used for, what aims and purposes and motives are served, where power and authority are located. Others in the composition community echo this concern. Richard Ohmann, for instance, has long criticized composition textbooks for treating student writers as though they were isolated, cut off from any cultural, political, or social contexts. Ohmann's *Politics of Letters* extends this critique to most contemporary teaching.[59] Similar critiques of the asocial and alienating nature of composition instruction appear in the works of Charles Yarnoff, David Bartholomae, Charles Bazerman, Patricia Bizzell, and particularly James Berlin.[60]

Other work has recently focused on context and on the communal aspects of learning. In particular, Shirley Brice Heath's ethnographic studies demonstrate how writing and reading must

---

57 Mas'ud Zarvarzadeh & Donald Morton, *Theory, Pedagogy Politics: The Crisis of "The Subject" in the Humanities*, 15 BOUNDARY 2: A JOURNAL OF POSTMODERN LITERATURE AND CULTURE, 1, 14-15 (Fall, Winter 1986-87).
58 *See* Myers, *supra* note 46, at 166.
59 *See* RICHARD OHMANN, POLITICS OF LETTERS (1987).
60 *See* Charles Yarnoff, *Contemporary Theories of Intervention in the Rhetorical Tradition*, 41 COLLEGE ENGLISH 552 (1980); David Bartholomae, *Inventing the University*, in WHEN A WRITER CAN'T WRITE: STUDIES IN WRITER'S BLOCK AND OTHER COMPOSING-PROCESS PROBLEMS 134 (Mike Rose ed., 1985); Charles Bazerman, *Scientific Writing as Social Act: A Review of the Literature of the Sociology of Science*, in NEW ESSAYS IN TECHNICAL AND SCIENTIFIC COMMUNICATION: RESEARCH, THEORY AND PRACTICE 156 (Paul Van Anderson et al. eds., 1983); Bizzell, *supra* note 34, at 213-43 (1982); Patricia Bizzell, *Foundationalism and Anti-Foundationalism in Composition Studies*, 7 PRE/TEXT 37-56 (1986); BERLIN, RHETORIC AND IDEOLOGY, *supra* note 35.

be seen as developing within a social context in which talk plays a major role.[61] David Bleich's *The Double Perspective: Language, Literacy, and Social Relations* examines the ways in which learning is situated in and beyond our classrooms;[62] his chapter on "Collaboration Among Students" offers particularly useful (and concrete) advice. At the Center for the Study of Writing, Linda Flower and her colleagues are working to relate the cognitive factors in composing to their social contexts.[63] Still others, focusing on professional and work-related writing, stress the importance of social and political contexts in such writing.[64]

The early work of Elbow and Bruffee has been augmented in this decade by a large and growing body of scholarship on collaborative learning, much of it linked to the National Writing Project and to writing across the curriculum movements.[65] In addition to the work of LeFevre[66] and Gere,[67] we now have major studies by Collette Daiute[68] and colleagues on collaboration among young school children,[69] by Anthony Pare and his colleagues on collaboration in high school settings,[70] and by the authors represented in Bouton and Garth's *Learning in Groups*,[71] to name only a few. This interest in, and growing commitment to, principles of collaborative learning grows out of, and is informed by, the philosophical tradition on which Bruffee's work builds. And, whether its advocates are aware of it or not, this tradition implicitly calls into question perceived notions of writing as inevitably and inherently *individual* and of intellectual property rights as belonging to radically individual selves. Whatever the strengths of the "collaborative learning" or "social constructionist" movement in composition studies may be, until scholars pursue the

---

[61] SHIRLEY B. HEATH, WAYS WITH WORDS: LANGUAGE, LIFE, AND WORK IN COMMUNITIES AND CLASSROOMS (1983).

[62] DAVID BLEICH, THE DOUBLE PERSPECTIVE: LANGUAGE, LITERACY, AND SOCIAL RELATIONS (1988).

[63] READING-TO-WRITE: EXPLORING A COGNITIVE AND SOCIAL PROCESS (Linda Flower et al. eds., 1990)

[64] *See, e.g.,* WRITING IN NON-ACADEMIC SETTINGS (Lee Odell & Dixie Goswami eds., 1985); Janis Forman & Patricia Katsky, *The Group Report: A Problem in Small Group or Writing Processes?*, 23 J. OF BUS. COMM. 23-35 (1986).

[65] See John Trimbur, *Collaborative Learning and Teaching Writing, in* PERSPECTIVES ON RESEARCH AND SCHOLARSHIP IN COMPOSITION 87 (Ben W. McClelland & Timothy R. Donovan eds., 1985) for a review of work on collaborative writing.

[66] *See* LEFEVRE, *supra* note 19.

[67] *See* GERE, *supra* note 9.

[68] *See* Collette Dauite, *Do 1 and 1 Make 2? Patterns of Influence by Collaborative Authors*, 3 WRITTEN COMM. 382-408 (1986).

[69] *Id.*

[70] *See* Anthony Pare, *How It Works: A Group-Authored Assignment*, 7 INKSHED 5-7 (1988).

[71] *See* LEARNING IN GROUPS, NEW DIRECTIONS FOR TEACHING AND LEARNING 14 (Clark Bouton & Russell Y. Garth eds., 1983).

full implications of collaboration for these traditional notions of authorship and authority, they will fail to answer—or even to address—the questions with which we opened this essay.

III. THE CHALLENGE OF COLLABORATIVE WRITING

The work on collaborative learning surveyed here emphasizes the ways in which knowledge is constructed among members of communities. The recent attention given to collaborative *writing* might thus seem a natural extension or a subset of collaborative learning theory. Yet as the preceding pages have suggested, collaborative learning theory has from its inception failed to challenge traditional concepts of radical individualism and ownership of ideas and has operated primarily in a traditional and largely hierarchical way. Students in collaborative learning situations may work together on revising or on problem solving, but when they write, they typically continue to write alone, in settings structured and governed by a teacher/authority in whom final authority is vested. Studies of collaborative *writing*, on the other hand, make such silent accommodations less easy to maintain and as a result offer the potential to challenge and hence resituate collaborative learning theories.

Much of the work on collaborative writing has focused on the world of work. Studies by numerous authors examine collaborative writing in a number of job-related settings.[72] Others have attempted to build collaborative writing into classroom contexts.[73] In a 1986 survey, Hallie S. Lemon found that composition faculty at Western Illinois University use collaboration at every stage of the writing process, including drafting.[74] Exten-

---

[72] *See, e.g.*, MARY B. DEBS, COLLABORATION AND ITS EFFECTS ON THE WRITER'S PROCESS: A LOOK AT ENGINEERING (1983); Janis Forman, *Computer-Mediated Group Writing in the Workplace*, 5 COMPUTERS AND COMPOSITION 19 (Nov. 1987); Stephen Doheny-Farina, *Writing in an Emerging Organization: An Ethnographic Study*, 3 WRITTEN COMM. 158 (1986); Faigley & Miller, *supra* note 36, at 557.; Geoffrey Cross, Editing in Context; An Ethnographic Exploration of Editor-Writer Revisions at a Midwestern Insurance Company (1988) (unpublished Ph.D. dissertation, Ohio State University). Two publications have recently devoted special issues to the subject of collaborative writing. *See* 38 TECHNICAL COMM. (Nov. 1991); 53 THE BULLETIN (Assoc. for Business Communication) (1990).

[73] *See, e.g.*, Deborah Bosley, A National Study of the Uses of Collaborative Writing in Business Communications Courses Among Members of the ABC (1989) (unpublished Ph.D. dissertation, Illinois State University); Sharon Hamilton-Wieler, *How Does Writing Emerge From the Classroom Context? A Naturalistic Study of the Writing of Eighteen Year-Olds in Biology, English, Geography, History, History of Art, and Sociology* (available in ERIC, Retrieval No. ED 284 209); KAREN SPEAR, SHARING WRITING: PEER RESPONSE GROUPS IN ENGLISH CLASSES (1988); CHARLES R. COOPER, RESPONDING TO STUDENT WRITING, THE WRITING PROCESS OF STUDENTS (Walter Petty & Patrick Finn eds., Report of the First Annual Language Arts Conference, State Univ. of N.Y. at Buffalo, 1975).

[74] *See* Hallie S. Lemon, Collaborative Strategies for Teaching Composition: Theory

sive research on this kind of "shared document" collaboration is being carried out by members of a research team[75] in an effort to define kinds of collaborative writing and to describe the processes involved in such group writing tasks. Among their studies is an important case study of collaborative writing groups.[76] Also at the college level, O'Donnell and his colleagues have conducted experiments which support the claim that group-produced documents are perceived as "better" than those individually produced.[77] In a study of writers in seven contexts,[78] Stephen P. Witte identified four forms of collaborative writing and concluded, among other things, that across these seven contexts "writing became increasingly more collaborative and collaborative in different ways."[79] Thomas L. Hilgers[80] and Daiute[81] have explored the uses of collaborative writing with younger children.

Nevertheless, as Allen and her colleagues point out, because "very little detail is known about collaborative writing processes in general . . . there is a need for in-depth study of the features of collaborative writing [defined as] a situation in which decisions are made by consensus."[82] We would add that much more careful attention needs to be given to just what is meant by "consensus" and to the ways consensus is or is not achieved. John Trimbur begins such an exploration in "Consensus and Difference in Collaborative Learning," in which he builds on the work of Habermas to argue that we must "distinguish between consensus as an acculturative practice that reproduces business as usual and consensus as an oppositional one that challenges the prevailing conditions of production" by providing a "critical instrument to open gaps in the conversation through which differences many emerge."[83] Joseph Harris extends this critique of consensus and

---

and Practice, Unpublished Paper Delivered at the Conference on College Composition and Communication (St. Louis, Mar. 1988).

[75] This research team began their work in a Purdue University Ph.D program.

[76] *See* Meg Morgan et al., *Collaborative Writing in the Classroom*, 50 THE BULLETIN 20-26 (1987) (Assoc. for Business Communication).

[77] Angela M. O'Donnell et al., *Cooperative Writing*, 2 WRITTEN COMM. 307 (1985).

[78] The seven contexts include: junior high school, high school, upper-division undergraduate, doctoral students, a chemist, a general manager, and a civil engineer.

[79] Stephen P. Witte, Some Contexts for Understanding Written Literacy 2-3, Unpublished Paper Delivered at the Right to Literacy Conference (Columbus, Sept. 1988).

[80] *See* Thomas L. Hilgers, On Learning the Skill of Collaborative Writing, Unpublished Paper Delivered at Conference on College Composition and Communication (New Orleans, Mar. 1986).

[81] *See* Dauite, *supra* note 68.

[82] Morgan et al., *supra* note 76.

[83] John Trimbur, *Consensus and Difference in Collaborative Learning*, 51 COLLEGE ENGLISH 602 (1989).

offers an argument for "community without consensus" in his *Idea of Community in the Study of Writing.*[84]

Our own work has attempted to explore the varying and sometimes conflicting definitions of collaborative writing[85] and to identify the characteristics of effective collaborative writing as well as its varying modes.[86] In our study of collaborative writers in seven professional organizations, for instance, we identified the following factors that serve to affect the degree of satisfaction experienced by collaborative writers in their jobs:

1. the degree to which goals are clearly articulated and shared,
2. the degree of openness and mutual respect characteristic of group members,
3. the degree of control writers have over the text,
4. the degree to which writers can respond to others who may modify the text,
5. the way credit (direct or indirect) is realized,
6. an agreed upon procedure for resolving disputes among group members,
7. the number and kind of bureaucratic constraints (deadlines, technical or legal requirements, etc.) imposed on the writers, and
8. the status of the project within the organization.

Further questioning of our research subjects led to an emerging profile of effective collaborative writers. They are flexible and respectful of others; attentive, analytical listeners; able to speak and write clearly; dependable and able to meet deadlines; able to dispute and share authority, to lead *and* to follow; open to criticism but confident in their own abilities, and ready to engage in creative conflict. As we sketched in this profile, however, we gradually became aware that collaborative writing on the job occurs in varying modes. The dominant mode our research revealed emerged as highly structured and hierarchical, with power and authority distributed vertically in the hierarchy, and with productivity and efficiency as primary goals. A much less frequent mode of collaboration also emerged, however, one that we refer to as "dialogic." This alternate mode of collaboration is loosely structured, participants' roles are fluid, and the problem

---

[84] *See* Joseph Harris, *The Idea of Community in the Study of Writing*, 40 COLLEGE COMPOSITION AND COMMUNICATION 11 (1989).

[85] LUNSFORD & EDE, *supra* note 2, at 14-16.

[86] *Id.*

of articulating or reaching goals is of great importance.[87] Identifying these varying modes helped us to see how dramatically collaborative writing on the job offers theoretical challenges to
traditional notions of originary authorship and radically individual intellectual property rights. Yet, in practice, such collaborative writing often gives the authority and intellectual ownership
to "the boss" or the leader, without question, particularly in a
rigidly hierarchical mode. In a number of cases, however, and
particularly in those involving dialogic modes of collaboration,
the writers involved were aware of at least a working sense of
shared authorship, shared authority, and shared intellectual
property, one far different from the traditional definition of a solitary, originary *author* holding individual intellectual property
rights.

This review of research on collaborative writing suggests,
first of all, that we need more and better studies of the processes
and varieties of collaborative writing. It also points up, however,
some directions that seem increasingly clear. First, collaborative
writing offers a strong potential challenge to the hegemony of
single, originary authorship and intellectual property and thus
presents a series of challenges to higher education in general and
to the teaching of writing in particular.

IV.   Implications for the Composition Classroom

Closest to home is the challenge to traditional classroom format and to the teacher's role. Our classrooms most often continue to vest power and authority in the teacher. At best,
students are in apprenticeship to authority; they do not help constitute it.[88] Richard Ohmann acknowledges this challenge when
he probes the issue of student "powerlessness" in our classes:
"The writer's situation is heavy with contradictions. She is . . .
invited both to assume responsibility for her education and to
trust the college's plan for it; to build her competence and to
follow a myriad of rules and instructions; to see herself as an autonomous individual and to be incessantly judged."[89] As one
concrete way of contesting such alienating tensions, Ohmann
uses collaborative group interviews, including one of himself.
Ohmann notes:

---

[87] For a more complete description of these modes, see LUNSFORD & EDE, *supra* note
2, at 133-36.

[88] *See* Jane Tompkins, *Pedagogy of the Distressed*, 52 COLLEGE ENGLISH 653 (1990).

[89] *See* OHMANN, *supra* note 59, at 252.

This underlies their ownership of the writing task in two ways. First, it demystifies my role in the class, opening up my goals and values as a subject for inquiry on the students' terms, taking them off the secret agenda. Second, it changes the relationship of their writing to what I have said in class, turning the latter into material for analysis and criticism rather than the graven words of authority.[90]

But even in the most collaborative of our classrooms, the authority to organize and evaluate rests with the teacher. As John Trimbur notes,

Even when I'm not in the room, my authority remains behind, embedded in the very tasks I've asked students to work on . . . . If anything, I have never felt more powerful than in the collaborative classroom precisely because I know much more about what's going on, how students are thinking about the issues of the course, what language they are generating to talk about these issues and so on:[91]

As Foucault's work suggests, collaborative writing itself constitutes a technology of power, one we are only beginning to explore.[92] As we carry out such exploration, as we investigate the ethics of collaboration and the ways in which collaborative writing challenges traditional power relationships, we need to bring students into these discussions, asking them to work with us to examine how authority is negotiated, shared, distributed. At least potentially, we could argue, collaborative writing holds out the promise for a plurality of power and authority among teacher and students, what Ohmann calls an "opening up" of the classroom.[93]

The hierarchical bases of power in our classrooms, of course, reflect the larger structure of our educational institutions. Most university calendars, divided neatly into semesters or quarters, reflect a positivistic approach to learning: knowledge is "packaged" into discrete segments and dispensed to passive recipients, fast-food style, through four years. Such a system represents students as isolated units, all of whom learn in similar ways and at similar speeds. The time necessary for group cohesion to occur, for the examination of group dynamics involving consensus and dissensus to take place, much less for a consideration of

---

90 *Id.* at 256.
91 *See* Trimbur, *supra* note 83, at 602.
92 *See* Foucault, *supra* note 38, at 141.
93 OHMANN, *supra* note 59.

the issues at stake in seemingly simple questions such as "Who is the author of this essay?" or "Who is responsible for these words?" is not easily found in such a system. The research and scholarship reviewed here strongly suggests that just as we must rethink our roles as teachers in a collaborative writing classroom, so also must we rethink our use of time in the college curriculum. At the very least, we must become aware of how such things as the use of time reflect assumptions and traditions that no longer fit with our educational goals.

We could of course point out other institutional constraints that militate against a pedagogy of collaboration. Most notable is no doubt traditional classroom design. Large, cavernous lecture halls in which students see only the backs of other students' heads and classrooms whose bolted down desks face dutifully toward the slightly raised lectern in front present major stumbling blocks to collaborative learning and writing. Institutional practices, bound as they are in ideology, may prove even more intractable to change than will classroom settings. Among these, the examination system seems particularly problematic. This system, barely a hundred years old, is rooted solidly in positivistic assumptions: knowledge is objectifiably knowable and can be measured and counted. Such a tradition, of course, goes hand in hand with the conception of a solitary, sovereign—and usually male—writer with individually "owned" property rights. This view of knowledge calls for a "controlled" testing situation and valorizes the hard data such situations yield as "proof" of success or failure. Testing as we know it is by definition a-contextual and anti-social, anti-communal, as far from a collaborative activity as could be imagined. In such a system, students must do "original" work, and they are individually judged on individual "quality of mind." Unfortunately, the dependence on and infatuation with mass testing at all levels of the educational system seems only to be growing, as evidenced most recently by a call from The National Council of Education Standards and Testing for yet another and more rigorous round of national exams for America's students.[94] Yet the movements discussed here all question the very foundations on which such testing and grading practices rest.

The institutional reliance on testing "norms" and the ideology it reflects can be found replicated, not surprisingly, in the writing classroom, where concerns over individual perform-

---

[94] Dennis Kelly, *National Standards*, USA TODAY, Jan. 24, 1992, at D1.

ance—and especially over plagiarism—can become near obsessions. Certainly collaborative writing calls such obsessive concerns into question and reveals the formalist, positivist, and individualist ideological assumptions on which common notions of plagiarism rest. But do such questions obviate the very notion of plagiarism? If not, how can we help students construct a more sophisticated and enabling understanding of this concept? Teachers of writing may best begin, it seems to us, by taking a rhetorically situated view of plagiarism, one that acknowledges that all writing is in an important sense collaborative and that "common knowledge" varies from community to community and is collaboratively shared. From this perspective, attribution of sources becomes not a means of avoiding the heinous sin of plagiarism, but of building credibility or writerly *ethos*, of indicating to readers that the writer is a full collaborative participant in the scholarly conversation surrounding whatever topic is at hand. Clearly, teachers wishing to implement a pedagogy of collaboration will need new ways of evaluating the process of collaborative writing and the products produced thereby.

Our current sense is that a thorough re-examination of the grounds of testing and grading practices in higher education in general and composition classes in particular will have to follow rather than precede curricular reform. And in this area, the research on collaborative writing reviewed here may have a more immediate impact. In spite of the reform efforts of Heath, Emig, and others, the current curriculum is still based on a model of content coverage: classes must clip along, "covering" a certain number of units in a certain number of days. But this model is under increasing attack on a number of fronts and for a number of reasons. Most obviously, it is simply no longer possible for any one person to "cover" all the material in any field, even a fairly narrow one. Less obvious but equally important is the growing realization that what we "teach" in this inexorable drive to cover a content area is not necessarily or even probably what is learned. Here the research in collaborative learning theory is clear and unequivocal: real learning occurs in *interaction* as students actively use concepts and ideas or strategies in order to assimilate them. The pedagogical implications are equally clear: less may well yield *more* in terms of learning. What follows from this line of reasoning is the need to reconsider course structure in terms of assignments that will engage students in interaction and in collaboration with their teachers and other students. What is much less clear is whether teachers are willing or able to make the next logical and necessary step—to move from such collaboration to collaborative *writing*. Doing so challenges, as we have shown, very deep-seated beliefs in radically individual ways of knowing and in the writing pedagogies accompanying such beliefs.

Yet the time seems particularly ripe for teachers of writing to accept this challenge and to explore further the questions raised in the opening section of this essay. The work summarized here as well as the research we have conducted barely scratches the surface in terms of understanding the full range of collaboration, of exploring its dangers as well as its potentialities, of establishing an ethics of collaboration. For teachers of writing, however, the most immediate need is for a pedagogy of collaboration, one that would view writing as always shared and social; writers as constantly building and negotiating meaning with and among others; and evaluation as based at least in part on a "range of selves" and on communal efforts. Articulating such a pedagogy of collaboration, we believe, would advance efforts on a number of fronts to reconceive intellectual property and selfhood and to value these reconceived notions in a way that is commensurate with the idea of a postmodern democracy.

THE AUTHOR IN COPYRIGHT: NOTES FOR THE LITERARY CRITIC

MONROE E. PRICE* AND MALLA POLLACK**

A collection of essays, largely by literary critics and comparativists, is the occasion for asking more about the legal definition of "authorship" than has traditionally been the case. Our task, in a sense, has been to respond, to try to determine how courts and Congress have come to define, or failed to define, this seemingly obvious concept. We have sought to trace authorship in legal analysis, particularly in copyright, and have tried to determine whether the definition of authorship, for purposes of copyright law, turns on anything more than the judge's perception of the nature of the work produced.[1]

Quite fortuitously, while our essay was in gestation, the Supreme Court, for the first time in a century,[2] and the second time in two, uttered its Delphic mysteries on this very question, albeit in the peculiar way that American judges have of answering broad questions from very narrow perches. The Court, on this occasion, spoke to the seemingly banal question of whether the particular "expression" as presented in the hefty volumes we call "telephone books" is the subject of copyright. The Court determined that telephone books have no bard, at least not the common style of pages as we know it. That is the teaching of Justice O'Connor in *Feist Publications v. Rural Telephone Service*,[3] a case that purports to provide an authoritative view of authorship. Justice O'Connor's opinion, grounded in a body of experience and judicial discourse, frames the question of who is an author. This opinion is consistent with the tradition of our courts whereby decisions emerge from a history of prior treatment of the question.[4]

---

* Professor of Law, Benjamin N. Cardozo School of Law. B.A., 1960, L.L.B., 1964, Yale University.
** Clerk for Honorable Ruth Bader Ginsburg, D.C. Cir. B.A., 1975, State University of New York, Albany; J.D., 1991, Benjamin N. Cardozo School of Law.

[1] This article is the result of an invitation from Peter Jaszi and Martha Woodmansee to give a paper at Case Western Reserve University. Our thanks to them for inviting us and to Professor Arthur Jacobson of Cardozo School of Law and Peter Hayward of St. Peter's College, Oxford, for commenting on the essay.

[2] For counting purposes, we are conflating the Trade-Mark Cases, 100 U.S. 82 (1879) and Burrow-Giles Lithographic Co. v. Sarony, 111 U.S. 53 (1884).

[3] 111 S. Ct. 1282, 1286 (1991).

[4] Also not surprising is an absence of any reference to the literary debates over the nature of authorship. This omission is apparently by choice, not by mere belief that law lives only in law libraries. *See* Simon & Schuster v. New York State Crime Victims Bd.,

Despite the representation that such a history exists, surprisingly little has been written on the subject in the judicial treatment of copyright. True, the Constitution, which serves as the foundation for copyright legislation, offers Congress the power to protect only the writings of "authors,"[5] and the copyright statute itself only protects "original works of authorship."[6] Perhaps this absence is attributable to the fact, noted by Benjamin Kaplan in his great and wonderfully short history, that the author was only a convenient hook upon which to hang the privileges of the publisher.[7] Still, we should hope to describe and understand so important a hook.

Feist confronted Justice O'Connor with a pattern of facts that could be placed in a familiar context, at least familiar to lawyers. The plaintiff, presumably, had gone to a great deal of trouble to assemble the names, addresses and phone numbers for its phone book.[8] The defendant, who published a regional book incorporating numbers from a group of other books (all of which the defendant was licensed to use, except those of the plaintiff), had reaped where he had not sown; or, to use another frequent judicial metaphor, had benefitted by the sweat of another's brow.[9] One question raised by this case was whether the stuff of phone books constituted non-protected "facts" as opposed to the work of an "author."[10] Justice O'Connor easily dealt with that aspect of authorship, reiterating that facts are not copyrightable, whether they come in molehills or mountains. The amount of work involved in assembling the facts does not enter into the legislated equation.

As to facts, regarding the sweat of a putative author's brow,

---

112 S. Ct. 501 (1991) (Son of Sam statute case decided by O'Connor in December 1991 mentioning such non-legal sources as Malcom X's autobiography and The Confessions of Saint Augustine). But perhaps it is non-legal *analysis* of the world that is not considered—or considered and rejected as unsure footing. Roe v. Wade, 410 U.S. 113 (1973), used then-current medical knowledge. *Roe* was criticized for reading changing scientific dogma into the Constitution. *See, e.g.*, ARCHIBALD COX, THE ROLE OF THE SUPREME COURT IN AMERICAN GOVERNMENT 113-14 (1976).

5 U.S. CONST. art. I, § 8, cl. 8.

6 "Copyright protection subsists, in accordance with this title, in original works of authorship . . . ." 17 U.S.C. § 102(a) (1988).

7 *See* BENJAMIN KAPLAN, AN UNHURRIED VIEW OF COPYRIGHT (1968).

8 This may be an inaccurate presumption. The names, addresses and telephone numbers are supplied by would-be subscribers during the normal course of requiring telephone service. As Justice O'Connor notes, "Rural obtains subscriber information quite easily." *Feist*, 111 S. Ct. 1286. This information would have to be coordinated for billing. With today's computer technology, reassembling it into directory format hardly seems incredibly laborious.

9 The "sweat of the brow" or the "industrious collectivism" doctrine is traced in *Feist* to a misreading of the 1909 Copyright Act. *Id.* at 1291-92.

10 Feist, 111 S. Ct. at 1287.

Justice O'Connor saw no room for debate. On another question, however, analysis was necessary, and it was analysis that yielded insight into the requisites for authorship. Even if facts are not copyrightable, compilations or collections may be, if, but only if, the mode of compiling or collecting is itself "original," or the act of authorship. Perhaps some arrangements in telephone books demonstrate sufficient originality for protection, but not the garden variety book that lamely assembles names in alphabetical order, following them with addresses, and then, after a discreet space, with the number of their telephone device. Surprisingly, Justice O'Connor used the sledgehammer of constitutionality to kill the flea-sized modicum of originality and authorship represented by the plaintiff.[11]

What is important about *Feist*, for our purposes, is the gap that it discloses between the legal and the literary debate over the notion of the author. Elsewhere in this issue, those skilled in the history of criticism reflect upon the evolving treatment of authorship outside of legal analysis. It is fairly clear that the idea of author as romantic, creative hero, as the genius of homo sapiens, the person whose stroke of genius is the basis for civilization—an idea that is reflected, often in legal discourse—has been the subject of intense debate and criticism. Ideas of originality, so central to Justice O'Connor's analysis,[12] are highly suspect among modern literary critics. Indeed, the very idea of authorship is often perceived to be part of the general hierarchy of power that ought to be destroyed in the interest of creating a newer and better society.

For us, this dichotomy between law and literature raises several important questions. Is there something about law and legal analysis that requires a different approach to the notion of authorship than that which persists in literary criticism? The literary critic, awash in movements that deny the nineteenth-century model of author, sees the problem of text and attribution in ways that are fundamental to the nature of society. For the modernist,

---

11 *See* Marci A. Hamilton, *Justice O'Connor's Opinion in Feist Publications, Inc. v. Rural Telephone Service Co.: An Uncommon Though Characteristic Approach*, 38 J. OF COPYRIGHT SOC'Y, U.S.A. 83 (1991). Professor Hamilton asserts that the decision was uncharacteristic of Justice O'Connor's jurisprudence, which ordinarily exhausts the possibility of statutory interpretation before resorting to constitutional hermeneutics. As to the lack of illumination, suffice it to say that few are equipped, without poetic tendencies of their own, to summarize the difference between what is "original" and what is not. *See, e.g.*, Nichols v. Universal Pictures Corp., 45 F.2d 119 (2d Cir. 1930) (Learned Hand's formulation of the abstractions test). Indeed, this article exists because of the structural problem of defining authorship itself.

12 *Feist*, 111 S. Ct. at 1287-89.

perhaps, all work is collaborative, all work is derivative. For those who see the world as representation, who see every account as a construction of events, rather than the event itself, there can be no true distinction between "facts" and the mental creations.   For the law-trained judge, the task is different. The subtext for the lawyer is the search for underlying principles of liberty and freedom, not for source, influence and social construct. At the very least, how authorship is defined brings us into intimate contact with notions of freedom—freedom of expression, freedom to publish history and commentary. Congress purports, pursuant to the constitutional mandate, to expand protection in order to encourage creative work. But if we expand protection too broadly or in unproductive ways, creativity may be stymied by constraining the use and interplay of ideas. In a society that deals more and more with the production, bundling and trade in information, how that information is constrained and characterized will determine the structure of competition, the opportunity for entry and the cost of engaging in intellectual and practical advances. The "idea-expression" distinction exemplifies the problem: copyright is said to protect the skin of ideas, not the ideas themselves; but, if anything is clear from history, it is the murkiness of this distinction.[13] Almost every issue now litigated, from fair use to the definition of minimum creativity, has these questions of importance to the shape of an advanced information society as subtext. As is true in virtually any debate about

---

[13] *See, e.g.,* Richard A. Jones, *The Myth of the Idea/Expression Dichotomy in Copyright Law,* 10 PACE L. REV. 551 (1990) (the traditional dichotomy is superfluous and misleading since there is no such thing as an unexpressed idea; the correct distinction is between unprotectable and protectable expressions); Alfred C. Yen, *A First Amendment Perspective on the Idea/Expression Dichotomy and Copyright in a Work's "Total Concept and Feel,"* 38 EMORY L.J. 393 (1989) (copyright dodges First Amendment problems by limiting only the use of expression; however, this is insufficient because the decisions on the bounds of expression are premised on mere instinct and the resulting uncertainty of outcome creates a chilling effect). Consider the current debate over this basic distinction as applied to computer interfaces. *See, e.g.,* Lotus Dev. v. Paperback Software Int'l, 740 F. Supp. 37 (D. Mass. 1990) (menu command structure is copyrightable as expression even though it is useful); Daniel J. Fetterman, *The Scope of Copyright Protection for Computer Software: Exploring the Idea/Expression Dichotomy,* 36 COPYRIGHT L. SYMP. (ASCAP) 1 (1986 competition, printed 1990) (advocating wide protection of design, structure and organization of computer programs to match that of other literary works); John H. Pilarski, *User Interfaces and the Idea—Expression Dichotomy, or Are the Copyright Laws User Friendly?,* 37 COPYRIGHT L. SYMP. (ASCAP) 45 (1987 competition, printed 1990) (The apparently conflicting decisions on the boundary between idea and expression in computer programs actually follow consistently the traditional balancing policy of encouraging progress by public availability of material while providing incentives through protection of new creations.); Steven R. Englund, Note, *Idea, Process, or Protected Expression?: Determining the Scope of Copyright Protection of the Structure of Computer Programs,* 88 MICH. L. REV. 866 (1990) (calling for more detailed analyses of the programs to limit protection to those elements which are not unprotectable ideas or processes).

the scope of copyright, beneath the doctrinal struggle are profound arguments about democratic theory and the production of ideas. The definition of authorship is no exception.

The lawyer works by analogy, the literary critic from a different context. Take patent law for example. For the critic, patent does not provide a relevant context for constructing an author. But for a law-trained scholar, patent law would be the first place to look for guidance. In the mind of the lawyer, patent is a close relative to copyright. Both derive from the same constitutional phrase,[14] and the Supreme Court has accepted the rationality of

---

[14] "The Congress shall have Power . . . To promote the Progress of Science and useful Arts, by securing for limited Times to Authors and Inventors the exclusive Right to their respective Writings and Discoveries . . . ." U.S. CONST. art. I, § 8, cl. 1, 8. The intended relationship between the two subjects of the clause is unknown. The intellectual property clause was submitted on September 5, 1787, by Brearley, for the Committee on Unfinished Business, in response to a suggestion by James Madison "[t]o secure to literary authors their copyrights for a limited time," and to two suggestions by Charles C. Pinckney "[t]o grant patents for useful inventions" and "[t]o secure to authors exclusive rights for a certain time." ARTHUR T. PRESCOTT, DRAFTING THE FEDERAL CONSTITUTION 529 (1968). No debate is recorded. 1 JAMES MADISON, THE DEBATES IN THE FEDERAL CONVENTION OF 1787 WHICH FRAMED THE CONSTITUTION OF THE UNITED STATES OF AMERICA (Gaillard Hunt & James B. Scott eds., 1987); ALAN LATMAN ET AL., COPYRIGHT FOR THE NINETIES 5 (Robert A. Gorman & Jane C. Ginsburg eds., 3d ed. 1989).

    Several rejected alternatives on the same general subject are known.

    MADISON: It should be provided that the government have power to encourage by premiums and provisions the advancement of useful knowledge and discoveries.

    PINCKNEY: Power should be given the government to establish public institutions, rewards and immunities for the promotion of agriculture, commerce, trades and manufactures.

    PINCKNEY: The government should have power to establish seminaries for the promotion of literature and the arts and sciences.

    MADISON: Congress should be enabled to establish a university in the place of the general government, and should possess exclusive jurisdiction over the institution. It should be specified that all persons might be admitted to the university and to its honors and emoluments, without any distinction of religion whatever.

JAMES MADISON, CONSTITUTIONAL CHAFF: REJECTED SUGGESTIONS OF THE CONSTITUTIONAL CONVENTION OF 1787, at 64 (Jane Butzner comp., 1941). Madison's later defense of the clause is not very helpful:

    The utility of this power will scarcely be questioned. The copyright of authors has been solemnly adjudged, in Great Britain, to be a right of common law. The right to useful inventions seems with equal reason to belong to the inventors. . . . The States cannot separately make effectual provision for either of the cases, and most of them have anticipated the decision of this point, by laws passed at the instance of Congress.

THE FEDERALIST No. 43, at 186 (James Madison) (THE ENDURING FEDERALIST, Charles A. Beard ed., 1948). Elliot's compilation includes no indexed mention of discussions on this clause. See generally JONATHAN ELLIOT, DEBATES IN THE SEVERAL STATE CONVENTIONS ON THE ADOPTION OF THE FEDERAL CONSTITUTION (1941).

    Besides the lack of information on the framers' intent, we have the additional problem, common to all constitutional discussions, of deciding the importance of that intent. In the words of James Madison, "[a]s a guide in expounding and applying the provisions of the Constitution . . . the debates and incidental decisions of the Convention can have no authoritative character." Letter from James Madison to Thomas Ritchie, Sept. 15,

illuminating copyright problems by looking to previously created patent solutions.[15] Also, a lawyer would note that while the copyright statute breezes by authorship without a careful definition, the patent statute denies protection to anyone except the original inventor.[16] The case law is rich with quarrels over priorities[17] and detailed statements of the minimum in action and understanding needed to qualify for the title "inventor."[18] One must both "conceive" of the invention and "reduce it to practice."[19] Actual reduction to practice is physical operation of the claimed invention for its intended purpose. Constructive reduction to practice is filing a patent application showing the discovery and its use.[20] "Conception" consists of "formation in the mind of the inventor, of a definite and permanent idea of the complete and

---

1821, *quoted in* LEONARD LEVY, ORIGINAL INTENT AND THE FRAMERS' CONSTITUTION 1 (1988). Later writers have expressed widely disparate views. *See, e.g.*, Ronald Dworkin, *The Forum of Principle*, 56 N.Y.U. L. REV. 469, 490 (1981) (framers may have intended to delegate power to future population to make decisions); Frank H. Easterbrook, *Legal Interpretation and the Power of the Judiciary*, 7 HARV. J.L. & PUB. POL'Y 87, 94 (1984) (courts should not add restrictions to the Constitution); H. Jefferson Powell, *The Original Understanding of Original Intent*, 98 HARV. L. REV. 885, 948 (1985) (by "framers' intent" the Framers meant the intention of the sovereign parties, not of the writers of the Constitution); Mark V. Tushnet, *Following the Rules Laid Down: A Critique of Interpretivism and Neutral Principles*, 96 HARV. L. REV. 781 (1983) (interpretivism assumes an undemonstrable historical consensus). *See generally* LEVY, *supra* (overview of opposing theories).

[15] *See, e.g.*, Sony Corp. of America v. Universal City Studios, 464 U.S. 417, 439-42 (1984) (using the patent definition of a "staple article of commerce" to decide a copyright issue).

[16] "A person shall be entitled to a patent unless—

. . . .

(f) he did not himself invent the subject matter sought to be patented . . . ." 35 U.S.C. § 102 (1988). One can, of course, assign one's rights to a patent and the statute has a special provision allowing a non-inventor to apply when an inventor exists under certain limited special circumstances.

> Whenever an inventor refuses to execute an application for patent, or cannot be found or reached after diligent effort, a person to whom the inventor has assigned or agreed in writing to assign the invention or who otherwise shows sufficient proprietary interest in the matter justifying such action, may make application for patent on behalf of and as agent for the inventor on proof of the pertinent facts and a showing that such action is necessary to preserve the rights of the parties or to prevent irreparable damage; and the Commissioner may grant a patent to such inventor upon such notice to him as the Commissioner deems sufficient, and on compliance with such regulations as he prescribes.

35 U.S.C. § 118 (1988).

[17] Squibs on "anticipation" (the existence of the invention before the applicant's discovery) and "priority of invention" (who among rival claimants was the first to invent) fill over sixty pages of the United States Code Annotated. 35 U.S.C.A. § 102 (West 1984 & Supp. 1992) (annotations to 35 U.S.C. § 102).

[18] *See, e.g.*, Lutzker v. Plet, 843 F.2d 1364, 1366 (Fed. Cir. 1988) ("Generally, the party who establishes that he is the first to conceive and the first to reduce an invention to practice is entitled to a patent thereon.").

[19] *Id.*

[20] Hybritech Inc. v. Monoclonal Antibodies, Inc., 802 F.2d 1367, 1376 (Fed. Cir. 1986), *cert. denied*, 480 U.S. 947 (1987).

operative invention, as it is hereafter to be applied in practice."[21] Conception is an understanding of what you have created; an understanding present in a mind. One must bring to the Patent Office not just an operative machine, but an understanding of how that machine will be useful. "[P]eople conceive, not companies . . . ."[22] This centrality of inventorship in patent law is in severe contrast to the marginality of authorship in copyright.

Why is this reasoning persuasive to the lawyer or judge, but worth nothing to the literary critic? One answer might be that the critic's task is different from the judge's. The role of the legal institutions may be reduced to providing a set of traffic rules for commercial transactions. The test of the rules is whether traffic moves, whether transactions are completed, whether investments are made and whether innovations take place with adequate frequency. If the rules perform these tasks, then the lawmaker feels vindicated, whether or not the rules embody principles that are philosophically or morally defensible. A rule that prohibits scholars from publishing the contents of the letters of the famous may be criticized because the rule limits scholarship and the growth of knowledge. That is the important question, not the abstract issue of whether a letter is subject to copyright or not. We ask whether patents can be held in living organisms, but the answer turns on the encouragement of science, not on issues of abstract truth.[23] For the lawyer, the experience in patent law involves mental gymnastics that are similar to those in the copyright sphere. As a matter of efficiency, the patent field is thought to produce precedents.

The Sisyphean task of the lawyer is to fit the messiness of life into categories of legal rule. Doctoral candidates may spend years studying the relationship between one painter and another, in terms of iconography, or color or placement of verticals and horizontals on the canvas. But the aesthetician's range of influence has to be reduced, in the legal process, to the category of plagiarism *vel non*. For the critic judging the work of Sherrie Levine, the artist, whose work consists of the reinterpretative ap-

---

[21] *Id.*

[22] New Idea Farm Equip. v. Sperry Corp., 916 F.2d 1561, 1566 n.4 (Fed. Cir. 1990). We have been unable to locate any cases crediting conception, or invention, to non-humans—including computers or monkeys.

[23] *See* Monroe E. Price, *Reexamining Intellectual Property Concepts: A Glimpse Into the Future Through the Prism of Chakrabarty*, 6 CARDOZO ARTS & ENT. L.J. 19 (1988). *See also* Edward L. Andrews, *U.S. Patent on Genetic Codes, Setting Off Furor*, N.Y. TIMES, Oct. 21, 1991, at A1, A12 (U.S. Government decided to patent genes without waiting to discover their functions).

propriation of other artists, the standard for judging stretches into realms of intention, of context, of the power of the artist to use the work of others in her own process of critical commentary. For the lawyer, categories are often reduced to merely two: this is an act permitted, or this is an act forbidden.

In any act of writing or creation, there are various levels of purpose or intention. The physical act of placing marks on paper, as an example, may be involuntary or accidental. At the time the mark is made, the intention to create may be absent. For some artists, the purposeful selection of accidental transactions constitutes their work. Other artists and poets have sought intentionally to incorporate and capture chance in their work. Here there is intention, even though it is sometimes the intention to appear unintentional. Sometimes intentionality follows the act, as opposed to being contemporaneous with it. An artist, by characterizing a thing as art, joins his or her intention to an otherwise finished object. In some part, the intention is to change the object from the mundane, the utilitarian, to the domain of art. Consider Duchamp's *Fountain*, the artistic selection of a mass-manufactured urinal. Sometimes, we believe that because the artist is an artist, what he or she calls art becomes art.[24] Judge Leval, in his Brace Lecture on fair use, sought to differentiate the homely note tacked on a refrigerator door.[25] These may be scribbles done under the impulse of communication, with no thought of their entry into the system of art; yet, at a later point, because of the identity of the scribe, they may become art.

But this Article is about law and by authors trained primarily in law. We have turned not to the literary critics, but to the history of copyright decisions, to determine how legal analysis has approached the question of authorship. We intend to deal with these questions in far greater detail elsewhere, but our own narrative of that history—our authored construction, as it may be put—suggests several paradigms for thinking about the author. The easiest construction of authorship is any mark[26] on a piece of paper, or some other medium, by a person.[27] This is the interpre-

---

[24] *See infra* note 35 (Dickie's Definitions).

[25] Pierre N. Leval, *Toward a Fair Use Standard*, 103 HARV. L. REV. 1105, 1119 (1990).

[26] There's trouble right here, since the definition requires some objective manifestation. An argument could be made for a copyright law that protected ideas as well as expression, or for a copyright law that was based on the principle that there is no meaningful distinction between ideas and their physical, or close to physical, expression.

[27] "Copyright protection subsists . . . in original works of authorship fixed in any tangible medium of expression . . . ." 17 U.S.C. § 102(a) (1988). Whether authorship should be limited to human beings, we leave aside and assume that only human beings are authors. But computers are coming up fast, *see, e.g.*, Pearson, *Copyright in Computer*

tation which is most at odds with Justice O'Connor's view in the *Feist* decision, since it requires hardly any originality. A second construction of authorship would require that the author manifest, through some objective notion of intent, that he or she wishes to be considered an author for purposes of copyright and that the particular work is related to that conception of authorship. The third construction would have the law turn on a social definition of who constitutes an artist, a version of the law that would rely on an external determination of the protected class and then reward that class for its membership, not necessarily for its individual product. We have called these tests, respectively: the objective, intentional and aesthetic tests.

From our review of the literature, it seems that something like an objective test has had great appeal. It seems most suitable in a community thoroughly suspicious of line-drawing based on the nature of the work produced or the intention of those creating it. Any stroke of work, no matter how created or by whom, would be the subject of protection. The objective test is agnostic as to the nature of the work, agnostic as to the nature of the creator, and agnostic as to the purpose, if any, behind the work's creation. To be sure, the infringement of some works may be more important than the infringement of others, but that is an issue for determining damages, or whether to issue an injunction.[28] Refinements on the objective test could require, at a minimum, that the stroke be by a human conscious of making the mark, or that it have some minimum level of creativity, or otherwise begin to import small qualitative distinctions. American copyright law has often had objective impulses, particularly because of a fundamental distrust of aesthetic determinations by judges.[29] While the copyright law nominally requires originality and something which differentiates the work from the mundane and the useful, the objective tendency in American law has deemphasized these defining qualities. Because Americans tend to distrust judicially

---

Generated Programs, 1987 ABA Sec. Patent, Trademark & Copyright Law Rep. 181 (authorship of program created by a master program), and we anticipate claims from the champions of animal rights. *See, e.g.*, D. MORRIS, THE BIOLOGY OF ART: A STUDY OF THE PICTURE-MAKING BEHAVIOR OF THE GREAT APES AND ITS RELATIONSHIP TO HUMAN ART (1962).

28 On the importance of separating rights from remedies in copyright see Honorable James L. Oakes, *Copyrights and Copyremedies: Unfair Use and Injunctions*, 18 HOFSTRA L. REV. 983, 992-97 (1990) (existence of infringement should not automatically settle issue of whether injunction should be issued).

29 *See, e.g.*, Bleistein v. Donaldson Lithographing Co., 188 U.S. 239, 251 (1903) ("It would be a dangerous undertaking for persons trained only to the law to constitute themselves final judges of the worth of pictorial illustrations . . . .").

determined definitions of art, they are more comfortable with eligibility standards based on more formal criteria, such as: is the work reduced, in some way, to paper—or "fixed," to use the more technical term.[30]

One can explain the objective test as an extension of the oxymoron of objective intent familiar from contract law. We do not deal with what the author subjectively (*i.e.*, actually) intended.[31] Rather, we deal instead with what a person observing the author's actions would have thought he intended. This paradigm only makes sense if the observer needs protection, as he does in contract where one relies on what he observed. This copyright paradigm establishes the constitutional clause as a contract between the public and the author. This analogy, however, is seriously flawed. The public acted to set up copyright *before* the author wrote;[32] the public did not act in reliance on its observation of the author's production. The only actor who responded to the author's creation was his competitor, a later author or publisher. This competitor must decide if the earlier author had created a protected work or one he could safely mine for additions to his own creation. This reliance, however, rests more on the interpretation of court actions than on those of the original author. The more logical outcome of copyright as contract is the economic paradigm.

The test of economic intentionality also prevailed in American history. Until 1978, copyright law turned, to a remarkable extent, on the expressed intention of the author to make use of the system of copyright. Generations of lawyers were taught to ask whether the work carried the necessary signal of intention to seek the umbrella of statutory protection (the now-disestablished "c" in a circle).[33] The most charming aspect of the economic test is its democratic access to copyright and its joinder to the simple manifestation of intention incorporated in the notice requirement. No one had to be certified to be entitled to copyright; any

---

[30] To be copyrightable a work must be "fixed in any tangible medium of expression." 17 U.S.C. § 102(a) (1988).

[31] *See, e.g.*, Armstrong v. M'Ghee, 1795 Add. 261 (County Ct., Westmoreland, Pa., 1795) (contract for sale of horse enforced though intended as a joke).

[32] Motivation of the individual author seeking protection is also not clearly required. *See infra* note 38 and accompanying text.

[33] "Cure," the saving of a work which otherwise fell into the public domain by publication without notice, was allowed by the 1976 Revision which controlled works created from January 1, 1978. 1976 Copyright Act, Pub. L. No. 94-553 § 405, 90 Stat. 2541, 2578 (codified as amended at 17 U.S.C. § 405 (1988)). The need for notice on new works was eliminated in 1988. Berne Convention Implementation Act of 1988, Pub. L. 100-568 § 7(e), 102 Stat. 2853, 2858 (codified at 17 U.S.C. § 405 (1988)).

idea of subjective intention was fulfilled by the objective formalities that clearly demonstrated a desire to accept society's offer of a monopoly over the work for a limited term in exchange for the work's publication. One might argue that it is not only irrelevant, but almost impossible to define the specific intent to be "an author," rather than the general intent physically to record an idea, or otherwise take the simple actions required to move a pencil across a paper, a brush across a canvas or fingers across a machine. We shall assume that a person (leaving aside corporations or other artificial entities) can entertain a specific intent to be something which we call "author." The notion of being an author embraces and celebrates such an intent. Indeed, the concept of copyright is enriched and rationalized by an approach that provides some legal substance to the concept of authorship. But note that the intention central here is the intention to profit from the system—not the intention to create masterpieces.[34]

The aesthetic test, seemingly so different from the general history of copyright, has a logic that might bring it closer to the work of the literary critic, though with opposite conclusions. At least it looks to the world of the arts as the standard for determining who should be entitled to protection. Only "artists and authors," perhaps self-defined,[35] but more likely defined by the National Academy of Arts and Sciences, would be entitled to the incentives provided by copyright protection or some other device. This group, "authors," would be identified as the group professionally devoted to making a livelihood from writing and painting, and they should be honored, protected and supported. Think of the Japanese experience of protecting human "national treasures" in the way that America protects landmarks. Copyright is not the most efficient or credible way of doing that: supporting the authors and artists by providing protection for their

---

[34] Few things were below the originality level of copyrightability if they complied with the formalities. *See, e.g.*, Bleistein v. Donaldson Lithographing Co., 188 U.S. 239, 251 (1903) (uninspired circus posters are copyrightable); Magic Mktg. v. Mailing Servs., 634 F. Supp. 769, 771-72 (W.D. Pa. 1986) (phrases and bold lines on envelopes are not copyrightable). True genius would forfeit copyright protection if statutory formal requirements were not met. Letter Edged in Black Press, Inc. v. Public Bldg. Comm'n, 320 F. Supp. 1303, 1311 (N.D. Ill. 1970) (Chicago Picasso not protected due to publication without proper notice).

[35] At least one modern aesthetic philosopher makes the creator's self-identification central to the artistic nature of a piece. To George Dickie "[a]n artist is a person who participates with understanding in the making of a work of art," and a "work of art is an artifact of a kind created to be presented to an artworld public." GEORGE DICKIE, THE ART CIRCLE: A THEORY OF ART 80 (1984). A person's own decision to enter his creation into the public forum of works criticized as art by interested observers is the central act which transmutes an artifact into an art object.

works. A society could—and many do—go further, and directly
support the artists. Those classified as artists should be supported whether or not they produce physical works of art in any
particular year. The person, not the work, should be the fulcrum
for incentive.[36] In the United States, the closest analogy we have,
from the perspective of the federal government, is the National
Endowment for the Arts, and "peer review" is the mechanism
used here for definition and determination of eligibility.[37] Our
most recent expansions of protection shy away from the aesthetic
test—even though both were prompted by The Berne Convention. We added an indirect subsidy by supplying European-style
extra rights, moral rights, to a limited number of works of special
characteristics.[38] This new federal legislation, however, carefully
refrained from tying this added protection to judgments of artistic merit about specific works—the act instead deals in special
categories of works.[39] Similarly, the recent expansion of protection to architectural works deals with quality only indirectly by
excluding from coverage "individual standard features" of protected entities.[40]

For a very long time, the economic intentionality test most
nearly characterized American attitudes. In a society that relies

---

[36] For a discussion of such a system, see MIKLOS HARASZTI, THE VELVET PRISON: ART-
ISTS UNDER STATE SOCIALISM (G. Konrad trans., 1987). Of course, changes in government can strand artists who have become dependant on such a system of subsidies. *See,
e.g.*, Henry Kramm, *Freed From Censorship, Culture in Hungary Now Suffers Lack of Security*,
N.Y. TIMES, Dec. 11, 1991, at A20.

[37] 20 U.S.C. § 954 (1988). The Chairperson of the National Endowment for the Arts
acts upon recommendations made by the National Council for the Arts, whose members
are "private citizens . . . widely recognized for their broad knowledge of, or expertise in,
or for their profound interest in, the arts." *Id.* § 955.

[38] Visual Artists Rights Act of 1990, Pub. L. No. 101-650, 104 Stat. 5128 (to be codified at 17 U.S.C. §§ 101, 106A, 107, 113, 301, 411, 412, 501, 506 (1988)). This act
grants the rights of attribution and integrity, *id.* § 603 (to be codified at 17 U.S.C.
§ 106A), to works of visual art. A "work of visual art" is defined as

> (1) a painting, drawing, print, or sculpture, existing in a single copy, in
> a limited edition of 200 copies or fewer that are signed and consecutively
> numbered by the author, or, in the case of a sculpture, in multiple cast,
> carved, or fabricated sculptures of 200 or fewer that are consecutively num-
> bered by the author and bear the signature or other identifying mark of the
> author; or
> (2) a still photographic image produced for exhibition purposes only,
> existing in a single copy that is signed by the author, or in a limited edition of
> 200 copies or fewer that are signed and consecutively numbered by the au-
> thor, with certain listed exceptions.

Id. § 602 (to be codified at 17 U.S.C. § 101 (1988)).

[39] Some states' moral rights statutes do incorporate quality distinctions, Louisiana
and New Mexico, for example. LA. REV. STAT. ANN. § 51: 2152 (West 1987); N.M. STAT.
ANN. § 13-4B-2 (Michie 1989).

[40] Architectural Works Copyright Protection Act, Pub. L. No. 101-695, § 702(a), 104
Stat. 5133 (1990) (to be codified at 17 U.S.C. § 101 (1988 & Supp. 1990)).

on the economic test, the status of the creator (an approved artist or author) is not the determinant of protection, but more fundamentally the relationship of works of art to the marketplace. Copyright law exists as an exception to the First Amendment prohibition on laws limiting speech, but it does so for a specific reason.[41] The Constitution, taken as a whole, recognizes that protection of works of art is necessary in order to encourage their production. A fundamental reading of the copyright clause suggests that we would be a poorer society and world without patents and copyrights because the incentives for creativity would be wanting. Clearly our patent law follows this paradigm: only the premier inventor can obtain a patent;[42] he must do so by timely approaching the Patent Office with proofs of his entitlement;[43] his failure to make this bargain dedicates the invention to the public despite the work of later reinventors.[44] This economic

---

[41] Congress is not forced by the First Amendment to grant copyright monopoly to all works. "The first amendment does not protect the right to copyright," according to Ladd v. Law & Technology Press, 762 F.2d 809, 815 (9th Cir. 1985). More fully, this case held that the deposit requirement is neither a taking prohibited by the Fifth Amendment, nor a tax on expression barred by the First Amendment. Presumably any formality that is rationally related to the constitutional purpose of "promoting the public interest in the arts and sciences," *id.* at 814, can be congressionally imposed as the price of copyrightability.

[42] *See* 35 U.S.C. § 102(f) (1988); text quoted *supra* note 16.

[43] *See* 2 PETER D. ROSENBERG, PATENT LAW FUNDAMENTALS §§ 13.01-.08 (2d ed. 1991) (contents of patent applications).

[44] This statement is a generalization; certain types of old work do not destroy "novelty" for the patent statute which has a very detailed list of statutory bars to protection.

A person shall be entitled to a patent unless—

(a) the invention was known or used by others in this country, or patented or described in a printed publication in this or a foreign country, before the invention thereof by the applicant for patent, or

(b) the invention was patented or described in a printed publication in this or a foreign country or in public use or on sale in this country, more than one year prior to the date of the application for patent in the United States, or

(c) he has abandoned the invention, or

(d) the invention was first patented or caused to be patented, or was the subject of an inventor's certificate, by the applicant or his legal representatives or assigns in a foreign country prior to the date of the application for patent in this country on an application for patent or inventor's certificate filed more than twelve months before the filing of the application in the United States, or

(e) the invention was described in a patent granted on an application for patent by another filed in the United States before the invention thereof by the applicant for patent, or on an international application by another who has fulfilled the requirements of paragraphs (1), (2), and (4) of section 371(c) of this title before the invention thereof by the applicant for patent, or

(f) he did not himself invent the subject matter sought to be patented, or

(g) before the applicant's invention thereof the invention was made in this country by another who had not abandoned, suppressed, or concealed it. In determining priority of invention there shall be considered not only the respective dates of conception and reduction to practice of the invention, but

test, however, raises important questions about the relevance of intention and its presumptions. Must the author be personally motivated by the incentive or should all authors receive protection because the copyright system motivates them as a group?[45] Here, again, the complexity of copyright in a free society presents itself: how does one calibrate a legal structure so as to provide adequate incentives for creativity without, at the same time, discouraging the inventive scholarship that comes from the exploitation of existing ideas?[46]

Where is the *Feist* decision in this continuum? Recall that Justice O'Connor finds that the plaintiff has no claim, that the telephone book has no author for the purpose of invoking copyright law. More than an objective test is clearly required, though how much more is not certain. Justice O'Connor conflates the two meanings of "originality." On the one hand, originality relates to origins, and an author is the origin of the work. On the other hand, originality has come to mean more, and this additional meaning is important to the Court: originality implies a modicum of creativity, something thought of, the product of some element, however modest, of human genius.[47] Nor is the *Feist* Court adopting the economic intentionality test. Indeed, there is no question that the plaintiff sought to be part of the copyright system by manifesting its intention to publish a work that would have the maximum protection possible. These were

---

also the reasonable diligence of one who was first to conceive and last to reduce to practice, from a time prior to conception by the other.
35 U.S.C. § 102 (1988).

[45] The group approach was endorsed in Hutchinson Tel. Co. v. Fronteer Directory Co., 770 F.2d 128 (8th Cir. 1985) (holding specific telephone directory copyrightable even though it was clearly not motivated by the copyright monopoly, but rather by the desire to maintain its telephone service monopoly), *overruled on other grounds by* Feist Publications, Inc. v. Rural Tel. Serv., 111 S. Ct. 1282 (1991) (holding white page telephone directories not copyrightable because of lack of originality). The group approach is also suggested by the cases on "usefulness." The Constitution speaks of the "useful Arts," U.S. CONST. art. I, § 8, cl. 8. Copyright has been upheld for specific "useless" items because the system of copyright is itself useful. *See, e.g.*, Pacific and S. Co. v. Duncan, 744 F.2d 1490, 1498-99 (11th Cir. 1984) (upholding copyright for broadcasts which could not be repeated because the tapes were destroyed), *cert. denied*, 471 U.S. 1004 (1985); Jartech, Inc. v. Clancy, 666 F.2d 403, 405-06 (9th Cir.) (upholding copyright for obscene materials), *cert. denied*, 459 U.S. 826 (1982).

[46] Jessica Litman has suggested (1) that the American copyright system is based on an inaccurate myth that authors create *ex nihilo* and (2) that a large public domain is the safety valve needed to prevent this myth from overstressing the reality of authorship. Jessica Litman, *The Public Domain*, 39 EMORY L.J. 965, 1023 (1990).

[47] The third meaning of originality particular to copyright requires that the work be conceived without copying, as to its creative margin, a pre-existing work. To use a well-worn example, if an author were to write the same words in the same order as they appear in one of Shakespeare's plays, but did so without any reference to Shakespeare, they would be "original."

not accidental writings, like letters or off-hand notes. Oddly, the decision is closest to the aesthetic test: the *Feist* Court wants a living, breathing author;[48] without one, there cannot be the "originality" demanded. The most striking element of *Feist* is that it places the judge, once again, in the position of judging the quality of the work.

What should the law of authorship look like? As important as is the question of who an author is to the literary critic, the absence of legal analysis may suggest its relative unimportance in copyright law. The image of the author, however, can be fashioned from other doctrines. Doctrines such as work for hire, fair use, joint authorship and originality all inform us more readily about what the law thinks of authors than the interpretation of the word itself. All of these questions deal with the outer husk of authorship. They presume there is an author and debate only its identity. It has taken *Feist*[49] to suggest again that the inner husk of authorship can be dealt with directly.

Why focus on the author as opposed to the writing or the fair use? The arguments against are clear. Trying to determine who is an author has the general tendency to implicate the aesthetic test, one that has been so strongly eschewed by American law. There are fundamental difficulties in defining authorship by examining the intention of the creator of the work. To be sure, a definition of authorship that rests on an intent to have one's writing protected is a definition that springs from the very purposes of the constitutional copyright clause. This protection serves as an incentive for engaging in the process of producing a protected writing. But intention is also problematic, for it implicates the judge too much in a search that has little relationship to the creative process. Perhaps a person who writes and sends a letter with the recognition that the recipient can give it to a library and make it available to researchers should not be considered an "author" under the copyright law unless there is strong evidence to the contrary. Perhaps this is the reason men and women acting in their official capacity for the government are not authors under the copyright law.[50] Under this view, authorship would erect a standard independent of the nature of the writing. Only a work by an author could be considered a protected writing.

It would be tempting to argue that a tougher definition of

---

[48] One can also read *Feist* as merely requiring a *work* of a certain level of "originality" and assume such a work implies such an author.

[49] *Feist*, 111 S. Ct. at 1282.

[50] 17 U.S.C. § 105 (1988).

authorship is better because it confines the scope of copyright and expands the zone of material available to be copied and used in a free society. But that argument would prove too much. We might favor an independent definition of authorship because of some collective feeling that the zone of protection is too broad, or that accession to the Berne Convention by eliminating the need for formalities raises questions of additional constraint. Our own impulses for finding a definition of authorship arise from concerns about the pressure on the fair use doctrine. Our belief is that the tremulousness among publishers, particularly regarding critical biographies, stems from too broad a definition of copyrightable material and too narrow a definition of what constitutes fair use. The strains within the Second Circuit stem from its overuse of the fair use doctrine. One solution, and one that has almost been accomplished, is to obtain a broader definition of what constitutes fair use, either through the courts[51] or through Congress.[52] Another approach is to reduce the zone of copyright itself. Since the Supreme Court has just strongly reiterated the primacy of originality, courts are justified in rechanneling the American legal discussion of copyright from the centrality of the object to that of the author.

American copyright law before the Berne Convention was open to criticism for its mediation among the three paradigms mentioned—the objective, the intentional and the aesthetic. Within them, however, a long-time balance existed in which the concept of authorship could have been situated, even implicitly. What is increasingly clear, however, is that the traditional formalities of American law are declining and serving less and less as a meaningful line between what should be protected and what should not be protected. Notice is no longer required.[53] Without notice, or the expression of intent to opt into a system of copyright,[54] the objective approach, unalloyed, may yield too

---

[51] Several recent cases can be seen as judicial attempts to widen the narrow reading of the fair use provisions in Salinger v. Random House, Inc., 811 F.2d 90 (2d Cir.), cert. denied, 484 U.S. 890 (1987) and New Era Publications Int'l v. Henry Holt & Co., 873 F.2d 576 (2d Cir. 1989), cert. denied, 110 S.Ct. 1168 (1990). See New Era Publications Int'l v. Carol Publishing Group, 904 F.2d 152 (2d Cir.) (using published/unpublished distinction), cert. denied, 111 S.Ct. 297 (1990); Wright v. Warner Books, Inc., 748 F. Supp. 105 (S.D.N.Y. 1990) (using, inter alia, loopholes of paraphrase, banality, factuality, failure to show economic harm and unclean hands).

[52] S. 1035, 102d Cong., 1st Sess. (1991), a pending revision of 17 U.S.C. § 107 (1988) introduced by Senator Simon, would make the unpublished nature of a work less central in the fair use analysis. 137 CONG. REC. S5649 (daily ed. May 9, 1991); 137 CONG. REC. E. 1821 (daily ed. May 16, 1991) (House version).

[53] 17 U.S.C. § 405 (1988).

[54] Registration certainly does not fulfill this function. Copyright exists before regis-

wide a swath of protection. Publication is not a dividing line between what is protected and what is not.[55] Even the concept of fixation is soft around the edges.[56] The concept of originality, once a source for separating the sheep from the goats, no longer usefully performs that function.[57] In addition, decisions that fail to distinguish between copyrightable works of art and objects of mere utility have blurred the precincts of art.[58]

The Berne Convention tradition may mean, in important respects, more of a tendency toward the aesthetic standard. The very essence of American copyright law differs from the romantic Europeans with their exotic neighboring rights, personal rights, and moral rights. For them, the act of creation is central to the very notion of protection; to us, with a perspective that integrates copyright with property rights rather than with human rights, the source of the property seems far less relevant.[59]

Copyright law in the United States is shifting toward the European model, but it is still entrapped in the ideology of its

---

tration. 17 U.S.C. § 408(a) (1988). Furthermore, while useful, registration is merely voluntary in most cases. *See* M. LEAFER, UNDERSTANDING COPYRIGHT § 7.4 (1989) (providing an overview of registration).

55 All "fixed" works are protected. 17 U.S.C. § 102(a) (1988). Gone is the 1909 Act's outcast category of unpublished works that were relegated to common law protection. 17 U.S.C. § 102 (repealed 1976; eff. Jan. 1, 1978).

56 Courts protect video games despite their wide variations and user input. *See, e.g.*, Williams Elecs., Inc. v. Artic Int'l, Inc., 685 F.2d 870, 874 (3d Cir. 1982) (holding play mode of video game copyrightable). *See* MELVILLE NIMMER & DAVID NIMMER, NIMMER ON COPYRIGHT, § 2.18[H][3][b](1991) (providing an overview of video game cases).

57 Few items are below the level of originality. Plebeian topical songs are protectable. Henderson v. Tompkins, 60 F. 758, 763-64 (C.C.D. Mass. 1894) (protecting the song "I Wonder If Dreams Come True" over a charge of triviality). *But see* Magic Marketing v. Mailing Serv. of Pittsburgh, 634 F. 769 (W.D. Pa. 1986) (denying copyright protection for envelopes with a solid black stripe and the phrases "telegram," "gift check," "priority message," and "contents require immediate attention"). White page telephone directories with listings in standard alphabetical order were only recently placed outside the pale. Feist Publications, Inc. v. Rural Tel. Serv., 111 S. Ct. 1282 (1991). Perhaps this is an indication of the revival of the originality requirement as a meaningful barrier to protection.

58 *See, e.g.*, Kieselstein-Cord v. Accessories by Pearl, 632 F.2d 989 (2d Cir. 1980) (holding decorative belt buckle is copyrightable); National Theme Prods. v. Jerry B. Beck, Inc., 696 F. Supp. 1348, 1353 (S.D. Cal. 1988) (holding designs for masquerade costumes copyrightable, even though the items are useful articles, because their details result from artistic—not function driven—decisions. *But see* Esquire, Inc. v. Ringer, 591 F.2d 796, 805 (D.C. Cir. 1978) (holding overall shape of lighting fixture is not copyrightable), *cert. denied*, 440 U.S. 908 (1979). The usefulness limitation may be applicable only to "pictorial, graphic, and sculptural works." 17 U.S.C. § 102(a)(5)(1988). Computer programs are, however, useful and protected. *See* Malla Pollack, Note, *Intellectual Property Protection for the Creative Chef, Or How to Copyright a Cake: A Modest Proposal*, 12 CARDOZO L. REV. 1477, 1487-89 (1991).

59 American law, therefore, protects publishers to encourage the marketing of works created by others. *See, e.g.*, Zechariah Chafee Jr., *Reflections on the Law of Copyright: I*, 45 COLUM. L. REV. 503, 509-11 (1945) (need for publishers' business expertise in distributing works necessitates protection for others than the Constitution's named beneficiaries: authors.)

American past. If this is the case, as we believe it is, then strains in judicial decision-making should become increasingly clear, strains that follow from applying a familiar ideology to a changed legal landscape. The shift, in the world of The Berne Convention, is toward attention to the privileges of being an author. Our objective model of copyright is dissolving and a struggle is under way for another body of jurisprudence to take its place. The saga of the telephone book is merely one aspect of that process.

APPENDIX
INTELLECTUAL PROPERTY AND THE
CONSTRUCTION OF AUTHORSHIP

A Conference Sponsored by
The Society for Critical Exchange
April 18-21, 1991
Case Western Reserve University   Cleveland, Ohio

Arch(e)-Authors

Moderator: Susan Eilenberg, English, State University of New York, Buffalo

Margreta de Grazia, English, University of Pennsylvania
Shakespeare in Quotation

Caroline Gebhard, English, Grinnell College
Forging an Author's Signature: Harriet Beecher Stowe's Creation of a Male Persona

David McWhirter, English, University of Pennsylvania
Constructing Henry James: Authorship and Authority in the New York Edition

Thomas Pfau, English, University of Wisconsin
Author(iz)ing a Collective Subject: Lyric Form, Moral Speech, and the Social Performance of Wordsworth's "Ode to Duty"

Laura J. Rosenthal, English, Florida State University
Disembodied Shakespeare: The Author as Ghost

"Authorship," Repression and Revolution

Moderator: Raymond Birn, History, University of Oregon

Bryan Bachner, Law, City Polytechnic of Hong Kong
When All Is Said and Done: Conscience, de Man, and the American Dream

John C. Dolan, Rhetoric, University of California, Berkeley
James MacPherson and Hugh Blair: The Expropriation and Foreign Transfer of Third-World Literary Property

Catalin Mamali, Communication Studies, University of Iowa
Scientific Authorship in a Totalitarian Society

Benjamin Moore, English, University of Iowa
Reforming Authors: Literary Proprietorship and Social Authority in Early Modern England

Writing as Collaboration

Moderator: Andrea A. Lunsford, English, Ohio State University

Anne Ruggles Gere, English, University of Michigan
Common Properties of Pleasure: Texts in Nineteenth-Century Women's Clubs

David Gewanter, English, University of California, Berkeley
"Daffodils" and Authority: Wordsworth's Collaborative Lyric

Wendy J. Gordon, Law, Rutgers University
Reality as Artifact

Jeff Masten, English, University of Pennsylvania
Seeing Double: Collaboration and the Interpretation of Renaissance Drama

James L. Pethica, English, Wolfson College, Oxford University
Contested Parentage: Yeats, Lady Gregory and Collaborative Authorship

Origins of Authorship

Moderator: Martin Elsky, English, Brooklyn College, City University of New York

John P. Feather, Library and Information Studies, Loughborough University
From Rights in Copies to Copyright: The Recognition of Authors' Rights in English Law and Practice in the Sixteenth and Seventeenth Centuries

Lawrence Needham, English, Oberlin College
Beauty and the Beast: Monstrous Texts, Mimic Writing, and Romantic Authorship

Mark Rose, Humanities Research Institute, University of California, Irvine
The Author in Court: Pope v. Curll *and the Idea of Literary Property*

Susan Stewart, English, Temple University
Crimes of Writing

David Sanjek, English, Fordham University
"Don't Have to DJ No More": Sampling and the "Autonomous" Creator

The Professionalization of Writing

Moderator: Mark Rose, Humanities Research Institute, University of California, Irvine

Martin Elsky, English, Brooklyn College, City University of New York
Francis Bacon: Failed Courtiership and the Retroactive Construction of Authorship

Nancy Glazener, English, University of Pittsburgh
The Professional v. the Storyteller: Ideologies and Politics of Authorship in the Fin-de-Siècle U.S.

Charles Johanningsmeier, English, Indiana University
American Fiction Authors, the Associated Literary Press, and the Rise of Authorial Free Agency in the Late Nineteenth Century

James C. Keil, English, Howard University
Melville's Authorship: Reading, Imitation, Writing, and Originality

Joseph F. Loewenstein, English, Washington University
Milton's Talent: The Authorial Icon in the Tonson Era

Beyond "Authorship"

Moderator: Gary Lee Stonum, English, Case Western Reserve University

David L. Lange, Law, Duke University
At Play in the Fields of the Word

Andrea A. Lunsford, English, Ohio State University
Literacy, Intellectual Property, and the Status Quo: Scenes for Writing in the Academy

Authors in the Marketplace

Moderator: Lawrence Needham, English, Oberlin College

Raymond Birn, History, University of Oregon
Rousseau and Literary Property: From the Discourse on the Origin and Foundation of Inequality *(1755) to* Emile *(1762)*

N.N. Feltes, English, York University
International Copyright: Structuring "the Condition of Modernity" in British Publishing

Richard A. Fine, English, Virginia Commonwealth University
Copyright and the Controversy over the American Authors' Authority

Peter Lindenbaum, English, Indiana University
Milton's Contract

William B. Warner, English, State University of New York, Buffalo
The Institutionalization of Novelistic Authorship in England: The Battle Between Samuel Richardson and the Irish Printer George Faulkner

Resurrecting the Author

Moderator: Peggy Kamuf, French and Italian, University of Southern California

Eve Tavor Bannet, English, University of South Carolina
"Invention de l'autre": The Resurrection of the Author in French Deconstruction of the 1980s

Gail Gilliland, Institute for the Humanities, University of Michigan
The Moment of the Subject: Motherhood and Authorship in a Deconstructive Age

Cheryl Walker, Modern Languages, Scripps College
Persona Criticism and the Death of the Author

Monroe Price, Dean, Benjamin N. Cardozo School of Law
Intentionality in Copyright Law

Marie-Pierre LeHir, Modern Languages, Case Western Reserve University
Authors v. Playwrights: The Two Authorship Systems of the Old Regime and the Repercussions of Their Merger

"Authorship" in Popular Culture

Moderator: Wendy J. Gordon, Law, Rutgers University

James P. Saeger and Christopher J. Fassler, English, University of Pennsylvania
Pericles, Theatrical Authority, and Authorship in Early Modern England

Marvin D'Lugo, Foreign Languages, Clark University
Authorship and the Concept of National Cinema in Spain

William Rothman, Communications, University of Miami
The Conditions of Authorship in Film

Eve Shelnutt, English, Ohio University
Authorship and Individuality: Does It Matter Anymore?

History of Fair Use/Fair Use of History

Moderator: David Van Tassel, History, Case Western Reserve University

Diane Conley, attorney, Akin Gump Strauss Hauer & Feld
Author, User, Scholar, Thief: Fair Use and Unpublished Works

Kevin Dunn, English, Yale University
Information, Incorporation, and Intellectual Property in Commonwealth England

Karen Burke LeFevre, English, Rensselaer Polytechnic Institute
The Tell-Tale Heart: "Fair Use" (?) of Unpublished Texts

L. Ray Patterson, Law, University of Georgia
Understanding Fair Use

The Inevitability of Plagiarism

Moderator: Martha Woodmansee, English, Case Western Reserve University

Mark Freeman, Psychology, College of the Holy Cross
Stolen Words and the Predicament of Originality: The Case of Helen Keller

Jim Swan, Center for the Study of Psychoanalysis and Culture, State University of New York, Buffalo
Touching Words: Helen Keller, Plagiarism, and Authorship

Comments: Margreta de Grazia, English, University of Pennsylvania

The Ontology/Technology of "Authorship"

Moderator: Jessica Litman, Law, Wayne State University

Coburn Freer, English, University of Georgia
Changing Concepts of Literary Ownership in the English Renaissance

Meredith L. McGill, English, Johns Hopkins University
Wheaton v. Peters *and the Materiality of the Text*

Marlon B. Ross, English, University of Michigan
Authority and Authenticity: Scribbling Authors and the Genius of Print in Eighteenth-Century England

Pamela Samuelson, Law, University of Pittsburgh
Some New Kinds of Authorship Made Possible by Computers and Some Intellectual Property Questions They Raise

Marian Keane, Film Studies, University of Colorado, Boulder
Stanley Cavell's Concept of Medium and Individual Mastery

The Future of Copyright

The Honorable Ralph Oman, Register of Copyrights, United States Copyright Office

Authorship in International Perspective: Legal Reverberations East and West

Moderator: Peter Jaszi, Law, The American University

William P. Alford, Law, Harvard University
To Steal a Book Is an Elegant Offense

James Boyle, Law, The American University
A Theory of Law and Information: Copyright, Genes, Blackmail, and Insider Trading

Comments: Yuanyuan Shen, Law, University of Wisconsin, Madison

Extensions of "Authorship"

Moderator: Marilyn Edelstein, English, Santa Clara University

Rosemary Coombe, Law, University of Toronto
Author/izing the Celebrity: Publicity Rights, Postmodern Politics, and Unauthorized Genders

Jane Gaines, English, Duke University
Bette Midler and the Piracy of Identity

Helen Liggett and David Perry, Urban Studies, Cleveland State University
Constructing Moses: Building the City

Thomas Streeter, Sociology, University of Vermont
Broadcast Copyright and the Bureaucratization of Property

Alfred C. Yen, Law, Boston College
The Interdisciplinary Future of Copyright Theory

From Originality to Forgery

Moderator: Susan Stewart, English, Temple University

Julie C. Hayes, Modern Foreign Languages, University of Richmond
Plagiarism and Authorship in Eighteenth-Century France

Gerhard Joseph, English, Lehman College, City University of New York
Construing the Inimitable's Silence: Pecksniff's Grammar-School and International Copyright

Jessica Litman, Law, Wayne State University
Copyright as Myth

John Sutherland, Literature, California Institute of Technology
Me-Tooism and Free Trade in Ideas

Max Thomas, English, University of Pennsylvania
Editing, Authorship, and the Production of a Renaissance Commonplace Book

Martha Woodmansee is Associate Professor of
English at Case Western Reserve University and
Director of the Society for Critical Exchange.
Peter Jaszi is Professor of Law at Washington
College of Law, The American University.

Library of Congress Cataloging-in-Publication
Data
The Construction of authorship: textual
appropriation in law and literature/Martha
Woodmansee and Peter Jaszi, editors.
ISBN 0-8223-1382-0 (cl).
ISBN 0-8223-1412-6 (pa).
1. Copyright. 2. Plagiarism. I. Woodmansee,
Martha. II. Jaszi, Peter.
K1420.6.C66 1994
346.04'82—dc20
[342.6482]   93-32347CIP